D1707925

EASY
WRITER

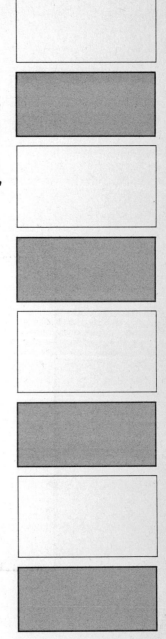

EASY WRITER

A PROCESS AND SENTENCE-COMBINING APPROACH TO COLLEGE WRITING

THIRD EDITION

DIANNA CAMPBELL
University of Michigan

HarperCollins*CollegePublishers*

Sponsoring Editor: Mark Paluch
Project Coordination and Text Design: York Production Services
Cover Design: Kay Petronio
Cover Photo: Comstock Inc.
Production/Manufacturing: Michael Weinstein/Paula Keller
Compositor: York Production Services
Printer and Binder: Courier Companies, Inc.
Cover Printer: The Lehigh Press, Inc.

EASY WRITER: A PROCESS AND SENTENCE-COMBINING APPROACH
TO COLLEGE WRITING, Third Edition

Library of Congress Cataloging-in-Publication Data

Campbell, Dianna S., 1949–
    Easy writer : a process and sentence-combining approach to college
writing / Dianna Campbell. — 3rd ed.
        p.   cm.
    Includes bibliographical references and index.
    ISBN 0-06-041157-0
    1. English language—Rhetoric.   2. English language—Grammar—1950–
    I. Campbell, Dianna S., 1949
II. Title.
PE1408.C2824   1993
818′.042—dc20   92-22559
                                                              CIP

92   93   94   95   9 8 7 6 5 4 3 2 1

To the memory of my grandmother,
Anna Karbarska Szczur, 1894–1991, my source

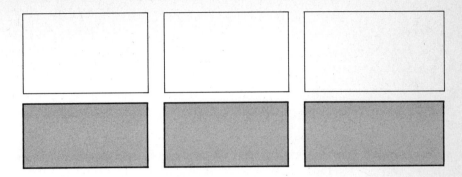

Contents

To the Teacher   *xiii*
To the Student   *xv*

SECTION I   THE WRITING PROCESS

CHAPTER 1   Prewriting and the Writing Process   3
WATCHING STUDENT WRITERS AT WORK   3
THE FIVE PARTS OF THE WRITING PROCESS   3
CREATING IN THE PREWRITING STAGE   4
FREEWRITING   6
LAST WORDS ON PREWRITING   11

CHAPTER 2   Special Concerns: Becoming Concrete and
Specific and Establishing Point of View   12
USING CONCRETE AND SPECIFIC LANGUAGE   12
ESTABLISHING POINT OF VIEW   19

CHAPTER 3   Description and Narration   22
DESCRIBING PEOPLE   22
DESCRIBING PLACES   28
EXERCISES FOR DESCRIPTIONS OF PEOPLE AND PLACES   35
WRITING NARRATIVES   37
IDEAS FOR NARRATIVE WRITING   57

CHAPTER 4   Special Concerns: Considering Diction and
Addressing Audiences   61
DICTION   61
AUDIENCE   72

CHAPTER 5   Exposition: Writing Definitions and Comparison/
Contrast Essays   81
DEFINITION ESSAYS   83
COMPARISON/CONTRAST ESSAYS   101
TIPS ON COMPARING AND CONTRASTING   106

CHAPTER 6   **Special Concerns: Problems of Logic and Paragraph Organization**   111
LOGIC   111
PARAGRAPH ORGANIZATION   117

CHAPTER 7   **Persuasion: Writing Cause and Effect Essays and Documented Arguments**   136
CAUSE AND EFFECT ESSAYS   137
DOCUMENTED ARGUMENTS   151
DOCUMENTING YOUR SOURCES   157
EXAMPLES OF STUDENT WORK   165

SECTION II   SENTENCE COMBINING AND EDITING SKILLS

CHAPTER 8   **Introduction to Sentence Structure**   183

UNIT 1:   *Basic Clause Patterns*   183
SIMPLE SENTENCES—THOSE WITH ONE CLAUSE   184
FINDING VERBS IN CLAUSES   184
FINDING SUBJECTS IN CLAUSES   186
FINDING ELEMENTS THAT COMPLETE THE VERB   186
SUMMARY OF BASIC CLAUSE TYPES   190
REVIEW OF UNIT   194

UNIT 2:   *Taking a Closer Look at Subjects*   195
NOUNS   196
PRONOUNS   198
NOUN SUBSTITUTES   199

UNIT 3:   *Taking a Closer Look at Predicates*   201
VERBS   201
MORE ABOUT COMPLETING ELEMENTS IN THE PREDICATE   205

UNIT 4:   *The Modifiers*   206
ADJECTIVES   206
ADVERBS   207
APPOSITIVES   208
PREPOSITIONAL PHRASES   211

UNIT 5:   *Review*   213
EXERCISES   214

CHAPTER 9 **Strategies for Combining Clauses and Punctuating Sentences** **221**

UNIT 1: Compound Sentences 222
PUNCTUATING COMPOUND SENTENCES 222
OTHER USES OF THE COORDINATING CONJUNCTIONS 223
A NOTE ON *FOR* AND *NOR* 223
EXERCISES 224
LINKING MORE THAN TWO CLAUSES 228

UNIT 2: Complex Sentences 228
COMPLEX SENTENCES MADE WITH SUBORDINATING CONJUNCTIONS 228
COMPLEX SENTENCES MADE WITH RELATIVE PRONOUNS 232

UNIT 3: Making and Punctuating Phrase/Clause Combinations 242
MULTIPLE PHRASES 245
ABSOLUTE PHRASES 246
PHRASES IN COMPOUND AND COMPLEX SENTENCES 247
"LANGUAGE MEDICINE" 248

UNIT 4: Other Useful Comma Rules 248
USING COMMAS IN A SERIES 248
USING COMMAS IN ADJECTIVE PAIRS 250
FOUR MORE USES OF THE COMMA 252

UNIT 5: Reviewing Commas 253
EXERCISES 254

UNIT 6: Using Semicolons 258
THE BASIC FUNCTION OF THE SEMICOLON 258
USING SEMICOLONS WITH LOGICAL CONNECTIVES 261
A LESS COMMON USE FOR THE SEMICOLON 263

UNIT 7: Using Colons 264
FOR LISTS 264
FOR EXPLANATIONS 268

UNIT 8: Cumulative Review Exercises for the Comma, Semicolon, and Colon 269
A SIMPLE WAY TO REVIEW AND WARM UP 269
A NOTE ON PUNCTUATING DIRECT QUOTES 270
WHAT THESE EXERCISES ARE REALLY ABOUT: CREATING SENTENCES, NOT JUST PUNCTUATING THEM 270
PUNCTUATING LONGER PIECES 275

UNIT 9: Using Dashes 279
GUIDELINES 280

*UNIT 10: Cumulative Review of the Comma, Semicolon,
Colon, and Dash*   284
EXERCISES   284

*UNIT 11: Miscellaneous Punctuation: Quotation Marks,
Hyphens, and Apostrophes*   291
IMPORTANT NOTE FOR STUDENTS AND TEACHERS   291
QUOTATION MARKS   291
HYPHENS   304
APOSTROPHES   307

CHAPTER 10 **Solving Common Problems in Combining and
Punctuating Sentences**   317

UNIT 1: Run-ons and Comma Splices   317
DON'T USE A COMMA TO SOLVE A RUN-ON   318
THE ROLE OF PRONOUNS   320
THE ROLE OF THE ADVERB *THEN*   320
EXERCISES   320
EDITING FOR RUN-ONS AND COMMA SPLICES IN CONTEXT   324

UNIT 2: Fragments   330
INTENTIONAL FRAGMENTS   330
TYPES OF FRAGMENTS   330
EDITING FRAGMENTS IN CONTEXT   335

UNIT 3: Misplaced and Dangling Modifiers   342
MISPLACED MODIFIERS   343
DANGLING MODIFIERS   344
EXERCISES   345

UNIT 4: Problems in Coordination and Parallelism   350
COORDINATION   350
PARALLELISM   352

UNIT 5: Passive Sentences   356
AN EXERCISE   356
JUSTIFIABLE PASSIVES   358
FINDING PASSIVE SENTENCES IN CONTEXT   358

CHAPTER 11 **Solving Problems at the Word Level**   366

UNIT 1: Subject–Verb Agreement   366
THE STANDARD PATTERN   367
IMPORTANT POINTS   369
MORE EXERCISES   371

UNIT 2: *Consistency of Verb Tense*   377
TENSE PROBLEMS: A SOURCE OF INCOHERENCE   378
WHICH VERB TENSES TO USE   378

UNIT 3: *Adding -d and -ed Endings*   386
THREE IMPORTANT TENSES   387
MODAL AUXILIARIES   388
PASSIVES   388
SPELLING CHANGES   389
ADJECTIVES MADE FROM VERBS   389
SUMMARY   389
AVOIDING COMMON ERRORS   391

UNIT 4: *Forming Plural Nouns*   396
NOUN MARKERS   397
WHEN THERE IS NO NOUN MARKER   398
SPELLING CHANGES   398
EXERCISES   400

UNIT 5: *Pronoun Problems*   403
PRONOUN–ANTECEDENT AGREEMENT   403
PRONOUN CASE   409

UNIT 6: *Homonyms and Other Easily Confused Word Pairs*   410
EXERCISES   416

UNIT 7: *Capitalization*   422
EXERCISES   423

CHAPTER 12 **Exercises in Sentence Combining**   428
HOW SENTENCE COMBINING WORKS   428
REVERSING THE PROCESS   429
DON'T LET IT BE BUSYWORK—AND OTHER IMPORTANT INSTRUCTIONS   429
EXERCISES   430

Answer Key   *439*
Sources   *453*
Index   *461*

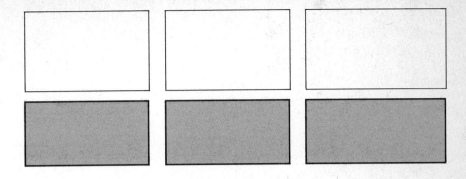

To the Teacher

This edition of *Easy Writer,* with a new section on the writing process, is a radical departure from earlier editions. The enlarged scope represents the reflections of twenty years of teaching writing and, more importantly, is made possible by the generosity of many hundreds of students from the University of Michigan in Ann Arbor and Mount Mary College in Milwaukee, many of whom have allowed me to include their writing—both the hard struggles of early drafts and the solid achievements of later ones.

The new material in section I combines a process approach that emphasizes the various stages of writing—from prewriting through revision—with a more traditional approach that is oriented toward methods of conceptualizing and structuring writing projects. Working with a wide variety of topics, assignments, and drafts, your students will repeatedly move through a messy, challenging, exciting, and ultimately effective sequence—one in which they *create, shape, write, revise,* and *edit.* This approach, as recursive and unpredictable as it is, works well for students who come from many backgrounds and who begin college with dramatically different levels of skill. The combination of a *process* approach (with its emphasis on the stages through which the writer moves) with a *product* approach (highlighting types of writing projects or modes of discourse) draws students into the excitement of writing but also offers some stability, a set of flexible frameworks that most can employ with good, often great, results.

The book helps students use traditional formats, including narratives, descriptions, definitions, comparison/contrast essays, cause and effect essays, and documented arguments, while acknowledging how frequently these modes overlap and combine. Students see, for example, that a successful documented argument might have a narrative opening and rely heavily on methods of comparison and contrast.

Here student writing *is* the reading. It provides the models, so your students see, not polished professional pieces, but drafts of student writing as they actually evolve. Some drafts are more successfully revised than others, but they are all instructive in some way. The student writing also exposes readers to controversial views and unexpected perspectives; readers may be inspired by some essays and angered by others. Suffice it to say that the writers are American college students, and their work reflects what's on their minds. I hope that these pieces will stimulate lively class discussions for you, as they have for me, and will evoke equally strong writing in response.

If you've used an earlier edition, you'll notice that the traditional *Easy Writer* material, which now comprises section II, has been expanded and reordered. The new material—whether it's on plural nouns, the dash, or the rarer uses of the semicolon—was created in response to teacher requests. What you see in the new format, including changes in sequence and a shift to more standard grammatical terminology, seems to work best for the greatest number of student writers.

The design of this book allows students to be engaged in sections I and II simultaneously, perhaps working with all or most of section I, but choosing—on the basis of their strengths and weaknesses and your guidance—what they need from the editing material in section II.

This edition is updated and more ethnically and culturally inclusive than ever before. Because of the contributions of so many students from backgrounds richly diverse in race, ethnicity, religion, and class, it was a pleasure and an education to move further in this direction.

An *Instructor's Manual* for this edition is available; it contains more student writing, discussions, exercises, and tests.

Finally, my thank yous. I am grateful for help from many highly valued colleagues, especially Bazel Allen, Andrea Banks, Nick Collins, Shirita Hightower, Marcy Nolen, Dawne Owen, Ralph Story, and Enid Zimmerman of the Comprehensive Studies Program at the University of Michigan, and all of my colleagues at UM's English Composition Board. Also, thanks to Saiful-Islam Abdul-Ahad and Gail Nomura of UM's History Department, Anita Norich and Stephen Sumida in English, and Kim Hill in Anthropology. Special thanks to Gay Reeves of Milan Middle School.

I will always be deeply indebted to my wonderful former colleagues at Mount Mary College, especially Sisters Joan Cook, David Marie Mueller, Hester Valentine, Mary Warner, and Luetta Wolf, all School Sisters of Notre Dame, Ed Torrance, and the late and dearly missed Teddy Morton.

I am also deeply grateful to Terry Ryan Meier, my co-author on earlier editions, and to the many reviewers who helped shape the final version of this text through their suggestions. They are Margo L. Eden Camann, DeKalb College; Donna Cheney, Weber State College; Lorne Coughlin, Champlain Regional College; Carol Joyce Fokine, Portland State; Rose Lynn Greene, Watterson College; Betty Jo Hamilton, Bakersfield College; Jessica Harris, Queens College; Margaret Meyer, Ithaca College; Jane McCollough, St. Petersburgh Jr. College; Jane Paznick, Borough of Manhattan C.C.; Ted Walkup, Clayton State College; and Janet Wall, Laney College.

Loving thanks to my husband Richard, our children, Chris and Caitlin, my sister Charlene Sethney, and Molly and Dick Campbell. Sincere gratitude also goes to Angela Gladfelter at York Production Services and Mark Paluch at HarperCollins, both of whom have shown me no shortage of patience.

Dianna Campbell

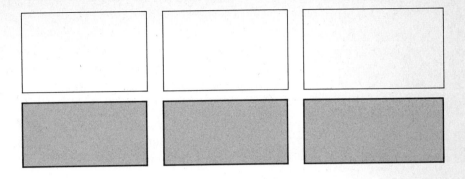

To the Student

If you want to be a better writer, follow the advice of the Nike commercial: *Just do it*. Start now and don't stop: Write, write, and write some more. As Isaac Bashevis Singer, a master novelist and short-story writer, once said, "The wastepaper basket is the writer's best friend." In fact, that's the theme of this book, which is very much revision oriented. To get better, you'll write, throw it out, and write again. But each time you'll move forward. In these pages, you'll see the work of many students who did likewise—who tried and tried again, often revising a second, third, and fourth time to get closer to what they wanted to say. You'll watch them—and yourself—becoming clearer, stronger, and more compelling as you both create, shape, write, revise, and edit.

Many of the students who have generously allowed me to share their writing with you did not come into the college writing classroom thinking they were exceptional writers. Some did little writing before college, or they wrote but encountered the same frustrations over and over—whether it was having trouble getting started or being criticized for writing run-on sentences or "going off on tangents." But as you watch their drafts evolve, you'll see that they had plenty of potential as writers all along. (And, of course, what they accomplished here is only the beginning.)

You'll see an interesting mix of writing in this book—some pieces still in need of considerable revision and other pieces on a par with the writing of professionals. To discover your potential, which may surprise you, you'll need to settle in for some very hard work, because with writing, as with so many things in life, those who exert the greatest effort usually make the most progress. It's not uncommon to see hard-working students who began their college careers not entirely sure if they would make it to their sophomore year end up not only graduating but going on in teaching, medicine, law, business, social work, engineering—wherever their dreams and energy carried them. As student writers, they may not have started out with the most creative or well-developed first drafts, but they revised more often and more thoroughly than most. They are the ones who realized that writing is both an art and a skill; it takes the *mind* and the *heart*.

What are your goals as you begin your work in this book? Naturally, everyone's goals will be different, but you will have one held in common with everyone else who commits to the difficult, life-expanding process of growth as a writer. That goal is best illustrated by this anecdote: When, very early in this century, the famous photographer and gallery owner Alfred Stieglitz first saw the art of the great Georgia O'Keeffe, whom he later married, he shouted, "At last—a woman on paper!" That's something of the feeling you will have when you've really begun to grow into the writer you want to be: "At last—*me* on paper!" You will know that you've come as close as you can to expressing and recording the best of you.

And the process does not have to stop. The writer in you can keep growing all through college and all through life; you can continue to revise and improve forever. English teachers love to see their students come down with "revision fever," but do heed a word to the wise: Keep your perspective and your sense of humor. If you've given it your all, the due date is here, and it's time to hand it in, *hand it in*. Sure, someday you might revise that essay one more time, but for now, it has to be good enough. Just say to yourself, as Steve Martin once did, "I think I did pretty well, considering I started out with nothing but a bunch of blank paper."

Dianna Campbell

SECTION I

THE WRITING PROCESS

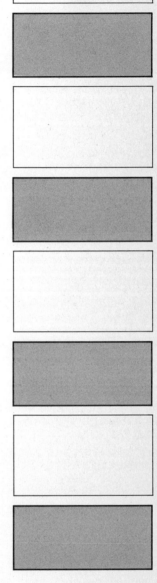

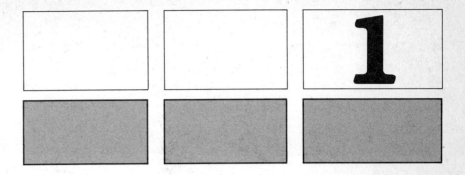

Prewriting and the Writing Process

Watching Student Writers at Work

Section I of *Easy Writer* is based largely on the idea of students teaching students. What you'll see here is not flawless writing (which often is not terribly helpful to students anyway), but it's wonderful writing—writing that's alive, quirky, unique, struggling, growing, messy, improving, sometimes fantastic. These traits are what we can expect to see when we look at writers at work. And, somehow, students seem to learn things from watching each other that they could never learn from a teacher alone. Not infrequently, for example, someone walks into my office with a dazzling revision of a paper that was going absolutely nowhere in its first or second draft. When I ask what happened, it's amazing how often the answer is something like, "Well, after I heard So-and-So read her paper in class, it just hit me what I really wanted to do with this."

The Five Parts of the Writing Process

We'll also pay a great deal of attention throughout both sections of this book to the parts of the writing process. Basically, successful writers do five things: *create, shape, write, revise,* and *edit.* These five things, or stages, together form the writing process. Writers most often follow these stages roughly in the order in which they are listed here, but writers also can change the sequence in which they are done, do them more than once during a given writing project, or do more than one at the same time. Picture the writing process as a series of loops that stretch forward but also somehow double back, each picking up and connecting to the one before.

The first and last stages—creating and editing—are the only ones that can be performed by a writer or taught by a teacher in a way that is completely separate and distinct from the other stages. And even creating and editing frequently occur out of sequence. But these two have more distinct borders than do the other stages, and so each is handled on its own terms: Creating material to write about, also called *prewriting,* is the main subject of this chapter. Editing, which can mean many different things depending upon the skills of individual students, is the concern of all of Section II.

The other stages—shaping, writing, and revising—are much less distinct. They blend into one another. For example: You select material from whatever you generate during prewriting, and these first choices begin to give shape to what will eventually be the final product. You write and write, continuing to shape and reshape, trying various ways to say things and experimenting with alternative sequences of information. Then you revise by adding, deleting, and shifting material. These actions can be done in distinct stages during the writing of one paper, and then as a massive burst of sustained activity during the writing of the next paper.

When students are first exposed to the idea of breaking the writing process into its sometimes hard-to-see stages, they are often resistant because it looks like more work. But it's really not. The truth is that writing is easier, not harder, if you understand these separate stages. In writing, it's self-defeating to try to do everything at once: You're cooking up some creative ideas when you stop to change a comma to a dash. Then you think about whether or not you should indent for a new paragraph, and you change that dash back to a comma. You start to wonder if you're getting off the track when you realize you don't have enough evidence to prove your point, and then you find two subjects that don't agree with their verbs. You decide to ask for an extension on the assignment.

Writing doesn't have to be so tough. First things first. Once you've become more process-oriented, you'll realize that you don't need to worry about organization until long after you have some good ideas to work with, and you don't need to worry about punctuation until you've solved problems of organization.

The two most distinct stages in the writing process—prewriting and editing—are also the two most essential for those students whose fear of failure keeps them from becoming solid writers. Even for those students who don't worry about how to begin or how to correct errors on the surface of their papers, these stages are vital; they simply lead to a better final product, no matter what kind of writer you are.

Creating in the Prewriting Stage

In prewriting, writers do all the activities that help them launch the writing process. Prewriting is everything you do so that the night before a deadline you're not staring at a blank sheet of paper or a darkened computer screen, grinding your teeth and asking, "What can I say?" and "How long does this thing have to be?" Prewriting not only defeats the last-minute "writing-as-torture" syndrome, but it can make the process of writing a gradually unfolding adventure. Even when it doesn't work that spectacularly, it's a big help to students who have never liked to write, have often missed deadlines, or have failed to complete required assignments. For those students, prewriting makes writing doable.

Starting Early

When you get an assignment, you'll do yourself an enormous favor if you start early. Writers need time to let ideas "cook." Mystery writer Agatha Christie once said, "The best time for planning a book is while you're doing the dishes." For you, the best time to plan writing might be when you're fixing your hair, running a couple of miles, working on your car, or pushing your child on the swing at the park. Anytime when you are engaged in a mostly physical activity, your mind can play with ideas, images, bits of dialogue, ways of proving a point, and possible structures for a piece of writing. Then as soon as possible, you can record your inspirations. Don't worry that they might turn out to be false leads. That's the beauty of prewriting—even a false lead is not a waste of time. It might not take you where you thought you were going, but it will take you *somewhere*—to a new idea, a truer image, a clearer bit of evidence, or a fuller awareness of what you really believe and what you want to communicate to your readers.

Talking It Over

In the first stage of planning a paper, don't neglect a valuable resource: your family and friends. You might be surprised how many different slants you can get on a topic by sharing your early thoughts with the people close to you. They can be a prism through which you see all sorts of different colors and angles of your topic. They also give you—through their questions—an early idea of what your readers might need to know to follow your thinking; in other words, they help you to anticipate ways to guide and satisfy your audience.

Keeping a Journal/Scrapbook

One of the best things a writer can do is to keep a combination journal and writing scrapbook and write in it for a few minutes four or five times a week. Although your journal entries normally will not be geared toward one specific writing project, as you browse through your journal, you'll often find good ideas for papers and how to develop them. If you keep a journal, you'll rarely have to say, "I can't think of anything to write about." You're probably full of fresh, quirky ideas; it's just that these ideas get lost in the rush of everyday life. Keeping a journal is a way to record your thoughts and the events in your life. Then, when you need to recollect them, you simply open your journal.

In addition to writing entries about what's going on in your life and in your heart, you can save newspaper and magazine clippings, write down lyrics from songs, describe music videos, record bits of overheard dialogue and quotes—anything and everything that you might be able to use someday in a paper. (For media products—books, newspaper stories, quotes from songs, and so forth—make sure that you include the full reference information in case you eventually use one of these items in a writing project that requires documentation of sources.)

Your teacher may ask you to keep a journal and hand it in every two weeks or so. If your journal includes writing that is too personal to share, let your teacher know. Most teachers who encourage journal writing are careful to develop policies that respect a student's right to privacy.

Freewriting

Freewriting is probably the single best way to get going on a topic because it frees you from any pressure to think logically or coherently, back up your points with evidence, or watch your spelling, word choice, or sentence structure. In freewriting, you write anything and everything that comes into your mind, never stopping to change or correct a thing. It's an intense burst of output—pure, raw writing—and usually it's done for no more than ten minutes. But even after only ten minutes, you might feel played out the first few times you try it.

Freewriting helps to break down the reluctance to write, which is usually based on fear of failure. First, freewriting helps you get used to the physical and mental act of writing. Second, when you're freewriting, you discover—if you didn't know it before—that you have a good mind, a unique style, and a lot to say. Freewriting also helps the perfectionist and the procrastinator (often the same person) because it lets you jump in and start anywhere, instead of waiting for that perfect essay to spring to life full-blown on your legal pad or computer screen.

In some freewriting assignments, you'll have complete freedom to write about whatever is on your mind. Other times, your writing teacher might offer a word, a quote, a question, a riddle, a current news story, a song, a household object, or a work of art as a stimulus. Or you might do your freewriting on the subject of your next paper. No matter what the subject of the exercise is, the important thing is to write nonstop for the full ten minutes. Keep your pen or pencil in continuous motion. When you can't think of anything to write, make loops, write zeroes, or draw squiggles. The important thing is **don't stop.** Keep your pen moving and your juices flowing. When you have anything to say—whether or not it connects with what you've written already—say it. In freewriting, it doesn't matter at all if you "get off the track." In fact, you might find that the new track is a more interesting place to be. And maybe later you'll see links between the tracks—connections or crossties that could become the basis of a writing project.

In freewriting, you can use disconnected words or phrases or whole sentences—it doesn't matter. (Some writing teachers call the activity *brain-storming* when students write in words and phrases and *freewriting* when they write in sentences. We'll call all free-flowing output activity—no matter how you do it—freewriting.) For now, forget about sentence structure, punctuation, usage, spelling, and organization. If sentences generated during freewriting happen to turn out well-formed and properly punctuated without any great effort on your part, that's fine. But at this stage, an overconcern with correctness can prevent you from creating with power and fluency. First things first; the mechanics become important later, during the editing stage. Polishing a final draft is very important and takes considerable skill (see Section II), but it's clearly not part of the *creating* process. The point of freewriting is to generate ideas and images and to experience the production of language. Don't make good ideas and fresh images wait while you decide whether to use a comma or a semicolon. Great material has a funny way of disappearing.

Your teacher will probably encourage you to do a lot of freewriting while you're using this book—sometimes in class and sometimes at home. Some freewriting assignments will lead to larger, more formal writing projects, while others will be just for exercise. The more you do it, the more helpful this activity will become. It's best, in fact, if every writing project starts with freewriting.

Let's look at some examples. Both of the following sets are based on student reaction to dramatic news events; in each case, students wrote for ten minutes. Only spelling errors have been corrected so the samples are more readable.

SET A: *ON THE WAR IN THE GULF*

These freewritings were produced by four students in an introductory composition course on January 16, 1991, the day the United States went to war in the Persian Gulf.

> War and destruction lost lives killing murder destruction no peace killing hate territory religion people dying catastrophe murder Hussein U.S. die villain G.I. murder horror body bags destruction murder desert ships planes horror destruction God help us All people places things madness Holy War religion terror longlasting peace no war destruction madness going on people dying stop must stop where will it end it will not end continuous forever script Armageddon the end forevermore destruction Syria Jordan Iraq Britain Europe people dying war missiles aircraft carriers planes bombs submarines destruction war no peace everlasting continuous Israel war bombs neverending continuous outrageous friends family dying ships crazy won't end many wars to come not over it won't stop this is the end won't end war destruction madness terror Congress Bush protestors rallies activists pro and against terror Middle East neverending oil refineries bombs

> There has to be some relief for the soldiers in the gulf on this day because the waiting is over and the conflict has begun. I felt so anxious waiting on board ship as we cruised down the coast of Vietnam. It was quiet and dark on the ship we were all engaged in our private thoughts. But "Would we be in the 'returning alive' group?" was not a question that once occurred to me—as I look back, at 19 years old you still think nothing can happen to you. Like all the accidents that I walked away from before in cars and motorcycles. OOOOOOOOOOOOOOOOOOOOOOOOOOOOO OOOOOOOOOOOOOOOO As we cruised down the coast we watched the flickering lights dance on the nighttime scene. OOOOOOOOOOOOOOOOO OOOOOOOOOOOO When we did dock

> War, war, war, why? Is it necessary or not. Why. Is Bush doing the right thing. Will our troops be protected. Will the citizens of Iraq be OK? Why. Many questions. Will all of our loved ones be OK? Will their loved ones be OK? Why must this go on? Just because Saddam or whatever his name is refuses to leave? It's a terrible thing. I don't want the war because no matter who gets killed the point is that someone will. Whether that person is dear to me or not I still care. Thou shalt not kill, thou shalt not kill. What are they thinking about? PEACE, peace! Please don't kill my son, says a mother. Please don't kill my fellow African

Americans, says another African American. Why must the blacks always be on the front line? My heart

> WAR. It is a small and dangerous word with a big devastating meaning. It's always been a part of history, but now it's part of our present. It's our turn. OOOOOOOOOOOOOOOOOOOOOOOO I can say I'm sorry and write about it, but I don't think that will help I wish it did. It's just me sitting in a classroom and I'm afraid of this war. I'm really scared. But I will never get close to knowing the great fear that all those soldiers and people in the Middle East must be feeling, War war war war war war war war war. We are already used to hearing this word so when someone says we are going to war we can say, "Oh yeah I heard."

Why So Few Digressions?

When freewriting, writers often veer from one point or subject to another, in a style close to free association. For example, a student might start out responding to a sketch of an old woman in this way: "Her face is extremely wrinkled and lined. 000000000 The wrinkles make me think of how much I hated camp when I was little. We had to make our beds so perfectly that the counselor couldn't find a wrinkle in the sheets."

In the samples on the gulf war, you didn't see much of the veering away that is normal in freewriting. Why do you think there were so few digressions in the freewritings produced on this particular day?

SET B: *ON MAGIC JOHNSON AND THE HIV VIRUS*

These moving and often intense freewritings were created by four first-year college writers within a few days of Magic Johnson's announcement that he had contracted the HIV virus.

> No one can really believe Magic has been diagnosed w/ the HIV virus. It is a shock to the world. Magic is from Lansing and everyone at home knows him. He sometimes even walks down Grand River w/o a million bodyguards. He went to State. My best friend's sister was for a couple of months dating Magic. Wow! My mom—who teaches 2nd grade (at the time)—had Magic come speak to her class. He is so big. But so nice—like a big, brown bear. We all know Magic around Lansing for something or other. When we started to see his 500 or whatever # black Mercedes w/ tinted windows we knew it was him. At home though we kind of all called him Earvin. A local newscaster—famous in the capital area—labeled him Magic some years ago and it stuck. I babysat his son before. He lives with his mom on West _____ Street. Everett [Johnson's old high school in Lansing, Michigan] is filled w/ Magic's old shoes, vest, jersey, etc. I love Magic. But I am not sad. We all must die. I get mad when people talk like he is dead. He is O.K.—just he can't play pro b-ball. I am so sad about Magic. Magic magic magic magic magic. I just looked on John's paper. I guess that would be called "Freewriting cheating." But I want to know how other people feel about Magic. He has done lots for basketball. I wish he could be in the Olympics. How tragic all of this is—it is really a blow to my system. I am very upset. And he just got married and is expecting. I hope they find a cure fast. Maybe this will make people—wake up, wake up

Unfortunately, Earvin Johnson has contracted the HIV virus. OOOOOOOOOOOOOOOOOOOOOOOOOOOOOOOOO It took this act for aids awareness to become heightened in this country. For so long people have thought that Aids could never happen to them. With a pro sports figure contracting this disease maybe now society will understand that any person can contract the HIV virus. It is sad to see that this country would not deal with the issue of Aids until a celebrity contracted the disease. Gay people were seen as dispensable and worthless. The president refused to deal with the issue, but when Magic got the disease even he responded with a supportive attitude. Is your life worth nothing unless you are famous. That is what society has told all those who have died from AIDS. Now that the Magic man has the disease, maybe, no, I am sure that efforts to find a cure will increase. It is sad that his life had to serve as an example for all of us to not follow. OOOO OOOOOOOOOOOOO Hopefully he will be able to teach young children to practice safer sex and maybe no one else will be forced to go through the rough times Magic has ahead of him.

"Magic" my brother why you. I couldn't believe it. The 1st time I heard about it I thought somebody was cracking a joke or something. I just couldn't believe it. What happened? I thought you were smarter than that, man! Why? You were the greatest. You had it all except the Olympic Gold Medal & you were about to get it. Now you can't because you made a silly mistake. What about your kid? And your wife? What she must be feeling. You don't deserve aids I want to tell you that I think you can beat it. Remember your name—"MAGIC." It's going to take Magic to beat this thing. We are all praying for ya! Hang tough. The NBA. What does everybody think. I know I feel for you. Your life isn't even half over. Now you have HIV +. OOOOOOOOOOOOOOOOOOOOOOOOO OOOOOOOOOOOOOOOOOOOOOOOOOOOOOOOOOOOOOOOOOOOOOOOOOOOO peace #32 M. J. OOOOOOOOOOOOOOOOOOOO The Lakers OOOOOOO You handled it so well. It's like you don't even care. OOOOOOOOOOOOOOOO OOOOOOOOOOOOOOOOOOOOOOOOOOOOOOO

I remember I was combing my hair and looking in the mirror when there was an announcement on the radio that said, "Magic Johnson has been diagnosed with the Aids virus." I turned towards the radio in shock, my first assumption was that the radio was making a joke. Then the announcer went on to say that Magic would hold a press conference at 6:00 P.M. I sat in my chair stunned in silence. I started thinking about all of the people I have had sex with. I started thinking about the times I had unprotected sex. I turned around to my desk, picked up my bible and I began to cry. All I kept thinking about was that if Magic Johnson caught it, then so could I. All types of thoughts started running through my mind. How could I have been so stupid. My first reaction was to call my mother. I needed positive reassurance. I was getting all worked up on the phone I asked my mother was she sure that my tests had come back negative (I have already taken the AIDS test twice to make sure everything is o.k.) She assured me that the test was negative both times. I started feeling better. My roommate and I went to the cafeteria to eat dinner. Magic Johnson's name was heard throughout the cafeteria. No one could believe what had happened. Some friends of mine got in a really heated discussion. We were all having the same "What if I have it?" feelings. Even though I have taken the test it still doesn't prove anything. It takes a long time for the virus to show. Magic Johnson has brought me to a hard decision. It's going to be a *long* time from now before I have sex again. And before I do, we are both going to take the test

When You're Hot: Essaylike Freewriting

Sometimes you really get lucky with freewriting. The spirit moves you, and your output seems in some way complete, whole. You're "on," and in ten short minutes—or maybe ten plus a few more devoted to quick fix-ups—you have produced a short, effective essay. Here's a great example, which was written in less than fifteen minutes. Of course, Mike could continue to revise and perfect it, but what are its virtues as is?

Now You See Him, Now You Don't—It's Magic
Mike Miranda

1.   For eleven years, he electrified crowds with the no-look pass, the give-and-go, and his million dollar smile. He will be remembered as a 6'9" giant who played the game with the finesse and agility of a 6'4" guard. The NBA is a victim of the HIV virus; they have lost one of the greatest athletes ever to lace up a pair of sneakers. Not only did they lose an athlete, but a great personality that represented the NBA in every positive aspect. A true sportsman and a true gentleman, Magic never fell short in either category. The fact that Earvin Johnson has the HIV virus does not erase any positive effects he has had on millions of people across the world. His image isn't tarnished, but rather the realization that no one is untouchable is made that much more evident. Everyone makes mistakes, even Magic, and as costly as the mistake is, Magic is now on a different crusade. This crusade is not to win another NBA title but to save lives.

2.   I've seen Magic's sincerity when it comes to compassion and caring for others around him. If anyone can make the world aware of a virus that is killing millions, it is Earvin—a star who treats everyone else as a star, an equal. He has a heart of gold, and this I know. I've been witness to the smile that has touched American hearts. As an usher at the Forum, I had the pleasure of meeting this man, this legend. He made everyone feel comfortable, like a neighbor. He was more than nice—he personified the word friendly.

3.   Pat Riley, former Laker coach, recently recalled a story from his early coaching days. The Lakers were playing on the road and Riley instructed the team to head to the locker room while he headed for the team coaching box. He went up a dark staircase and had the feeling he was being followed. He finally came to a part of the staircase that was lighted and there was Magic and the rest of the Laker team behind him. Riley said, "I thought I told you guys to go to the locker room." Magic responded, "You're our leader and we will follow you wherever you go." Well, now Magic is the leader, with a much bigger team, and it is time for him to lead the way.

Freewriting, Class Discussion, and Privacy

As you no doubt perceived while reading the sensitive material in parts of sets A and B, freewriting is a very private kind of warm-up activity. Freewriting, especially when produced at the start of a class period, can lead to great class discussions, but students must never be pressured to share their freewriting with others.

Last Words on Prewriting

This chapter has discussed just a few of the many techniques of prewriting. When you receive an assignment, the important thing is simply to do it—just jump in and start thinking, talking, and writing. Leave shaping, refining, and editing for later. And don't lose your confidence because you don't immediately find your prewriting output valuable or usable. Some of it will be; some of it won't. Listen to the words of the great short story writer Katherine Mansfield: "Looking back, I imagine I was always writing. Twaddle it was too. But better far write twaddle or anything, anything, than nothing at all." Mansfield had to write some "twaddle" in order to write some terrific stuff; you will too.

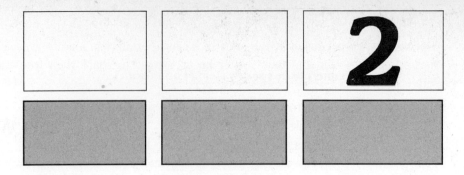

Special Concerns: Becoming Concrete and Specific and Establishing Point of View

In this chapter, we'll examine two areas that are important for description and narration—the subjects of chapter 3—but that also have important implications for other types of writing projects.

Using Concrete and Specific Language

A major weakness in much of what students write is that it's too abstract and general. What you want to strive for is just the opposite: to be as *concrete* and *specific* as possible.

An abstract word represents something that you can't touch, see, hear, taste, or smell. You might say it's an "idea word." For instance, *love* is abstract, while *kiss* is concrete. Abstract words appeal more directly to the mind, while concrete words appeal primarily to the senses. So there's no mystery why readers value concreteness in writing; it's what adds flavor and spice. Concrete language gives the reader the feeling, "Now we're getting down to it. Okay, I get the picture." By themselves, abstractions are neither pleasing nor convincing to most readers, but they're fine when supported by concrete language.

In good writing, the language also tends to be more specific than general. Something general is very broad and often too inclusive; something specific is more narrowed, limited, precise. For example, saying "I can't stand certain people" is very general; but saying "I can't stand people who are only interested in pushing their own agenda" is more specific. Specificity appeals to us as readers for the same reasons that concreteness does: Both satisfy a natural human desire to see things from the inside.

Exercise One

Circle the more concrete or specific item in each pair.

1. gesture   salute
2. sweet things   maple syrup
3. prostate cancer   illness
4. bad habit   nose picking
5. TV show   TV sit-com

6. *Murphy Brown*   TV sit-com
7. flowers   geraniums
8. lending $10   a favor
9. attack   rape
10. tennis   sport

Of course, abstract words are not to be avoided entirely; it would be impossible to discuss ideas and feelings without them. But writers often overuse abstract language because it comes more easily to mind. Thinking of a concrete way to say something, a way that can bring readers to the scene and let them decide things for themselves is more difficult than producing an abstraction. If, for example, you write that you met a "handsome man," how much does that really communicate to readers, individual tastes being as varied as they are? Others might not think the man was handsome at all. Furthermore, whether they would agree or disagree, they can get little pleasure from the abstraction *handsome,* but a great deal of pleasure from a concrete description.

When abstract language is used where concrete language would have been preferred, the abstract words seem to report on the scene from a distance; people, things, and events are pre-processed and explained. It's as if the writer has said, "Well, I guess you had to be there" and ignored the task of taking us there. But when concrete words are used, the reader is brought to the scene; the words re-create the original experience. Wherever possible, you want to let readers in on the action: Help them to see what you saw, taste what you tasted, hear what you heard. Then they can decide for themselves; they can make their *own* abstractions and generalizations. And this is important not only in descriptive and narrative writing but in all your writing. Even in research papers, using concrete and specific words will make your explanations and arguments vivid and will strengthen your selection of evidence.

Exercise Two

With concreteness and specificity in mind, evaluate and discuss the use of language in these excerpts from early and later drafts of the same paper. As you read, circle words or phrases that appeal to you. Ian describes a typical workday in the West Indies. If you've never been to the West Indies, which excerpt takes you there?

EXCERPT A   *From a First Draft*
Ian Crick

1   It is eight o'clock in St. Vincent; the alarm goes off and you wake up. You look outside to see what the weather is like. After discovering that the day is beautiful, you open the window to smell the morning breeze. You then get dressed and make some tea to drink with your breakfast. It is Monday morning and you have to be to work soon. At

2

eight-thirty you hurry to the bus stop, giving yourself time to get to work. On your way to work, you look outside the window of the bus, admiring the same sights you see every day. You get to work with time to spare, and before you know it lunch time is here.

You go down the street from where you work to eat at your regular spot. After lunch you return to work, and the second half of the day seems to go by much slower.

EXCERPT B   *From a Later Draft*
Ian Crick

1

It is eight o'clock in St. Vincent; the alarm goes off and you wake up. The sun is shining and the ground is dry. You open the window to smell the morning breeze. You get dressed and make some tea to drink with the bread you baked yesterday. It's Monday morning and you have to be at work by nine o'clock—another day as a secretary. At eight-thirty you hurry out to the bus stop, giving yourself thirty minutes to get to work. On your way to work, you look outside the window of the bus and admire the sights you see every day: lily flowers growing next to the street, an old man sitting on a stool singing a joyful song, and children walking to school dressed in their clean white shirts. You get to work with minutes to spare, and before you know it, it's lunch time.

2

You go down the street from where you work to eat at your regular spot—Hannah's Snacket. You order a beef roti with sliced baked potatoes and some sorrel to drink. After lunch you return to work, and the second half of the day seems to go by much slower.

A Little Can Go a Long Way

Often a single vivid word—just the right word—can make a sentence. It might be an unexpected verb, a snazzy adjective, a crisp, hard noun, or a wry phrase. Novelist and critic John Gardner pointed out that young writers sometimes make the mistake of trying for near-total originality and freshness. But if everything in a piece of writing—or even in a single sentence—were completely new and unfamiliar to us, we wouldn't be able to grasp the writer's meaning. We need the familiar to make sense of the unfamiliar.

So try for occasional originality, but take the pressure off; don't try to make every sentence a zinger. Even if it were comprehensible, it would seem forced and "overwritten." Much of what we write—whether it's to move the reader from one idea to the next or to get a character in or out of a room—is workmanlike stuff that simply has to be done. And, in any event, it's against a relatively plain background that a gem will really shine.

What's the gem in this sentence, taken from a story by Clyde F. Turner II?

That morning, instead of being at the football game, I was stuck pushing a tremendous load of groceries in a rickety shopping cart, trying to keep up with my mother as she skirted from one aisle to the next.

More on Becoming Concrete and Specific

Let's look at a few more examples of how student writers use concrete and specific language to create interest and to be more compelling. The first translates a lackluster abstract statement—"I knew how to manipulate my father, and he spoiled me"—into more interesting images:

EXAMPLE A
Lisa M. Barksdale

>   My father would buy me whatever I wanted—whether it was a bag of my favorite chewy red licorice or a sky blue ten-speed bike. All I had to do was shed a few salty tears.

Instead of explaining, Lisa creates pictures that will take many readers back to childhood—either to their real childhood or to the one they wish they'd had.

How about the next example for bringing to life a pitcher's dream?

EXAMPLE B
Jason H. Harrison

>   I pitched for three innings. . . . My arm was like a 90-millimeter automatic handgun shooting bullets into the glove of my catcher. My curveball had the batters' heads falling off and rolling around home plate. I loved every minute on the mound.

Next, a writer describes a nightmare about his first day of high school and makes a charming admission. Which words take you to the scene?

EXAMPLE C
William Campbell

>   My new clothes smelled of a department store. The shirt was starchy; I hated the way it felt. My pants were also starchy, and the crease looked as if it had been ironed all night. I felt like a walking pole. The stiffness was a force surrounding my body. My shoes were as white as snow. They squeaked when I walked. This was one day of school that my parents were not going to attend. I didn't want the other students to think I was a momma's boy, which I am.

In example D, the writer's younger self and other children in church have just been chastised by the minister for their unruly behavior. Now the narrator, while fearful about making the big step toward baptism, sees—for the first time—a possible payoff. Evaluate her use of concrete and specific language.

EXAMPLE D
Yolanda R. Taylor

>   When the minister opened the doors of the church, half the front row got up. Girls in their pretty dresses, white shoes, and ponytails, and boys in their black suits, white shirts, crooked ties, and scuffed shoes, joined the church. The others stayed in their seats as quiet as mice, because they had already been baptized. I sat on the pew with my slip hanging, my knees knobby, and my ponytail unbraided— contemplating what I should do. I was eight years old and had never been baptized. I felt it was something that I had to do. Maybe if I joined

the church my mother would not be angry with me for my behavior. She might even take me to the Dairy Queen. I decided to do it.

In the final example, a writer describes the work of a Burger King pro. Maybe it's a fascination with systems or processes, but whatever it is, Americans love to know the inside scoop: How do things get done? What goes on behind the scenes? Concrete language is needed to answer these questions. Especially notice the writer's snazzy use of verbs. Circle those that are not the run-of-the-mill word for a particular action.

EXAMPLE E
Roderick D. Moore

1   One employee named Genny was fast and efficient and had seventeen years of experience. She could take a Whopper and a bun and make it look so appetizing that my taste buds watered at the sight.

2   She had the routine down: She layered two thin slices of American cheese on top of the meat and placed it in the microwave. While the bottom heated up, she dressed the top bun. She quickly swiped the bread with thick, creamy white mayonnaise and then sprinkled on crisp fresh green lettuce. Effortlessly she glided two thick ripe slices of red tomato onto the lettuce. Beep, beep! The sound of the microwave pierced the air. She whipped the Whopper out of the microwave and put it in its carton, as little clouds of steam piped from the meat into the air. The steam slowly evaporated, leaving behind the aroma of char-broiled burgers. She added four thinly sliced pickles to the striped burger, along with several swirls of Heinz ketchup. Then, for the grand finale, she sprinkled chopped onions so evenly that the hungry customer would taste some in every bite. It was no mystery to me why Burger King was the second most successful fast-food restaurant in the world.

Exercise Three

Practice writing more concretely by translating these abstract statements into terms that appeal to one or more senses.

1. The man became very angry as circumstances developed and he realized that once again he would have bad luck at the grocery store check-out counter.
2. The meal was heavenly; everything was simply perfect.
3. My first paper is going to be about the most exciting, terrific, wonderful fantasy I've ever had.
4. I remember the sights and sounds of my happiest birthday.
5. There were certain aspects of the old house that made me feel that no one had been in it for a long, long time.

Exercise Four

After writers identify and value concrete images, they have to give the images shape—find a measure of form—in order to use them. This is an exercise to help you focus your concrete and specific language. It's a first step toward creating a controlling purpose and later a thesis—the main idea a writer wants to express or prove in a piece of writing.

Students are given 20–30 minutes for Steps 1 through 3.

Step 1: Each student selects one object from a table full of objects that the teacher has brought to class. (Or each student could be asked to bring something.) These objects might include feathers, photographs, rocks, candles, small sculptures, seashells, toys, souvenirs, earrings, medallions, pressed leaves, a fresh flower, an old baseball, scarves, wrapped candy, or fruit in a variety of shapes, sizes, and conditions. Things that have been around a while usually provide more potential for this exercise because they have a little character, a history.

Step 2: Students examine the object until a *dominant impression* forms. If you want to do some freewriting to discover this impression, you may. Or you can look at the object and handle it until an idea hits you. The point is not to write a perfectly polished, well-organized paragraph, but simply to select something central from all your thoughts about the object—to find a focus for a piece of writing.

Step 3: Next, the writer describes the object so that the reader can understand how the dominant impression was formed. You don't write "This feather is beautiful" if none of the concrete details you mention support the notion of beauty. **The dominant impression must be logically connected to the qualities of the object.** The writer's job is to communicate this "fit" to the reader.

Step 4: At the next class, students share successful examples.

Student Examples

Both writers of the following examples happened to pick up a child's toy. Each writer gives a lot of concrete detail, but which one is much more successful at communicating a dominant impression and suggesting how it was formed?

EXAMPLE A   *A Rag Doll*

> The first impression this most colorful rag doll gives me is the sense of being scared. The doll has a weirdness about it that makes me think of voodoo. The doll is very imaginative. I can tell that whoever made it knew what they were doing and exactly how they wanted their finished product to be. The colors of the doll are pink, black, blue, yellow, beige, brown, orange, red, white, aqua, and green. The skirt is purple, red, pink, green, blue, and black. The face consists of a red smile, black eyes, and aqua cheeklines. The skirt is a drab yellow, and it is the only thing on the piece of work that is not eye-catching. Finally, this rag doll seems as if it's capable of hurting you. The reason? The way it looks. It's pretty in a way. It grabs your imagination and makes you wonder if it really is a doll.

EXAMPLE B   *A Stuffed Toy Kitten*

As I hold it in my hand, the look on the kitten's face makes me feel like a small child with a new toy. But I feel a little silly because I'm too old to play with toys, and here we are smiling at each other. The kitten smells like whoever owned it was probably eating cookies straight from an old ceramic cookie jar. The kitten is a dull beige with a little red mark on its head. A child probably wanted to see what the kitten would look like in another color but then changed his mind. Its emerald green eyes with black centers remind me of the marbles I used to play with. The nose makes me think of a strawberry-flavored Sunburst candy. The whiskers look like miniature untwisted licorice sticks. This little cat makes me want to run down to the corner candy store.

Exercise Five

Evaluate the use of concrete and specific language in this short excerpt from a piece of writing. How successful is the writer in communicating a dominant impression of a person she never met? What helps her create the aura of the old days?

Anna McWhorter
Chrisalle M. Wilson

1   I wish I could have met Anna McWhorter, but she died many years before I was born. Anna, a full-blooded Cherokee, was the mother of twelve children, and one was my Grandma Pearl. It's through Grandma Pearl's memories that I have an idea of my great-grandmother.

2   She was a medium-sized woman, about 5'5" and 135 pounds. She wore two French braids, one plaited on each side of her head, and they hung down to her hips. Her hair was charcoal black, silked with highlights of gray. Her eyes were very deep and keen. She had a broad nose, full lips, and high cheekbones. Her skin was the color of cinnamon.

3   Anna had her ways; she could be very strict. She used to make my Grandma Pearl and her five sisters and six brothers eat so much oatmeal that they came to hate the smell of it. She had strong ideas about medicine that she had inherited from *her* mother. Anna breastfed all her children and tied a string of herbs around her babies' necks to relieve the pain of teething. When they suffered from colds, she rubbed goose grease on their chests to relieve congestion. Another remedy for colds was to give the children sugartits; a sugartit was sugar, butter, and a small amount of turpentine rendered into a cube form.

4   Anna McWhorter's first love was to be a mother and raise her children, but periodically she was a schoolteacher in a church on a hill, and she washed and ironed clothes for many of the townspeople. She and her husband had a small crop of corn, and she made quilts from the feedbags that had held feed for their pigs. She lived 86 years of her life smoking Pall Mall cigarettes and doing patchwork, and when she became ill and died in 1956, she left behind many traits and memories for the McWhorter family.

Establishing Point of View

Sometimes we can get a new slant on a piece of writing by using an unexpected *point of view.* Point of view simply means who is speaking—who is telling the story or narrating the essay.

Establishing point of view involves deciding whether to use the first person pronouns (such as *I, me, my*) or the third person pronouns (such as *he, him, she, her*). It allows you to tell a story, not as you lived or observed it, but as another character did. In other words, establishing a point of view can mean anything from putting yourself in the writing as *I* or as a *she* or a *he* to creating the voice of another—real or imagined—person to speak for you.

In various selections in section I, writers have chosen unusual points of view or shifted from one point of view in an early draft to a different point of view in a later draft. Sometimes such a shift brings an entire work to life. By experimenting with point of view, you can imbue your writing with life, warmth, bitterness, excitement—almost any quality you can imagine—but especially with an air of authenticity. You can give the reader the sense that, yes, this is the real thing, this is life—you've captured it.

Let's look at one good example. Here the writer decided very early to let her subject—her mother—tell the story in her own words.

Portrait of a Strong Black Woman
Dora R. Robinson

1   It's often the small incidents in life that make or break a person. To honor my mother, a woman of great love and courage, I have chosen one small episode from her life. *Here is my mother's story in her own words:*

2   I met your daddy when I was fifteen, and when I graduated from high school I wanted to get married to him, but I also wanted to go to college. Since your grandma didn't have the money to send me to college and because she felt I needed more experience in the real world, I joined the army. At first, Aunt Winola and everybody was telling me they didn't want me in the army because they said those women were prostitutes. But Momma told them, "She could be a prostitute right here without even joining the army. I know my baby, and she's got too much character for that." She felt I could be in the army if I wanted to. That made me feel good.

3   The army is where I got my values together. This was the first time I had been to the South, and never before had I been confronted with blatant segregation. I was stationed at Fort McClellan, Alabama, for basic training, and from there I was transferred and ordered to take a train to the new station with Clary, a white girl, who was also from up North. So when I got to the train station, I met Clary and was going to catch a cab with her to the U.S.O. club, an officers club, since we had time before catching the train. But once we were in the cab, the driver just kept circling the block. Finally he asked us where we were from. After we told him, he said, "I knew y'all weren't from here because colored folks don't ride in the same cab with whites."

4   He wouldn't take us to the club, so he drove us back to the train station. At the station, a white security guard walked up to me and said,

"What do you think you're doing? Can't you read? That sign says, 'COLOREDS UPSTAIRS, WHITES DOWNSTAIRS.' Go where you belong!" I told him that I didn't see the sign because I wasn't used to signs. Then I found a telephone and called home crying, and Momma said, "Just get on that train and get out of there." So Clary and I got on the train. But then the ticket man told me, regardless of my orders, I couldn't get on the white train with Clary, but she could board the colored train with me.

5   When she boarded the coach with me, all the Black people on the train stopped what they were doing and stared at Clary, thinking she must be colored if she was in that coach. When we sat down, a little boy walked up to Clary and just stood there with a runny nose. Clary reached in her purse and pulled out a handkerchief, wiped his nose, sat him on her lap, and said, "Hi." Everyone in the coach looked relieved. This, I believe, was the reason I learned not to resent whites because from that moment I knew they were not all the same.

After telling more about this period in her mother's life, Dora switched from her mother's point of view to her own and attached this conclusion:

6   As Alice Walker once said, "We're rich because we have those women [heroic women like Rosa Parks, Fannie Lou Hamer, and others.] And I don't mean just black people are rich. I mean human beings are rich. . ." (qtd. in Lanker 24). I have great respect for my mother, who enriches the world, and with these small fragments of her life, I honor her as the life-enhancing force that she is. I honor my mother as the embodiment of strong Black womanhood.

Work Cited

Lanker, Brian. *I Dream a World: Portraits of Black Women Who Changed America.* New York: Stewart, Tabori & Chang, 1989.

Discussion

Imagine how this story about Dora's mother might have sounded if Dora had used her own point of view—perhaps the more conventional point of view. Let's convert just a small section, the second paragraph:

2a   My mother met my father when she was fifteen, and when she graduated from high school she wanted to get married to him, but she also wanted to go to college. Since my mother's mother did not have the money to send my mother to college and because my grandmother felt her daughter needed more experience in the real world, my mother joined the army. At first, my mother's Aunt Winola and other people told her that they didn't want her to join the army because they said the women in the army were prostitutes. But my grandmother told them that my mother could be a prostitute right where she was without joining the army. My grandmother said she knew her daughter, and she knew that her daughter had too much character to do that. My mother's mother felt that my mother could be in the army if she wanted to. That made my mother feel good.

What advantages did Dora create by telling the story from her mother's point of view? What is gained in terms of tone, warmth, characterization, feeling for time and place, and sense of authenticity? What other differences do you see between paragraphs 2 and 2a?

Dora uses a small bit of research in her conclusion. Handling quotes and citations is taught in Chapter 7.

Point of View Exercises

Practice shifting your point of view, choosing from among the six options listed after the following excerpt. After you write, analyze how the shift in point of view might have affected the facts and details you thought of including, your feeling of freedom to say what you wanted to say, and the directness or immediacy of the final product.

But before you begin, read John's clever description of tea time from the tea bag's point of view.

Pip Pip: It's 12:00 O'Clock
John Dilligard III

1   Ah, it feels good—good not to be couped up in that dark square pit with the rest of those losers. My day has finally come. I thought it'd take forever for me to get out, but freedom is mine. Yeah, buddy, I'm really glad I . . . hey, did you hear that? Bong! There it goes again! It's coming from that square thing with the numbers and sticks on it. I wish it would stop. Ah, there . . . twelve times and it stopped. Hey, look at that big moving thing with the grabbers on the sides. Boy, it looks stupid. It's coming this way. Damn, I hope it didn't hear me. Hey man, what you doin'? Let go of my neck! Turn me loose! Hey, don't put me in there—it's too hot, plus I can't swim. Help, HELLLP. SPLASH!

2   "Pip, pip, old boy, it's tea time."

Options
1. Describe a cat's experience of getting brushed; a shark's experience of spotting and getting or missing its prey; an ice cube being popped out of a tray and into a drink; or the life and times of a toenail clipper—from the point of view of the cat, shark, ice cube, or clipper, respectively.
2. Describe a birth from two points of view, choosing from the mother's, father's, doctor's or midwife's, or baby's.
3. Describe part of a religious service from the point of view of a completely naive, "taken in" member of a congregation. Then paint the scene again, this time from the point of view of the clergyman or clergywoman conducting the service—a person who is in reality corrupt and crafty.
4. Describe a nightclub scene from the point of view of a young person who is thrilled to be there for the first time. Describe it again from the point of view of a disc jockey who has worked there five nights a week for three years.
5. Describe a protest at an abortion clinic from the point of view of a right-to-life protester. Then describe it again from the point of view of a woman who has gone there to have an abortion.
6. Describe yourself from your mother or father's point of view; then switch to a close friend's point of view.

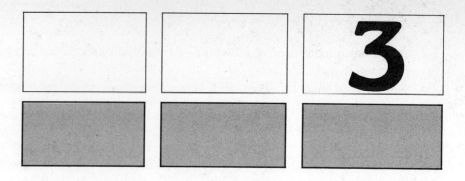

Description and Narration

In this chapter, we'll work on writing about people, places and stories.

Describing People

Human beings are endlessly fascinating to each other, and, because of that simple fact of human nature, they are a great subject for writing practice.

In description, there is so much you can do if you think past the "driver's license" level: hair color, eye color, height, and weight. Most of the time, who cares about that statistical information, anyway? It's usually wiser to focus on something special, something that might reveal a bit of truth about the character or situation of the person you're describing: knobby-fingered workers' hands; almond-shaped eyes; a heart-shaped hairline; trembly, crackling knees; a little tummy on an otherwise model-thin woman. Look for the specific and the unexpected. In description, that's the mother lode.

It's also important to establish a *controlling purpose* or *organizing principle* for your description—or for any writing project other than prewriting or personal writing, such as a journal entry or a letter to a friend. Your description should center on some basic impression or idea you want to convey. This will help you select and order your concrete/specific material.

Small Pieces

Let's begin with a wonderful thumbnail description of a great-grandmother's habit. As you read, mark concrete/specific detail that appeals to you and think about how the description evokes a small boy's fascination.

EXCERPT A   *Old, Wise, and Snappy*
William Campbell

Grandma Trixie, my great-grandmother on my father's side, dipped snuff. This is very common for people of the South. When I was little and she came up North to visit, she would send me to the store to buy the kind with the Indian on the label. She would open it up, smiling like a child unwrapping a lollipop. It smelled like prunes and burnt leaves. She would dig down deep into the pouch and, with her long thin fingers, pull out a wad of snuff. I watched her from a distance, seeing pieces of tobacco lodged between her teeth and trying to make myself think of something delicious like ice cream or candy. She would chew on the tobacco for a while, smacking and wiping an occasional drip off her lip. Then she would scoot forward in her rocking chair, lean over, and spit into an open tin can. The chewed snuff would hit the can with a thump. She knew I was somewhere. She would smile and say, "Someday you'll be dippin' snuff, too!"

Next are two paragraphs from different sections of an essay describing one of the writer's high school friends. What does Daniel do to help readers quickly form the two pictures of Joe? (*Joe* is not the friend's real name.) Which images are most helpful to you?

EXCERPT B   *The Alienation of Joe*
Daniel Friedenzohn

PARAGRAPH 1

Joe lived in an upper-middle-class suburb and attended a highly respected high school. He had a great social life, was active in the school's French club and tennis team, and got very good grades. He was never satisfied with an A — and always questioned teachers to find out why he missed a problem on a test. He played good-natured tricks on his friends and was the matchmaker in our group: He could always fix you up with one of his many female friends. Joe was never happier than when he was helping out someone who needed his "expert" advice. Whether it was the math problem on page 100 or the girl who sat next to you in English, Joe was there to help.

PARAGRAPH 2

By the end of his junior year, weed, acid, and alcohol had robbed him of everything, and had robbed us of him. All of Joe's friends knew he had a drug problem. In just a period of months he had deserted practically everyone he had grown up with. Still, he called me weekly. But now he was asking *me* for help with his schoolwork. He lost weight, let his hair grow, and became careless about personal hygiene. Finally, he lost touch with reality. He stopped speaking to people, and he didn't care what they said to him. After his second attempt to commit suicide—by walking into a busy street—Joe called me from a restaurant. I tried to talk to him about why he wanted to end his life, but he just sat in the booth staring at his glass of water. He mumbled a few words at a time; then his mouth just dropped open.

An Essay-Length Description of a Person

Let's examine fuller attempts to describe people. Our first descriptive essay creates a powerful and moving portrait of the writer's great-grandmother. What sensory details arouse your interest and bring you to the various times and places? Please mark them as you read.

How does Darilís use the point of view of herself as a little girl to add richness and an unsentimental sense of reality to her essay? What is the controlling idea or mood of the piece?

It's not customary for students to comment on the process of writing as they are writing, as Darilís does in her concluding paragraph, but is the technique justified here? Why or why not?

Darilís revised her essay several times and with great success, but if she were to revise once more, what would you like to see her do?

Adiós, Mamá Sara
Darilís García

1   "¡Adiós, Mamá Sara! Nos vemos el proximo domingo" ("Good-bye, Mother Sara! I'll see you next Sunday"), I had said to my great-grandmother on that late Sunday afternoon.

2   "A pañe, a pañe" (Sara's slang for "God be with you"). "Quieres unas bolitas de algodón?" ("Would you like some cotton balls?") she asked me on my way out. I don't know why she offered me the cotton balls; perhaps she thought a nine-year-old could make a game with them. But I do know that she was an unselfish woman who always put other people first.

3   Sara Colón Rivera was a typical Puerto Rican woman by the standards of her time: Her place was in the home. She had twelve children—eight boys and four girls—but one of the girls died shortly after her birth. Sara suffered from diabetes but was still able to cook, wash clothes, and sew for the people who meant the most to her—her husband and eleven children. As time passed, her children grew up and moved out to start their own families. Because times were tough in Puerto Rico during the early 1950s, Sara's children moved to the United States to make a better living, and they left their children behind for her to take care of until the families could be reunited. In her fifties, Sara once again became a mother—this time to seven young children whose voices, laughter, and cries filled her home as those of her own children once had.

4   Then in 1971 her husband died; at the age of 69 Sara was left alone in a small town named Juncos. Since she finally had the chance, Sara started to grow old. Her daughter Lydia, my grandmother, went back to Puerto Rico from New York to live with Sara now that she was entering her old age.

5   In her early seventies Mamá Sara seemed to have an attitude towards me, but I was only seven at the time and maybe I had an overactive imagination. After we left her house late on Sunday afternoons and returned to ours, I would be so mad because I had felt so left out of the conversations that my mom, my grandmother, and my great-grandmother would have—the traditional gossipy conversations every Sunday afternoon after church. In a small room that my great-grandmother and my grandmother shared, these conversations would go on for an hour or two. The room had two beds that were enclosed by mosquiteros (mosquito netting). My grandmother's mosquitero was pink, and my great-grandmother's was aqua blue. Between the two beds, against the wall, was a trunk. My great-grandmother would sit on her bed, my grandmother on the trunk, and my mother and I on my grandmother's bed. They would talk about everything and everyone—from what they did, to why they did it, and who they did it with. As I look

back on those days, I think it might have been all in my head, the idea that she had an attitude towards me. As I got older, she seemed more friendly, more loving towards me. Even though I was only nine and still a kid, she actually talked to me as a real person.

6 But soon, during a physical at the hospital, doctors found that my great-grandmother had liver cancer. For a year this poor 81-year-old woman was in and out of hospitals. During her final days all she wanted was a cup of coffee. Then finally on December 2, 1983, her pain ended. Peace and tranquility took over for the doctors. But she never got her wish—to have that last cup of coffee.

7 I do not remember my reaction to the news; all I remember is the following day. A lot of people offered my family and me their condolences for Sara's death. "Lo siento mucho!" ("I'm very sorry!") I remember not wanting to see her in the casket. After some time I finally got up the nerve to look. Seeing her lying there looking so beautiful reminded me of leaves that fall from the trees. One day they are so green and full of life, and the next day they are yellow and orange. Even though they look so pretty, everyone knows once they are swept away, you will never see them again.

8 December 5, 1983, the day of her burial, is mostly a blur in my mind. Maybe I do not want to remember that day so she will still live in my memory the way she used to be—so sweet and humble. "Si compañía venía a la hora de la cena Mamá Sara le daría su plato" ("If company came during dinner time, Sara would give up her plate"), my mother once told me. At the funeral I could not cry; I tried to force myself, but I couldn't. I don't recall the lowering of the casket.

9 I don't remember much about that December 5. But I do remember Sara very well. In the eyes of this nine-year-old, the word *great* in front of *grandmother* fit Sara perfectly. Her beautiful smile with her perfect white teeth lit up a room like the rising sun on an early summer morning. Her long, soft white hair reminded me of the cotton balls she offered me that Sunday afternoon. She was a friendly woman who had a warm cup of coffee and some nice warm bakery bread just waiting for any neighbor who wanted it. She wasn't a wealthy woman. All she could make for dinner was rice and beans, but it was the best rice and beans I ever had.

10 Until this day I cannot remember if I took the cotton balls she offered me, but I hope I did. It bothers me that I misunderstood my great-grandmother and wasted all those years thinking that she was mean when I should have been enjoying her company and her wisdom. "Un amigo es un peso en el bolsillo, si no está roto" ("A friend is a dollar in your pocket—if your pocket is not ripped"), Mamá Sara used to say.

11 It troubles me that I cannot recall being at the cemetery, but what hurts me more is that I could not cry at the funeral. I could cry watching a sad movie, but I could not cry for my great-grandmother. But while writing this paper, I was finally able to cry. Typing it, I had to stop a couple of times to wipe the tears. While reading over my work, I realized just how much I miss her and that she will always live in my heart and mind. It took me eight years to cry over Mamá Sara, but for me it is not a cliché to say "better late than never."

A Description of a Person in Two Drafts

In our next description, we'll see how a writer develops material through successive drafts. This essay begins in relatively abstract terms and evolves into something much more concrete and much more successful. An unexpected feature of this description may be the fact that the writer's interest is never in the physical details of his subject's appearance. What details do interest the writer? Mark the best details, especially in the later draft.

What is the controlling purpose or organizing principle of each draft?

Other major improvements were made in the movement from the first to the second draft. How many can you spot? Mark strengths and weaknesses, including punctuation and other technical skills, as you read both drafts.

DRAFT A   *The Black Father Described*
Chessada Laney

1   For many years people have wondered what it is to be a black father. Is a black father just a man who gives a child life through the biological process? If you listen to the media and all the negative stereotypes about him you would think so. Is a black father a person who neglects their family all the time to hang with friends and drink? Some would say that is normal and predictable of the black father. Well I will tell you exactly what it means to be a black father. A black father is a man who has had to struggle with adversity his whole life yet he never blamed anyone for his situation. He is the man who lost his mother at the age of twelve. Which left his father, sister and himself to run a farm with no other help. Living and working on a farm is no easy task for anyone. When you're twelve though and have to work in the fields all day, life can be unbearable. In this situation you have no choice but to grow up very quickly. Since he has to work all day and since school is five miles away he has no choice but to drop out of school in the sixth grade.

2   Three years later his father remarries but three other kids also come with the new marriage. There really is no money or room left for this young man so he decides to leave home. At the age of seventeen he leaves home a small farm in North Carolina for New York City with nothing but a few changes of clothes and twenty dollars left. He knows nobody in his new town and has no place to sleep. He obtains odd jobs and finds somewhere to stay on a day-to-day basis. After six months of living in such a fashion he decides to join the army. After serving in the army for three years he goes back to New York. He is able to get a job and a place to live. Soon he gets married and starts a family. This black father knows that to get anywhere and make money he has got to go back to school. He is able to work at his job and support his family and go to school at night. All black fathers are not like what the media and society wants you to believe; that he will run out on his family and his responsibilities. For example, when his wife loses her job he works longer hours to support his family. Finances is not the only thing that makes the black father stand out. The black father is a man who is always there to talk to his children about any problems that they may have. He is the man who teaches his children values and to appreciate what they have no matter what others possess. The black father is a man who tries to lead by example and if he makes a mistake he admits it. He is the man who comes and visits his sick four-year-old son every day for a month in the hospital even if he did just work for fourteen hours straight. He is a man that can take care of his eleven-year-old son when his wife is hospitalized for six weeks. He does cooking,

cleaning, food shopping, and makes sure his son goes to school on time. He can do all this when many other men cannot even support themselves never mind someone else.

3   The black father is a man who after a long day's work has enough time and energy to help his granddaughter with her homework. He is the man that knows how to sacrifice. After working on a job twenty years he doesn't retire when he wants to because he is trying to put his son through college. A black father is a man who helps raise five kids to the best of his ability always having enough love and time for everyone. So when the media or anyone tries to describe the black father negatively I don't believe all the things they say. When a person asks me what a black father is or what he should be like I tell them they should be like my father who I feel represents all that a black father was meant to be.

DRAFT B   *The Black Father Described*

Chessada Laney

1   "Every man is innocent until proven guilty." This is one of the basic rights that all people supposedly have living in the United States. But this right is not given to all people. Because of the many stereotypes that exist in the United States, many people are presumed to be guilty of certain things simply on the basis of their skin color.

2   The way the black father is portrayed by every part of the media, one would think that he is guilty of being totally useless to society. The stereotypes of the black father are very prevalent in our society. I am not saying that there are no black fathers who give credence to these stereotypes, but they are in the small minority. The media have told their version of the story of the black father. Now, from firsthand experience, I will tell mine.

3   One of the most common stereotypes of the black father is that he is irresponsible and that he doesn't support or take care of his family. I disagree with this depiction of the black father. My father, Malcolm Laney, *does* assume his responsibilities and supports his family. When my mother lost her job, for instance, my father worked longer hours to make up for the lost income. My mother was out of work for six months, and my father worked overtime for the Mass Transit Authority of New York City during that whole period. He received time-and-a-half working those extra hours. But the media rarely show this kind of situation; they show a black father running out on his family or abandoning them, putting them on welfare.

4   My father also takes care of the family in other ways. When I was four years old, I was hospitalized for a month because of epilepsy, and my father came to see me every day, even after working a fifteen- to seventeen-hour shift. If you believed the stereotype of the black father, you would think of a father who never went to see his son and didn't want to be bothered with a sick child.

5   On another occasion my mother was sick, and my father took care of the family. She was hospitalized for six weeks, and my father ran the house while she was in the hospital. My father cooked spaghetti, spinach, stuffing, rolls and other good meals, just like my mother. He cleaned, did the food shopping, and made sure I got out to school on time. The stereotypical black father would have bought McDonald's once a week, told his kids to fend for themselves, and let the house fall apart.

6   Another stereotype of the black father is that he is lazy, uneducated and doesn't want to work honestly for a living. My father, even at a very young age, worked long hours and did extremely strenuous work. His mother died when he was only twelve years old. After my grandmother died, that left my grandfather, my aunt, and my father to do all the work on their farm in North Carolina. My father worked in the fields picking cotton, tobacco, and all types of vegetables. Because he had to work in the fields and the school was five miles away from the farm, my father was not able to go to school much of the time. He went to school usually about three months of the year, yet later he managed to go to college and earn a degree in business administration. The stereotypical black father would never have tried to go to school but instead would have ended up on the streets somewhere with nothing to show in life.

7   Society has another stereotype of the black father, which is that he is focused on himself and his own pleasure and doesn't care about the future generations. My father cares a great deal about the future generations of our family. After a long day's work he sits down and helps his seven-year-old granddaughter with her math homework or spelling. He also takes her to the track at Elmont High School, and they run together. My niece usually runs two laps and then sits down to play; my father runs ten laps, and then they walk home together. With these shared moments, my father is giving his granddaughter a precious gift: a positive image of black men that she will never forget.

8   Further proof of how much my father cares about the future generations of my family is the sacrifice he made for me. After working all his life for New York's Mass Transit Authority, my father was eligible to retire this past year. But he decided to delay retirement to put me through college.

9   The media, racism, and the ignorance of people have created these stereotypes of the black father. I know of many other black fathers who are just like my father, and *they* are the ones who are typical of the vast majority of black fathers in the United States. If a person asked me to show him what most black fathers are like, I would show him my father—a hard-working, loving, caring man who takes care of his responsibilities, a man who is completely unlike the black father that the media have tried and convicted. I would show him Malcolm Laney.

Describing Places

Descriptions of places can be as interesting as descriptions of people. In our first example, a portrait of the *barrio* of a major American city, what is the writer's controlling purpose and is it well supported by concrete and specific detail? What appeals to you most about Enrique's essay? Does he help you see his neighborhood in a new way? If so, how? What—if anything—would you add, delete, or move?

The Barrio
Enrique Humberto Olachea

      The names of all individuals, streets, parishes and schools have been changed.

1   7:30 A.M. The alarm goes off. Time to get up for work and check the obituaries. So begins another day in the Barrio. It is a morning not unlike most others. As usual, you wonder if all your friends are still alive.

2   The Barrio isn't the greatest looking place. Most of the homes were built over forty years ago, but they're very solid. Most people try to keep their houses looking as good as possible or fix them up better than they were. But right next door could be a house with people who don't care how it looks. A good number of houses are being replaced by vacant lots. A prime example is two blocks from my house where two small streets intersect. On three corners there is nothing for three to five lots, depending on where you stand. There were once houses and a long, two-story apartment building at this intersection. Now there is only a party store on the fourth corner.

3   The Barrio is not a bad place. It is full of hardworking, proud people of all races. Contrary to popular belief, there are not many people on welfare in the Barrio. Most people are too proud to accept handouts and will work almost anywhere to provide for their families. There is also strong camaraderie in the Barrio, which shows in how the community comes together to help people. When the Lucajvich house burned, they received help from the people of Divine Savior Church. Everyone pulled together again when the Coranado house burned down. People are always willing to help.

4   There is a lot of crime in the Barrio. Prostitutes can be seen on Main Street all hours of day or night, and they are nothing like the glamorous prostitutes Hollywood gives us. Here most of the prostitutes are excessively skinny, and their tight clothing does little for them. Their faces have a gaunt look that can't be hidden under any amount of makeup. But in a perverse way, the prostitutes can be classified as practically the only professionals in a Barrio of mostly laborers.

5   The break-ins aren't always at night anymore, and drug deals are no longer discreet. A new trend is to steal aluminum siding off houses to sell for scrap, and the victimized houses aren't always abandoned. The money from the sale is either for buying drugs or paying back money owed to dealers.

6   Drugs have taken their toll. J. Ortero died of a drug-related heart attack at the age of 17. This guy was everyone's friend. He had no enemies; no one didn't like him. Now he's dead.

7   Daniel Stearn was killed in a shoot-out when he and his boys sold drugs to an undercover cop. He was only 22. He had graduated from Divine Savior High School in 1984 with his whole life ahead of him. At the funeral I knew that this shouldn't be. He looked intensely alive lying there in his favorite Adidas suit. He had no reason in the world to be in that box; he should've been with his girlfriend making out or cruising with his buddies. He should have been anywhere but there. There was nothing I could say to the family and girlfriend he left behind.

8   Seeing the drug dealers walking in the streets sometimes makes me feel like getting a gun and becoming a vigilante. The cops can't do anything because the law protects the dealers, and it doesn't look as if the dealers will kill each other off very quickly in the drug war. But people in the Barrio are becoming brave. In a handful of incidents people have overrun a crack house and kicked the dealers and users out. The first was a house on Apple. The next was on France Street. It's

illegal to take the law into your own hands, but what are you supposed to do if strange and sometimes violent people are always coming to the crack house next door? The police can't or won't do anything, and your family is threatened. Some people believe that your only alternative— and admittedly it's not a great one—is to attack.

9   My street is one of the main streets in the Barrio, and the traffic flows at all times of the day. What disgusts me most is how the drug dealers cruise the streets in their loud, ugly cars. One dealer drives an '88 Mercury Cougar; it's maroon with gold trim and matching mag wheels. He had a spoiler mounted on the trunk. To top it off, he had "Pump Me Up" painted on the lower half of the doors. It is one of the ugliest cars on the road. Even the cops know he's a dealer, but he hasn't been caught yet. There's also a black Jeep Wrangler around the barrio. It has silver trim and matching mag wheels and some of the largest aircraft lights I've ever seen. The logo on his door is "Paid In Full." The back of the jeep is all speakers. These cars are meant to impress, and sadly they do. The flash of cash lures many, but those who are lured don't remember the ones who have died.

10   Two dealers, Antonio and Samuel, used to go to my school. As young children we were friends. Samuel's father had been a dealer himself but was sent to prison; then it wasn't too long before Samuel took up the business. Soon he was a semi-major dealer. In my junior year of high school, Samuel was in rehab. He was pretty straight for a while, but the last I heard he was back in the business.

11   Antonio's story is not much different. After tenth grade he dropped out to devote more time to his trade. Like his friend Samuel, Antonio was also a semi-major dealer. Antonio was shot in the head while he and a friend were making a deal with an undercover cop; miraculously, he survived the shot. Now he walks with a cane.

12   Then there are the burnouts who call the Barrio streets home. Malooby paints the most vivid picture. He fried his brain on acid about twenty years ago. Now he dresses as a Middle-Easterner from about the time of Christ. Everything from the long shaggy beard right down to the sandals looks very authentic. He roams the Barrio endlessly, looking for food in the trash. Only his unaccented English gives his nationality away.

13   And there are others. A mother and son known as "the odd couple" have been in the Barrio about as long as Malooby. They can be seen every now and then walking along Main. Every time I see them, they are wearing the same clothes. There is another family that has lived on welfare for generations. They have been in the same house on Cross Street for decades. The only legacy passed from father to son is the welfare checks. They and many like them are the ones who wander the Barrio looking for a handout, returnable bottles, or souls to save.

14   Three gilded gates of hope stand in the Barrio. They are the schools: Central and Milton, public schools, and Divine Savior, a Catholic school. Within their walls are young people who know enough about life to want something better than the Barrio. Within them are also dealers, hookers, and others with no particular plans. It's a motley crew, but a strange camaraderie exists between them. They stick up for each other because they are all they have.

15   Divine Savior and Central are predominantly Hispanic; Milton is mostly Black. The city schools are nowhere near good schools, and the schools of the archdiocese are not much better. Divine Savior is the

best in the area, which doesn't say much; the kids get an education, but the facilities are so outdated it's pitiful. Despite this, a percentage of each senior class graduates. Others go on to get their G.E.D. or enter the military. The rest can be seen somewhere on the streets of the Barrio.

16   These kids are the great hope of their parents, most of whom are Mexican, Puerto Rican, or Cuban immigrants. They have worked hard all their lives just to get *into* the Barrio. For most of them, the Barrio is far better than what they had in the old country. Still, they know there is a better place and if they can't get there, then they hope that at least their children can. They want their children to live the life they have only dreamed of. But considering the realities of the Barrio, they also hope that their offspring will simply *live*.

17   The children also have dreams. Some want families; others want to be rich; almost all want to get out of the Barrio if it's the last thing they ever do. Many of them don't think too much about the problems of the world; their biggest concern right now might be how to cover up a zit or a hickey. Others worry about finding a job or choosing a college. They have as many hopes, fears, and dreams as their parents. While some don't care about the future, others are ambitious and want to see what's out there.

18   Finally, there are illegal immigrants in the Barrio. Just how many isn't known. But they all have a common fear that doesn't discriminate against age or sex: It's called *la migra*, immigration. *La migra* is the only thing that can send them back to what they escaped from, which could be anything from poverty to certain death. Although they may not be much better off here, they definitely don't want to return to where they came from. While some are lucky in evading *la migra*, others are not. *La migra* had been looking for Anna and her family for two months; they were found recently and ordered back to Mexico. Friends of theirs are using lawyers to try to get them legalized. If that doesn't work, they will go back to Mexico and cross again into California after a while.

19   For now the Barrio will remain the same. Who knows if the situation will improve? A fight for change is going on in the mayor's office and on the streets themselves. People are starting to have the courage to improve their situation. With luck, the courage will not fade. But for now, things will be the same: The dealers will cruise the streets, loud music will blast, hookers will walk, dreamers will dream, and the unlucky will die. This is the Barrio.

Now we'll look at two drafts of a description of a place. As you read the first draft, in addition to thinking about controlling purpose and supportive concrete detail, also consider this question: What is it about the mix of information the writer wishes to convey that makes it a challenge for the writer to organize the material? What factors, including skill issues addressed in section 2, make draft B so superior to draft A?

DRAFT A   *Colombia: The Country of Beauty and Character*
Sally Barajas

1   Colombia, what does this South American country mean to the average American? Drugs, chaos, cartels, death? Colombia has much more to offer than these poor media-imposed images. It is a country

with vast natural resources and has a national character that will amaze the average American. Colombia's national character will induce the American to reconsider the past tales of this South American nation, and introduce a new perspective of the country.

2   Cartagena and San Andrés are examples of the beauty this country has to offer. These cities, with rich, deep, blue waters, unpolluted beaches and gorgeous climate, is best suited for year-round fun. The beauty of this country has been recognized by tourists worldwide. I met an American couple, in Colombia, scuba diving in the clear blue waters. They had stated that Colombia was one of the best locations they had been to scuba dive. The cities are alone, extremely gorgeous, but the exports of Colombia are better examples of the region's beauty.

3   Colombia exports many popular goods worldwide. Many believe cocaine is the country's only "export," that is clearly not true. Emeralds, praised for its finest quality, are shipped to every corner of the globe. The deep green, nearly flawless, gems have been categorized as the finest in the world. The coffee, needless to say, is the richest in the world. The wild, exotic flowers are simply breathtaking. Watching these delicate and lovely flowers being picked from a huge field, is an awe-striking sight to see. The bright colors of the flowers, the rich coffee, the precious export of gems—all simply wipes the mind of the ill image Colombia has been given. Instead of dwelling upon the tourist image, I want to focus upon the Colombian national character. What makes this group of people so interesting and diverse than those of the United States?

4   Colombia differs greatly from the United States. The people's values, customs, life-styles, music and dance, are extremely different than Americans. The strength and perseverance of the Colombian nation will force anyone to look upon the Colombian people with awe and respect.

5   Colombia has never had a problem with racism like the United States has. Distinction between races is very minimal. Here, in the U.S., when the average American speaks to another person, what does he/she notice first? They notice what color they are, whether they are African American, Hispanic, Indian, etc. In Colombia the people speak to one another without noticing their color, they only notice the persons for themselves. Actually, in Colombia, the "darker" you are the more lovely in their eyes. Therefore marriages between people of "darker" skin tones and "lighter" skin tones occur without hesitation. In fact these deep-rooted values have been passed on to my own family. My sister Jenny is going to marry an African American man. Our family did not even blink at this, whereas others (Americans) noticed immediately, some even criticized.

6   African influences in Colombia are most notable in the music and the dances, traditional and modern. The rhythmic and melodious beats, the shaking of the maracas, the deep beat of the drums, are all tools which are very significant and prevalent of the influences in music. The Cumbia and Mapale are two, of many dances, which blend in the influences of music and dance together. The traditional dance, the Mapale, has taken the form of African dances, these are most popular in the mountain regions. The Cumbia, which is most popular in the coastal regions, has a higher degree of musical influence than African dance elements.

7   The Colombian life-style is much more relaxed than the American life-style. Colombians take time for everything and are not as worried,

pressured, or tense as Americans. During the day, three main meals are served and eaten. Time is taken to eat and digest. During the afternoon, local shops, businesses, and schools close several hours for lunch. The food is eaten and afterwards a *siesta* or, in English, a nap or break is taken. This allows the food to digest and makes the individual less tense and rushed. (I really believe Americans need this custom in their lives, we are far too tense and rushed.) Although many may believe this is a very lazy attitude, it really is not. Hours are extended to serve business purposes and important, serious, matters are handled with the utmost sincerity.

8   There is also an aspect of Colombian life which is very humorous. The art of bargaining, or *regateando*, is a fine art which even I picked up on during my brief visits in Colombia. Believe me when I say that it is a true art; whenever you obtain something for less money, it *is* an art! It is very funny walking through a marketplace in Colombia, while all the slick transactions are made. Watching my Grandmother arguing with a young man about the price of fruit is indeed a very funny sight. The rationale here in the United States is "More money must mean it is better!" In Colombia, they do not succumb to those false ideals. Bargaining is a way of life, especially since the economy demands of it.

9   The most amazing aspect of this South American nation is the perseverance and strength of the people against the malignant drug cartels. An *extremely small* percentage of Colombia consists of the drug cartel. Colombia is a strong country that wants the drug dealers tried, convicted, and imprisoned for their hideous crimes. Even after the abductions, bombings, and murders of judges, public officials, police officers, newspaper columnists, and innocent bystanders, the people have persevered and continue to demand justice. It is impossible for the drug cartel to "buy" the Colombian people. The people realize the evil and destruction of allowing these monsters to roam freely. This is why they seek the maximum punishment for these criminals. How do you think the United States public would react to the same situation? I doubt they would have the same diligence and strength.

10   The nation and people of Colombia have been misrepresented to the American public. The country's perseverance, customs, resources, values, and life-style have all been viewed negatively. I hope a brighter, newer image of a beautiful and wonderful country has been shed upon. Colombia is a nation that should be viewed with respect and admiration. The people and the nation have earned it.

DRAFT B   *Colombia: The Country of Beauty and Character*
Sally Barajas

1   Colombia—what does this South American country mean to the average American? Drugs, chaos, cartels, death? Colombia has much more to offer than these poor media-imposed images. It is a country with vast natural resources and has a national character that would amaze the average American. Colombia's national character would induce the American to reconsider the past tales of this South American nation and adopt a new perspective on the country. I, as the daughter of an immigrant family, have witnessed the true Colombian nation and its people. I also, as an American citizen, have witnessed the false images portrayed in the U.S. media.

2   The most amazing aspect of this South American nation is the perseverance and strength of the people against the malignant drug cartels. An *extremely small* percentage of Colombia consists of the drug cartel. Colombia is a strong country that wants the drug dealers tried, convicted, and imprisoned for their hideous crimes. Even after the abductions, bombings, and murders of judges, public officials, police officers, newspaper columnists, and innocent bystanders, the people have persevered and continue to demand justice. It is impossible for the drug cartel to "buy" the Colombian people. The people realize the evil and destruction of allowing these monsters to roam freely. This is why they seek the maximum punishment for these criminals.

3   Another virtue of Colombia is that it has never had a problem with racism like the United States has. Distinction between races is very minimal. Here, in the U.S., when the average American speaks to another person, what do they notice first? They notice what color they are, whether they are African American, Hispanic, Indian, etc. In Colombia, the people speak to one another without noticing their color; they notice the persons only for themselves. Actually, in Colombia, the darker you are, the more lovely you are. Therefore marriages between people of darker skin tones and lighter skin tones occur without hesitation. In fact, these deep-rooted values have been passed on to my own family. My sister Jenny is going to marry an African American man. Our family did not even blink at this, whereas others (Americans) noticed immediately, and some even criticized.

4   The Colombian life-style and daily activities differ greatly from those of the people in the United States. Colombians are much more relaxed. They take time for everything and are not as worried, pressured, or tense as Americans. During the day, three main meals are served and eaten. Time is taken to eat and digest. During the afternoon, local shops, businesses, and schools close several hours for lunch. The food is eaten and afterwards a *siesta* or, in English, a nap or break is taken. This allows the food to digest and makes the individual less tense and rushed. (I really believe Americans need this custom in their lives. We are far too tense and rushed.) Although many may believe this reveals a very lazy attitude, it really does not. Hours are extended to serve business purposes, and important, serious matters are handled with the utmost sincerity.

5   There are also other aspects of Colombian life which are very humorous and interesting to watch. The art of bargaining, or *regate-ando*, is one. *Regateando* is a fine art which even I picked up during my brief visits in Colombia. It is very funny walking through a market-place in Colombia while all the slick transactions are made. Watching my grandmother arguing with a young man about the price of fruit is indeed a very funny sight. I could not believe it when I watched her starting to argue with the grocer. Imagine a tiny old woman nagging a young man to lower the price. Before I knew it, she had struck a deal with him for half the original price. I was completely shocked—she actually did it! Soon I was doing it too—just like a native Colombian. Now believe me when I say that it is a true art: Whenever you obtain something for less money, it *is* an art! The idea here in the United States is "More money must mean it is better." In Colombia, they do not succumb to that false idea. Bargaining is a way of life, especially since the economy demands it.

6   The people of Colombia celebrate and express their feelings through dance and fiestas or parties. The people dance with so much emotion and endurance that on my trips I have soon grown tired just watching them. The rhythmic beat of the drums and the constant shaking of the maracas hypnotize the people into an instant dance mood. It is so much fun just watching them; it is even better participating in the dances yourself!

7   Just as the beauty of Colombia is represented through the life-style of the people, the country itself sparkles with beauty. The cities of Cartagena and San Andrés are examples of the beauty this country has to offer. These cities, with unpolluted brown sandy beaches and rich deep blue waters, are best suited for year-round fun. The climate of the region is not excessively hot; it is moderate and one can walk comfortably throughout the city. The cities are extremely gorgeous. White Spanish villas rest near the beaches; from the villas one can watch fuchsia sunsets on the ocean and feel the gentle evening summer's breeze coming in across the water. A walk on the cobblestone streets and among the Spanish castle ruins is the perfect ending to a romantic dinner at one of the wonderful restaurants by the ocean. Watching the fishermen reel in the evening's catch, knowing that it will become your dinner, is very exciting.

8   The vending of exotic fruit in brilliant colors of bright pink, deep green, and golden yellow can be seen on every street corner in the cities, but the exports of Colombia are even better examples of the region's beauty. Colombia exports many popular goods worldwide. Emeralds, praised for their finest quality, are shipped to every corner of the globe. The deep green, nearly flawless gems have been called the finest in the world. The coffee, needless to say, is the richest in the world. The wild, exotic flowers are simply breathtaking. Watching these delicate and lovely flowers being picked from a huge field is an awe-inspiring sight. The subtle peach and orange tones are rare and precious in orchids, but they seem to come to life more in their dramatic pinks, reds, yellows, and other colors I didn't even know existed. The most exciting aspect of being in the fields is watching the hard-working men and women carry huge racks of flowers on their backs. Their bodies are encompassed with the flowers: The workers and the flowers seem to become one.

9   Colombia has been misrepresented to the American public. The country's perseverance, customs, resources, values, and life-style are unknown or viewed negatively. In reality, Colombia is a beautiful, wonderful country, a nation that should be viewed with respect and admiration. The people and the nation have earned it.

Exercises for Descriptions of People and Places

The best topic ideas for describing people and places will come mostly from you, because you are the one who knows who you know, who and what intrigues you, where you've been, and where you'd like to go. But the next two exercises provide some suggestions to help you in your search. After you settle on a topic, start with freewriting and move through all the stages of the writing process.

People

Choose from among the following topic ideas for describing people, or think of your own idea. Some of these possible topics are realistic, while others are oriented more toward fantasy and fiction.

1. A major influence on you—a parent, grandparent, or teacher, for instance.
2. A person who defies stereotypes about the group to which she or he belongs—such as a single parent, a pro wrestler, a three-times-a-week bowler, an accountant, a radical feminist, an only child.
3. A person you thought you knew well until something happened that allowed you to see that person in a deeper, richer way.
4. A person you know who—because of the person's boundless energy, lack of emotion, or for another reason—makes you think of a cyborg or an android. This is somebody about whom you've wondered, "Is this person really human? Do we belong to the same species?"
5. Someone who has undergone a big change—for example, a child before and after placement in a good foster home, a grandparent or neighbor before and after the onset of Alzheimer's disease, a friend who has undergone a successful year or two of psychotherapy, or anyone who has fallen in love.
6. The person you most wanted to be like when you were in the third grade, or the person you feared most when you were in the sixth grade.
7. A relative from the distant past—for example, the first person in your family ancestry to immigrate to or be brought to America. Imagine what he or she looked like, felt, wanted, missed, and consider what it would be like if he or she could see you, a dear descendant, now.
8. A public person in his or her private life—for example, Dan Quayle talking to himself about his image, Alice Walker having coffee with a friend, Amy Tan thinking of scenes for her latest novel, or Andrew Dice Clay trying to get a date.
9. Anyone transformed into something else: For example, you sometimes hear people say, "If Larry Bird were a black player in the NBA . . ." Well, what if he were black? Or what if Madonna were a man—what would she be like? How would an older Michael Jackson be as a grandfather? What if your high school principal were president—running the United States instead of one school?
10. Your mother and father when they first knew each other.

Places

Choose from among the following topic ideas for describing places, or think of your own idea. Some of these possible topics are real places, while others are more or less fictional, imagined places.

1. A public place that has taken on a very personal meaning for you—for example, a public park; a swimming pool; a county building; a certain room in a museum; a playground; a toolshed; a small patch of grass, weeds, and wildflowers near the railroad tracks where you used to play as a kid; a place

where a parent works, such as a mother's law office, a father's bunk at the fire station.

2. A place about which your feelings have changed over time—for example, your old bedroom at home after you've been away at college for a while (it might be a den by now or a younger sibling's bedroom); a hospital you had driven by many times but had never entered until you needed the services of its emergency room; or the public library you visited first as a child and then as a student.

3. The way other people's houses struck you as distinct and complete worlds when you were a child. (I recently overheard my seven-year-old daughter Caitlin asking her friend Martina, "Isn't it funny how every family's house has a different smell?")

4. A scene in your home, in the street in front of your house, in the country—anywhere you happened to be—both during and after a severe headache or other illness.

5. Your apartment a few hours before special guests are to arrive and then the moment they actually do arrive; or the living room of a Yuppie couple, who are used to the childless life, before the birth of their first child and then ten or twelve months later.

6. A farmstead when it was an active, working farm and later, after it has been deserted.

7. The place where a friend or family member is buried—as seen during each of the four seasons of the year; or a place where you'd choose to be buried or have your ashes scattered.

8. The one place you'd choose if you had to be confined to a single spot for the rest of your life. Would it be the most romantic, glamorous place you can imagine? The place with the most books? With the best home entertainment system? The best fishing? The highest mountains? Toughest golf courses?

9. Typical fantasy settings shown often—with small variations—in music videos and in some advertisements (such as for beer).

10. A place that—more than any other location—reveals something essential about the character of someone you know well—for example, your father's workroom or garage, stuffed with a million and one tools, including countless duplicates; your grandmother's pantry, stocked with enough canned food to take a small town through World War III; a friend's bathroom closet, which never has more than one scrunched up tube of toothpaste and a single, half-used roll of toilet paper; your uncle's lake cottage, closed up for the winter; the bedroom (or even just the top of the dresser) of an elderly woman, never married or now widowed.

Writing Narratives

One of the best first steps toward writing strong essays of *all* types is to immerse yourself for a time in writing description and narration. Not only does this give you a chance to learn how many fascinating experiences you've had and how many complex people you've known, but it also allows you to freshen your insights, and, as stated earlier, to practice using more concrete and specific language. But perhaps the greatest step toward strong writing you can take is constantly trying to write *with* or *for* a controlling purpose. I say *with* or *for* because sometimes you have a controlling purpose in mind as you begin to write. Other times, you are unsure about your main point or the mood you want to convey, and then you are writing *for* a controlling purpose. You are struggling toward it, knowing that the process of writing—with all its various stages of prewriting, shaping, revising, and so forth—will take you there.

All your work in creating concreteness, focus, and coherence in writing that is primarily descriptive and narrative is of great value in itself, but it will also pay off enormously when you begin to write exposition and argument. Narration is simply storytelling, and as you begin to tell your stories, you will find that you have choices about your controlling purpose. For one student telling one story, the controlling purpose may grow quite naturally out of the narrated experience; but for another student telling another story, the controlling purpose may be something that needs to be imposed from outside—by some sort of an ordering mechanism.

In this part of chapter 3, we'll look at several student narratives. You'll notice that description and narration are almost inseparable. In the descriptive essays you read earlier, from time to time you saw bits of narration. Likewise, in these narratives, you'll see wonderful chunks of description. Examine the essays for clear controlling purposes and concrete and specific detail—and, of course, for whatever else comes to mind, such as sequence of information, realistic dialogue, a clever opening or ending, sentence structure or length, and basic skill issues. But most of all, enjoy.

In the first narrative, we're taken on a wild ride by a spunky twelve-year-old. Watch how Clyde's colorful and precise use of language creates the humor and authenticity of the story. Mark examples that especially appeal to you. A brief discussion follows.

My First Drive Through the Jungle
Clyde F. Turner II

1   Have you ever gone against your parents' wishes and ended up seriously regretting that you did? Of course, you have. Everyone has done something that their folks warned them about. Take me, for instance. I was considered by most to be an intelligent and responsible kind of guy. So intelligent and responsible, in fact, that I was allowed to drive at the very tender age of twelve. I wasn't using the main thoroughfares, of course—just driving up and down Rutland, the street in front of my house, with astonished friends watching me pass by. That was enough for me.

2   Predictably, there were those who were insanely jealous of me. More specifically, Peter, Alonso, and Little John—three of the roughest characters on my block. The three of them had tried many times in the past to embarrass and harass me, and my driving did not bring us any closer. The three decided to band together and make my life miserable at every opportunity.

3   Unfortunately for me, the guys happened to be the top members of the neighborhood gang I belonged to, the Black Aces. The Black Aces were made up of all of my friends and all the "in" people in the neighborhood. As the top members of the gang, Peter, Alonso, and Little John had the power to put on trial anyone they felt was threatening the Black Aces' code of honor or reputation. So, to get back at me, they held a meeting at Little John's house to officially kick me out of the gang. Needless to say, I was furious. I had done nothing wrong and was getting kicked out of the gang for no reason at all. The guys didn't even have the decency to tell me themselves! They had one of their desperate hopefuls inform me of my dismissal. The more I thought about it, the angrier I became. From that point on, I began making mistake after mistake.

4   At home, I sat on my bed wondering what I could do to get back at the three top dogs of the gang. I remember my mind racing, searching for the perfect payback, propelled by that deadly force known as revenge. Then a thought hit me. What made these guys want to get rid of me in the first place? The fact that I drove my father's stick-shift car, of course! So, to get back at them, I thought, why don't I just take driving one step further and take the car out on the road? Have the radio up loud and really show them up. "Yeah," I said to myself, "that's what I'll do."

5   I jumped off the bed and went to work setting my plan into motion. I learned from my younger brothers that my mother and father would be gone for dinner the next night. That whole night I carefully planned everything from what time I would leave (so my brothers wouldn't know) to the direction I'd be traveling. I even planned what song I'd play as I roared past my enemies in one silver streak. As I slept that night, all I could dream about was how their faces would look when they saw me pass, playing my favorite song, "Beat Box" by The Art of Noise, on full blast.

6   I was taking an extreme risk. The car was only three months old and, as I mentioned earlier, I had driven it only up and down my street. And I haven't mentioned what type of parents I have. Although not excessively strict, they are firm believers in the practice of spanking their kids for disobedience. My father had told me many times never to drive without his permission, especially not his brand new silver LeCar. If he found out about this, I would probably not be able to sit down for a week without feeling remorse for my wrongdoing.

7   Finally night came, and I quickly headed out to begin my adventure. Quietly I sneaked out of the house and got into the car. Without turning on the engine, I shifted the car into neutral and felt it begin to slide slowly down our inclined driveway. Once out in the street, I turned on the headlights and the engine and headed for the main street, known in those parts as Grand River.

8   Slowly, with the seat almost all the way back, I cruised down Rutland, looking for any observers to honk at. A feeling of complete control was in my grasp as I approached the corner of Grand River. With the ease of a smooth criminal, I slipped in my cassette and calmly shifted into second. All done in one breath. Confidence was mine.

9   Until I came to a screeching halt at the corner.

10   On Grand River, between the hours of 4:00 and 6:30 P.M., the center lane normally used for making left turns becomes another lane—for rush hour traffic. Many people who live near the street know that

during rush hour, Grand River is transformed into a virtual autobahn of tired workers in a rush to get home—many people, that is, except me. I had never driven on a main street before and had no idea that anybody would ever go 55 m.p.h. on a 35 m.p.h. street.

11   Cars of all shapes, sizes, makes, and models whizzed by at incredible speeds, merging into a flurry of blue, gray, and red streaks that could not be crossed or interrupted. I felt a stab of fear, and panic followed fast. My mind warned me to turn the car around and go home, but my pride wouldn't let me.

12   After what seemed like hours, the traffic finally slowed to a complete stop. The jungle was at rest! I was momentarily saved by a red light. Quickly I made a right turn and tried to flee from the crouching mechanical beasts behind me. As I sped down the street, my mind was in a whirlwind, wondering what to do. Again I heard a voice telling me to go home, but I ignored it, somewhat shaken but still blinded by revenge.

13   I was on my way to the car wash where the Black Aces usually hung out. I looked further up the street and saw the guys talking and breakdancing on the corner near the car wash. The only thing on my mind was to see their faces as I cruised by them. I regained my cool demeanor and turned up the radio a bit more. An enormous smile spread across my face while the whole gang, including Peter, Alonso, and Little John, watched with burning jealousy as I slowly drove by with one hand on the wheel. I had done it! Or I thought I had.

14   Suddenly I heard a loud horn. I looked to my left and saw in my side-view mirror a blazing white Lincoln going way too fast! My only reaction was to turn sharply to the right. If I had made that turn a half-second sooner, I'm sure that Lincoln Continental wouldn't have scraped the side of my father's car. Tires screeching, it careened onto the corner, parting the members of the Black Aces like scared fish. In those few seconds I experienced a combination of fear, horror, and terror that no man should ever have to face.

15   I pushed on the brakes with all the force a terrified twelve-year-old could give. My father's three-month-old, now tarnished silver LeCar slid off the grass onto the residential street and stopped, throwing me against the steering wheel.

16   Finally at rest, I waited a moment to think about what I had just done and what was going to happen to me. I looked down the street for the Lincoln that had hit me. All I could see was the back of the car, now speeding even faster, and disappearing down Grand River. I turned the engine back on and shifted into first. If only I had listened to my conscience! I slowly creeped further up the street, mostly to spare myself the embarrassment of the gang watching me check my car for injuries. Once safely away from the scene, I stopped to check the damages. Unbelievably, the Lincoln had left only a long scratch along the back near the bumper.

17   I got in the car and quietly drove home. It was a miracle that my father didn't even notice the blemish until a week later. But, as expected, I got one of the whippings of my life and was pulled from driving for a month. As for the Black Aces, I tried my best to avoid them so I wouldn't be reminded of the incident. Unfortunately, some of my friends still belonged to the gang, and they did their best to remember it for me and will not hesitate to this day to tell my story to anyone who may or may not care to listen. Looking back on that incident, I realize

that my moment of revenge was not worth all of the anxiety and terror I felt, not to mention the whipping I received, and since that day I've always listened to my conscience and never sought revenge—at least not in somebody else's car.

Discussion

In paragraph 8, Clyde writes that he slipped a cassette into the car's tape player "With the ease of a smooth criminal." In an earlier draft he had written that he performed this action "With the grace of a swan." Why is his revision such a good one? What other uses of concrete language and bits of imagery fit so well with the voice of a twelve-year-old poised on the dividing line between boyhood and manhood, determined to impress his friends but fearful of his father's wrath?

While "My First Drive Through the Jungle" focuses mostly on one day, the next narrative begins with the events of one day and then fans out to include events both before and after. With his excellent detail, the writer helps bring us into his narrative in a powerful way. One technique he uses is called the "bookend effect" in which something about the first and last paragraphs matches; together, the introduction and conclusion have the effect of a pair of bookends. This is also called "closing the circle"—coming back at the end of the work, however briefly, to some point, word, or bit of imagery from the beginning. How does Junaur accomplish this?

Ever Dearest Gardener
Junaur Alojipan

1   The icy days of winter are fast approaching. Every green plant and garden will soon be covered with a glistening coat of freezing ice and snow. The lush green vegetation will wither away and leave the gardens—once alive with sparkling colored vegetables—as barren as an Alaskan tundra. Gardens, especially at the end of the season, always remind me of my dad and that day in December two years ago.

2   It was three days before Christmas; everything was going great. The house was decorated with all the usual Christmas ornaments. The tree was trimmed with rainbow-colored lights, sparkling streamers, and all the cards we had received from as close as Royal Oak and as far away as Manila, Philippines. And that familiar aroma was in the air—the aroma of the traditional foods the Alojipan family always enjoyed this time of the year: cooked pancit (noodles with meat and mixed vegetables), steamed rice, oven-roasted pork, and fresh baked bibinka (a sticky Filipino cake). This was going to be a great Christmas.

3   I had just come home from a wrestling meet; the Redskins varsity team had won. I was in a great mood; this victory just added the icing to my Christmas holiday. Everything was perfect. I was singing and cheering as I came into the house. I called my mom to tell her my good news, and she walked out from her room to meet me. As I was about to tell her we had won, I noticed something wrong, something different about her. She was usually very worried that I would get hurt during one of my meets. This time, however, she didn't ask me any of her usual questions: How did your day go? How was your meet? Did you win? Did

you get hurt? Are you tired? Her eyes were red and puffy as if she had been rubbing them for hours. Instantly it struck me that something must have happened to my dad. He had been sick off and on for two years. He had been in and out of the hospital during this time. Now he was in the hospital because something was wrong with his kidney treatment. The doctor had told Mom and me that Dad would be out by Christmas. But before I could ask her anything, she said, "Papa died this morning." Those four words hit me hard, like a sledgehammer slamming my chest full force. For a brief instant I hoped that my mother had said something else or that she was wrong. She wasn't. But the reality did not sink in until later when I saw my relatives entering the house crying. Papa was dead; he wasn't coming back.

4   The next three hours were mass confusion. Relatives poured into the house to give their condolences. The house was filled with the cries of my mother and my aunts. Their cries sounded like the sirens during a tornado drill. I cried too—almost all night. I spent all that night comforting my mother, trying to ease her pain.

5   Christmas, usually a happy time of giving and loving one's family, changed suddenly from a joyous and happy occasion to a bleak and dismal wake. My uncle tried to ease our pain by giving the traditional family Christmas party, but it failed. It was strange and terrible to see my uncle trying to cheer everyone up and my mom in the corner of the room crying. My dad wasn't there anymore sharing the festivities with us. There was an empty feeling as if someone had ripped a hole in our hearts, and the hole could not be filled.

6   From that time on, I was expected to "fill my dad's shoes." Many of his responsibilities fell on me, a burden I often thought I was very unprepared for and unable to handle. All the things that he had done and I had taken for granted, I now had to do. This included going shopping, cooking our meals, and fixing whatever was not working around the house. I now had to learn to do these things. I was fortunate that my uncle taught me how to do certain things like change light switches. I found a job at school in the audio-visual department so I would be less of a burden to my mom financially. I had to reduce the time I spent with my friends. I couldn't go to as many football and basketball games because of my new responsibilities. Trying to fill my dad's shoes at a young age was a difficult and many times not a pleasurable task.

7   The garden in our backyard is not what it was when my dad was alive. With Mom working all the time and me away at college, it is pretty much neglected. When he was alive, the tomatoes seemed to be bright crimson jewels growing out of stems. But now there is only a single solitary tomato plant in our garden. I wonder what he would say if he were here today to see what has happened. He would probably lose his temper as he often did, go to the garage, take out his gardening tools, and get to work.

8   I miss Papa. I miss the way we used to argue about trivial things such as which gas station to go to, what type of gas to get (he would always get the cheapest kind anyway), or who should drive to the grocery store. I miss going to the Tigers games with him. I wish that he would have been there for my high school graduation.

9   I didn't realize how much I would miss him. Most of all, I miss seeing him working in his vegetable garden and seeing his lush green leaves and the bright yellow-orange flowers of his squash plants. Much like a plant needs a gardener to nurture it, my mom and I needed the

support and nurturing of my dad. He tried to teach me, but I was never interested in gardening when he was alive. Now I wish I had listened and tried. But ever dearest gardener, someday I will.

Our third narrative is an excellent one of a slightly different kind. The writer tells a series of small, compelling anecdotes which together communicate her experience of growing up.

Why do Molly's individual stories have such power for most readers? What concrete details help you enter the world of her childhood?

Does her sequence of information persuade you to see things as she saw them? Are you more apt to see things her way at the end than at the beginning?

Why is her conclusion—in spite of its brevity—so satisfying?

Becoming Asian American
Molly Jung Bidol

1   It began in Korea when I was three years old and a passerby found me, along with my four-and-a-half-year-old brother, Jon, crying in Taejon Railroad Station. Not knowing what to do for us, the passerby referred us to Chungboo Office, which was similar to an American police station. No one claimed us, so we were sent to an orphanage and put up for adoption. A few months later, a white couple in America adopted us. On 18 September 1974, Jon and I arrived at Chicago's O'Hare Airport to begin a new life. Thus, as a young child, I was suddenly and almost completely transplanted into another culture.

2   Growing up was hard for me. I think that where I grew up played a significant role in this. I was raised in a conservative, predominantly white middle-class Midwestern town. Being Korean, I felt self-conscious and alienated in this small, sometimes insensitive, and often unaccepting community.

3   My parents knew that our initial transition into American life would be difficult. But they thought that once we became accustomed to the culture and the language, we would be okay. They believed in a color-blind society. To them it didn't matter that we were Korean, and they didn't think it should matter to anyone else either. But we do not live in an ideal society, and race, color, and ethnicity do matter.

4   From a very young age, I was made to feel as if I didn't belong. Once at a playground, for instance, some kids came up to me and started taunting, "Chinese, Japanese, dirty knees, look at these." On *Chinese*, they pulled the corners of their eyes up. On *Japanese*, they pulled the corners of their eyes down. On *dirty knees*, they pointed to their knees. And on *look at these*, they pointed to their chests. I didn't know what the taunt meant; I just knew that they were making fun of me because I was Korean. But I didn't understand why. Yet it made me feel ashamed and insecure about myself.

5   My life as a Korean adoptee was filled with questions and doubts about who I was. Deep down inside, I always knew that I was different or at least looked different. But I didn't want to be different. Sometimes I would look into the mirror and pull my upper and lower eyelids open with my fingers to try to make my eyes look wider. I also tried to make my nose pointier by pushing it up. I was always disappointed when I couldn't figure out how to get these changes to stay.

6   My physical appearance wasn't the only thing I wanted to change. I wanted to change my name, too. In elementary school, kids always wanted to know everybody else's middle name. Why this was so important I don't know. I guess kids are just funny like that. Anyway, I never wanted to tell people what my middle name was. I hated it so much that sometimes I would lie and pretend that I didn't have one, and other times I would just say that it started with the letter "J" and let them guess. Of course, I knew that they would never get it because it was my Korean name. One time I convinced everyone that it was Jane. That didn't last long though; I'm not a very good liar. Somehow the truth always manages to get out. Finally I became worn down and exasperated with their questions, and I just told them. "Jung," I said, "that's my middle name." I said it quietly and kind of mumbled over it, partly because I was ashamed of it and partly because I wasn't really sure how to pronounce it since I didn't know anybody who spoke Korean. I thought it was an ugly sounding name; apparently they thought so, too. They looked at me with disturbed faces and exclaimed, "What?" as if this strange foreign word had hurt their ears. However, they made me repeat it five times to make sure they got it, and then they started saying it back to me. I hated hearing it aloud, and it never sounded right when they said it, either; I always tried to correct them. Why couldn't I just have a nice "American" middle name like everybody else?

7   Sometimes I deluded myself and pretended that I was white. It was at these times that I totally avoided looking into mirrors; then I could deny that I was Asian. Occasionally, friends would make that denial easier for me. One friend and I used to joke that I was more "American" than most Americans. I could eat more hot dogs than all of my friends. I was really proud of that. To me it proved that someone had finally noticed the hard work I had put into trying to be "American." Even though I was Korean on the outside, I was definitely "American" on the inside. I wanted to believe that so much that sometimes it was a shock to me when I looked into the mirror and saw that I wasn't white—I was Korean.

8   When I was about twelve, I had a friend, Jennifer, whose younger sister, Sara, was also an adoptee from Korea. Sara, who was about five years younger than I, used to follow me around when I was at Jennifer's house and say how cool it was that we both liked the same things and that we were both Korean. I remember her saying, "You like pickles? Well, I like pickles, too," as if the fact that we both liked pickles intrinsically bonded us. Her comments made me very uncomfortable. My friend and I laughed them off as if they were silly things to say. I didn't want to be reminded that I was Korean and that I was different. Sara's identification with me was something I couldn't handle. Years later, I still feel guilt because she needed someone, as I had, to show her that it was okay to be Korean. I wasn't at ease about being Korean, so I wasn't comfortable with anyone who looked up to me because I was.

9   It's been seventeen years since my transplantation, and I am now able, in my third year of college, to celebrate being Asian American. It was with the help of my Asian American friends that I have come to understand and conquer my own internalized racism. And now I take pleasure in knowing a seven-year-old Asian American girl who tells her mother, a professor of mine, that when she grows up, she wants to be like me.

The next story is a fascinating and subtle narrative exploration of American and Indian identity. Interweaving dialogue with small bits of narration and description, the writer takes us with him on a train headed from Calcutta to Bombay where, in the second-class compartment, he discovers a small society, a temporary world of its own. A glossary follows the narrative. See discussion questions at the end.

Storytrain
Shyam Maskai

1   "This man is also going to Bombay. He said that he would help you out. And don't worry, I travel second class all the time—it's fun." I watched as my friend's uncle stepped off the train and back onto the platform, after asking for the tenth time if I had enough money for the trip.

2   "Hi, my name's Gotham. So this is your first time riding a train in India?"

3   "No, I've traveled on trains here before but never in second class. My name's Shyam."

4   "So you live in the States?"

5   Nobody had told him; it was obvious that I did. He asked me where my family was from. "My extended family lives in Bombay, but I live with my mother, father, and sister in Michigan."

6   "Where?"

7   "Detroit."

8   "Oh yes, Debt-troit. Are you Gujarati?"

9   "No, Cutchi Lohana."

10   "Oh, you're Lohana, so am I."

11   I looked at the three men who sat facing me on a long bench three feet away, a bench which at night would convert into two beds. The bottom of the back lifted out and then was hung from the ceiling by two chains. There was a third bed on top. The train started, and we jerked back and forth as if we were on strings pulled by a drunken puppeteer.

12   I looked through the window. It was covered by a grill that was completely rusted, and pieces were chipping off. Through the lines of rusted steel I could see the train pull out of the station. Out of the corner of the window I could see bunches of people filling and spilling off the platform waiting for other trains. Most of those people were not actually going anywhere, but every person who was traveling had a contingent to see him off.

13   "Shyam, would you like some food?"

14   "No thanks, Rajeesh." Three other people were going from Calcutta to Bombay, in addition to Gotham and me, and they were all eating homemade food that one had brought for the trip.

15   "It's really good—my wife made it. Just have a little."

16   I shook my head. The ticket collector came by, and we discovered that four people had the same seating assignment.

17   "Don't worry," Gotham reassured me, "this happens all the time; the ticket wallah will sort it out." And he did, in a few short seconds. I looked out the window; a monsoon rain had begun. Scattered streetlights lit endless sheets of rain. The water pounded the train, and pools and rivulets formed on the ground outside.

18   A man put a cup of dhai above me on the bunk. Plop, the white dripped down my yellow t-shirt, blue jeans, and Birkenstocks. He was "very, very sorry" and cleaned everything up. Rajeesh gave me a towel. *The Hitchhiker's Guide to the Galaxy* recommends that you shouldn't go anywhere without a towel. For some reason I always forget.

19   I decided it was time for bed. I climbed to the top bunk and lay down. On my right was the same type of grill that I had seen on the window. It separated me from the guy sleeping on the bunk in the next compartment. All I could see was his back. On my left was a fan, covered by another rusty grill. I couldn't imagine what it'd be like turning it on—that stuff would fly everywhere.

20   "Shyam, come down, I've saved a seat for you." I looked down, and morning light had filled the train. The bench was full, except where Gotham had set some newspapers. The train stopped as I climbed down. Suresh, another of the Bombay travelers, took everyone's water bottles from the wall and stepped out onto the platform to fill them up. He appeared in the window; lines of rust crossed his face. "Anyone want some chai?" After he took the order, Suresh disappeared in the crowd, pushing and being pushed.

21   The aisle of the train was filled with people surging through. Hawkers moved among them, their voices bobbing above all the other noise in the train. "Dhai Warah, Dhai Warah, Dhai Warah." A boy who looked two years younger than I balanced food on his head. Samir, the fourth man going to Bombay, stopped him and bought food for us. Behind him, people got on and off, climbed up and down. Then I caught sight of a man much older than I, dragging himself along by his arms. He was begging for money, which many people gave him, including me. People flowed around him as he made his painful, slow way down the aisle.

22   Rajeesh ate some bhath and turned to me. "Shyam, I have something to ask you. Why do you have your hair like that—is that the style in the States? And the earring?"

23   I started my automatic defensive response that I had formulated back home, but Gotham cut in. "You know, before the English came, many Indians had long hair and earrings." I had known about the earrings—people kept their wealth in jewelry so it would be safe on their body—but I hadn't known about the hair. I was excited because now I had another argument for my grandfather and my family. I looked more Indian than they did.

24   Rajeesh continued to press the point. "But that was then, and this is now. We must live in today's world."

25   Gotham pointed to Rajeesh's dhoti, which is a style my grandfather also wears. "That's hundreds of years old. Why do you keep wearing that?" One whole side of the train started to laugh. I didn't know all those people were listening.

26   At the next stop, the aisles filled up and people rushed through again. Just before the train left the station, a man in a saffron robe got on, obviously some kind of sadhu. He had a beard and hair that spilled over his shoulders and onto his chest. He took out a tambourine and started to beat a rhythm, and then in a high-pitched voice, started singing. His whole body shook. Our side stopped and watched him. Out of the corner of my eye, I could see a couple of legs keeping time.

27   "What's he saying, Gotham?"

28   "He's singing songs about Krishna."

29   When the music stopped, I walked to the end of the compartment. The door was open and the land rushed by, but I could see only a doorway's worth. Holding onto the side rails, I leaned into the outside. The air blew right through me. (I learned this trick from dogs—they always stick their heads out of car windows. I do it when my friends are driving; it's too hard when I'm at the wheel.) I saw a farm pass by and women hunched over, dressed in blue, red, and yellow saris. A row of trees, like palms except much taller, swayed back and forth at the edge of the field. Later I found that the coconut-like shell of the fruit of this tree has four compartments inside, each one bearing a sweet morsel.

GLOSSARY

bhath	rice
chai	tea
Cutchi Lohana	an Indian ethnic group
dhai	homemade yogurt
Dhai Warah	Indian junk food
dhoti	a strip of cloth, usually white, wrapped around the waist and thighs (Mahatma Gandhi is often pictured dressed this way.)
Gujarati	an Indian ethnic group
Krishna	a Hindu deity
sadhu	religious leader
wallah	the person in charge of something; one who performs a specific duty or provides a service

Discussion

How does Shyam juxtapose the American elements of his identify with the Indian ones? What concrete details characterize him as American? As Indian?

What does he include to allow us, the readers, to share his experience and help us feel we are there in some sense, each of us an American in India, too?

How does he quickly characterize his friend's uncle and each of the Bombay travelers?

When you see the word *compartments* in the last sentence, describing the tree's fruit, do you recall its earlier use? What might Shyam be suggesting by using this word? What is significant about the fact that the fruit contains *four* compartments? And does their sweetness relate to anything else that Shyam may have found unexpectedly sweet on this journey?

Finally, let's look at two narratives in their before and after drafts. Mark the strengths and weaknesses in both of Becky's drafts, and then see the discussion at the end.

DRAFT A   *Great-Grandma*
Becky Gastman

1   "I finished my homework, Mom," I triumphantly shouted.
2   "That's great, Becky," Mom called from upstairs where she was finishing putting away the laundry. "Get your shoes on, and we'll go to Elias Brothers for dinner."

3   I was looking forward to a weekend filled with fun and excitement. With my older brother away at his friend's for the weekend, I was going to spend my time eating out with my mom, listening to my pop music tapes, and watching my favorite cartoons. My girlfriend, Julie, invited me to her sixteenth birthday party on Saturday night. All in all, life could not have seemed brighter.

4   While my mother was turning on lights and closing drapes, I was standing in front of the mirror putting the finishing touches on my hair. Suddenly the phone rang. My mother screamed that she had it, so I continued to brush the knots out of my long, curly hair.

5   After a while, Mom came rushing down the stairs. She was weeping so hard that she couldn't even talk. She motioned me to follow her, so I obediently placed my brush down and went into her room. I wondered anxiously what terrifying news that phone call brought. I could see my mother struggling to regain her composure. Finally, after taking some deep breaths, she began to speak.

6   "Becky," she whispered my name in a voice as strained as a rubber band impending to snap.

7   "What's wrong, Mom? Who called? What happened?"

8   Then, in words that rushed out faster than water gushing from a faucet, she said, "It was Grandma from Pittsburgh. Great-Grandma Doe is in the hospital. She's dying. The doctors say she has only 24–36 hours to live."

9   I was stunned. Great-Grandma couldn't be dying. She was a vibrant, independent woman. She was the one who easily walked up the two flights of stairs to her apartment while the rest of us had to stop to catch our breath. She was the one who stuffed the turkey for Thanksgiving and did the crossword puzzles with no mistakes. She could even solve all the puzzles on "Wheel of Fortune" before the answers were shown. Great-Grandma couldn't be dying. A sense of unreality settled over me.

10   I remember vividly the next few hours were like hell for me. My mother threw herself in a frenzy of phone-calling while I haphazardly packed my suitcase. It was arranged that I would sleep at Julie's house for the weekend and then I would go to my dad's for as long as my mother would be gone. For breakfast I ate a bowl of my favorite cereal, which was Frosted Flakes, but for some reason it lost its palatable sweet taste that I always remembered. While gazing endlessly at the missing child notice on the milk carton, I suddenly felt so frightened and confused. I pictured my own face in that photo, knowing well the fear of losing people who are loved. Flashbacks to my early childhood were racing in and out of my mind like a train moving at full speed. The weight of my pain felt like massive rocks pressed upon my weak shoulders. All this, and I was only a young woman of sixteen.

11   I was suddenly startled by Mother's familiar voice. She made her reservation to fly to Pittsburgh early the next morning. After two hours of preparation, Mom finally drove me to Julie's house. Her hands were white from so tightly grasping the steering wheel, and her whole body was unnaturally stiff. I kept praying we wouldn't have an accident.

12   "I'm sorry." Those were the consoling words with which my girlfriend greeted me.

13   "It's okay," I mumbled, although deep down inside of me I knew it wasn't.

14   My mom held me tightly, kissed me goodbye, and left. For a while, I just sat in my friend's room thinking about everything and nothing at all.

15   Saturday was such a draining day, it felt like a week. We went to see *Pretty in Pink,* a John Hughes film. I thought it would take my mind off things, but I couldn't even get a smirk on my face during the funny parts of the movie. Images of Great-Gram kept appearing on the screen.

16   When we returned back to Julie's house, I couldn't help myself from glaring at the telephone. Since that Friday night, the shrilling sound of the phone ringing became my worst enemy. I dreaded that one call I was expecting from my mother.

17   That moment came much sooner than I imagined. "It's for you," Julie's dad said. My mouth felt dry as cotton. Blood rushed straight to my face and filled my cheeks, feeling a good cry was coming.

18   "What do you mean, it's over?" I asked with a shaky voice.

19   "Great-Grandma died a peaceful death this morning. She couldn't respond, but I know she heard me telling her how much we all loved her."

20   I hung up the receiver. Slowly the tears began to stream down as I remembered all the precious times I had visited Great-Gram in Pittsburgh. I pictured sleeping at her apartment, lying next to her watching TV, and sharing a huge bowl of peanut butter ice cream with nuts on top. I could hear her telling me how beautiful and special I was. I felt so warm and secure when she held me in her gentle arms. I cried, not being able to understand that I would never see her again.

21   She was my cherished great-grandmother. She was a strong woman of valor. I'll remember her for her generosity, kindness, and vibrant personality. I'll always hold a special place in my heart for her, and she will forever be in my memory.

DRAFT B   *Great-Grandma*
Becky Gastman

1   "I finished my homework, Mom," I shouted triumphantly.

2   "That's great, Becky," Mom called from upstairs where she was putting away the laundry. "Get your shoes on, and we'll go to Elias Brothers for dinner."

3   With my brother away, I was looking forward to a weekend of fun and excitement. I was going to spend most of my time with my mom: eating dinner out, window shopping at the Orchard Lake Mall, and watching rented movies on the VCR. My girlfriend Julie had invited me to her sixteenth birthday party on Saturday night. Life could not have seemed brighter.

4   While my mother turned on lights and closed drapes, I stood in front of the mirror putting the finishing touches on my long, curly hair. Suddenly the phone rang. My mother yelled that she had it, so I continued to brush out the knots.

5   After a while, Mom came rushing down the stairs, weeping so hard that she couldn't speak. She motioned for me to follow her, so I put down the brush and went into her room. I wondered anxiously what terrifying news that phone call had brought. My mother struggled to gain her composure, and after some deep breaths she began to speak.

6   Her words came gushing out: "That was Grandma from Pitts-

burgh. Great-Grandma Doe is in the hospital. She's dying, Becky. The doctors say she has only twenty-four to thirty-six hours to live."

7   I was stunned. Great-Grandma couldn't be dying: She was my greatest role model, a Jewish woman who had survived the Holocaust and then found the strength and courage to mourn six million Jews who died because of their religion. Not only did my great-grandmother lose most of her family in World War II, but she also lost her loyalty to her native country, Russia. Yet she managed to find the stamina to flee Russia, leaving behind her husband, who had already been taken away by the Nazis. Great-Gram and her two children were extremely fortunate to miss the arrival of the soldiers who took her husband; she and her little ones had been in the forest, preparing a hiding place for when times got more dangerous. When they returned home, they found their village deserted; the Nazis had cleared out all the Jews they could capture.

8   After they discovered their village empty, she and her children escaped quickly with only the clothing on their backs and a small sum of money. They returned to the forest where they stayed in hiding—living underground with other Jews—for almost a year.

9   During all the time in the forest, nobody could speak loudly or walk outside the hiding place. All they had to eat was raw potatoes, carrots, and grass. They could urinate only during the deep dark hours of the night. The most horrifying times were when they could hear bombs exploding a couple miles away. Almost every night, Great-Gram woke up in a cold sweat from the recurring nightmare that the Nazis would find her and the others. Waking in fear, she would hear the bombs.

10   Her lifelong dreams were shattered, and her future crumbled before her eyes. She would never again see her loving husband, watch her children grow up in peace in their native country, or live a long plentiful life of stability. But despite the odds against her, she had one important force to help her survive: her faith in God. After eight months of hiding underground in the forest, she found out that she and her children could escape to the United States. They received false passports, and a cattle truck took all the Jews who had been in hiding to the last boat out of Russia. Great-Gram prayed to God that she and her children would be safe. With hope in God and a lot of luck, they managed to be the last ones to get on the boat. Her children held onto her as the boat set sail. There was barely anywhere to move because the boat was crowded with thousands of strangers who were also searching for safety and a better life. The long, draining trip lasted a week but seemed endless.

11   When they arrived in the United States, they had to remain strong. Their destination was Pennsylvania, where she knew of a distant cousin. With great difficulty, they tried to leave the painful times behind. God gave them the gift to begin a new life.

12   Great-Gram never remarried, but she found joy in watching her son and daughter grow up to be successful people with families of their own. She was happy living the rest of her life in a one-bedroom apartment in Pittsburgh, making homemade quilts. I once asked her how she could still find it within herself to see the beauty in life. She answered with a saying I will never forget: "When you get to the end of your rope, don't give up. Tie a knot and hang on."

13   She hung on. In fact, Great-Gram amazed us all with her zest for life. She was the one who easily walked up two flights of stairs to her

apartment while the rest of us had to stop to catch our breath. She was the one who stuffed the turkey at Thanksgiving and did the crossword puzzles without making any mistakes. She solved all the puzzles on "Wheel of Fortune" before the answers appeared on the TV screen.

14   She had been through so much that maybe a part of me thought she would live forever, that she would cheat death again. But, of course, that couldn't be. The hours after my grandmother's phone call were like hell. My mother threw herself into a frenzy of phone-calling while I packed my suitcase haphazardly. It was arranged that I would spend the weekend at Julie's house and then go to my dad's for as long as my mother was gone.

15   The next morning while I was sitting at the kitchen table, the missing child notice on the milk carton caught my eye, and I felt frightened and confused. I pictured my own face in the photo, suddenly knowing the fear of losing a loved one. I wondered why the people we care about are the ones who have to leave. Flashbacks to my childhood raced in and out of my mind, and my youth seemed so temporary. I tried to picture what death felt like, but nothing came to my mind. I couldn't come to terms with the idea that Great-Gram was really dying.

16   My mother made her reservation to fly to Pittsburgh the next morning and drove me to Julie's house.

17   "I'm sorry," Julie said as she met me at her front door.

18   "It's okay," I mumbled, although, of course, deep down I knew it wasn't.

19   My mother held me tightly, kissed me, and left. For a while, I just sat in my friend's room, thinking about everything and nothing.

20   Saturday felt like forever. We went to see *Pretty in Pink,* a John Hughes film. I thought it would take my mind off things, but it didn't. While I watched, Molly Ringwald's face faded out from the screen, and images of Great-Gram laughing like a young girl appeared and reappeared.

21   When we returned to Julie's house, I couldn't keep my eyes from the phone. Since the night before, the shrill sound of the phone had become my worst enemy. I dreaded the call I was expecting. It came much sooner than I had imagined it would. "It's for you," Julie's dad said. My mouth felt dry as cotton, and blood seemed to rush to my face and fill my cheeks.

22   "Great-Grandma died a peaceful death this morning," my mother told me. "She couldn't respond, but I know she heard me telling her how much we all love her."

23   I hung up the receiver, and the tears streamed as I remembered the precious times we had shared when I visited Great-Gram in her apartment in Pittsburgh. I pictured myself lying next to her, watching TV and sharing a huge bowl of peanut butter ice cream with nuts on top. I could hear her telling me how beautiful and special I was. I felt so warm and secure when she held me in her gentle arms. I could see her in the pink and white sundress she loved to wear on sunny days in July.

24   She was my cherished great-grandmother—a strong woman and a woman of valor. After all the hardships she lived through, she still found peace within herself. I'll always admire her for having the strength to continue to believe in God after losing so much. When I face my own hardships in life, I'll remember Great-Gram's life and her wisdom. I'll always hold a special place for her in my heart, and she will remain forever in my memory.

Discussion

This is a fascinating set of drafts—and a good example of what makes overworked English teachers love teaching. First, you probably noticed several small skill issues that appear in draft A, most of which are resolved nicely in draft B.

But much more importantly, you can see that in the first draft Becky leaves out what is really the heart of the story and instead relies on word choices and imagery to create drama and convey her sense of admiration for her great-grandmother and her grief over the woman's death. In draft A, Becky shares plenty of interesting concrete information, but many of these details—the great-grandmother walking up two flights of stairs more easily than her younger relatives, stuffing the Thanksgiving turkey, solving puzzles in the newspaper and on TV—are not facts that can really help the reader accept a key idea that is asserted at the end of draft A: that Becky's great-grandmother was a woman of valor. The draft A details are interesting and highly visual, but they don't support the controlling idea; they don't help the reader share the writer's view. In short, they are not persuasive.

Because of the writer's uncertainty about how it would fit within the frame of the narrative (the story of the weekend Becky discovered this news), she at first omitted what might easily be called "the real story"—a heroic woman's survival during the Holocaust. But when she read the draft in class, other students wanted to know why Becky considered her great-grandmother a woman of valor. In response to that curiosity came the very satisfying additions and reworkings of draft B. Her essay became a narrative within a narrative.

Becky also deleted a number of clichés from draft A—for example, a rubber band about to snap. Making these deletions was easy for Becky once she found her true controlling purpose. Is there material still in draft B that you would encourage her to delete if she revised again?

With these changes, the rather general story of the great-grandmother's *death* in draft A became the more specific, richer, and more powerful story of her *life* in draft B—a profound transformation.

The last set of narrative drafts, written just weeks before the collapse of the Soviet Union, offers a fascinating glimpse at the excellent transformations made by a student who takes the revision process seriously. Please mark strengths and weaknesses as you see them; then see the discussion at the end.

DRAFT A   *A Hot Dog Vendor*
Michael G. Weiskopf

1   As I stepped off the plane into the cold, damp air, I was filled with a feeling of disbelief. Here I was with twenty of my classmates exiting a plane in the Soviet Union. It seemed almost unbelievable that only a few short weeks before, I had seen a show on television which made me want to travel to the Soviet Union. My mind was sent back to the night in which my desire to travel to the U.S.S.R. was realized.

2   It was a school night like any other. I was watching television with my parents, trying to convince myself to go to my room and do my homework. I decided that I would watch one more show before retiring

to my room and my books. Perhaps it was fate, or maybe it was just coincidence, but the last show I chose to watch was "Head of the Class," a sit-com which profoundly influenced me. In this episode the I.H.P. kids go to the Soviet Union to take part in an international knowledge contest. Much of the show dealt with how incredible an experience it was for all the kids in the class and how beautiful the country was. The experience of the actors on television really hit home with me, and I said to myself, I could do that and I want to do that. When I mentioned the idea to my parents not more than thirty seconds after the show had ended, they were excited as well.

3   Suddenly I was brought out of my flashback episode by the comments of one of the students behind me. His name was Jeff Pike, and he was verbally expressing the feeling of awe and amazement which we all felt. As my mind returned to the present, I realized that the group had made its way down the metal stairs of the plane and we were now walking on solid ground, foreign ground, communist ground. We were really here, standing in the country which for almost my entire lifetime had been portrayed as America's worst and most powerful enemy. I still could not believe I was here.

4   This sense of awe would be with me the whole trip, but it was quickly lessened by the necessity of going through customs and picking up my baggage. As I made my way through the airport grounds, it was very apparent that this was a different country, a country controlled by its military. As we walked across the gray pavement of the landing field, we passed many soldiers. They said nothing. They stood motionless yet intimidating. The soldiers were tall and trim, their long gray woolen overcoats were perfectly fitted, not a medallion or crease out of place. Their appearance was tidy and finished, to the point of being scary. The soldiers' faces were taut and weathered, obviously from many hours of exposure to the harsh winters in Leningrad (St. Petersburg), and they stared straight forward with no sign of emotion. This emotionless stare was one of meaning, for when I looked into these soldiers' eyes, I saw a look of power, a look which said, "I can do anything." This was the first time I had encountered a look such as this, but it surely would not be the last time. The soldiers' overall appearances were intimidating, and I felt as though I had to watch my step. I also realized why Americans feared Soviet soldiers. The feelings of awe and fear which had risen up inside of me since seeing these soldiers had also arisen in the minds and bodies of my classmates, for we all walked silently and reverently past the soldiers. It was this first encounter which gave me a strong sense of the power of the military in this country.

5   As my classmates and I toured the country, I found that after seeing one museum and one palace, you have seen them all. What I did find very interesting was how the people of this country lived. At this time the Soviet Union was two or three years into Mikhail Gorbachev's perestroika. The underground or "black market" had become a huge business, one run mostly by Soviet teens. In talking and dealing with these black marketeers, I have learned much about how people really lived in this country. These teens dressed in Western styles and spoke exceptional English. They all wanted our Western clothes, music, and especially our views. These people wanted to know anything and everything about American life and American life-styles. They were very modern in their thinking, and they wanted to have better lives than their parents and grandparents. All the traders were exuberant

and energetic, ready to take on the world and change their lives. The marketeers believed that trading on the black market was their road to a better life.

6   The other people whom I encountered here were of different generations than the marketeers. They had lived most of their lives under the repressive governments of hard-line communist party leaders. These other generations of people comprised a majority of the people I encountered in the streets. These people dressed in plain, drab clothes. The streets were crammed with people walking to shops or to jobs. An overview of the busy streets of Moscow showed huge crowds of people dressed in long skirts, loose-fitting pants, and untailored shirts and blouses. The clothing was all either black, brown, green, or some off-shade of the above. The people were packed into the streets like bees in a hive. At many shops along the streets, there would be long lines, sometimes two or three blocks long. Here, short stout women wearing babushkas and carrying bags of household or personal goods would stand in line for hours to buy food from government-owned stores. All these people who stood in line and walked the streets everyday had a look about them. Their faces were worn, and their motions were slow and without any feeling. Unlike their children or their grandchildren, these people seemed to have long ago given up on the idea of changing the world. They seemed content to survive the way things were.

7   After meeting and talking to both generations of people and watching them go about their daily business for a while, I began to think about *us* and *them,* the U.S. and the U.S.S.R. One day as I walked down a side street talking with both my trip leader and the group's tour guide, something simple yet incredible happened. I bought a hot dog from a street vendor and as I watched the man behind the cart prepare my hot dog, I thought about the hot dogs I bought outside of Tiger Stadium before a ball game, and I realized that a hot dog vendor is a hot dog vendor, regardless of where he lives or works, or what political ideology his government believes. In the simplest terms, I realized that people are people, flesh and blood, regardless of where they are born.

8   With this realization, I suddenly felt at ease in the Soviet Union, but at the same time I felt very angry. I was angered by the fact that two governments who oppose each other in political belief would knowingly teach their people to hate the other. For Americans, the cold war painted a sick and unrealistic picture of the Soviet Union, and it did the same for Soviets' views of Americans. To hate a whole country, just because of the beliefs and actions of a government which the people did not control, was extremely ignorant. From the realization that people are just people trying to get by and survive, I also realized that all we see and hear in our world is not true, and that only I can decide for myself how things "really are."

9   My trip to the Soviet Union was one of the most eye-opening experiences of my lifetime. I can surely say that I would not be the person I am today had I not seen this country and its people.

DRAFT B   *Retitled POWER TO THE PEOPLE*
Michael G. Weiskopf

1   As I stepped off the plane into the cold, damp air, I was filled with disbelief. Here I was with twenty of my classmates exiting a plane in Leningrad, the Soviet Union. As the group made its way down the metal

stairs of the plane, I realized that we were walking on solid ground—foreign ground—communist ground. We were really here—in the country which for almost my entire lifetime had been portrayed as America's worst and most powerful enemy. I could not believe I was here.

2   This feeling of disbelief was quickly lessened by the necessity of going through customs and picking up my baggage. As I made my way through the airport grounds, it was very apparent that this was a different country, a country controlled by its military. We passed many soldiers as we walked across the gray pavement of the landing field. They said nothing. They stood motionless yet intimidating. The soldiers were tall and trim; their long gray woolen overcoats were perfectly fitted, not a medallion or crease out of place. Their faces were taut and weathered, and they stared straight forward with no sign of emotion. When I looked at these soldiers' eyes, I saw a look of power, a look that said, "I can do anything." This was the first time I encountered this look, but it surely would not be the last time. I felt as though I had to watch my step, and I realized why Americans feared Soviet soldiers. We were all intimidated by these menacing figures. We walked silently and cautiously past them. It was this first encounter that gave me a strong sense of the power of the military in the U.S.S.R.

3   Once in the terminal, we were stopped in a long hallway that had red marble floors and was completely enclosed by plain gray-framed windows that overlooked the landing strip. At the end of the corridor were four or five black booths, and in front of each one stood two Soviet Customs officials. Each of us had to go into one of these booths before we could officially enter the country. Once someone entered the booth, the door would shut. No one could see or hear what was happening inside the booths. I thought that we were going to be interrogated or strip-searched. As it turned out, all that happened to any of us was that we were frisked and swept over with a hand-held metal detector.

4   The trip was basically to be a sight-seeing tour of the country. The palaces and museums were works of art in themselves, with ornate gardens and gold-covered walls and ceilings. However, two stops along the tour left a deeper and more lasting impression on me. The first was Red Square, a square adjacent to the Kremlin wall. In this square are two of the most impressive sights in Moscow: Lenin's Tomb and the Memorial to the Unknown Soldier. Tourists and Soviet citizens alike would wait in a line four or five blocks long just to get a thirty-second look at the embalmed body of Lenin, the man who founded the Communist Party in Russia. The tomb constructed in his honor was a box of black marble. Inside the tomb it was very dark, with just enough light to illuminate his body against the black background. He rested on a white silken bed supported by four marble pillars. His body was perfectly preserved; the fresh red flowers on his chest contrasted strongly with the pasty white of his face. We were allowed only a few seconds to view the body, and then the soldiers silently hurried us out. Lenin's power was still real.

5   The Memorial to the Unknown Soldier also strongly suggested the government's awesome power. The memorial is a large bed of black marble with the Soviet flag draped over the front corner of the stone. Atop the marble base, a metal tripod houses an eternal flame. I visited this place two or three times during my stay, but it made the most powerful impression on me during my one nighttime visit. The

darkness fell like a black velvet curtain behind the monument. As the cold wind whipped through the square, the flickering orange-red flame illuminated the stone in quick bursts of light. The erratic backlighting gave the illusion of the red flag fluttering in the wind. I know I have not seen a more beautiful or more powerful display in my life. As I studied this monument, I was once again struck by the idea of power. The fire and stone, symbols of the force and beauty of nature, and the red and black, a stirring contrast of basic, elemental colors—for me, these images created another tribute to the country's great power.

6   Later we visited the Lenin Museum, an entire building dedicated to one man's life and ideas. Here I was again confronted with the look of power I had first seen in the soldiers' eyes at the airport. There were many photographs of Lenin, either giving speeches or leading parades. His eyes were dark and close together; he was partially bald, exposing a larger than average forehead that made him appear rather fierce. All together, his look said, "I can do anything." This look was more than determination; it was a look that lay somewhere between genius and insanity—it was the look of pure power.

7   But along with many pictures of Lenin, something else caught my eye. It was a sculpture that once again embodied power but this time went way beyond the kind of imposed power I had seen and felt in so many other images. It was the bronze sculpture of a factory worker. In a country where the worker is the most important part of the economy, it is not surprising that a steel worker would be immortalized in art. What moved me about this work was how it was presented: The sculpture showed a strong man at work. He wore no shirt, which exposed his perfectly defined physique. His muscles were flexing and straining as he lifted his piece of metal. This man was symbolic of the greatest power of the Soviet Union—the power of its people.

8   In 1989, all the power of this great country was controlled by the few people who ran its government. Now, almost three years later, it seems incredible how much change can occur in such a short time. With the democratic reforms taking place in the Soviet Union, it seems that the power of this country is finally being returned to its people. From the stout little women dressed in their babushkas and their drab green and brown clothes to the young, enthusiastic and very Western-ized teens who trade on the black market, like the steel worker immortalized in bronze, these people are the true possessors of power in the Soviet Union. The power of this nation is truly the strength of its people, people who have been oppressed for seven decades, yet who still have the strength to demand their rights.

Discussion

You can see that Michael's first draft was an interesting but somewhat unfocused account of his trip to the Soviet Union. Yet students were fascinated when he read it in class, and several stayed afterwards to hear more about things not included in the essay—more about the teenagers, their interests and tastes, partying and drinking in the Soviet Union, the political mood at the time of the trip, and so on. After the class, Michael had even more ways to go with his paper, not fewer. So he had some difficult decisions to make.

In draft B, you see not just a little fixing of errors here and there, but a major *reconceptualization*—which is what revision most often should be. In rethinking and narrowing his purpose, and then expanding his evidence to fulfill the new purpose, Michael moved from a fairly standard "let me tell you about my trip" approach, loosely following chronological order, to a much more sophisticated and compelling narrative piece on power in the Soviet Union. This is often the way students move from lackluster to superb narrative essays as they find a worthy controlling purpose.

Did Michael lose anything valuable in the move from draft A to draft B? You might believe that he did. But remember, there's always another paper coming up. You can't do everything at once. And as far as this paper is concerned, Michael mostly gained.

Ideas for Narrative Writing

With help from the following suggestions, choose an episode or chapter in your life as a focus for your narrative writing. The ideas listed might call to mind other possibilities that only you could think of—and of course, such ideas often are the quirkiest and the best.

1. *A triumph:* This might be when you read your first grown-up book; saved the day in a local ball game; won a contest at school; landed a good role in a play or a solo in a concert; figured out how to deal with the neighborhood bully; broke a bad habit; drew out a shy, reclusive person; outsmarted a parent.

2. *A mistake or wrongdoing:* Did you tell a lie? Take a candy bar from the corner store? Dump your baby sister out of her stroller? Cheat on a test? Overcharge for babysitting? Sneak into a movie? Discover pornography? Buy or sell a controlled substance? Betray a trust?

3. *A rite of passage:* You shaved for the first time; wore an athletic supporter for the first time; bought your first bra; had to shower in gym for the first time; had your first menstrual period; went on your first date; gave birth; breastfed your baby; drove your first car; got engaged, married, or divorced; cooked your first meal; had to place an older relative in a nursing home; attended your first funeral; survived your first day on your first job; celebrated your baptism, confirmation, bar or bat mitzvah, or other religious ceremony.

4. *The survival of a new experience—strange or funny, embarrassing or wonderful, exhilarating or devastating—but definitely instructive and life-altering:* For example, you were mistaken for a member of the opposite sex, or you found out someone you thought was a man was really a woman (or vice versa); you had to go through testing for some type of illness; you worked at a homeless shelter; you gave or refused to give money to a person on the street; you felt confident in a course yet failed the first major test, or you were scared to death but aced the first major test; you were assaulted; you had to appear in court; you met a doppelgänger (your double, someone who bears an uncanny resemblance to you); you broke someone's heart, or someone broke yours; your best Valentine's Day fantasy or your worst Halloween nightmare came true.

5. *An important adjustment:* Perhaps your family took a trip somewhere—or your parents went on a trip and left you home—and during this time you experienced a sort of growth spurt, emotionally, socially, or physically; with the birth of a sibling, you lost your only-child status in the family; you moved into a new neighborhood or school; you moved into a dorm room and were assigned to share a room with a member of a different race, religion, or sexual orientation; you lost or made a close friend; you lost a dear relative or became close to (or reconciled with) a relative with whom you had not been close before.

6. *The discovery of a new talent:* You realized you had a special gift or enthusiasm for drawing, painting, sculpting, writing, ice-skating, running, rapping, playing tight end, canoeing, backpacking in the wilderness, playing the flute, learning tae kwon do, speaking Norwegian, doing the breaststroke, working in a medical lab, learning Sign language.

7. *A revelation:* A family secret came out (somehow you learned why everybody always stops talking when Aunt Clara walks into the room); you realized why you've always feared a certain person or gravitated toward another person; you learned the real story behind the little scar on your left knee; you discovered you were adopted.

Deciding About Very Personal Topics

When you're selecting an idea for narrative writing, you should realize that it's a bad move to choose a topic if you would be reluctant to provide the details needed to make that topic come to life. If it's too personal, painful, or embarrassing, and you would not want to share it with your writing teacher or co-writers in class, avoid it. A good teacher does not want to invade your privacy, and for you to benefit from practicing narrative writing, you need to be completely free to write whatever comes to mind. You don't want to be in the situation where your teacher says, "You need to be more concrete and specific," and you reply, "But I just can't be—it's too personal." Save such topics for your journal.

Getting Started

Now begin prewriting activities on your story idea. Mull it over; record scattered thoughts, images, and questions; and, if you can, do things to take you back to the time when the episode occurred—maybe look at old photographs or listen to music from that period. If you wish, discuss the story idea with others—family members, friends, classmates, your teacher, or keep your idea to yourself if you have a hunch that sharing it might lessen its intensity. Many professional writers believe it's absolutely essential to be closemouthed about their ideas before publication, but on this point student writers and professionals seem to part company. For professionals, talking about ideas often drains the ideas of energy. But for many students, sharing ideas is empowering, probably because they find it so helpful to see potential reader interest.

Freewriting and Narration

The next step is freewriting about your idea. In this part of the process, let yourself go and write whatever comes—even if it takes you far afield from what you first imagined as the heart of the story. Try to pull out all possible images and ideas associated with the episode and put them on paper. You never know what you might use.

Concentrate on all the sensory details—the sights, sounds, tastes, smells, textures—you can recapture. Start by picturing yourself at the age you were when the episode occurred. If you were very young when it happened, estimate how tall you were then and try to picture how the world must have looked from that vantage point. Some sensory details you might remember with great certainty; others you might make up, using artistic license. Thinking of the people involved in the incident, try to recall what they might have been wearing, how their hair was styled, and where they might have been going to or coming from on a typical day back then. For example, if your mother was a key player in the story, try to remember a particular outfit she could have been wearing that day. A dress? Blue jeans and a sweatshirt? If she was wearing a sweatshirt, was there a logo or design on it? How about her shoes? Were they broken-in brown leather sandals or fresh-from-the-box white Reeboks with blue trim? Or was she wearing black patent-leather high heels with scuff marks on the back of the right heel from where her shoe met the floor under the gas pedal?

Try to think of how you talked at the time. Recall expressions that were "in" and that could lend realism to the scene. Or try to remember expressions that other characters typically said (maybe Uncle Joe always prefaced his announcements with "Here's the scoop"). What music might have been playing in the background? What sit-com might have been on the television? What was in the news? Whose face might have been looking out from the cover of a popular magazine sitting on the coffee table?

If you are describing an outdoor scene, what billboards might have been in the background—and what products were they advertising? What commercial buildings were nearby? Were their signs electric or neon? Were cars nearby? What kinds? What were people doing on the street? Were kids skateboarding or roller-blading? Or were they just hanging out?

If the episode took place on a farm, what season was it? How was the weather? Were the farmers in the fields planting, combining, or harvesting? Or was it too wet or cold to work in the fields? If the crops were in, how did they look? What animals were in view? Were they newborn? About to give birth?

Think details! See your pen and paper or your computer as a movie camera. With them and with the pictures you create, you're saying to the reader, "Let me take you there."

After Freewriting

Be prepared to exclude some things—maybe even some great things—generated during the freewriting stage. They just might not fit. Other bits you'll save and expand. You should end up working with whatever helps you communicate your controlling purpose and whatever adds visual interest or puts the reader in mind of the time and place. If you can't find a good use for things developed in the freewriting stage, let them go. Then, with a controlling purpose (or at least a desire for one) in mind, begin to shape your material, write, revise, and, finally, edit.

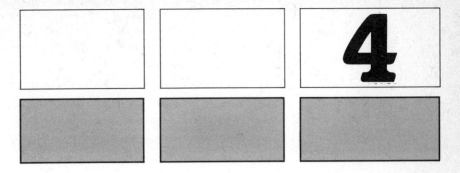

Special Concerns: Considering Diction and Addressing Audiences

In this chapter, we'll work in two areas that can make the difference between an average college writer and an outstanding one: *diction* and *audience*.

Diction

The difference between the right word and the nearly right word
is the same as that between lightning and the lightning bug.

Mark Twain

Good use of diction—a writer's choice of words—is important for all writers. We will not focus here on the plain and simple use of the "wrong" word. For example, in the statement, "The two candidates represent their perspective districts well" the writer meant "respective," not "perspective." Similarly, a student might write, "The ideal that disabled people face discrimination every day suddenly meant something new to me." The writer meant "idea," not "ideal."

If you frequently make this kind of diction error, then you need to find ways of paying more attention to language: Read more, browse in a good dictionary a few times a week, listen carefully to spoken language, and, *especially,* keep a list of the misuses that your teachers and other supporters are able to spot for you. Chances are it will be a short list, but it will contain words that are used—and therefore can be misused—often.

Clichés

You know that good writers strive to be concrete, to appeal to the senses, and, whenever possible, to avoid vague, abstract, and overly general language. And yet these worthy goals sometimes lead to a problem that's just as bad as too much abstraction and generalization, and that is using *clichés*. To say, for instance, that "a bird in the hand is worth two in the bush," or that a piece of news "hit me like a ton of bricks" might call up visual images, but most of us have heard these expressions so many times that they've lost their power. Clichés are worn-out, dead uses of language, and they really don't help us picture things.

It's not only famous sayings that become clichés. In narrative writing, for example, it's best to avoid "Tears streamed down my face," "Tears rolled down my cheeks," "I froze in my tracks," "My heart pounded wildly," "My heart almost stopped," "My mind went blank," "It was a day I'll never forget," "I learned a valuable lesson," and all other sentences that you can safely bet almost everyone in your class or writing group could also work into *their* stories. If you're considering using a phrase anyone could use—regardless of the specific tale he or she has to tell—then you can safely assume it's been used before—probably many times.

"So what if it's been used before?" you might ask. Well, a writer is not likely to hook a reader with run-of-the-mill language—words and phrases that readers have heard a thousand times. Your story was *new* when it happened—at least for you. You need to work hard to find the language that can convey that newness. It's not easy replacing sentences like "Tears streamed down my face," but it's worth the effort. If you can't come up with a fresh, concrete way to make your point, it's often better to settle for something simple: In this case, "I cried" beats "Tears streamed down my face."

Avoiding clichés is important in other types of writing, too. If your ideas and opinions are worth writing about, they are also in some way new, fresh, and alive. Again, you need to find language to carry that freshness and life. Statements such as "In today's society, we have made great progress" and "We must all learn to cooperate in this modern world of ours" are clichés that might appear in expository and argumentative writing. So are expressions of the opposite view: "There is no hope of changing anything in this oppressive society" and "Most people could not care less about these critical issues." The first two statements, in addition to being vast generalizations, express what novelist and critic John Gardner called the "Pollyanna" style—everything is sunny and terrific—while the latter two statements express the spirit of what Gardner called "disPollyanna"—the cynical attitude that says, "To hell with everything. *I* know the truth, of course, but who listens to me?" Both are basically clichéd ways of viewing the world.

Sometimes students ask, "How do you know what's a cliché and what isn't?" And this brings up an ironic point: Many of the expressions we now consider clichés were originally recognized as brilliant verbal constructions. Think of Shakespeare's "To be or not to be—that is the question" or "All's well that ends well." These lines still exemplify brilliant uses of language, of course, but by now many of us have heard them so often that they no longer hit hard (unless we hear them spoken in a first-rate theatrical performance).

So the ability to recognize clichés is a product of exposure. It has a lot to do with how much and how well you read and listen. Lack of exposure is why some adults still use certain expressions—"Give me five!" "Heavy!" "Solid!"

"Fresh!"—long after teenagers have gone on to something new. For the most part, the older folks do not hear slang often enough to realize when it's lost its power of newness. (They start to catch on when they see the pained looks on the faces of their offspring.) Of course, it's really a little more complicated than this because—as every teenager knows—the appropriation of slang by adults is one of the main reasons it loses its power and must be replaced.

The point to remember is this: **Strive for language that lives and breathes.** Clichés are dead. Let your words reveal the specialness of *you*—your life, your experience, your worries, your wisdom. This anecdote from poet Gwendolyn Brooks says it best:

> "It is the morning of our love." It seemed like a beautiful, simple way to start a love poem, but it was a mistake. I tell poets that when a line just floats into your head, don't pay attention 'cause it probably has floated into somebody else's head. Sure enough I found it in another poem. So now I don't use that and the poem begins, "In a package of minutes, there is this 'we' " which is a line I struggled over. So I don't expect to see it anywhere.

Language That Stereotypes and Insults

Other language to be avoided is the kind that stereotypes and insults. In spite of social and political gains for so many groups (and perhaps also *because* of the gains), there is still a great deal of this type of language used. In its most obvious form, it's sometimes called "hate speech," and debates rage on as to how much it should be protected under the First Amendment. But it exists in subtler forms, too, and is sometimes used unintentionally. Recognizing language that stereotypes and insults is one of the most crucial tasks of developing good diction.

Offenses ranging from the slightly irritating to the truly grievous are committed regarding gender, race, ethnicity, religion, age, sexual orientation, physical appearance, and physical or mental disability. References to "Bible-thumping Baptists," "pushy Jews," "dumb Polacks," "lazy Mexicans," "limp-wristed fairies," "beefy broads," "dried up old geezers," and "retards," for example, are simply slurs, and they are absolutely indefensible in any context.

Like clichés, this kind of language represents tired, worn-out thinking; it's also overgeneralized and inaccurate. Sometimes stereotypes and insults occur, not in overt slurs, but in less obviously offensive uses of words. A writer, for example, who unconsciously assumes that all secretaries and nurses are female and, therefore, always uses the feminine pronouns to describe people in these lines of work, is simply in error. We all know that it's also inaccurate to make automatic use of the masculine pronouns for administrators and doctors. But such stereotyping through language stills goes on, and it can be especially harmful to impressionable children, limiting their aspirations and flexibility.

Sometimes mistakes are made innocently, resulting simply from a lack of facility with the language or topic. In these cases, a dictionary, thesaurus, or other reference work, such as an encyclopedia, can help a writer find acceptable substitutes. Compare this amusing set of sentences from two drafts of the same paper:

DRAFT A

> An example of eroticism in art would be an old painting in which naked fat ladies appear.

DRAFT B

> An example of eroticism in Renaissance art is a Botticelli painting of a voluptuous, full-bodied woman.

Often, the use of insulting or stereotyping language is somewhat subtle, although it is usually quite apparent to the targeted group. Newspaper stories, for example, sometimes use verbs with negative or childlike connotations to introduce quotes by women or to describe women's speech: for example, "She complained shrilly," "She screeched," "She whined," "She nagged," "She pouted," and "She chirped." These can be found in contexts where it is very doubtful that the writer would have made the same diction choices had the subject been male. For a man, writers more often use relatively neutral verbs, such as, "He said," "He recalled," and " He announced."

Where contentious issues are concerned, writers probably can't be perfect, but they can try to be sensitive. For example, the term *minorities* offends some readers, who would prefer the writer to use *people of color*. Likewise, some writers have strong political reasons for using *Latino* rather than *Hispanic*, while others, including some of Mexican or Puerto Rican descent, prefer using *Hispanic*.

These examples are offered as a reminder that language is emotional, political, explosive—and always fascinating. The important thing is not to let these concerns hamstring you, but simply to try to be fair in your writing, to be just, to honor the humanity of those you write about, and to treat your subjects with the same sensitivity and respect you would want for yourself. And when someone else's use of language offends you, speak up.

"Thesaurus-ese"

When writers translate their own language into words from a dictionary or thesaurus (a book of synonyms), they are guilty of using *"thesaurus-ese."* One anecdote explains "thesaurus-ese" vividly: I once had a student who wrote, "My mother's biggest dream was to be corporeally appropriate." Of course, I had no idea what it would mean to be "corporeally appropriate," so when he stopped by my office one day, I asked him to explain. "Well," he said, "Mom always wanted to be physically fit, but she never quite made it." Okay. Naturally, I asked him why he hadn't written it the way he had just said it. "Well, that would have been stupid," he replied. "Just those little words—'physically fit'? No way. See, I wanted this paper to sound really good, so I looked up *physical* and I found *corporeal*, and then I looked up *fit* and I found *appropriate*. That's what she wanted to be—corporeally appropriate."

This student had his own distinctive style, but he didn't see that it had any place in what he called "school writing." Getting him to go with his own language once in a while—or just to put his thesaurus down—was no easy task. But eventually he started to trust himself. Even if you discover that your diction needs fine-tuning, it's easier to strengthen and build on your own authentic style than to fall into bad habits and later have to "undo" language that wasn't yours in the first place and wasn't any good in the second.

It's not that you should never consult a dictionary or thesaurus. They're valuable tools—just don't go overboard. Develop your own voice, and value your own language. Don't assume that every word you would say in conversation must be changed just because you're writing it down or you've never heard your teachers say something in quite the same way. The first thing that comes out of your mouth might sometimes be the freshest, most original, powerful, and accurate way to say what's on your mind. (This is true in spite of all that we've said about the value of revision.) Let your teacher and your co-writers in class see the real you. To be a good writer, you have to take plenty of risks. Don't hide behind the horrendously formal, vague, pretentious language that so many students think English teachers want to hear. (And, unfortunately, a *very* small number of wrong-headed teachers do, so that perpetuates the problem.) If you want to increase your vocabulary, do it gradually. Often, you'll need to have many exposures to a new word before you can really make it your own and begin to use it well. If you're unsure, don't force it.

Inappropriate Shifts in Diction

There is no word that's never usable; whether a word is right for a given sentence in a given piece of writing depends on the writer's purpose, style, and audience. Where does the diction shift into "inappropriate" in this passage?

> One thing that I learned in the process of becoming a man was that sex was, for the most part, the culmination of a desire felt by two people to jump each other's bones, and I realized that I would have to approach this sensitive issue with greater respect and maturity.

Somehow the writer loses credibility by using the expression "jump each other's bones." It's not that the phrase could never be used in writing; in fact, it might work perfectly as part of a dialogue in a narrative. But here it's a lapse; it doesn't fit with the overall style and message of the passage.

Some shifts in diction have unintended comic effects. One student wrote, for example,

> Although the transmission of most sexual diseases is considerably lessened by the use of a condom, sexually active people must face the fact that the condom is not all it is pumped up to be.

If the writer is trying to be funny, great—she succeeded, at least for this reader. But if she's attempting to make a serious point in a research paper, she needs to revise "pumped up."

Here are two examples that show slang or casual, colloquial diction used to good effect. In the first, the writer is reliving her greatest moment on the basketball court during tournament play.

> Running down the court, I received an awesome pass from my teammate. I dribbled a couple of times and made a sweet lay-up right in my opponent's face. As I rose in the air, I was geeked. I couldn't be stopped.

An "awesome pass"? Sure, it sounds just right. Would "a carefully executed pass" be better? Of course not. A "sweet lay-up"? Why not? Who wants to hear about a "highly effective lay-up"? She was "geeked"? Okay, so maybe in a few years readers won't know what "geeked" means. But this student was writing for her classmates in 1991, and in 1991 they needed no explanation.

Now if, in the middle of a traditional biology research paper, the same student wrote about "awesome findings," "sweet experiments," and "geeked scientists," she'd need to think about revising. It's all a matter of context—the right word for the right occasion.

Let's look at our other example.

> I don't see why film directors don't produce movies that tell the truth about Vietnam. I had to find out the hard way in history class. My history teacher was telling about the casualties from the war and concluded that because the Americans had more casualties than the Vietnamese, the United States lost the war. That night I read my history book to see for myself if he was right—he was. I kept quiet about my "jackass of the year" feeling. Thanks, Rambo!!!

In this passage, the writer does a great job of evoking the naïveté of the high school kid who suddenly realizes popular culture has led him a bit astray—at least on one point of recent American history. His breezy, colloquial language is perfect. The medium (his language) fits the message.

Wordiness

Wordy passages contain more words than are necessary to communicate the message. Often at the heart of wordiness is the writer's reluctance to reveal how simple his or her point is. And yet simple can be beautiful, strong, elegant, truthful. Another cause of wordiness is exhaustion. When the language gets loose and repetitive, you can often sense that the writer has tired. Instead of taking a break and coming back fresh, the writer stuck with the job too long and started to grope for words, repeat phrases, and use five lines to say something that could have been said in two.

Here are three classic examples of wordiness. What can be deleted from each? Remember: **Less is more.**

EXAMPLE A

> The offensive and defensive formations in basketball and baseball lead me to another contrasting point about the sports of basketball and baseball. In basketball there are always five players on offense and on defense. In baseball there is a feeling of one man on offense having to face a defensive squad of nine players by himself. Of course, there is moral support from the rest of the team for a player stepping up to bat and facing the others, but in my opinion, the feeling described

in the previous sentence sums up my feeling when I step up to bat on offense.

EXAMPLE B

The letters were written as a constant reminder, reminding us to remember the good times in the past and prepare for the good times up ahead.

EXAMPLE C

It was discovered from many experiences that my grandfather was a poor manager of money, but yet and still, although he had these money problems and gambling and so on, the marital relationship between my grandfather and grandmother has given me something to look forward to as far as marriage is concerned, an inspiration for my own marriage in the future.

Inexactness and Ambiguity

Sometimes the problem is not that a writer uses too many unnecessary words, but that just one or two words give an unintended or simply vague impression. If your ideas are important to you, then you need to find the words that can convey them as accurately as possible. For example, consider how the following statement is subject to more than one interpretation. Then, let's try some exercises.

The flexible admissions practices and academic standards of women's colleges in the United States have been without precedent in higher education.

Exercises on Diction

Exercise One

Paying special attention to diction, compare these in-class responses to the question "What is beauty? Define it in any way you wish." (These responses were written in twenty minutes.) How does the choice of words affect the clarity of each piece and your interest in it? Rank the pieces in order of their appeal to you as a reader.

EXCERPT A
Michael Z. Matthews II

When most people think of beauty, they think of physical appearance. Though physical attributes are a contributing factor, the attitude of a woman is the major part of her beauty. A woman should be happy with herself. She should be able to take constructive criticism graciously but remain secure. A beautiful woman is a generous woman. She constantly shares both material things and wisdom, but she never lets people take advantage of her. A beautiful woman possesses infinite knowledge. She is not always educated in schools, yet the world has taught her survival. A beautiful woman is very confident. She knows that she has the capacity to accomplish what she wants and needs out of life. A beautiful woman has class. You might not always agree with her, or you might not even like her, but because of the way she carries herself with dignity and style, you will always respect her. A beautiful woman is a good teacher. She never has problems sharing her knowledge. She is beautiful because she has the ability to give and receive love.

EXCERPT B
A. Nonymous

Beauty is the maximizing effect a person or object has that makes it appealing to the subjective character of a person. The instinctive quality that designates the subject as beautiful is that it has the superiority to capture one's attention and keep it at a standstill for long intervals of time. Although the reasons for justifying that something is beautiful can often be directed toward the shape or color of the subject, the mysterious part about beauty is that it is often impossible to explain its appealing qualities. While it might not be stated as the synonym to perfection, one who believes that a subject is beautiful will often attribute it to perfection.

EXCERPT C
Andrea L. Bell

Beauty is a hot summer day at the beach. Every summer I go to Long Beach Island, New Jersey, where I spend every waking moment observing the beach life. I can envision the brownish-white sand seeping through my toes while I slowly walk off the dunes heading toward the water. My goal is to enter the ocean water. The water is green with specks of seaweed and jellyfish floating around in it. Dead horseshoe crabs are lying on the edge of the water while the waves wash upon the shore. There are young children playing in the sand digging for sand crabs while teenagers surf on boogie boards in the ocean. In the distance, water-skiers and sailors enjoy the rocky waves. The fishermen attempt to dodge the swimmers and skiers. Perhaps they are afraid of hooking one of them. As I shift positions, I notice hundreds of people walking, playing ball, building castles, and enjoying a relaxing day at the beautiful beach.

Exercise Two

The following sentences—or parts of them—lack clarity. Rewrite them, using the clearest language possible. Some parts are obscure enough that you might feel as if you're being asked to be a mind reader. But it's instructive to realize that these are actual examples from some very sharp students—students who, at least for a moment, lost sight of the importance of using language to make things *clear.*

1. Pornography is the epitome of the manifestation of the urges and underpinnings of popular culture in a society in which delayed gratification and the thoughts of self-control and looking for deeper relationships are not there.

2. In the limelight of a woman's right to her privilege of privacy is the fact of whether or not she can provide proper prenatal care to her unborn child if she is a drug user; this is in relationship to other privacy issues for women such as the question of if they should be legally allowed to work in factories where they are exposed to such contaminants as lead, which could affect a fetus, if the woman is of an age where she could possibly become pregnant, regardless of whether or not she actually is.

3. Televised aggression provides children with information about how to express aggression or take risks along with plenty of different deeds.

4. To disadvantaged American ethnic groups, completion of a higher education meant upward mobility economically, culturally, and socially. It also meant a hard struggle with preexisting conditions—a struggle that led as rapidly to a decline in enrollment, or dropout, as it led to the increase.

5. Another argument against prayer in public schools is that many different religions are practiced by many different people who attend the public schools, and many people think this could have an adverse effect on the youth in the public schools.

Exercise Three

In this exercise, we'll look at writing that is clear but wordy. We know exactly what the writer means, but the sentence contains more words than it needs to. The sentence could be crisper, tighter, stronger, livelier.

Rewrite the following sentences, slashing whatever you can, and allowing the meaning to come through more vividly.

1. Spike Lee's movies, such as *Jungle Fever* and *Do the Right Thing*, show us how in today's society we have a very long way to go before we can even begin to say that this society is willing to look at the deep social problems that we still have as a society as a legacy of racial injustice.

2. Our society throws away billions of nonrecyclable products made from plastics, which are not recyclable, daily.

3. In any human endeavor, on the basis of trial and error one is able to isolate the problem and change the factors that hindered one's performance in an attempt to achieve one's goal.

4. Some of the same people who claim to be religious because of their good works are some of these same people who do such things as lie on financial aid forms or in order to receive more money, cheat on their spouses, taxes, or exams, gossip, and degrade other people.

5. During the later days of the 1960s, it was believed by many individuals—both in and out of the music scene—that the messages that rock and roll could convey musically to the world could change crucial negative aspects of the worsening state of the world.

Exercise Four

Rewrite these two longer items, again to eliminate wordiness. Both are excerpts from student writing.

1. According to experts on sexual aggression, rapists have a great difficulty within themselves in terms of identifying their own anger and making the distinction between what is in reality a feeling of anger and what is actually sexual arousal, and they desperately need help in not letting these feelings become blended as one.

2. In traditional Chinese culture, a young couple can have sex only after they are married. Otherwise, they are not considered to be good normal people, and their relatives, friends, and especially their parents, will feel shame for them because of how they are behaving and how they are not acting normal. In the case of a girl, if she has sex before she is married, she may lose all of her girlfriends because if her girlfriends still keep in the relationship with her as they did before, others may think that the girlfriends are the same kind of girl as she is. So to avoid all these possibilities of things being seen as not normal and all this trouble, if a girl begins dating, her parents may send her brother or sisters to go with her, to make sure that everything is okay. So if you fall in love with a Chinese girl in China, don't mention about sex until you get married.

Exercise Five

This is an exercise in using freewriting when you're faced with a cliché in an early draft. You know you want to change the cliché, but to what? Before you try the exercise, look at the following examples.

Here are a few quickly conceived substitutions for the cliché "Tears streamed down my [or someone else's] face." How do they differ from the cliché?

- The tears popped out of his eyes like coins out of a slot machine.

- I could feel the tears coming, but I held back: I was wearing mascara—not the waterproof kind—and I was determined not to look like a raccoon.

- Teardrops made hot rivers run down both cheeks and up under his nose.

- They say "A man ain't supposed to cry," but then I thought, "Who's 'they'?" So I let loose.

- She refused to cry. Blinking back the tears, she imagined she could feel them trickling down the inside of her skull. She was a tough lady.

- Salty tears poured into the corners of my mouth. I was a pitiful, snuffling mess. Fumbling in the bottom of my purse, I found one tissue—wadded up around a hard lump of grape gum.

Now you try it. Choose one of the following clichés and write three substitutions for it, using fresh, concrete language. Aim for roughly the same meaning. Use your own paper.

They knew that someday their ship would come in.
My mind went blank.
I froze in my tracks.
He could have eaten a horse.

It hit me like a ton of bricks.
She was as cute as a kitten.

Exercise Six

The following sentences, from student papers, present a mixed bag of diction problems. In some cases, you might find more than one type of problem per sentence. Revise them, rewriting each as needed.

1. Indeed, before I made the acquaintanceship of one particular female, Ms. X, I had never comprehensively considered a relationship with a woman outside of the dimension of its sexual content. I began to reflect back upon past episodes and brief encounters of an erotic nature, whereas I could not even remember the lady's name the next morning.
2. More than 100 years after the heinous crime of slavery, African Americans are still waiting, struggling, practically begging for financial reparations which are past due, while the U.S. government gets a big laugh out of what has to be a joke for even being proposed.
3. A recent trend in the thought patterns of young people today is leading them back to some professions and occupations long considered taboo by the Yuppie, including the fine arts, teaching, and even carpentry and painting. The main idea that is being brought about in young minds is that it is all right to follow one's heart.
4. Rap, I believe, can bring these two groups—blacks and whites—together, if only to educate them that the differences between them are not that different because rap is political and educational more so than musical.
5. After Law 936 was passed, agriculture and the fishing industry in Puerto Rico went down the drain to the point where there is no way to create self-sufficiency.

Exercise Seven

This exercise also contains a mixed bag of diction problems from student writing. You may find an item or two that you believe needs no revising. Revise each sentence, or explain why you believe it should not be changed.

1. Although in today's society there are many forces that are trying to down the Miss America program, it is still beneficial in the accomplishing of women's objectives, especially in the sense of the potential for scholarship money earned.
2. Guillermo Gómez-Peña, an artist and writer, believes in the belief that the average or typical Anglo thinks of Hispanics as not real people but rather, on the other hand, as symbols, images, and metaphors that are mostly symbolic.
3. Among the many theories that have arisen during the last two centuries for the explanation of the cause of the asthma attack, the oldest and most widely discussed theory has continuously been the nervous theory, in which the condition of an asthma sufferer is thought to be brought on by a nervous condition.

4. My mother looked worried, but I just excused her looking that way for her normal behavior of her always being worried about something.
5. It is time to recognize the severity of the problem of all the garbage we are filling the landfills with and look for a solution.
6. People who blow off the concept of airline deregulation do not take into account the fact that it has great benefits to the consumer, especially increased flexibility in routes, schedules, and fares.
7. As a Mexican American, I can say with no hesitation that Black people have taken more shit than anyone else in America, and throughout it all they have come up strong and never given up on their fight for equality.
8. For those who choose to abstain from sex, they have to face the pressure from their partner if it is not a decision made by both. They also have to prepare themselves for the possibility of being rejects, which is part of reality.
9. I further realized that the crime scene in the city had gotten out of hand, and more and more youths had become sitting ducks in a game of chance and murder.
10. Although today's society is now accepting the fact that many young people have sex before marriage, because of campaigning for sexual awareness, sex before marriage is still not something which is encouraged in our society.

Audience

One of the reasons good writers are careful about diction is that they consider their audiences. Thinking about who your audience is—in other words, who will be reading your story or description, or who will be listening to your explanation or argument—is an important part of writing, not only because it governs your choice of words, but also because it helps you decide the amount and type of detail to include, the type of evidence to provide, how fully to develop your points, and how to organize your points.

Are you preaching to the already converted? Or to a sworn adversary—someone who can barely stand to consider your proposal for a moment? To someone with a great deal of experience in your subject area or to a complete newcomer? To an adult or to a child? If you doubt for a moment that audience is a real-life issue, watch lawyers pitch their closing arguments to a jury, each attorney trying to use the exact points, language, and tone that will strike the right chord with jurors.

You might think that the issue of audience doesn't matter much because you're always writing for the same one anyway—your teachers. In one sense, that's true: Right now, a great deal of your writing is being judged and graded by teachers. Later, in your career, much of it might be evaluated by a boss or supervisor. But even given these realities, it's very helpful for a writer to "think audience." If you're creating a paper on the Civil War, for example, is it for an introductory American history survey course taught by a generalist? Or is it for an upper-level course taught by a specialist in Civil War history? To an extent, the answers to these questions may dictate how you narrow your topic, the kind of research you do, and how much evidence you provide.

There is another important reason for being sensitive to audience:

Sometimes we are so immersed in our own lives and interests that it's easy to forget or to fail to imagine what readers—people who have not lived the same life and may not share the same interests—need to know about a subject in order to be persuaded to accept our controlling purpose. What needs to be explained? Are you so close to your subject, such an expert on it, that it's difficult to imagine others not knowing what you know? This is frequently the case, and, unless you remind yourself to be attentive to audience, ironically, your own expertise may lead to odd gaps in your writing.

Another benefit of considering your readers is that writing to a very specific audience may free the writer to say things in a more powerful or intimate way. Picturing a particular audience, the writer may feel creative juices flowing—ideas rushing in, memories flooding back.

Let's look at two student writers successfully addressing two different audiences. The first example, written in letter form, shows how a writer's voice changes when the audience shifts from parent to peer. Mark any of the writer's specific changes that you find interesting or effective.

EXAMPLE A *A Date Told in Two Voices*
Angela Kendrick

Dear Mom,

1   I met this really nice young man named Daryl at a fraternity party, and I think you would really like him. He's from Chicago and he attends Michigan State University. He's 20 years old, tall, and very cute. He is a very intelligent and well-mannered young man.

2   I had a chance to meet his family, and they seem to be very nice. His father works for Ford, and his mother works for the city of Chicago. He is the oldest of three children. He has a sister who is 16 and a brother who is 14, and they all get along great. He is such a good role model for them to follow.

3   He has a variety of things that interest him. He is planning to go into engineering. He loves playing basketball, football, and golf during his free time. He listens to all types of music, but he concentrates more on jazz. He is really into learning about his black culture and heritage. He enjoys going to historical and musical plays for knowledge and enjoyment. I think he could have a good influence on my life. I am really glad I met him.

4   Last week we went out on our first date. We went to dinner and a movie, and it was really nice. He was such a gentleman. He opened doors for me and pushed in my chair for me. He did everything a gentleman would do. For dinner we had steak and shrimp with wine. We had a nice intelligent conversation and started to get to know each other. After the movie, we took a drive through the park, and then he brought me back to the dorm. He gave me a kiss good-bye on the cheek, and then he left. He was very sweet, and yes, he did bring me home at a decent time. I will have to bring him home one day so you can meet him. Well, that's all for now. I'll write soon.

Love,
Angie

Dear Tia,

1   Girl, I met this cute guy named Daryl at a fraternity party. He is light-brown skinned with hazel eyes and pretty, deep dimples. He has wavy hair and heavy dark eyebrows. He's about 6'2," with sexy bowlegs and a nice body. I mean muscles are everywhere. He has a pretty mustache with not too little and not too much—it's just right.

2   Well, getting to the story, we went out last week. We went to Mountain Jack's and to the movies to see *Child's Play 3*. The date was so perfect. He was such a gentleman. The food was good, and the conversation was going: We had so much in common. We talked about what he was interested in, and what I was interested in, and the interest we had in each other. Girl, you know I was smiling ear to ear.

3   After the movie, we took a drive through some park in Ann Arbor. He had a slow jam tape playing with Guy, Johnny Gill, and Luther Vandross as we drove around. He had it going on. Then we stopped near a lake and took a walk along the water. We held hands and talked a little more. Then the time was right. The moon was shining on the lake. I was looking at him, and he was looking at me. Then it happened. Girl, it was so good. It was so nice and gentle, and it lasted a long time, too. His lips were so soft and wet. It was a kiss I will always remember. After that, we just hugged each other and watched the water.

4   It was getting late, so he decided to take me back. During the ride back to the dorm, our conversation was still going. We got along as if we had been friends for years. Then he walked me back to my room, gave me another long good-night kiss, and told me he would give me a call the next day. He is such a sweet guy; you'll have to meet him. Well, that's all for now. I'll write you again after our next date.

Your #1 Cuz,
Angie

The next example, a very different two-audience project, shows how the writer successfully shifts from an "in-the-know" reader to a reader who—quite understandably—might need a little more help. How do we see that the writer accurately calculates the needs of each audience? In which summary does she reach *you* most successfully? Why? After this example, let's try some audience exercises.

EXAMPLE B   *Summary of a Lecture in Biological Anthropology 161*
Euniece Lashawn Dixon

For a student enrolled in the course but absent from the lecture.

1   Today's lecture discussed animal and primate behavior from a sociobiological perspective. We applied what we learned from previous lectures and assumed that the underlying genetic basis of behavioral phenotypes which successfully reproduce will be passed on to future generations. Thus, those individuals with genotypes coding for behaviors that enable them to have higher reproductive success than other individuals are said to have higher fitness and ultimately pass on their genes at a faster rate.

2   The first type of behavior discussed was altruism. An "altruist"

acts in the interest of others at a cost to himself. Ground squirrels demonstrate this behavior. The squirrel acting as the altruist in a situation that threatens the fitness of all individuals in the group is usually killed (cost), but others in the group are saved (benefit).

3   Altruistic behavior is favored by natural selection when and only when the benefit divided by the cost is greater than one over the coefficient of relatedness, $b/c > 1/r$. If an ego makes the ultimate sacrifice and four siblings benefit, each sibling has a one-half chance of distributing the allele for altruism into the gene pool, thereby increasing the frequency of that allele.

4   The other type of behavior discussed was infanticide among nonhuman primates. Langurs, for instance, live in social groups comprised of one or two reproductive males, several reproductive females, and their offspring. Males without mates live in bachelor groups. Members of the male coalitions will on occasion attack and take over the troop. The male lasts as head of the troop for only about two years before he is overthrown. Because the new reproductive male is anxious to produce his own offspring, he commits infanticide. This is a behavioral strategy that allows the adult male to maximize his fitness.

5   Infanticide takes place among nonhuman primates in situations in which the adult male has a short tenure, the members of the species are nonseasonal breeders, there is a long lactation interval, and there is little female choice.

6   If we imagine there is an allele for infanticidal behavior, it would increase in frequency relative to the allele for patient behavior. Therefore, a father who has previously displayed infanticidal behavior will then pass on his infanticidal genotype to his own offspring, ultimately increasing the allele for infanticidal behavior in the gene pool.

7   Altruism and infanticide are phenotypes subject to natural selection. Their biological significance is determined by the reproductive success of individuals displaying the behaviors vs. those individuals displaying alternative behaviors. It is most likely that both phenotypes are adaptive.

For a college student who is not enrolled in the course and has not taken it previously.

1   In today's lecture, Professor Kim Hill used the theory of evolution to explain two types of animal and primate behavior: altruism and infanticide. First, it's necessary to realize that *alleles* are different forms of genes that affect a specific trait. Because we know that evolution is a change in allele frequency in a population from one generation to the next, we can assume that in order for phenotypes— or observable characteristics—to be passed from one generation to the next, individuals must have children. Individuals with genotypes allowing them to acquire more resources or mates, or better avoid predators, etc., are more likely to have children, thus passing the genetic basis of such traits to future generations. (*Genotype* means the genetic makeup of an individual or group.) Consequently, such individuals pass on their genes at a faster rate.

2   The first type of behavior discussed was altruism. Altruism is a behavior in which an individual "alarm giver" selflessly warns other members of his group about life-threatening situations. Ground squirrels demonstrate this behavior. The squirrel who acts as the alarm giver is often killed, but other members of his group are saved.

3   Because relatives share the same genes, it is possible that the gene for alarm calling will spread even though the alarm giver is killed. This is because the individuals that were saved are related to the alarm giver and probably share the altruistic gene. For example, if four of the alarm giver's brothers and sisters were saved, each one of those siblings has a one-half chance of carrying the allele for alarm giving and perhaps contributing it to the gene pool—the total set of alleles in the population—therefore increasing the number of alleles for alarm giving.

4   The other type of behavior discussed was infanticide among several animals. Take langurs, for instance. Langurs are a type of monkey that lives in India. They live in groups made up of one or two adult males, many adult females, and their offspring. The adult male mates with all of the adult females in the group. This adult male stays head of the group for about two years. Males without mates live in all-male groups. From time to time, a male langur from outside the initial group will start a fight with the male who is already part of the group. If he wins, he gets the females and becomes head of the group. The defeated male is usually killed or is forced to move on and find another group to try to take over. Once head of the group, the new adult male attacks and kills the babies that were fathered by the previous male. The new male behaves as if he knows that he doesn't have long before another male will come along and take over the group, so he is anxious to have his own children. Killing the babies is nothing personal; it's necessary if he is to contribute to the gene pool.

5   Infants are killed among langurs and other animals when four conditions exist: (1) the male is going to be in the group for only a short time (about two years); (2) the species reproduces all year round; (3) infants have to depend on their mother for a long time; and (4) females do not have much to choose from when it comes to males.

6   The allele for child killing is dominant over the allele for patient behavior. Therefore, a father who has shown child-killing behavior will pass on his genes for child killing to his own children. The allele for child killing is ultimately increased in the total set of alleles in the population.

7   Alarm giving and infant killing play a big role in how genes are inherited from one generation to the next. Just how big a role is determined by the ability of the individual to have children and pass on genes that design the nervous system that produces this behavior.

Exercise One

Choose two of the following options to practice adjusting your writing to meet the needs of different audiences. Just as the "imagined writer" shifts when you change points of view, the "imagined reader" shifts when your audience changes.

Later, in class, share the results and analyze how you and your co-writers geared your writings toward different audiences. As the imagined audience shifts, do you also see shifts in purpose, diction, tone, amount of detail, sequence of information, average sentence length, and/or sentence structure?

1.   Explain the April 30, 1992 verdict in the Rodney King police brutality case and its aftermath to two different audiences, for example, to your peers and then to a six-year-old child, or to an audience that has experienced police brutality and to an audience that has not.

2. Describe how to cook something—either a bakery item, such as home-made bread or cherry pie with a lattice crust, or a main dish, such as beef Wellington or jambalaya—to someone who cooks as well as you do; then describe the process again to someone who's never boiled water.

3. Imagine that you are a psychiatrist talking within the privacy of a psychotherapy session to someone who was severely abused in early childhood. You are trying to help your patient understand the source of his or her low self-esteem and see how the past is still affecting the present. Then imagine that you are the same psychiatrist sharing this case study in a formal presentation to colleagues at a professional conference.

4. Create a short speech commemorating the arrival of Christopher Columbus in the New World. Write it first for an audience of Italian Americans; then write it again to be delivered to an organization of Native Americans.

5. Imagine that last night you celebrated a holiday or holy day or performed the rites of a ceremony or custom that is particular to the racial, ethnic, or religious group to which you belong. First, write a letter about the event to a relative who belongs to the same group but was not able to be with you last night. Second, describe the event again, this time for an audience that knows little or nothing about your racial, ethnic, or religious group.

6. Describe the plot of a new R- or X-rated movie (or the lyrics of an explicit and controversial new song) to someone you know won't be offended by either the content or the language; then describe the plot or lyrics again to someone who you assume has a different sensibility, for example, your grandfather, your straight-laced aunt, or a priest, minister, or rabbi.

7. Write a letter to a sister, brother, or childhood friend about something you both did in the past—for example, a great vacation the two of you took out West, a special party you both attended, or a game you played together when you were little. Then describe the same thing to an outsider, someone who did not share the experience.

8. Explain a process you know well to another person who also knows it well. Then explain it again to someone who knows almost nothing about it. The process could be anything from an intricate play in a football game to the democratization of Eastern Europe.

Exercise Two

Knowing how to appeal directly to an audience is one of those wonderfully practical writing skills that can have major payoffs both in and out of the classroom. The following, for example, is a brief, effective personal statement that accompanied a student's application to Columbia University's Medical School. (Applicants were limited to approximately 250 words.) In what ways might Sivaram's essay appeal to a range of "physician readers"? In what way might it appeal to the medical teaching staff of Columbia in particular?

Personal Statement/Medical School Application
Sivaram Rajan

1   Deciding to become a physician was a gradual and deliberate process. Certain appealing qualities—technical challenges, altruism,

and potential for social impact—are intrinsic to the profession and have strongly influenced and solidified my decision.

2   My experiences accompanying and observing my father, a general surgeon, made the challenges of medicine vivid and clear. During his rounds, my father interacted with patients, nurses, and technicians, so I saw the importance of his interpersonal skills. In surgery, I was impressed with the depth of knowledge one must integrate and apply, as well as the need for concentration, resolve, and stamina. These demands will always challenge me and engage my interest.

3   In addition to these factors, the altruistic nature of the profession is compelling. Medicine is not about building cars, maximizing profit, or settling divorces; it is about helping people live longer, healthier, and more fulfilling lives.

4   The medical profession also has great potential for social impact. As an Asian Studies major with an honors concentration in Cambodian history, I took a keen interest in the plight of the Cambodian people and developed a strong desire to work in refugee camps on the Thai-Cambodian border as part of my clinical rotations. When I saw on Cable News Network that Columbia sent medical students to this region, I knew the school was ideal for my objective. The comments from the students indicated that it was an extremely gratifying experience.

5   As a physician, I expect to apply my knowledge and skill to socially conscious action. I firmly believe that the greatest satisfaction in medicine is obtained not only through the technical challenges, but also by providing health care where it is most needed.

Exercise Three

Here, with elegant descriptive detail, the writer tells about an important Thai custom. Is Salina addressing an audience that is already quite familiar with Loykatong? What evidence supports your answer?

Loykatong
Salina S. Chinnukroh

1   Loykatong is a traditional Thai festival celebrated each year on December 15, the date on which the full moon appears. As the moon reflects on the river, Buddhists of Thailand gather along the banks to pay respect to the god of water. Because of the necessity of water to all living creatures, this god is honored by a holiday.

2   The river represents a wishing well. But instead of throwing money down a well and making a wish, Thais say a prayer that includes a wish and then place the Loykatong, or paper lotus, on the flowing river. The brilliantly colored lotus is handcrafted with the utmost care and detail. Upon its petals, intricate designs of religious symbols are painted. Candles are placed in the middle of the Loykatong to serve as a light to guide it on its journey down the river. The people gather along the river, and each person makes a wish and lights the candle, illustrating the vivification of the dream. Thais make moral, not material, wishes: for health, happiness, and security.

3   Families and friends together watch the lights flickering on the water in hopes of catching a glimpse of a place where their wish is reality.

Exercise Four

Who is the principal audience for the essay, "Am I a Black American?"? At what point does this become clear? Why does Adanna address her essay to this audience? What specific things does she do to make her case convincing to this audience? Does she succeed? Why or why not? Imagine the essay if it were written to a more general, nonspecified audience. How would it be different? Would it lose anything?

Am I a Black American?
Adanna Chioma Amanze

1   At my dinner table, there are no recollections of a mother by the name of Africa, whose children were wrenched from her fertile arms. Instead, as the rice is passed, there are only recollections of those children who were nourished by her rich milk. These joyful spirits were my ancestors who were never chained to the white man's soil. Am I a Black American? In my living room, there are never heated discussions about segregated schools, buses, bathrooms, or drinking fountains. There is little talk of the triumphant freedom marches. Am I a Black American? When guests walk into my home, they are not met by the eyes of Martin Luther King; it is the militant face of my great-grandfather, the Chief of Emii, that greets them. Am I a Black American? My last name does not define a white man's trade; it is not Baker, Taylor, or Carpenter. My name is Adanna Chioma Amanze, which defines me as God's first child in my family. My brother and sister's names are Emeka and Ngozi, not Thomas and Jennifer. Am I a "true" Black American? I am Black, born and raised in the United States, but I am also a true and proud Nigerian.

2   As a young child, I was often ridiculed for various reasons: my name, the "funny" accent of my parents, and the assumption that my brothers and sisters in Africa ran around half-naked and lived in huts. You may snicker at these insults and simply brush them off, but that is to be expected; you would not understand. As a young Black American child, were you ever ridiculed because your family was from Montgomery, Alabama, or anywhere down South, for that matter?

3   When I was younger, like a fool I hid behind the shield that shouted, "I was born in the United States, and therefore I am an American." However, through the years, these shouts became more like whispers as I began to define my individuality. Unlike many Black Americans, my heritage does not lie in the American South; it resides in the motherland, Africa. My family is from Owerri, Imo, and is a member of the Ibo tribe; in this tribe our native tongue is not English; it is Ibo. The clothing we wear, the food we eat, the greetings we speak are all a part of our tribal customs. My culture is not the aroma of sweet potato pie for the holidays; it is the scent of a Nigerian soup that tickles your nose. My culture was never the perms or curls, but the braids and natural Afros. When someone leaves my home, my culture sends them off not with a simple wave good-bye, but with the blessing of the hands. My culture is tribal costumes, not blue jeans. It was my culture that defined slavery as a punishment for the "untouchables"—criminals who were put to work as servants—not as the stripping away of one's individuality or the denunciation, brutalization, or oppression of an entire race.

4   My Nigerian culture has always been a strong backbone for me, yet I sometimes feel that it cannot fully support me; it is not enough. Many times I have found myself on the outside looking in. I may be the silent one as people speak about their parents' and grandparents' involvement in the civil rights movement. I may be the one who suddenly looks up when the teacher declares that all of our ancestors were slaves. I may be the one who does not fully understand segregation, but I do fully understand discrimination. I may be the one who is aware of, but still does not fully relate to, all of the African American struggles of the past. What I do know is the history and the struggles of a Nigerian. I understand all of the civil wars fought among tribes, the poverty, the oppression by the government, and the lack of opportunity that sent so many, including my mother and father, far from their homeland. But many African American traditions still remain a mystery to me. It is not a lack of awareness or a lack of emotion that prevents me from a fuller understanding; it's the lack of the deeper understanding that perhaps can come only from the oral traditions of Black Americans, traditions that have been passed down from many generations.

5   Although I often have seen it as "the Black American versus me," as I evolve I see that this view must evolve also. There is and will always be one unifying social fact: race. Ultimately we are all sitting at the same dinner table, regardless of where our roots are or how deep they are. As Malcolm X knew, we are one: The concerns of African Americans are the concerns of Africans, and theirs are ours. We are all daughters and sons of the same Mother, even if she could not hold and comfort us all.

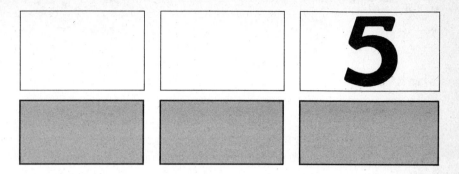

Exposition: Writing Definitions and Comparison/ Contrast Essays

In this chapter, we'll work with expository writing, also called *exposition*. Basically, the purpose of expository writing is not to tell a story or describe anything but to *explain*. Although expository essays often include some narration and description, their focus is on explanation.

It's actually easier to show differences between expository writing and narrative or descriptive writing than to explain them, so let's begin by looking at a fascinating pair of essays. In each, Giovanni writes about the transformation of his New York City neighborhood. In the first case, he *describes* and *narrates* what he sees; he *shows* us the transformation. (Note that a glossary follows the first essay.) In the second, he mostly *explains* what he sees; he *tells* us what happened to Washington Heights, using his own first-hand knowledge and a little bit of research. (If you are unfamiliar with research writing, citations, such as the one given in the second essay, will be explained in chapter 7). Together, these brief essays offer a clear demonstration of the difference between narrative/ descriptive writing and expository writing.

Washington Heights—A Narrative/Descriptive Essay
Giovanni Cruz

1   It's a little past seven, and I have just finished eating arroz con bacalao, batatas, y pastelitos. The most relaxing part of the day has arrived; it's time for me to check up on what my Dominican neighborhood is up to. I sit down by my bedroom window sill and watch the sun settle down to the east as it turns the day golden brown. It's a sweltering summer day, and a long line indicates that business for the lady on the corner is prosperous. She scrapes away at a giant block of ice placed in a cart and then molds the crystals into a cone-shaped icy. Depending on one's taste, she'll pour coconut, pineapple, or tamarind

juice over it, finally preparing a Frío Frío. As I continue to look around, I see the older men with straw hats smoking their pipes and playing dominos around a small table. Most of the older women are inside watching their Spanish novelas. The younger kids dash across the stream of an open fire hydrant to cool themselves off while Caribbean merengue rhythms blare into the air from car speakers. A group of teenage guys stand beneath a tree and flirt with the girls passing by. The atmosphere is full of festivity and excitement.

2   Suddenly shots ring out, and a siren screams. A blue police car with the emblem *NYPD* races in pursuit of a gold-trimmed Mercedez-Benz 190. The placid atmosphere is broken, and everyone scatters. Welcome to New York City's Washington Heights, which drug dealers have made a notorious place to live. Fun time is over, and I close my window until the next day.

GLOSSARY

arroz con bacalao, batatas y pastelitos	rice with codfish, sweet potatoes, and meat patties
Frío Frío	a Caribbean icy
merengue	Dominican music
novelas	soap operas
tamarind	a tropical fruit

Washington Heights—An Expository Essay
Giovanni Cruz

1   In the mid-1980s the Washington Heights community, a predominantly working-class Dominican neighborhood in upper Manhattan, underwent major transformations. It experienced several socioeconomic changes: Certain individuals became wealthier, the values of its youth changed, new immigrants from the Dominican Republic arrived in greater proportions, the level of violence increased dramatically, and English increasingly gave way to Spanish. The changes that took place are of great interest, but even more important is the culprit behind the changes. As a Dominican who grew up in Washington Heights, I witnessed the community's transformation, and I blame these disturbances, to a great degree, on an inexpensive, enticing, and lethal product—crack. Its proliferation within my community not only changed Washington Heights but virtually destroyed it.

2   Crack—made easily with cocaine, baking soda, and water—infiltrated our cities and spread like wildfire. According to Gordon Witkin in *U.S. News & World Report*, some of the creators of crack were "anonymous kitchen chemists and drug traffickers in the Caribbean and later in the United States, who used rudimentary science and marketing savvy to help hundreds of small-time criminals set up crack operations" (44). This lucrative and illegal commodity was irresistible to many inner-city youth living in areas with few high-paying jobs. "Nowhere did crack grab hold as tightly as it did in the northern Manhattan area called Washington Heights, a teeming neighborhood with a distinctly Caribbean flavor" (49). In fact, police named one area resident, described as "a street-savvy Dominican immigrant in his mid-20s," as "the marketing genius behind the spread of crack in New York's Washington Heights, the city's first big market" (48).

3   The crack dealing business soon became dominated by Dominicans, and many of those who sold it profited greatly. "The drug-dealing
Dominicans, like their many legitimate shop-keeping counterparts,
proved to be ambitious and well organized" (Witkin 49). Dominican
drug dealers could be seen in fancy clothing driving BMWs and Lotus
Esprits. Others kept a low profile by laundering their profits in
Dominican banks and investing in other businesses back on the island.
The luxuries enjoyed by many of these drug-dealing criminals became
very attractive—particularly to the youth.

4   Many teenagers saw the material rewards that the drug trade
offered and quickly became involved. It seemed more logical to make
six hundred dollars a night than to earn only one-fourth that much in
a week. Many of the more good-looking women soon began to associate
with those who were "living large." I can recall how many of my
friends were frustrated because a lot of the attractive women went out
with drug dealers. Many students dropped out of school to sell drugs;
education took a back seat to crack. Gold necklaces and a Mercedez
Benz with tinted windows replaced family values.

5   Everyone in the Dominican Republic knew about the traditional
American dream, but drug dealing was a new and more efficient way of
fulfilling it. More Dominicans—some with the intention of holding a
legitimate job and others with the idea of making it big in the drug
world—arrived in sizable numbers. Many of the new immigrants who
became drug dealers were males in their 20s and 30s. The English-
speaking youth called these newcomers "hicks." The "hicks" were very
ambitious, but at the same time incredibly dangerous. The level of
violence in Washington Heights increased dramatically.

6   Washington Heights became Dodge City. Soon police sirens could
be heard every night as gunfights broke out among drug dealers. The
risks in this business are higher than those in any other because, in
the drug world, people's lives are always at stake. New and ambitious
dealers often fought over a client; this usually resulted in a funeral.
Children could no longer play on the sidewalks late at night because of
the parents' fear that their child might be showered by a hail of bullets.
Meanwhile, frenzied crack addicts roamed the streets.

7   Sometime around 1985, crack infested Washington Heights, and
it had severe effects. The community experienced more than simple
changes; it underwent a revolution.

Work Cited

Witkin, Gordon. "The Men Who Created Crack." *U.S. News & World Report*. 19 August
1991: 44–53.

Definition Essays

We'll be working with two types of expository essays in this chapter: *definitions*
and *comparison/contrast essays*. For now, we'll focus on definitions. To find good
topics for writing definitions, think about what you know. Finish the sentence, "I
could tell you everything you'd ever want to know about _____ ." Or fill in
the blank: "If you want the truth about _____, just ask me."

Another topic might be a subject about which you've always been curious.
You're not sure what something is, but you want to find out about it? Here's a
good chance to do research on the subject.

Whether you're an expert or an interested party, you should have little or no trouble forming a controlling purpose for a definition essay. In expository and persuasive essays, the controlling purpose is often called a *thesis*. We'll use both terms here to refer to what you want to prove in a paper—the idea that unifies your project and helps you decide what to put in and what to leave out.

Ideally, you'll choose to define something because you have strong views on what it really is and, maybe, because you think it's time for other people to hear you out on this topic. You have something special to say about it. If you don't have this attitude, then you don't have a good topic. Keep looking.

You can define a relatively abstract term or a very concrete one.

Abstract Choices

If you choose an abstract subject, you'll need to make it come to life by translating it into concrete terms in your essay. Here are some more or less abstract topics: trouble, love, motherhood or the ideal mother, fatherhood or the ideal father, abuse of a certain type, good humor, comedy, self-sacrifice, loneliness, jealousy, commitment in a marriage, patriotism, multiculturalism, political correctness, femininity, feminism, masculinity, the men's movement, machismo, an obsession of any type, grief, obscenity, compassion, racism, sexism, homophobia, education (not only in the sense of "book learning"), success, failure, evil, God, soul, America, apartheid, bad luck, liberation theology, the guilt of the survivor, a hero, style, innocence, beauty—or, more specifically, the meaning or standard of beauty for American women, good karma, bad karma, mysticism, the artistic sensibility.

Concrete Choices

Many writers find it difficult or boring to try to translate an abstract subject into concrete terms. For these writers, it's wiser to choose more specific, concrete topics for their definition essays. In fact, student writers are generally much more enthusiastic about concrete topics, especially current ones.

Here are some relatively concrete topics for definition papers, and they should give you ideas for many more: life as a member of a Latino family; Ukrainian cooking; small-town life; the ideal high school; rap music; jazz; the essence of any big city—Chicago, Miami, Milwaukee, Seattle, New York, Minneapolis, San Francisco; nouvelle cuisine; a neighborhood—in the truest sense of the word; the ultimate wilderness camping trip; the blues (music or mood); the community college spirit; the special ambience of a women's college; the ambience of a trade or technical college; the significance of a religious or secular holiday; the ultimate birthday party for a girl or boy of a specified age; the beauty of baseball, softball, curling, throwing the discus, or any other sport; what it means to be a Big Ten athlete or a wheelchair athlete; what it means to be a telephone salesperson, a dedicated pianist, a nursing home attendant, or a volunteer; what it means to be the big sister, the little brother, the oldest child, or the only child in a family; a near death experience; attributes of the perfect kindergarten teacher; the ghost-dance phenomenon in American Indian history; the meaning of the religious life or the celibate life; the ingredient that makes

_____ America's quintessential team in a given sport; the original spirit of the U.S. labor movement; the life of the migrant farm worker.

How to Define a Term

Of course, you begin a definition essay the same way you begin any other writing project—with freewriting and/or other prewriting activities. But, no matter what your topic, you might want to go beyond your own notions and experience. If, for example, you decide to define the term *obscenity,* which legal scholars have been trying to define for decades, you might do some research, summarize their attempts, and conclude with your own definition, which may or may not agree with any of the several definitions you discovered in your research. As a starting point, you can research any topic—whether abstract or concrete. Look up your topic in the dictionary, encyclopedia, the index of a book of famous quotes, or your library's card catalog or computer system. Interview classmates or others to see how they define the term you have chosen. You do this sort of research mostly to gather background information and form an idea of how your understanding of a subject compares with how others have defined it. Some of this research you may end up using in your paper; other information may simply serve to get you going. (When it comes to writing your paper, however, try *not* to begin with the dictionary definition. This practice has become a cliché and, while it may be appropriate on occasion, you usually can do better.)

You'll need a good plan for organizing your paper. You can organize a definition paper in any number of ways. You can focus on one well-developed example or offer several, even many. Or you can define your term by comparing what many people mistakenly think it is to what you *know* it is. You can give your paper a structure in a variety of ways—as long as you have a thesis, or controlling purpose, in mind and you are very concrete about proving it or illustrating its truth. The definition essays included here show a number of methods of development.

Then you'll write the paper, revise it, and edit it. Of course, these processes sometimes will occur in unexpected sequences. But do save the bulk of the revising—and certainly the editing—for the end. Stir up those fresh ideas and capture them on paper before you get bogged down in worrying about how the final product will look.

Don't Worry About Switching Modes

Let's say you pick the topic *homophobia.* What if you get in the middle of writing your paper and you think, "Oh, no—I'm supposed to be doing definition, but this is turning out to be more of a cause and effect paper"? Well, so what if it is? If you have a reasonable teacher—and most writing teachers are more than reasonable; they're known for their flexibility and creativity—this will be no problem. Why shouldn't a writer who wants to define homophobia be free to consider its causes or effects or both? Wouldn't most readers be interested in why some people fear the life-styles of gay men and lesbians and in how such fear affects their lives? In many instances, inherent in the very act of defining a term is the necessity to examine its causes and effects. In other cases, particularly when you are attempting to correct a common misunderstanding about what something is, you'll inevitably be comparing and contrasting (appearance versus reality, superficial understanding versus deeper understanding) as you define.

All of this mode switching is perfectly fine. Look at it as just one more of life's messy realities. In writing—as in love, politics, art, sports, and almost every aspect of human endeavor—things cross and crisscross in endless and amazing ways. No matter what the assignment, the principal motivation of a good writing teacher is always to help students create a strong paper, not a strong paper of a certain type, in which the writer can never veer from a preordained pattern or set structure. That would be ridiculous—it would be valuing the coffee cup over the coffee.

Let's look at some interesting definition essays. In all cases, you'll see that we haven't left narration and description behind entirely. Elements of each are visible from time to time, as is often the case in good expository writing.

In our first definition essay, University of Michigan center Eric Riley lets us know that it's not *all* fun and games being a Big Ten athlete. What structure did Eric use to organize his material? What details help you see his subject from the inside?

The University of Michigan Basketball Player
Eric K. Riley

1   While walking through the Diag (a diagonal walkway in the center of the U of M campus) yesterday, this guy came up to me and said, "Man, you think you're bad because you play b-ball. I'll beat you any day—come on!" I had no response and kept walking. "Oh, I see you *ain't* that bad—come on!" So I laughed him off and walked on. This is something that wouldn't happen to most students. It happened to me because I'm 6'11" and I was wearing my varsity jacket. This is just one type of confrontation I encounter frequently because I am a University of Michigan basketball player.

2   Many people have their own ideas about U of M basketball players. Some people think we are special because we are in the public eye. Still others think we are dumb jocks who take classes like basket weaving. The most common assumption we encounter is that we are stuck on ourselves or real cocky. But all of these definitions of us are incorrect.

3   A U of M basketball player not only plays basketball but is a student as well. Our lives as athletes are not similar to the lives of other students. We practice 25 hours a week and often stay up very late to do homework we could not complete earlier. This routine is very hard to follow because after practice we are so tired that all we want to do is sleep.

4   We are also stopped constantly while walking to class by strangers who want to talk. We listen to everyone's opinion on how our team can be better. We are always being disturbed while we're eating at restaurants on campus. We have to attend important functions and act nice to important people who we sometimes do not like. We are often harassed and have to be careful not to get into fights because if we do, it will be in the *Daily* (the UM student newspaper) the next day.

5   As U of M basketball players, we meet many women who seem interested in dating us. This might sound great to most guys, and it is—sometimes. However, sometimes this can be confusing. When we get serious about a woman, we are never sure whether she is really interested in who we are as people or in what we do.

6   Some teachers label us as dumb jocks before they get to know us. We miss two or more classes a week for road games, and sometimes teachers will not excuse us. The teachers who stereotype us as dumb jocks think we are just skipping their class. While traveling, we have to study in hotel rooms and on airplanes. We never get quality study time on the road.

7   After all I've said about being a U of M basketball player, you may be saying, "Damn! It's not as good as I thought it was." But there are a few advantages, too. Without basketball, most of us would not have the opportunity to get a higher education. Most of our families are poor and could not afford to send us to the community college down the street, let alone the University of Michigan. We also realize that other students pay a lot of money for tuition, books, and living arrangements. So do not think we are not grateful for free tuition, because we are!

8   U of M basketball players also get treated better than other students. Some people we don't even know treat us as if we are their friends. Here's an example: I went to Little Caesar's for some pizza and asked for something that cost $4. When I realized I had only $2 with me, the guy said, "Oh, that's all right, take it—as long as you guys win another NCAA championship." I wish people would treat every student on campus like they treat us. If they did, our school would be great.

9   Another advantage is that we travel all around the United States to play games. Last year we spent ten days in Maui, Hawaii. We have also been to Chicago, New York, and Seattle. This year we are going to Las Vegas and Boston. During these trips we have a chance to meet famous people like pro basketball players; we've met Magic Johnson, Joe Dumars, and Roy Tarpley. Last year we also met President Bush and Vice-President Quayle.

10   Another aspect that is really positive for us is that we do not have to join a fraternity to make friends as some do. All of us are best friends, and we like to think of ourselves as family. When we are on the court, we must work within a unit and count on each other. This brings trust within the team. This trust and brotherhood also carry off the court. We go to the bar together. We stick up for each other. And if one of us has a problem, the rest of the family is willing to listen and help out.

11   There's a kind of pride we have in being University of Michigan basketball players that we will have for the rest of our lives. It is more than the National Championship gold rings, and it is more than our letter jackets. We will leave this university with the pride of knowing we pushed ourselves both mentally and physically for four years of our lives, and we survived.

How would you like to get all dolled up, look absolutely smashing, and then stand around and do nothing for three hours? Our second definition essay takes us inside a world few of us would ever enter otherwise. What concrete details does Kristi use to create a vivid picture of her experience? Does she anticipate well what most of us would like to know?

Standing Still: The Life and Times of a Mannequin Model
Kristi A. Kirk

1   The small dressing room reeks of cigarette smoke and coffee. Half of us puff on thin brown cigarettes which we gracefully position between skeletal fingers. Some models gossip amongst themselves,

while others leaf through the latest issues of *Vogue, Elle,* and *Cosmo.* The dressing room is the size of the average dormitory room. The problem is that it has to be shared by sixteen females and store racks and racks of the latest styles from the greatest houses.

2   Sixteen of us have exclusive modeling contracts with Jacobson's Department Store. Today, for a special in-store promotion, our assignment is to mannequin model. We are all accustomed to strutting catlike down a runway, but mannequin modeling is something different. It means standing or sitting in some awkward position for a couple of hours—possibly while being harassed if an onlooker discovers your true identity.

3   The requirements to be a mannequin are tough. The average model for this job has to be 5′9″ to 5′11″ and not half a pound over 120. She also must have perfect posture and an extra-long neck.

4   My favorite part of the job is the preparation. After waiting in the cramped dressing room, we are taken individually into an even smaller room where a team of makeup artists, manicurists, hairstylists, and fashion experts creates that glamorous look.

5   First, I am stripped down because no underwear is permitted. This is to prevent a panty line from showing; a mannequin's look is to be flawless, and an unsightly panty line would destroy the illusion. Two people dress me while another woman clips my toenails and fingernails. A man wearing a long ponytail and a series of earrings does my hair. He doesn't like the way it's behaving, so he pulls a wig from his bag to create a look to his satisfaction. Meanwhile, another person is outlining my lips and eyes, applying new lashes, and stroking blush on my cheekbones. Layers and layers of foundation are applied to my face and hands. If I wear a short-sleeved top, then foundation is also applied to my arms. It is important that I look as much like a mannequin as possible. After what seems like an eternity, I am finally ready. As I glance in the mirror before I go to my station, I look like a Barbie Doll: made-up, plastic, artificial, and phony.

6   My assigned station is on the second floor in the women's designer suits. I am wearing a Perry Ellis original in black with sheer nylons and three-inch heels. My companion is a girl named Molly who is also wearing a Perry Ellis suit, except hers is red. Molly looks as fake as I do. Our advisor has informed us that we can change positions only every fifteen minutes. Today our shift will last for three hours. All I can think of is how hungry I will become during the next three hours. Molly sits with her legs crossed while I stand. I shift my body weight to one side and cock my hand against my hip. The advisor removes the screen that keeps Molly and me hidden while we change and position ourselves. Ta da! Here I am for the world to see—I am a mannequin! Of course, it is essential that I never move. Which means no coughing, sneezing, or laughing. A method I use for staying focused and not cracking up is to lock my eyes onto a specific spot on the floor. The rest is a mental game.

7   The first five minutes go by . . . I am having a lot of fun. My smile is radiant. I feel pretty in all of my makeup and clothes.

8   The next five minutes . . . I am hot and beginning to sweat. A light is shining directly on my forehead. Oh, no. A little boy just discovered Molly is a "real" person. I hope he doesn't figure me out. I hope . . .

9   "Ma, look," shouts the little boy to his mother, who is comparing designer suits on the next rack, "these ladies are real!" Soon a

gathering of about ten people forms—all because of this loud-mouthed boy. It is amazing how many people stop to look. I can tell Molly is disturbed. I am too, and I feel myself beginning to blink faster. The little boy starts picking at my nylons. He is truly enjoying himself. I, on the other hand, want to kick him away and tell the other people to stop staring. Finally the crowd begins to disperse. I breathe a sigh of relief.

10   The last five minutes . . . New shoppers casually stroll by. Nobody even notices I am a mannequin. I am so bored I want to scream. My stomach growls. The light is still hot and shining in my face. I think my left leg is going to sleep. I remember how fun it was to get all dressed up, and now all I want to do is go home. My smile is not quite as radiant. Out of the corner of my eye, I see my advisor; she is carrying a screen for us to be hidden behind as we change positions. She places the screen around me and Molly. "Whew," I think to myself, "fifteen minutes is finally up!" I shake out my legs and arms. I drop my smile.

11   "Now, time to change positions," our advisor directs.

12   As I change positions, I am exasperated. Fifteen minutes down—two hours, forty-five minutes to go. I am bored to death. My face begins to itch underneath all that foundation. I think to myself how much I would like to be relaxing in sweatpants and a T-shirt right now. I guess the boredom goes with the territory. Mannequin modeling is a job I love and hate simultaneously. I wonder if Christie Brinkley started out like this.

In the next definition essay, the writer introduces us to a subject that few Americans know much about. What techniques does Adriana use to take us *inside* her culture? What gives this paper its exuberance and zest? Does each paragraph have its own recognizable purpose? What are the strengths of her structural plan? What would you ask her to do, if anything, if she were to revise one more time?

Entre y Tome Asiento (Come and Take a Seat)
Adriana Peljovich

1   My name is Adriana Peljovich, I was born in Miami Beach, Florida, on May 4, 1973, and I am a Jewban. I know it is a word foreign to most ears, but for me and many others in Miami Beach it is an everyday term. The word *Jewban* simply means a Cuban Jew. My race is Hispanic, and my religion is Jewish. I take extreme pride in being a Jewban because Jewbans are like no other. We share qualities that most Americans and even most Cubans or Jews cannot relate to.

2   Since I arrived at the University of Michigan, I have realized that both my Jewish and Cuban background have molded me into a unique individual. In my family's case, which is typical of most Cuban Jews, they were living in Poland in 1917, a year when the number of pogroms against the Jews was rising rapidly. Unlike others who came to the United States to escape anti-Semitism, my grandmother's family fled to Cuba. It was in Havana that my beautiful grandmother married my grandfather and gave birth to my mother. My grandmother, the daughter of an observant Jew, found herself forced to assimilate into the Latin culture, so she and her family taught themselves Spanish through television and radio. Eventually the Jewish traditions and customs my family followed had to end because of Fidel Castro's

communist takeover of Cuba. Left with no alternative, most Cuban Jews escaped to Miami Beach. So the European Jews who had transplanted themselves into a Hispanic culture were destined to enter the United States to create one more beautiful piece of the American mosiac.

3   What makes Jewbans so different from other Americans? And how do Hispanic and Jewish traditions blend? I learned in Hebrew school that Jews always lived together whether it was in Europe or anywhere else, even during the Middle Ages and earlier. They lived in ghettos or shtetls, which were Jewish communities. What was important was that they were all together. Similarly, Hispanics value unity and togetherness. Being Jewban means keeping in close contact with family and friends. It means attending huge dinners where people who are technically your friends are referred to as "Aunt" and "Uncle." In both the Latin and Jewish family, the circle of people is valued most.

4   Being Jewban means having a love of language. It means being bilingual and being envied by all your American friends. Being Jewban means having your grandmother ask, "Adri, vus makhste? Vi azoy lernste zikh?" ("Adri, how are you? How are your studies?"), and responding, "Abuela, recuerde que es inglés o español o hebreo porque yo no entiendo yiddish!" ("Grandma, remember it's either English, Spanish, or Hebrew because I don't understand Yiddish!") Being Jewban means being loud; it means feeling so embarrassed when your father yells out the prayers in shul that you elbow him in the ribs and tell him, "Papi, no somos sordos." ("Dad, we are not deaf, please lower your voice.") Being Jewban means trying to express the beauty of the Jewban culture but having a difficult time doing so.

5   Being Jewban also means uniting in good times and bad. It's planning surprises at weddings and bar/bat mitzvahs for your closest friends. Every time my parents' Jewban friends get married or have a party, all their friends get together and create a song and dance. Jewbans thrive on happiness and celebration where they can express huge outbursts of energy and emotion. And being Jewban means not only uniting in times of joy, but also in times of sorrow. When my family found out that my brother Steven was diagnosed with leukemia, we heard from people I did not even remember. During his hospitalization in Ann Arbor, nurses always had to tell us to "shut up" and to remember that so many visitors were maybe not in Steven's best interest. Not only did friends, family, and our rabbi come to visit my brother, but the walls in his room were covered with cards and donations made to our synagogue in honor of Steven's recovery. Being a Jewban means having fellow Jewbans at your side whenever you need them.

6   Being Jewban also means that a mix of generations will always support you and remind you how precious you are. It means knowing that wherever you are, you are loved unconditionally. It means having your grandparents drop by with a jar of your favorite homemade herring—the one with the huge chunks of carrots and onions. It means being told by your parents' friends in the Jewban community, "Adri, has cambiado tanto. Antes eras una niña chiquita y ahora eres una mujer preciosa." ("Adri, you have changed from a young girl into a beautiful woman.") Being a Jewban means belonging to one of three Cuban Hebrew Congregations in Miami Beach and—through the help of older members—bringing the joys of the past into the future.

7   But most importantly, being Jewban to me means having the most wonderful family in the world: two brothers who call me at nine in the morning to wish me good luck on my math exam and parents who work their hardest so we can go to the college of our choice. Being Jewban is feeling warm inside every time I say the words *Jewish* and *Hispanic* in the same sentence. It means a mixture of cultures that thrive on unity, love, loudness, celebration, tradition, and family. It means being the luckiest girl in the world who loves to sit down and talk about her heritage all day long. To fulfill my Jewban upbringing, I will raise a family with the Jewban customs I have learned to love. My children will learn Spanish and go to Hebrew school. In essence, to me, being Jewban means the good fortune to know that I am different and that I have a whole group of Cuban Jews whom I consider my family.

Here is one young woman's powerful and moving attempt to define the African-American female experience. What are the essay's assets? How is it organized?

Being Born a Black Woman Is . . .
Yolanda R. Taylor

1   I strongly resent growing up in a society where being born a woman puts me at an automatic disadvantage. I often ask myself why this is. All women should be held in high esteem because we carry the future of the world in our wombs. You may, therefore, ask why I write about being a *black* woman. The answer is simple: Black women encounter prejudice that goes beyond gender to include race. My feelings about being born black are as strong as my feelings about being born a woman. Like many other blacks, I ask myself time and time again, "Why must I be judged on the color of my uniform and not by my performance in the game of life?" Being a black woman, I find myself in double jeopardy. The only hope for change in our society must begin by facing the truth of our history and listening to the black woman of the past and present.

2   I am the first generation of black women in America. For me, being a black woman has meant being beaten and brought to a foreign land in chains. Those were my people on the slave ships Mary and God's Gift. I am the black woman who jumped overboard to free myself from the unknown horror in what the captain called the New World. I am one of the thousands who were stolen from their native African soil. As a result, my children do not know the beauty of the Motherland. They are ignorant of their native languages, family names, heritage, and culture. They do not know whether they are the descendants of great African kings and queens or fierce warriors. I am the black woman who was raped by a stranger. My children's skin has been lightened over the years by force, not choice.

3   It was my children that were taken from me at birth and sold for cheap labor. I am the one who scrubbed and cleaned "Miss Ann's" floors. I am the woman who moaned all night when "master" hung my son from the big oak tree in the hills of Tennessee. Every time I close my eyes, I see my son's lifeless head in the noose and all the fight gone from his dark body. I am the black woman who set up the Underground Railroad, which helped hundreds of slaves escape to freedom in the

North. It was I, Harriet Tubman, who put my life on the line and answered the cry for freedom. I am the black woman of the distant past.

Decades later, I am regarded as a second-class citizen in a socially, economically, and educationally unequal society. "Separate but equal" laws prevent me from drinking from the same water fountains as whites and prevent my children from attending white schools. It is my children who receive an inferior education. Tired of being separated and segregated, I am the black woman who was arrested because I refused to give my seat to a white man on the bus. I, Rosa Parks, am the woman who sparked the Montgomery, Alabama, bus boycott.

5   I am the darker sister whose hair is not as straight, whose nose is not as pointed, whose lips are not as thin as white society and the media dictate. I am the black woman who cannot get a job as an elevator operator because my complexion is too dark. I am the lighter sister—the outcast of the black race. It is thought that I am not black enough because of my light hair and eyes. I am labeled a "wanna be." Yes, I am a "wanna be"; I "wanna be" accepted by my darker brothers and sisters.

6   I am the widow of a black minister who gave his life to the civil rights movement. I am the black woman who raised his children and held our family together. I am the woman he turned to for inspiration and support. I, Coretta Scott King, nurtured the great dream that united an entire race of people. I symbolize the black woman of the not-so-distant past.

7   In the late twentieth century, I am a black woman trying to raise four children on welfare. I am uneducated and unemployed. The only job I can get pays minimum wage, which is barely enough to pay the babysitter. I could go back to school, but who would watch my children? That is why I never questioned my son when he started bringing home money. It comes from an illegal source, but it pays the bills and feeds my other children. He is regarded as just one more kid who has lost his way in society. Yet he is my only hope, my salvation.

8   I am the black girl who was raped in New York and left with racial slurs on my body. Many Americans did not believe my story, and those who did were not powerful enough to have the perpetrators punished. I, Tawana Brawley, am the black girl on whom America turned its back.

9   I am the woman who was tired of being silent, so I sought a way to express myself. I turned to writing. I, unsatisfied with hearing *his* story, wrote my own story. I am Maya Angelou. I am the great-granddaughter, the continuation of the black race in America, tomorrow's promise. I am accomplishing things that I once only dreamed about. I, Carol Gist, am the first black Miss USA. I represent *all* American women.

10   I am a college student at Hampton University, completing my master's degree in education. My dream is to educate and uplift the black race—to stop the cycle of teen pregnancy, drug use, illiteracy, and violence that has troubled my race in the last decade. My sisters and I represent the future of black women.

11   This is the black woman's story, and many of its chapters have separated her from women of other races. Her story is one not often told in the history books that read like fairy tales: "It was a land of plenty, overflowing with opportunities." Opportunities for whom? Not for black women. It is time to listen to the real story—the story of a great race of people who were not only slaves but were an indispensable and instrumental force in building America. The black woman's time has come.

Finally, let's look at two essays in their "before" and "after" drafts. In the first case, as you read draft A of Kimberly's "Track," mark problems that you would attempt to solve in a later revision if you were the writer. Then read draft B and see if she had the same ideas—and the same solutions. A discussion follows.

DRAFT A   *Track*

Kimberly A. Cook

1   The definition that the dictionary gives for track is: sports performed on a track, as running and jumping. This by no means does track any justice. If that was all there is to track everyone would be doing it—track is much more than running and jumping on a track.

2   Track requires that a person gives of herself physically, emotionally, and mentally. She must be willing to give 150 percent in each.

3   Track is practice. Practice is running, running, and more running—six times a week, two hours a day. It is running two miles—just as a warm-up. Then running a total of six additional miles as sprints. Last, but most certainly not least, running another two miles—as a cool down. How does one accomplish all of this in two hours you ask. You are pushed to do so. You are pushed to complete each event in a specified amount of time; sometimes seeming impossible to do. You are pushed to complete ten 100-yard dashes in 12–15 seconds each, ten 200-yard dashes (1/8 of a mile) in 25–30 seconds each, and four 400-yard dashes (1/4 of a mile) in 60 seconds each. Track is doing all of this day after day, afraid to think of tomorrow, for you might not make it through today. Track is waking up at five o'clock Saturday morning—after running a track meet that lasted until 11:30 Friday night—to make it to practice at 6:45 A.M.

4   Track is getting bundled up in every piece of clothing that can be found, to run in -30 degree weather. Track is running on ice and in snow, too numb to think about how long you have been running. Track is trying to find the coolest clothing you can, to run in 90-degree weather for practice. Track is running as hard and fast as you can while sweat pours down your face stinging your eyes and open pores. The sweat pouring from your whole body feels like every drop of water you've ever tasted leaking from invisible holes in your body, pushing you closer to dehydration. Track is trying to run the last 10 yards, in practice, when you dig deep within yourself to pull forth that extra burst of energy—only to find emptiness.

5   Track is waiting, in shorts and a tank top, for the starter to give the commands: runners to your marks—set—BANG! The gun sounds and you're off running against the wind as it sides with the rain—slapping you in the face, whipping up under the paper-thin shorts, and making giant water puddles for you to splash in. Finally you cross the finish line and looking around you see that you are the first runner to cross. You stand there with a smile of triumph peeking through the strands of dripping wet hair covering your face and knowing that it wasn't all for nothing. Track is sitting in the bleachers, not so eagerly awaiting your next race, freezing in your sopping wet sweats.

6   Track is running to the restroom every fifteen minutes while waiting for your event to come up. Then arriving at the starting line only to feel the bowels churning and your bladder instantly refilling.

Track is waiting in the set position for the gun to go off, knowing that you have no chance of beating your opponents—or even worse, knowing that you can and should beat your opponents by giving nothing less than 110 percent and running a time that you ran only one other time in your whole track career—at practice, under absolutely no pressure.

7   Track is being ahead in a race, closing in on the last 10 yards and suddenly feeling the sharp, piercing pain of the shinsplints you had hoped would not surface. The closer you get to the finish line the sharper the pain, yet you want to stay ahead so you try to ignore it—crossing the finish line you collapse in what is now triple the pain.

8   Track is running the first leg of a relay with the heavy pressure of gaining a lead for your relay team weighing you down. It is the relief you feel when you pass the weight along, as you pass the baton to the second leg of the relay. Track is standing in the ready position, as the anchor of the relay, watching as the baton is passed from person to person, and feeling the weight of keeping the lead getting heavier and heavier until it is finally passed on to you. It is the eagerness of the chance to bring the relay team into first as you wait to receive the baton. It is the humiliation of knowing in your heart that there is no way humanly possible for you to avoid finishing last, running as the anchor, yet still running as fast as you can.

9   Track is running in your third consecutive event with the sun beating down on your back, shinsplints bolting through your legs, cramps slicing through your stomach and crossing the finish line first, only to be told that one of your relay team members got the team disqualified.

10   Track is consistently tying and finally beating the fastest runner on the team. It is constantly defending your new title as the fastest runner on the team. It is finally getting comfortable and confident with this title at the end of the season only to find that there will be incoming freshmen to compete with next season. It is watching your title threatened, then taken away by the very freshmen that you coached and encouraged to become as good as they are.

11   Track is earning a varsity letter four years in a row and various team honors and championships. It is participating in the meet that the team finally, after seven agonizing and humiliating years, defeats a long-standing rival.

12   Track is going through practice after practice struggling to finish; experiencing sometimes triumph and success, and sometimes defeat and failure; gaining a varsity letter and winning team championships; being stressed during senior year with everything that comes along with it, not wanting to continue to run.

13   Track is ending your career by not going to the state meet and letting your relay team down because you are just too sick and tired of track to run your last race. It is later hearing, but not wanting to believe, that your relay team could have had a chance if you had shown up—and living with the consequence of never knowing yet always wondering, "Could I have made that difference?"

DRAFT B   *Track*
Kimberly A. Cook

1   The *Scribner-Bantam English Dictionary* defines track as "sports performed on a track, as running and jumping." This definition by no

means does any justice to track. If that was all there was to track, everyone would be doing it. Track is much more than running and jumping. Track requires that a person give of herself physically, emotionally, and mentally. She must be willing to give 150 percent in each area.

2   Track is, however, the sport that gets pushed into the small corner of the sports page—underneath the forecast of the basketball championships, and squished between the long article about last night's softball game and an advertisement for a sporting goods store. It is the sport that basically gets what is left over—after football, basketball, and swimming—in scholarship money. Track is the sport in which the teammates are often the only spectators and supporters.

3   Track is practice. Practice is running, running, and more running—two hours a day, six days a week. It is running two miles—just as a warm-up, then running a total of six additional miles as sprints. Last, but most certainly not least, it is running another two miles—as a cool down. How does the runner accomplish all of this in two hours? She is pushed. Her coach pushes her to complete each event in a specified amount of time. She is expected to complete ten 100-yard dashes in 12–15 seconds each, ten 200-yard dashes (1/8 of a mile) in 25–30 seconds each, and four 400-yard dashes (1/4 of a mile) in 60 seconds each. Track is doing all of this day after day and not stopping to think of tomorrow, for if she does, she might not make it through today. It is running the last ten yards in practice and digging deep within to pull forth that extra burst of energy—only to find emptiness. Track is waking up at five o'clock Saturday morning—after running a meet that lasted until 11:30 Friday night—to make it to practice at 6:45 A.M.

4   Track is getting bundled up in every piece of clothing that can be found, to run in -30 degree weather. It is running on ice and in snow when she—as a long-distance runner—is too numb to think about how long she has been running. Track is trying to find the coolest clothing she can, for practice runs in 90-degree weather. It is running as hard and fast as she can while sweat pours down her face, stinging her eyes and open pores. The sweat pouring from her whole body feels like every drop of water she's ever tasted leaking from invisible holes in her body, pushing her closer to dehydration.

5   Track is running to the restroom every fifteen minutes while waiting for her event to come up, then arriving at the starting line only to feel her bowels churning and her bladder refilling. Track is waiting for the starter to give the commands: "Runners to your marks—set—BANG!" The gun sounds, and she is off running into the wind as it sides with the rain against her—slapping her in the face, whipping up under the paper-thin shorts, and making giant puddles for her to splash in. Track is focusing only on the finish line, never turning to see where her opponents are—for fear of losing crucial seconds and falling behind. It is finishing the race and looking around to see that she is the first to cross the line. It's the smile of triumph peeking through the strands of dripping wet hair covering her face as she realizes it wasn't all for nothing.

6   Track is a hurdler waiting in the set position for the gun to go off, knowing that she has no chance of beating her opponents—or knowing that she can beat them only if she gives nothing less than 110 percent and runs a time that she ran only once before in her whole track career—at practice, under absolutely no pressure.

7   Track is running the first leg of a relay with the pressure of gaining a lead for her relay team weighing her down. It is the relief she feels as she passes the burden. Track is standing in the ready position as the anchor of the relay—the last leg—watching the baton being passed from person to person and feeling the weight of keeping the lead getting heavier and heavier until it is finally passed to her. It is the eagerness of the anchor who waits for the chance to bring the relay team into first. It is the humiliation of the anchor who runs as fast as she can yet knows that there is no way humanly possible to avoid finishing last.

8   Track is consistently tying and finally beating the fastest runner on the team. It is a runner constantly defending her new title as the fastest runner on the team. It is finally getting comfortable and confident with this title at the end of the season, only to find that there will be incoming freshmen to compete with next season. It is watching her title threatened, then taken away, by the very freshman that she coached and encouraged to become as good as she is.

9   Track is a sprinter sitting in the bleachers, not so eagerly awaiting her next race, freezing in her sopping wet sweats. Track is running her third consecutive event, putting forth all that she has, and crossing the finish line first—only to be told that one of her teammates got the team disqualified.

10   Track is being ahead in a race, closing in on the last ten yards and suddenly feeling the sharp, piercing pain of the shinsplints she hoped would not surface. The closer she gets to the finish line, the sharper the pain, yet she wants to stay ahead so she tries to ignore it. Then, crossing the finish line, she collapses in what is now triple the pain.

11   Track is earning a varsity letter four years in a row and various team honors and championships. It is participating in the meet in which the team finally, after seven agonizing years, defeats a long-standing rival. Track is going through practice after practice, struggling to finish, sometimes having success and triumph, other times defeat and failure. It's one more stress during an already stressful senior year.

12   Track may be a runner ending her career by not going to the state meet and letting her relay team down because she is just too sick and tired of track to run her last race. It may be hearing later, but not wanting to believe, that her relay team could have had a chance if she had shown up—and always wondering, "Could I have made the difference?"

13   For those who take it seriously, track is a learning experience. It is learning how to work with others as a team: encouraging and praising or correcting and critizing one another when needed. It is learning how to take the good with the bad, success with failure. It is learning how to deal with triumph and defeat. Track is a lesson in life: who you are, who you want to be, and what you need to do to become that person.

Discussion

This is a great set of drafts for student writers to study. Kim had some problems in draft A and came up with very inventive solutions in draft B.

First, a note about sentence structure. You probably noticed right away that in both drafts Kim uses a single sentence pattern over and over: "Track is this" and "Track is that." In some papers, this would become monotonous and be a drawback; in fact, you might find it too repetitive for your taste even here. But it's important to realize that Kim made a conscious choice of this style. Track is many things, and she's defining the sport by a process of accumulating facts and observations.

The great virtue of draft A is that Kim has a lot of knowledge and emotion about her subject. She uses interesting, specific information and some colorful, concrete language. But the essay as a whole is arranged in almost random order. Some paragraphs hang together, and others do not. Overall, there is no strong, clear organization in the first draft, but there's great potential.

Also, a challenging pronoun problem appears right away: How should the writer refer to the track runner? In draft A, Kim begins with the pronoun *she* in paragraph 2, then switches first to *one* and then to *you* in paragraph 3. Kim stays with *you* for most of the draft until the last paragraph, when the track runner becomes *I*. This may seem a minor issue, but in reality it's an important one to resolve. Pronoun switching can make a paper seem loose and unfocused, lacking in coherence. In the first draft, Kim is in the position all writers find themselves in once in a while: She will have to decide which pronoun will serve her purposes best and then stick with it. It's not a case of right or wrong; the only error here is inconsistency.

Another problem is that some of the paragraphs in draft A don't have their own distinct identity. One cannot say that each paragraph is about a different aspect of track. Look at draft A, paragraph 4: All the material in this paragraph revolves around a single subtopic—except for one sentence. Which sentence veers away?

In draft A, the sentences are sometimes not as tight as Kim wanted them; this is especially true in the second half of the draft (paragraph 8 is a good example). Punctuation is another issue she needed to address.

How did Kim jump over these hurdles in her revision? First of all, she switched to the pronoun *she,* which was a very effective change. It's true that all of this information about track probably applies to males as well as to females, but Kim had the female track athlete in mind as she wrote, so why not use *she?*

The shift to *she* created coherence, but it also added drama and a greater sense of solidity to draft B. With this switch, things fell into sharp, dramatic focus. Suddenly we are able to see a woman runner, a woman hurdler. We watch all that she does, all the effort, joy, and disappointment. It rings true.

You probably noticed two entirely new paragraphs in the revision: paragraph 2 on track's second-class status in the media and in terms of scholarship support, and paragraph 13, a new conclusion that stands back from all the subdefinitions in a reflective and all-inclusive way.

By a number of seemingly small changes, Kim worked some magic that makes us recall the last sentence of draft B: She took what was, figured out what she wanted it to become, and made the transformation happen.

Finally, let's work with one more set of definition drafts. Here the writer defines the hobby of car collecting. As you read Salig's first draft, mark its strengths and weaknesses and try to predict what he might do in his revision. Then read draft B and see how his essay actually did evolve. A discussion follows.

DRAFT A   *Collecting Old Cars*
Salig Ram Hutchins Sharma

1   Why should anyone want to collect cars? This has puzzled countless observers, many of whom have never seemed completely satisfied with any of the explanations. Old cars are often unkempt and cumbersome, a small number of them can take up an awful lot of space, and they're, well, not new. The ultimate madness as the puzzled non-collector sees it is that someone may spend good money—in some cases very good money—on an old car and then hardly ever use it. Why, well it's probably something like what Louis Armstrong meant when somebody once asked him about jazz, "If you have to have it explained to you, you probably won't understand anyway."

2   But, explanations of a sort do exist. One thing that makes cars different from most other collectibles is that they are active not passive things. With coins, stamps, furniture, paintings, etc., the objects of our attention usually lie, sit, or hang there while they accept our interest and respect. Cars can sit around also but they are at their best when they are doing something. Cars are very lively things, generating sounds, sights, and a kind of physical involvement that conventional artifacts can never give us. They are equal parts of technology, history, dreams, and art. Anyone who might regard the automobile as frivolous or unimportant should be reminded that few other creations of man have had so profound an effect on the lives of everyone in civilized society during this century, or have given us such mobility, such opportunity, and such freedom.

3   Perhaps cars fascinate us so because they're endowed with so many human characteristics, admirable and otherwise. Cars are very like living things, with identities and personalities as evident and varied, and variable, as any group of people you ever knew. In cars one can find treachery and pretense, impatience and inexhaustible, doglike devotion. Some never seem to be satisfied no matter how much money and attention they get. And like people, while some manage to get by on their looks alone, the most honored of them are admired for their style, their accomplishments and engineering.

4   Like most things, car collecting isn't what it used to be. What was once a peaceful, genteel hobby enjoyed by knowledgeable men and women is now overrun with crooks and con artists of every imaginable type, all scrambling for a piece of the action.

5   The boom began in the seventies, following the groundswell that had been building for ten or fifteen years before. A Model J Duesenberg (1929–1935), one of the greatest of all American automobiles, would change hands for $1,700 in 1959, and for $35,000 in 1969. Today one could cost you a million or more. It's the old story of supply and demand. The number of people involved in car collecting has expanded tremendously, while the number of cars remains more or less constant.

6   As rapid as the growth of car collecting has been recently, it's probably going to continue to expand throughout the Nineties, barring

some kind of economic calamity. It's no news that Americans have idolized the automobile during its 100-year life span. In its limitless variety and indispensable utility, it has touched us all, and played no small part in building this nation.

7   But sadly, the generations of cars that have been so many things to so many of us are not to be followed by more of the same. Cars from now on are going to be increasingly efficient, first and last, and if you find this prospect unexciting, that's only because it is. One feels truly sad for those who will grow up from now on, never knowing the drama and delight that were once a natural part of the automobile; when cars were so different from one another that, if you were really good, you could stand on a street corner with your eyes closed and identify every one that passed by sound alone. Perhaps all that variety won't go out of the automobile, but most of it will, and it's not coming back. This is why old cars are so precious.

DRAFT B   *Collecting Old Cars*
Salig Ram Hutchins Sharma

1   Why would anyone want to collect old cars? This has puzzled countless observers, many of whom never seem completely satisfied with any explanation. Old cars are often unkempt and cumbersome, a small number of them take up an awful lot of space, and they are, of course, not new. The ultimate madness, as the puzzled noncollector sees it, is that someone might spend good money—in some cases very large sums—on an aged vehicle and then hardly use it. In explaining collecting to the noncollector, one is reminded of what Louis Armstrong said when somebody asked him to define jazz: "Anyone who has to ask will never know."

2   But explanations of vintage car collecting do exist. One thing that makes cars different from most other collections is that they are active as opposed to passive. With coins, stamps, furniture, and paintings, the objects of our attention usually lie, sit, or hang while they accept our interest and respect. Cars can sit around also, but they are at their best when they are being driven! Cars are very lively things, generating sounds, sights, and a kind of physical involvement that ordinary objects could never give us. Technology, history, dreams, and art—these are all part of an automobile. Anyone who might regard the automobile as frivolous or unimportant should be reminded that few other creations of man have had so profound an effect on the lives of everyone. In civilized society, during this century, these objects have facilitated our mobility, provided opportunity, and promoted our physical freedom.

3   Perhaps cars fascinate us so because they are endowed with so many human characteristics, admirable and otherwise. Cars are very like living things, with identities and personalities as evident and as varied. In cars one can find treachery, pretense, impatience, and inexhaustible, dogged devotion. Some never seem to be satisfied no matter how much money and attention they get. Like people, while some manage to get by on their looks alone, the most honored of them are admired for their style, their accomplishments and engineering.

4   But like most things, car collecting is not what it used to be. What was once a peaceful, genteel hobby enjoyed by knowledgeable men and

women is now overrun with crooks and con artists of every imaginable type, all scrambling for a piece of the action.

5   The boom began in the seventies, following the groundswell that had been building for ten or fifteen years. A Model J Duesenberg (1929–1935), one of the greatest of all American automobiles, would change hands for $1,700 in 1959, and for $35,000 in 1969. Today one could cost you a million or more. It's the old story of supply and demand. The number of people involved in car collecting has expanded tremendously while the number of cars remains more or less constant.

6   As rapid as the growth of car collecting has been recently, it is probably going to continue to expand throughout the nineties, barring some kind of economic calamity. It's no news that Americans have idolized the automobile during its 104-year life span. In its limitless variety and indispensable utility, it has touched us all and played no small part in building this nation.

7   But sadly, the generations of cars that have been so many things to us are not to be followed by more of the same. Cars from now on are going to be increasingly efficient—first and last. If car lovers find this prospect unexciting, that's because it is. Modern manufacturers operate under the constraint of diminishing resources that has caused an overall move towards efficiency. Dwindling oil reserves and the subsequent high cost of gasoline have necessitated the move from the V-12 and even V-16 engines of the past to the less thirsty V-6 and 4-cylinder engines of the present. Because of our concern with fuel consumption, a car's bodywork, which was once fantastic, aesthetically pleasing and limited only by the designers' imagination, is now dictated by cold aerodynamic equations. The use of robotics and the high cost of skilled labor have done away with the hand-built automobile of the past. With the hand-built automobile's demise, we lose such touches as hand-cut felt insulation between dashboard and gauges, and the small squares of leather hidden between wood and metal wherever the two meet on such cars as the Mercedez-Benz of the 1950s and 1960s.

8   One feels truly sad for those who will grow up never knowing the drama and delight that were once a natural part of the automobile. Cars were so different from one another that, if you were really good, you could stand on a street corner with your eyes closed and identify every one that passed by sound alone. One might hear a 1932 SJ Duesenberg with its characteristic high-pitched whine from its centrifugal supercharger, or the conspicuous absence of almost any sound at all coming from a 1935 Auburn 851 Speedster stopped at the traffic light.

9   During the last six years I have been involved in the painstaking restoration of a 1969 280SE Cabriolet Mercedez-Benz. This work has shown me the character that older automobiles have when compared to the generic cars of today. This certain quality of great old cars is difficult to sum up in words, but it can be seen in the expressions of awe and amazement on the faces of the young and old at any classic car show. This is why old cars are so precious and should be preserved.

Discussion

Salig's drafts give us a superb example of how to enrich and develop a paper through expanded detail and plain old polish—especially a little extra TLC in the diction and punctuation departments. Space constraints do not allow us to examine intermediate drafts, but it's useful to note that Salig's beautiful final product is the result of a lot of hard work—not just two drafts, but four.

What are Salig's most interesting and creative ideas about cars? Does he make you think about cars in a new way? If so, how?

Some paragraphs in draft B are polished but not changed much in their content. Others are expanded greatly. Where are the radical expansions in draft B? How do these add substance and depth to his essay?

Where are you helped by changes in wording or the insertion of punctuation? Improvements in both areas—the content and the surface—help keep us focused on the interesting ideas and enthusiastic style of the writer.

Note that in draft A the Louis Armstrong quote at the end of the introductory paragraph is actually a paraphrase. In draft B, Salig uses the famous quote in the exact form attributed to Armstrong.

In paragraph 4 (of either draft), Salig may have piqued your interest regarding how "crooks and con artists" have worked their way into the world of vintage car collecting. Does he satisfy that interest in paragraph 4 of draft A or B? In a later part of the paper?

For you as a reader, where has Salig done his best work in transforming his paper? What more could a reader want?

Comparison/Contrast Essays

Another form of exposition borrows one of the basic and universal operations of the human mind: comparing and contrasting. People compare and contrast other people, things, events, ideas—just about everything. When we shop, we compare two heads of lettuce: They're the same price, but one is larger, while the other is a little fresher. *Which head should we buy?*

We might compare two people we're dating: They're both very attractive, but one is more fun than the other. However, the one who's more fun is also less reliable. *Whom should we choose?*

We might compare two wars: The war in Vietnam and the war in the Persian Gulf were both tragic events, but the American people, as a whole, gave little support to one and substantial support to the other. One war was protracted while the other was over quickly. Soldiers returning from one were spit upon, while those returning from the other were lauded as heroes. So the two wars appear to be quite dissimilar, with the war in the Persian Gulf seeming to be the "preferable" war. If asked, most Americans would probably say, "If we have to go to war, that's the way to do it." Yet could it be, as some observers have suggested, that the war in the Persian Gulf was just as devastating as the war in Vietnam but did not seem so to many Americans because there were so few American casualties (although so many on the Iraqi side)? Could it be that, ultimately, the war with Iraq will have negative consequences as long-term and far-reaching as the war in Vietnam? *What are the instructive similarities and differences between America's two most recent wars?*

In all three examples, we are comparing and contrasting *for a purpose.*

(Often, by the way, people use the word *compare* to mean both—comparing and contrasting.) Keeping a clear controlling purpose is the most important thing you need to do when writing in this format. When you are asked to compare and contrast two things, don't do it just to be doing it. Don't say, "Apples and oranges are both fruit, but apples are red, green, or yellow, while oranges are orange." You know what your reader is going to think—and with good justification: "Yeah, so what?"

A good comparison/contrast paper is not only an exposition but also an argument. However, your teacher often does not give you the argumentative focus. You must create it for yourself. The writer must push a point, and this point is the paper's controlling purpose or thesis; it's the reason the writer is comparing and contrasting two items. Maybe you want to show that one thing is, quite simply, better than another. That's often a good, natural controlling purpose for a paper of this type. But your purpose might be more complicated. You might want to show how two things that seem so much alike are actually radically different when examined closely. Or, conversely, you might want to show how two public figures, for example, who seem so different are, at heart, much the same in some essential way.

If you keep it argumentative, the comparison/contrast format can be a very useful tool in a wide variety of courses and situations. And your papers will often practically organize themselves; you won't have to sit and think, "Should I put all the similarities first, and then go to the differences?" (This is sometimes a useful approach, sometimes not.) "Or should I say everything I know about *X* and then everything I know about *Y*?" (Always a bad idea: It makes your readers do too much work, because they have to remember everything about *X* until they get to the discussion of *Y* and then practically make the comparison or contrast themselves.)

If you have an argumentative purpose in mind for your paper, just go ahead and start writing: The similarities and differences that are important will often come up in natural, logical spots in your draft. If not, you can cut and paste later. By having a purpose for the comparison/contrast, you don't need to wonder, "Should I raise this point or that?" Raise a point if it's essential to your argument—or so interesting or riveting that you can't bear to leave it out.

One last note: Just as comparison/contrast writing overlaps with argument, it also overlaps with other formats, for example, definition. A writer might try to define what a subject *is* by showing the reader what it is not. Such a paper might try to define the essence of actress Susan Sarrandon by showing how she is unlike most Hollywood actresses and more like a certain type of European character actress.

The Pepsi Project

In 1989, the pop singer Madonna appeared in a two-minute commercial for Pepsi that cost the company $5 million to make. The commercial was set to the music of her then popular single "Like a Prayer." At almost exactly the same time that the commercial came out, Madonna's music video for "Like a Prayer" also debuted. The video was controversial, touching on the issues of race, sex, and religion. According to newspaper reports, Pepsi officials were very concerned that negative fallout from the video would hurt Pepsi's image, even though the commercial and the music video were separate entities, and Pepsi had had nothing to do with the creation or financing of the music video.

In a summer writing course, my students and I watched the commercial and the longer music video several times and had enthusiastic, intense—and sometimes loud—discussions about them. I asked my students to put themselves in the position of a top-ranking Pepsi executive who had to persuade other executives either to pull the commercial or to keep it on the air. (In reality, Pepsi executives quickly decided to pull the $5 million commercial from any broadcast stations that also showed the music video.)

In this writing assignment, it was natural for students to compare and contrast the commercial and the music video to make their arguments. Although the final essays varied a great deal in ideas presented and in structure, in each case, the writer's organizational plan grew naturally out of a clear controlling purpose.

Of the many thoughtful, lively, and fun-to-read comparison/contrast papers that resulted from this assignment, two are printed here. One says yes; the other says no. Which one persuades you? Why? Also, what was gained by the writers putting themselves in the shoes of an executive of a major corporation? Evaluate the voice each writer used.

Pepsi's Prayer
Marcus A. Williams

1   Recently Pepsi's marketing division designed and produced a new two-minute commercial featuring Madonna's single, "Like a Prayer." The commercial cost over $5 million to produce, but we willingly paid the price.

2   The commercial's chief theme is centered on the slogan "Pepsi: The Choice of a New Generation." Madonna is shown with a Pepsi in her hand, watching a tape of her eighth birthday party. The flashbacks to the birthday party are filmed in black and white to reinforce the feeling of a home movie. The commercial also features scenes of people drinking Pepsi and dancing in the streets with the grown-up Madonna; these scenes portray a very positive outlook on life—of which Pepsi is a very vital part. All the while, Madonna's "Like a Prayer" is playing in the background. The commercial ends with the eight-year-old Madonna holding up a Pepsi bottle to the camera as if to propose a toast. The adult Madonna, who is watching the home movie on her big-screen television, whispers, "Go ahead. Make a wish." The young Madonna blows out the candles on her cake.

3   The commercial is powerful, not only because it effectively sends a message that Pepsi has been around for years, but also because it implies that people have always liked Pepsi. When the viewer sees the older Madonna drinking a Pepsi and watching a home movie of the young Madonna drinking a Pepsi, he concludes that people everywhere have always drunk Pepsi, and he feels he wants to drink it, too. When the little girl blows out her candles upon Madonna's command, a subliminal message is sent: "Make a wish. Madonna's wish—to become a star—came true because she had a Pepsi in her hand." This associa-

tion with success encourages people to drink Pepsi, which is what an advertisement is supposed to do. As Executive President of the Marketing Division, I am very optimistic about how much our company stands to gain from this investment.

4   But the concern that my fellow executives express is not over the commercial. Their concern is with Madonna's music video for "Like A Prayer," which in some ways coincides with the Pepsi commercial. In the music video, Madonna takes a very strong stand against an issue that almost everyone tries desperately to avoid. She takes a stand against racism, and for that she is to be commended.

5   The music video has a very strong plot in which Madonna witnesses a robbery where a woman is brutally beaten by a gang of youths. A young black man comes to the aid of the woman, but then he is taken to jail when the police find him at the crime scene, even though he has committed no crime. Madonna uses the scene to express a conflict within herself—the same conflict we all should experience when we witness injustice. She struggles with the question of whether or not she should tell the police what she knows.

6   After this central part of the plot is established, Madonna uses several powerful scenes to get her point across. She appears several times singing in a field full of burning crosses. At a quick glance, one might conclude that she is being portrayed as an advocate of the Ku Klux Klan. But in a second, more focused view, one can see that she is communicating a message: If she does nothing to stop this black man from being punished for a crime he did not commit, then she is no better than the KKK. This, to some extent, helps her to figure out what she is going to do. What some of our executives are worried about is that such a powerful message might put a lot of people on edge with their own conscience. In other words, viewers may think about times when they failed to live up to their ideals, feel guilty about their behavior, and then associate their guilty, negative feelings with Pepsi, making them less apt to buy the product.

7   Another controversial scene in the music video shows Madonna going into a church for consolation in her struggle for peace of mind. In the church, encased in a shrine is a statue of St. Martin de Porres, a sixteenth-century saint who is the patron of the poor and the homeless. He has a serene, almost sad look on his face. As Madonna gazes at the statue, it seems to come alive. The statute walks out of its casing, looks Madonna in the eye, and leaves the church, as if to say, "It's *your* decision. It's up to *you* to do the right thing." She is left alone to figure out her dilemma. She picks up a dagger that was in the case with the statue and, feeling a sharp pain in her hands, drops it—only to discover stigmata in her hands. The stigmata represent a horrible truth that is very relevant to the story: For justice to be served, someone must suffer. When Madonna witnessed the robbery earlier, one of the perpetrators gave her a sinister stare that said, "Now that you have seen what happened, what are you going to do about it?" The sinister white man is representative of the larger white community looking at her to see what she will do—the right thing or the wrong thing? In this case, as in the case of Jesus, the one who does right is the one who suffers.

8   The video also contains a scene in which Madonna is falling through the sky; her fall is broken by a black woman who supports her, then lifts her back to where she wants to be. This scene clearly

exemplifies Madonna's personal views on blacks: She feels that blacks are not a people to be discriminated against, but rather to be respected; they are a people who have something to offer this society. It is this respect that motivates her to go to the police station and vindicate the innocent black man.

9   What it all comes down to is this: Even if some consumers view Madonna's "Like a Prayer" video in a negative light and then criticize our organization because she advertises for us, still a greater portion of the community will see the video for what it is—a solid, thoughtful anti-racism statement. It takes a strong company to stand behind Madonna in her controversial campaign. Even though her views may upset some people, these views are positive and need to be upheld. As a leader and a major corporation, Pepsi has a responsibility to take a stand—with Madonna—against racism.

Pepsi's Pratfall

Lisa M. Barksdale

1   Good afternoon, ladies and gentlemen. We are here today to decide whether or not our Pepsi advertisement featuring Madonna should be pulled from television. After thoroughly reviewing the commercial and the music video, both of which use the song "Like a Prayer," I feel strongly that there are several controversial issues that will not be well accepted by the public if we keep our commercial on the air and allow people to associate Pepsi with everything that is in the video. In spite of the fact that we have spent millions of dollars on this campaign, I firmly believe that we should pull the commercial from television.

2   Let's take a close look at the commercial and the music video. First, the commercial appeals to the general audience: children, parents, and grandparents. It shows Madonna as a child drinking Pepsi at her birthday party. The young Madonna dreams of future success. In intercut scenes, people are dancing around and having fun with both the young Madonna and the older one. The film flashes back to when the young Madonna is about to blow out the candles on her cake. Then the older Madonna says, "Make a wish." The young girl blows out the candles. Finally, the Pepsi emblem is displayed on the screen with the motto "The Generation Ahead."

3   The music video "Like a Prayer" differs from the commercial in dramatic ways. In the music video, Madonna witnesses the attempted murder of a young woman by some men. Soon after they stab her, the men flee from the scene. A young Black man runs up to the woman to see if she is all right; the police arrive and immediately arrest the young Black man. Because she fears the result of her actions, Madonna does not immediately tell the police what she knows about the crime. Instead, she goes into a nearby church to try to resolve the turmoil she is experiencing and make a decision: Will she tell what she saw and allow an innocent man to go free, or will she allow herself to be intimidated by hoodlums? In this dreamlike scene, a statue of St. Martin, a Black saint, comes to life, gently kisses her forehead, and whispers words of encouragement in her ear. Also in the dream, Madonna, who appears to fall through the air, is literally lifted up by the female reverend of a gospel choir.

4   An analysis of the commercial and the video shows that there are

certainly some positive aspects of both. As for the commercial, it is very lively, and it commands the attention of the audience. With all the dancing, singing, and celebrating, the commercial gives a clear and decisive idea of the message Pepsi is trying to express. The message is simply this: As a child, Madonna drank Pepsi and dreamed of success; her success came true and, as an adult, she still drinks it. We went into this project with the idea that a commercial featuring Madonna would make other children want to drink Pepsi and become successful, too.

5   The music video, which is not as simple and clear-cut as the commercial, contains several deep and meaningful messages. First of all, it expresses the belief that we should not contribute to the racism already present in society by being indifferent to people wrongly accused. For example, Madonna is reluctant to divulge the truth about the attack on the woman for fear of the consequences, but eventually she overcomes her fear. Second, Madonna uses Blacks and Caucasians interacting together in the music video; the video suggests that these races can work and play together. Finally the video evokes the feeling that we should trust in God, and everything will turn out positively. For instance, Madonna uses St. Martin, a female reverend, and a gospel choir to provide the enlightenment to help her see that she needs to do the right thing.

6   But in spite of the positive factors in the music video, there are other points that cannot be overlooked because there is a great likelihood that they will offend the public. First, the fact that Madonna is scantily dressed in the church will not look good for our company's image, especially when we are using the theme song of the video, "Like a Prayer," for our commercial. Yes, it is true that this is the Madonna that everyone is familiar with, but do we really want to be associated with a pop star in a low-cut dress sashaying up to a young choir boy and caressing his cheeks with her bosom almost in full view? Second, there is a symbolic association between St. Martin and the young accused Black man, but it is not apparent at first glance. This could cause much confusion and misunderstanding by the audience. Finally, much of the imagery used is complicated—especially the stigmata and the burning crosses. Any members of the viewing audience who judge the video on the basis of its complicated exterior without making an in-depth analysis of its true meaning are probably going to be offended, and their anger might be aroused again when they see the Pepsi commercial featuring the same star and the same music.

7   We, as a company, should not risk our image over this commercial. We must keep in mind the great potential for negative publicity that could result in protests and boycotts. We could very well lose more than the $5 million that we originally invested in the project. If protests are initiated by conservative religious groups or others, we could lose a lot of support from our customers; moreover, our image could be irreparably damaged. Although it will be quite a loss to our advertising budget, it will be more beneficial to Pepsi in the long run if we do not associate our company's name with Madonna's music video.

Tips on Comparing and Contrasting

When you compare and contrast, remember three important points: (1) **be interested in your topic**; (2) **give it limits** (broad topics may need to be narrowed); and (3) **work toward a thesis,** usually an argumentative one, that will control what goes into the essay.

What Can Be Compared

Comparison and contrast focuses on two items that are both similar and different. Of course, you can't compare a television newscast to a statistics course or a crystal bowl. It would be difficult, too, to make a logical comparison between a television newscast and a situation comedy, even though they're both television shows. If such a comparison concluded that the sit-com is better because it's funnier, so what? The newscast was never supposed to be funny. Obviously, it is not fair to compare two things that set out to achieve different purposes. A sit-com may be compared to another sit-com, and one newscast may be compared to another newscast. Within those guidelines, refinements can be made; for example, a sit-com with a focus on teenagers might be compared to another sit-com with a focus on teenagers; one station's local newscast might be compared to another station's local newscast.

Sizing Down

Think creatively and look inside large subjects for smaller, more original, and more doable ideas. For example, students often consider comparing and contrasting two well-known people, such as Malcolm X and Martin Luther King, Jr. There's a lot of merit to this idea because of the two men's essential similarities—both were important twentieth-century leaders, both were African Americans, both worked tirelessly for social justice, and both were assassinated. And there is at least one major difference between them—their respective methods of making their visions a reality. But still, Malcolm X versus Martin Luther King, Jr., is an awfully big subject. People could write entire books comparing these two men, and there are many books available on each man alone. It would be very difficult to do justice to either man in an essay.

With such a subject, student writers must set some limits, focusing not on the broad picture but on a smaller, more promising topic. For example, one student might compare these two men on a single point, such as their language or rhetorical style, the influence of their wives, or their ideas about women and women's rights. Another student might drop King altogether and instead compare two phases in Malcolm X's life—perhaps before and after his imprisonment or before and after his first trip to Mecca.

Ideas for Topics

If you have an argumentative purpose for doing so, you can compare and contrast two politicians; two feminist leaders; two athletic teams or two players on one team (make sure they play the same position); two leading actors; two movies by the same director, or two movies on the same theme; an old television show and its remake (for example, the old "Star Trek" and the new one); any movie and its sequel; anything that has come out in both television and movie form (for example, *The Addams Family* or *Batman*); two novels, stories, plays, or poems by the same writer, or two works of literature on the same theme; a man's approach versus a woman's approach to something (baby care, planting a garden, changing the oil in a car, lecturing to a class, serving as a circuit court judge); two computer programs that are supposed to do roughly the same thing; two video games (for example, Mario Brothers and Mario Brothers 2) or two video game systems (for example, Super Nintendo and Sega Genesis, or Sega Genesis and Turbo Grafx 16); black rappers and white rappers; male rappers and female rappers; two heavy metal bands; Take Six, a male *a cappella* group, and Sweet Honey in the Rock, a female *a cappella* group; two methods of making pottery; two types of beauty or charisma—possibly as personified by two different people; the early stages of the U.S. labor movement and the current state of the movement.

Don't forget about the possibilities that no one but you could discover. From the trivial and the quirky to the serious and profound, some of the best topics are ones that express your individuality and the ways you've developed as a human being. No one but you knows what you've read, what movies you've seen, what hobbies you've taken up, where you've been, and what you've been observing. Brainstorm on the choice of a topic itself, and you might be surprised at how many terrific options you have. You can do just about anything you want, as long as you have the enthusiasm to express what you know or to find out what you don't know and a reason for comparing and contrasting. Remember: You need to have something to prove.

Equal Time for Similarities and Differences?

Should a writer give equal time to the similarities and the differences when comparing and contrasting items? This is a common question students ask and, as it suggests a concern with fairness, it's not a bad question. But the answer is no. It's hard to imagine why it would ever be necessary to write an equal number of words or paragraphs on how two things are alike and how they're different. The idea is to write what you *need* to write to fulfill your purpose, your reason for comparing and contrasting the two chosen items (people, policies, movements, whatever). This need will differ from paper to paper and from student to student.

Notes on Organizing

There are many good methods of organizing a comparison and contrast paper. You'll discover all kinds of logical ways to proceed as you try different strategies, examine your classmates' drafts, and browse through newspapers and your favorite magazines, noticing how professional writers work in this mode.

One to Avoid: Lumping

There is one organizational method that you should avoid: This is the overly simplistic pattern of saying everything you know about X, then turning your attention in the other direction and saying everything you know about Y. A paper of this type ends up as two big unappealing lumps. For example, let's say that you've found an argumentative reason to compare two leading American actresses: Meryl Streep and Sally Field. The last thing you want to do is to write everything under the sun about Streep first, then to write everything you know about Field. Your readers will have to work too hard, because they'll need to remember all the information you gave about Streep in "lump 1" and then connect it to related points you give about Field in "lump 2." This format also tends to make writers repeat themselves as they struggle to help their readers remember how X (in our example, Streep) rated on respective points that they're now raising in relation to Y (in our case, Field).

Picking Your Points

Better than lumping your information is to pick out a few points or bases for comparison. For example, your paper might compare and contrast Streep's and Field's work in comedy, their work in drama, their charisma or star quality, and their apparent willingness to stretch or try unusual roles. By focusing on your bases for comparison, you can devote one section of your paper to each category. Each section might be one paragraph that is devoted to both Streep and Field, or two paragraphs, one on Streep and the other on Field. This depends, at least in part, on how much you have to say. The length of a paragraph may often be one-half to two-thirds of a double-spaced page. If a paragraph is much longer than two-thirds of a page, the reader will find it easier, visually, if you break it in two—assuming there's a logical way to do that. In our example, of course, there is a logical way because you're writing about how two different people stack up in one area.

Here's another question students sometimes ask: If you use the two-paragraph system (for example, you begin your paper with one paragraph on Streep as a comic actor and one paragraph on Field as a comic actor), do you always have to present the subjects in the same order (Streep first, Field second) for all your points? No, of course not. Do what's logical, what sounds right to you. Play it by ear. The paragraph police will not arrest you.

Picking your points is not the only way to organize a comparison and contrast paper, and sometimes it's not the best way, but it's a good one to know.

Similarities and Differences

Another format to consider is exploring the *similarities* between X and Y and then exploring the *differences* between them (or vice versa). This is a good approach if you want to argue that things *seem* alike (or different) but are not.

Let's say that you've decided to compare Yellowstone National Park in Wyoming, Montana, and Idaho to Glacier National Park in Montana. You want to show that, in spite of the fact that the parks seem very much alike and are often spoken about in one breath, they're in fact quite different and, because of these differences, Glacier is the superior park. This would be a lively, surprising thesis for a number of reasons, including the fact that Yellowstone is the most famous and possibly best-loved of our national parks.

You could write about the similarities between the parks first: They're both out West; they both have bears, bighorn sheep, Rocky Mountain goat, elk, moose, beautiful birds, and fabulous fishing; they both have gorgeous vegetation; each is rich with history. But soon you'd turn your attention to how the parks are different and how these differences ultimately favor Glacier. Yes, you could admit, it's true that Yellowstone has geysers, hot springs, and a herd of bison, but Glacier has more spectacular mountains, it's the home of the breathtaking Going-to-the-Sun road, it's less spoiled and less commercialized than Yellowstone, and fewer people visit Glacier than visit Yellowstone.

Last Words

With these notes in mind, settle on a topic; do some freewriting; then select from your freewriting and begin to shape, write, revise, and edit your comparison/contrast essay.

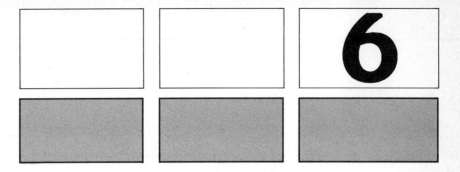

Special Concerns: Problems of Logic and Paragraph Organization

In this chapter, we'll look at two issues that are critical to solid writing: strong, clear logic and well-focused, coherent paragraphs.

Logic

No matter what you're writing, you need to check that your logic is clear and solid. Let's look at seven issues of logic and logical expression that often come into play in student writing.

Target Positions, Not People

Avoid attacking people when you are discussing their ideas, policies, or positions. Consider, for example, the sentence, "There is no reasonable way that the American people can be expected to follow the foreign policy leadership of a president who can't even admit he colors his hair." What does the issue of natural versus dyed hair have to do with a president's ability to execute sound foreign policy? While it may be true that the issue of honesty might be relevant here, it would be wiser for the writer to move to the heart of the matter and examine what's wrong with that particular president's foreign policy.

An attack on a person—especially when the focus should be on an issue associated with that person—is a cheap shot, and it raises the suspicion that the writer has no real case.

Don't Go Overboard

When people have strong feelings about things, they often overstate their case by what is termed *overgeneralizing*. For example, if you've recently been badly hurt by a member of the opposite sex, it's tempting to say, "Men are dogs" or "Women are heartless," even though your best self knows better. It's undeniable that *some* men are dogs and *some* women are heartless—at least some of the time. But if you're going to write "Men are dogs," then you might as well write "*All* men are dogs," because that's the effect your statement will have. You are unfairly characterizing all members of a group.

To solve the problem of overstating or overgeneralizing, pare down your statement to what you can actually stand behind and defend. One way to do this is to use *qualifiers*, which limit the scope of a statement. Qualifiers that can tame wild generalizations include *most, many, some, a few, usually, often, sometimes, in some cases, in many cases, in most cases, probably, generally, normally*, and *for the most part*. You also can use verbs that state things more accurately. For example, you might write, "Backyard swimming pools *can cause* neighborhood squabbles and terrible tragedies" instead of "Backyard swimming pools *cause* neighborhood squabbles and terrible tragedies," which implies "in all cases."

When teachers suggest revisions for sweeping statements, students often respond, "Well, that's what I meant; anybody would know that." It's good to give the reader credit for having common sense, but why count on the reader to *assume* that you are a careful, strong, fair-minded thinker when you can *prove* you are by choosing your words more carefully? Write in a way that accurately reflects the good ideas and sound judgments you're offering.

While you need to be on guard against overgeneralizations, don't let the use of qualifiers make your writing weak; you don't *always* need to hedge your bets. Some general statements are true. For example, "Serious followers of Judaism believe in the sanctification of life through ethical and moral behavior." This is a general statement about a large group of people, but it is not an overgeneralization because it is true: To be truly Jewish in the religious sense means to believe in this basic tenet. Other examples are "Babies need TLC," and "Human beings have a natural desire to be treated with respect." These statements are always true.

Also, be aware of the fact that even sentences with qualifiers can be tremendous overgeneralizations and ridiculous statements. For example: "*Most* men who are florists, hairstylists, or choir directors are gay." "Psychiatrists *usually* need more help than their patients." "Kids in junior high school are *generally* intolerable." Qualifiers don't help these statements at all.

Evaluate the following statements from student writing. Which ones are overgeneralizations, and how could you fix them?

1. People who wear $100 athletic shoes have no values.
2. Students who come to college learn that they do not write on the college level.
3. After people marry, the trust between them becomes more intense.
4. Whenever one person has caused the death of another, capital punishment is not only a just verdict, it is the only reasonable verdict.
5. Old people need love and attention just as young people do.

6.   Love—that hot wet stuff. We're all in search of it, yet most single people sit home alone every Friday night.

Make Sure That a Reason Is Really a Reason

In a book review, Abraham Lincoln once wrote, "People who like this sort of thing will find this the sort of thing they like." If you've got a sense of humor like Abraham Lincoln's, you might be able to get away with writing sentences that go in a circle. But if you're trying to make a serious point—be careful. Watch out for statements that *seem* to give a cause for a condition, but in reality just restate the condition.

Consider, for example, the sentence, "Stereotypes will always prevail in our society as long as we continue to be biased in our thinking." Is this any different from saying, "We'll always have stereotypes as long as we have stereotypes"? The sentence *seems* to give an explanation for stereotypes, but any sharp reader will see that it really doesn't. This kind of redundant sentence means next to nothing.

For some student writers, meaningless redundancy is a slippery and recurring problem, so here are a few more examples to consider. Try to rewrite any three.

1.   This being a chauvinistic world we live in, dominance over women is a common attitude among men.
2.   The Japanese have made it extremely difficult for U.S. firms to establish themselves in Japan by simply not allowing it to happen.
3.   The Education Department projected that the number of teachers will rise from 2.7 to 3.2 million between 1989 and 2001; this rise is attributed to more people entering the teaching field.
4.   It got terribly cold because the temperature dropped.
5.   He was a real hero to me because I had always admired him.
6.   The reason drugs are so prevalent and young people are under so much pressure to take them is that dope is everywhere, and wherever they go, someone is pushing drugs at them.

Does One Thing Really Lead to Another?

As a writer, you have to be very careful when you try to establish causes and effects. Try to imagine where there might be holes in your argument. Consider the following excerpt from a paper on the effects of divorce on children.

EXCERPT A

Many people try to avoid divorce because they want to stay together for the children, but then they often feel hatred toward each other and go through unnecessary troubles for the sake of their children. Therefore, the parents suffer more by staying in the marriage than the children would have suffered if the parents had decided to get a divorce.

It's true that some parents stay in a bad marriage for the sake of the children, but does the writer give any evidence to support the conclusion that, in these marriages, the parents suffer *more* than the children would have suffered had the parents split up? In fact, is it likely that any evidence could be found to support such a conclusion? Could the suffering of parents and the suffering of children be measured and compared? Are there other problems in the logic of excerpt A? What revisions would you make?

In relating cause and effect, writers often ignore potential causal factors (either by being unaware of them or by not citing them) or assume that what happened earlier—simply because it happened first—caused something that happened later. But often (not always, of course), the two happenings are completely or largely unrelated. For example, consider this excerpt:

EXCERPT B

>   The Smiths finally bought a Nintendo, and within twelve months little Billy had to repeat a grade and the parents were in divorce court.

Did a video game system cause all this trouble, as the writer seems to imply? If so, how does the writer know for sure? What other factors might have been involved?

Beware of Mixing Issues

It's hard enough proving just one point; it's a real mess trying to prove two or three points at a time. Keep things separate. Read the following excerpt from a paper arguing against smoking in the workplace.

EXCERPT A

>   One co-worker who smoked claimed that smoking helps smokers increase their work capacity. This can't be true because they're still damaging their own and others' health.

Isn't it possible that both things could be true—that smoking could give smokers a short-term boost but also be destructive to their health and to the health of others? These are two different issues, and each one needs fuller development. What are the mixed issues in this excerpt?

EXCERPT B

>   One way to correct the problem of alcohol and drug abuse in the airline industry is to forcibly administer a test to determine the level of alcohol or drugs in the blood of every pilot before he or she is allowed to fly. This idea may sound unethical, considering how expensive it could be.

Remember That "Society" Is Not Your Neighbor Down the Block

The final two points have more to do with the expression of an idea than with its logic.

Sometimes students write as if an organization or society itself were a person, attributing to it acts, thoughts, and speech. In student writing, this problem most often appears when the word *society* is used. One student wrote, for example, "Society has to take into consideration that success in life does not necessarily mean acquiring great masses of money." And another wrote, "Society thinks women have it so hard, but it has no sympathy for how rough it is to be a man in the 1990s." These sentences are imprecise and oversimplified—they make it seem as if we could change society's mind if we could just get her to sit still and listen. In essence, they are personifying society.

Personification happens with other words, too. Any abstraction or collective noun that signifies people lends itself easily to personification. For example, be careful of statements that begin "The women's movement thinks . . ." or "The scientific community acts as if . . ." Try to be more precise about *who* thinks and *who* acts.

Check Conjunctions

Conjunctions are more than little globs of glue; they not only attach clauses to one another but they also create meaning. Check to see if you have clear, logical conjunctions to show relationships between your clauses. As an exercise, try to revise these examples:

1. Most children are very frightened by overbearing, aggressive adults, *unless* they are also confused by this behavior.
2. Living with Harriet was an unforgettable experience *because* now the tables are turned, and I am living without her.
3. Americans should not make television a basis for entertainment and leisure *where* television should be used in a more moderate way.
4. *Because* I was her ninth child, my mother had some difficulty conceiving me.

Exercises on Logic

Let's work with more examples from student writing. The examples are excerpts from freewriting practice, in-class projects, and assigned stories and essays. Some are not so bad; others are outrageous. And you might find a couple of the examples are so funny that you'd kind of hate to change them, but consider: What if the writer did not intend a comic effect? Try to rate how effective each statement is based strictly on logic.

Exercise One

What, if anything, is wrong with the logic or logical expression of the following statements? You may see more than one problem in some items.

1. One child in the neighborhood read a newspaper story about the sadistic treatment of animals and then set fire to a newborn kitten; that's why the newspapers shouldn't print these stories.

2. The civil rights movement thought that it was time to say "No" to the lingering mentality of the Jim Crow laws.

3. On moral grounds, he disapproves of homosexuality, so of course he could never contribute any money to AIDS research.

4. President George Bush and his wife Barbara Bush both came down with the same rare thyroid condition while he was in office, so it must have something to do with the water in the White House or something else they were both exposed to.

5. The Detroit Pistons have no talent because they depend completely on brute strength and strong-arm tactics; they're a bunch of thugs who can't set a pick, make a pass, or dunk a ball to save their souls.

Exercise Two

Again, evaluate the logic or logical expression of each statement. Identify any problems.

1. The Chicago Cubs haven't won the World Series for ages because they just can't stop losing; they can't get on top of things; they absolutely cannot win. Let's face it: They're losers.

2. Women just look at babies and melt; men are more into their jobs than their families.

3. Elvis Presley was a first-class nothing; people thought he was a big deal when in reality he was just another white guy ripping off black musicians. The dude couldn't even sing, and everybody knows it.

4. Society says that it's so important to care for children properly, yet society pays child-care workers ridiculously low wages.

5. Then there is [a singer], who can't sing for [expletive deleted]. I have to turn the radio off every time I hear her. The minute I read somewhere she was into the environment, that was when I realized I never really cared about the damn whales in the first place.

Exercise Three

Evaluate each statement on the basis of logic or logical expression and identify any problems.

1. Teenagers can't stand the way their parents are always telling them what to do and never giving them any credit.

2. For a lot of people, contact lenses are a tremendous hassle because they're just so inconvenient.

3. Other countries have practically no athletic talent compared to the United States because just look at the Olympics: If the Americans had let their pro athletes play for all these years like a lot of other countries, everybody else would have had their butts kicked clear across the continent. Nobody except the U.S. would have won a thing.

4. Prayer in the public schools is a sensitive issue for Americans when people consider religion such a private affair and see the United States

as a Christian nation, yet everybody wants diversity and fairness for Jews, Muslims, and atheists, too.
5. Golf is a boring game in which very little happens because people go out there on the course, get bored, and do what? That's right—practically nothing.

Paragraph Organization

A good paragraph, no matter where it is in an essay—the introduction, body, or conclusion—doesn't always need a topic sentence, which is sort of a mini–thesis statement. But it *does* require a definite purpose, what the French call a *raison d'être,* or reason to exist. There must be a reason why it's one paragraph, not two, or why the material in it is not incorporated as part of another paragraph. Why is this paragraph a unit by itself? What is its job? If you don't have good answers to these questions, you don't have a paragraph.

Paragraphs represent steps or units in the thought process of the writer. They're part of a larger whole, building blocks inside stories and essays. Although it's unusual to discuss them out of context, there *are* things we can learn from looking at them this way. In this section, we'll examine individual paragraphs—both strong and weak—from the three major parts of papers.

Introductory Paragraphs

Pascal once said, "The last thing that we find in making a book is to know what we must put first." The same thing can be said for making an essay or story. The way we begin is important—so important that we often don't discover how to do it until the rest of the paper is finished.

The following two paragraphs exemplify some of the *worst* ways to begin an essay.

EXCERPT A

> In today's age of scientific knowledge, there have been many medical discoveries by scientists. Some of these have to do with the nature of the brain. The brain is a tremendous center of information. More funding is needed to study the human brain.

EXCERPT B

> There have always been many social problems throughout history. In today's society there are still many problems. One of them is the lack of acceptance of people with a different sexual orientation. This is a problem that needs to be addressed, and it needs to be addressed now.

It almost seems as if these writers are thinking, "Let me see how *bland* and *general* I can get." These writers think that they have to show how their topics fit into "the big picture." Taking such an approach in your introduction is usually a mistake. Often, you *don't* need to show how your topic fits into a bigger picture. And if you do need to relate your subject to a larger framework, you often can do so later in the paper. Making broad statements with phrases such as "in today's society" creates a boring beginning. The last thing you want your reader to think after reading your introduction is, "Do I have to read this? Maybe I'll go for a walk first. Are there any chocolate chip cookies left? I wonder what's on TV."

A good introduction sets the intellectual stage and the tone for the rest of the paper. Many times, it announces a thesis (the idea the paper will try to prove) or it hints at a thesis that the writer will reveal gradually. By announcing or hinting at a thesis in an introduction, the writer is appealing to the *mind* of the reader. In other papers, usually narratives or descriptions, the introduction does something more subtle and difficult to define: It evokes a feeling or creates an image or impression that will be expanded on throughout the work. When writers use such an approach in their introductions, they are appealing to the *heart* of the reader.

A good introduction invites the reader in. It's as if the writer is saying, "If you follow me closely, I won't waste your time. I'll delight you, intrigue you, make you think, help you see something in a new way, maybe make you change your mind. If you give me some time, I won't let you down." Thus, whether it's one paragraph or several, an introduction acts as a contract between writer and reader, promising a journey for both.

Let's look at some successful introductions. The first one is self-explanatory.

INTRODUCTION A   *Pain for Vanity*
Daniel R. Cauterucci

1   A man is browsing through a fashion magazine and finds himself attracted to an advertisement for a new mascara by Revlon. The ad depicts a woman's eye—a dark, deep blue eye outlined by thick black lashes. The man is attracted by the picture and wonders what thoughts and dreams lie behind that captivating feminine eye.

2   What actually lies behind the image, however, is another eye, one now scarred and blistered by the chemicals that were used in making and testing the mascara. Chemicals used in cosmetics must be tested to protect consumers, and a common method is testing on animals. Animal testing, however, causes great suffering and disfigurement and is not needed to ensure the safety of cosmetics. There are several alternatives that can be used in today's laboratories.

Daniel's introduction is a great example of the kind that both interests us and clearly states a thesis or lets us know where the writer is headed: Interest is created by the first paragraph, and the thesis is stated in the second. In the first paragraph he appeals to our hearts, and in the second he appeals to our minds. You won't always see the two tasks performed in such a distinct way. Sometimes introductions merge their appeals.

Next is a very interesting and unusually long introduction.

INTRODUCTION B   *Oh Contraire, My Brother*
Lester Reffigee

1   We see it in the movies—a pimp layered in five gold chains, his wide-brimmed orange hat leaning to one side, gaudy rings on each finger, and a long-length dog fur that flows as he walks. His prostitute is dressed in high-heeled yellow patent leather shoes, fish-net panty-hose, a micro-mini red leather skirt, and a bolero-cut rat fur. Neither one of these two characters can form or articulate a complete sentence.

2   We see it on television. A young girl, no more than fourteen, unable to bend down to tie her shoes because of her big belly, swollen not from too much bacon, but from pregnancy. The father unknown, the baby unwanted.

3   We read about it in the papers. On the corner of Black Street and Hail, a teenage boy is gunned down and his $300 leather coat is stolen. The victim lives but is unable to function as a normal human being.

4   We see it in our neighborhoods. A squadron of police surround an abandoned-looking house, babies cry, and neighbors peek while a drug bust is in progress across the street from our home. Men, money, and marijuana are taken down to the station.

5   Our cities are inundated with negative images of black people, and our youth are soaking it up like sponges. Yet, despite what many may believe, these youth possess high levels of self-esteem. How is it that black youth still view themselves in a positive manner, and how does this high level of self-esteem affect their achievement in academics? Recent psychological studies have attempted to answer these questions.

6   In her research on self-esteem, Beverly Hendrix Wright investigates the relationship between personal and racial self-esteem. . . .

Lester's introduction is a little longer than most, but you can see that it's provocative and effective, creating within readers a tremendous "need to read." With the vivid, grim pictures of the first four paragraphs in their mind's eye, many readers will be wondering—maybe for the first time in their lives—how it is that so many young blacks can see these images day after day and still develop strong self-esteem. Readers are primed and ready to follow Lester as he develops his thesis by giving a guided tour of psychological research on the interrelatedness of race, self-concept, and good parenting.

Finally, let's look at the introduction from two drafts of the same paper.

INTRODUCTION C   *Rain of Terror: The Environmental Challenge of the Decade*
Salig Ram Hutchins Sharma

EARLY DRAFT

A chemical disease is deteriorating the face of North America and Europe. This disease is commonly called acid rain. Acid rain is caused by the emissions of sulfur dioxide and nitrogen oxides from the combustion of fossil fuels. An array of natural sources, such as volcanoes, mud flats, etc., emit sulfur dioxide into the atmosphere. Although in comparison to industry's share, their contribution to the problem is quite small.

LATER DRAFT

> Acid rain has emerged as the most important and controversial environmental problem of the decade. Unlike the toxic wastes at Love Canal or the radioactive hazards of Three Mile Island, the substances that cause acid rain—sulfur and nitrogen oxides—are found throughout nature and are, in fact, part of nature's essential plan. But the burning of fossil fuels has released these substances into the air in quantities that dwarf nature's output and that have upset the balance in nature on a planetary scale. Acid rain is also more than an environmental issue: It has devastating effects on the economy and creates intense regional conflicts.

The introduction in the early draft does not state a thesis and does little to arouse a reader's interest. Can you see how much more pulled together the revised introduction is? It's much clearer and more accessible. Salig lets us see where he's headed and states what he wants to argue, namely, that acid rain is a more important problem than most of us realize because it affects not only the environment but also the economy and regional politics.

The revised introduction doesn't do anything terribly dramatic to arouse interest in the subject, yet in class discussion students invariably agree that it *is* much more inviting than the earlier version. By adding concrete references to Love Canal and Three Mile Island and by using the verb *dwarf* the writer shows us that he knows what he's talking about. The new draft evokes authority and a passionate interest in the subject. Its words pack a punch.

Paragraphs in the Body

There is basically only one thing to say about paragraphs in the body of a paper: Each must have its own reason for being. In the body of a paper, most paragraphs do one of two things: They make a *point,* or they serve as a *transition.* Although it's uncommon for a good paragraph to be just one or two sentences, and more likely for it to run from roughly one-third to two-thirds of a double-spaced typed page, there are few hard and fast rules in writing. A transitional paragraph might well be only one or two sentences in length. For example, a pivotal sentence such as, "There is another side to this story," could be set off as a paragraph by itself, placed between the two large chunks of material that present two sides of the story. The essential thing is for each paragraph to have a purpose.

Weak body paragraphs are predominantly of two types: those that have problems with focus and those that skimp on evidence or development.

Poor Focus

Good paragraphs are *planned;* they rarely just happen (although the more you practice, the faster you'll be able to plan them). In one type of weak paragraph, the writer goes on and on, never focusing on one point. The reader may sense, "Whatever comes, comes." Teachers usually judge such paragraphs as trying to do too much, but often the real problem is that the writer didn't try to make them do anything. The writer didn't plan the purpose of the paragraphs, and so they simply drifted on and on.

Here, for example, is a paragraph from the body of a paper that attempted to define discrimination but that, in spite of some excellent points, never found a strong, clear thesis. It's not surprising that the problems in the piece as a whole are reflected in individual paragraphs.

> Discrimination is both covert and overt. A handicapped person is denied access to facilities that she requires to do her job successfully. Another handicapped person who cannot walk is turned down for a job as a computer analyst because the prospective employer believes that he will be unable to perform at the same level as someone who is not handicapped. These are examples of overt discrimination. Homosexuals are now the victims of overt discrimination in areas such as housing, and covert discrimination in fields such as employment. In an era when people are being called on to provide a "kinder and gentler nation," people should feel morally obligated to be more accepting of others with varying sexual orientations. However, the public has yet to accept homosexuality in general. Therefore, homosexuals are being discriminated against in all aspects of society.

This paragraph starts out with a focus: The writer appears to be planning to show how discrimination is both overt and covert (although that in itself is a very tall order). Soon, however, the focus is diffused, and the point is lost. What assertions are left undeveloped and in need of explanation?

Weak Evidence or Development

Even if a paragraph has a good, strong purpose, it will be weak if the writer does too little to achieve that purpose. Without enough explanation or the support of convincing examples, a purpose, no matter how strongly stated, will remain undeveloped.

In the following two excerpts from a paper on double standards for men and women, the writer's purpose in each paragraph is fairly clear, but she does not do enough to develop those purposes.

EXCERPT A

> Sexism is also sometimes experienced in the work force. A woman may be qualified and not get a job just because she is a woman, or she may get the same job as a man, yet the man is sometimes paid more.

EXCERPT B

> When a boy is born, a father is usually needed. A single mother may not be as strict as a father. The child may lack discipline and may turn out to be a delinquent. Without a firm hand in the household, he may turn to crime and drugs.

Both of these paragraphs move too fast. The writer takes large leaps from one sentence to the next. She needs to slow down. These are enormously complex issues, and nothing is accomplished by glossing over things. But the purpose of each paragraph is clear. We have no questions about what's on the writer's mind. Our only question is why she stayed on such general turf. Why didn't she develop these ideas more precisely, give examples and evidence?

Again, the paper from which these are excerpted lacked a clear thesis. Remember, a single paragraph often is a microcosm of the paper in which it appears. So if you have a lot of difficulty making your individual paragraphs hold together, reexamine your paper as a whole. Does it have a tight thesis?

Powerful Paragraphs

We've looked at problems; now let's look at successes. The following paragraphs come from the bodies of two very different papers, but whether from a narrative about a personal episode in the writer's life or from a research paper, a good paragraph hangs together. It has unity. It does one thing, accomplishes one purpose within the larger effort of the story or essay. (Of course, in some pieces a paragraph may accomplish more than one goal, but it has to accomplish at least one.)

The first example comes from a paper defining the essence of being short. What makes this paragraph effective?

BODY PARAGRAPH A   *Being Short Means . . .*
Regina C. Hathaway

> The world was not made for short people. We're discriminated against wherever we go. If you've ever ridden on a bus, you know that the handrails are so high that it is almost impossible to reach them. I guess short people are just supposed to fall since we're "so close to the ground." Even clothes are not made for short people. There aren't very many places where you can find petite clothes that fit. You usually have to cut, hem, take up, or roll up. And, of course, when I drive a friend home from school, I often hear the crack, "Are you sure you can see over the steering wheel? Maybe you need a telephone book."

The format here is basic: a topic sentence and a few examples to show its truth. This is not a complicated format, but it's very effective. The material about the bus, clothes, and steering wheel all contribute to proving the truth of the first sentence: "The world was not made for short people." This is a well-done paragraph of a classic type. All paragraphs don't have to be this clear-cut, but they all do have to hang together in some sort of way.

What makes the next paragraph effective?

BODY PARAGRAPH B   *Women in Music Videos:*
Victims or Victors?
Stephanie S. Wright

> Some people condemn music videos because of the negative, stereotypical roles that exploit women. One of the most common stereotypes in videos is the sultry woman with the 36-24-36 figure, dressed scantily in tight-fitting clothes and portraying the sex object of

the male performer. One of the members of 2 Live Crew, in the video "Me So Horny," displays the sexist behavior so commonly found in videos as he lounges in his robe, watching a woman undress and chanting, "Me so horny, me so horny." But now, some female artists are creating new images of feminine control and power. Janet Jackson, for example, wears black military gear as she commands her army of dancers. A more complex example is seen in the video "Expression" as Salt-N-Pepa, wearing sequined bras, chant "I'm in command!" Like an African monarch, Queen Latifah sports her lavish headdresses and says, "I order you to dance for me!" In "Ladies First," looking powerful and dominating, she sends the message that women can stand on their own. Many female performers have shunned the stereotype of the sex object to show the emergence of women with strength and power.

Stephanie's paragraph answers one charge: that music videos are bad because they portray women in a sexist way. Notice how she first wisely acknowledges that there *is* some basis for the charge and then shows, with a number of good examples, how the picture of women in music videos is changing. The business of this paragraph is clear: It sets forth an accusation and answers it.

Some writers, especially those who follow more of a newspaper style, might have broken body paragraph B into two paragraphs. (Newspaper copy breaks into new paragraphs for every possible reason, to keep stories as easy to read and accessible as possible.) That would be fine, as long as the break came at the one natural spot for it. Where is that spot?

Concluding Paragraphs

It's important to end your paper on a strong note. Your ending is your last chance to make your case. Take some time and do it right.

Weak Endings

This paragraph, from a paper comparing the virtures of baseball to those of basketball, is a classic example of the weak conclusion:

EXCERPT A

> I hope that I have effectively used history, traditions, rules and officiating, mechanics, and my opinions to present a comparison and contrast of baseball and basketball that is both informative and interesting.

The conclusion of your paper is not the time to *hope* you wrote a good paper. It's your last chance to *make* it a good paper—wrap it up, hit home, say something memorable. Excerpt A reads as if the writer is thinking, "Thank goodness that's over. I'm outta here."

The second example, which is from a paper in support of the rights of lesbian mothers, mirrors the problem of the type of introduction that generalizes about "today's society."

EXCERPT B

> This country is full of close-minded people. In other words, they are ignorant of new cultures that are brought to or born in the United States. Must we attack every new culture as if it were a threat to our old and accepted culture? This is childish! In this modern world of ours, we really should accept every culture, new and old, for what it is and not for what we want it to be.

As you can see, excerpt B is vague, a little preachy, and contains at least one generalization that the writer probably does not want to support, namely, that "we really should accept every culture, new and old, for what it is . . ." For one thing, who is "we"? For another, can you think of any culture—one that existed in the past, one that exists now, or one that could be imagined in the future—that reasonable people (assuming this is what the writer means by "we") would *not* want to accept?

This sort of all-purpose conclusion could be tacked on—but with equally little success—to almost any paper. Notice that it says nothing about lesbians, their roles and rights as mothers, the possible effects on children, or anything at all specifically related to the argument of the paper. It just says people are close-minded and should try to do better. That's not going to convince too many readers. It's also not going to help them remember this paper for long—even if it was a powerhouse up until the conclusion.

Another thing you don't want your conclusion to do is straddle the fence. Even if your issue is very complex and you have considerable sympathy for the other side, you need to be clear and decisive at the end. Does the following conclusion from an argument essay on the subject of using animals in scientific research leave you with a firm impression about the writer's thesis?

EXCERPT C

> Scientific research is perhaps the major means by which the sum of human knowledge has been expanded. Though many people have benefitted from the medicines and surgical techniques made possible by animal research, there has often been disagreement over the methods used by science to reach its ends. Animal research has been viewed as both an absolute necessity for scientific progress and as a cruel and immoral exploitation of animals.

Strong Endings

A good conclusion—normally only one paragraph in length but, as in the case of introductions, sometimes longer—gives a feeling of closure to a paper. A writer might achieve this feeling by summing up major points, by creating an especially vivid image, or by stating a well-expressed final sentiment.

Summaries   Some conclusions unnecessarily sum up all of a paper's major points. This can be repetitive, boring, and sometimes even insulting to your reader. A summary conclusion works well only in a paper where the points have been numerous and/or complex—in other words, where it's a good bet that the reader could use a quick explanation or reminder of all that the writer has covered. The points of the paper from which the following excerpt was taken were not complex or confusing, but there were a lot of them. The writer wanted to put them all together for the reader, and she did so in a summary-type conclusion that works well.

CONCLUSION A *What Is a Christian?*
Tiffanie L. Lang

> The term *Christian* is rich with meaning. It stands for a belief, a relationship, and a way of life. To be a Christian means more than just going to church or being good. It means having a special relationship with Christ and in daily life always trying to please Him and be more like Him. Christians don't simply *believe* that there is a God and then do whatever they want to do. They do what pleases God, which is to praise Him, live a holy and separated life, show brotherly and sisterly love, and tell others about Him. All those who proclaim Christianity but live the way they want and not the way God wants, should consult their Bibles. A Christian is not someone who simply has a belief or a ritual; it is someone who also lives a special way of life.

Here is another good example, this one from a fairly complex paper discussing three options for the future of Puerto Rico.

CONCLUSION B *Puerto Rico's Future*
Clarissa Morales

> The people can follow the lead of Carlos Romero Barcelo and vote for statehood; or they can say yes to Rafael Hernández Colon and remain a commonwealth; or they can support the philosophy of Ruben Bérrios and become an independent nation. Whatever status they choose, it will bring with it many pros and cons for both Puerto Rico and the mainland. There are three options, but the people can give life to only one. It is going to be very interesting to see what the Puerto Rican people choose to do and how the American people will react to the possibility of the United States flag bearing one more star.

Quotes Sometimes writers end their papers by using someone else's words. If the person quoted is also an authority on the subject, so much the better.

The use of a quote is very effective if it lends something new: not in the sense that it brings up a new point that the writer should have made in the body of the paper, but rather in the sense that it puts a powerful spin on what the writer has been saying all along.

In the following conclusion, this end-quote device is used with excellent results. Conclusion C ends a paper in which the writer has traced the transition of rap music from its early preoccupation with egotistical and personal themes to a later concern with race and social justice. The writer has chosen a quote that is longer than most used in conclusions, but it's definitely not *too* long, because it provides a beautiful setup for the writer's final and most powerful observation about the ultimate value of a certain kind of rap.

CONCLUSION C   *Rap Music—Then and Now*
Marcus A. Williams

Rap music, in its present forms, strengthens and uplifts the minds of blacks. It provides a positive sense of what being black is, and it enlightens blacks about what can be done to change the way things are. In the 1960s James Baldwin, in "A Talk to Teachers," said

> There is something else the Negro child can do, too. Every street boy—and I was a street boy, so I know—looking at the society which has produced him, looking at the standards of that society which are not honored by anybody, looking at your churches and the government and the politicians, understands that this structure is operated for someone else's benefit—not for his. And there's no reason in it for him. If he is really cunning, really ruthless, really strong— and many of us are—he becomes a kind of criminal. He becomes a kind of criminal because that's the only way he can live. Harlem and every ghetto in this city—every ghetto in this country—is full of people who live outside the law. They wouldn't dream of calling a policeman. They wouldn't, for a moment, listen to any of those professions of which we are so proud on the Fourth of July. They have turned away from this country forever and totally. They live by their wits and really long to see the day when the entire structure comes down.   (qtd. in Simonson and Walker 6–7)

Rap provides an alternative to living outside the law. The alternative is to spend your time learning what it is to be black. Once you know, teach someone else. Knowledge is king—that's rap's message, and that's the message every black kid in this country needs to hear.

Closing the Circle   A good conclusion can come in a number of forms, but it always provides a finishing touch, something that gives a sense of closure or completion. And sometimes it picks up on some element of the introduction—an image, a special word, a question, a quote—and returns to it in the end, not simply by repeating it, but by doing something different with it. This technique, called *closing the circle* or *creating a bookend effect,* invariably polishes a piece of writing. (For one example, see the narrative "Ever Dearest Gardener" by Junaur Alojipan in chapter 3.) Read professionally written feature articles closely, and you'll see that, whether the subject is sports, fashion, music, science, video games, or mental health, professional writers often end their pieces by closing the circle. It may sound like a gimmick, but if it works for people who are paid to write, why shouldn't student writers try it? (But, as you know, a clever ending can never save a poorly written paper. The whole piece has to click.)

Here's an example of closing the circle from a student's narrative paper. Between the introduction and the conclusion, Becky tells a tale of first love—shared dinners, movies, afternoons at an amusement park, and a magical night at her cousin's Bat mitzvah—and its ending—the phone call breaking off the relationship, the support from her parents and friends, the process of starting to date again, and the journey of personal growth from dependent girlhood to independent womanhood.

Bass Shoe Box
Becky Gastman

INTRODUCTION

   I sit in solitude, on the floor in the middle of my walk-in closet. As I pull out the hidden Bass shoe box from the corner of my storage shelf, it brings forth feelings of sadness and nostalgia. I lift the cover to look at all the mementos I had saved throughout the nine months when we were together: a prom picture inside a heart-shaped frame, a concert ticket to Pink Floyd, tear-stained tissues, the gold ankle bracelet he gave me for my birthday, the Valentine's card that said so little but meant so much. To anyone else, these would simply be objects, nothing more. But for me, each is a remnant, a memory that is still precious.

CONCLUSION

   I close my eyes, and the music [of the night at the Bat mitzvah] swims back to me. I hear the band playing that sad, sweet melody. Alive and on fire, we stare into each other's eyes. Just the two of us, slow-dancing to a love song that seemed to have no end. I open my eyes, and the reality of the present returns. Lifting the cover of the shoe box, I take one last hard look at the memories of my first love. Gently I close the box and put it back in its familiar corner of the storage shelf, maybe for the last time.

Exercises on Paragraph Organization

Exercise One

Here are two paragraphs from different sections of a paper comparing and contrasting Michael Jackson and Prince. Each paragraph is rich with interesting information, but which one is more successful in stating a clear purpose and offering evidence in support of that purpose? Make notes on your ideas for revising the other paragraph.

Images of Michael Jackson and Prince
Roxanne Bowen

1   Both Michael Jackson and Prince have enjoyed gold and platinum albums, although Prince was constantly criticized because of his early lyrics and thus had a more difficult time reaching the level of success that Michael Jackson enjoys. Prince is considered by many, including his critics, to be one of the most creative and gifted songwriters and musicians ever, mainly because he has created so many different styles of music. Each of his albums has been totally different from the last. Prince has also discovered other talents. He has helped many other performers get their start by writing songs for them and creating looks for them. He has worked with or discovered artists such as Sheena Easton, Sheila E, and Vanity. He also started his own record company, Paisley Park. Michael Jackson is considered by many to be one of the most gifted and natural dancers that the music industry has seen. He electrifies his audiences with his unusual moves and charisma. He won an Emmy for singing his number one single "Billie Jean," and

introducing a dance called the "Moonwalk" on the "Motown 25" television special. The dance immediately became a favorite all over the world, even though very few people could actually do the dance. Unlike Prince, Michael Jackson does not write and produce all his albums; however, he has a great deal of input in everything he does. Both individuals are perfectionists when it comes to making music and performing. They have both received American Music lifetime achievement awards, and that is quite an honor because both men are only about 30 years old.

2   To their credit, the two artists, with their unique styles of dress, have played a role in setting fashion trends among America's youth. Michael Jackson, with his trademark "Jeri Curl" hairstyle, single white sequined glove, and short pants that show off his white sequined socks, has influenced the dress of many young people. When he appeared on the cover of "Thriller" and in the music video for the album, Michael Jackson look-alikes instantly began to emerge. Prince has set many fashion trends as well with his trademark high-heeled boots, feminine ruffled white shirts and colorful, uniquely designed suits. His look is a bit more daring than Michael Jackson's because it's more feminine and a bit flashier. Prince look-alikes are almost as common as Michael Jackson look-alikes.

Exercise Two

Sometimes just a single sentence needs to be revised because it is too small or too large in its scope. The following paragraph is from a solid, well-done paper defining the experience of a pianist. Which sentence attempts to comment on the entire contents of the paragraph but does so in a way that is too limited and not quite accurate? Rewrite it, making it more inclusive.

Piano Passion
Sina L. Lewis

At least once in an amateur's career and more than once in a professional pianist's career, a recital is expected. For me, recitals are one of the most enjoyable moments. First of all, I pick pieces that interest me, one from each period: Baroque, Classical, Romantic, and Twentieth Century. Then I practice and memorize the music; this takes about four months. Finally, it is the night before the recital; this is the worst time. Strange things go through my mind: What if I forget how to play? What if I fall off the stage? I hope they like me. These doubts usually stay in my mind until after I perform that day. Then I'm totally surprised: The audience loved me, and my parents, relatives, teacher, and even total strangers congratulate me.

Exercise Three

In this exercise, and in the next one, you'll examine paragraphs within the context of a complete essay. The following essay has a clever introduction and conclusion that create interest and open and close the circle. After you've finished reading the essay, try to imagine it without paragraphs 1 and 9. Can you see how Reneé's description of a segment in the television show "In Living Color" might hook readers and pull them in on a subject that they might not be interested in otherwise? Also check to see whether each paragraph in the body

of the paper has a clear purpose and enough development of or support for that purpose.

West Indian Immigrants and African Americans
Reneé A. Alli

1   It is Sunday night, and you are in front of the television enjoying the half-hour comedy, "In Living Color." A segment of "Hey Mon," the story of the hard-working Hedleys, comes on, and you sit back, ready to be amused. Ol' Pop has countless jobs: He's a pilot, an undertaker, a security guard, judge, priest, surgeon, and coffin maker—and he continues to fill out job applications. Mom, a nurse, secretary, and homemaker, still has time to serve as every necessary assistant to her husband. All this goes on while their "lazy" son is only a security guard, waiter, paper boy, taxi driver, gardener, and general gofer. As the segment comically portrays a West Indian family from an African American point of view, do you ever wonder how much of the skit is an accurate description? The show is a comedy, so exaggeration is inevitable, but can you pinpoint where the exaggeration stops and reality begins? As a West Indian immigrant to the United States, I believe I can.

2   A West Indian immigrant is anyone who has emigrated from an island in the Caribbean. He or she may be of East Indian, African, or European descent, or a mixture of any or all of these, and most West Indians are from racially diverse backgrounds. In fact, racial diversity is the source of the pride, unity, and equality that exist among all the people of the Caribbean. This is what gives rise to the familiar Caribbean spirit shown in television commercials advertising the Bahamas, Jamaica, and other Caribbean Islands. In the Caribbean spirit, people are friendly and relaxed, yet diligent and motivated to be successful and prosperous.

3   Although the Caribbean Islands provide a beautiful place to live and are home to very successful people, they are a part of the Third World and do not provide many opportunities. The problems are numerous: It is difficult to obtain a decent college education; adequate suitable housing is not available; the food supply fluctuates along with prices, depending upon weather and other factors; and poor health conditions result from the lack of good health insurance and the high cost of medical services. It is not surprising that many West Indians emigrate for the benefit of themselves and their families.

4   When these Caribbean families come to the United States, they are greeted with a plethora of opportunities, and they try to take advantage of each one. But the first thing they must do is adjust to the United States and its culture. This entails finding a racial group with which to identify. This process is shocking to West Indians because never before have they had to value the importance of one distinct race.

5   Many of the West Indian immigrants who come to the United States are considered African Americans. This might seem a simple and natural fact, but when an individual is made up of three or four racial groups and comes from a culture in which diversity is celebrated, it is difficult to limit himself or herself to one specific racial category. In the United States, I was surprised to discover a general rule of thumb: If a person has a drop of black blood, he or she is automatically considered black. I found myself in a dilemma when I

came to the United States. Having a mother of East Indian descent and a father of black and white parentage, in the United States I fall into the racial classification of black. But I was raised by my mother in the Indian culture; therefore, I experienced difficulty in accepting a single racial category, and I found it odd to be considered black when I was quite ignorant of African American culture.

6   So that is the first step: identifying with one race. The next hurdle is to confront the stereotypes targeted against that racial group. For a West Indian this usually means taking on the oppression, racism, and inequality that exist for African Americans in this country. As people of mixed race, West Indian immigrants make the transition from being a majority who enjoyed equal opportunity in the Caribbean to being a minority who must try to overcome oppression in the United States. In addition, we must become familiar with African American culture and traditions, and adapt accordingly to fit in. This is difficult for two reasons: First, how do you adapt to a new culture without sacrificing your own? And second, how do you accept another culture without seeming phony?

7   One painful aspect of the transition is the realization that many African Americans think West Indians come to the United States to steal their culture and opportunities. But this is not the motive of West Indians. When they are categorized as black, they ultimately take pride in being united with brothers and sisters of African descent. When African Americans fail to realize this, unnecessary competition and hostility are the result.

8   The relationship between African Americans and many West Indians has historical roots that can be traced to the Motherland of both groups. During the 1700s the Triangular Trade System of slavery involved the capture and theft of many Africans from their homeland. Most slaves were taken to America, but en route many were left on the small islands in the Caribbean to be trained to work long hours at manual labor. This is the principal reason for the great population of black West Indians. The difference between West Indian culture and the culture of African Americans is a result of the different ways each group had to adapt to their new surroundings. Given this history, African Americans and West Indian immigrants to the United States should try to coexist peacefully because they have experienced similar challenges in the past, and in the present, in the United States, they face uphill battles as an oppressed minority.

9   To a certain degree, the African American depiction of the West Indian immigrant in the "Hey Mon" skit is valid. Like the superemployed Hedleys, most West Indian immigrants are motivated to overcome any hurdle at any expense to get decent jobs, educate their children, and achieve success. They want all that this country has to offer, but they don't want to steal opportunities from the African Americans who have fought oppression for centuries. On the contrary, the greatest desire of West Indian immigrants is to unite with African Americans to overcome racial oppression and achieve the good life.

Exercise Four

Finally, let's look at two drafts of a documented argument essay. As you read Dora's first draft, make notes. Then form small groups and discuss with your

co-writers how you could use what you know about paragraph construction to reorganize and revise the draft. (You may find other problems in draft A also.) Next, read Dora's very successful revision carefully and see how many of your ideas matched hers.

DRAFT A   *The Legalization of Drugs*
Dora R. Robinson

1   What can be done about the drug problem? There have been frequent proclamations of war and dramatic increases in government resources and funding against the sale and use of drugs in recent years totaling $8 billion yearly (Benoit 32). However, despite these attacks to end the drug problem, there are many indications that the problem is not going away and may even be growing worse. During the past year alone, more than thirty million Americans violated the drug laws on literally billions of occasions (Benoit 32). Many politicians and government officials have brought up the issue of legalization of drugs as a solution. Abundant evidence suggests that legalization may well be the best strategy for tackling the drug problem.

2   The cheapest and cleanest way to reduce drug-related crime would be to do away with the laws that make drug use a crime. Thus to legalize drugs. Producing, buying and selling, and consuming controlled and banned drugs is itself a crime in the United States. If the legalization of drugs were to occur, these activities would obviously no longer be crimes. Relations with Latin America would be improved. Some advocates say that the effort to stop drug smuggling is poisoning American relations with important nations such as Colombia and Mexico, who both have been unable and unwilling to stop or crack down on the drug trade. If legitimate companies took over the production and distribution of drugs, then violence in the drug industry would end. Competition among these companies would reduce the monopolizing power the pushers have over many addicts who do not have alternative suppliers. Because of these companies, addicts would not have to go into bad areas and neighborhoods for drugs. Also, defective drugs would be less common, therefore causing a decrease in hospital patients, and the spread of the AIDS virus from contaminated needles would decrease. Today over 50 percent of all people with AIDS in New York City, New Jersey, and many other parts of the country, as well as the vast majority of AIDS-infected heterosexuals throughout the country, have contracted the disease directly or indirectly through illegal use (Hamill 27). If drugs were legalized, clean syringes could be provided by legal businesses. Money from this business could be used for medical treatment for people who really need and want to be cured, such as pregnant women. Crimes committed by drug users such as robbery and burglary, as well as drug-dealing, prostitution and running numbers to earn money to purchase high-priced drugs would decline because if legalization of drugs were to occur, drugs to which they are addicted would be significantly cheaper. Even if excise taxes were placed on drugs to discourage its use, they would probably still be cheaper than they are today. Crimes by the drug traffickers occur because of the drug market being illegal. Illegal markets tend to breed violence not only because they attract criminally-minded individuals, but also because participants in the market have no access to legal institutions to resolve their disputes. This illegal drug market has led to the demorali-

zation of neighborhoods and communities. Legalization of the drug market would drive the drug-dealing business off the streets and into legal, government-related, tax-paying stores. This would lead to the diminishing of the financial temptations that lure so many, especially youth, into the drug-dealing business.

3   However, many argue that legalizing drugs would only make the situation worse. They believe cheap, available drugs would increase addiction, legalization would lead to the sale of synthetic drugs or derivatives like crack without any understanding of their effects, health costs of drug abuse, estimated at $60 million annually, would increase, and removing the legal strictures could make drug use socially acceptable. But, in response to this, there are reasons to believe that none of the currently illicit substances would become as popular as the already legalized substance, alcohol, even if legalized. Alcohol has long been the principal intoxicant in most societies, including many in which other substances have been legally available. Its popularity could possibly be due to the fact that it quenches thirst, goes well with food, and promotes appetite as well as sociability. Moreover, none of the illicit substances can compete with alcohol's place in American culture. Because of the fact that we have learned something from our past experiences with alcohol, as well as tobacco abuse, it is reassuring to believe that legalization of drugs will not lead to an increase in drug abuse levels. For instance, we know that consumption taxes are an effective method of limiting consumption rates. We know that bans on advertising can make a difference. This is also true of government measures such as restrictions on time and place of sale, prohibition of consumption in public places, packaging requirements, crackdowns on driving under the influence, and laws holding bartenders and hosts responsible for the drinking of customers and guests. Also, government-sponsored education programs about the dangers of cigarette smoking have deterred many children from beginning to smoke. It is therefore possible to avoid repeating the same mistakes of the past in designing an effective plan for legalization. Anyway, there is good reason to doubt that many Americans would use drugs even if given the chance to do so legally. Legalization could not *lead* to the sale of synthetic drugs and synthetics without any understanding of it because this already exists. If legitimate businesses took control of the drug market, drugs would be less detrimental to society. Many "street" drugs have additives that are sometimes not what the user believes it is and therefore possibly leading to even more harmful effects. The health cost increase could be funded, as stated before, by the money not used for the war against drugs and the money made by the business.

4   Drug use—whether legal or illegal—is going to occur. It is something very abundant in society and is no way hidden from reality. In other words, if people want to use drugs, they will use drugs whether or not they are legal.

5   It is important to stress what legalization is not. It is not a beckon for drug dealers to surrender, but rather a means to put them out of business. It is not an endorsement of drug use, but rather a recognition of the rights of adult Americans to make their choices free of fear of criminal sanctions. It is not to discard the "Just say no" approach, but rather to appeal to government to provide assistance and positive inducements, not criminal penalties and more repressive measures in support of that approach. It is not even a call for the elimination of the

criminal justice system from drug regulation, but rather a proposal for the redirection of its effort and attention.

6   There is no question that legalization is a risky policy, since it may lead to an increase in the number of people who abuse drugs. But this is a risk, not a certainty. My favor of legalizing drugs does not indicate that I approve of addiction and drug use. Most importantly, drugs should not be available to children legally or of course, illegally.

7   Legalizing drugs is a way to combat the many severe problems created by the ban of these drugs, such as unnecessary crimes and deaths, and if correctly legalized through the use of age restriction laws, among other laws, could effectively improve some of the damaging conditions in American society.

DRAFT B   *The Legalization of Drugs*
Dora R. Robinson

1   What can be done about America's drug problem? In recent years there have been frequent proclamations of war and dramatic increases in government antidrug programs, which now total $8 billion yearly (Benoit 32). However, despite these attacks on drugs, there are many indications that the problem is not going away and may even be growing worse. During the past year alone, more than thirty million Americans violated the drug laws on literally billions of occasions (Benoit 32). Many politicians and government officials have proposed legalization of drugs as a solution. Abundant evidence suggests that legalization may well be the best strategy for tackling the drug problem.

2   Producing, buying and selling, and consuming controlled and banned drugs—all these activities are crimes. The cheapest and cleanest way to reduce drug-related crime is to do away with laws that make drug use a crime—thus legalizing drugs. If drugs became legal, these activities would obviously no longer be crimes.

3   There are four major benefits to legalizing drugs:

4   *First,* if companies took over the production and distribution of drugs, then violence in the drug industry would end. Competition among these companies would reduce the monopolizing power the pushers have over many addicts who do not have alternative suppliers. Because of legal sources, addicts would not have to go into bad areas and neighborhoods for drugs, and innocent people would not be hurt because they happen to live near a crack house.

5   *Second,* crimes committed to earn money to purchase high-priced drugs—crimes such as robbery, burglary, prostitution, numbers running, and drug dealing itself—would decline because if drugs were legalized, they would become much cheaper. Even if excise taxes were placed on drugs to discourage people from using them, they would probably still be cheaper than they are today. Crimes by the drug traffickers occur because the drug market is illegal. Illegal markets tend to breed violence not only because they attract criminally-minded individuals, but also because participants in the market have no access to legal institutions to resolve their disputes. The illegal drug market has led to the demoralization of neighborhoods and communities; however, legalization of the drug market would drive the drug-dealing business off the streets and into legal, government-regulated, taxpaying stores. This would diminish the financial temptations that lure so many, especially youth, into the drug-dealing business.

6   *Third,* defective drugs would be less common, and therefore there would be fewer health problems related to drug use. The number of hospital patients suffering from bad trips and other drug-related illnesses would decrease. Also, the spread of the AIDS virus from drug users' contaminated needles would be slowed. Today, over fifty percent of all people with AIDS in New York City, New Jersey, and many other parts of the country, as well as the vast majority of AIDS-infected heterosexuals throughout the country, have contracted the disease directly or indirectly through illegal drug use (Hamill 27). If drugs were legalized, clean syringes could easily be provided by legal businesses. Also, money from legal drug companies could be used for medical treatment for people who really need and want to be cured, such as pregnant women.

7   *Fourth,* relations with Latin America would improve. Some advocates say that the effort to stop drug smuggling is poisoning American relations with important nations such as Colombia and Mexico, both of whom have been unable or unwilling to stop or crack down on the drug trade. It is important for the United States, which gets many of its resources from other countries all around the world, including Latin America, to keep good ties with other countries for trade purposes. It is also important to keep good relations with Latin America because we have many immigrants from that part of the world who contribute greatly to the culture and society of this country.

8   However, many argue that legalizing drugs would only make the situation worse. They believe cheap available drugs would increase addiction, increase health costs, which are now estimated at $60 million annually, and make drug use socially acceptable (Kondracke 16). But, in response to this, there are good reasons to believe that none of the currently illicit substances would become as popular as the already legalized substance, alcohol.

9   Alcohol has long been the principal intoxicant in most societies, including many in which other substances have been legally available (Benoit 34). Its popularity could possibly be related to the fact that it quenches thirst, goes well with food, and promotes appetite as well as sociability. Moreover, none of the illicit substances can compete with alcohol's place in American culture. Because we have learned something from our experiences with alcohol and tobacco abuse, it is reasonable to believe that legalization of drugs will not lead to an increase in drug abuse levels. For instance, we know that consumption taxes are an effective method of limiting consumption rates (Benoit 34). We know that bans and controls on advertising can make a difference. This is also true of government measures such as restrictions on time and place of sale, prohibition of consumption in public places, packaging requirements, crackdowns on driving under the influence, and laws holding bartenders and hosts responsible for the drinking of customers and guests. Also, government-sponsored education programs about the dangers of cigarette smoking have deterred many children from beginning to smoke (Benoit 35). Thus, lessons learned from dealing with alcohol and cigarette abuse can be used to design an effective plan for the legalization of drugs.

10   It is important to stress what legalization is not. It is not a beckoning for drug dealers to surrender, but rather a means to put them out of business. It is not an endorsement of drug use, but rather a recognition of the rights of adult Americans to make their choices

free of fear of criminal sanctions. It is not to discard the "Just say no" approach, but rather to appeal to government to provide assistance and positive inducements, not criminal penalties and more repressive measures. It is not even a call for the elimination of the criminal justice system from drug regulation, but rather a proposal for the redirection of its effort and attention.

11   There is no question that legalization is a risky policy, since it may lead to an increase in the number of people who abuse drugs. But this is a risk, not a certainty. Support for the legalization of drugs does not indicate approval of addiction and drug use. Most importantly, drugs should not be available to children, legally or illegally.

12   Drug use—whether legal or illegal—is going to occur. Legalizing drugs is a way to combat many of the severe problems associated with drugs, such as crimes and unnecessary deaths. With careful planning, the legalization of drugs could mean a major improvement in American society.

Works Cited

Benoit, Ellen. "Drugs: The Case for Legalization." *Financial World* October 1989: 32–36.
Hamill, Pete. "Facing up to Drugs: Is Legalization the Solution?" *New York* 15 August 1988: 20–28.
Kondracke, Morton. "Don't Legalize Drugs: The Costs Are Still Too High." *The New Republic* June 1988: 16–20.

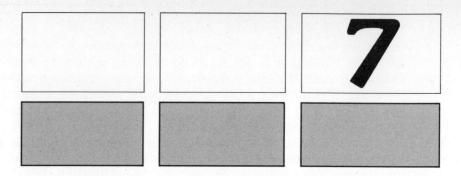

Persuasion: Writing Cause and Effect Essays and Documented Arguments

All writing—with the exception of journal entries and other jottings you make for your eyes only—is by its very nature persuasive. For example, when we write narratives, we want the reader to experience the story the way we experienced it. That's why we work so hard to make our ideas, images, and language fresh and powerful. We want the reader to say, "Yes, it was thrilling," or "Yes, it was tragic," or "Yes, it was almost too complex for words." When we describe something, we want the reader to see it the way we saw it. When we define a concept, we're trying to persuade the reader to accept our definition. When we compare and contrast two ideas, we want the reader to see how alike or unalike the two ideas really are. In all of these public types of discourse, the aim is to persuade; we're always writing with a *rhetorical* intent. We want to have an impact on people. That's communication.

So why is this particular chapter headed "Persuasion" if we've been attempting to persuade all along? Basically, it's because in the two types of essays we will discuss here—cause and effect essays and documented arguments—the writer goes about the business of persuasion in a much more explicit and direct way. When we write about what causes what, or how a certain action will probably have predictable effects, our intent is usually to say either, "People shouldn't do such and such because if they do, this is what's going to happen," or "This is what causes a positive, desired outcome, so let's go ahead with it." The point of a cause and effect paper is to go beyond explaining for its own sake; the point is to persuade. The same is true of documented arguments, which are essays that argue a certain position and show the strengths and weaknesses of opposing stances by presenting research.

There are other types of essays that persuade directly. But knowing how to write these two types is a major asset for college students, so we'll look at them in depth.

Cause and Effect Essays

Considering causes and effects is one of the most natural modes of thinking and writing. When we're about three years old, we start asking, "Why?" and "What if . . . ?" Even at this tender age, it's natural to wonder about causes (why?) and effects (what if?).

You'll be assigned many papers of this type in a wide variety of courses during your college career, even though it's possible—even likely—that your professors will rarely call them "cause and effect essays." What they *will* do is ask you to write on the causes of sickle cell anemia, or the effects of pornography, or the reasons why the poet Keats is often rated above his contemporary Shelley. Or your teacher might say, "Write a ten-page paper on the destruction of the world's rain forests." In this case, it would be up to you to think, "Okay, I'll make this a cause and effect paper, and I'll try to develop the thesis that the destruction of the rain forests is principally caused by . . . or that the worst effects of the deforestation of the South American jungles will be . . ."

What Gets the Emphasis

In cause and effect papers, you can emphasize or focus on either causes or effects, or you can explore both. (Of course, this depends on how an assignment is worded and how much latitude you're given.) For instance, if the subject of gangs interests you, you can write an essay that emphasizes causes and try to answer one or more of these questions: Why do kids join gangs? Why do so many gangs become violent? Why do communities tolerate their formation? Or you can turn your attention to effects and explore these questions: What happens to kids when they join a gang? What happens to communities? Some writers, if they have the time, energy, and flexibility in terms of paper length, might tackle all of these questions in one paper, but that paper would have to be quite long to be thorough. As you know, normally it is best to limit your focus so that, within that tighter focus, you can do in-depth work.

Topic Ideas for Cause and Effect Papers

Here is a short list of suggestions for paper topics. These suggestions should give you a rough idea of what's doable and help you to generate other ideas. You can probably address some of the topics entirely from your own experience. Others may require some reading or other type of research. Many cause and/or effect topics lend themselves to both approaches—the writer can bolster or contrast personal testimony with information culled from research.

Ideas that Emphasize Causes

1. A recent report said that the math skills of American kids are so poor that half of all eighth graders score just above the level of fifth-grade proficiency. What's behind the American weakness in mathematics?
2. What causes addictive behavior in any one of its various forms—for instance, alcoholism, drug abuse, or obsessive romantic or sexual relationships?
3. What causes bulimia and anorexia nervosa? Why do these health problems hit teenage and college-age women especially hard?
4. Why do so many people love soap operas? Are they just fun, or do they fulfill deeper needs?
5. A preference for the term *sexual orientation* rather than *sexual preference*, which has been expressed by many lesbians and gay men, suggests that one's sexuality is not entirely something that one chooses. Is this true? What causes a person to be heterosexual, homosexual, or bisexual? What do scholars in relevant fields say?
6. Why are children so fascinated with dinosaurs?
7. Why do so many people, especially teenagers, love scary movies?
8. Why is moviemaker Oliver Stone so fascinated with the sixties? Or why does any director, writer, artist, or musician return again and again to the same subject?

Topics that Emphasize Effects

1. What effects, if any, does the "political correctness" movement have on freedom of speech in American colleges and universities? (For this, you could do library research plus interview teachers—especially the most radical on both the left and right—at your own institution.)
2. What were the effects of growing up where you did—in a big city or in a small town, in the suburbs or on a farm, on an Army base or on an Indian reservation?
3. What are the effects of growing up with a sister or brother (or other family member) who faces a special challenge such as Down's syndrome?
4. How does television affect children? Is it really the culprit it's generally thought to be?
5. What are the effects of the practice of tracking (grouping children on the basis of perceived ability) in the schools?
6. What were the effects of the birth order of you and your siblings?
7. How did Professor Anita Hill's testimony affect Americans' understanding of sexual harassment?
8. How did a change in one family member's life affect your whole family? (The family member might have gone to college or entered the military, given up smoking or drinking, lost fifty pounds, started a new job, or remarried.)

Topics that Involve Both Causes and Effects

1. What caused the Berlin Wall to come down (or the Soviet Union to dissolve)? What have been some of the main effects?

2. What is special about Spike Lee as a film director? What causes his work to stand out the way it does? What influenced him to grow in the directions he has taken? And how does his work affect people's perception of issues?

3. Why are children attracted to high-powered water guns, such as the Super Soaker, and what are the effects of playing with these toys?

4. Who are pornography's major users and how does pornography affect their sexual behavior?

5. What causes "hate speech," and should it be protected by the First Amendment?

6. Recent studies show that holding children back in school is often a harmful practice, causing them to do less well academically and be more likely to drop out. Statistics also show that, in some school systems, race is a big factor in determining who repeats a grade. What are the causes and effects of this practice?

Creating the Paper

Once you have a topic, the next step is to develop a thesis. This may come quickly when you're first freewriting, or it may be a long and slow process, requiring much thinking, writing, and research. And your thesis may change once or twice while you're thinking about and researching the issue. No matter when you settle on it, eventually you must have a thesis, a purpose for your exploration of a cause and/or effect. Then you can proceed through the usual rough, overlapping, and sometimes recursive stages: selecting from the material generated in the prewriting process, shaping it, writing, revising, and editing it.

Examples from Student Writing

Let's look at successful cause and effect essays from three students. The first, which both students and teachers have found powerful and fascinating, looks at the drug problem from a slightly different angle. By graphically showing the tragic effects of drug dealing, T.S. Hughes argues that readers should "just say no" not simply to the practice of using drugs but to the even more sinister practice of selling them.

What are the essay's greatest strengths? Do you think any parts of the essay should be revised? How? Also, as you read, ask yourself if this essay should include researched facts, such as statistics or quotes from scholarly experts? See the discussion at the end.

Life in the Fast Lane
T.S. Hughes

(**Note:** All names in this essay have been changed.)

1   Many attempts are made to inform the public of the dangers and risks of using illegal narcotics such as cocaine, crack, and marijuana. For example, elementary children are taught to "Say No to Drugs." The same slogan is printed on candy boxes in our neighborhood stores. The harmful effects of drugs are advertised through billboards, television

commercials, sit-coms, and magazines and newspaper articles. This information is very important for the public to know and understand, but there is one flaw: Why isn't the public more concerned about the drug dealers, also known as "dopemen," who are supplying the public with drugs? So many children see only the drug dealer's "fast money" and material possessions. Children have to be taught to say "No!" to *selling* drugs as well as to *using* them.

2   Some might argue that if children are told to say no to drugs they will automatically say no to selling drugs also. But I disagree; If that were true, there wouldn't be as many drug dealers as there are. In my high school, approximately one in every seven males was selling drugs, and many of those dropped out of school. Children ask themselves why they need education when the drug trade can provide everything they could possibly want in life. But children don't see all of the risks and consequences of being a "dopeman." In fact, in some communities most children see the dopemen as role models.

3   The majority of my male friends are dopemen. I grew up with them, and now I am watching them destroy their lives. I worry about them every day as they deal in the illegal exchange of narcotics for money. They get their supply of drugs from various places which are unknown to me and push their drugs on as many people as possible. Their lives are based on money and power.

4   I have done everything I could to persuade these friends to escape the drug world. I have tried talking to them, and I have tried not talking to them. Neither strategy worked. I finally realized that for them to stop selling drugs, they would have to want to stop themselves. But I continue to be their friend because I grew up with most of them, and they became a part of my life. A lot of them are the best friends I could have, except for the fact that they live in the drug world. I will stick by them and be there to help them when I can. I cannot desert my friends when I know that they have a serious problem. All I can do is be there for them and try to understand why they are jeopardizing their lives and polluting the lives of others.

5   I know drug dealers as young as ten and as old as thirty. Members of the various age groups present themselves differently. For example, a dopeman usually looks more conservative as he gets older. The younger ones wear track suits and gym shoes and are "draped in gold," while the older dopemen favor three-piece suits with alligator shoes and matching attache cases. In or out of their Jaguars, BMWs, Mercedez Benzes, Legends, Accords, and trucks, they are easily recognized.

6   Dopemen are under constant surveillance by the FBI, often because they get themselves in trouble with the law by buying expensive things without having a legal job and paying taxes. For example, a drug dealer named Tony left his home one morning and noticed a strange white van parked on the opposite side of the street; the man behind the wheel wore sunglasses and looked suspicious. When Tony returned home, the van was still there. Tony felt someone was watching his every move. After a few days the van suddenly disappeared, and Tony thought he was safe. A few days later he began making drug transactions over the telephone again. But while Tony was in the streets, the FBI had tapped his phones and every room in his house. The FBI recorded a conversation and used it as evidence in court to lock Tony and a couple of his associates in prison. He is still serving time.

7   Dopemen are often swarmed by women, commonly known as "sackchasers," who are interested in only one thing: the dopeman's "sack" of money. Tina was a fifteen-year-old girl who was obsessed with material things. A twenty-three-year-old dealer named Mike was her current boyfriend, and he gave her everything she asked for. He bought her a new Honda Accord, an apartment, a new wardrobe, coats, purses, and gold. She left home and dropped out of school, but after she broke away from her family, he began to spend less and less time with her. The time he did spend was filled with sex, followed by brutal beatings and sometimes an apology weeks later. This continued for months until she announced she was pregnant. His visits gradually got further apart, but she was determined to have the baby to get him back into her life. She believed that he would take care of her and the baby forever. But during her seventh month, Mike was killed for selling someone bad cocaine. They shot him repeatedly as he was leaving his home. They put him in his car and drove him far out into the woods, leaving his body there to rot. Tina now has a baby with no decent place to live. Her parents have disowned her, and she is depending on other dopemen to take care of her and her baby.

8   Charles was another good friend of mine who involved himself in the drug world. I had known him since I was fifteen; we went to the same school and were in many of the same classes. When I was a sophomore, he was a senior. When he graduated, we still had a close relationship. He always referred to me as his "little sister." He always came to get me if I needed a ride somewhere, and he bought me something to eat if I was hungry. He was always there to listen to me and give me advice, but he would never tell me what was troubling him.

9   One day he picked me up from school. When I reached the car, I noticed four bullet holes on the door. I got in anyway. When we left the school grounds, I asked him why there were bullet holes on the side of the car. He looked at me as if he didn't know and sped toward his home. When we got there, we saw three bullet holes in the front window. He told me to go to the corner and take a cab home; he gave me some money, kissed me on the cheek, and told me not to worry about him. I walked down the street as he entered his house. From the corner telephone booth, I watched nervously as I called the police. When they arrived, the house was vacant and the back door left standing open. Days later the police found Charles in the alley. His body was covered with blood, rats, and flies. He had died from three bullet holes to the head.

10   My most tragic and painful memory of the drug scene is the story of Darrin. I had known Darrin since I was about eight years old and he was eleven. Like Charles, Darrin also treated me like a little sister. As we grew older, he continued to look after me. He was always concerned about who I went out with, and he said he would kill anyone who harmed me in any way. I loved Darrin as a brother, and it hurt me so much to see him destroy his life as a drug dealer. The more he involved himself in drugs, the less I wanted to see him. In time Darrin started to realize he was hurting me and everyone else he loved, so he decided to stop selling drugs. Months went by, and day by day he started breaking away from the scene. Then one day two guys came to Darrin's house demanding money that they said he owed them from a drug deal the week before. But he had not been involved in any recent drug deal. The confrontation took place in front of Darrin's house, and when he tried

to enter it, they wouldn't let him. They began to argue very loudly until Darrin's mother came to the door. She told the boys to leave and started to pull her son into the house. Someone pulled out a gun and shot Darrin's mother four times in the chest and Darrin once in the right leg. She died instantly as she fell back onto Darrin. The guys ran to the car and left.

11   Darrin searched everywhere for the guys who killed his mother. His life became distorted, and once again he began to sell drugs. I begged him not to get involved, but it seemed as if I were talking to another person; he looked at me as if he didn't really know who I was. He moved out of his house and rented an apartment. That was the last I ever heard from him. Months later, I saw Darrin on the street, and he just looked at me without saying anything. I learned that he was dealing with a different crowd this time; he was so far into selling drugs that his whole perspective on life had changed. He set up drug connections throughout the city and made bundles of money. His partners saw that he was making more money than they were, and in their jealousy they set him up on a fake deal. He was told to meet them somewhere, and when he arrived he was shot so many times that he was barely recognizable. His funeral was in March 1989.

12   Drug dealers live a fast life and approach a fast death. I have seen whole families destroyed and lives ruined because people involved themselves in the distribution of drugs. Since many of my closest friends died because of drugs, I feel insecure about establishing close relationships with others. I feel that when my friends die they take a part of me with them until eventually I am also destroyed mentally and physically.

13   Too many children are blinded by the material wealth that the dopeman possesses. They rarely see or hear about the outcome of a drug dealer's life. They rarely know of the fear in which a drug dealer lives. The dopeman continually looks over his shoulder and retraces his tracks. The law is his enemy as well as the people he calls his associates. Children must know that selling drugs is just as life threatening as using drugs. Children must learn the consequences of being a drug dealer or a sackchaser because so many are getting caught up in the fantasy world that drugs have created.

Discussion

When we discussed "Life in the Fast Lane" in class, some students asked, "When do you know you need research for support in a cause and effect paper?" Usually you need it when the subject matter is completely or substantially outside your sphere of experience, exposure, or expertise. For my students, this paper was a great example of one in which the insertion of a statistic here and there (or another type of documented fact) would have been unnecessary, maybe even ridiculous. This writer is relating her own experiences; her expertise is firsthand. In this case, no library sources were needed.

Our second essay, a very strong, controversial paper by Jonathon Sung Bidol, is an exploration of both the historical causes and psychological effects of language choices. If this issue is new for you, to what extent is Jonathon successful in opening your eyes to his point of view? If this is an issue you've considered before, does he give evidence that supports or reverses your earlier position? If so, what specifically is that evidence?

Who are the two major audiences for his essay? Is he equally effective in reaching both? Why or why not?

Jonathon has included some researched information. Has he used it effectively? If he revised again, what would you like to see him do?

"Oriental": Their Word, Not Ours
Jonathon Sung Bidol

1   *Ching Chong Chinaman, chink, gook, zipperhead, jap, nip, yellow monkey, dothead, chink-a-moto*—Asian Americans have been victimized by these obviously offensive and derogatory racial slurs. But what about the term *Oriental?* Why is *Oriental* accepted and used by some, but offensive and derogatory to others? To understand the racist nature of the term *Oriental*, some background information is needed. Where did *Oriental* come from? Who originally used it and for what purpose? What are the implications of this term today?

2   The word *Oriental*, as originally conceived and used by Europeans, referred to a place and culture east of Europe, known today as the modern Arab world. However, when most Americans conceptualize *Oriental*, they make associations with China, Japan, and occasionally Korea. But while Americans and Europeans may think of different geographic locations and peoples when using the word *Oriental*, the images and connotations of the term remain the same. *Oriental* conjures up images of exoticism, mystery, inscrutability, inexplicability, inferiority, strangeness, weirdness, the foreign, and the sinister. As Edward W. Said so aptly puts it in his book *Orientalism*, "There are Westerners, and there are Orientals. The former dominate; the latter must be dominated, which usually means having their land occupied, their internal affairs rigidly controlled, their blood and treasure put at the disposal of one or another Western power" (36). The truth of Said's comments was most obviously manifested during the second half of this century in the wars waged by the imperialistic United States government in Korea and Vietnam. Besides these overt acts of American aggression, countless other covert acts can be cited. The infiltration of American hegemony into Indonesia, the Philippines, and Cambodia—in the form of unequal trade agreements, military presence, and CIA-funded death squads—is a prime example.

3   The word *Oriental* is used by most Americans to describe a people, place and culture that are considered inferior. Anything "Oriental" is considered "the Other," that which does not belong and can never be considered part of the "superior" American culture. While this may seem an extreme view, the term does manifest itself in subtle and insidious ways. Take, for example, "Oriental" rugs, "Oriental" lamps, and "Oriental" food; these things are considered exotic, curious, and strange by the vast majority of people in America. "Oriental" products are aberrations from the "normal" experiences of the average American and are not considered anything more than curiosities or adventures in experimentation. So when one applies the term *Oriental* to a woman or man, a girl or boy, rather than a lamp or a rug, the connotations of "otherness" are not suddenly lost.

4   During the late 1960s in the United States, people who traced

their ancestry to the Asian continent began to question the term *Oriental* as it applied to them, Asians in America. They realized that while the term *Occidental*—as a reference to the West—had fallen out of favor, the term *Oriental* was still commonly used. Why was this so? Who had created these terms and for what purpose? As Asians in America began to develop an increasing awareness of their role in American society, they realized that *Oriental* was an archaic white man's term. It had been imposed upon Asians in Asia by outsiders and was used in America to describe a group of people who were considered foreigners. All the connotations of the term *Oriental* reduced Asians in America to less than human in the eyes of others as well as in their own eyes. Asians in America further realized that they were not confined to the imposition of these one-dimensional stereotypes.

5   In light of these revelations, something had to be done about the term *Oriental.* On the road to claiming the power of self-determination, a group of California college students in the late sixties decided to name themselves *Asian Americans.* They recognized that language is a tool of power and that the system created by white heterosexual men—because they have the most power—controls the meaning of words. By rejecting *Oriental* and all of its racist connotations and creating the term *Asian American,* Asians in America were able to redefine themselves on their own terms. In choosing *Asian American,* these students asserted their Asianness, but more importantly they claimed their Americanness.

6   Through many years of struggle, Asian Americans have worked to make their self-proclaimed name known to the general public. *Asian American,* far from being used solely on college campuses, has been gaining wider acceptance and is now the term used by the government, as evidenced in the 1990 census questionnaire. While the increased use of *Asian American* is a good sign of progress for Asians in America, the recalcitrance of *Oriental* is a disturbing reminder of continued inequality.

7   There are Americans, including too many Asian Americans, who believe that *Oriental* is not offensive or derogatory and, in fact, maintain that it accurately describes Asians in America. This points to some serious issues in the Asian American community. Who defines us? Who controls our destiny? The Asian American community must not passively accept the imposition of stereotypes like the "model minority." We must instead challenge the one-dimensional images that the white supremacist system inflicts upon our community. Furthermore, Asian Americans must reject the imposition of perpetual foreigner status—and claim our role in the composition of American society.

8   By redefining ourselves as Asian Americans and denouncing the term *Oriental,* we take control of our own lives. In understanding and explaining *Oriental* in its historical and social context, Asian Americans reject the stereotypes associated with the word and also realize how it has been used as a tool of the white supremacist American hegemony. Thus Asian Americans become subjects of their own lives rather than objects of others' false notions.

Work Cited

Said, Edward W. *Orientalism.* New York: Vintage Books, 1978.

The next essay moves readers into the world of the migrant worker—a world that did not disappear with John Steinbeck's powerful novel *Grapes of Wrath* or Edward R. Murrow's classic documentary *Harvest of Shame*. Is Socorro's emphasis mainly on causes, effects, or both? What concrete details create the tremendous power in her work? How could she improve the organization? Where could she cut material and combine sentences? Finally, why did this project present unusual challenges in verb tense?

El Norte

Socorro Nieto Garza

1   As I grew up, I saw my parents work in the fields, and I decided that I would not stay a migrant forever. My parents say that I am fortunate to have been able to see them struggle as migrants because now I will not choose to live as they did. Unfortunately, my parents were the ones to set an example for me. This example began when they were in Mexico and heard about the high paying jobs in the United States. Because of these jobs, in 1970—uneducated and illegally—they came to the United States. My aunt and uncle, who had come to America a few years before, helped my parents out by providing them with a place to stay. At first my dad had unstable, low paying jobs, mostly as a fisherman in the southern parts of Texas and California. Then in 1971 my eldest sister was born in the United States. This allowed my parents to become legal Mexican-American citizens and to head where everyone else was going—"El Norte." From then on, my parents, my two older sisters and two younger brothers, and I have worked as migrants, traveling from place to place, following the seasonal harvest.

2   The seasonal harvest has taken us to many different cities and states in the United States. My family and I always travel together in a truck, often with three or four persons in the front and the rest in the back. It usually takes us two days to get to our destination. The night before we go on the road, my mother prepares food—usually flour tortillas with fajitas and fruit—that lasts us throughout a day. It saves us money and time from stopping at restaurants and having to wait on our orders. Like many migrants, we usually spend our first night at Hope, Arkansas. It is a place especially for migrants to stay while traveling. Air conditioning and furnished rooms are offered to us at lower rates than in any other hotel. After enjoying a comfortable place to sleep, we start our next day on the road at 4:00 a.m. My dad is the only one in my family that drives when we are traveling, so by the second day he is tired of driving. This is why, after we run out of the food my mother prepared, we stop to eat at restaurants while he stays in the car and rests. After this we move on until we reach our destination. We usually travel two or three days, and because of the cramped conditions, these are the worst days for us.

3   Once we get to our destination, my oldest sister Janie, who speaks the best English and is the most outgoing member of the family, always contacts the boss. If it is a weekday, my parents would enroll us in school. The first day of school is always difficult because as a result of not knowing anyone, I do not know what to expect. Although there has always been a student in every school polite enough to introduce himself or herself and offer friendship, many just stare as they pass by. It seems as if every time I start getting accustomed to a new

place—whether we are planting, pruning, or picking—soon it is over, and my family moves to another area and starts all over again. It is hard to go to several schools in a year. Maybe it is because I always think about the negative things that can happen to me on my first day of school instead of the positive ones. Also, I never know if I will get to see the new friends I made in each school again.

4   But there is something worse than the hard conditions of traveling and starting over in so many different schools: Working in the fields is what I despise most about being a migrant. In the sixth grade, I started working on weekends and vacations. Instead of looking forward to vacations like most children, I dreaded them. The tomato plants in Florida had an awful smell, and we had to bend down to prune them. It was really hot, and my family and I worked from sunrise till sundown. Lots of times what kept me going were my terrific daydreams. I'd pretend to be a superstar working in the fields, taking a short break from her Hollywood life. After work, all I felt like doing was resting, but then I had to help my mom make dinner and clean the house that was provided by our boss. My mom was good at reminding me that I was no movie star—at least not yet!

5   In our travels, we have worked in Florida, New York, South Carolina, Wisconsin, California, Michigan, and many other states. Michigan was the state I especially hated going to work in because there we picked pickles during the summer. Picking pickles was the hardest job I ever did. We woke up at 6:00 a.m. every day, ate a simple breakfast, packed our lunch, and—half asleep—headed towards the fields. Each one in the family would get two rows of pickles, one on each side. To pick them, we would have to bend down, pick one row, put the pickles in the bucket, then pick the other side, do the same, and keep moving forward. When our buckets were filled, we poured the pickles into a wheelbarrow that my dad would then dump into a large box. Even though I hated this job, I liked the amount of money we earned. For every box filled, we were paid $30.00. My dad made sure we did our jobs better and quicker than any other workers. In Michigan we earned more money than in any other state and also worked harder for it. By the time we were finished, our backs ached so badly that all we wanted to do was go back to our one-room shack that had only two bunk beds, a refrigerator, and a stove. We had an outhouse and a shower room located outside that we shared with other migrant neighbors.

6   We came to know about higher-paying jobs like the one in Michigan from our bosses on an earlier job or from social workers. Social workers play an important part in migrants' lives. They are people who know how to do their jobs right. For instance, I have worked in jobs that do not provide restrooms or clean homes, even though there is a law stating that they must be provided. To make sure bosses obey laws like these, social workers go into the fields or camps and fight for our rights. I think of them as the voice for migrants since we are unable to stand up for ourselves because of the fear of losing our jobs. I looked up to them for caring and not giving up on strangers. They have inspired me to hope to become a social worker and help my own people.

7   Migrant workers can be taken advantage of in so many ways. Bosses think that because most migrants are illiterate and from Mexico, they can abuse their power over us. It is easy for people to take advantage of others who are uneducated. In order for this not to

happen to me, I must get an education. I recall times when I felt anger at my parents for raising me as a migrant. Why did *I* have to get up so early to work on weekends and vacations when other teenagers got to sleep or go to summer camp? But my father's answer always comforted me: "Socorro," he would say, "now you know why education is important. Without it, you'll be a migrant all your life." I will continue college until I graduate. My children will not be forced into migrant work, but will be educated, and hopefully our family will be able to improve the quality of life for migrant workers who have no choice.

8   These are the words of a migrant!

Finally, let's examine a cause and effect essay in two drafts. As you read the first draft of "Coming of Age in Vietnam," ask yourself what its greatest strengths and weaknesses are and what Don might alter in his rewrite. Then read the revision and see how many of Don's fine changes in concrete detail, organization, development, and editing you can find. Mark them for class discussion.

DRAFT A   *Coming of Age in Vietnam*
Don A. Hennings

1   Why do very young men choose a life in the military? How does this decision at a young age affect the rest of their lives? What are some of the realistic benefits? What are the risks involved?

2   I can understand the motivation of people that immigrate to the United States, they do so because it offers them the opportunity to improve the quality of their lives. Their homelands are troubled places politically, that offer very limited prospects economically. Oftentimes there were conditions that put their very lives at risk. Such is the current case with the Kurds of Iraq, and such was the case with the Vietnamese people during and shortly after that war, and surprisingly, those same kinds of motivations existed for me in Detroit in 1963. Without the prospect of flight to another country, young men of the ghettos often choose a life in the military.

3   I was motivated by fear that if I remained on the east side of Detroit, my fate would be locked into the depression and poverty cycle of the ghetto. I knew that education was important, but I had no real prospects of going to college, even though I had chosen a "college preparatory" curriculum in high school. My realistic job opportunities existed only in the automobile factories, and to reach those opportunities I had to navigate the alcohol, drugs, and the violence that accompanied life in my neighborhood.

4   My family was on "the welfare," and the state only provided bare necessities. Food stamps bought our food, a clothing allowance paid for our clothing, and a Good-Fellow box for Christmas, with two shirts (usually plaid), a toy, and some underwear, had made for delightful and exciting holidays for me as a youngster. I was able to earn five dollars on weekends working for Mr. Higby at the corner store, a little more by running errands or shoveling snow in the winter. My friends were older than me, and occasionally I could borrow a piece of clothing (a Hi-Lo shirt or a Banlon sweater) from them. This added a little variety to what I wore to school every day. But I was getting older and I wanted things that my mom could not provide for me. She had her hands full

trying to raise nine children, pretty much by herself. So I asked her to sign for me to go into the military. She knew as well as I that life in the military held more promise for me than Detroit's "Black Bottom." As a condition of her agreeing to sign the paperwork that gave me permission to join the army, my mother made me promise to finish high school while in the service.

5   I entered the United States military. I trained and worked as a weapons specialist for two years in Hawaii, and the jungles of Okinawa. I then requested and was granted permission to attend training as a helicopter mechanic, and shortly after my eight months training, our entire unit and all of our equipment was loaded onto ships and we sailed across the Pacific Ocean to a place I could not pronounce.

6   We entered Vietnam coastal waters at night; we could hear explosions and see flashes of light that we knew were exploding shells and munitions. We had arrived in Saigon, all 3500 of us, after a three-and-a-half-week ship ride. I lived in that country for two years. I was with the 420th Transportation Battalion. Our job was the repair and maintenance of Huey helicopters. Hueys were the predecessors of today's Apache helicopters. They were heavily armed with grenade launchers, 60-caliber machine guns, and rockets. Occasionally one would get shot down, and we would have to go into the jungle and recover the "ship" if possible, or totally destroy it.

7   Binh lived in Pleiku, South Vietnam, she was our mama-san. She washed our clothes, changed our linen every Tuesday, she made our beds, she shined and cleaned our boots and shoes. Binh was one of the perhaps 100 men and women from the local villages that were hired to do the domestic kind of work around the camp. This inexpensive labor left us free to work in our specialities. They worked in our kitchens, they filled our sandbags, and generally provided cheap labor. They were glad to have the work, and we were glad to have them.

8   Binh was also pregnant, she had come to work every day and I was used to seeing her that way. Then one day when she came to work she was not pregnant any more. I was shocked that she had given birth to that child and returned to work the very next day. I had been the oldest of nine children; I had been with my mother during some of her later births of my sisters and brothers. I knew that childbearing could be a physically exhausting experience. I think it was during this time that I started to thinking and perhaps even feeling beyond the language barrier, and I realized that I liked this person that I saw every day, tending to my affairs. I began to talk to her and know her. We talked about children, and she told me that she had them so that they could take care of her in her old age. She told me about her husband and her life. I often worried about her during the nights when she would leave the compound and return to her village. Because it was at night that most of the attacks by the Viet Cong came. I began to realize during those days in that country and in others since that time that people are pretty much the same the world over. Once you get by the language barrier, and into the hearts and minds of people, you quickly realize that they were no different than us. They loved their mothers, fathers, and children. They feared and worshipped a God. They laughed, cried, sang, danced, and did all the other things I did. They were of my family, the family of man, and if they could, they too would risk all they had for the opportunity of a better life for themselves and the children.

9   The military remains a viable option today for young men that can't find jobs and don't have any real chances of getting into college. Unfortunately, the price can sometimes be life itself.

DRAFT B   *Coming of Age in Vietnam*
Don A. Hennings

1   Between October and December 1988, I lost three relatives to the Detroit city streets: my brother Felix, age 24; my nephew Antonio, age 24; and my nephew David, age 19. All three died of gunshot wounds. In 1990, another nephew was sentenced to ten to fifteen years for shooting to death a young man who had tried to rob him of the crack cocaine he was selling. Other than the personal shock of these incidents, they are not uncommon in Detroit's "Black Bottom," my old neighborhood and a place that, to this day, remains a killing ground for many a young black man.

2   Wanting to escape this kind of environment and not having many other viable options, young men often choose a life in the military. I was motivated by fear when I joined the military in 1963—fear that if I remained on the east side of Detroit, my fate would be locked into the depression and poverty cycle of the ghetto. I knew that education was important, but I had no real prospects of going to college, even though I had chosen a "college preparatory" curriculum in high school. My realistic job opportunities existed only in the automobile factories, but to reach those opportunities I had to navigate the alcohol, drugs, and violence that accompanied life in my neighborhood. And even if I were fortunate enough to find work, I could expect to get somebody pregnant, probably a few times; then I would be locked into the welfare/ child support scenario which was its own kind of hell.

3   My family was on what we called "the welfare," and the state provided only the bare necessities. Food stamps bought our food, a clothing allowance paid for about four pairs of pants per year, and a Good-Fellow box for Christmas, with two shirts (usually plaid), a toy, and some underwear, made for delightful and exciting holidays for me as a youngster. I was able to earn five dollars on weekends working for Mr. Higby at the corner store and a little more by running errands or shoveling snow in the winter. My friends were older than I, and occasionally I could borrow a piece of clothing (a Hi-Lo shirt or a Banlon sweater) from them. This added a little variety to what I wore to school every day. But I was getting older, and I wanted things that welfare could not provide for me. My mother had her hands full trying to raise nine children, pretty much by herself. So, because I was only seventeen and still a minor, her signature was required on my application before I could go into the military. She knew as well as I that life in the military held more promise for me than the Bottom. As a condition of her agreeing to sign the paperwork that gave me permission to join the army, my mother made me promise to finish high school while in the service

4   I entered the United States military and within the first two years I delivered on my promise to my mother: I tested for and received my GED (Graduate Equivalency Diploma). In addition, I trained and worked as a weapons specialist for two years in Hawaii and the jungles of Okinawa. I was granted permission to attend training as a helicopter

mechanic, and shortly after my ten months training, our entire unit and all of our equipment were loaded onto ships, and we sailed across the Pacific Ocean to a place I could not pronounce.

5   We entered the coastal waters of Vietnam at night; we could hear explosions and see flashes of light that we knew were detonating shells and munitions. The gambling, idleness, and frivolity that had filled three Sundays on board ship were suddenly replaced with almost total silence, as we all stood on the starboard side, each with his own private thoughts. All of us probably wondered if we would ever leave this place alive. We knew that the casualty rate was in excess of 100 men per day.

6   We arrived in Saigon, all 3,500 of us. Play time was over; it was time to get down to the business of war. We had to build our shelters, which were thirty-men tents erected on concrete slabs, with an opening at both ends and flaps on both sides to allow air to circulate when it wasn't raining as it did daily during the monsoon season. When we had a chance to sleep, we fell into our bunks in our boots and clothes, exhausted from the rigors of the day and oblivious to the constant firing of the artillery battery next door. If there was a hell, this had to be it.

7   With the 420th Transportation Battalion, our job was the repair and maintenance of Huey helicopters, the predecessors of today's Apache attack helicopters. They were called "gunships," and they were heavily armed with grenade launchers, 60-caliber machine guns, and rockets. Occasionally one would get shot down and we would have to go into the jungle and recover the ship if possible, or totally destroy it.

8   After about six months in country and after most of the logistical work of setting up was done, I was transferred from Cuchi to the airfields of Quinhon. This base was more established, and they hired local people to work during the day. Binh, my mama-san, washed our clothes, changed our linen every Tuesday, made our beds, and cleaned and shined our boots and shoes. Binh was one of the perhaps 100 men and women from the local villages that were hired to do domestic work around the camp for about $5 a day. This inexpensive labor left us free to work in our specialties. They worked in our kitchens, filled our sandbags, and generally provided cheap labor. They were glad to have the work, and we were glad to have them.

9   Binh, who was pregnant, had come to work every day, and I was used to seeing her that way. Then one day when she came to work she was not pregnant any more. I was shocked that she had given birth to that child and returned to work the very next day. I was the oldest of nine children; I had been with my mother during some of the births of my sisters and brothers. I knew that childbearing could be physically exhausting. I think it was during this time that I began to think and perhaps even feel beyond the language barrier, and I realized that I cared about this person that I saw every day, tending to my affairs. I began to talk to her and know her. We talked about children, and she told me that she had them so that they could take care of her in her old age. She told me about her husband and her life. I often worried about her during the nights when she left the compound and returned to her village because it was at night that most of the attacks by the Viet Cong came. Knowing Binh, I realized that the Vietnamese were no different from us. They loved their mothers, fathers, and children. They feared and worshipped a God. They laughed, cried, sang, danced, and were

more similar to me than different. They were of my family—the family of man.

10   Today the military remains a viable option for young men who can't find jobs and don't have any real chances of getting into college. They don't have to die or live a diminished life in the "Black Bottoms" of America. But unfortunately, the price of the military experience can sometimes be life itself. Such was the case for Clifford Johnson, Carlos Jelks, Steve Johnson, and the entire second platoon, twenty-eight of my very good friends who got caught in an ambush and died without me. But I was lucky: For me, in spite of the horrors of Vietnam, the military meant a chance for a larger life.

Documented Arguments

Research—a little for flavor, or a lot for substance—can be used with excellent results in many types of papers. One important and often-assigned paper that includes research is the *documented argument*. In a documented argument, the writer explores an issue in depth and then, on the basis of the writer's own ideas and information gathered through research, builds a compelling case in favor of a thesis.

The most important thing to know about research writing is that it is *not* something entirely new. It is very much like the writing you've been doing. All along, you've been working with a central focus or dominant image in your narrative and descriptive writing projects. And in your expository and persuasive writing, you've had a controlling purpose or thesis. In documented arguments, you also work to prove a thesis.

So what's different? Only this: In papers that contain research, you do not rely exclusively upon your own mental processes and the evidence you have experienced or observed in your own life. You also employ other types of evidence, such as facts, statistics, charts, graphs, quotes, and paraphrases (other people's ideas put into your own words). Your evidence comes from your *sources,* such as newspapers, magazines and periodicals, books, television and radio shows, recordings, and interviews. You refer to your sources to help you prove the truth of your argument and to show that you are aware of and understand the positions of those who disagree with you.

Sources must be *cited*. This means that in your paper you need to give full credit to the people and publications you use to convince readers of your thesis. Later in this chapter, two simple systems of citing sources within the paper and listing references at the end of the paper are explained.

Staying in Charge

The most important thing to remember when writing a documented argument is this: **Never let your sources control your paper.** If you do, you'll end up with a cut-and-paste job. In this kind of weak, ineffective paper, researched material is *presented* rather than *used* by the writer. The writer "cuts" materials from their original sources and "pastes" them together to create a paper. The reader then has to do all the mental work, putting the various bits of evidence together and making a case. And most readers don't want to work that hard—and they shouldn't have to. The heavy work is supposed to be done by the writer.

The writer must do more than type up research and hope that it speaks for itself. Research *can't* speak for itself. The problem with a cut-and-paste research paper is that the writer disappears. But for the essay to work, the writer (meaning the writer's intellect) must stay evident, arguing a position and controlling the researched evidence, not being controlled by it. Because you will be controlling what evidence appears in support of your argument, you probably won't use all of your research findings. If you feel compelled to include every note you took, to work it in somewhere, anywhere, then you're allowing yourself (and your paper) to be pushed around and overwhelmed by what others have said about your topic. **Let your evidence back you up, not beat you up.** Argue what you want to argue, then support your case with your findings. When it comes to research, if you can't use it, lose it.

Developing a Tentative Thesis

How do you start a writing project of this kind? The first step is to find a doable project that really interests you—that is, of course, if you have been given the freedom to pick your own topic or adjust an assigned topic to suit your interests. If a teacher assigns you a topic or gives you a list of topics from which to choose, you might ask if you can have greater latitude. If you do ask this, be sure to have a specific proposal in mind. Your teacher may not let you adjust the topic, but asking won't hurt. Most teachers will admire your initiative even if they can't say yes.

Whenever you have the freedom to choose or modify your topic, you can identify a good thesis by developing a list of general topics, narrowing them down, and then constructing thesis statements about them. This is a valuable prewriting exercise for documented argument papers and for all types of research writing where you have the freedom to define the limits of the topic. You'll be surprised at how many narrower topics and thesis statements you'll be able to list for each general topic. You'll get especially good results with this exercise if you work with other writers in a group. Here's an example:

> *General topic:* Problems in education
> *Narrowed topic:* Tracking (ability grouping)
> *Thesis:* Tracking should be abandoned because it creates more problems than it solves.

It's important to note that not just any sentence about the narrowed topic will be a thesis statement. These sentences, for example, are *not* thesis statements:

> Tracking is widely practiced in America.
> Many math teachers believe tracking is a necessity.
> Some parents of children in the "lower" groups hate tracking.

Why aren't these sentences thesis statements? Because they are not arguable. Where could you go with them? How could they control the scope and content of a paper?

This three-part exercise is one way to limit a broad topic and find a good, arguable slant on it. You want to avoid wasting precious time researching enormous general topics such as, "The images of women in advertising and the media and how these images have affected women's self-concepts in the twentieth century." There's no way any writer could treat a topic such as this in anything less than a book; in fact, a series of books might be required to do justice to the topic. And even in a book, the writer would have to narrow the topic into subcomponents to create chapters and, within those chapters, probably would create sections and subsections to discuss smaller theses.

Exercise

Take five of the following general topics and narrow them. Then turn your narrowed topics into thesis statements. Make sure that each thesis statement is actually arguable.

General Topics

Love	The police	Kindergarten
Golf	Medicine	Florida
Depression	Clothing.	War
Movies	Beer commercials	Smoking
Race	High school proms	Adoption
Sibling rivalry	Eating disorders	Salespeople
Telephone answering machines	Juvenile offenders	Parents
	Canada	The Dallas Cowboys
Cats	Computers	Jokes
The spread of AIDS	Student newspapers	Drunken driving
Nervous habits	Sexuality	Rock concerts

Starting Your Research and Taking Notes

Once you have narrowed your topic and focused on a tentative thesis, you can start your research. Your thesis is tentative for now because the position you intend to argue may change as you do more and more research. Lively thinkers remain open to the possibility of changing their stance. Their research may uncover evidence that convinces them to adjust their position or even to switch sides.

If your topic has been in the news, start a clipping file on it. (Clip relevant articles from your own newspapers and magazines, or photocopy them from the library's collection.) Then, using the card catalogs, bibliographies, and whatever computerized systems are available, begin to explore the holdings of your college or university library and possibly other libraries in the area. Don't hesitate to ask a librarian for help if you are new to research work or unfamiliar with a facility. Most librarians love to point students in the right direction and troubleshoot when necessary. Besides, it's their job.

When you find a source (book, magazine, newspaper, journal) that seems relevant to your narrowed topic, read as much of it as possible. If you don't have time to read an entire book, use the index to identify the parts that relate most directly to your research. Be sure that you don't take quotes out of context, however.

While you're reading, take notes on large notecards or on separate pages of a legal pad. Record one major point (fact, quote, or paraphrase) on each card or page. Underneath, on the same card or page, write any thoughts you might have about how or where you might use this bit of information in your paper. If a good idea comes to you as you're reading, jot it down then. If its use doesn't occur to you during research, don't worry—you'll figure out how best to use it later. Clearly separate the researched data from your own comments by drawing a wavy line between the two sections or marking them in some other way.

The important thing is to create a system for your research note taking and stick with it. Don't cause yourself grief by taking scrunched up, indecipherable notes. This is *not* the time to try to save paper. If you're a dedicated environmentalist, use the backs of old sheets of recycled paper. But write on one side only, and don't run your items together. You want separate points on separate cards or sheets so that later you can lay them out and shuffle them around to discover connections and create a good sequence for your material.

When you take notes, keep a careful record of what you've taken down as a direct quote and what you've put into your own words. In your notes, insert double quotation marks around anything that you copy in its exact wording and label it "DQ" for direct quote. When you take down the essence of an idea but not its original wording, write "PARA" for paraphrase next to your rewording. A paraphrase is also called an *indirect quote*.

Also precisely record everything you might need for your reference list. For each quote, paraphrase, statistic or fact you write out in your notes, list the author, complete title (of book or of both article and periodical), publisher, date and place of publication, and the page number or numbers where the information appeared. For a more complete list of what you'll need for citation purposes (not only for books and articles but also for musical recordings, television shows, personal interviews, and so forth), see the section on documenting your sources later in this chapter.

Honoring the Opposition

As you collect your research, remember to examine opposing views. Some students mistakenly think that the only research material they can use is material that directly supports their viewpoint. However, if you can find documentation of *other* positions (those viewpoints with which you disagree), research it to (1) ensure that your position is correct and (2) allow yourself to fairly depict and address opposing views in your paper. Sometimes a direct quote from the opposition can do wonders to clarify your own position and show exactly where and why you part company with others.

Imagine yourself as a lawyer arguing a case in court. You'll look naïve and unprepared if you cannot respond to the best arguments of the opposition. More importantly you'll probably lose your case. As an attorney or as an argumentative writer, you need to anticipate what the other side (or sides, as there are often more than two sides to an issue) will come up with. And, like an attorney, the smart argumentative writer treats opponents with respect—even when dismantling their arguments. Remember, it's the *honorable* opposition. (And you never know when your reader is a member of that opposition.) If you rudely attack or belittle opposing arguments or treat them too lightly, you might appear defensive, as if, deep down, you doubt your ability to answer them. Be gracious and tough. Take the position: "Give me your best shot; I can handle it. I've thought this through and done my research, and I believe what I am saying. This is a complex issue, so you will have some good points, but I have some that are even better."

To understand the benefits of honoring the opposition, compare the approaches of two teenagers trying to persuade their parents to extend their curfews. One says, "You idiots! You dictators! You pair of controlling neurotics—you deserve each other. You worry about the weirdest stuff, and you never let me do a _____ thing. You treat me like a big baby. I don't know where you're coming from, and you clowns know zip about me." The other says, "I understand what you're worried about. I know you want the best for me. You want to protect me from all the dangers out there, and I know those dangers are real. But please listen to the way I see it . . ." Who has the better chance of staying out later?

Caution: Sometimes in trying to show good faith toward the opposition, students go overboard. Showing open-mindedness and respect for other views doesn't mean being wishy-washy or vacillating about your viewpoint. Consider this example from the middle of an essay that argued that baseball is America's greatest sport:

> For the one type of crowd that feels the game of baseball is useless and has no meaning, we must accept their opinion and somewhat agree with them. We recognize that baseball is not an action-packed sport like football and basketball. It has about as much excitement as golf.

A writer can respect the opposition without agreeing with it or in any way undermining his or her own position. You'll see how this is done in some student essays presented later.

Avoiding Plagiarism Problems

Plagiarism is using someone else's published words or ideas without giving them credit. At most colleges and universities, the penalties for this practice are very high, ranging from failure on the assignment to expulsion from the institution. Even if you change the wording but use someone else's reasoning, you need to give that person credit. Many students seem unaware of this and believe that if they change a word here and there, they can use someone else's ideas without acknowledgement. This is an erroneous practice that lands many students in trouble. It's very difficult to prove that plagiarism was accidental or a result of inexperience in research writing. When identified, the act of plagiarism appears intentional and devious. **Always be meticulous about giving other people credit.** Many students are not: A recent study conducted at Ohio's Miami University found that slightly over 90 percent of the students surveyed admitted to having plagiarized written work. Studies conducted elsewhere show similar trends.

Over the years I, along with many other teachers, have encountered students who omitted citations because they worried that their own writing (both the ideas expressed and the expression itself) would look inferior next to the writing of their sources. So they claimed their sources' material as their own. In the remote possibility that this mind-set is also yours, then consider not only that plagiarism is a flagrant ethical violation with serious penalties but also this point: *Your* intelligence develops a thesis, and *your* skill finds and assembles the words and facts of experts and authorities into a powerful, convincing argument. These are demanding tasks, and they are the ones that will be evaluated. You can afford to be magnanimous. Your teacher will credit you for your hard work, so you also must give credit where credit is due. The bottom line is this: If you are proud of your intellect, you will not even consider behaving unethically in doing your academic work.

Turning Research into Writing

Students often divide the task of doing a research paper into two completely distinct jobs: collecting material and writing the paper. Quite a few of us (certainly not only student writers) have trouble finishing the first part and moving into the second. A sort of writer's block begins to form: "I don't know where to start." "I have too much stuff." "I have no idea for the intro." "Can I have a few more days?" "Maybe if I keep reading, I'll run into something that'll pull it all together." (Right—maybe you'll win a million dollars in the lottery, too.) When this happens, you must realize something very important: All the time you've been doing your research, you've really been writing. You've been "in process." Researching and writing are not two entirely distinct stages; they overlap considerably. You've taken notes from several sources; collected facts, statistics, and quotes; and jotted down your ideas on their potential uses. The notes to yourself might even constitute a rough outline. Pulling all your research and ideas together into a formal paper is, in large part, simply making a record of the intellectual work you've already done.

You might begin writing by using your cards or sheets of notes to experiment with different organizational plans: Lay them out on a large table or on the floor and arrange them into different sequences until you find one that looks like an effective way to prove your thesis. On the basis of that configuration, you can make a tentative outline.

Or you might just jump in and start writing. If you work on a word processor, it's very easy to begin a paper, knowing that later you can move around paragraphs and whole sections (in a sense, this is the high-tech equivalent of laying out your research notes on the floor or table).

Do whatever works. Try different techniques, and eventually you'll discover a system that works well for you. (This system might even include a ritual, such as wearing a certain pair of blue jeans or drinking coffee from one particular mug whenever you write. Writers do have their odd ways.)

Just make sure that you *stay in charge* of your research. Don't allow yourself to make a point that you know doesn't really belong in your essay simply because you found a great quote or a quirky fact to back it up. You need to be disciplined. Write a documented argument as you'd write any other paper with a good controlling purpose, but instead of relying solely on your own well-considered thoughts or personal anecdotes as evidence, use your research findings to back yourself up.

Documenting Your Sources

As noted earlier, when you use other people's words or ideas to prove your point or to show the thinking of those with whom you disagree, you must give credit to the source of your information. You do this by making a brief citation in the paper itself and then including a list of more complete information about all your sources at the end of the paper.

College teachers often ask you to use one of two simple reference systems. We'll look at one system in some detail and at the other quite briefly. (Never mix them. Use *one* style.) If you need more extensive instructions for a particular project or if you're required to use a method not discussed here, you can refer to a variety of publications devoted to research writing, including the most recent editions of the *MLA Handbook for Writers of Research Papers* and the *Publication Manual of the American Psychological Association*. Your teacher can direct you to the most helpful source.

When Do You Need to Cite a Source?

Before we look at the two systems, let's make sure that you know when it is necessary to provide a source. After all, you already knew some of the things your sources told you before you began your research. So what do you need to cite? First, you must give the source of all material you quote directly, that is, whatever you repeat using someone else's exact words. But often you need to provide a citation for other reasons. A good rule of thumb is this: If the information is something that the "man or woman on the street" can be assumed to know and you're not using someone else's exact words, then you usually don't have to give your source. But **if the information is in any way specific or technical enough so that it is not part of collective knowledge or conventional wisdom, then the source should be given.**

Let's look at an example. In the Summer 1989 issue of *Journalism Quarterly,* Lauren Kessler, a professor of journalism at the University of Oregon, made a point about cigarettes and the media. Let's imagine for a moment that she had written this:

> Cigarettes are widely advertised in the United States, and they make a great deal of money for various branches of the media.

Would Kessler have needed to give a source for this information? It's hard to imagine why. We all know that cigarettes are heavily advertised and that the media do not carry these ads out of the goodness of their heart, but because they make big bucks by doing so. This is common sense.

Now let's look at what Kessler actually did write:

> As the most widely advertised consumer product in America, cigarettes brought $1.5 billion into the media's coffers in 1983.

Did she need to give a source for this information? Yes, for two reasons: (1) many people may not know that cigarettes are more heavily advertised than any other consumer product in this country (especially considering that they are not advertised on television), and (2) few of us would know the exact amount of money ($1.5 billion) that cigarette advertising made for the media in one specific year. So Kessler gave the reader the exact source of her information:

> R. Hutchins, "A Review of the nature and extent of cigarette advertising in the U.S.," in *Proceedings of the National Conference on Smoking and Health* (New York: American Cancer Society, 1982), pp. 249–262.

By doing this, Kessler made it easy for an interested party to track down her source and get more information on the same subject.

The MLA Parenthetical Citation System

A widely used and easy-to-learn citation system is the one created by the Modern Language Association (MLA). (This is the system followed by the students whose works appear in this book.) In this system, the writer follows a few clear guidelines and relies on common sense to figure out special situations. Instead of using a number to refer the reader to a footnote or endnote, the writer includes some brief source information in the text itself—usually the author's last name and a page number. This information is placed within parentheses, usually just before ending punctuation.

A Work by One Author

Let's imagine that the following excerpt is from a section of your paper in which you quote from page 620 of Martha Banta's book *Imaging American Women: Idea and Ideals in Cultural History*:

> Sex in advertising is nothing new. "Sexuality was clearly a marketable product by the 1890s, both as an item for direct sale and as a come-on for the readers of the tabloid press" (Banta 620).

The citation "(Banta 620)" tells your reader that the direct quote comes from page 620 of a work by someone with the last name of Banta. No punctuation is used between the author's name and the page number.

If readers want more information right away, they can turn to the end of your paper, where they will find a section labeled "Works Cited." In this section, you have listed all your sources in alphabetical order. Among them will be this entry:

Banta, Martha. *Imaging American Women: Idea and Ideals in Cultural History.* New York: Columbia University Press, 1987.

The "Works Cited" page is discussed in greater detail later. For now, let's return to the parenthetical citations within the paper itself.

Returning to our example, suppose you had used Banta's name in setting up the quote. Then, you would drop her name from the parenthetical citation:

> Banta points out that sex in advertising is nothing new: "Sexuality was clearly a marketable product by the 1890s, both as an item for direct sale and as a come-on for the readers of the tabloid press" (620).

If you quote from more than one work by the same author, include the name of the relevant work (in a shortened form, if possible) in the citation. For example, Banta is also the author of *Failure and Success in America,* so if elsewhere you quoted from that book in your paper too, then your in-text citation here would be

> Sex in advertising is nothing new. "Sexuality was clearly a marketable product by the 1890s, both as an item for direct sale and as a come-on for the readers of the tabloid press" (Banta, *Imaging American Women* 620).

Notice that in all these cases the parenthetical citation is placed *before* the period. The exception to this is when you use the single-spaced block form for quotes that are longer than four typed lines. Then you place the citation within parentheses two spaces *after* the end punctuation mark of the quote. (Your papers, including shorter quotes, are usually double-spaced.)

A Work by More than One Author

If you are quoting from a book or article by two authors, simply use both names with *and* between, for example, "(Smith and Jones 251)." If you have three authors, use commas as in any list, for example, "(Larson, Randall, and Payne 43)." If you have four or more authors, name only the first one and then use the Latin abbreviation *et al.* (meaning "and others") before the page number, for example, "(Belenky et al. 120)."

A Corporate or Anonymous Author

If the author is not a person but a corporation or institution, list the corporation in the parenthetical citation instead of the author's name. If the work has no named author, use the title of the work in place of the author's name.

An Indirect Source

If you find that you must quote someone as quoted by another person, you need to indicate that your quote came from a secondary source. For example,

> Francisco Goya, an early Spanish master of modern art, once said, "Phantasy abandoned by reason produces impossible monsters; united

with her, she is the mother of the arts and the origin of their marvels" (qtd. in Storr 67).

This citation indicates that you didn't find Goya's words in a work by Goya, but rather as quoted in the book *Solitude: A Return to the Self* by Anthony Storr.

A Multivolume Work

If in your paper you quote from a work that has more than one volume, your parenthetical citation must include the appropriate volume number followed by a colon and a space before the page number. For example, here's how to indicate a quote from page 452 of the second volume of *God's Playground: A History of Poland* by Norman Davies:

> Of the massacre of Polish officers in the Katyn Forest, Davies has said, "In Polish eyes, this one crime has become the symbol for countless other, unrecorded atrocities committed by the Soviet Union against the Polish nation" (2: 452).

In the MLA system, arabic numerals are used whenever possible. Use roman numerals only when necessary, such as in reference to the page number of a preface or introduction. Numbers of volumes, chapters, sections, and so forth should be arabic.

Quotations from Poems, Plays, Sacred Texts, and Novels

When you quote from poems, plays, or sacred writing, you need to cite the numbers of acts, scenes, and lines or the chapters and verses (always moving from larger to smaller). By using these identifying numbers rather than the usual page numbers, you're allowing your readers to find the quote even if they do not have the same edition of the poem or play or the same version of the sacred text. In the following example, the first four lines of a poem are cited.

> In "I Knew a Woman," Theodore Roethke delights with double meanings:
>
> > I knew a woman, lovely in her bones,
> > When small birds sighed, she would sigh back at them;
> > Ah, when she moved, she moved more ways than one:
> > The shapes a bright container can contain!   (1–4)

In "Works Cited," the writer should include the full information about the book in which the Roethke poem was found, even though the page number was not cited in the text.

When you quote a passage from a play, the numbers of the act, scene, and lines are separated by periods with no spaces on either side. For example the citation "(2.1.15)" means the second act, the first scene, line 15. Again, use arabic numerals.

When you quote from the Bible, it's traditional to use a colon between chapter and verse. While that style is still acceptable, the MLA system suggests that the writer use the same approach as for passages from plays. Thus, a reference to the third chapter, verses 1 through 5 of the Book of Ruth can be indicated in either of two ways: (Ruth 3.1–5) or (Ruth 3:1–5).

If you quote from a novel, it's best to give the chapter number after the page number. Separate them with a semicolon. This helps the reader who may have a different edition of the novel find your quote. Here's an example:

> Later the narrator of Ellison's *Invisible Man* tells us, "I'd no more have to speak than Paul Robeson had to act; they'd simply thrill at the sight of me" (399; ch. 19).

The "Works Cited" Section

The "Works Cited" section follows the text of your paper. If your conclusion ended on page 9, type **Works Cited** (no underlining and no quotation marks), centered, one inch from the top of page 10. Let's look at how to set up some of the most common types of sources listed in a "Works Cited" section.

Books or Selections from Books

Remember how the Banta book was set up in our previous example of a listing on the "Works Cited" page?

> Banta, Martha. *Imaging American Women: Idea and Ideals in Cultural History.* New York: Columbia University Press, 1987.

Notice that there are three blocks of information in the listing:

1. the author's name (last name first), followed by a period;
2. the name of the book, underlined and followed by a period; and
3. the place of publication, followed by a colon; the publishing company, followed by a comma; and the year of publication, followed by a period.

This pattern is used for most references. Skip two spaces after the author's name and after the author's work. Indent five spaces for all lines after the first. In the following list, note how the format is adapted to suit various situations.

A book by two or three authors (Note that the second author's name is not reversed.):

> Sanders, Thomas E., and Walter W. Peek. *Literature of the American Indian.* Beverly Hills: Glencoe, 1976.

A book by four or more authors:

> Belenky, Mary Field, et al. *Women's Ways of Knowing: The Development of Self, Voice, and Mind.* New York: Basic Books, 1986.

A book by a corporation or organization:

> The University of Chicago. *The Chicago Manual of Style.* 13th ed. Chicago: The University of Chicago Press, 1982.

A book with an editor:

> Burack, Sylvia K., ed. *The Writer's Handbook.* Boston: THE WRITER, INC., 1987.

A selection within an anthology (Cite the author of the selection used; the editor of the anthology is given after the book title. Remember to give inclusive page numbers.):

Elliot, Grace. "Marie-Antoinette at the Opera, July 1792." *Eyewitness to History.* Ed. John Carey. Cambridge: Harvard University Press. 1987. 247–248.

An unpublished dissertation (Note that the title is in quotation marks.):

Campbell, Richard A. "Narrative, Myth and Metaphor in '60 Minutes': An Interpretive Approach to the Study of Television News." Diss. Northwestern University, 1986.

Articles

Let's first look at an entry for a newspaper article. Note that the number given after the colon at the end of the entry is the page number.

Schoemer, Karen. "Johnny Cash, An Enduring American Icon." *The New York Times* 3 May 1992, sec. 2: 27.

If a newspaper article is not signed, begin with the title of the article. If the paper comes out in various editions, give the edition (for example, "late ed." or "Midwest ed.") after the date and before the section and page number. If, for example, a newspaper story begins on page 10 and continues on pages 15–16, use the notation 10+. If the paper's title does not contain the name of the city in which it is published, include the city in brackets after the name of the newspaper, but don't underline or italicize it. If the quoted material is from an editorial, type *editorial* before the name of the newspaper. Set off *editorial* between commas. Follow the same procedure for a *cartoon* or a *letter* appearing in a newspaper.

Now let's look at how other types of articles are listed on a "Works Cited" page.

A book review:

McGrath, Peter. "Anatomy of a Catastrophe." Rev. of *Dreadnought*, by Robert K. Massie. *Newsweek* 25 Nov. 1991: 57.

An article from a magazine (Give inclusive page numbers for the article.):

Cohn, Bob, and David A. Kaplan. "How the Defense Dissected the Tape." *Newsweek* 11 May 1992: 36–37.

An article in a journal with continuous pagination (Note the volume number follows the journal title and precedes the year of publication, which is in parentheses. The issue number is not given for a journal that is continuously paginated.):

Gonzalez, Hernando. "The Evolution of Communication as a Field." *Communication Research* 15 (1988): 302–308.

An article in a journal with separate pagination (Here "24.3" means volume 24, issue number 3.):

Unger, Arthur. "Barbara Walters: 'I Can Ask Them But I Can't Answer Them.'" *Television Quarterly* 24.3 (1990): 5–17.

A signed article in a reference book (Basic, well-known reference works are done as simply as the following example, with no volume number and no page number listed. If the reference book is obscure, however, give more information, including the name of the editor, the number of volumes, place of publication, publishing company, and year of publication.):

Weinberg, Alvin M. "Nuclear Energy." *World Book Encyclopedia.* 1988 ed.

Other Source Materials

The following is a list of other types of sources you might use in your research. A sample entry is given for each type.

Movie (Underline or italicize the title.):

Citizen Kane. Dir. Orson Welles. RKO Studios, 1941.

Television or radio show (If the writer, director, or producer is known, his or her name and title follow the show's title. If an episode title is known, place it first and enclose it within quotation marks.):

World of Audubon: Mysterious Elephants of the Congo. WTBS, Atlanta, Georgia. 30 November 1991.

Musical recording (Here, "Arista" is the label, and "ARCD-8628" is the catalog number.):

Franklin, Aretha. "Someone Else's Eyes." *What You See Is What You Sweat.* Arista, ARCD-8628, 1991.

Interview (Be sure to state whether the interview was conducted in person, by mail, or in a phone conversation.):

Sethney, Charlene. Personal interview with author. 16 June 1977.

Lecture (If possible, include the title of the lecture within quotation marks.):

McDonald, Elizabeth. Class lecture. Psychology 566. University of Texas, Austin. 21 September 1990

Two or More Works by the Same Author on the "Works Cited" Page

If you have more than one work by the same author, don't repeat the author's name. Put the works in alphabetical order and, after the first use of the author's name, use three hyphens and a period. For example,

Percy, Walker. *The Moviegoer.* New York: Avon, 1960.
---. *The Thanatos Syndrome.* New York: Farrar Straus Giroux, 1987.

Endnotes with Parenthetical Citation

Numbered notes may also appear in a paper that has parenthetical citations. You might do this for one of two reasons: (1) to give extra information that the reader would find interesting but that is not relevant to proving your thesis; and (2) to refer the reader to several other sources. All you need to do is insert a raised arabic number at the appropriate spot in your paper and then include your endnote after a matching raised number on a page labeled "Notes," which is placed between the last page of your paper and the first page of "Works Cited."

The APA System

The citation style of the American Psychological Association (APA) is often used in the social sciences. It differs from the MLA parenthetical citation system most notably by emphasizing the year of publication. In the parenthetical citations in text, the year of publication is inserted after the author's name. Commas and "p." or "pp." (for "page" or "pages") are used in this style. For example, in the following sentence the student writer refers to a book by one author:

> One scholar in the field noted that "Freud's triad remains equally relevant in the application of psychoanalysis to the behavioral sciences, and to the humanities" (Erikson, 1964, p. 43).

If Erikson's name had been used in setting up the quote, the citation after the quote could be "(1964, p. 43)." Or, equally acceptable in the APA style, the date could be given immediately after the writer's name, with the page number appearing alone after the quote.

> Erikson (1964) noted that "Freud's triad remains equally relevant in the application of psychoanalysis to the behavioral sciences, and to the humanities" (p. 43).

For works with three or more authors, list all of their names the first time you cite them in the text. In subsequent in-text citations, use the last name of the first author and *et al.* (If a work has seven or more authors, use *et al.* after the first author's name even in the first citation.)

At the end of the paper, APA style calls for an alphabetized section of sources labeled "References." Again, the date is given prominence; it follows the author's name. The reference to Erikson would look like this:

> Erikson, E.H. (1964). *Insight and responsibility.* New York: W.W. Norton.

Note that, in APA style for reference listings, initials are used for the author's first and middle name, and only the first word in a work's title or subtitle (plus any proper noun) is capitalized. The date appears within parentheses.

Sample References

In the following list, references that appeared in the section on the MLA citation style for "Works Cited" have been reworked to mirror the APA style. Notice that an ampersand (&) is used instead of *and*. This symbol is used in the in-text citations and in references at the end. Notice also that the names of journals and newspapers are capitalized conventionally and that neither the word *page* nor the abbreviations *p.* or *pp.* are used in journal references. Indent three spaces for all lines after the first line in an entry.

A work by more than one author:

Sanders, T.E., & Peek, W.W. (1976). *Literature of the American Indian.* Beverly Hills: Glencoe.

An article in a newspaper (Note that no quotation marks are used around the article title.):

Schoemer, K. (1992, May 3). Johnny Cash, an enduring American icon. *The New York Times,* p. 2: 27.

An article in a journal with continuous pagination:

Gonzalez, H. (1988). The evolution of communication as a field. *Communication Research, 15,* 302–308.

An article in a journal with separate pagination (Note that the volume—24— is underlined, and the issue number—3—is enclosed within parentheses.):

Unger, A. (1990). "Barbara Walters: 'I can ask them but I can't answer them.'" *Television Quarterly, 24* (3), 5–17.

Page Headings in the APA System

One notable feature of the APA style is that it requires the writer to create a shortened title for his or her paper, center it in the lower part of the title page (which in this system is numbered as "page 1") and then repeat the short heading in the upper right-hand corner of each page of the essay. This allows the title page with the student's name to be removed for the convenience of the teacher who wishes to read papers without knowing who wrote them.

Examples of Student Work

Three Strong Essays

Let's examine three documented arguments. The first one, which appeals to the intellect and the heart, is an excellent essay on the sensitive subject of surrogate motherhood. Look for a clear thesis, convincing evidence to support it, exploration of opposing views, and helpful citations. (All five student essays conform to the MLA parenthetical citation style.) In addition, check for the things that are important in *any* essay: concreteness, flair, logical paragraphing, a strong sequence, an introduction that creates a need to read, and a satisfying conclusion.

Surrogate Motherhood
Tiffanie L. Lang

1   In the United States today, about fifteen percent of all couples of childbearing age face fertility problems ("Surrogate Mothers" 68). Because the process of adoption takes such a long time and has become more difficult, many of these couples are turning to an alternative method of having children: surrogate motherhood. This is the process in which an infertile couple contracts another woman to be impregnated with the husband's sperm. After the woman has the child, the child is returned to the natural father and is then legally adopted by his wife.

This process may sound like a wonderful way to help infertile couples have the babies of their dreams, but it actually causes more pain than it is really worth. Although surrogate motherhood has some positive effects, it has a greater number of negative ones. Surrogate motherhood is a complex idea that fails to take into account the feelings of everyone involved and the problems that arise as a result of the process. Thus surrogate motherhood should be outlawed in America.

2   Surrogate motherhood involves many controversial and emotional issues that may arise and have great effects on the parties involved. If the child is born handicapped or retarded, neither the couple nor the surrogate may want the baby. Or suppose the couple decides not to have a baby through surrogacy after the surrogate has already been artificially inseminated. The result will be another child being born into this world without the love and care of a real family. Also, the surrogate may change her mind either during or after her pregnancy and want to keep her unborn child, which in turn will lead to a custody battle over the child and cause much pain, sorrow, and grief to both the surrogate and the infertile couple.

3   There is also the possibility that the surrogate process will go smoothly and that initially everyone will be happy, but that years later, the adoptive mother will have difficulties raising a child who was conceived by her husband and another woman. Also when the child becomes older and discovers the process by which he was conceived, he may want to find his natural mother and live with her. This would cause problems between the parents and their child and also between the parents and the surrogate. Therefore the results of surrogate motherhood may make an infertile couple happy, but there are so many possibilities for people to be hurt that the chance that couples take is not worth the pain that may be caused. A surrogate mother who appeared on television talk shows using the pseudonym Elizabeth Kane said, "All you're doing is transferring the pain from one woman to another, from a woman who is in pain from her infertility to a woman who has to give up her baby" (qtd. in "Surrogate-gate" 36).

4   Surely, Mary Beth Whitehead, the surrogate mother in the nationally known "Baby M" case, would agree with Miss Kane's view. In the Baby M case, William and Elizabeth Stern contracted Mrs. Whitehead to have Mr. Stern's baby. It was widely reported that the Sterns paid the agency that arranged the contract $7,500, nonrefundable (Novak 406). They also agreed to pay all of the medical bills and presented Mrs. Whitehead with an offer that set out these conditions:

> (1) All risks belonged to her; if anything went wrong with her or the baby during the pregnancy, she was to receive *nothing;* (2) in case of miscarriage she was to receive *nothing;* (3) between the sixteenth and twentieth week, her baby would have to be tested for "physiological abnormalities"; at this point, (4) if "physiological abnormalities" were discovered, she would be obliged "upon demand of William Stern" to have an abortion; (5) if the abortion were demanded by William Stern, William Stern would pay her a big-hearted $1,000; and (6) with the delivery and surrender of a healthy baby for possession by the Sterns, Mrs. Whitehead would receive—at the point of sale—$10,000.   (Novak 406)

5   This contract is cruel and immoral. It was wrong for the Sterns to claim the right to tell Mrs. Whitehead, who was willing to have a baby for them, that all risks belonged to her, and if something happened during her pregnancy, she would receive nothing. A miscarriage is a painful event that would have been out of Mrs. Whitehead's control; thus, in the case of a miscarriage, she should have been offered some sort of compensation. Also there was the possibility that Mrs. Whitehead would be forced to have an abortion. Not only would it be immoral to demand this of her, but it would also be dangerous. A woman should be able to decide for herself whether or not she will have an abortion. Many aspects of the contract do not treat Mrs. Whitehead fairly, nor do they treat the unborn baby fairly. The greatest injustice to the baby, of course, is the baby's fate if physiological abnormalities are found. This is the fatal flaw in surrogate motherhood: It fails to respect the feelings and the humanity of everyone involved. This birth-marketing tactic can negatively affect everyone; it even tends to negatively affect our society as a whole.

6   One aspect of birth marketing is that the baby is bought and sold as if the baby were a commodity. More than 100 years ago we decided that we did not want people to be bought and sold in this country. But today, with the rise of surrogate motherhood, we are doing to babies the same thing that was done to the slaves: We are treating them as objects, not as people. Mrs. Whitehead was to be paid $10,000 for a live baby or $1,000 if the baby were aborted. Therefore, she was not being paid for the services she was rendering, but rather for delivering a live child. There was a time when life was considered priceless; now we are putting price tags on it. Exactly how much is a life worth? To have a baby through surrogate motherhood, the average fee is $22,000, about half of which is paid to the surrogate (Arking 56). Rita Arditti, faculty member of the Union Graduate School, states in an article in *Social Policy,* "Surrogate motherhood . . . turns children into commodities, making them objects that can be bought, sold, or returned if defective" (46).

7   Another aspect of surrogacy is the way in which the surrogate mother is demeaned and downplayed. She is never viewed as the natural mother of the baby when that is what she really is, but instead she is labeled a substitute and a baby maker. The surrogate is not usually allowed to form a relationship with her child because the child is not recognized as hers but as the father's alone; she is nothing more than an incubator for his sperm. She receives sperm from him and gives a baby back to him. "Based on the idea of supremacy of the sperm, Baby M has only one parent, the father, and the mother's genetic and nurturant contribution and the experience of birth are ruled out of the picture" (Arditti 43). Surrogates have even been viewed as prostitutes because they sell the use of their bodies to men who can afford to pay them enough money. Surrogates are rarely acknowledged for who they really are: They are the natural mothers of the children just as the fathers are the natural fathers. The women also rarely receive any credit for being *real* women with feelings, feelings that could become very strong for the children they carry inside for nine months and finally bear through a delivery that may be painful but joyous. Instead, they are treated as baby-making machines.

8   A third aspect of the baby trade is the way it reflects class

distinctions. Contracts are drawn mainly between upper-middle-class couples and working-class or lower-middle-class women. Because surrogacy is so expensive, poorer infertile couples cannot afford it. When choosing candidates for surrogate motherhood, companies that make such arrangements operate on the principle that poor women are more likely to "behave." Dr. Howard Adelman, a psychologist who screens women for Surrogate Mothering, Ltd., in Philadelphia, told *OB/GYN News:* "I believe candidates with an element of financial need are the safest. If a woman is on unemployment and has children to care for, she is not likely to change her mind and want to keep the baby she is being paid to have for somebody else" (qtd. in Corea 229). Just as the poor have always been hired to clean the houses and care for the children of the rich, today, members of the upper-middle-class are hiring the poor to have their children. Critics predict that surrogacy will lead to a "breeder class" of poor women who rent their wombs to the wealthy. Thus, "commercial surrogacy can thrive because of class differences and exploitation of poor women" (Arditti 44).

9   Another negative factor is the way surrogate motherhood undermines the family. The family is supposed to be a sacred unit, but surrogacy reduces it to a business: Genes from a man are placed into a woman, not his wife, in order to produce a baby which is then returned to the father for a fee. Why is it so important for a child to have the genes of at least parent? Obviously, our society is not supporting the right kinds of values if we place so much emphasis on genetic makeup. Parenting means loving and caring for a child, not preserving one's genetic line. Thus a couple should be able to parent a child whether the child has the genes of one, two, or neither of the parents. Genetics don't create love. If they did, there would be fewer children in state agencies. As one expert commented, "Human reproduction should be firmly placed in the matrix of personal sexuality, marital love, and family bonds" ("Surrogate-gate" 35).

10   Proponents of commercial surrogacy claim that women have always had babies for other women, often referring to the case of Sarah and Hagar in the Old Testament. Genesis 16 states that Abraham's wife, Sarah, could not bear children; thus Abraham had a child by Sarah's maid, Hagar. What proponents fail to mention is that after Sarah later became pregnant through a miracle and bore her own son, Isaac, Hagar and her son were cast out into the desert. Thus the surrogacy did not create a loving, happy family, but resulted in great suffering by the woman who bore a child for someone else and her son.

11   Surrogacy may seem to be a wonderful alternative for infertile couples, but the negative effects are so far greater in number than the positive effects that it should be outlawed. Infertile couples should continue to seek children who need either to be adopted or cared for as foster children. One of the lawyers in the Baby M case called surrogacy a "terrible practice," adding, "there's so much potential harm that it shouldn't even be considered by rational people" (qtd. in Arking 55). Surrogate motherhood is a process which markets babies as commodities, demeans women who act as surrogates, exploits poor women, and undermines the family. It also creates the possibility of leaving all parties involved with deep emotional scars. "In the case of commercial surrogate motherhood, the line should be drawn under the word NO" ("Birthmarketing" 692).

Works Cited

Arditti, Rita.   "The Surrogacy Business."   *Social Policy* 18.2 (1987): 42–46.
Arking, Linda.   "Searching for a Very Special Woman."   *McCalls* June 1987: 55–56.
"Birthmarketing."   *Commonweal* 114 (1987): 692.
Corea, Gena.   *The Mother Machine.*   New York: Harper and Row, 1985.
Novak, Michael.   "Buying and Selling Babies: Limitations on the Marketplace."
   Commonweal 114 (1987): 406–407.
"Surrogate-gate."   *Commonweal* 114 (1987): 35–36.
"Surrogate Mothers."   *The Futurist* 18 (1984): 68.

In the next essay, the writer uses a variety of research material to support his strongly expressed view of one incident of apparent corruption—or at least ethical laxity—in American government. How well does Jeremy use his research? Is the essay well-organized, and does each paragraph have its own agenda? How well does Jeremy make clear explanations and strong diction choices in building a successful argument? Does he examine and answer objections to his position?

The "Perkolator" Brews Another Scandal on the Hill
Jeremy Kloubec

1   News of crooked dealings has surfaced on Capitol Hill once again. It seems that members of Congress have been writing bad checks that were routinely covered by the House Bank. Since September of 1991, these checks—from the top 66 offenders alone—have amounted to a total of almost $11 million (Salholz, "Caught" 29). While some members may have been unwitting dupes in the scandal, others have definitely abused their privileges. For instance, Robert Mrazek, a representative from New York, wrote 927 bad checks and held a negative balance that exceeded his monthly paycheck for 23 consecutive weeks (Salholz, "Wreckage" 38). Ineptitude on the part of Congress is nothing new to the American people; however, during a recession, it is very disillusioning to have the country's leaders mishandling money.

2   A peculiar twist to this story is that "Rubbergate," as it has been called by the media, possibly involved no violation of the law. (Investigations continue, and it is too soon to tell.) The House Bank is a cooperative in which the payroll of the members is cashed. Money is then borrowed against the next month's payroll. The bank remains solvent only if other members leave their money in the bank so it can be borrowed against. In one sense, no bad checks were written since the bank always had enough money to cover them. Also, it's true that this privilege has been available for more than 150 years (Rowan 11). However, when congressmen and women write 8,000 bad checks in one year, people start to question the integrity of the bank and the members who use it (Salholz, "Caught" 26). To some, it would seem that the House Bank's motto is, "It is better to give than to receive."

3   What illegalities may have been involved in the House Bank transactions? A special investigation is probing possible fraud and check-kiting by members of Congress. Check-kiting is the act of depositing a check of more than $100 with the intent to defraud, and this offense carries a maximum three-year jail sentence (Salholz, "Caught" 28). Also, an unusual number of bad checks were written

before the last November election and repaid in the second week of that month. This could mean that money was illegally transferred into re-election campaign funds and repaid after election day (28). These interest-free loans could help a faltering campaign and aid an incumbent in a bid to keep his or her seat.

4   The scandal does not stop there. The House Post Office is also under investigation. Evidently, large quantities of stamps were purchased with personal and campaign checks; the stamps were then returned in exchange for money. This could be a form of money laundering. The day before this story broke, House postmaster Robert Rota hastily resigned his position (Ellis 32). He was not alone in being suddenly unemployed, however. Jack Russ, the House sergeant-at-arms who oversees Bank transactions, also retired as the check-bouncing story broke. It raises suspicions of wrongdoing when two individuals not accused of any crime decide to retire on the advent of an investigation of check bouncing.

5   Some observers claim that members of Congress need interest-free loans and other advantages so that they can live more easily and concentrate on running the country. But—even without overdrawing their accounts—they already enjoy many perks that the average citizen does not. Parking, for example, is free in every location because parking tickets cannot be assessed against a member of Congress. Food is basically free: The unpaid tab at the House Restaurant totaled over $300,000 in a recent nine-month period (Salholz, "Caught" 26). Health care is also socialized for the members of Congress, who will not create a bill so that the average citizen can enjoy the same luxury. Factor in free use of the gym and free plants from the U.S. Botanical Garden (26). To this wealth of perks, tally additional gifts from Political Action Committees. It is hard for the American people to believe that—with all these extras—the members of Congress are short on money.

6   The saddest commentary on the House banking scandal is that it is nothing new to the public. It has become almost a common occurrence for some congressperson to be violating some rule. Many Americans might overlook minor infractions if Capitol Hill were generally perceived as operating for the common good. But this is not the case. In a recent *Newsweek* poll, Congress was judged "ineffective" by 78 percent of Americans who were surveyed, and 75 percent answered "No" when asked if Congress understands the concerns of the average person. Sixty percent believed that events have "gone too far" and that some "new blood" is needed in Congress (Salholz, "Caught" 29).

7   Some members of Congress abused the check-writing privilege because they could get away with it. Whether or not their activity was illegal, they clearly put themselves out of touch with the people. It is also hard to believe that anyone who writes over 700 invalid personal checks in one year can help create a solid fiscal policy for the nation. Americans need to re-evaluate the perk system and do some serious housecleaning in Congress. The nation requires new, qualified leaders who understand the average citizen and will stay within clear ethical bounds. As columnist David S. Broder has said, the House must once again become "an effective and accountable legislative body—not a personal plaything for its members" (15).

Works Cited

Broder, David S.   "House's checks and balances have gone awry." *Detroit Free Press* 19
     March 1992, sec. A: 15.
Ellis, David. "Checkmate for the Speaker?" *Time* 30 March 1992: 32.
Rowan, Carl. "A scandal of politics and hype." *Detroit Free Press* 18 March 1992, sec.
     A: 11.
Salholz, Eloise. "Caught in the Act." *Newsweek* 23 March 1992: 24–29.
---. "Wreckage on the Hill: The Body Count Begins." *Newsweek* 30 March 1992: 38–39.

In our third essay, the writer creatively blends modes of expression to build a compelling case for more awareness of one of the most horrifying crimes—the sexual abuse of children. Through her creation of narrative/descriptive material—in the form of Amy's journal—Hakeemeh humanizes and clarifies a painful subject.

How effectively does Hakeemeh blend her narrative/descriptive material with the more traditional expository and argumentative passages? Does she use her research well? Does she look at opposing viewpoints, or is this one case in which there is no "other side"?

Childhood Sexual Abuse: From Victim to Survivor
Hakeemeh Montgomery

1   A great deal of misunderstanding surrounds childhood sexual abuse, especially incest. Most people think of it as a taboo that does not exist. But incest is a real problem that involves real people, and to understand it, people must become familiar with the feelings of those involved. Researchers have done many case studies of survivors of incest. One such study was done on Amy, a 19-year-old who was sexually abused by her stepfather for five years. As part of her therapy, she began to express herself through a journal. *Her entries will appear here in italics.* By considering the words of a survivor and the opinions of academic experts, readers may gain a fuller understanding of the issues surrounding incest.

2   *At first he would just stand by the bed and touch me. Later, he began asking me to touch him—sometimes with my hand and other times with my mouth. I hated that, and I would cry the whole time. He didn't seem to notice. Eventually, he wanted more, and at the age of 15, I lost my virginity to my stepfather—unwillingly. I never resisted because I knew that I was no match for him. I taught myself to detach my mind from my body. I could actually see myself from the corner of the room. I saw the little girl crying in bed, and I felt sorry for her.*

3   Most often, a child victim of incest is misunderstood. Some people feel that the child brought it upon herself for acting or dressing too provocatively around her father, stepfather, brother, or uncle. The offender often claims that the child made the initial step and that he was simply doing what she wanted. Some challenge a child's story by accusing her of lying, trying to get attention, or trying to get back at her abuser for some unknown reason. And others put the responsibility of incest on the child by saying that she had ways out of the situation: She should have told someone, left home, or asked her abuser to stop. But the actions of the adult must not be forgotten in these situations; the responsibility of incest should never be placed on a child. She is the naive one, the one who is supposed to be nurtured and cared for. How

can anyone expect her to behave like an adult when she is not one? Furthermore, most children do tell someone, leave home—possibly for short periods of time—and tell their abusers to stop. These methods rarely work. Amy, for instance, tried to get out of her situation by telling someone:

4   *I told Mom when I was twelve, but somehow Dad convinced her that I was a troubled child seeking attention—the subject was dropped, but the abuse continued.*

5   "Too frequently a child has reported the situation to an adult who refuses to believe the child" (Fortune 166). If one adult did not believe her, why would others? "When a victim has asked for help from an adult and not been believed, she readily concludes that adults in general cannot be trusted" (Fortune 167). As for the option of leaving home, at the age of eight or nine, when abuse generally begins (Bierker 146), where would a child go? Her last alternative is to confront her abuser and tell him to stop. Yet most victims "feel that they have no right to refuse a parent's wish to use them sexually . . . a child wants to continue being provided for and may fear that she will be abandoned if she resists the sexual activity" (Bierker 146).

6   *Sometimes, when he was done and I would get up crying, he would ask me what was wrong. I told him that I didn't like to do those things with him, and he would say, "Okay." Later, he would tell me that I was not his special little girl anymore—I would feel so lonely. He always knew that he could come back to me that night because I wanted to be loved.*

7   Children who have been victims of molestation have to develop coping mechanisms. One of the most common is detachment. Amy, for example, could mentally detach herself from her body and watch the abuse take place from another part of the room. By doing this, she reduced some of the emotional strain. To friends and family, victims who use detachment may sometimes seem insensitive, and physical signs of their abuse often are not evident. But this does not mean that a child is "tough enough to handle it"; the victim is simply learning how to be a survivor. Child victims may also cope by misbehaving or underachieving in school, being hypersensitive, and sometimes even committing suicide. They may have friends, but "the victim seems isolated from her peers . . . and may feel older and more experienced than them as well" (Fortune 166).

8   As adults, survivors may "bounce from one sexual partner to another with little emotional involvement or caring for their partner's needs" (Bierker 148). This behavior is directly related to how children deal with abuse: by detaching physical sex from its emotional significance (Hopkins 17). Without counseling or therapy, children can grow up to face a number of problems in adult life: They may become abusers of their own children, avoid relationships or enter into abusive ones, spend years in mental institutions, or take their own lives.

9   *I finally decided to tell a friend. She told her mother, and with their support, I pressed charges against Dad. Because he plea bargained, I didn't have to go through a trial and testify. He was sent to prison for three years for criminal sexual conduct in the second degree. Mom didn't believe me—again—and stood by Dad the entire time. I lived in a girls home for a couple of months, and then I was placed into a foster home until I went to college. It was pretty hard for me to deal with my emotions, but therapy helped. I never went back home.*

Now I live a normal life as a college student, and FINALLY, Mom believes me.

10   All cases do not have a happy ending in which the "bad guy" goes to jail and everyone lives happily ever after. Often, if the father is prosecuted, "the mother's reaction is not to show sympathy or alarm but to blame the girl for having sent her father to prison. The family is broken up, Social Services is needed, and the other children are possibly put into care" (Hopkins 16).

11   *Mom was allowed to keep the kids, but she had to have a hearing to determine if she was unfit for allowing my abuse to go on for so long. She had to go through therapy, along with the rest of the family, but I still don't think she really understands. As soon as Dad gets out of prison, I know that Mom is going to let him come back home. My little sister will be eleven by then—the same age I was when he started molesting me.*

12   Incest is not only a problem of the poor or the unemployed; it is widespread and affects people of all racial and social backgrounds. In 1983, statistics showed that "38% of females and one out of every ten males will be sexually molested by the age of 18. At least 50% of all child sexual abuse occurs in the family as incestuous abuse" (Fortune 164). These numbers should shock society into dealing with the problem. Victims should receive therapy, and abusers should be punished to the full extent of the law. After prison, they too should be mandated to attend therapy sessions. The problem will not go away by locking abusers up or taking children out of the home. Rehabilitation—for all those involved—is the key. To protect children, society must begin to understand how incest and other forms of child sexual abuse occur, why they occur, and how to stop them from occurring again.

13   *I really wish I would have had someone to talk to, so that maybe I could have stopped it from happening. I have always felt like it was my fault, but now I know that I was only a child. He was responsible for himself and for me—but he is sick, and I had to be the adult in the situation. I am a survivor.*

Works Cited

Bierker, Susan B.   *About Sexual Abuse.*   Springfield, Illinois: Charles C. Thomas Publisher, 1989.

Fortune, Marie M.   *Sexual Violence: The Unmentionable Sin.*   New York: The Pilgrim Press, 1983.

Hopkins, June, ed.   *Perspectives on Rape and Sexual Assault.*   London: Harper & Row, 1984.

Two Approaches to One Assignment

As you've seen, writers approach argumentative tasks from many directions and write in a wide variety of styles. Some stand close to their research and use their findings in a very specific way that calls for careful citation. Others stand back from the specifics of the case and paint their picture with a broad brush. Some argue more from the mind, others straight from the heart. Wise writers develop a variety of skills so they can adjust their approach from project to project, as dictated by subject matter, mood, and intended audience.

The following essays are by two students who were assigned the same research project: to evaluate the Sioux Indians' claim to the Black Hills. Students were asked to argue for or against the Sioux's right to the land itself or to financial compensation for the loss of it. Both students began by watching a PBS "Frontlines" documentary on the subject, "In the Spirit of Crazy Horse." Then they read much of the same research and, as it happened, formed similar theses about the case. But they wrote their papers in radically different styles—each successful and pleasing in its own way.

In the first essay, you'll see a careful student historian at work. Bishari Bivins stands close enough to the facts so that his style necessitates careful documentation, yet you'll notice that, even in a very traditional academic style, he is able to write with great passion.

In the second essay, you'll see a completely different take on the same subject. Mila Stephens is a highly creative thinker who backs up from her research and argues here as she might in a conversation at the dinner table.

As you read the essays, look for the strengths of each, note your own reactions, and imagine how other readers might react to the two styles. If you were given the same assignment, what questions about the requirements of the assignment might you ask your teacher before choosing a writing style?

Note: Terms became somewhat problematic in this project. The Sioux most prominently involved in the case are the Teton Sioux. In addition, many Sioux prefer the name *Lakota,* but students used the traditional name *Sioux* because that was the term they found almost universally in their research sources.

Decades of Dishonest Dealings with the Teton Sioux
Bishari Bivins

1   The Black Hills are a majestic land, abundant with game and blessed with some of nature's most beautiful scenery. This area in southwestern South Dakota and eastern Wyoming is a land with the power to relinquish a body of all its troubles. When man first laid eyes on the Black Hills, they left him in awe. Those who came in contact with the Hills were subdued into worshipping their beauty. And that is exactly what the Sioux Indians did. They worshipped the Black Hills, which were the center of their religion and their lives.

2   In the late 1770s, three factors forced the Sioux to move west from what is now Minnesota: the expansion of the white settlers, hostilities from Indian tribes that had an advantage in arms resulting from trade with the Europeans, and the fact that the Indians' primary food source—the buffalo—was being driven west (Benson 5). By 1814 the Teton Sioux gained control of the Black Hills by defeating the Kiowa; later they expanded their empire into present-day Wyoming and Montana by overpowering the Crow Indians (Lazarus 7).

3   When the European settlers reached the Black Hills, the Sioux retaliated with violence, but still homesteaders came into the area to find farmland and other resources, especially gold. America was growing, and the government wanted the land of the Sioux Nation for expansion and economic purposes. The new Americans, with help from the military, systematically dispersed or killed off most of the buffalo on the plains around the Black Hills (Lazarus 42–43). Then, with their main food source gone, the Sioux became dependent on rations from the U.S. government. With the promise of rations, along

with bribes of liquor and money, and also with guns in their faces, the Sioux were forced into signing the Manypenny Agreement of 1877 which forfeited all of their territorial rights to the Black Hills.

4   But the Manypenny Agreement violated earlier agreements with Native Americans in general and with the Sioux in particular. For example, in the Northwest Ordinance of 1787 the United States had promised that the "utmost good faith shall always be observed towards the Indians; their land and property shall never be taken from them without their consent . . ." (qtd. in Lazarus 11). Manypenny also violated a treaty that the chiefs of the Sioux Nation—except Crazy Horse and Sitting Bull—had made with the American government in 1868. This treaty set aside for the Sioux all of present-day South Dakota west of the Mississippi, including the Black Hills, and specified that no Sioux land could be sold without the consent of three-fourths of all adult Sioux males. But the commissioners of the Manypenny Agreement collected the signatures of only ten percent of the adult Sioux men (Lazarus 92). So the agreement was not legally valid because it did not meet the terms of earlier treaties. Therefore, the transfer of the Black Hills to the U.S. government is null and void. For this reason—since 1877—the Teton Sioux have wanted the Hills back, and technically the land still belongs to them.

5   In this battle, the "conquered people" rationale has been used by those who oppose the Sioux Nation's claim. This rationale argues that throughout history stronger nations have always conquered weaker nations and seized their land in the process. According to this line of reasoning, what the United States did to the Sioux is no worse than what the Sioux did to the Kiowa and the Crow (*In the Spirit of Crazy Horse*). But the chiefs of the Sioux Nation had not made any treaties or promises—as the U.S. government had—to the people whom they conquered. Treaties are supposed to be words of honor never to be broken. The U.S. government did exactly the opposite of what it was supposed to do under its own laws: America dishonored its word.

6   In 1923 Ralph Case, a lawyer for the Sioux, filed the first legal claim against the taking of the Black Hills. The case ended in 1954 when it was dismissed by the Indian Claims Commission, which concluded that the U.S. government had been justified in taking the gold-filled hills for public use and for the well-being of the nation's economy (Lazarus 204).

7   After this setback, the Sioux sought financial compensation for the violation of their Fifth Amendment rights. That amendment to the U.S. Constitution states that private property cannot be taken for public use without just compensation. In 1974 a Court of Claims handed down a decision in favor of the Sioux, specifying that through the Manypenny Agreement the United States had taken the Hills in violation of the Sioux Nation's Fifth Amendment rights. The Sioux were awarded $17,533,484—the estimated value of the Hills in 1877—plus five percent interest dating from 1877 to 1974, an approximate total of $106 million (Lazarus 374–75). The historic decision was affirmed by the U.S. Supreme Court on June 30, 1980, and the longest-running legal claim in the history of our nation seemed to be resolved at last (Lazarus 401).

8   But the claim didn't really end there because the Sioux's tribal government decided not to touch the money but rather to demand the return of the Hills themselves. Over 100 years ago, the lives of the Sioux were shattered when the Black Hills were taken from them; their

culture, religion, and customs were stripped away. Many still live in an American limbo of poverty, depression, alcohol, and drug abuse, and some Sioux spiritual leaders believe that nothing will improve until the people can once again live and perform sacred ceremonies in their ancestral home (*In the Spirit of Crazy Horse*).

9   There is no question that the U.S. government knew what would happen to the Sioux if the Black Hills were taken away. Despite this, Congress bypassed humanity, ethics, and morality for greed. In this regard, the United States is responsible for the emotional distress, drug abuse, poverty, and high suicide rate among this group of Native Americans. Recently, in an unrelated case, the media reported that a man was awarded over $100 million because a surgeon injected the wrong solution into his left eye, which he then lost. Yes, the surgeon is guilty of malpractice. The United States is also guilty of bringing unnecessary hunger, malnutrition, drug addiction, and death to the Sioux. If a person can receive $100 million for one eye, what would be just compensation for damage to and loss of thousands of lives over several generations?

10   The Sioux's chances of getting the Black Hills back are minute. It would mean the displacement of many non-Indians, and the United States would not tolerate a "separate nation" within its borders, which is the way a Native American—owned Black Hills might be perceived. The best the Sioux can do is to take the money, which has now accumulated to about $300 million (Lazarus 427), and get on with their lives instead of waiting for the return of the Black Hills. This money could be used to improve Sioux life and buy back sections of sacred land from non-Indian landowners.

11   If we as Americans want to practice a true form of democracy, how can we allow the government of our great country to escape serious questioning on its dishonorable, unethical, and immoral dealings with the original owners of this land? The Black Hills, along with their religion and customs, were all the Sioux people had, and the U.S. government took it all away. Ironically, our government sends millions of dollars overseas to try to fix problems that it had no part in creating. It's upsetting to know that the same government is not as willing to address the problems of the Sioux—problems it did create. The people of America should become familiar with the Sioux claim to the Black Hills and should support the Sioux in collecting every penny owed them.

Works Cited

Benson, Douglas S. *The Black Hills War 1876 to 1877: A History of the Conflict with the Sioux Indians.* Chicago: D.S. Benson, 1983.

In the Spirit of Crazy Horse. PBS Frontlines Series. WTVS, Detroit, Michigan, 18 December 1990.

Lazarus, Edward. *Black Hills, White Justice: The Sioux Nation Versus the United States 1775 to the Present.* New York: HarperCollins, 1991.

The Orphaned Sioux
Mila L. Stephens

1   You are born with a mother, someone who gives you life and helps you sustain it. You are born with the understanding that your mother is yours, and in some circumstances you are forced to share her services, time, and attention, but you can tolerate that. Now let's suppose that you are sitting at home one night reading a book when a funny-looking man named Thomas Jefferson knocks at your door and

says that he just bought your mother from a guy named Napoleon for fifty cents. The thought of someone *owning* your mother seems impossible. Selling her seems even more impossible, especially for fifty cents; she's worth way more than that. In fact, there's no way to put a price on your mother—*she's priceless.* For a while, you feel secure because your mother is considered the worst cook in the neighborhood and Jefferson already has a mother of his own. He assures you that—even though technically he owns your mother—you can keep her "for as long as the grass shall grow and the waters run."

2   But one day, word gets out that your mother makes a delicious meatloaf, and Jefferson comes to take her away. He pulls out a gun and offers you a teddy bear to shut up. You reluctantly shut up and accept his offer. When you are a little older and the teddy bear is worn and tattered, you decide you want your mother back.

3   This scenario may seem farfetched, but something quite similar happened to thousands of people more than a hundred years ago. The Sioux Indians had their mother—the Black Hills, the Paha Sapa, the "heart of everything that is"—taken from them. Through the Louisiana Purchase, the United States bought land between the Mississippi River and the Rocky Mountains from Napoleon for about $15 million (Dethloff 506)—a deed completely incomprehensible to the Native Americans who had lived on the land for thousands of years before the arrival of the Europeans. Left orphans, a large number of Sioux Indians have been forced into one small corner of our country with two "nannies"—welfare and alcoholism.

4   Today, at a time when many people think of the United States as the police and "fighter for justice" everywhere, the longest-running legal case in our nation's history is still unresolved. On June 30, 1980, the U.S. Supreme Court "settled" the case of the *United States v. Sioux Nation of Indians* by upholding a lower court's award of more than $106 million to the Sioux (Lazarus 385 and 401). The Sioux desperately needed this money then, and they still need it now. Eight out of every ten Sioux adults are without jobs; many are on ADC (Aid to Dependent Children) or some other form of welfare (*In the Spirit of Crazy Horse*). But these poverty-stricken people rejected the $106 million settlement because of their conviction that they would be better off if they once again lived and performed sacred ceremonies in the land that is their mother. Should the Black Hills be returned to the Sioux if they will not accept monetary compensation for their historic loss?

5   Many of the Sioux believe that in the Manypenny Agreement of 1877, which terminated Sioux ownership of the Black Hills, the Hills were "taken by a gun." They say that their ancestors were tricked by mistranslations, liquor, and force. Lazarus quotes Joseph Black Spotted Horse, a Sioux elder, as many years later recalling, "At the door there was a company of soldiers with guns with bayonets. Further back towards the fort, all the cannon were turned toward us. I think this was done to scare us" (92). Historians also note that the Treaty of 1868 was violated when the signatures of far fewer than three-fourths of all adult male Sioux were collected. Only Sioux chiefs and headmen signed.

6   Those who oppose the Sioux Nation's claim to the Black Hills look at the situation in a variety of ways. Some believe that the land taken from the Indians was desperately needed for the survival of the American economy; it was hoped that the gold in the Black Hills would pay off the national debt (Lazarus 78). But even if the United States had

a severe need for that gold, it still was not theirs. Others say that the rations the Sioux received in the Manypenny Agreement kept them from starvation. But they never would have been facing starvation in the first place if the new immigrants and the government had not run off the buffalo and disrupted Native American life in a variety of ways. One of the most compelling arguments comes from the non-Indians who now call the Black Hills home. Many have been there for generations, and they don't believe that they should have to give up their homes, farms, or businesses. As they see it, the Black Hills belong to *everyone*.

7   I believe that the Black Hills should be returned to the Sioux, but this is highly unlikely. Where government promises are concerned, the Sioux should take their cue from the African-American community—most Blacks stopped looking for their forty acres and a mule a long, long time ago. It is generally agreed that the wrongs of the past should be made right, but many Americans realize that the only way for a group of people to "bounce back" is to take the future into their own hands. The Sioux Indians should accept the settlement money offered by the U.S. Supreme Court and *help themselves.* They should buy their *own* land and build their *own* schools to educate their *own* children to run their *own* businesses. The Sioux have been seriously wronged, but it would cost too many people too much to set the harm completely right. These Native Americans should take the money, which is more than any other of this country's mistreated ever got. The history of the West has been called "a tragedy with no permanent winners" (Mathews 34), but it doesn't have to be a perpetual tragedy for the Sioux. Their mother is gone and gone forever, but like many other motherless children, they can grow up and flourish without her.

Works Cited

Dethloff, Henry C. "Louisiana Purchase." *The World Book Encyclopedia.* 1988 ed.
In the Spirit of Crazy Horse. PBS Frontlines Series. WTVS, Detroit, Michigan. 18 December 1990.
Lazarus, Edward. *Black Hills, White Justice: The Sioux Nation Versus the United States 1775 to the Present.* New York: HarperCollins, 1991.
Mathews, Tom. "The Custer Syndrome: What's the Right Answer to 'Who Owns the West'?" *Newsweek* 30 September 1991: 34–35.

Topic Ideas for Documented Argument Essays

To practice writing a documented argument, choose from the following topics or use the following list to help you think of your own topic. Remember that a topic alone is not enough: You need to develop a working thesis and remain open to changing your position if your research findings alter your thinking.

1. Date rape—some argue that this is a more complex issue than it appears.
2. College athletes and sexual assault. (A good starting point is Gerald Eskenazi's article "When Athletic Aggression Turns into Sexual Assault," in the sports section of *The New York Times,* June 3, 1990.)
3. Female "buddy movies"—are they a welcome or destructive addition to an old genre? (A great starting point would be to see *Thelma and Louise,* the first movie of this type.)
4. Whether financial reparations should be made to African Americans for the suffering caused by slavery and the aftereffects of slavery.

5. Chico Mendes and the Amazon rain forest. (Two good sources are *The Burning Season* by Andrew Revkin and *The World Is Burning* by Alex Shoumatoff.)
6. The medical ethics of one specific issue—for example, euthanasia or doctor-assisted suicide; the intentional conception of one child to save the life of another, such as when a perfect match for a bone-marrow transplant is needed; or liver transplants for alcoholics or recovering alcoholics.
7. The car industry and trade practices between the United States and Japan.
8. Women and makeup. For example, one could argue that women should resist societal pressure to wear makeup, that wearing makeup should be a matter of individual preference, or that companies should not be able to demand that their female employees use cosmetics (recently, an airline fired a woman employee for refusing to wear makeup).
9. Federal funding and freedom of expression in art.
10. Automation, robotics, and the implications for human workers.
11. The controversial idea of creating a vast "Buffalo Commons" to solve the economic, natural-resource, and population problems of the Plains states. (A good source is "The Poppers and the Plains," by Anne Matthews in *The New York Times Magazine*, June 24, 1990.)
12. The notion that the gender gap between girls and boys may not be closing after all or may not be closing fast enough.

Here are other ideas to help you choose your topic and build your thesis:

- food colorings and additives;

- acid rain;

- the safety of nuclear energy;

- rights of stepparents and stepchildren;

- value of joint custody;

- any battle over Native American treaty rights;

- rap music and freedom of speech;

- controversial uses of technology in music;

- golf country clubs that discriminate against blacks and other racial minorities, Jews, and women;

- same-sex marriages (in other words, should states and religions recognize them?);

- medical experimentation on animals;

- genetic engineering;

- disposal of toxic waste;

- the sanctuary movement for refugees from Latin America;

- ethnic intimidation crimes (for example, the murder of Yusuf Hawkins and others who have ventured into what some considered "the wrong neighborhood");

- police brutality in the age of the home video camera;

- legislation for racial balance in jury selection;

- parental consent for minors who seek abortions;

- media images of women (for example, in the notorious Budweiser beer television commercials), or media images of any group (Chinese Americans, Italian Americans, the elderly, teenagers, and so forth);

- affirmative action and preferential hiring or admissions policies;

- methods of discipline in the home;

- best methods of raising great kids;

- kindergarten for four-year-olds, or all-day kindergarten;

- prayer in the public schools;

- the legalization of drugs;

- the value of colleges for women only;

- the value of black colleges;

- military institutes for men only;

- the adoption rights of single people;

- the adoption rights of lesbians and gay men;

- transracial adoption;

- women in combat;

- the need for national health insurance;

- American Indian mascots or logos for college athletic teams;

- AIDS testing for medical professionals;

- "safe sex" practices (for example, how safe are they?);

- sex education (for example, should the schools encourage abstinence?);

- mandatory retirement;

- term limits for members of Congress;

- bias against women in science (for example, some say that male bias is an inherent part of the traditional scientific method);

- the death penalty for capital crimes; and

- salaries for professional athletes.

SECTION II

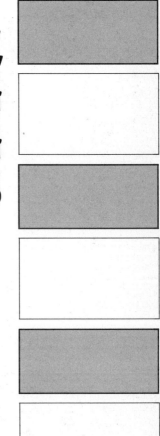

SENTENCE COMBINING AND EDITING SKILLS

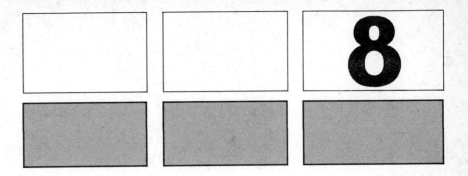

Introduction to Sentence Structure

In this second section of *Easy Writer*, you'll be learning some of the most valuable writing skills. Your work in this section can help your writing achieve a level of excellence. First, in this chapter, you'll focus on the components of simple sentences—those with only one clause. It's natural for a college student to feel that looking carefully at clauses and their components, subjects and predicates, is taking a step backward. However, you don't want your writing, which is almost certainly growing increasingly strong in logic, creativity, and structure, to be underevaluated because of distracting surface flaws. Both avoiding and editing surface flaws will be much easier once you've developed a working knowledge of a few basics—especially the structure of the clause. So try to be patient. Later, you'll see that it was your careful work in this chapter that enabled you to improve your sentence structure and punctuation and to master a number of other rules and conventions that polish your writing.

UNIT 1: Basic Clause Patterns

Some college students can define a sentence, and some can't, but no doubt you know a sentence when you see one. Read the following choices and circle the letter of the one that is a sentence.

a. Noses entire people's throughout grow lives their.
b. Their grow lives throughout people's noses entire.
c. Grow lives their people's entire throughout noses.
d. People's noses grow throughout their entire lives.

Each of the four sequences contains the same words, but only one sequence makes *sense*—and that one, as you knew instantly, is d. Sequence d makes sense precisely because the words in it are arranged in the form of a sentence. Your ability to recognize the sentence so easily shows how natural the sentence pattern is and how much intuitive language skill you already have. Try to formulate spoken sequences of words that are *not* sentences, and you'll realize it's hard to do.

Simple Sentences—Those with One Clause

Luckily, for most of us it is much more important to be able to recognize and produce good sentences than to define and analyze them in the precise, meticulous way that linguists must. But in order to make good sentences and avoid certain types of errors, we need to develop a basic working definition of a sentence. Let's start by looking at why sequence d is a sentence.

Sentences are made up of *clauses*—sometimes just one clause, sometimes more than one. This chapter focuses on *simple sentences*—those that contain only one clause. In later chapters, you'll work with sentences that contain more than one clause.

A clause is a subject plus a predicate. The *subject* of a clause names something, such as a person, object, place, or idea. The subject is usually one or more nouns or pronouns. The subject might also be a noun substitute (a word that isn't a noun but works like one in a particular context).

The *predicate* makes a statement about the subject by telling something about that person, object, place, or idea. The predicate tells one of two things about the subject: It tells that the subject is performing an action, or it states the condition of the subject.

Finding Verbs in Clauses

The easiest way to analyze a clause is to look first at the predicate, the part of the sentence that makes a statement about the subject. The most important part of the predicate is the *verb*.

Action Verbs—Visible and Invisible

You probably know that most verbs show some kind of action. Sometimes this is *visible action,* as in *she swims* or *they kissed.* At other times, it is *invisible action,* as in *he forgot* or *we decided.*

The verb in our original example sentence—sequence d—shows visible action. Draw a line beneath the verb and write *v* above it.

People's noses grow throughout their entire lives.

If you identified *grow,* you're correct. That's the word that shows the visible action of the subject. What's the subject doing? In this sentence, it's growing.

Linking Verbs

Other verbs, such as *is* and *seem,* don't show an action, but instead show a subject to be in a certain *condition* or a state of being. They do this by *linking* the subject to a word or words in the predicate. These verbs are, quite logically, called *linking verbs*.

Let's look at two example sentences:

The woman is an intern.
The students seem confident.

In these sentences, the woman and the students are not performing actions, but they are in a state of being or a condition. We might say that, in the first case, the woman is in the state of being an intern and, in the second case, the students are in the condition of being confident.

There are many common linking verbs, such as additional tenses of the verb *to be (am, are, was, were, will be, has been, have been, had been,* and others) and the various forms of the verbs *appear, become, feel, look, smell, sound,* and *taste.*

The Role of Context

Some verbs are action verbs in one context and linking verbs in another. A couple of examples will make this clear. In sentence a, is the italicized verb describing an action or a condition?

a.   I *smelled* the familiar fragrance of Chanel No. 5 in the living room.

In a, the verb form *smelled* is describing an action, the action of the subject (*I*) smelling. Now notice the very different meaning of the same word in sentence b.

b.   The rotten chicken *smelled* terrible.

In b, the subject (*chicken*), is *not* performing an action; you don't picture a chicken running around sniffing the air. What the verb in b shows is that the chicken is in a certain condition—namely, the condition of smelling bad.

In the blanks provided, label the verb in each of the following sets of sentences as either *action* or *condition*.

1a.   I *felt* the green velvet. _____

  b.   I *felt* sick. _____

2a.   We *tasted* every chocolate in the box. _____

  b.   The salad dressing *tasted* strange. _____

3a.   You *appear* tired. _____

  b.   The ghosts *appear* suddenly in the middle of Act II.

[ANSWERS: 1.a. action;   b. condition;   2.a. action;   b. condition; 3.a. condition;   b. action.]

If the idea of linking verbs gives you trouble, think of them this way: In 1b the verb *felt* might just as well be the verb *was*. To say "I *felt* sick" is basically the same thing as saying "I *was* sick." The words are not the same, but they mean approximately the same thing, and they both show the condition of the subject. On the other hand, to say "I *felt* the green velvet," as in 1a, is not at all the same as saying "I *was* the green velvet."

Here are two more examples to consider: To say "The cherries *taste* great" is roughly the same as saying "The cherries *are* great." And to say "The group's first song *sounded* bad" roughly equals saying "The group's first song *was* bad." The cherries don't perform an action, and neither does the song.

A Review of Verbs

Now you know the two main types of verbs:

1. those that show the *action* of the subject (and that action might be visible or invisible), and
2. those that show the *condition* or *state of being* of the subject by *linking* it to something in the predicate.

Finding Subjects in Clauses

Let's return again to our original example sentence:

People's noses grow throughout their entire lives.

To find the subject, you simply have to ask yourself, "What grows?" Draw a line beneath your answer and label it *s*. You're correct if you identified *noses*. The word *noses* is the *simple subject* or the *key word* within the complete subject. The complete subject of any sentence is the simple subject or key word plus all the modifiers attached to it. Here, the complete subject is *People's noses*. But what is actually growing is noses, not people.

Throughout our work with clauses, we'll focus on the key word or words within the complete subject because that's what is most directly tied to the predicate. A key word is what the predicate makes a statement about. And, in the present tense, it's the simple subject with which the verb must agree. For a variety of reasons, not the least of which is subject–verb agreement, you'll find that being able to spot the simple subject of a clause is an essential skill.

Finding Elements that Complete the Verb

In the sentence *People's noses grow throughout their entire lives*, nothing is needed to complete the verb *grow*. In other words, even though four words follow *grow* in the sentence, those words are not needed for sentence structure.

They're needed for the writer's meaning, of course, but not for completing the clause. The subject and verb (*noses grow*) make a certain kind of sense and give a feeling of completeness all by themselves.

But there are other verbs that by themselves cannot make a complete structure with a subject. Consider these subject and verb combinations:

> They desire
> She said
> The tree was
> People need
> Bill kissed
> They are
> Tourists want

These sets leave you hanging, wondering: They desire what? She said what? Bill kissed whom? In each case, the verb needs a word or words to complete its meaning. The words that do this job in the predicate of a clause are called *complements* and *objects.* We'll look at their basic types.

Subject Complements

One important kind of complement is the *subject complement,* which follows a linking verb. A subject complement is a noun, pronoun, adjective, or adverb of place that follows a verb in a clause. (We'll examine these parts of speech after we establish this overview of clause structure.) Here are some sentences in which the subject complements are underlined and labeled *sub com:*

                          sub com
a.   Martha Aliaga is a superb <u>math teacher</u>.

The subject complement *math teacher* answers the question, "Martha Aliaga is what?"

                              sub com
b.   The juniors are our <u>representatives</u> on the committee.

The subject complement *representatives* answers the question, "The juniors are what?"

                    sub com
c.   James feels <u>wonderful</u>.

The subject complement *wonderful* answers the question, "James feels how?"

In sentences d through f, write *v* above the verb and label the subject complement *sub com.*

d.   Yolanda appears interested in the project.

e.   That was it.

f.   The gifts were there.

[ANSWERS: d. v = appears, sub com = interested;   e. v = was, sub com = it; f. v = were, sub com = there.]

Direct and Indirect Objects

Direct Objects

Linking verbs are not the only kind of verb that needs completion. Another type of verb that needs completion is a kind of action verb called the *transitive verb*. This is a verb that carries or transfers action from the subject before the verb to the object after the verb. It makes a transition or a bridge from one part of the clause to another.

The words that complete the meaning of transitive verbs are called *direct objects*. They follow action verbs and answer the question "What?" or "Whom?" A good example is *I need you*: *You* is the direct object of the verb *need*.

Do all sentences with action verbs have direct objects? To answer, let's return one more time to the first sentence we considered: *People's noses grow throughout their entire lives.* This sentence has an action verb, but it doesn't have an object. The verb *grow* doesn't need one; *noses grow* has a sense of completeness without anything else. No one would ask you "Noses grow *what?*" They just grow. Although *grow* shows action, here it is not a transitive verb; it's an *intransitive verb*. It does not move or transport action from the subject to the object. So some action verbs are intransitive, and all linking verbs are intransitive.

In our earlier sentences a through f, we saw only linking verbs, because linking verbs are the only kind that are followed by subject complements. In sentences g through j, we'll see only action verbs, because action verbs are the kind that take direct objects. In these sentences, we'll label the direct object *do* and underline it. Here are two examples:

                     do
g.   We passed <u>the collection basket</u>.

The direct object *collection basket* answers the question, "We passed what?"

              do
h.   Frank paid the <u>money</u>.

The direct object *money* answers the question, "Frank paid what?"

In sentences i and j label the verbs *v* and the direct objects *do*.

i.   The sisters swindled the company.

j.   Susan loved Ralph.

[ANSWERS: i. v = swindled,   do = company;   j. v = loved,   do = Ralph.]

One quick way to double-check if a word is a direct object is to try using it as the subject of a passive version of the same sentence. If it *is* a direct object, it will work as the subject. For example, the active sentence *We passed the collection basket* becomes the passive sentence *The collection basket was passed by us.* And the active sentence *Frank paid the money* becomes the passive sentence *The money was paid by Frank.* Double-check sentences i and j by rewriting them as passive sentences, with the direct objects becoming subjects.

[ANSWERS: i. The company was swindled by the sisters.   j. Ralph was loved by Susan.]

If your sentence has a linking verb and a subject complement, you won't be able to transform it from active into passive. This transformation works only with sentences that contain direct objects. (We'll go into more detail about passive sentences later.)

Indirect Objects

Sometimes the predicate of a clause also contains a word that is *indirectly* affected by the verb. This word is called the *indirect object,* and it comes before the direct object. **The indirect object tells to whom or for whom an action is done.** We'll use *io* as the abbreviation for indirect object.

            io   **do**
k.   We passed <u>the boy</u> <u>the collection basket</u>.

We passed what? The basket. To whom? To the boy.

            io   **do**
l.   Francie sent <u>Eduardo</u> <u>the money</u>.

Francie sent what? The money. For whom? For Eduardo.
Label the verbs *v*, direct objects *do*, and indirect objects *io* in sentences m and n.

m.   I wrote you a letter.

n.   The woman gave her cousin a small farm in Norway.

[ANSWERS: m. v = wrote, do = letter, io = you;   n. v = gave, do = farm, io = cousin.]

If you are having difficulty keeping direct and indirect objects straight, reconsider sentence k. Did we pass the boy from person to person? Or did we pass the collection basket? Which word is *directly* affected by the verb *passed?* You're right—it's *basket*—the direct object. The word *boy* is only *indirectly* affected, so it's the indirect object.

    Some common verbs that are followed by both indirect and direct objects are the forms of *bring, buy, give, lend, offer, sell, send,* and *write.* Try writing a few simple sentences with these verbs, and you'll probably automatically create clauses with both indirect and direct objects. For example, complete these sentences:

I bought _____ (io) a _____ (do).

We sent _____ (io) twenty _____ (do).

The college offered _____ (io) a good _____ (do).

Object Complements

Some direct objects need a little something extra. They themselves need to be completed by an *object complement*. This word clarifies the meaning of the verb in a sentence or makes the meaning richer. The object complement always follows a direct object, and it helps to complete a direct object by identifying or modifying it.

Object complements are often found in clauses with verbs such as *appoint, choose, consider, elect, make, name,* and *think*. These verbs have one thing in common: They all roughly mean *to make* or *consider*.

We'll use *ob com* as our abbreviation. Here are some examples:

                   do   **ob com**
o.   We painted the <u>town</u>   <u>red</u>.

Can you see how sentence o means roughly the same as "We *made* the town red"?

                   do   **ob com**
p.   Gerald called his <u>mother</u> <u>a saint</u>.

Sentence p is similar to "Gerald *considered* his mother a saint."

Label the verb *v*, direct object *do*, and object complement *ob com* in each of these sentences:

q.   The members elected Onda president.

r.   The judge considered 2 Live Crew's song obscene.

[ANSWERS: q. v = elected, do = Onda, ob com = president;   r. v = considered, do = song, ob com = obscene.]

Like subject complements, object complements can be nouns or adjectives. Clauses with object complements don't occur as often as the other types of clauses we've examined.

Summary of Basic Clause Types

There are five basic types of clause.

1.   Subject + Verb

                  s   **v**
    Example: The children played.

2. Subject + Linking Verb + Subject Complement

   s   v   sub com

   Example: You are beautiful.

3. Subject + Verb + Direct Object

   s   v   do

   Example: Roosevelt inspired everyone.

4. Subject + Verb + Indirect Object + Direct Object

   s   v   io   do

   Example: Samantha sold her friend an antique ruby ring.

5. Subject + Verb + Direct Object + Object Complement

   s   v   do   ob com

   Example: Marvin called his lab partner a witch.

A NOTE ON ANSWERS

As you've already seen, when you're asked to answer a question or fill in a blank within explanatory material, the answers are given immediately after the questions. This enables you to decide whether you're following the explanations well and, if you're having some problems, to go back and reread or mark passages to discuss with your writing teacher.

Answers for some other exercises begin on page 439. The exercises with answers given at the back are starred. You can correct these exercises on your own so you will know right away if you're having difficulty. Your teacher will give you the answers for other exercises. Whatever you do, don't look at the answers before you do an exercise.

* **Exercise One**

In the following simple sentences, label the subject *s*, the verb *v*, the direct object *do*, the indirect object *io*, the subject complement *sub com*, and the object complement *ob com*.

   Hint: Most students have the greatest success if they look for the verb first.

   Remember: The subject complement follows a linking verb and appears in a sentence where the verb helps to show the condition of the subject. Direct objects appear only in sentences that have action verbs. When object complements are present, they follow direct objects.

1. His motive was mysterious.

2. I bought the suit.

3. The woman in the second row coughed.

4. Caroline gave Steven a choice.

5. The nectarines feel ripe.

6. Music lovers named Aretha the Queen of Soul.

7. The patient slowly improved.

8. The teacher lent Katherine a tape.

9. She made the skirt very short.

10. His father frosted the cupcakes.

Now check your answers to exercise one and review any areas where you had problems.

If you had trouble with this first exercise, don't worry. We've covered a lot of material; don't expect to absorb it all quickly. Keep practicing identifying sentence parts, and soon you'll be able to label a sentence almost without thinking.

Exercise Two

Label the parts of these simple sentences. Use *s* for subject, *v* for verb, *do* for direct object, *io* for indirect object, *sub com* for subject complement, and *ob com* for object complement. Again, try finding the verb first.

1. Students amaze their teachers.

2. Hot air rises.

3. Christopher painted the border black.

4. Amelia Earhart disappeared.

5. He is fascinating.

6. The dances were new.

7. That experience taught me a lesson.

8. Angelica aced the test.

9. Our new mayor made the problems worse.

10. David bought everyone a bagel.

A NOTE ON MULTIPLE PARTS

In the remaining exercises you may find clauses with more than one key word in the subject or more than one verb, complement, or object. In the following sentences, use the blanks provided to identify the multiple parts that appear in italics:

a. *Rose, gray,* and *white* are her favorite colors. _____

b. He *loves* and *respects* her. _____

c. The little girl is *curious* and *spunky.* _____

d. I bought *fudge, cashews,* and a *newspaper.* _____

e. The architect gave her *clients* and the entire *audience* a real surprise. _____

f. The release of the movie made him *rich* and *famous.* _____

g. The decision *surprised Isaac* and *angered Anna.* _____ _____

[ANSWERS: a. three key words in the subject;   b. two verbs;   c. two subject complements;   d. three direct objects;   e. two indirect objects; f. two object complements;   g. two verbs (*surprised* and *angered*) and two direct objects (*Isaac* and *Anna*).]

A NOTE ON THE CONTENT OF EXERCISES

So far, in addressing the most basic issues of clause structure, we've worked with very elementary sentences. Now we can use material that's a little more complex and certainly more interesting. As noted in To the Student, wherever possible, the writing skill exercises are based on true, researched material on a wide variety of topics. The following, for example, is a two-part exercise on the career of baseball pitcher Nolan Ryan.

Exercise Three   *   PART A

Label the parts of the following simple sentences, using *s* for subject, *v* for verb, *do* for direct object, *io* for indirect object, *sub com* for subject complement, and *ob com* for object complement. *Remember:* Find the verb first.

1. Serious baseball fans consider Nolan Ryan a superb major league pitcher.

2. Year after year, Ryan endures and improves.

3. According to statistics, the typical major league pitcher shows hitters his best stuff

   at age 30.

4. But a recent baseball season was Ryan's twenty-fourth in the big leagues.

5. He was 43 years old and better than ever.

6. Control problems became a thing of the past.

7. According to the radar guns, at this point in his long career, his fastballs sometimes

   reached speeds of 100 miles per hour.

8. Ryan's amazing fastball made his curveball more effective.

9. Batters braced for the heat.

10. Then he slipped them the curve.

PART B

Use the labels _s_ (subject), _v_ (verb), _do_ (direct object), _io_ (indirect object), _sub com_ (subject complement), and _ob com_ (object complement) to identify the parts of these sentences:

1. Early in his twenty-fourth season, in mid-May, doctors diagnosed a stress fracture in Ryan's back.

2. After a three-week rest, the "elderly ace" won five of six starts.

3. On his fifth day off the disabled list, the native of Refugio, Texas, threw the sixth no-hitter of his career.

4. In that game, Ryan denied the world champion Oakland Athletics a victory.

5. Later in the same summer, the Rangers pitcher enjoyed his 300th career win and joined an elite circle of twenty 300-plus lifetime winners.

6. His gutsy performance made Ryan the darling of fans in Texas and all throughout the baseball-loving world.

7. Ryan's staying power is almost miraculous.

8. The veteran hurler constantly fights injuries.

9. Teammates call his daily exercise routine amazing.

10. On a typical day he lifts weights, runs wind sprints, rides a stationary bike, and performs underwater exercises.

Review of Unit

Let's take stock of where we are. You've learned about subjects and verbs and about the different kinds of words that follow verbs and complete the predicate of a clause.

You've worked briefly with the five main patterns of the simple sentence, the sentence with only one clause. Each of these five patterns involves a slightly different type of predicate.

Linking verbs are followed by subject complements, and the whole job of the predicate in clauses with linking verbs is to show the condition or state of being of the subject.

You've seen action verbs used alone, when the verb is intransitive, and with objects when the verb is transitive. Sometimes direct objects need a little completion, and for that job we have object complements.

By working closely with these sentence parts, you've developed a good basic sense of what can make up the clause. Let's try one more exercise to solidify what you know before we move on.

* Exercise Four

Here are ten simple sentences on assorted topics. Label the key parts, using _s_, _v_, _do_, _io_, _sub com_, and _ob com_.

1. Tu Dil Hil I is the ancient Apache name for the sacred Salt River in Arizona.

2. "Yo! MTV Raps" draws MTV's largest daily audience.

3. In the years just after World War I, chicken-shaped trucks brought hungry Americans "Chicken Dinners," a nut-roll candy bar.

4. The cosmetic industry uses about 4,000 different raw materials in its products.

5. Amish quiltmakers are famous for their love of vibrant colors, such as purple, black, teal, and magenta.

6. George Bush vomited and collapsed at a state dinner in Japan.

7. Jack Agueros is the author of _Halfway to Dick and Jane: A Puerto Rican Pilgrimage._

8. In the movie _Dick Tracy_ Madonna played the roles of Breathless Mahoney and The Blank.

9. Harvard law students recently elected 28-year-old Barack Obama the first African American president of the prestigious _Harvard Law Review._

10. About 36 million Americans over the age of 18 walk almost every day for exercise.

UNIT 2: Taking a Closer Look at Subjects

This unit takes a closer look at the subject of the clause. Simple subjects or key words within complete subjects are nouns, pronouns, or noun substitutes. The key word might be a single noun, a single pronoun, or a combination of the two. Write _s_ over the key words in the subject of each clause in these sentences:

a. Shirley Maclaine is an actress.

b. Warren Beatty is an actor.

c. Shirley Maclaine and Warren Beatty are sister and brother.

d. He and she are sister and brother.

e. Shirley Maclaine and he are sister and brother.

[ANSWERS: a. the noun *Shirley Maclaine;*   b. the noun *Warren Beatty;*
c. the nouns *Shirley Maclaine* and *Warren Beatty;*   d. the pronouns *He* and *she;*
e. the noun *Shirley Maclaine* and the pronoun *he.*]

Nouns

You might remember that a noun is the name of a person, place, thing, or idea. In this definition, the word *thing* means a concrete noun, something you can touch or experience through one of the senses, and the word *idea* means an abstract noun, something that you can't touch, something intangible.

These nouns are arranged in their respective groups:

Persons	Places	Things	Ideas
accountant	kitchen	butter	success
welder	garage	sweater	identity
doctor	movie theaters	magazines	problems
mothers	city	frame	memories
criminal	Idaho	toothpaste	cheerfulness
Santa Claus	Disneyworld	Kleenex	Judaism

As you can see, nouns can be singular (one) or plural (more than one). Some are capitalized, and some are not.

The Noun-Marker Test

All of the listed nouns, except the capitalized ones, can follow the words *a, an,* or *the,* which are called *noun markers,* because they signal or "mark" the appearance of a noun. For instance, you can say *an accountant, the kitchen, the butter,* and *a success.* But you cannot get the same complete effect by saying *a beautiful* or *the scary,* because *beautiful* and *scary* are adjectives, not nouns. In fact, it was the seventeenth-century educator and linguist, Bathsua Makin, who first pointed out that one way to define an English noun is as a word that can be preceded by *a, an,* or *the.* She also was the first to note that nouns, unlike adjectives, can differ in number, as in *a good movie* and *good movies.*

The Subject Test for Nouns

Another way to see if a word is a noun is to try to use it as the subject of a sentence. If a word can be used in this way, it's either a noun or a pronoun. (And the pronouns that can be used as subjects of sentences make a relatively short list. We'll discuss them soon.)

Let's say, for instance, that we want to see if *decorate* and *decoration* are nouns. We can try each as the subject of a sentence:

a.   The *decorate* lit up the room.
b.   The *decoration* lit up the room.

This test quickly shows us that *decoration* is a noun but *decorate* is not. If you need to practice identifying nouns, try the next two exercises.

*   **Exercise One**

In each of the following pairs, one word is a noun and one is not. Use the noun-marker test or the subject test to decide which one is the noun. You can do this orally or write the sentences on your own paper. Then circle the noun in each pair.

1.   begin, beginning
2.   prediction, predict
3.   organization, organize
4.   liar, lied
5.   gently, gentleness
6.   decide, decision
7.   allow, allowance
8.   reliability, rely
9.   collection, collect
10.   defy, defiance

If you had any problems with this exercise, try the next one.

Exercise Two

Use the subject test or the noun-marker test to determine which word in each of these pairs is the noun. Circle the nouns.

1.   agree, agreement
2.   identify, identification
3.   surprise, surprising
4.   govern, government
5.   isolation, isolate
6.   necessity, necessary
7.   classify, classification
8.   amaze, amazement
9.   observation, observe
10.   nervousness, nervously

Most of the nouns in exercises one and two are idea nouns; they're abstract. Notice how often they have the same word endings. Here are five common noun suffixes: *-ance, -ity, -ment, -ness,* and *-tion.*

You've learned that a noun is a word that can be used as the subject of a sentence. But that doesn't mean that nouns can't appear in other positions; in fact, you've already worked with many nouns that have been used as direct objects and subject complements.

Pronouns

Pronouns are words that take the place of nouns. We use them to avoid repeating a noun over and over. For example, instead of writing, "*Dancing* is a popular form of exercise. *Dancing* burns up 200 to 400 calories per hour," a student might want to change the subject of the second sentence to the pronoun *It,* which, in the context, would clearly mean dancing.

Here's another example: "Compared to men, American *women* historically have been less well paid. In fact, during the past four decades, *women* have received 40 to 43 percent less than men for similar efforts." In the second clause, a writer might use the pronoun *they* to avoid the close repetition of the noun *women.*

This chapter focuses on the pronoun's ability to function as a subject. But pronouns can do all sorts of other things in sentences, too. Let's look at three groups of pronouns that can be used as subjects of independent clauses. (Later we'll look at pronouns that can be subjects of dependent clauses.)

Personal pronouns	Demonstrative pronouns	Indefinite pronouns
I	this	anybody
you	that	anyone
he	these	anything
she	those	everybody
it		everyone
we		everything
they		nobody
		no one
		nothing
		somebody
		someone
		something

It's not necessary to memorize these pronouns in their three groups, but it's essential to know that they are pronouns and can be the subjects of sentences. In fact, if you, like so many college students, have a tendency to write an occasional comma splice or a run-on (two very common errors), then knowing that pronouns can be subjects of independent clauses will help you improve one technical aspect of your writing.

Exercise Three

On your own paper, write ten brief sentences, each one having a pronoun as its subject. Choose pronouns from each of the three groups.

Noun Substitutes

In addition to nouns and pronouns, other constructions can work as subjects. These are words, phrases, or clauses that perform the same job as a noun. (You already know what a clause is. A *phrase* is any series of two or more words that is less than a clause. A phrase might have a subject-type word or a word from the verb category, but it won't have both.)

Let's look at a few examples of the main types of noun substitutes. In each case, a phrase does the same job a one-word noun could do.

Infinitive Verb Phrases

An infinitive verb phrase is any verb preceded by the word *to*. Examples are *to walk, to sing, to dream*. Look at this sentence:

> *To decide* is to take a risk.

Here, the verb phrase *to decide* works like a noun and acts as the subject of the sentence. You can make a rough equivalent of this sentence by using a conventional noun as the subject:

> A *decision* is always a risk.

Here's another example. This time the verb is followed by an object:

> *To complete the sculpture* is my goal.

Do you see how the words *To complete the sculpture* function as a noun, serving as the subject of the sentence? The sentence could just as easily use a traditional noun form and read this way:

> The *completion of the sculpture* is my goal.

Gerund Phrases

A gerund is a verb that ends in *-ing* and works as a noun. In fact, we already used a gerund—the word *Dancing* in the sentence *Dancing burns up 200 to 400 calories per hour.* A gerund phrase is simply a gerund plus other words attached to it. Here's an example:

> *Planning an overseas trip* takes a tremendous effort.

You can see that the subject here is roughly equivalent to the noun subject in the sentence:

> A *plan for an overseas trip* takes a tremendous effort to create.

Here's another example:

> *Struggling through puberty* can seem like a full-time job.

Again, the subject—the gerund phrase *Struggling through puberty*—has about the same meaning as the subject of this sentence:

> *The struggle through puberty* can seem like a full-time job.

Prepositional Phrases

You probably know that most prepositions are direction or relationship words such as *at, behind, inside,* and *toward.* A prepositional phrase is a preposition plus the noun or pronoun that follows it. Prepositional phrases can also work as subjects:

> *Before breakfast* is a good time for a walk.
> *Under the boardwalk* was the place to be.

Clauses

Infinitive verb phrases, gerund phrases, and prepositional phrases are common constructions that can do the job of a noun. Therefore, they can be subjects of clauses. (They can also be objects of verbs.) But these are not the only noun substitutes, just the most common ones. Other constructions can act as nouns. As this example illustrates, a whole *clause* can act as a subject within a larger clause:

> *What really gripes me* is wilted brown lettuce in a high-priced salad.

Can you see how the subject in this sentence is similar to the noun phrase *My complaint* or *My pet peeve?*
Here's another example:

> *That he should care so much* makes all the difference in the world.

The subject here is similar to the nouns in *His concern* or *His affection,* isn't it?
    You don't have to be too concerned about the names of these constructions. But it is important to remember

1. what the job of the subject is (to present a topic for the predicate to make a statement about by showing the subject's action or condition), and
2. that nouns, pronouns, or a variety of other substitutes acting as nouns can do that job.

*   **Exercise Four**

Find the subject of each sentence. Draw a line under the subject and write s above it. (It will help to find the verb first.) All the subjects here are drawn from

the noun substitute category. If you wish, label the different types of noun substitutes.

1. To work hard today is to believe in tomorrow.

2. Banning the book will do no good.

3. To say yes to Kit was to say no to happiness.

4. What the world needs now is love, sweet love.

5. At the very beginning of a string of commercials is a good time to get a snack.

6. Tracking students into so-called ability groups often creates great damage of both an intellectual and an emotional nature.

7. To kiss him once is to know divine ecstasy.

8. That you would revise this paper four times impresses me.

9. Outside that crazy office is where she wanted to be.

10. What a racist or sexist joke reveals about its teller is quite astonishing.

UNIT 3:   Taking a Closer Look at Predicates

In this unit, we'll look more closely at the part of the sentence that makes a statement about the subject—the predicate. This means examining verbs and their completing elements in a little more detail.

Verbs

As noted earlier, verbs either show the action—whether visible or invisible—or the condition of a subject. Those that show the condition of the subject do so by linking the subject to a complement that follows the verb.

Another important fact is that verbs change in form to communicate changes in time. These various forms are called a verb's *tenses.* Sometimes forming a verb tense involves nothing more than the addition of an ending; for example, adding a *-d* or *-ed* ending can form the past tense of a regular verb. But other times it involves the addition of a *helping verb,* which is simply a verb that helps another verb form a particular tense or a mood. Helping verbs include forms of the verb *to be* such as *is, are, was, were,* and *will be.* They also include forms of the verb *to have* such as *has, have,* and *had.*

Other helping verbs are the modal auxiliaries: *can, could, may, might, shall, should, must, will,* and *would.*

There are also helping verbs that give extra emphasis to the predicate: *do, does,* and *did.*

When a verb joins up with a helping verb, what's formed is a *verb phrase*. For example: *is living, are visiting, will be reviewed, has answered, could remember, might sing,* and *did pay*. Other verb phrases contain more than one helper. Examples are: *will have been dedicated, should be invited,* and *may have promised*.

Regular Verbs

The past tense of regular verbs is formed by adding *-d* or *-ed*. For example, the present tense *I smile* becomes the past tense *I smiled. They want* becomes *they wanted*. Most verbs are regular verbs.

Irregular Verbs

Irregular verbs do not follow the same pattern. To change the tense of an irregular verb, you do not add *-d* or *-ed*. The base form might not change at all, it might take a spelling change other than the addition of *-d* or *-ed,* or it might change only in its pronunciation.

Here is a list of the most common irregular verbs. You may want to commit this list to memory or consult it as necessary. The list shows the three most often used forms of verbs: the base verb, the past tense, and the past participle. The past participle is the form of verb that is used with the helper *has, had,* or *have* (as in our list) or with a form of the verb *to be,* such as *is, are, was,* or *were*.

A helpful way to practice forming the tenses of irregular verbs is to have someone read the base form to you and for you, in answer, to give the past and past participle. For example, a friend reads, "Today I *do* it," and you reply, "Yesterday I *did* it" and "I *have done* it." This method can help you quickly identify which verbs you need to study.

Base Verb	Past	Past Participle
be (am, is, are)	was, were	(have) been
bear	bore	(have) borne
beat	beat	(have) beaten *or* beat
become	became	(have) become
begin	began	(have) begun
bite	bit	(have) bitten
blow	blew	(have) blown
break	broke	(have) broken
bring	brought	(have) brought
build	built	(have) built
burst	burst	(have) burst
buy	bought	(have) bought
catch	caught	(have) caught
choose	chose	(have) chosen
come	came	(have) come
cost	cost	(have) cost
creep	crept	(have) crept
deal	dealt	(have) dealt

dive	dived *or* dove	(have) dived
do	did	(have) done
draw	drew	(have) drawn
drink	drank	(have) drunk
drive	drove	(have) driven
eat	ate	(have) eaten
fall	fell	(have) fallen
feel	felt	(have) felt
fight	fought	(have) fought
find	found	(have) found
fit	fit *or* fitted	(have) fit *or* fitted
fling	flung	(have) flung
fly	flew	(have) flown
forget	forgot	(have) forgotten *or* forgot
forgive	forgave	(have) forgiven
freeze	froze	(have) frozen
get	got	(have) got *or* gotten
give	gave	(have) given
go	went	(have) gone
grow	grew	(have) grown
hang (to suspend)	hung	(have) hung
hang (to kill by hanging)	hanged	(have) hanged
have	had	(have) had
hear	heard	(have) heard
hide	hid	(have) hidden
hit	hit	(have) hit
hold	held	(have) held
hurt	hurt	(have) hurt
keep	kept	(have) kept
know	knew	(have) known
lay (to place or put down)	laid	(have) laid
lead	led	(have) led
leave	left	(have) left
lend	lent	(have) lent
lie (to recline or rest)	lay	(have) lain
lose	lost	(have) lost
make	made	(have) made
mean	meant	(have) meant
meet	met	(have) met
pay	paid	(have) paid
put	put	(have) put
read*	read	(have) read
ride	rode	(have) ridden
ring	rang	(have) rung

---

*The base form (present tense) of *read* is pronounced with a long *e,* as in *reed*; the past and past participles are pronounced with a short *e,* as in *red.*

rise	rose	(have) risen
run	ran	(have) run
say	said	(have) said
see	saw	(have) seen
sell	sold	(have) sold
set	set	(have) set
shake	shook	(have) shook
shine (to emit light or distinguish oneself)	shone	(have) shone
shine (to polish)	shined	(have) shined
sing	sang	(have) sung
sink	sank	(have) sunk *or* sunken
sit	sat	(have) sat
sleep	slept	(have) slept
slide	slid	(have) slid
speak	spoke	(have) spoken
speed	sped	(have) sped
spend	spent	(have) spent
stand	stood	(have) stood
steal	stole	(have) stolen
sting	stung	(have) stung
strike	struck	(have) struck
swear	swore	(have) sworn
swim	swam	(have) swum
swing	swung	(have) swung
take	took	(have) taken
teach	taught	(have) taught
tear	tore	(have) torn
tell	told	(have) told
think	thought	(have) thought
throw	threw	(have) thrown
wear	wore	(have) worn
win	won	(have) won
wind	wound	(have) wound
write	wrote	(have) written

* **Exercise One**

For the following sentences:

    a. **Write *s* over the key word or words in the subject.**

    b. **Write *v* over the verb or verb phrase. (Create your own marking system to show that an element contains more than one word.)**

    c. **Label other structurally important elements in the predicate—if there are any—using the abbreviations *sub com, ob com, do,* and *io.***

   1. According to a recent study, even mild sleep deprivation can prevent the retention of new and complex knowledge.

2. For centuries, the tongue, with its various colors, textures, and patterns, has given doctors a mirror of the condition of the rest of the body.

3. By November 1964, Malcolm X had made three trips to Africa and had altered his position on the possibility of black and white cooperation and harmony.

4. *Nintendo Power* magazine is published every other month.

5. In his later works, Vincent van Gogh painted his suns a brilliant yellow.

6. Competition has been defined as mutually exclusive goal attainment.

7. Perhaps Chester F. Carlson should have named his invention, the copying machine and forerunner of the Xerox machine, after himself.

8. Standard male mannequins wear size 40 regular.

9. Since the beginning of the last Ice Age, the size of human teeth has been decreasing at the rate of one percent every 2,000 years.

10. According to experts in nutrition, most people with occasional mood swings should blame their diet, not their ancestry or sheer bad luck.

More About Completing Elements in the Predicate

In Unit 1, you learned about the different kinds of completing elements that help a verb make a clearer or fuller statement about a subject. You learned that subject complements follow linking verbs; direct objects and indirect objects follow certain action verbs; and object complements follow some direct objects.

The completing elements you worked with earlier were simple—usually a single noun, pronoun, or adjective. Now we'll examine more unusual objects and complements. Three sources of unusual objects and complements are infinitive verb phrases, prepositional phrases, and gerunds and gerund phrases.

An infinitive verb phrase is any verb in its base form preceded by the word *to*. Here infinitive verb phrases are used to complete verbs:

a. He loves *to fly*.
b. She plans *to compete*.
c. They want *to surrender*.

These examples show prepositional phrases used as completing elements:

d. The students went *over the notes*.
e. He is *without resources*.
f. The child abuser was *beneath contempt*.

Here gerunds—nouns formed from verbs with *-ing* endings—and gerund phrases serve as completing elements in the predicate:

g. We attempted *placing the bets.*
h. I like *playing tennis.*
i. The director requests loud *singing* on the next number.

In j through l, identify the completing elements as infinitive verb phrases, prepositional phrases, or gerunds.

j. He went *riding.* _____

k. He went *to ride.* _____

l. He went *for a ride.* _____

[ANSWERS: j. gerund;   k. infinitive verb phrase;   l. prepositional phrase.]

UNIT 4:   The Modifiers

Up to this point, we have focused on the parts that form the *kernel* of the clause: the simple subject, the verb, and the completing elements such as complements and objects. These parts can be visualized in another, structural way: They form the skeleton of the clause.

Now we're going to turn our attention to the parts that *modify,* or *describe,* the kernel. These words can be thought of as decorations, because they elaborate on the essential parts of the clause. They add flesh to the skeleton. Sometimes, however, these modifiers are themselves part of the kernel, namely, when they serve as completing elements after verbs.

We'll discuss four types of modifiers: *adjectives, adverbs, prepositional phrases,* and *appositives.*

Adjectives

Adjectives, as you know, are words used to describe nouns and pronouns. In English, adjectives usually precede the words they describe. Here are some examples:

a. This is an *aggressive* team.
b. She has a *terrific* attitude.
c. It is a *beautiful* sculpture.

But, as you know, adjectives also can follow the words they describe *if* they are used as complements. For example:

d. This team is *aggressive.*
e. Her attitude is *terrific.*
f. The sculpture is *beautiful.*

* **Exercise One**

Circle the adjectives in the sentences below.

1. She sat on the polished oak desk.
2. The biggest problem seemed small.
3. He feared a negative reaction to his best work.
4. I heard a deep, raspy voice.
5. The persistent inflation called for drastic measures.
6. Our supporting evidence was historical.
7. We fished in the crystal waters and hoped for big pike.
8. The tallest man in the group served old-fashioned blackberry pie to the ladies.
9. The final assignment was difficult and challenging.
10. I was struck by the dramatic contrast between her sunburnt arms and pale white face.

You might have noticed how certain words can be adjectives in one context and nouns in another. For example, in sentence 8 the word *blackberry* is an adjective because it describes the pie. But what is the same word in this sentence: "I found only one moldy *blackberry* in the box"? That's right—it's a noun; here, we're talking about an actual blackberry, not something that is described as blackberry in flavor or type.

Exercise Two

Circle the adjectives in the sentences below.

1. Hot buttered popcorn was sold from a rickety red wagon.
2. The fizzled fireworks sent the disappointed crowd home before ten o'clock.
3. A roll of sticky, twisted transparent tape sat on the dusty windowsill.
4. Her manner was sassy and impatient.
5. The little kids might eat frosted banana cake.
6. An industrious woman ran a well-stocked shop.
7. His coffee tasted bitter and old.
8. That young man was my true hero.
9. The discussion group took up the subject of damaged relationships and possible ways to heal them.
10. Your deadlines are unrealistic.

Adverbs

We usually think of adverbs as words that modify verbs and end in -*ly*. Many adverbs do. But they don't have to end in *ly,* and they can describe other modifiers—both adjectives and other adverbs. Our focus here is on basic sentence structure, however, so we will discuss only how adverbs modify verbs.

Adverbs can appear almost anywhere in a sentence. In the blank following each of these examples, write in the verb that the adverb modifies or describes:

a. The children sucked their thumbs *loudly*. _____

b. I tiptoed *quietly* into the corridor. _____

c. *Eventually* we learned the truth. _____

d. The doctors *later* spoke to the press. _____

e. She spends too much time *there*. _____

f. The secretary delivered the package *here* in the early

evening. _____

[ANSWERS: a. sucked;   b. tiptoed;   c. learned;   d. spoke;
e. spends;   f. delivered.]

Some adverbs tell *how* an action is done: *How* did the children suck their thumbs? *Loudly. How* did I tiptoe into the corridor? *Quietly.*

Another group of adverbs tell *when* an action happens: *When* did we learn the truth? *Eventually. When* did the doctors speak to the press? *Later.*

A third group of adverbs tell *where* an action happens: *Where* does she spend too much time? *There. Where* did the secretary deliver the package? *Here.*

Adverbs don't have a great bearing on sentence structure. So we'll end our discussion of adverbs with just one more note. It is important to realize that adverbs sometimes appear in the *middle* of verb phrases. Label the verb phrases and the adverbs in these sentences:

g. Texaco Star Theater was consistently rated a number one show in the

early years of television.

h. One of every four American women in the work force can, unfortunately,

expect poverty in her old age.

[ANSWERS: g. The verb phrase is *was rated,* and the adverb is *consistently;*
h. The verb phrase is *can expect,* and the adverb is *unfortunately.*]

Appositives

Appositives are another kind of modifier. They are noun phrases that follow and describe other nouns. Although they can appear after any noun, in this chapter we'll look at how they often follow the simple subject of a clause. Here are some appositives that describe various U.S. presidents:

a. Calvin Coolidge, *the thirtieth president,* walked a pet raccoon on a leash.

b. Jimmy Carter, *a former peanut farmer,* was undone by the hostage crisis in Iran.
c. Andrew Johnson, *a skilled tailor,* made most of his own clothes.
d. Ronald Reagan, *a former actor,* took the role of president in 1980.

You can see how each appositive is a noun phrase that follows and describes another noun. You also can see that when appositives are used in this position—between the simple subject and the predicate of a clause—they are set off by commas.

Exercise Three   * PART A

The following ten simple sentences, like the example sentences, contain bits of information about U.S. presidents, and each one has an appositive. For each sentence:

a. Label the structurally important parts of each clause: the simple subjects, verbs or verb phrases, complements, and objects.
b. Draw a wavy line under the appositive in each sentence and set it off with beginning and ending commas.
c. Write the kernel of each clause on the line provided. Remember that the kernel omits all the modifiers and contains only the structural essentials of the clause.

1. George Washington the first president of the United States loved peanut soup.

    Kernel: _____

2. John Quincy Adams the sixth president liked swimming in the nude in the Potomac River every morning at five o'clock.

    Kernel: _____

3. Zachary Taylor a career officer in the army for most of his life voted for the first time at the age of 62.

    Kernel: _____

4. James Buchanan president from 1857 to 1861 was a bachelor throughout his entire life.

    Kernel: _____

5. Abraham Lincoln an extremely persistent individual won the presidency in 1860 after eight election losses in a row.

    Kernel: _____

PART B

Directions: Continue to do the same: Label the structurally essential parts of the clause, draw a wavy line beneath appositives, and enclose each appositive within two commas. Then write the kernel on the line provided.

1. Ulysses S. Grant general of the Union Army in the Civil War disliked rare meat because of his extraordinary fear of blood.

   Kernel: _____

2. William Taft a 325-pound commander-in-chief became stuck in the White House bathtub several times during his administration.

   Kernel: _____

3. Franklin D. Roosevelt president throughout most of the Great Depression of the 1930s was very superstitious about the number thirteen.

   Kernel: _____

4. John F. Kennedy a graduate of several speed-reading courses could read almost 2,000 words a minute.

   Kernel: _____

5. Gerald Ford the thirty-eighth U.S. president had been a professional model at one point in his life.

   Kernel: _____

   Note: Adjective and adverb phrases also can follow and modify the subject of a clause. Like appositives, these phrases are set off by commas when they appear between the subject and verb of a clause. For example, in this sentence an adjective phrase describes the subject:

a.   The child, *intelligent and strong,* took after her parents.

Here, an adverb phrase is the modifier:

b.   The woman, *cautiously at first,* planted the seeds under a thin layer of reddish dirt.

Prepositional Phrases

Prepositional phrases are probably the most difficult modifiers to learn because there are so many of them. Before we define these phrases, let's look at an example. Underline the modifiers in this phrase:

the high cost of textbooks

The word *high* is obviously a modifier—an adjective, to be precise. But the words *of textbooks* make up another type of modifier—a prepositional phrase. The words *of textbooks* describe the noun *cost* just as surely as the adjective *high* does. We are talking about a high cost, not a low cost. Similarly, we are talking about the cost of textbooks, not the cost of banana splits. So *of textbooks* is a prepositional phrase that works as an adjective.

Here's an example of a prepositional phrase that acts as an adverb:

The boy dialed 911 *in a panic.*

How did he dial the number? He dialed it *in a panic,* not in a cool, calm frame of mind. In other words, *in a panic* modifies the verb *dialed.*

Prepositional phrases also can describe *where* an action was done. For example:

The man wrote his novel *at a seaside hotel.*

Or they can describe *when* an action was done. For example:

My mother graduated from law school *in May.*

As you'll see in the following list, most prepositions can be thought of as *direction* or *relationship* words. The noun or pronoun that follows a preposition is called the object of the preposition. Taken together, the preposition and its object form a prepositional phrase. An important thing to know in editing your work is that **the subject of a sentence will never be inside a prepositional phrase.** Knowing this fact will help to solve problems of subject–verb agreement, a topic we will review later in the book.

Here is a list of the most common prepositions, each used in the context of a prepositional phrase. The words in italics are the prepositions.

about the introduction	*above* his head
across the border	*after* recess
against his principles	*along* those lines
among ourselves	*around* our city
at the time	*before* the meeting
behind her	*below* the ice
beneath the top layer	*beside* her mother
between two slices	*beyond* tomorrow

by them	*despite* my wishes
down the path	*during* the first minute
except you	*for* my children
from his grandmother	*in* the spirit
inside his mind	*into* the grocery store
like a winner	*near* her heart
of the joke	*off* the top
on the dresser	*onto* the floor
out the door	*outside* the solar system
over the noodles	*past* his house
since her graduation	*through* the middle
throughout the poem	*to* my office
toward the future	*under* it
underneath the books	*until* winter
up the steps	*upon* her entrance
with love	*within* your lifetime
without regrets	

There are also *phrasal prepositions*. These are prepositions that are made up of two or more words. Here are a few examples, again given in the context of a prepositional phrase. The phrasal prepositions are in italics:

according to Mark	*along with* fried clams
because of my sister	*except for* him
in addition to the readings	*in case of* emergency
in place of the party	*in spite of* your absence
instead of television	*out of* luck
up to par	*with reference to* the letter
with regard to your request	

* **Exercise Four**

Use the labels *s, v, sub com, ob com, do* and *io* to mark the key parts of the following simple sentences. Draw a wavy line under appositives and cross out prepositional phrases and other modifiers. Then write the kernel on the line provided.

1. Robin Burns, the highest-paid woman in the United States, is the chief executive

   officer of Estee Lauder USA.

   Kernel: _____

2. During the early part of his career, Babe Ruth pitched.

   Kernel: _____

3. In 1981 the number of foreign tourists in the United States exceeded the number of

American tourists in foreign countries for the first time in the memory of record keepers in the travel industry.

Kernel: _____

4. For some strange reason, the color of raspberry popsicles has always been blue.

Kernel: _____

5. The Treasury Department of the United States dry-cleaned soiled money during the administration of President Woodrow Wilson.

Kernel: _____

6. According to experts in animal behavior, a female tree frog instinctively recognizes the connection between the volume of a male tree frog's song and his physical strength and vigor, prime factors in his desirability as a mate.

Kernel: _____

7. The headquarters of the McDonald's Corporation in Illinois has a 700-gallon burger-shaped waterbed.

Kernel: _____

8. The decaying organic matter on the floor of a forest is *duff*.

Kernel: _____

9. The average size of the winner of the male division of the Boston Marathon over the years is 5 feet and 7 inches and 135 pounds.

Kernel: _____

10. Ironically, country singer Hank Williams's last record before his death in 1953 at the young age of 29 was "I'll Never Get Out of this World Alive."

Kernel: _____

UNIT 5:   Review

Here are exercises that will help you draw together and review the information and skills you've learned in chapter 8. It's essential to have a strong sense of clauses in order to do well in the following chapters, so, if necessary, review units 1 through 4 before you begin the following exercises.

Exercises

Exercise One   *   PART A

Here is a series of simple sentences exploring a question of interest to many: Do women and men love in the same way? Some of the information given is derived from "How Women Love," an article by Dr. Joyce Brothers. (For the full citation for this and other sources, consult Sources at the back of the book.)
Show the key parts of each clause by doing the following:

a. **Use s, v, sub com, ob com, do and io to label the key parts of each clause.**
b. **Cross out the various types of modifiers.**
c. **If it's helpful, write out the kernel of each clause.**

1. Many students of love throughout the centuries have been poets, philosophers, psychologists, historians, and just plain folks.

2. Some of these observers from diverse times and places have noticed profound differences between men's and women's ideas about love.

3. According to the experts, women make decisions about love much more slowly than men.

4. For one study, field-workers from a research organization took a stopwatch to a singles bar.

5. There they made an amazing discovery.

6. According to their observations, the average man's intentions with respect to the pursuit of a relationship with a woman were formed within seven seconds.

7. Women are generally much slower and more cautious in the love arena.

8. One underlying reason for the quicker male response is the relative importance of visual stimuli.

9. Men, in contrast to women, generally seem more concerned about the physical characteristics of the opposite sex, at least initially.

10. Women, on the other hand, most often judge men attractive or unattractive on the basis of less tangible qualities, such as their probable suitability as fathers.

PART B

Follow the directions given in part A to do this part of exercise one.

1. The accuracy of research studies and projects on a subject like love is debatable.

2. However, certain trends offer us a fascinating glimpse into the differences between men and women.

3. Generally, a woman's feelings of love for a man are slower in their formation than a man's feelings of love for a woman.

4. However, a woman in love more often reports classic romantic symptoms such as giddiness, exhilaration, and a sense of increased physical health.

5. According to studies, at the end of a romance, the intensity of suffering among males and females differs dramatically.

6. Men in general endure greater heartaches than women upon the occasion of a breakup.

7. In fact, men commit suicide three times more often than women at the end of love relationships.

8. Complicated factors cause this greater devastation among males.

9. Because of childhood experiences, many men, in their search for love, seek an all-approving and affirming woman and neglect the development of other relation-ships with family and friends.

10. In the event of a breakup, these men unfortunately may not enjoy the comfort of a network of supporters.

Exercise Two

First read the sentences on the contribution of Mrs. Rosa Parks to American history. Then:

a. **Use the labels *s, v, sub com, ob com, do* and *io* to mark the key parts of each clause.**
b. **Cross out modifying material.**
c. **Write the kernel of each clause on your own paper if you find this practice helpful.**

This is a long exercise; your teacher may ask some students to do only some of it and others to complete all six parts. *It's essential that each part be corrected, discussed, and understood before proceeding to the next.* This information is collected from a wide variety of sources.

* PART A

1. Rosa Parks is without a doubt the mother of the Civil Rights movement in America.

2. On a cold December 1, 1955, in Montgomery, Alabama, that movement was born.

3. Mrs. Parks, a skilled seamstress, had been altering men's clothing at the Montgomery Fair department store.

4. Completely exhausted from her long day at work, she felt sharp pains in her shoulders, back, and neck.

5. She climbed the steps of a Montgomery city bus, paid her fare, and took a seat next to a black man and behind several white riders.

6. According to her own testimony in an interview years later, Mrs. Parks immediately recognized the bus driver.

7. J.P. Blake, the driver that day, had ejected Mrs. Parks from a bus years earlier in 1943.

8. Soon no places on the crowded 36-seat bus remained.

9. Blake wanted Mrs. Parks's seat for a white male passenger.

10. That she and three other black passengers move to the back of the bus was his exact demand.

PART B

1. Eventually the others did move.

2. Mrs. Parks, a 42-year-old woman with plenty of experience in similarly demeaning situations, quietly but flatly refused.

3. The bus driver's order made her extremely angry.

4. In fact, according to her description of the event years later, her seat was actually in "no man's land," a section between the one for whites and the one for blacks.

5. The entire bus became absolutely silent.

6. Blake issued a threat.

7. He cited the local segregation codes and claimed emergency police powers.

8. He said that he would have her arrested.

9. She replied, "You may do that."

10. Blake left the bus and contacted the Montgomery police.

* PART C

1. At the Montgomery police station, Mrs. Parks was booked, fingerprinted, and jailed.

2. Immediately after her call home, Mrs. Parks's mother contacted E.D. Nixon.

3. Nixon, president of the Alabama branch of the first major black trade union, the Brotherhood of Sleeping Car Porters, was a well-known and dedicated local black activist.

4. Nixon and Clifford Durr, a trusted white lawyer, immediately became involved and posted bail for Mrs. Parks.

5. Mrs. Parks, E.D. Nixon, Clifford Durr, and Virginia Durr, his wife, arrived at the Parks home and were greeted by Mrs. Parks's immensely relieved husband, Raymond Parks, a barber, and Mrs. Parks's mother.

6. After a great deal of joyful talk and celebration, Nixon and the Durrs explained the case's possible use as a test of local segregation laws.

7. Mrs. Parks discussed the situation with her husband and mother.

8. Both wanted an end to the incident and were very upset.

9. Raymond Parks greatly feared the possibility of his wife's further incarceration.

10. But once again, just as on the bus, Mrs. Parks courageously chose the path of resistance.

PART D

1. Nixon and the Durrs left the Parks home and quickly contacted key members of the community.

2. Nixon called Reverend Ralph Abernathy, the minister at his church, and Reverend Martin Luther King, Jr., the minister at Montgomery's Dexter Avenue Baptist Church.

3. At the same time, Jo Ann Robinson, a professor of English at Alabama State University and a leader of the political affairs committee at Reverend King's church, heard the news and called other professional and church women.

4. The women met in offices at Alabama State around midnight.

5. There, throughout the night, Jo Ann Robinson and her friends developed a plan of action and wrote and revised a letter of protest.

6. Their main problem was a lack of access to radio and newspapers.

7. In the dark of night, they polished their letter to the community and duplicated it on university mimeograph machines.

8. Aware of the risks of these activities at a state-funded university, the women gave one another a promise of silence.

9. The women leafletted the community and requested a one-day bus boycott in a show of solidarity with Mrs. Parks.

10. By the end of the next day, the women's leaflets had saturated Montgomery's black community.

* PART E

1. On the following Monday morning, Mrs. Rosa Parks was convicted.

2. Immediately, the entire black population of Montgomery began a complete boycott of city buses.

3. Meanwhile, the Montgomery Improvement Association (MIA), a protest and support group, was formed with Dr. Martin Luther King, Jr., at its head.

4. With the help of the MIA, the Montgomery bus boycott became a long-term success.

5. A planned one-day action quickly ballooned into something much bigger.

6. Some people formed car pools and gave their friends and neighbors rides.

7. Others pedaled their bicycles or simply walked.

8. During the boycott, black cab companies charged their customers bus fare rather than the traditionally higher cab fare.

9. Through a wide range of events, people raised money for gasoline and tires.

10. Boycotters endured for 381 days and denied the local bus company enormous profits.

PART F

1. The struggle in Alabama continued.

2. Finally, on November 13, 1956, the U.S. Supreme Court affirmed an earlier decision of a special panel of three judges.

3. Focusing on the laws for segregation on public transportation, those three judges had declared Alabama's state and local segregation laws unconstitutional.

4. The work of Mrs. Parks, Dr. King, and thousands of other people was a great success in and of itself.

5. But most historians also consider this episode the beginning of the Civil Rights movement in America.

6. On a personal level, Mrs. Parks's life changed greatly as a result of her heroic role in this momentous event in American social history.

7. For one thing, she lost her tailoring position and left the South.

8. In Detroit, she became a special assistant to U.S. Congressman John Conyers and held that position for a quarter of a century.

9. In addition, she and her husband founded and still administer the Rosa and Raymond Parks Institute for Self-Development.

10. Rosa Parks, an American hero, continues in the struggle for social justice in America.

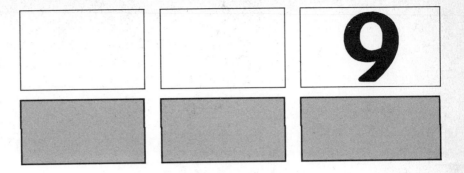

Strategies for Combining Clauses and Punctuating Sentences

Up to this point, we have been working with sentences that have only one clause, but now we are going to take up sentences that *combine* clauses.

Simple sentences definitely have their place in writing. For example, they can be very useful for creating an abrupt, staccato effect. But if you rely too heavily on simple sentences and use them where there's no special rhetorical purpose for doing so, your writing will be choppy and disconnected, seeming, at times, to have been produced by someone younger or less sophisticated than you are.

Think about the exercises in chapter 8 where we worked with only simple sentences, for example, the ones discussing Nolan Ryan, Rosa Parks, or the differences between men and women in love. If you took those sentences out of the form in which they appear (numbered lists), grouped them into paragraphs, and typed them as essays, you'd have a real problem. Why? Because the same sentences that worked well in list form would seem choppy and monotonous in essay form. While a long list of sentences with only one clause worked well in an exercise for helping us get a handle on sentence structure, sentences that combine some clauses in ways that show the relationships between the various facts and judgments asserted make better essays for two reasons: *variety* and *logic*.

It's not difficult to combine clauses. In fact, several of the sentence-combining techniques that you'll work with in this chapter are already, to some extent, part of your automatic language patterns. But here you'll learn to become *conscious* of the conventionally accepted processes for combining clauses and the value of those processes. Your work in this chapter will give you a number of good options for making smooth, logical connections between thoughts.

Our first focus in this chapter is on a number of the accepted ways to combine clauses. But certain classic sentence problems—especially *comma splices, run-ons,* and *fragments*—occur as a result of missteps in the process of basic sentence combining, so it's logical to look at those problems in this chapter, too.

UNIT 1:   Compound Sentences

One of the most natural ways to combine clauses is to link them with a conjunction. The easiest conjunctions to work with are the *coordinating conjunctions.* Seven words are usually listed in this category, and they should be memorized:

Coordinating conjunctions

and	or
but	so
for	yet
nor	

When a coordinating conjunction is used to link two clauses, each clause is considered *independent.* In other words, neither one becomes subordinate to the other or dependent upon the other. In terms of the emphasis the writer gives the clauses, they remain on a fairly equal level.

Punctuating Compound Sentences

In a compound sentence, a comma is inserted at the end of the first clause, right before the conjunction. The traditional rule states that, when both clauses in a compound sentence are very brief, this comma may be omitted. But some options—including this one—are really just one more thing to remember; in other words, they may be more trouble than they're worth because they make whatever rule you're learning more complicated. So, because it is never wrong to use a comma between the clauses of a compound sentence—whatever their length—and it is usually necessary or helpful, just do it. Develop the habit of consistently using the comma in a compound sentence.

Another reason to use the comma even in a short compound sentence is that the comma often helps to avoid confusion. Consider this sentence:

I dropped off Raymond and Benjamin appeared out of nowhere.

A comma after *Raymond* will help the reader avoid a split-second confusion. Without the comma, the reader might think that you dropped off both Raymond and Benjamin and that you accidentally omitted the subject of the verb *appeared.* In other words, the reader might mistakenly think *Benjamin* is a direct object of the verb *dropped off* when it's really the subject of the verb *appeared.* Remember: Make it easy for your reader.

Here are some more examples of compound sentences. If it helps you to see the two clauses in each sentence, label the key words:

a. Type O is the most common blood type in the world, *and* type AB is the rarest.

b. The life expectancy of the average white person in the United States is 74.4 years, *yet* it is only 68.3 years for the average black person.

c. Radio City Music Hall in New York was once the largest indoor movie theater in the entire world, *but* not a single movie has been shown there since 1979.

Other Uses of the Coordinating Conjunctions

All seven words that work as coordinating conjunctions also can be used to do other jobs in sentences. So don't automatically use a comma before each of these seven words without stopping to think about how the word is being used. For example, in these sentences *and* and *but* do not join clauses, so a comma should not be used in either one:

d. Red *and* blue are two of the three primary colors.

e. Parenthood is a wonderful *but* difficult challenge.

In sentence d, *and* joins two nouns used as subjects—*red* and *blue*. In sentence e, *but* links two adjectives. Use a comma *only* when one of the seven words is doing that larger job: joining clauses.

A Note on *For* and *Nor*

The meanings of most of the coordinating conjunctions don't need any explanation, but it should be pointed out that when the word *for* is used as a conjunction it means roughly the same as *because*. In other words, it's not the *for* in "This letter is for you," but rather the *for* in the slightly old-fashioned sounding "I would rather travel in my youth, *for* someday in the future I may have the money but not the health."

In compound sentences that use the conjunction *nor*, you'll see that the subject and verb of the second clause are inverted. In other words, the verb (or at least the helping verb of a verb phrase) will appear before the subject, just as in a question. For example:

f. Vincent Van Gogh did not sell more than one painting during his entire lifetime, *nor did he receive* the least bit of positive attention from the art world.

In the second clause of sentence f, half of the verb phrase *did receive* is placed before the subject *he*. Instead of the usual word order of *he did receive*, here we have *did he receive*. Here's another example, this time with a single-word verb rather than a verb phrase:

g.   You couldn't work that fast, *nor could I*.

Exercises

* ## Exercise One

Read the following sentences, which discuss a variety of topics. Some are simple sentences (one clause), and some are compound (two clauses). Then

   a.   insert a comma where it belongs in each compound sentence;
   b.   write *simple* or *compound* in the blank after each sentence.

If a sentence gives you trouble, label the key words in its clause or clauses. You might even want to write out the kernels on your own paper. Soon you'll have the sentence figured out.

1. The average American family's evening meal takes 32 minutes and 40 percent of all households in the United States eat their main meal of the day with the TV or VCR on. _____

2. Years ago baseball players were typically recruited directly from the minors or from high school teams but now most play college baseball and then move on to the big leagues. _____

3. "I never ever ran from the Ku Klux Klan and I shouldn't have to run from a black man." (line from Kool Moe Dee, "Self-Destruction") _____

4. The Roman god Janus could look both backward and forward at the same time. _____

5. Real pearls require regular exposure to daylight or they eventually lose their luster and become dull. _____

6. The distribution of women doctors is highest among pediatricians and psychiatrists and lowest among surgeons. _____

7. Writers in their twenties and thirties often get discouraged by failed publication attempts and high stacks of rejections letters yet the most productive age for published prose writers is actually 43. _____

8. "Maybe Baby" was a big hit for early rock and roll's Buddy Holly and his mother wrote the lyrics. _____

9. Americans do not spend as much each year on eye research as on eye makeup nor do they spend as much on child protection services as on toys. _____

10. Philadelphia's Anna Jarvis wanted to honor her late mother in a special way so she began a letter-writing campaign and inspired the modern version of Mother's Day. _____

Exercise Two   PART A

Read the following sentences on a government policy that proved to be a disaster for Native Americans. Then

   a. **insert a comma where it belongs in each compound sentence (label the clauses if that helps you tell simple from compound sentences); and**
   b. **write *simple* or *compound* on the line provided.**

1. The federal government in the late nineteenth century did not wish to preserve the traditional Native American way of life so some government officials decided to make Indians farmers. _____

2. In 1887 the U.S. Congress adopted the General Allotment Act. _____

3. This legislation was sponsored by Senator Henry L. Dawes of Massachusetts and it is also known as the Dawes Act. _____

4. The Dawes Act broke up large tribal land holdings and distributed parcels of land to individual Native Americans. _____

5. Some allotments were as small as 40 acres but others were as large as 160 acres or a quarter of a section. _____

6. Assimilation of Native Americans into the mainstream of American society was the purported goal and some historians consider the allotment policy well-intentioned and benevolent in its original design. _____

7. The intentions of some of the act's supporters may have been good yet the results were extremely destructive and tragic. _____

8. The most basic problem with the allotment policy was its disregard for the Native Americans' intense desire to keep their lands intact and communal in nature. _____

9. Another problem involved the Native Americans' inexperience with U.S. laws and legal procedures and this difficulty later allowed thousands of "grafters" to swindle them out of their allotted lands. _____

10. One principal result of the Dawes Act was the sudden availability of great land at bargain prices. _____

* PART B

Continue as in part A: Insert a comma in every compound sentence and label each sentence *simple* or *compound*. Label key words if you find that helpful.

1. The government decided to give a standard 160-acre share to each "head of a family" and smaller parcels of land to unmarried men and children but this plan also caused trouble. _____

2. This method of assigning allotments often caused problems for women and children traditionally had their own property rights in a good number of Indian societies. _____

3. Many Native Americans tried to prevent the legislation or they fought against it after its enactment. _____

4. Sitting Bull visited the Crows of Montana in the winter of 1886–87 and urged them to resist the division and allotment of their land. _____

5. Many Native Americans in the West and Northwest wanted first to consult with one another and then to express their opposition in Washington but government agents forcibly kept them on the reservations during this time. _____

6. The military officer at the head of the Pine Ridge Agency defended the right of the

Sioux to resist allotment of their range land and he predicted the degradation and even extinction of the people under the Dawes policy. _____

7. Through the General Allotment Act, the Wahpeton and Sisseton Sioux of the Dakota Territory lost 660,000 acres of their land in the rich Red River Valley of the North and the Choctaws and Chickasaws lost 3.5 million acres in the South. _____

8. Untold numbers of Native American families were swindled out of their lands and they and their descendants suffered the most extreme poverty and demoralization. _____

9. Often they were reduced to squatting on the remaining allotments of friends or relatives or they set up camp on church property. _____

10. In 1934 a sad chapter in American history ended with the abandonment of the allotment policy and reform measures finally began. _____

Exercise Three

Create six of your own compound sentences, choosing one option from each of the following numbered groups. Use your own paper, and don't forget to put the comma in after the first clause.

1. Write a compound sentence using *and* to link clauses about
   - two things that intrigued or pleased you about a place to which you've traveled or
   - two things people like about you.
2. Write a compound sentence using *but* or *yet* to link clauses about
   - one thing you admire and one thing you don't admire about a certain celebrity or a movie you've seen or
   - one thing you like and one thing you dislike about rap, heavy metal, jazz, new age, or your parents' favorite music.
3. Write a compound sentence using *or* to link clauses about
   - two possible scenarios for your future or
   - two alternate uses for a large sum of money you've just acquired.
4. Write a compound sentence using *nor* to link clauses about
   - two things your parents won't let you do, or you won't let your children do, or
   - two fears a parent might have about a child who has not learned enough math to deal with the practical realities of adult life.

5. Write a compound sentence using *so* to link clauses about (1) a hope or goal and (2) a plan of action to make that hope or goal come true. For example,
   • the desire to get in shape and a plan to do it or
   • the goal to earn the highest grades you've ever received and a plan to do it.
6. Write a compound sentence using *for* to link clauses, the second one of which explains the cause of something. For example,
   • the decline in SAT scores and its likely causes or
   • the reason why a new wave of immigrants to the United States usually must fight terrific battles for acceptance and respect.

Linking More than Two Clauses

The conjunctions we've looked at in this unit are most often used to connect two clauses, but they can be used to connect more than two clauses within one sentence. How many clauses, for instance, do you see in this sentence? Insert a comma or commas where appropriate:

Several dates throughout history have been used to commemorate the birth of

Jesus Christ but December 25 was adopted by Bishop Liberius of Rome in 354

and it has been considered the official date ever since.

[ANSWER: The sentence has three clauses. A comma should be inserted after *Jesus Christ* and after *354*.]

Connecting three clauses with coordinating conjunctions is perfectly okay, but you probably want to avoid doing it too often or connecting more than three clauses in this way. The risk is a flatness or lack of variety in your sentence structures. That's why we're going to work with several other options for combining clauses.

UNIT 2:   Complex Sentences

Complex sentences are another way of combining clauses. We'll look at two important types in this unit.

Complex Sentences Made with Subordinating Conjunctions

Subordinating conjunctions can do a little more than coordinating conjunctions can do. They can attach clauses by appearing at the start of the first clause or at the start of the second. The clause that is headed by a subordinating conjunction is *subordinate to* or *dependent upon* the other clause. It can't stand alone as a sentence but rather is dependent upon another clause for a sense of completeness or independence. The other clause is called the *independent* or *main* clause. By using subordinating conjunctions, a writer can choose to put emphasis on the information in either the first or second clause of a sentence.

In this example, the subordinating conjunction (the word *when*) is placed directly before the second clause, making it the dependent one:

a.   An album is considered "gold" *when* at least 500,000 copies have been sold.

In sentence b, we have the reverse: dependent clause first, independent or main clause second.

b.   *When* at least 500,000 copies have been sold, an album is considered "gold."

Not all complex sentences made with subordinating conjunctions can have their clauses reversed, but many can.

Complete the following complex sentences using the subordinating conjunction *because*. The dependent clause is already given; use the blanks provided to supply an independent or main clause:

c.   _____

      because I ate too much during the holidays.

d.   *Because* I ate too much during the holidays, _____

      _____.

When to Use a Comma

You may have noticed that a comma normally is used between the clauses in these sentences when the dependent clause is first. Generally, a comma is not used when the subordinating conjunction is in the middle of the sentence. (The rule here is opposite to the rule for coordinating conjunctions.)

The conjunction *although* is the most consistent exception to this rule. When *although* is used to link clauses, a comma usually is placed between the clauses; it doesn't matter if *although* is used before the first or second clause.

But that's an exception. The general rule is this:

When a dependent clause is first, use a comma between clauses;
when an independent clause is first, use no comma.

Subordinating Conjunctions to Memorize

The following is a list of some of the most common subordinating conjunctions. Some are single words and others are phrases, but they are all used to link clauses by making one dependent upon the other.

Subordinating conjunctions

after	if	when
although	since	whenever
as	so that	where
as long as	that	wherever
as soon as	though	while
because	unless	why
before	until	

Although the emphasis in this book is not on memorization, it *is* a good idea to know the coordinating and subordinating conjunctions. Compound and complex sentence structures already appear in your writing with great frequency, so you need to know the relevant punctuation rules. An easy way to accomplish this is to copy the lists of conjunctions and the rules that appear in boldface in this chapter onto a card or piece of paper and tape that card or paper to your bathroom mirror, refrigerator door, or any place where you'll see it often. Read the lists and rules aloud every chance you get, and before you know it, you'll have them down.

Now let's try some exercises.

* **Exercise One**

Do the following:

   a. **Circle the subordinating conjunction that connects the clauses.**
   b. **Insert the correct punctuation. Some sentences may call for no further punctuation. (Treat quotes as you would treat any other sentence.)**
   c. **Label the key parts of the two clauses in each complex sentence if you need to in order to see the two clauses.**

1. Although the New York Mets had the worst team batting average in baseball in 1969 they still won the World Series that year.

2. Tattooing was not known in the Western hemisphere until Captain Cook returned from his voyage to Tahiti.

3. "When I want to read a good book I write one." (a boast from Benjamin Disraeli, former Prime Minister of England)

4. Aretha Franklin decided to become a singer as soon as she heard the great Clara Ward's "Peace in the Valley" at a relative's funeral.

5. "If my horse can't eat it I don't want to play on it." (Philadelphia Phillies' retired first baseman Dick Allen's comment about Astroturf)

6. Isaac Bashevis Singer continued to chronicle Jewish life in the Old World and the New after he won the Nobel Prize for literature in 1978 at the age of 73.

7. Unless a condom can stretch beyond 1.5 cubic feet it will not meet current quality-control testing standards in the U.S. prophylactic industry.

8. Because ice cream contains so many calories eating it will actually make a person warmer rather than cooler.

9. It is a national tragedy that 25 million Americans are illiterate or almost illiterate in the 1990s.

10. "When he hits you you have to take inventory." (Washington Redskins' quarterback Jay Schroeder's reaction to being sacked by New York Giants' Lawrence Taylor)

Exercise Two

Read through the sentences in exercise one and try to switch the order of the two clauses in each one. You'll see that some can be switched, and some cannot. In reverse order, some sentences may lose in gracefulness, style, humor, or proper emphasis, and some simply may not make sense.

Find *three* sentences in which the clauses can be reversed, write them down in the order that is the opposite of the way they appear in the exercise. Then adjust your punctuation accordingly. Use your own paper, please.

Exercise Three

Using five different subordinating conjunctions, write five subordinate or dependent clauses. Find a partner and exchange papers with him or her. Complete your partner's sentences by adding an independent clause to each. Then decide whether the sentences you just completed need commas inserted and, if so, insert them. Exchange again so that you have your original paper. Check the sentences for logic and punctuation. Discuss any problems, inserting combinations, or special cases.

A Final Note

You may have noticed that some of the words listed as subordinating conjunctions were also listed as prepositions earlier in this book. There are many words in the English language that have multiple functions. Make sure that a word is actually being used as a subordinating conjunction before you apply the punctuation rules you have learned.

For each of the following sentences, label the word in italics as either *conj* for conjunction or *prep* for preposition.

1a.   I read the paper *before* breakfast.

 b.   I read the paper *before* I ate my biscuits and sausage.

2a.   He didn't speak a word *until* his fourth birthday.

 b.   He didn't speak a word *until* he turned four.

3a.   *As* she dressed in her clown suit, she dreaded the upcoming party.

 b.   She dreaded going to the costume party *as* a clown.

[ANSWERS: 1a. prep,   b. conj;   2a. prep,   b. conj; 3a. conj,   b. prep.]

Complex Sentences Made with Relative Pronouns

Another kind of complex sentence is formed when you use a *relative pronoun* to produce a dependent clause. A relative pronoun replaces the normal subject of a clause and creates a subordinate clause that refers to a word in an earlier part of the sentence (that word is called an *antecedent*). For now, we'll work with two important relative pronouns: *who* and *which*. The word *which* is used to refer to nonhuman subjects, and *who* is used to refer to human subjects.

Relative clauses must be combined with independent or main clauses in order to make well-structured sentences. (The only exceptions are questions such as "Who is that?" or "Which did you buy?") Use this rule to combine relative clauses with main clauses:

> **In a complex sentence, a relative clause will either (1) follow the main clause or (2) be embedded in the main clause between its subject and predicate.**

To see how a complex sentence can be formed by creating a relative clause to follow a main clause, let's look at a sequence of two simple sentences:

1a.   People should avoid a high level of lipids. They are found in meat, olives, and peanuts.

Say you want to combine these two sentences so that you have a longer, more fluent structure. You scan through the coordinating and subordinating conjunctions, but find none that is just right for linking these two bits of information.

That's when you turn to the relative pronouns and change the subject of the second clause (*They*) to the relative pronoun *which,* and add a comma where the period was. Then you'd have a good complex sentence:

1b.   People should avoid a high level of lipids, *which* are found in meat, olives, and peanuts.

The main or independent clause in sentence 1b is *People should avoid a high level of lipids;* the relative subordinate clause is *which are found in meat, olives, and peanuts.* When the relative clause follows the main clause, you normally use a comma between them.

A Problem to Watch Out For

Sometimes using a relative pronoun to link clauses can cause a slight problem to arise. Let's take another pair of two simple sentences:

2a.   The first movie version of *Frankenstein* came out in 1910. It was produced by inventor Thomas Edison.

What happens this time when you change *It* to *which* and combine the two clauses to make a complex sentence? Do you see a problem in the resulting sentence?

2b.   The first movie version of *Frankenstein* came out in 1910, which was produced by inventor Thomas Edison.

This sentence makes it sound as if Thomas Edison produced the year 1910, doesn't it? The clauses in 2a can't be combined in the same way as the clauses in 1a. One of the things you need to do with relative clauses is make sure that they are placed as close as possible to the word that they modify.

　　　To combine the clauses in 2a logically, we need to do something a bit more complicated: We need to insert the relative clause between the subject and predicate of the main clause. To do this, we first must pull apart the subject and predicate of the main clause:

2c.   The first movie version of *Frankenstein*   came out in 1910.

Then, into that opened spot, we can embed (or insert) the relative clause— because it most logically describes *the first movie version of Frankenstein.* And here's our result, a well-structured complex sentence:

2d.   The first movie version of *Frankenstein,* which was produced by inventor Thomas Edison, came out in 1910.

　　　When the relative clause sits between the subject and predicate of the main clause, you usually set it apart from the main clause with two commas. (At times you use no commas; we'll work with such examples later.)

Exercise Four

Combine each set of sentences by doing the following:

    a.   Make sentence b a relative clause. In other words, change its subject to *which* or *who.*

    b.   Then embed that clause between the subject and predicate of the main or independent clause, which is always sentence a. Use the lines provided to write out the new combination.

    c.   Enclose the embedded relative clause within a pair of commas.

1a.   Bo Diddley has been called the godfather of rap.

  b.   He was using spoken taunts and boasts in his recordings four decades ago.

_____

_____

_____

2a.   Dr. Lynne Layton says that many of Madonna's young female fans see her as an embodiment of the diverse and seemingly contradictory aspects of femininity.

  b.   She is a professor of popular culture at Harvard University.

_____

_____

_____

3a.   Babe Ruth was the best-paid athlete in the world at the time.

  b.   He earned $80,000 in 1930–31.

_____

_____

_____

4a.   The $2 bill turned out to be a big fizzle.

  b.   It was initially greeted with a lot of fanfare.

_____

_____

_____

5a.   Sexual harassment was the issue in a locker-room case involving *Boston Herald* reporter Lisa Olson and the New England Patriots.
 b.   It is encountered by countless employees in the workplace.

_____

_____

_____

6a.   The family of Dr. Charles Leale recently loaned Leale's blood-stained shirt cuffs to the newly remodeled museum in Ford's Theatre.
 b.   He was the first doctor to reach the wounded Abraham Lincoln.

_____

_____

_____

7a.   The tip of the tongue is the most sensitive and yet the toughest part of the human body.
 b.   It can withstand temperatures up to 170 degrees.

_____

_____

_____

8a.   Cleopatra had some of them engraved on onyx and crystal tablets.
 b.   She wrote passionate love letters to Antony.

_____

_____

_____

9a.   Pretzels are said to be the original snack food.
 b.   They have been around for over 1,400 years.

_____

_____

_____

10a.   Helen Keller was not blind or deaf until shortly before her second birthday.

b.   She became an inspiration to so many people.

_____

_____

_____

A Variation: Reducing the Relative Clause

In some cases, the embedded relative clause can be reduced. Consider, for example, sentence 2 in exercise four:

> Dr. Lynne Layton, *who is a professor of popular culture at Harvard University,* says that many of Madonna's young female fans see her as an embodiment of the diverse and seemingly contradictory aspects of femininity.

This sentence can be reduced to

> Dr. Lynne Layton, *a professor of popular culture at Harvard University,* says that many of Madonna's young female fans see her as an embodiment of the diverse and seemingly contradictory aspects of femininity.

Both versions are correct; you can use either option. When you make this kind of a reduction, you turn the relative clause into something with which you've already worked in chapter 8: an appositive, a noun phrase that follows and describes another noun phrase.

Now you try it. Reduce the relative clause in sentence 6 in exercise four:

> The family of Dr. Charles Leale, _____
> _____ , recently loaned Leale's blood-
> stained shirt cuffs to the newly remodeled museum in Ford's Theatre.

More on the Punctuation of Relative Clauses

In the preceding examples and exercises, all the relative clauses have called for punctuation. This is because all of them follow very specific subjects that do not require the information in the embedded clause in order to be clear or precise. To understand this, let's take another look at the first sentence you formed in exercise four:

a.   Bo Diddley, *who was using spoken taunts and boasts in his recordings four decades ago,* has been called the godfather of rap.

In this sentence, you know for sure who the subject is—Bo Diddley—without any help from the information in the relative clause. If you omitted the relative clause and simply said *Bo Diddley has been called the godfather of rap,* you and your reader would still know that you're making a statement about Bo Diddley. There could be no confusion about who is the subject of the sentence.

But look at this sentence:

b.   A boy *who is only six years old* should not be left alone without a sitter.

Here you have another relative clause—*who is only six years old*—but an entirely different situation. If you dropped out the information in the relative clause, you'd have *A boy should not be left alone without a sitter.* And that, obviously, is not what this writer wanted to communicate. The writer did not intend to make a statement about any boy or a boy of any age. The average 13-year-old boy, for instance, could probably be home alone for a time without a sitter.

So *A boy* by itself is not the subject of sentence b in the way that *Bo Diddley* by itself is the subject of sentence a. The real subject of b is *A boy who is only six years old.* In b, the relative clause is so necessary to the proper description or identification of the subject that it can't be omitted from the sentence. In that kind of sentence, *you do not use commas around the relative clause.* It's an essential part of the subject and can't be broken off or set aside in a more or less casual way, which is what the two commas do.

To summarize:

If the information in the embedded clause is a necessary part of the subject of the main clause, leave the embedded clause alone—use no commas.

If the information in the embedded clause is *not* necessary for the reader's correct understanding of the subject of the main clause, show that the embedded clause is "extra" by setting it apart with two commas.

Hint:

Always judge the importance of the embedded clause in relationship to the word it describes—the *subject of the main clause*—not in relationship to the meaning of the whole sentence.

The rules for punctuating relative clauses are challenging for many writers, so here are a few sets of contrasting sentences to examine, punctuate, and discuss in class before you do an actual exercise. In each pair, one sentence will call for two commas and one will call for none. First, underline the embedded relative clause and write *s* over the subject of the main clause. Then decide whether or not to add commas.

1a.   Anthony Carson who has very poor eyesight left his glasses in the

classroom this morning.

b.   A person who has very poor eyesight must have washed this car.

2a.   All parents who have children with special learning problems should sign up

for the lecture by Dr. Teresa Smith on Tuesday evening.

b. My parents who love to travel as often as possible definitely should join your discount travel club.

3a. People who have an optimistic philosophy of life tend to live longer.

b. My youngest brother who has an optimistic philosophy of life might live longer than my older and more pessimistic brother.

4a. Your wonderful attitude about your work which never fails to impress me has earned you the respect of many other teachers, too.

b. The thing that impresses me most of all is your wonderful attitude about your work.

5a. Anyone who loves the Miami Dolphins will understand my point of view.

b. My best friend who loves the Miami Dolphins will understand my point of view.

[ANSWERS: 1a. Commas around *who has very poor eyesight,* b. no commas; 2a. no commas, b. commas around *who love to travel as often as possible;* 3a. no commas, b. commas around *who has an optimistic philosophy of life;* 4a. commas around *which never fails to impress me,* b. no commas; 5a. no commas, b. commas around *who loves the Miami Dolphins.*]

If you had trouble with any of these sentences, review the text to try to clear up your questions before you tackle exercise five.

* **Exercise Five**

Underline the embedded relative clause and write *s* over the subject of the main clause. Then punctuate the sentence correctly.

1. Women who have heart attacks are twice as likely as men to die within a period of two months.

2. President McKinley who took a car ride in 1900 was the first U.S. president to travel in an automobile.

3. The only one of the seven dwarfs who does not have a beard is Dopey.

4. Charlie Chaplin who was widely imitated once entered a Charlie Chaplin look-alike contest and came in in third place.

5. A child's first teacher who may be good or bad or in-between is certainly bound to have a strong impact.

6. "Everyone who works in the domain of fiction is a bit crazy. The problem is to render this craziness interesting." (a quote from film director François Truffaut)

7. Those who attended the Mad Hatter's tea party were the Mad Hatter himself, the March Hare, the Dormouse, and Alice.

8. My paternal grandmother who left Poland in her late teens never returned to her homeland.

9. "The man who does not read good books has no advantage over the man who can't read them." (Mark Twain)

10. Al McGuire who coached the Marquette University Warriors to an NCAA basketball championship before the start of his television sports-announcing career once gave this answer when asked how to make basketball more exciting: "Eliminate the referees. Raise the basket four feet. Double the size of the basketball. Limit the height of the players to five-nine. Bring back the center jump. Allow taxi drivers in free. And allow the players to carry guns."

Correct exercise five and discuss any problems before continuing.

Exercise Six

Underline the embedded relative clause and write _s_ over the subject of the main clause. Then punctuate the sentences correctly. All of these sentences are on TV trivia.

1. "In Living Color" which was choreographed by Rosie Perez from Spike Lee's film _Do the Right Thing_ was the first weekly television program to regularly feature rap music.

2. American children who are between the ages of two and five typically watch almost 33 hours of television a week.

3. January and February which are the coldest months of the year in the United States are also the heaviest months for television watching.

4. Mike Wallace who earned his reputation on the long-running CBS program "60 Minutes" started out in television doing cigarette ads and Fluffo shortening commercials.

5. An American who has reached the age of 15 has probably witnessed more than 13,000 violent deaths on television.

6. The television tower that can boast of being the tallest in the United States is the tower for KTHI–TV of Fargo, North Dakota.

7. Students who are enrolled in college watch one-third less television than any other group of people.

8. "Cheers" which was America's highest-rated show in the 1990–91 television season started out as the lowest-rated network program back in the early 1980s.

9. Vladimir K. Zworykin who is often called the father of television said at the age of 84 that his favorite part of a television set was the "off" button.

10. A person who wants to buy an issue of America's best-selling magazine will have to purchase a copy of *TV Guide*.

If the Relative Clause Follows the Main Clause

If the relative clause follows the main clause, as it did in one of the first example sentences—*People should avoid a high level of lipids, which are found in meat, olives, and peanuts*—you'll employ the same rationale for punctuation as you used for embedded clauses. But this time, of course, your choice will be between one comma and none at all. Consider sentences a and b:

a.   A good piano teacher would never demand that level of performance from Jessica, *who is only eight.*

Here you use *one comma* because the information in the relative clause is *not* needed to identify or clarify the word to which it relates. *Jessica* is precise. The information in the relative clause can be considered "extra" and can be set off with a comma.

b. A good piano teacher would never demand that level of performance from a girl *who is only eight*.

In sentence b, you use *no comma* because the information in the relative clause *is* necessary for the identification of the antecedent—the *girl*.

A Note on *Which* and *That*

In exercise five you made decisions about punctuating sentences that use the relative pronoun *who* to refer to a human antecedent. When sentences have pronouns referring to nonhuman antecedents, on the other hand, you'll find that the wording itself will give you a clue about whether you need to add a comma. What is this clue? Generally, the word *which* is not used when the situation calls for no commas. Instead, the word *that* is used. Most writers make this word switch correctly without even thinking about it.

Compare these two sentences:

a. A turkey, *which is traditionally served at Thanksgiving,* is easy to prepare.

b. A turkey *that is diseased* should never be served at your Thanksgiving meal.

In sentence a, we use *which* and two commas because the subject is *a turkey*—any turkey. But in sentence b we use *that* and no commas because the intended subject is not simply the word *turkey*. Try reading b aloud without the relative clause. Who would say *A turkey should never be served at your Thanksgiving meal?* The subject is obviously not a turkey in general, but a diseased turkey.

An Exception to the "Two or Zero" Rule

Normally, you do not put a single comma between the subject and verb of a clause. You don't split them up in that way. The only exception to this—and it comes up *rarely, if ever* in most students' writing—is when the sentence would be very difficult to read if the writer didn't point out where the subject stopped and the predicate started.

For example, can you tell where a single comma was used in the second line of this snide but humorous quote from the poet James Russell Lowell? Insert a comma, please:

Nature fits all her children with something to do;

He who would write and can't write can surely review.

The second line is hard to read, isn't it? It contains the kind of embedded relative clause that normally would take no punctuation because it's a necessary part of the subject. (The word *He* alone doesn't tell us much, does it?) To clarify the line, Lowell wisely violated the normal custom and inserted a single comma between subject and predicate, producing this:

He who would write and can't write, can surely review.

This kind of exception might come up once in a great while in your writing. But in the *Easy Writer* exercises, embedded relative clauses will always take two commas or none at all.

UNIT 3: Making and Punctuating Phrase/ Clause Combinations

As you learned in an earlier chapter, a phrase is a sequence of two or more words that lacks the full subject plus predicate content of a clause. A phrase might have a noun or a pronoun, or it might have a verb, but—unlike a clause—it won't have both. Mark each item below either *ph* for phrase or *cl* for clause:

1a.   in a red Corvette _____

  b.   when she rode in a red Corvette_____

2a.   they felt fine_____

  b.   feeling fine_____

3a.   hoping to see a meteor shower in Perseus_____

  b.   and we saw a meteor shower in Perseus_____

[ANSWERS: 1a. ph,   b. cl;   2a. cl,   b. ph;   3a. ph,   b. cl.]

What's the value of working with phrases? Precisely this: They add tremendous grace and variety to writing. While you're revising your papers, look for chances to recast a clause in a compound or complex sentence as a phrase.

Here we'll look at phrases in three basic positions: before, after, and in the middle of a clause. If a phrase comes before or after a clause, it is often set off from the clause with a single comma. If it's used in the middle of a clause, you'll generally need two commas. We'll call these *intro phrases, end phrases,* and *mid phrases.*

At times, it's your choice whether or not to set off a phrase. For example, you could put in a comma after the first word of this sentence, or you could leave it out:

Later he stopped over for a quick game of hearts.

Other times, the comma is a necessity. These times include sentences in which the first word is (1) *Yes* or *No;* (2) a number, such as *First* or *Second;* or (3) a person's name, such as *Chris* or *Caitlin.* A tag question should always be set off at the end of a clause. For example,

You like turquoise, *don't you?*
Canada should be able to rely on the United States for support, *right?*

Reading sentences aloud will help you decide whether their phrases need punctuation. A hard stop in oral reading is a pretty good sign that adding a comma in that position would help the reader understand the sentence more easily.

Read these two sentences aloud. In which one is a comma needed, and in which is it optional?

In the morning Lee said goodbye and disappeared.
Stunned Lee said goodbye and disappeared.

It's the second sentence that needs a comma. This is a little easier to read:

Stunned, Lee said goodbye and disappeared.

All of the examples and exercise items in the rest of this unit come from the wonderful 1984 novel, *Love Medicine,* by Louise Erdrich, a very gifted writer of Chippewa and German-American descent. As you examine the structure and figure out the punctuation of Erdrich's sentences, you'll enjoy the power of her eye and the vividness and originality of her language choices.

Note: The quotation marks you'd normally expect around direct quotes have been omitted here. This has been done to help you avoid distractions and focus on phrase and clause structure and your decisions about commas.

Here are some examples from *Love Medicine.* Underline the clauses. What's left will be the phrases.

Intro phrases

a. Driving north, I could see the earth lifting.
b. Sitting, she leaned down and rested her forehead on the top of the metal toilet-roll dispenser.
c. Until the end of time, death would be our rock.

Mid phrases

a. Lynette's face, stained and swollen, bloomed over the wheel.
b. He was handsome, good-looking at least, and could have been an Indian.
c. Her tan hair, caught in a stiff club, looked as though it had been used to drag her here.

End phrases

a. The snow was bright, giving back starlight.
b. We floated into the field and sank down, crushing green wheat.

c.   Grandma Kashpaw's rolled-down nylons and brown support shoes appeared first, then her head in its iron-gray pageboy.

* Exercise One

Insert commas where they would help to set off intro, middle, and end phrases in these sentences from *Love Medicine*. Underline the clauses and label their key parts if it is helpful for you to do so. Read the sentences *aloud* before you make your decisions about punctuation.

> **Note: The answer key for all the exercises in this unit shows the decisions that Erdrich made. In some cases, your answer may be different but also acceptable.**

1. Under the gray swirls and spots and leaves of the pattern I knew there was tar paper and bare wood that could splinter a baby's feet.

2. She puffed her cheeks out in concentration patting and crimping the edges of the pies.

3. Her breasts like overfilled inner tubes strained at her nylon blouses.

4. Gaining confidence he rolled down his window and gathered speed.

5. He drove with impossible slowness now hardly able to keep his course.

6. Like the quality of staying power this faithfulness was invisible.

7. The sun is setting in the windows black and red.

8. His grin flashed now wolf white and sharp in his big placid face.

9. Waiting for the elevator he flexed his nimble fingers.

10. Everything was on even the oven.

Exercise Two

Continue to follow the directions given for exercise one.

1. She pretended to sleep breathing evenly and pure.

2. Zelda sits bolt upright sniffing the air.

3. I jumped out not knowing what on earth to think.

4. The sky was an impenetrable liquid starless and grim.

5. She even took her sleeping breath with a certain rigid meanness holding it stubbornly and releasing it with small explosive sighs.

6. Outside the sun was hot and heavy as a hand on my back.

7. Her round face and chubby hands were a pale dough color cold and wet with shock.

8. Thanks to Grandma's toaster Gordie was probably spared.

9. It was important that he get a bottle several bottles to stop the rattling.

10. On Friday mornings I go down to the sloughs with my brother Eli and wait for the birds to land.

Multiple Phrases

In the remaining exercises you'll find some sentences that have more than one phrase to be set off for the reader. In a single sentence, you might use one comma to set off a phrase before a clause and another comma to set off a phrase after it. Or you might have two intro phrases, three end phrases, and so forth. Any combination may occur. Again, it's very helpful to read the sentences aloud to make good decisions about punctuation.

Here are some examples of Erdrich sentences with multiple phrases. Examine them before you try the exercises. To help you identify the phrases, underline the clauses:

a. Without considering, in an almost desperate shuffle, she took her bundle and entered the ladies' room.
b. Her hands are big, nicked from sharp knives, roughed by bleach.
c. And then she began to beat on the spools of the iron bedstead, knocking flakes of white paint off, making an unholy racket.
d. By all accounts, the drowned weren't allowed into the next life but forced to wander forever, broken shoed, cold, sore, and ragged.

* Exercise Three

Continue to add commas to set off phrases in these sentences from *Love Medicine*. Some have multiple phrases. A few sentences are quite difficult and could be punctuated in more than one way; don't get frustrated.

1. Muffled slogged in pillows she gripped the head bars.

2. Fearing thieves she took the bundle into the stall and held it awkwardly on her lap.

3. They had always been together like brother and sister stealing duck eggs blowing crabgrass between their thumbs chasing cows.

4. I stood in my kitchen packing apples in jars pouring the boiling syrup and cinnamon over them.

5. Flylike glued to him by suction we rode as one person whipping a great wind around us.

6. Solid in my good dress I was proud and could ask.

7. Something dark and wavering fringed like a flower's mouth was collecting in the room between us.

8. His eyes were black sly snapping with sparks.

9. I looked up at her hopeless.

10. Watching Zelda walk in front of me so sure of herself and thin with a cutting edge with a mind that wasn't made up with pure white anklets and careful curls I felt an amazement.

Absolute Phrases

Sometimes the phrase that needs to be set off is called an *absolute*. Although it's not a clause, it has some of the characteristics of a clause because it's often made up of a noun or pronoun that's followed by a participle.

However, a participle is not a verb that can function on its own to make a statement about a subject. A participle, in its present tense form, is a verb that ends in -*ing* (for example, *loving, deciding,* and *speaking*), or in its past tense form, is used with a helping verb such as *have* (for example, have *baked,* have *traded,* have *given,* and have *lost*).

The absolute phrases appear in italics in these sentences by Erdrich:

a. I heard the rush of air brakes, *gears grinding only inches from my head.*
b. He was so relaxed on his back, *hat tipped on his face,* that at first I did not think he was dead.

Notice that, in sentence a, if you changed the participle *grinding* to *grind* or *ground,* you'd be changing the absolute phrase into a clause. In sentence b, if you added the helping verb *was* to the phrase, you'd be turning it into a clause.

Find the absolute phrase in each of the following sentences and insert the required punctuation:

c. The giant cartoon outline of a cat eyes fringed in pink neon winked and switched its glittering tail.

d. Her mouth the lipstick darkly blurred now tipped unevenly toward his.

e. Jerking the baby up ankles pinned in the forks of her fingers she

repositioned the triangle of cloth under his bottom.

[ANSWERS: (The absolute phrases are in italics.) c. The giant cartoon outline of a
cat, *eyes fringed in pink neon,* winked and switched its glittering tail;   d. Her
mouth, *the lipstick darkly blurred now,* tipped unevenly toward his;   e. Jerking the
baby up, *ankles pinned in the forks of her fingers,* she repositioned the triangle of cloth
under his bottom.]

Phrases in Compound and Complex Sentences

In this unit so far, most examples have shown a phrase attached to a simple
sentence. But a phrase—or even several phrases—also can be used in a
compound or complex sentence, which will then need punctuation for at least
two different reasons. Let's look at this example from *Love Medicine:*

> *Like the butter,* there was a surplus of babies on the reservation, *and* we
> seemed to get unexpected shipments from time to time.

You can see that here we have an intro phrase, *Like the butter,* and we also have
a compound sentence formed with the conjunction *and* between the two clauses.
        Read aloud and punctuate each of the following sentences. Then label each
one as either *compound* or *complex.* (Label and underline clauses if needed.)

a. We held each other's arms tight and manly when we got to the bor-

der. _____

b. His thoughts swam between us hidden under rocks disappearing in weeds and I was

fishing for them dangling my own words like baits and lures. _____

c. When he thought of June for instance she was a young girl who fed him black

plums. _____

d. The hollyhocks were choked with pigweed and the stones that lined the driveway

always painted white or blue were flaking back to gray. _____

[ANSWERS: a. complex, has the conjunction *when,* needs commas before and after
tight and manly;   b. compound, has the conjunction *and,* needs commas before and
after *hidden under rocks,* after *disappearing in weeds,* and before *dangling my own
words . . . ;*   c. complex, has the conjunction *When,* needs commas before and
after *for instance;*   d. compound, has the conjunction *and,* needs commas after
pigweed and before and after *always painted white or blue.*]

"Language Medicine"

While you're writing and revising your essays—whether they're narrative, expository, or argumentative—from time to time, try some of Louise Erdrich's moves. Don't let yourself form clause after clause, creating an overload of simple sentences or an endless train of compound and complex sentences. Instead, reduce some of those clauses to phrases. A dose of this kind of "language medicine" can add strength and grace to your writing.

UNIT 4:   Other Useful Comma Rules

This unit will discuss several other important rules for inserting commas.

Using Commas in a Series

One of the most natural uses of the comma is for separating more than two items in a series, or list, within a sentence. The items might be three or more nouns, adjectives, verbs, prepositional phrases, or almost anything. For example,

a.   Donna Shalala, the chancellor of the University of Wisconsin in Madison, has said that the three major problems on college campuses today are *racial tension, alcoholism, and date rape.*

In any series, the comma before the word *and* or *or* that connects the last two items is optional. In sentence a, the comma between *tension* and *alcoholism* is required, but the comma between *alcoholism* and *and date rape* is optional. In this particular sentence, it wouldn't matter much if you used the final comma or not, but in some sentences it helps you achieve greater clarity.

Insert a comma or commas in the next example, which is a bit difficult to read correctly without the punctuation:

b.   Most psychoanalysts agree that jealousy is a complicated emotion that

stems from worry about losing something one already possesses wants to

possess or imagines possessing.

Can you see how important it is to insert a comma between *possesses* and *wants?* A comma would also be useful before *or,* but you can see that, unlike the first comma, it's not essential for clarity.

Exercise One   *   PART A

Add commas to separate items in a series in the following sentences. If commas are needed in these sentences for other reasons, they have been supplied already.

1. Jack Kemp once said, "Pro football gave me a good sense of perspective when I entered the political arena. I had already been booed cheered cut sold traded and hanged in effigy."

2. Gourmet cook Julia Child has boldly admitted that some of her favorite foods are hot dogs hamburgers tuna-fish sandwiches jawbreakers and licorice whips.

3. Arguing that it's not a good idea for one woman to stay home and raise one child on a full-time basis, Barbara Ehrenreich writes in her book *The Worst Years of Our Lives,* "No culture on earth outside of mid-century suburban America has ever deployed one woman per child without simultaneously assigning her such major productive activities as weaving farming gathering temple maintenance and tent building."

4. New Orleans's Neville Brothers are Aaron Art Charles and Cyril.

5. Joe Martinez Manuel Pérez Sylvester Herreras Macario García and José Mendoza López are five Mexican Americans who were awarded the U.S. Congressional Medal of Honor for their heroism in World War II.

PART B

Continue to follow the directions given in part A.

1. "Happiness is having a large loving caring close-knit family in another city." (George Burns)

2. According to *Rolling Stone* magazine, the Red Hot Chili Peppers headlined a rock festival that also featured several aspects of 1990s youth culture, including a tattoo artist a body piercer exhibits of art a collection of hot rods and "virtual-reality" and "cyberpunk" demonstrations.

3. Each year the American Council of Life Insurance estimates the economic worth of the average homemaker on the basis of his or her services as a housekeeper a nurse a purchasing agent a cook a chauffeur and an economist.

4. The five most common names in the United States are Smith Johnson Williams Brown and Jones.

5. Miller Davis Wilson Anderson and Taylor rank sixth through tenth among the most common American names.

Using Commas in Adjective Pairs

When do you use a comma between two adjacent adjectives? Let's look at two contrasting examples:

adj   adj   n

a.   She was a *beautiful old* woman.

adj   adj   n

b.   She was a *beautiful, fascinating* woman.

The adjectives in sentence a seem tightly connected—*beautiful* is describing *old woman*—so they don't take a comma. However, the adjectives in sentence b are more loosely connected—both *beautiful* and *fascinating* are describing *woman*—so they do take a comma. When you have two adjectives in a row, ask yourself this question: Could you insert the word *and* between them and still have a smooth-sounding phrase or sentence? If so, the adjectives should probably be separated with a comma. For example, "She was a *beautiful and old* woman" sounds a little odd, doesn't it? But "She was a *beautiful and fascinating* woman" sounds fine. Insert the comma where the *and* would appear. (But don't use the comma if you decide to keep the *and* in.)

Another way to decide whether a comma is needed is to switch the order of the adjectives and see if the sentence or phrase is still smooth sounding. If you can reverse the order of the adjectives, use a comma between them. For example, "She was *an old beautiful* woman" sounds a little awkward, while "She was a *fascinating, beautiful* woman" sounds all right.

Often the first test—Can you insert *and* between the adjectives?—is a better basis for your decision. If you look at these correct examples adapted from articles in a recent issue of *The New York Times Book Review* (Dec. 30, 1990), you'll see that, often, the "*and*-insertion" test more clearly indicates the need for a comma than does the "switching" test. The word *and* could easily be inserted between the adjectives in each example:

adj   adj   n

Andrei Sakharov is described as having a "great, courageous heart."

adj

Ernest Hemingway is described as journalist Martha Gellhorn's "fraudu-

adj   n

lent, drunken competitor" in World War II.

> $\overset{\text{adj}}{}\quad\overset{\text{adj}}{}\quad\overset{\text{n}}{}$
>
> Bertrand Russell is described as having done "powerful, original work in
>
> logic and mathematics."
>
> $\overset{\text{adj}}{}$
>
> Kate Chopin is described as having a preoccupation with "restless,
>
> $\overset{\text{adj}}{}\quad\overset{\text{n}}{}$
>
> dissatisfied women who yearn for freedom . . ."
>
> $\overset{\text{adj}}{}\quad\overset{\text{adj}}{}\quad\overset{\text{n}}{}$
>
> Ludwig Wittgenstein is described as desiring a "Platonic, childless union"
>
> with Marguerite Respinger.

More than any other punctuation rule you've learned so far, this one—at least in application—involves a "gray area." Whether or not to insert a comma between adjectives is often a judgment call, and on a particular item two very competent writers might differ. So you need to understand the intent of the rule but not to fuss too much about individual cases.

Let's try an exercise.

* Exercise Two

In the following sentence pairs, insert a comma between adjectives where needed. In each pair, one sentence will call for a comma and one will not.

1a. I bought an *interesting antique* book.

b. I bought an *interesting thought-provoking* book.

2a. He put the frozen yogurt in a *crisp crumbly* cone.

b. He put the frozen yogurt in a *crisp new* cone.

3a. She is a *patient well-trained* child.

b. She is a *patient three-year-old* child.

4a. We looked into the *sinister purple* shadows.

b. We looked into the *sinister bleak* shadows.

5a. Let's find an *inexpensive Italian* restaurant.

b. Let's find an *inexpensive unpretentious* restaurant.

Exercise Three

In each of the listed phrases you'll find two adjectives in a row. Insert a comma between adjectives where appropriate.

1. that cloudless windless morning

2. her perfumed bejeweled hands

3. a long menthol cigarette

4. the happiest suburban community

5. a dull orange glow in the sky

6. the washable cloth diapers

7. his kind caring face

8. a panicky hysterical feeling

9. two warm wool coats

10. their gleaming greed-filled eyes

* ## Exercise Four

In each of the listed phrases you'll find two adjectives in a row. Insert a comma between adjectives where appropriate.

1. his thick black stubble

2. your mysterious mischievous grin

3. a murderous sadistic wish

4. her nice little ways

5. their fancy rodeo shirts

6. a puckered red apple

7. the churning twisting river

8. a slick flat-faced salesman

9. the buzzing yellow arc lamps

10. an enthusiastic energetic teacher

Four More Uses of the Comma

You should know about four more uses of the comma.

Between City and State

Commas are always used between the name of a city and the name of a state, province, or nation. For example:

Zap, North Dakota
Newark, New Jersey
Winnipeg, Manitoba

Warsaw, Poland
Arkadelphia, Arkansas
Santiago, Chile

Normally, a comma also follows the state, province, or nation, unless the item falls at the end of the sentence or in some other position that requires a different punctuation mark. For example:

> I visited Santiago, Chile, in May.
> In May I visited Santiago, Chile.

In Dates

Commas are used to separate the day of the month from the year in a date. For example:

January 16, 1792
December 3, 2001

April 23, 1949
October 31, 1902

As in the case of city and state, a comma also is generally used after the year:

> On March 29, 1984, my daughter was born.
> My son was born on July 25, 1979.

In Cases of Direct Address

Commas are used in cases of direct address—sentences in which someone is spoken to or addressed and in which their name (or some form of it or substitute for it) is used. The comma sets off the person's name from the rest of the sentence. For example:

> *Lindsay,* how are you feeling?
> Please get in the car now, *Julia.*
> *Doctor,* let me thank you again.
> Give me a kiss, *you sweet thing.*
> *Man,* you better watch your step.

In Tag Questions

A comma is used to separate a tag question from the rest of the sentence in which it appears. A tag question is a little question "tagged on" at the end of a declarative sentence. For example:

> Your knee is bothering you again, *isn't it?*
> Her cousin arrived around midnight, *didn't he?*
> You'll join us for coffee, *won't you?*

UNIT 5:   Reviewing Commas

Before you begin these cumulative exercises on the comma, take time to review the rules and guidelines presented in units 1, 2, 3, and 4.

In the following exercises, you'll often find that you need to think about more than one rule or guideline per sentence. Before you begin, examine this example. Which two rules are called to mind by this sentence?

"Between the ages of 2 and 7, children reach conclusions about who they are, how they'll relate to other people, and how well they'll do in life." (Dr. Matti Gershenfeld)

Exercises

* **Exercise One**

Add commas where necessary or where they would be helpful to your reader. Some sentences may call for no commas. *Remember:* It's just as important to know when to leave commas out as to know when to put them in.

1. On January 25 1989 Michael Jordan scored his ten-thousandth point in the National Basketball Association and on January 26 1990 he became the Chicago Bulls' all-time leading scorer.

2. "It is a sin to believe evil of others but it is seldom a mistake." (a quote from American writer and critic H.L. Mencken)

3. When Bessie Smith sang songs became legends.

4. Michael Newman who was a protege of W.H. Auden and is currently an editor of *The Paris Review* has created The Poetry Processor and two other computer programs to help poets.

5. Arnold Schwartzenegger in a quest to terminate flab has said that women who follow a bodybuilding and weight-lifting routine will not normally run the risk of developing a masculine physique.

6. Contrary to myth there is no way to increase the body's rate of burning up one-half ounce of alcohol per hour not even with strong black coffee.

7. Johnny Ace an important figure in early rock and roll died backstage in the Houston City Auditorium on December 24 1954 while playing Russian roulette.

8. The percentage of Americans who believe that God performs miracles is 82.

9. According to research on the causes of alcoholism men drink because it makes

them feel more masculine and women drink because it makes them feel more feminine.

10. Catgut is actually derived from sheep not from cats.

Exercise Two

Add commas where necessary or where they would be helpful to your reader. The items here are, again, assorted bits of information.

1. Lupe Anguiano a civil rights leader has played an important role in the movement to gain equal rights and full participation for Mexican-American women.

2. Developed in Vienna Austria in the late 1920s Pez candy made a big hit in the United States in the 1950s when its famous automatic dispenser was introduced.

3. "A room without books is like a body without soul." (Cicero)

4. According to the *Guinness Sports Record Book* for 1990–91 the oldest person to earn a black belt in Tae Kwon Do which is a Korean form of karate is Lucille "Killer" Thompson of Danville Illinois who attained that level of expertise in 1986 when she was 90 years old.

5. Bruxism the habit of grinding one's teeth during sleep is also called bruxomania.

6. All U.S. currency is printed by the Bureau of Engraving and Printing in Washington D.C. in large crisp sheets of 32 bills.

7. Aaron Neville who has one of the great falsetto voices in pop music says that his love of falsetto started when he went to the movies as a child and heard the cowboys yodel.

8. Because the TV show "I Love Lucy" was so immensely popular in 1951 the Marshall Field's store in Chicago closed early on Mondays allowing its employees to get home in time to watch.

9. Caused by the sudden contraction of the diaphragm and the intercostal muscles that brace the ribs hiccups seem to serve no beneficial purpose.

10. Adults who have normal vision can discriminate 120 to 150 different colors across the visible spectrum.

Now let's look at sentences that appear in a larger context. These exercises might seem more difficult, but they really aren't. Just take the sentences one by one. If you know the comma rules and guidelines, you'll do fine. Larger-context exercises help you transfer new skills to your own writing.

* Exercise Three

Add commas where necessary or helpful in this short piece on shaving.

1   If you are a man who hates shaving but does it anyway the statistics-loving

2   American razor industry can provide you with an amazing array of facts to contemplate

3   during your daily ritual. A single whisker for example grows an average of 0.015 inch a

4   day. That doesn't sound like much but it comes out to 27.5 feet during the 75 years of

5   the average man's lifetime. Most men shave 5.5 times a week devoting almost 12

6   minutes to each shave. Over an entire lifetime that's 3,350 hours of shaving. The

7   average beard contains 15,500 hairs and covers a third of a square foot. A man who

8   saved all his clipped whiskers would have to wait 16 years before he collected a pound.

9   More than 73 percent of all American men use blades and shaving cream and the rest

10 use electric razors.

11 Although some people might think of shaving as a male activity American women

12 buy a wide variety of razors and other hair removal products and they generally begin

13 shaving before men. When the average American boy starts shaving at the age of 15 his

14 all-American sister has already been scraping and nicking for two full years.

Exercise Four

Add commas where necessary or where they would be helpful in this paragraph on the slowing of the earth's rotation.

1   Many centuries ago ancient Chinese seers foretold events by using bones and

2   tortoise shells. Now modern astronomers by examining the inscriptions on those bones

3   and shells are able to estimate the rate at which the Earth's rotation is slowing down.

4   Dr. Kevin Pang an astronomer at the Jet Propulsion Laboratory in Pasadena California

5   says that each day in the year 1302 was shorter by 47/1,000 of a second than each of our

6   days at the end of the twentieth century. Astronomers mathematicians East Asian

7   language professors and other scientists collaborated to study the shell and bone

8   remnants that were found in the excavation of the city of Anyang which was once the

9   capital of the Shang Dynasty. The remnants that they studied were as old as the

10   fourteenth century B.C. After the researchers found inscriptions that described a

11   particular eclipse they used computers to determine exactly when the solar eclipse was

12   seen and how fast the planet must have been spinning for the people in Anyang to see

13   the eclipse on that day.

* Exercise Five

Add commas where necessary or where they would be helpful in this brief paragraph on a sports first.

1   According to George Gipe's *Great American Sports Book* the first recorded

2   baseball game between a black team and a white team was played in Chicago Illinois on

3   July 9 1871. Before a crowd of five hundred the Uniques who were black beat the Alerts

4   who were white by a score of 17 to 16. The *San Francisco Chronicle* had this comment

5   on the historic occasion: "The play was creditable on both sides and the contest quite

6   exciting and close throughout."

Exercise Six

Add commas where they are necessary or helpful in these short paragraphs on pasta.

1   Americans now enjoy over two billion pounds of delicious nutritious pasta a year

2   outranking every other country except Italy in consumption of the Mediterranean

3   staple. Thomas Jefferson was the man who started the American version of the craze

4   when he returned from Naples in the eighteenth century with four crates of

5   "maccarony." Now there are over 150 varieties of pasta including spaghetti linguine

6   rigatoni fettucine mostacholli agnolotti and ziti just to name a few.

7   In addition there are almost as many pasta accessories available. Pasta-making

8   machines drying machines cutting wheels tomato presses ravioli crimpers and electric

9   cheese graters are some of the most popular luxury items bought by pasta lovers who

10 want to prepare theirs at home.

11   Is the final product good for you? Despite its undeserved reputation as a fattening

12 food pasta actually has about the same number of calories as potatoes. The trick is to

13 watch the calories in the sauces and cheese toppings. Low in both sodium and fat pasta

14 is healthfully high in calcium iron niacin phosphorous protein riboflavin and thiamine.

UNIT 6:   Using Semicolons

The Basic Function of the Semicolon

The basic function of the semicolon (;) is simple. A semicolon generally is used between independent clauses that are not linked by a conjunction. In other words, a semicolon is used where you could use a capital letter and a period but you don't want such a strong break between clauses. The period separates; the semicolon connects. Because the semicolon connects, it is used only when the information in the two clauses is related in some logical way.

Here are some good examples. Notice how the statements on both sides of the semicolon are related or balanced:

a.   Muddy Waters is often called the most influential blues performer in music history; Sister Rosetta Tharpe is frequently named the most influential gospel singer.

b.   The ratio of new engineers to new lawyers each year in Japan is ten to one; in the United States it is one to ten.

c.   The average eight- to twelve-year-old American child can name 5.2 alcoholic beverages; the same child can name only 4.8 U.S. presidents.

d.   At one time all hurricanes were named after women; now we are as likely to have an Arnold or a Bernie as an Anna or a Betty.

Sometimes what is on one side of the semicolon is not simply one independent clause but rather what might be called an independent combination. For example, before or after the semicolon, you might find a main and a subordinate clause combined. But you'll *never* find a subordinate clause alone. Consider these correct examples:

e. The person whose face is on the $1,000 bill is Grover Cleveland; the $100,000 bill shows the face of Woodrow Wilson.

f. The golden retriever is a common choice for a family pet because it bites less often than any other dog; the German police dog is a less likely choice because it bites more often than any other breed.

Some of the sentences in the exercises will have these independent combinations.

Exercise One

Use semicolons to punctuate these old vaudeville jokes.

1. Old mailmen never die they just lose their zip.

2. Bowling is a great game for kids it gets them off the streets and into the alleys.

3. Old magicians never die they just lose their hare.

4. He grew up on a really small farm it was so small that the cows had to give condensed milk.

5. My aunt is always complaining about the shape of her legs she says she has calves only a cow could love.

6. My uncle loves his new job as a bus driver he always did want to tell people where to get off.

7. I really don't know how smart my sister's fiancé is he just stayed up all night studying for his blood test.

8. My mother is the most modest woman in the world she is so modest that she pulls down the shade when she changes her mind.

9. Old truck drivers never die they just can't make the grade.

10. Old quarterbacks never die they just pass away.

Question for Discussion: Why do you think the old jokes in exercise one lend themselves to demonstrating the use of the semicolon? How would they sound if you added coordinating or subordinating conjunctions instead?

Exercise Two

Insert one semicolon into each sentence. If it's helpful to you to do so, label the independent clauses in these sentences. Punctuation that is needed for other reasons has already been added.

1. Upon his election in 1988 George Bush became the twelfth Episcopalian to occupy the White House more U.S. presidents have come from that religious denomination than from any other.

2. Small handguns cause about 22,000 deaths in the United States each year they also cause over 16,000 serious injuries.

3. Linda Bloodworth-Thomason, the highly successful writer and producer who created "Designing Women" and "Evening Shade," blames television for giving women a powerless image she maintains that most programming depicts women as cowardly, stupid, and untrustworthy.

4. Per capita, the biggest wine-drinking country in the world is Italy the major consumer of beer is Czechoslovakia.

5. The word *flirt* comes from *fleureter* this old French word means to touch lightly or move from flower to flower.

6. "A unanimous chorus of approval is not an assurance of survival authors who please everyone at once are quickly exhausted." (André Gide)

7. Jacqueline Cochrane, an American pilot, was the first woman in the world to break the sound barrier, which she did in a dive Jacqueline Auriol, a French test pilot, was the first woman to break the sound barrier with her plane in level flight.

8. *K* is the first call letter of most U.S. television stations west of the Mississippi *W* is the first call letter of most stations east of the Mississippi.

9. Many years ago Milton S. Hershey, the candy man, founded a school for orphans the school still retains 77 percent of the voting control of his company through ownership of stocks.

10. "We know through painful experience that freedom is never voluntarily given by the

    oppressor it must be demanded by the oppressed." (Dr. Martin Luther King, Jr.)

Using Semicolons with Logical Connectives

Sometimes, just after the semicolon, a writer will use a word or a phrase to help the reader see the nature of the relationship between the clauses. This word or phrase is called a *logical connective* or a *conjunctive adverb*. Let's look again at an example sentence from the beginning of the unit:

   a.   The ratio of new engineers to new lawyers each year in Japan is ten to one; in the United States it is one to ten.

Sentence a is fine as it is, but it might be even clearer to a reader if the writer added a logical connective to show contrast. Such an addition might result in sentences b or c:

   b.   The ratio of new engineers to new lawyers each year in Japan is ten to one; *however,* in the United States it is one to ten.

   c.   The ratio of new engineers to new lawyers each year in Japan is ten to one; *on the other hand,* in the United States it is one to ten.

Sentences d and e, which reflect slight variations in word order, would also be fine:

   d.   The ratio of new engineers to new lawyers each year in Japan is ten to one; in the United States, *however,* it is one to ten.

   e.   The ratio of new engineers to new lawyers each year in Japan is ten to one; in the United States, *on the other hand,* it is one to ten.

All five of these sentences are correct, and, in all cases, *it is the semicolon that you should think of as connecting the clauses.* Where logical connectives are used after semicolons, they function as an introductory phrase that precedes the subject of a sentence. They are not conjunctions. They don't link the clauses.

As you can see, a comma normally is used after the logical connective. If the logical connective is embedded, then two commas are used.

Here are some of the most common logical connectives that are used after semicolons. They are arranged in several groups, and those in each group are synonymous or closely related to each other in meaning:

- for example, for instance
- however, on the other hand
- nevertheless
- also, in addition, furthermore
- therefore, consequently, as a result
- actually, in fact, as a matter of fact
- then, now, later (and other adverbs of time)

Caution: It is *not* the case that every time you use one of the words or phrases just listed you'll necessarily use a semicolon with it. All of these words and phrases are used in other ways in sentences, too. If you use a semicolon, always check to make sure you have independent clauses on each side of it. Here are examples of how the same words and phrases would be used *without* semicolons:

a. We had counted on hiking this morning. The weather, *however,* did not cooperate with our plans.
b. Many people are going back to school later in life. My brother, *for example,* is now starting law school at the age of 37.

Remember: **There are no words or phrases that are automatically always used with a semicolon. You need to check for independent clauses.**

Exercise Three

Select *five* sentences from exercise two. Write them on your own paper and add appropriate logical connectives. Don't forget to add commas after or around the logical connectives.

* Exercise Four

Punctuate the following sentences on Elizabeth Cady Stanton, using semicolons and commas. Some sentences may call for no punctuation.

1. Elizabeth Cady Stanton was one of the shining lights of the nineteenth century she was also one of the first leaders of the movement for women's rights.

2. The emancipation of women was one of her major concerns the abolition of slavery was another.

3. In 1840 she and her husband traveled to London for the World Anti-Slavery Convention however the convention's delegates voted to exclude women.

4. For years Stanton continued to work for full human rights for blacks and women.

5. After the Civil War however she broke her connection with those who favored voting rights for black men but not for women of any color.

6. Later Elizabeth Cady Stanton joined ranks with Susan B. Anthony together they founded the National Woman Suffrage Association in 1869.

7. On behalf of women Stanton used all her persuasive powers on California's Senator Aaron A. Sargent as a result he sponsored a woman suffrage amendment to the U.S. Constitution in 1878.

8. That amendment was reintroduced and voted down every single year until 1919 then it was finally approved and officially became the 19th Amendment to the Constitution a year later.

9. One of the last talks given by Elizabeth Cady Stanton was entitled "The Solitude of the Self" it is considered one of the greatest essays in American literature.

10. In it Stanton argues that throughout life each human being is alone in an essential way consequently each individual should come to "own" as much of herself or himself as possible.

A Less Common Use for the Semicolon

Another use for semicolons can be helpful in your college writing, especially in more formal assignments such as research papers: The semicolon is also used to separate items in a list when commas are already used for other purposes within those items. This is true even when the items between the semicolons are not independent clauses. For example:

> "It was once said that the moral test of government is how that government treats those who are in the dawn of life, the children; those who are in the twilight of life, the elderly; and those who are in the shadows of life—the sick, the needy and the handicapped."   (Hubert H. Humphrey)

Exercise Five

On your own paper, write a sentence in the style just described, using semicolons to separate listed items that already contain commas. If you're stuck for subject matter, try making a list of three or four friends, and put in a little description of each.

Exercise Six

Choose *one* of the following items—either item a or item b—and, on your own paper, write a sentence that uses semicolons to separate items in which commas are already used for other purposes.

a. Write a sentence about famous Arab Americans. You can use this information: F. Murray Abraham, the actor, won an Oscar for his performance in *Amadeus*. George Mitchell is the majority leader of the U.S. Senate. Michael DeBakey is an innovative, world-class heart surgeon. Casey Kasem is a well-known figure in radio, television, and the music industry. Kahlil Gibran is famous for his philosophically-oriented poetry. Quarterback Doug Flutie won the Heisman Trophy. Ralph Nader has positively affected the life of each one of us with his crusades on behalf of consumers' rights. The pop singer Tiffany is of Arab-American descent also.

b. Write a sentence about the factors that made the February 9, 1964, appearance of the Beatles on "The Ed Sullivan Show" such a big event in the history of pop music. Roger Catlin of *The Hartford Courant* mentions as one factor the presence of television in a large number of homes. He also cites the heavy promotion that preceded the Beatles' appearance. An additional reason he mentions was the nation's need for escape and entertainment less than three months after the assassination of John F. Kennedy. Finally, he offers the skill, energy, and exuberance of the band itself as another explanation.

UNIT 7:   Using Colons

For Lists

Sometimes you will want to use a colon (:) to set up a list, but to do this, you need to create a special kind of sentence. You don't use a colon simply because you have a list. If that were the case, you would have been using them earlier in the chapter, when you worked with commas to separate items in a series.

Normally, in academic writing, the special kind of sentence that uses a colon before a list has a direct object or a complement after the verb and before the colon. This direct object or complement (or a word or phrase that functions in a similar way) appears in the setup—the part of the sentence that precedes the listed items. Following the subject and verb, the complement or direct object gives the setup a finished look and often sums up the common bond between all the items in the list.

First, let's look at what *not* to do. *Don't do this:*

Wrong: *Paul Robeson was:* a singer, an actor, a writer, an athlete, and an internationally acclaimed champion of human rights.

Instead of putting a colon right after the verb *was,* you'll need to create a more substantial setup to precede the listed items. Here are some correct revisions. Please label the subject complement (*sub com*) or direct object (*do*) in each setup:

Right: *Paul Robeson was many things:* a singer, an actor, a writer, an athlete, and an internationally acclaimed champion of human rights.

Paul Robeson was many men in one: a singer, an actor, a writer, an athlete, and an internationally acclaimed champion of human rights.

Paul Robeson played five major roles: a singer, an actor, a writer, an athlete, and an internationally acclaimed champion of human rights.

Note that it would be perfectly fine to write a version of this sentence with no colon at all. Writing "Paul Robeson was a singer, an actor, a writer, . . ." is correct. But *if* you decide to use a colon, then precede the items in the list with an *s–v–sub com* or *s–v–do* setup.

Which two of the following sentences are *incorrect?*

a. Penelope named the four dimensions: length, width, depth, and time.
b. The four dimensions are these: length, width, depth, and time.
c. The four dimensions are: length, width, depth, and time.
d. The four dimensions are the following: length, width, depth, and time.
e. The four dimensions include: length, width, depth, and time.

Errors with Including *and* Such As

A common error is the use of a colon after *including* or *such as*. When *including* or *such as* appears in a sentence that has a list, *no punctuation*—no colon, no comma—should be placed directly after either term. (Directly before *including* or *such as* you might have a comma or you might not; that depends on your judgment in each case.)

Study these examples:

Wrong: 1a. Lee had a number of close friends, including: Charles, Frank, Beth, Karen, and Roger.

Right: b. Lee had a number of close friends, including Charles, Frank, Beth, Karen, and Roger.

Right: c. Lee had a number of close friends: Charles, Frank, Beth, Karen, and Roger.

Wrong: 2a. Robin was considering several careers in the medical field, such as: doctor, nurse, medical technologist, or hospital administrator.

Right: b. Robin was considering several careers in the medical field, such as doctor, nurse, medical technologist, or hospital administrator.

Right: c. Robin was considering several careers in the medical field: doctor, nurse, medical technologist, or hospital administrator.

Just remind yourself that, to use a colon, you need a setup that sounds finished and is quite separate and distinct from the items in the list. *Including* and *such as* don't separate the setup from the items in the list; they form a bridge or transition to them. These terms are acceptable to use, but don't use them with a colon.

* **Exercise One**

Use colons and commas to punctuate the following items. Label the subject complement *sub com* and the direct object *do* to help you determine if a sentence has the setup needed for a colon. Some sentences may call for commas only.

1. Recently Video Storyboard Tests named the five most believable celebrities in television commercials Bill Cosby James Garner Bruce Willis Cher and Linda Evans.

2. When Kevin Costner's *Dances with Wolves* was released many critics called it the first truly sympathetic movie about Native Americans. But some film historians mentioned several earlier films with a pro-Indian point of view *The Vanishing American Massacre Broken Arrow The Big Sky Apache Run of the Arrow Cheyenne Autumn* and *Little Big Man.*

3. The five general categories of arthritis are rheumatoid arthritis osteoarthritis gout septic arthritis and ankylosing spondylitis.

4. Research at Ohio State University shows that eight- to twelve-year-olds use over 500 different stress-reducing techniques including nail biting lip chewing thumb sucking hair twisting exercising praying teasing and being aggressive.

5. The Olympic decathlon is made up of ten events the 110-meter hurdles the 100-meter dash the 400-meter dash the 1500-meter run the long jump the high jump the pole vault the javelin throw the discus and the shot put.

Exercise Two

Rewrite the items from exercise one that do not call for a colon as they are written and create setups that do call for colons. Use your own paper.

Exercise Three

Use colons and commas to punctuate the following items. Use the labels *sub com* for subject complement and *do* for direct object to help you determine if a sentence has the setup needed for a colon. Some sentences may call for commas only.

1. It's amazing how many great books were not widely read in their own time. These are some of the classics that never made the best-seller list the year they were

published F. Scott Fitzgerald's *The Great Gatsby* Ernest Hemingway's *A Farewell to Arms* and *The Sun Also Rises* Richard Wright's *Native Son* Carson McCullers's *The Heart Is a Lonely Hunter* James Baldwin's *Go Tell It on the Mountain* and Joyce Carol Oates's *Them.*

2. The planets include Mercury Venus Earth Mars Jupiter Saturn Uranus Neptune and Pluto.

3. Mental-health experts say that a certain degree of jealousy is normal and healthy. In its good aspect jealousy can increase alertness stimulate people and thrust them into action. But when it becomes sick or pathological jealousy is very destructive. Pathological jealousy has three interrelated causes low self-esteem feelings of inadequacy and lack of confidence.

4. The seven best poker hands listed in order from most to least valuable are the following a royal flush a straight flush four of a kind a full house a flush a straight and three of a kind.

5. In his book *The 100* Michael H. Hart listed his choices for the 100 most influential people who ever lived. Toward the top of the list Hart included figures such as Muhammad Jesus Christ Buddha Isaac Newton Confucius Johann Gutenberg and Albert Einstein.

Exercise Four

Rewrite the items from exercise three that do not call for a colon as they are written and create setups that do call for colons. Use your own paper.

When You See the Colon Used in Another Way

If you notice that a colon preceding a list sometimes appears right after a verb in some newspaper and magazine headlines and stories, don't be dismayed. (You'll even notice that it's sometimes used after a verb in certain headings in books.) That's just one of many small differences between the academic style and other styles of writing. When you write your college papers, use the academic style and create those nice, strong setups before your colons.

For Explanations

The colon has another very powerful use. After creating the same kind of *s–v–sub com* or *s–v–do* setup that you created to make a list, you can make an explanation. Look for the colon used this way in newspaper and magazine articles. Once you start looking for it, you'll find it all over the place. Good writers use it often because it's efficient and powerful.

In the following examples, notice that if the explanation is a full sentence, the first word of it may be capitalized. (It also may be left lower case. It's your choice, but be consistent throughout a single piece of writing.)

a. "The essential point is this: that profoundly deaf people show no native disposition whatever to speak." (Dr. Oliver Sacks, on the necessity of sign language)
b. A recent survey revealed one amazing thing: Respondents reported more guilt because of overeating than because of extramarital sex.
c. Many Americans shared a common reaction to the Rodney King verdict: rage.

Do you see how this use of the colon helps you say things in a powerful way and cuts down on wordiness? In a sense, the colon takes the place of words that say "Let me explain what I mean" or "Now I'm going to get specific."

* **Exercise Five**

Insert colons where they are needed. (Capitalize the first word in a full-sentence explanation if you prefer that style.)

1. The epitaph on comedian W.C. Fields's tombstone was his last one-liner "All things considered, I'd rather be in Philadelphia."

2. There is a simple reason for the exploitation of the endangered blue whale a single whale can yield up to 140 barrels of oil.

3. "It was the first female-style revolution no violence and we all went shopping." (Gloria Steinem's description of the fall of the Berlin Wall)

4. Glenn Cunningham set a new world record for the mile in 1934 after overcoming a significant disability he had lost all the toes on his left foot in a fire at the age of eight.

5. "When I think of the price she paid for 'this life,' I regard her as I do all of the other black women throughout history miraculous." (actress Cicely Tyson, on her mother)

Exercise Six

Follow the directions given for exercise five.

1. Students of Mark Twain's life have noticed an interesting coincidence Halley's Comet appeared in the year of his birth, 1835, and again in the year of his death, 1910.

2. Often, heart disease has only one symptom sudden death.

3. In 1990, Walter H. Annenberg, who made a fortune in the communication industry, gave more money to worthy causes than any other American. For instance, Annenberg contributed $50 million to the United Negro College Fund, but in order to get more people involved in the support of UNCF, he built in one catch his $50 million donation was contingent upon UNCF raising $200 million from other sources during a three-year capital campaign.

4. "The mystery story is two stories in one the story of what happened and the story of what appeared to happen." (Mary Roberts Rinehart)

5. In her book *On Being Human,* G. Marian Kinget, a leading scholar of humanistic psychology, opened one chapter with a beautiful example of alliteration "Like life itself, love looms larger than language."

UNIT 8:   Cumulative Review Exercises for the Comma, Semicolon, and Colon

For many students, it's relatively easy to use correct punctuation when applying the rules separately, but it's a different story when the same students look at their own writing and find any and every type of sentence turning up. For this reason, it's a good idea to do some cumulative exercises on what you've learned so far about sentence combinations and punctuation. This is the best way to ensure a good transfer of skills to your own writing.

The exercises in this unit provide you with practice on all that you've learned about commas, semicolons, and colons—the workhorses of punctuation. Before you begin, review the rules in units 1 through 7 if you need to.

A Simple Way to Review and Warm up

Here's a simple way to review the rules you've studied: Write a short, uncomplicated sentence that has two "chunks" of information. For instance, something like this would do fine:

He came to my house, and he brought some candy.

Then see how many different ways you can rewrite it, using what you've learned so far in chapter 9. For instance, you could create these variations, among many others:

a. He came to my house and brought candy.

b. He came to my house, bringing candy.

c. Bringing candy, he came to my house.

d. The man who came to my house this morning brought candy.

e. James Davis, who came to my house this morning, brought candy.

f. James Davis came to my house; he brought candy.

A Note on Punctuating Direct Quotes

Occasionally, you'll encounter direct quotes in the following exercises. When you do, treat them as you would any other sentence, with this addition: When a quote is introduced by a subject–verb combination, follow that introduction with a comma. For example:

1a.   *The boss said,* "If you do that one more time, I'll have to let you go."

2a.   *The employee replied,* "I'll make sure that I watch my step."

But if the introduction takes the fuller form of a subject–verb–direct object or subject–verb–complement sequence, then use a colon. For example:

1b.   *The boss issued a warning:* "If you do that one more time, I'll have to let you go."

2b.   *The employee made this reply:* "I'll make sure that I watch my step."

The setups for colons used to introduce direct quotes and for colons used before explanations, which you studied in unit 7, have the same formats.

What These Exercises Are Really About: Creating Sentences, Not Just Punctuating Them

As you work through the exercises in this unit, it's important to realize that you're doing more than just putting in punctuation marks. As you look at the structure of sentence after sentence, you're really continuing to absorb and solidify your knowledge of important, useful sentence types. Whenever you write while you're working with this material, make a conscious effort to think about the types of sentences you're constructing and watch the extent to which they match the structures here.

Let's start with some jokes.

* Exercise One

Add commas, semicolons, and colons where they are needed or where you think they would be helpful to the reader. Some sentences may call for no further punctuation, and some can be punctuated correctly in more than one way. (These may be some of the worst examples of humor you've ever come across, but even bad jokes might make practicing punctuation less painful.)

1. Harold had always dreamed of being an attorney for a nudist colony but there was just one problem they didn't allow suits.

2. Gertie spent months trying to get a new car for her husband but she finally gave up when she couldn't find anyone who was willing to make the trade.

3. Butchers are known to be funny because they're always cutting up.

4. Ernie the electrician down the block says that he has a valid professional reason for reading the newspaper every day he needs to keep up on current events.

5. It looked like a good match when the dentist married the manicurist but it wasn't long before they started fighting tooth and nail.

6. There's one nice thing about being the mother of an archeologist archeologists always love their mummies.

7. Any tree surgeon who is really dedicated to her work will go out on a limb for you.

8. When Barney announced that he wanted to become a chimney sweep his father said "Soot yourself."

9. If you're in the offshore drilling business it's always the same old thing oily to bed and oily to rise.

10. I could never understand why Oscar didn't become a great trombone player he was always a great one for letting things slide.

Exercise Two

Add commas, semicolons, and colons where they are needed or where they would be helpful to the reader. Here are a few more jokes to keep you groaning.

1. Elsie is a terrific baby doctor and she'll probably be even better when she grows up.

2. When Ralph started to play the electric guitar he never wore any underwear because he had been told that you really have to watch out for shorts.

3. Olive used to go out with a really good-looking big-hearted X-ray technician but after a while she just didn't see anything in him anymore.

4. Betty wants to be a great magician when she grows up even now she can just walk down the street and turn into a department store.

5. Floyd's paper is cleverly written but superficial maybe he believes that it's better to be glib than to perceive.

6. My aunt did so well in the logging business that she finally had to open up a branch office.

7. An electrolysist's motto is simple "Hair today gone tomorrow."

8. I knew a painter who wanted to do his mother-in-law in oil but he couldn't find a big enough vat.

9. I don't know how the night watchman earned his retirement benefits he never worked a day in his life.

10. Sylvia an old newspaperwoman finally went into another line of work she just couldn't make any money selling old newspapers.

* Exercise Three

Add commas, semicolons, and colons where they are needed or where they would be helpful to the reader. Some items may require no punctuation.

1. The philosopher Erasmus once lived in the city of Freiburg however he was compelled to move when the constant ringing of the church bells interrupted his studies.

2. Jupiter rotates faster than any other planet completing one rotation in about ten hours.

3. Ellen DeGeneres a stand-up comic claims that her grandmother started walking five miles a day when she was sixty. "She's 97 today" says DeGeneres "and we don't know where the hell she is."

4. Men who smoke cigarettes throughout most of their lives are likely to die 18 years earlier than men who never take up the habit.

5. "Good judgment comes from experience and experience comes from bad judgment." (W. Burnham, Dartmouth College coach)

6. In order from one to ten the most consumed foods in the United States are these milk and cream potatoes beef refined sugar canned vegetables fresh noncitrus fruits pork chicken eggs and fresh citrus fruits.

7. "As the World Turns" which premiered on April 2 1956 was the highest-rated show on any major television network for almost a decade.

8. According to *Newsweek* magazine Nebraska Arkansas Idaho and Utah have much healthier job-growth rates than most other states.

9. When men and women graduate from college they can expect to earn roughly the same salaries only if they majored in accounting or engineering in other fields men are still offered more money for the same work.

10. The National Institute on Drug Abuse offers us a shocking statistic over 75 million Americans take sedatives or tranquilizers.

Exercise Four

Add commas, semicolons, and colons where they are needed or where they would be helpful to the reader. Again, some sentences may require no punctuation.

1. Demonstrating his chivalry and good taste Liberace once refused to read a commercial message that asked "Girls do you have briarpatch legs?" The sponsor was not amused and Liberace's show was canceled.

2. Nuts are nutritious but they are not a low-calorie food for example a cup of almonds has 850 calories.

3. According to the *Dictionary of Misinformation* the U.S. Constitution says nothing about the president's cabinet in fact the cabinet is just an American tradition not a legal necessity.

4. *Rolling Stone* magazine called Sinead O'Connor "the first superstar of the nineties" she regards her commercial success as inexplicable because she says that her songs are so personal.

5. Bill "Bonjangles" Robinson was America's premier tap dancer but he could also claim another distinction Robinson held the world's record for running 100 yards backwards.

6. The word *pica* means a bizarre craving to eat substances such as dirt clay hair mothballs burnt matches and laundry starch. This compulsion is very rare but when it occurs it is often related to pregnancy or hysteria.

7. When female swimmers from an Eastern bloc nation were accused of steroid use at the 1976 Montreal Summer Olympics because of their allegedly deep voices their coach defended them by saying "We came to swim not sing."

8. Peter Falk who won so many hearts as the rumpled guy in the wrinkled trenchcoat was an accountant in real life long before he was Columbo on TV.

9. Known primarily as a popular psychologist Dr. Joyce Brothers first gained national attention when she appeared on "The $64,000 Question" in 1955 as an expert on boxing.

10. When Louis Armstrong was once asked for a definition of jazz he said that anyone who has to ask will never know.

Punctuating Longer Pieces

Now let's try some items that are a little longer. If you take the sentences in the following exercises one by one, which is what you need to do when you edit your own writing, you'll see that they are no more difficult than the sentences in the preceding exercises.

* ## Exercise Five

Add commas, semicolons, and colons.

1. Although most people associate croissants with the French those flaky little pastries are actually Austrian in origin. Invented in the seventeenth century croissants were made in the shape of a crescent because the bakers of Vienna wanted to celebrate the city's successful defense against the Turks. A crescent shape was a prominent part of the Turkish flag consequently an Austrian who ate a croissant was symbolically demolishing and consuming the enemy.

2. Alice Paul the founder of the National Women's Party marched on Washington with five thousand others in 1913 demanding the right of women to vote. Although their efforts were later successful on the day of the march the women and their supporters were laughed at spit upon hit and burned by the lighted cigars of bystanders. Paul was also the person who submitted the first version of the Equal Rights Amendment to the U.S. Congress ten years later.

3. When Berry Gordy founded the Motown record company in Detroit in 1963 few could have predicted how many musicians his organization would catapult to success. Some of the most famous acts on the Motown label were Diana Ross and the Supremes Martha and the Vandellas Gladys Knight and the Pips the Four Tops the Temptations Smokey Robinson and Jr. Walker and the All Stars.

Exercise Six

Add commas, semicolons, and colons.

1. Because human subjects became too hot and restless under the intense studio lights early television producers made Felix the Cat the first television personality. In a

1929 experiment they placed a statute of Felix on a turntable and transmitted the image all the way from New York to Kansas.

2. Dinah Shore a singer and actress once tried to claim an income-tax deduction for gowns that she had worn for television and other business-related functions. At first the Internal Revenue Service refused to allow the deduction but after she met with auditors and modeled her gowns for them the IRS reversed itself. The idea of the new IRS ruling was simple a dress can be claimed as a professional expense if it is too tight to sit down in.

3. In a recent study Swedish researchers attempted to use humor to help patients with painful muscular problems caused by minor depression. Six female outpatients met with three good-natured jolly nurses at a health-care center for 13 weeks. During the course of treatment they did nothing but watch funny movies listen to comedy records read comedy books and encourage one another to look for the humor in everyday life. There was one thing that they *didn't* do they didn't talk about their problems. The doctors who supervised the project devised a rating scale to keep track of patients' reactions for example a "4" meant a laugh and a "5" meant a hearty laugh. The researchers reporting their results in an article in the *Journal of the American Medical Association* claimed that humor was a significant help to the women in finding relief from their symptoms.

* **Exercise Seven**

Add commas, semicolons, and colons.

1. The Volstead Act which banned the manufacture transportation sale use and import or export of alcohol became the 18th Amendment to the U.S. Constitution in spite of a veto by President Woodrow Wilson. Prohibition became official on January 17 1920 and ironically that date was also Alphonse Capone's twenty-first birthday. Who was Alphonse Capone? Better known as Al Capone he was for many years

America's most celebrated criminal and he made a multimillion dollar fortune on bootleg whiskey. At its height his empire included brothels breweries gambling casinos and speakeasies. Capone who had a certain way with words once said "Everybody calls me a racketeer. I call myself a businessman. When I sell liquor it's bootlegging. When my patrons serve it on a silver tray on Lake Shore Drive it's hospitality."

2. Buddy Holly an important early figure in rock and roll became a sort of mythic figure and permanent symbol of the 1950s when he died in a plane crash on February 3 1959 while en route from Clear Lake Iowa to Fargo North Dakota. Along with Ritchie Valens and J.P. Richardson also known as "The Big Bopper" Holly originally had planned to travel by bus but at the last minute he and his companions chartered the ill-fated plane. Why were they in a hurry? They wanted to get to Fargo in time to do laundry and catch up on their mail before their next performance. Buddy Holly the co-composer and voice of "Peggy Sue" and "That'll Be the Day" was only 22 when he died.

3. Dr. James P. Comer a professor of child psychiatry at the Yale University Medical School is one of the brightest lights in education today. Dr. Comer was one of five children of an East Chicago steel-mill worker and after their father's early death all five children went on to complete college. After he graduated from the medical school at Howard University in Washington D.C. Dr. Comer entered the field of psychiatry looking for ways to alleviate some of the hopelessness and depression he witnessed among the poor in the nation's capital. His educational model which is now being implemented in many urban schools is based on a simple idea a good school is run like a good family. A school in the Comer model forms a "governance team" of parents teachers psychologists administrators and representatives from such groups as the cafeteria and custodial staffs. The team plans academic and social events that ensure a great deal of parent involvement and create an atmosphere in

which reading writing and math skills blossom right along with fuller richer self-esteem for the children.

Exercise Eight   PART A

Add commas, semicolons, and colons where they are needed or would be helpful in this description of a major study of the health of migrant farm workers in the United States.

1   According to a report in *The New York Times* a major medical research study has
2   begun in eight counties of northwestern Ohio. When it's completed it will be the first
3   comprehensive study of the health and working conditions of America's 2.5 million
4   migrant farm workers. The study which is funded by a grant from the U.S. Congress is
5   headed by Dr. Marion Moses an assistant clinical professor at the University of
6   California Medical School in San Francisco. Dr. Moses is an expert in environmental and
7   occupational medicine and one of the main tasks of her study is to give about four
8   hundred farm workers and their children a complete battery of tests in three areas
9   vision hearing and coordination. The point is to learn everything possible about workers'
10 potential for neurological damage from long-term exposure to pesticides and other toxic
11 chemicals that are used in modern farming.

12   All migrant farmers who are part of the study are year-round workers. They
13 follow a path of ripening crops moving from the Ohio vegetable fields in the summer to
14 Michigan's orchards in the fall and finally to Florida's harvest of vegetables and citrus
15 fruits in the winter and spring. In order to locate enough year-round workers to make
16 a valid sample Dr. Moses enlisted the help of Baldemar C. Velasquez the president of
17 the Toledo-based Farm Labor Organizing Committee. Velasquez who was recently
18 awarded a $265,000 MacArthur Foundation grant to continue his own work was able to
19 help Dr. Moses make arrangements with workers in farm labor camps and gain
20 permission for her medical units to set up their equipment and conduct their tests on
21 farmers' land.

*   **PART B**

Follow the directions given in part A.

1   Farm workers' unions have struggled long and hard for improvements in working

2   conditions for their members however field workers are still excluded from many of the

3   legal protections that apply to other workers. In addition to being excluded from the

4   federal minimum-wage law migrant farm workers as of the early 1990s are not

5   guaranteed the minimum standards for safety and health conditions that are promised to

6   other workers under the nation's Occupational Safety and Health Act. Even the

7   Environmental Protection Agency (EPA) which is charged with the task of overseeing

8   pesticide use falls short in its efforts to guard the health of migrant workers. The EPA

9   does have guidelines that require farmers who employ migrant workers to keep them

10   out of sprayed fields until the most acute toxicity of the chemicals has worn off. Those

11   guidelines however are often not enforced. Farm workers' organizations have docu-

12   mented many cases where migrants returned to the fields too soon and suffered

13   horrendous effects. One example involves the injury of more than eighty farm workers

14   in Florida when they returned to a vegetable field too soon after it had been sprayed with

15   phosdrin an extremely toxic insecticide. Phosdrin shares a number of components with

16   the nerve gas used in chemical warfare some of the workers sustained serious injuries.

17   The strongest impetus for controlling pesticides and other chemicals used in

18   agriculture now comes from consumer groups that are concerned about the chemicals

19   in our food especially in produce. But as Dr. Moses has pointed out the most immediate

20   and damaging effects are the ones suffered by those who labor in the fields. It is her

21   dream and her expectation that this major study will be the beginning of a serious

22   national effort to protect farm workers and in doing so protect us all.

UNIT 9:   Using Dashes

Some English teachers don't mention the dash (—) because they worry that their students will overuse it, substituting it for other punctuation marks that would be better choices. So here's a caution: Don't use the dash as a general substitute for commas, semicolons, and colons. If you do, you'll end up making a lot of mistakes. The dash can be a powerful aid to a writer, but only when it is used sparingly and in just the right spots.

Guidelines

1. **A dash is used to set off a list that appears before the subject of a sentence.** In example a, notice that the subject of the sentence is the word *all:*

   a. Yale, Harvard, Princeton, Dartmouth, Columbia, Brown, Cornell, and the University of Pennsylvania—all of the Ivy League colleges and universities are located in the Northeast.

   The names of the institutions that help us understand the meaning of the subject *all* are set off from the subject with a dash.

   The second example is from the writing of Edna Ferber, who lists some of the qualities of a writer's emotional life:

   b. "Dislike, displeasure, resentment, fault-finding, imagination, passionate remonstrance, a sense of injustice—they all make fine fuel."

   Notice that the subject is the word *they*. The items in the list, which tell what the word *they* means in this sentence, are set off with a dash.

2. **Two dashes are used to set off a list that appears in mid-sentence.** Here is a striking example from Glenn Collins of *The New York Times:*

   a. "Bette Davis—animated, acute and utterly self-possessed—was perched on a beige silk love seat in her hotel suite on Manhattan's East Side."

   Example b is from the book *Psyche as Hero: Female Heroism and Fictional Form.* The author, Lee R. Edwards, describes why heroism is a human necessity that can be achieved by either sex:

   b. "But if action is important primarily for what it tells us about knowledge, then any action—fighting dragons, seeking grails, stealing fleece, reforming love—is potentially heroic."

   Notice that these sentences are always readable without the material enclosed within the dashes. If a sentence doesn't read right without the material that is set off between two dashes, then you have a problem you need to fix.

   Also, remember that if a list appears at the *end* of a sentence, you use a colon, just as you did in unit 7. The dash (or a set of dashes) is used when the list is at the beginning or in the middle of a sentence.

3. **Two dashes are used to set off an explanation or a definition that appears in mid-sentence.** Example a is from an article about jazz musicians by Owen McNally:

   a. "The idea of a self-destructive element in artists—an ambivalent mix of the creative and the destructive—has long appealed to the popular imagination."

   César Chávez provides another example:

   b. "When you have people together who believe in something very strongly—whether it's religion or politics or unions—things happen."

Again, notice that the sentences make sense and are correctly formed without the material between the dashes. Remember: It's always a good idea to check for readability.

It might have occurred to you that in examples 3.a and b two commas would work as well as two dashes. So how do you choose? It's easy: *Dashes give special emphasis to whatever material they enclose.* Commas do not give any special emphasis to the material that they set off. Commas separate a midsentence phrase from the words that surround it, and that's all they do. Dashes help you *highlight* what appears between them.

4. **Two dashes are used to set off any interruption or break in thought or flow to which you want to give emphasis.** For example:
   a. Rap music—this is what my students are telling me, anyway—is absolutely here to stay.

   Example b is from TV writer and producer Linda Bloodworth-Thomason:
   b. "My father would grab my mother right in front of us, bend her over—I mean *all the way over*—and kiss her. They were not like the Cleavers."

   As examples a and b show, dashes can emphasize an aside or interrupting comment. If you want to do the opposite and *de-emphasize* an interruption, you can enclose it within parentheses.

5. **A dash can be used to set off a definition or explanation at the end of a sentence.** When a dash is used in this position, you really have the choice of using either a dash or a colon. For most good writers, the choice is made based on desired style—the dash has a breezier, less formal feel than the colon. But in these examples, either a dash or a colon would work:
   a. In a speech at Corn Hill Methodist Church on February 16, 1965, Malcolm X explained the motto of the Organization of Afro-American Unity—"By Any Means Necessary."

   When used this way, the dash, like the colon, signals an explanation. In example a the dash says, "Let me tell you what the motto was."

   The second example is from Mendele Mocher Sforim:
   b. "Respect the children of the poor—from them come most poets."

Note: If the keyboard of your typewriter or computer does not have a dash, then use two hyphens (--) to create a dash. Don't use a hyphen when you intend a dash. The hyphen has a completely different use (see unit 11).

When typing, you can close up around dashes or you can hit the space bar once before and once after a dash. In other words, using the Sforim quote again, either one of these styles is fine:

"Respect the children of the poor—from them come most poets."
"Respect the children of the poor — from them come most poets."

Be consistent: The spacing should be the same on both sides of the dash, and the same style should be used throughout an entire piece of writing.

* ### Exercise One

Insert dashes in the following sentences. You will find it very helpful to read these sentences aloud. Other punctuation has already been supplied.

1. Richard Rodriguez teaches at the University of California at Berkeley and is the author of *The Hunger of Memory: The Education of Richard Rodriguez.* He says that, for him, the writing process almost always begins with the same stage a period of brooding.

2. In her book, *Transforming Body Image: Learning to Love the Body You Have,* Dr. Marcia Germaine Hutchinson writes, "We are so busy obsessing over what is wrong with us whether it's our weight, misproportion, wrinkles, pimples, excess hair or functional limitations that we fail to develop our potential as human beings."

3. Sarah Vaughan was named the best female singer by *Downbeat* magazine for 18 years in a row. The music of Sarah Vaughan bebop was widely misunderstood before she made it an integral part of popular American music.

4. *Arrow to the Sun, Where the Buffaloes Begin, Sing Down the Moon, The Girl Who Loved Wild Horses,* and *The People Shall Continue* all five books are celebrations of the spirit of the American Indian, and all are written for children and young adults.

5. Writer Wallace Terry described Dr. Carroll Hardy, an associate dean at The College of William and Mary, in these words: "The students who know her black and white respect her, fear her and love her. They will tell you, 'A mighty fortress is our dean.' "

Exercise Two

Insert dashes in the following sentences. Again, reading the sentences aloud will be helpful. Other punctuation has already been supplied.

1. Paula Abdul, The New Kids on the Block, Bobby Brown, Hammer, Madonna, Janet Jackson, and the infamous Milli Vanilli these were seven very lucrative acts that *The New York Times* described as owing a large part of their success to "cute and catchy" music videos.

2. Military conflicts have erupted approximately two hundred times in U.S. history, and the war in the Persian Gulf the battle with Iraq over the fate of Kuwait marked the tenth time a conflict between the United States and another nation has escalated into an actual war.

3. The Cranes are the world-famous aerialists of the Moscow Circus. Vilen Golovko, the troupe's principal catcher, says that there is one thing that must exist between a catcher and a flier absolute and complete trust. "The catcher is responsible for the flier's life," says Golovko, "and he knows that."

4. Julia Alvarez, a writer and college English teacher, has an excellent reason a deep respect for readers that compels her to revise her poems and stories again and again.

5. A writer for *Rolling Stone* magazine made this comment about ZZ Top: "The group's live sound thunderous drums, fat bass and scandalously loud guitar is simply awesome."

* **Exercise Three**

Let's try one short exercise where you supply all the punctuation. You can choose from commas, semicolons, colons, and dashes.

1   In 1983 Ann Hopkins an attorney in the nationally-known accounting firm of Price

2 Waterhouse could make an impressive claim she brought her company more business

3 than any other candidate for partnership. But in spite of her success she was denied her

4 bid to become a partner in the firm. All of the other 87 candidates for partnership were

5 men and ironically it was her alleged "manlike" characteristics that were held against

6 her. Various complaints against Hopkins that she smoked cigarettes drank beer at lunch

7 cursed wore no makeup or jewelry carried a briefcase instead of a purse and walked like

8 a man held no weight with U.S. District Judge Gerhard Gesell who ruled that Price

9 Waterhouse was guilty of unlawful discrimination based on indefensible gender

10 expectations and sex-role stereotypes. He awarded Hopkins a partnership in 1990 and

11 ordered Price Waterhouse not to retaliate against her in any way. Although Hopkins

12 believed that some in the company were probably not pleased with her promotion she

13 decided as a divorced mother of three to accept the lucrative partnership in order to

14 recoup some of the costs of her seven years of litigation.

UNIT 10: Cumulative Review of the Comma, Semicolon, Colon, and Dash

The exercises in this unit will help you pull together all the punctuation skills you've learned or reviewed so far: the various uses of the comma, semicolon, colon, and dash. These exercises are quite challenging, and you'll find a number of spots where more than one punctuation mark could work. So expect some differences of opinion with classmates. You both might be right.

Exercises

Exercise One   *   PART A

Insert punctuation that is needed or would be helpful to readers, choosing from commas, semicolons, colons, and dashes. Some sentences may call for no punctuation. Here, the subject is rap music.

1. In the complex world of the 1990s there is no doubt about one simple fact rap is the fastest-growing genre in popular music.

2. There is however a certain degree of conflict and controversy about the roots of rap.

3. Some music critics point to the early influences of Gil Scott-Heron the Sugar Hill Gang and The Last Poets.

4. The soulful sounds of James Brown the cadences of gospel preaching the ritualized insults of the dozens and the storytelling tradition of the blues these are also thought to be major influences on rap.

5. "Toasting" a little-known influence of both Jamaican and African-American origin involves the improvisation of rhymes over the instrumental tracks of a record.

6. In examining the subject matter and lyrics of politically-conscious rap music other

observers point to African-American literary influences including poets such as Don L. Lee Nikki Giovanni and Imamu Amiri Baraka.

7. Some critics most notably Jon Pareles of *The New York Times* have observed that television has also had a major impact on the development of rap.

8. Pareles asserts that much of rap and television share certain characteristics fast-paced rhythms unexpected juxtapositions diverse material and frequent self-promotion.

9. But everyone who knows rap realizes that the television networks didn't invent it inner-city disc jockeys did.

10. Disc jockeys gave birth to rap which was initially expected to be a short-lived fad by experimenting in dance clubs in the late 1970s.

PART B

Continue to insert commas, semicolons, colons, and dashes where they are necessary or would be helpful.

1. Although the music of certain rap artists has taken its share of criticism for being violent hateful and obscene this form of music does have its defenders and sometimes they come from unexpected quarters.

2. For example Dr. Jewelle Taylor Gibbs a professor of psychology at the University of California at Berkeley points out that hostile rebellious rap is a reflection of the injustice and violence of the contemporary world.

3. It's essentially a result not a cause.

4. Dr. Sonya Friedman a psychologist and host of a national television show agrees pointing out that rap music makes an important statement about the tragic effects of inequity and the denial of human potential.

5. Like Gibbs Friedman maintains that people should pay more attention to the conditions that rap reflects and less to the language in which the conditions are framed.

6. Friedman says "What offends the ear ought to be offending the heart."

7. There are rappers of course whose purpose is to enlighten as well as entertain.

8. Public Enemy is one such group KRS-One and his Boogie Down Productions (BDP) are another.

9. In some of their work these groups encourage African-American pride and social responsibility.

10. Some like Queen Latifah rap about the great African civilizations and the major contributions of African Americans.

*   PART C

Continue to insert commas, semicolons, colons, and dashes where they are necessary or would be helpful to readers.

1. An important date in the evolution of politically responsible socially conscious rap is September 10 1987.

2. That's when Kool Moe Dee BDP Doug E. Fresh and others appeared at the Nassau Coliseum in Long Island New York.

3. Some so-called fans were not at the Coliseum for the music they were there to harrass and rob other concertgoers.

4. Before the night was over a number of people had been stabbed the few security guards who could be found reportedly did little to help.

5. One young man died when someone decided his gold chain was more valuable than his life.

6. By the next day representatives of three of the major branches of the media the newspapers radio and television had almost unanimously found their scapegoat for the tragedy at the Nassau Coliseum the music itself.

7. Because for so many people rap had become synonymous with violence a group of record-industry people joined with a number of rap groups and individual stars to

create something that eventually became known as the Stop the Violence Movement.

8. According to Nelson George who edited a recent book on this chapter in the history of rap the movement had three main goals to create awareness of the causes and costs of black-on-black crime to raise money for the fight against illiteracy and crime in the inner city and to show how rap could be used to build reading and writing skills in inner-city children.

9. Dozens of rappers from several major groups collaborated to create a record and music video called "Self-Destruction" which was filmed at a number of locations in Manhattan.

10. Before long "Self-Destruction" had sold over half a million copies generating more than $200,000 for community programs run by the National Urban League and creating the possibility of a new direction for rap away from the glorification of the self and toward the regeneration of the community.

Exercise Two   PART A

Insert commas, semicolons, colons, and dashes where they are necessary or would be helpful to your readers. Some sentences may call for no punctuation. Here, the subject is Native American women in traditional societies.

1. Throughout history Native American women have found purpose fulfillment power and prestige in a variety of ways.

2. Three spheres motherhood medicine and political life provided outlets for the creativity and drive of large numbers of women in traditional societies.

3. Paula Gunn Allen a Native American writer and literary critic has written extensively about the importance of motherhood in Indian life.

4. One of her most crucial points is this it is one's mother whose physical and psychic shape makes the next generation possible.

5. "Who is your mother?" is one of the most important questions one can ask of the Keres Indians of the Laguna Pueblo in New Mexico.

6. In this context the word *mother* means an entire generation of women not necessarily an individual who carried a baby in her womb.

7. To know one's mother is to know one's right relationship to earth and society it is to develop a positive sense of self that is based on memory and tradition.

8. This profound expansive concept of motherhood is not an idea exclusive to Paula Gunn Allen it is also a vital theme in *The Ways of My Grandmothers* by Beverly Hungry Wolf.

9. Annie Rides-at-the-Door Hilda Strangling Wolf Ruth Little Bear Paula Weasel Head and Molly Kicking Woman these are only five of the many wise women of the Blackfoot Nation who mothered Hungry Wolf also known as SikskiAki or Black-Faced Woman.

10. In her book Hungry Wolf writes about the philosophies legends heroic deeds and practical skills that helped these women pass the spiritual values of their mothers' generation to the author and her contemporaries.

* PART B

Continue to insert commas, semicolons, colons, and dashes where they are necessary or would be helpful to readers.

1. One area in which many American Indian women excelled was the practice of medicine and though obstacles included both age and gender many resourceful women found ways around them.

2. Women usually could not practice the art of medicine until they reached middle age or older and were freed from some of the demands of raising small children and the taboos associated with menstruation.

3. The Apaches believed that women were in their mental prime between 40 and 60 and this view reflects a common pattern in American Indian societies women usually gained power as they grew older.

4. It was also generally true that a woman regardless of her age could not enter the

profession unless her husband had practiced it and trained her to assist him in life and replace him in death.

5. Occasionally a woman gained her healing gifts after she had met two conditions first she had been chosen and instructed as the successor of an elderly woman doctor and second she had dreamed her own medicine-dream.

6. Pretty-shield a medicine woman of the Sore-lip clan of the Crows had her medicine-dream while she was mourning her beloved baby daughter's death.

7. Hoping to gain the power to help others and a reason to stay alive the future medicine woman wandered alone in the hills and mountains of Montana for more than two months eating very little and sleeping on the hardest ground she could find.

8. Finally according to Pretty-shield's account physical deprivation induced a dream in which a woman appeared and helped Pretty-shield ask for the power she needed this woman also gave her the ants as her helpers.

9. Lacking a Native American view of nature many readers might find it difficult to imagine how ants could assist a doctor but Pretty-shield believed firmly that they spoke to her throughout her life often directing her heart in the art of healing. (Incidentally Pretty-shield whose story is told in a fascinating oral history by Frank B. Linderman was the wife of Goes-ahead one of Custer's scouts at the Battle of the Little Bighorn on June 25 1876.)

10. Some medicine women employed techniques that are easier for the modern scientific mind to understand and accept for example Otsani a Blackfoot wise woman enjoyed great success using porcupine quills and cactus spines to perform acupuncture.

PART C

Continue to insert commas, semicolons, colons, and dashes where they are necessary or would be helpful to readers.

1. What contributions did American Indian women make to the political life of their tribes and nations?

2. Women's political involvement varied from tribe to tribe and nation to nation but in all of American history both Indian and non-Indian women have rarely enjoyed the power that they were able to exercise among the Iroquois in upper New York state.

3. Many historians believe that the concept for the union of states that eventually became the United States was based on the confederacy of tribes within the Iroquois nation.

4. Within the politically sophisticated Iroquois Nation which was a matrilineal society women's high status was manifested in two powerful ways their ownership of the land and their power to put men on the tribal council and take them off if they did not perform well.

5. When their political powers within the nation once were threatened Iroquois women successfully boycotted lovemaking and childbearing their concerns were soon heard.

6. Native American women also took direct action in other ways for example they sometimes joined and occasionally led men in battle.

7. In Pretty-shield's narrative the usually merry 74-year-old becomes irritated several times when she discovers that the interviewer's male informants have completely omitted accounts of women's courage in battle she insists that these true stories were well-known to every older Crow whether male or female.

8. *(See hint at end of exercise.)* Among the greatest Native American female warriors were these eight women Running Eagle a member of the Blackfoot tribe Chief Earth Woman who came from the Ojibwa people Lozen an Apache Ehyophsta who was a Cheyenne Old-Lady-Grieves-the-Enemy who was a Pawnee and finally Finds-them-and-kills-them The-other-magpie and Strikes-two all three of whom were Crows.

9. The Cheyenne have a saying a people cannot be conquered until the hearts of their women are on the ground.

10. By their own accounts Native American women have often found their hearts on the ground but never forever their contributions as mothers doctors and leaders testify to their indomitable spirit.

Hint for sentence 8: It might help to clarify this item if you have a list of the women's names as separate from their tribes and nations. The eight women warriors are Running Eagle, Chief Earth Woman, Lozen, Ehyophsta, Old-Lady-Grieves-the-Enemy, Finds-them-and-kills-them, The-other-magpie, and Strikes-two.

UNIT 11: Miscellaneous Punctuation: Quotation Marks, Hyphens, and Apostrophes

Important Note for Students and Teachers

In units 1 through 10, you worked with the punctuation marks—commas, semicolons, colons, and dashes—that are closely linked to various ways of forming clauses and combining them to create different sentence structures. This unit concerns one form of punctuation that is more loosely connected to sentence structure—quotation marks—and two that are not connected at all—hyphens and apostrophes. It may be best for some students to keep their focus on punctuation and sentence structure and skip this unit for now, proceeding directly to chapter 10. They can return to this material later or consult it as the need arises.

Quotation Marks

Double quotation marks (" ") show that you are using the words of others, and specific structures are used to set up or frame quotes.

There are two basic ways that you can present what others have said: (1) You can quote a person *directly*, using his or her exact words, or (2) you can quote *indirectly*, expressing the person's thoughts in your own words. An indirect quote is also called a *paraphrase*.

A direct quote is a presentation of another person's exact words. An indirect quote is a description or approximation of what another person said. Here is a *direct quote:*

Just before her death, Queen Elizabeth I said, "All my possessions for a moment of time."

As you can see, the direct quote has double quotation marks both before and after the queen's exact words.

Here, on the other hand, are two *indirect quotes* that provide the same information:

> Just before her death, Queen Elizabeth I said that she would trade all her possessions for a moment of time.
>
> In the last moments of her life, Queen Elizabeth I declared she would give up everything she owned just to live one moment longer.

The two indirect quotes should not have quotation marks because these quotes express the queen's idea but not her exact words.

Whether you quote directly or indirectly, you always *name the person you are quoting.*

Here is another example of a *direct quote:*

> In the last seconds of her life, Marie Antoinette stepped on the toe of her executioner and said, "Monsieur, I beg your pardon."

An *indirect* version of the same statement would be:

> In the last seconds of her life, Marie Antoinette stepped on the toe of her executioner and begged his pardon.

Write down something that someone close to you—a parent, good friend, or spouse—says frequently. First, write and punctuate it as a direct quote; then write it as an indirect quote.

Direct quote: _____

_____

Indirect quote: _____

_____

Should You Quote Directly or Indirectly?

How do you decide whether to quote something directly or to paraphrase it? The best advice is to use a direct quote if your source's exact words are essential to proving your point or if something is so aptly expressed that you couldn't say it better yourself. As French novelist Anatole France once said, "When a thing has been said, and well said, have no scruple: take it and copy it." Just remember: *If you copy someone else's words, make sure that you give full credit to that person.* (France may have had something a little less honorable in mind!)

As we discussed in section I, if you do not use quotation marks around direct quotes and if you fail to give credit to the person whose words you've used, you may be accused of plagiarism, which is a violation of academic ethics that carries with it very serious penalties at most colleges and universities. (Review chapter 7 if you need reminders on how to cite your sources.)

Creating and Punctuating "Tags"

Writers need to know how to create and punctuate the "tags" that identify the speaker of a direct quote. Most are introductory phrases, such as *He said* and *She remarked*. But sometimes tags appear after a quote, and occasionally they appear in the middle. Normally, a tag is set off with a comma or a colon. In some cases, no punctuation is used directly before and after quoted material. Let's look at examples.

Using a Comma

If the tag is simply a noun or pronoun and a verb, follow it with a comma. For example:

Devon said, "_____ ."
The lawyer concludes, "_____ ."
I insisted, "_____ ."

Tags also can appear after the direct quote. In such cases, use a comma at the end of the quote:

"_____ ," said Devon.
"_____ ," concludes the lawyer.
"_____ ," I insisted.

Sometimes a tag can interrupt a direct quote. Then you need *two commas*—one before and one after—and *two sets of double quotation marks*—one set to enclose the first part of the direct quote and another to enclose the second part. For example:

"For once in your life," Maggie pleaded, "could you please let someone help you?"

Notice that *Maggie pleaded* is set off from the quote with *two* commas.

When you place a tag in the middle of a quote, use a period and a capital letter if each part of the direct quote is a full sentence. Here's a correct example:

"My kids will know what to do," said the mother. "They're very independent."

Notice that the final double quotation mark goes *after* the end punctuation—whether that end punctuation is a period, question mark, or exclamation point.

Using a Colon

If you create a tag with a direct object or a complement, follow it with a *colon.* (This is the same rule regarding colons and their setups that you learned in unit 7.) Study the following correct examples and label the direct object (*do*) or subject complement (*sub com*) in each:

a. The press secretary issued this statement: "_____

_____ ."

b. Her opening line was prophetic: "_____

_____ ."

c. The baby's first words were highly unusual: "_____

_____ ."

d. One old man made a cutting remark: "_____

_____ ."

[ANSWERS: a. *statement* = do;   b. *prophetic* = sub com;
c. *unusual* = sub com;   d. *remark* = do.]

On your own paper, reword the earlier items about Queen Elizabeth I and Marie Antoinette so that you can insert a colon before the quotes.

Now, to test your understanding of how to punctuate tags, insert either a comma or colon into each of the following examples:

a. The police officer responded "_____ ."

b. The woman said only three words "_____ ."

c. "_____" said the philosopher.

d. Her exact phrasing was very original "_____ ."

e. My sister answered "———————————————— ."

f. The most annoying line in the song is this "——————————— ."

[ANSWERS: a. comma after *responded;*   b. colon after *words;*   c. comma
before the second double quotation mark;   d. colon after *original;*   e. comma
after *answered;*   f. colon after *this.*]

Using No Punctuation

Occasionally, neither a comma nor a·colon is used before a direct quote or a part
of a direct quote. In these cases, the writer has incorporated the quoted material
into his or her sentence structure in such a way that no punctuation is needed.
Here are two correct examples:

a. In a recent in-depth character study in *The New York Times Magazine,*
    comedian Robin Williams was described as "more than a shtick figure."
b. Ralph D. Story, in an essay on the Harlem Renaissance in *The Black
    Scholar,* calls Zora Neale Hurston "one of the great imaginative writer-
    folklorists in the twentieth century."

If part of another person's statement is worked into the writer's sentence in this
way, the first word of the direct quote is not capitalized (unless it is a proper
noun), and the quote is not preceded by a comma or colon.

Special Notes on Punctuation of Direct Quotes

Commas and periods are almost always placed *before* the double quotation marks
at the end of a direct quote. This is done simply to make things look okay on the
page: Periods and commas look weird when they appear after quotation
marks—as if they're hanging out in space.

But when you are inserting other punctuation marks—exclamation points,
question marks, semicolons, and so forth—at the end of a direct quote, you
really have to stop and think. These marks can go before or after the double
quotation marks, depending upon how they are used. If a question mark, for
instance, is part of the quoted material, then it goes inside. But if the larger
sentence (not the quoted material) is a question, then the question mark goes at
the end of the whole sentence. Sometimes both the quoted material and what
you might call your *framing sentence* are questions. Study these correct
examples:

a. "What do you think the jury will decide?" the defendant asked his lawyer.
b. The defendant asked his lawyer, "What do you think the jury will decide?"

In both a and b, the quoted material is a question, but the framing sentence in
which the quoted material appears is a statement.

Now look at this example:

c.   Did you actually say, "A bird in the hand is worth two in the bush"?

In c, the quoted material is a statement, but the framing sentence is a question. And, finally, analyze this one:

d.   Was it Ring Lardner who asked, "How can you write if you can't cry?"?

In d, which is an unusual case but one that will eventually come up in your writing, you have a question within a question. The quoted material is a question, so it gets a question mark, and the framing sentence also is a question, so it gets another question mark. (It *was* Ring Lardner, by the way.)

To decide where exclamation points should be placed at the end of direct quotes or framing sentences, use the same reasoning that you use when contemplating where to insert question marks.

Here's another small but important point: If a direct quote ends with a question mark or exclamation point, *omit the comma* that would normally go before the tag. These are correct examples:

"Are your intentions honorable?" Sam asked.
"Get a life!" the audience yelled.

Showing a Change of Speaker

In a dialogue, you are directly quoting more than one speaker. Start a new paragraph each time you switch from one speaker to another so your readers won't be confused, wondering who said what. Watch for examples of this style in the following exercises.

* Exercise One

Label each item *d* for direct quote or *i* for indirect quote. Then make any necessary changes in the punctuation of the direct quotes. These changes might involve inserting double quotation marks, commas, colons, or question marks, and correcting capitalization. The indirect quotes will not call for any changes. These items are samples of classic American humor.

1. _____ Groucho Marx once asked someone why he didn't bore a hole in himself and

   let the sap run out.

2. _____ Fondly recalling his parents, comedian Rodney Dangerfield once claimed they

   sent me to a child psychiatrist, but what can I say? That kid didn't help me at all.

3. _____ What are you rebelling against Marlon Brando was asked in the movie *The Wild Ones* in 1953.

What've you got he answered.

4. _____ An anonymous wit once said that a good herpetologist will always work for scale.

5. _____ Comedian Fred Allen was said to have remarked that television was called a medium because nothing on it was ever well done.

6. _____ Once on "The Muppet Show" two muppets were watching a television program about Swedish cooking. Did you find that interesting the first one asked the second one when the show was over.

No replied the second muppet. Actually I was smorgasbord.

7. _____ Years ago, the writer Oscar Wilde made a wonderfully cynical comment about Niagara Falls every American bride is taken there, and the sight must be one of the earliest, if not the keenest, disappointments in American married life.

8. _____ Ann Landers has said that the most unusual letter she ever received was from a woman whose husband had hidden her dentures so that she couldn't go out and vote for a Democrat.

9. _____ Here's a fellow comedian's description of Jack Benny he was not one who said funny things, but one who said things funny.

10. _____ A man asked the preacher do you save bad women.

Yes replied the preacher I surely do.

In that case responded the man would you save me two for Thursday night.

Exercise Two

Label each item *d* for direct quote or *i* for indirect quote. Then make any necessary changes in the punctuation of the direct quotes, following the directions for exercise one. The indirect quotes will not require any changes.

Sources for these memorable insults and put-downs include Nancy McPhee's *The Second Book of Insults* and Dorothy Herrmann's *With Malice Toward All.*

1. _____ Ludwig van Beethoven once said to a fellow composer I liked your opera. I think I will set it to music.

2. _____ I've had a wonderful evening Groucho Marx used to say but this wasn't it.

3. _____ An anonymous source is credited with saying that a day away from actress Tallulah Bankhead was like a month in the country.

4. _____ When a batch of young and apparently inexperienced officers arrived to help him on the front lines, the Duke of Wellington, who was eventually victorious over Napoleon at Waterloo, said I don't know what effect they will have upon the enemy. But by God, they frighten me!

5. _____ Making a small but startling adjustment on the old cliché, playwright Noel Coward once described another writer as every other inch a gentleman.

6. _____ George S. Kaufman at one time worked as a drama critic for *The New York Times*. One night, after seeing a new comedy, Kaufman reported that he had heard laughter in the back of the theater, leading him to conclude that someone back there must have been telling jokes.

7. _____ Kaufman was also an expert bridge player. Once, after his partner had butchered a hand, the partner asked Kaufman how would you have played it.

   Under an assumed name replied Kaufman.

8. _____ Winston Churchill once offered this summary of the character of General Bernard L. Montgomery in defeat unbeatable, in victory unbearable.

9. _____ Wilson Mizner was working on a script in Hollywood in 1933 when he received word that his brother Addison was dying in Florida. The next day, Addison Mizner received a telegram that read stop dying. Am trying to write a comedy.

   A little later, Addison, near death, received word that his brother Wilson was beginning to worry about his own health, especially about the possibility that he might be going deaf. What do you care wired Addison. You've heard every-

thing.

10. _____ Someone definitely got the last word on an old fellow in Nova Scotia, who is

buried under a tombstone that bears this inscription Here lies Ezekial Aikle. Aged

102. The Good Die Young.

✳ Exercise Three

Make the necessary changes in the punctuation of these items, which are based on old vaudeville routines. Again, your changes may involve inserting double quotation marks, commas, colons, or question marks, and correcting capitalization. (You will need to put in some commas for reasons unrelated to quotes; for example, commas should be added to compound sentences or instances of direct address.)

1. So I went to my doctor and he said have you ever had this before.

   I said yes I have.

   He said well you've got it again.

2. So I went to my doctor and I said doctor I broke my arm in three places.

   She said oh yeah well stay out of those places.

3. So I went to my doctor and I said doctor it hurts when I do this.

   He said well then don't do that.

4. So I went to my doctor and she said you're sick.

   I said I want a second opinion.

   Okay she said you're ugly too.

5. So I went to my dentist and I said I've got yellow teeth. What should I do.

   He said wear a brown tie.

6. So I went to my pharmacist and I said which way to the talcum powder.

   She said walk this way.

   I said if I could walk that way I wouldn't need the talcum powder.

7. So I went to my doctor and I said I got the bill for my surgery.

He said oh good.

I said yeah now I know why you were wearing a mask.

8. So I went to my doctor and I said now don't tell me I'm overweight.

Okay she said you're four inches too short.

9. So I went to my doctor and I said after this operation will I be able to play the violin?

He said certainly.

I said that's funny. I could never play it before.

10. So I went to my doctor and she said I've got some good news and some bad news.

The bad news is that you owe me $1,000 a month for the next 12 months.

So I said what's the good news.

She said you've got only six months to live.

Exercise Four

After you have corrected exercises one through three, go back and select any five direct quotes from those three exercises and rewrite them as indirect quotes. Use your own paper, please.

As you do exercise four, you'll see that some sentences are much more effective as direct quotes than as indirect ones while others do not suffer much or at all in the translation from direct to indirect.

What happens, for example, when the direct quotes from the movie *The Wild Ones* (see item 3 in exercise one) are reworked into indirect quotes? Do you lose something if you describe the exchange rather than give the exact words?

Exercise Five

Interview a student in your class, a friend, a colleague at work, or a member of your family. Write out your brief interview, using a combination of direct and indirect quotes. If you quote yourself asking a question, remember to start a new paragraph to show the change of speaker.

Using Single Quotation Marks

Single quotation marks (' ') are used to enclose a quote that appears within another quote.

Here is a quote from Eva Jessye, who was the choral director for the original Broadway production of *Porgy and Bess* and the first black woman to receive international acclaim as the director of a professional choral group. She's recalling her early days in New York City in the 1920s: "I was living upstairs and my little studio always had little concerts and things. A man knocked on my door and said, 'I'm from the electric company and I've been sent time and time again to cut off your electricity. But I stood out here and you were playing so beautifully, I couldn't do it.' "

If you used this passage in a piece of your writing, you would be quoting one speaker—Eva Jessye—who, in turn, is quoting another—the appreciative electrician.

* Exercise Six

Insert double and single quotation marks where needed in each of the following items. This time, to simplify things a bit, all other punctuation is already in place, and no corrections in capitalization are required.

1. Eva Jessye recalled one of the barriers that existed in the early days of her carrier: In New York at the radio they used to say, Well, we don't have any need for your music. They thought the Negro didn't know anything except spirituals. Radio was an area black people hadn't broken into and it hadn't been opened for them.

2. *Newsweek* magazine reported that after listening to negotiations over the dates of a meeting between two world powers, U.S. Representative Patricia Schroeder said, I feel like you're listening to a fight between two three-year-olds. No, I will not. No, I will. Na na na.

3. In *I Dream a World,* actress Cicely Tyson remembers how her mother taught embroidery to her children: She would buy these huge things, tablecloths, bedspreads—whatever—and she would give each of us a corner to work (the fourth corner was hers). When I get back, she would say, I want you to have finished this much right here. Today we each have several of these beautiful pieces— remembrances of Mama's efforts to keep her family harmonious.

4. In his book *Humor and Social Change in Twentieth-Century America,* Joseph Boskin explains, Although it is possible to categorize and characterize the diversity of humor, its nature and meaning remain elusive. E.B. White once wrote, Essentially, it is a complete mystery.

5. The women I meet are *so* self-absorbed, said comedian Garry Shandling in a recent

interview. For example, I met this blonde today at a barbecue. At least I *think* she

was blonde—her hair was on fire—anyway, she couldn't stop talking about herself.

You know, Help *me, I'm* on fire, put *me* out . . .

Exercise Seven

Write three sentences that call for single quotation marks to be used within double quotation marks. Here are some suggestions for subject matter: You could

a. **quote your father quoting his father;**
b. **quote your physics teacher quoting Albert Einstein;**
c. **quote your mother quoting one of her best friends;**
d. **quote a famous writer telling how he or she was inspired by a certain line from a poem, story, or novel; or**
e. **quote a movie critic in the newspaper quoting and commenting on a particular line from a new movie.**

A Note on Verb Tense

When you are quoting someone whose words appeared in print, you often have the option of using the present or past tense in your tags and in the surrounding text.

For example, imagine that the fourth sentence in exercise six appeared in an essay you were writing. Once you decide to say *Joseph Boskin explains,* then you are committed to staying with the present tense whenever you refer to Boskin's points. You might also write *Boskin maintains, the author concludes, he says,* and so forth in later references to this author's comments.

On the other hand, if you decide to go with the past tense and use *Boskin explained,* then again, all references should be in the past: *Boskin maintained, the author concluded,* and *he said.*

Many accomplished writers choose the present tense for tags, especially when writing about a work of literature. The reason for this is that the work of literature is considered alive in the present, not something that had validity only in the past, at the time the author wrote it.

Whether you choose present or past tense when quoting something in print, the most important thing is to be *consistent.* Random switches in verb tense can make a piece of writing look anything from slightly unpolished to positively incoherent. It's a small detail, but an important one. (See chapter 11, unit 2 for more discussion on verb tense.)

Setting Off Longer Direct Quotes in Block Form

If your direct quote will be *longer than four typed lines,* it should be set off from the rest of the text and put in *single-spaced block form.* There are several conventions that should be observed here:

1. In most cases, use a colon after the setup that introduces the block quote. If your introduction to the quote is less than a subject–verb–complement or

subject–verb–direct object sequence, use no punctuation. Don't use a comma to introduce a block quote. Use a colon or no punctuation.

2. Add an extra blank line above and below the block quote so that it's set off from the rest of the text visually.

3. Indent ten spaces from the left margin and leave enough space on the right so that the quote looks fairly centered.

4. If the block quote is just one paragraph, don't indent the first line any more than the ten spaces you already indented to form the left margin. If your passage consists of more than one paragraph, indent three extra spaces (altogether thirteen spaces from the left margin) at the start of each new paragraph of the direct quote.

5. Do not put double quotation marks around your block quote. The fact that you've set it off with larger-than-usual margins and single-spaced it marks it as a direct quote, making double quotation marks around the whole thing unnecessary. Any direct quotes that appear within the passage you're quoting should be set off with double quotation marks rather than single marks because no other double marks are being used.

The following is a correct example of how a block quote might be introduced and how it might look in a paper.

In his autobiography, Chief Luther Standing Bear of the Oglala Sioux

describes his people's traditional view of their land:

> We did not think of the great open plains, the beautiful rolling hills, the winding streams with tangled growth as "wild." Only to the white man was nature a "wilderness" and only to him was the land "infested" with "wild" animals and "savage" people. To us it was tame. Earth was bountiful and we were surrounded with the blessings of the Great Mystery. Not until the hairy man from the East came and with brutal frenzy heaped injustices upon us and the families we loved was it "wild" for us. When the very animals of the forest began fleeing from his approach, then it was that for us the "Wild West" began.   (qtd. in Sanders and Peek 176)

A Few Fine Points

1. If you quoted a shorter passage from Standing Bear (one that would not require single-spaced block form), you would enclose the shorter passage within double quotation marks and, where he used double quotation marks, you would switch to single quotation marks. For example:

> In his autobiography, Chief Luther Standing Bear of the Oglala Sioux writes, "Only to the white man was nature a 'wilderness' and only to him was the land 'infested' with 'wild' animals and 'savage' people."

2. If you omit material from a quotation because it is not relevant to your purpose, show that you're doing so by using *ellipsis* points (. . .). If you

omit words from within one sentence, insert the three periods with a space between each to show where the material has been omitted. Here is a correct example from Standing Bear's first sentence:

"We did not think of the great open plans . . . as 'wild.' "

If you want to omit material that is made up of the end of one sentence, the start of another, a whole sentence, or a paragraph or more, use *four* periods—the first one represents a normal period. When you use four periods, you need a grammatically complete sentence both before and after. Here is a correct example:

"Only to the white man was nature a 'wilderness' and only to him was the land 'infested' with 'wild' animals and 'savage' people. . . . When the very animals of the forest began fleeing from his approach, then it was that for us the 'Wild West' began."

Do not use ellipsis points when you have omitted something from the start of a quote and have worked the remainder of the quote into your own sentence structure. The fact that the quote starts out with a lowercase letter will show the reader that you dropped something from the beginning. This example is correct:

Standing Bear speaks of how his people believed that they were "surrounded with the blessings of the Great Mystery."

Never omit anything from a quote that radically alters the original speaker's meaning. In other words, be fair; don't take things out of context.

3. You may sometimes need to add something to a direct quote so that it makes sense to your reader. If you used the last sentence from the Standing Bear passage alone—without the rest of the passage or at least the preceding sentence—you would want to clarify the word *his* for your readers. *To do so, you'd insert the briefest possible explanation within brackets:*

"When the very animals of the forest began fleeing from his [the white man's] approach, then it was that for us the 'Wild West' began."

Don't use parentheses because they would indicate that the author, in this case Standing Bear, had made a parenthetical insertion in that spot. The brackets show that the addition to the quote is yours. These additions are made only for the purpose of clarification, not for editorial comment.

Hyphens

The hyphen (-) is very simple to use. It connects the syllables of a word that does not fit completely at the end of one line and has to be carried over in part to the next. But that situation is less frequent now as greater numbers of students are using computers to write their papers. (The computer automatically pulls the whole word to the next line.)

More importantly, hyphens are often used to connect two or more words to make a new word. For instance, in the sentence, "Let's look for a *worry-free* solution to this problem," you know that you don't mean *a worry solution* plus *a free solution*. In other words, *worry* and *free* are not functioning independently as they describe the noun *solution*. They have been put together to create a word that has a new and singular meaning of its own.

Hyphens can be used to join two or more words to create new nouns, verbs, and adjectives. Here are some examples of each.

Nouns	Verbs	Adjectives
well-being	double-check	half-baked
rat-a-tat-tat	second-guess	fair-minded
war-horse	shilly-shally	public-spirited
talking-to	ice-skate	rapid-fire
love-in	sweet-talk	well-groomed
mock-up	breast-feed	water-resistant
dressing-down	water-cool	X-rated
day-tripper	custom-tailor	well-fed
cease-fire	jury-rig	quick-witted

Checking the Dictionary

There are many times when you can't be sure if a word has a hyphen or not; you need to consult a dictionary. For example, you might expect that *rain check* has a hyphen because the two words—*rain* and *check*—function as one word, but it does not have a hyphen. Also, some words might seem likely candidates for the hyphen, but they are simply compound words. The nouns *superpower* and *breakdown* are good examples. Again, check the dictionary.

Creating Your Own Hyphenated Words

Occasionally, you might create your own words that call for a hyphen, especially in adjectival phrases. They won't be in the dictionary, but they may be valid nonetheless. For instance, you might describe a doll as *prune-faced,* or a society as *sex-crazed.* The novelist Walker Percy, for example, often used *death-obsessed* and *death-dealing* in writing about the spiritual problems of modern American culture. You won't find these words in the dictionary—with or without hyphens—but they were important words that Percy created to explain his thinking, and they called for hyphens.

When You Shift from One Part of Speech to Another

Some words call for a hyphen when they function as an adjective, but not when they function as a noun. Here are some correct examples to look over:

1a. bush league (noun)
 b. a bush-league play (adjective)

    2a.   day care (noun)
      b.   a day-care center (adjective)
    3a.   ice cream (noun)
      b.   an ice-cream cone (adjective)
    4a.   middle class (noun)
      b.   middle-class values (adjective)
    5a.   x ray (noun)
      b.   an x-ray machine (adjective) *or* to x-ray his arm (verb)

Similarly, sometimes an expression is two words when used as a verb, but hyphenated when used as a noun. For example, "The thief was planning to *break in* to her house" and "There was a *break-in* at her house."

Special Cases

Hyphens are *not* normally used after prefixes, but there is one exception: You often use a hyphen when the letter at the end of the prefix is the same as the letter at the beginning of the base part of the word. The purpose is to make the word easier to read. Examples are *co-op* and *de-escalate*. (Again, there are many exceptions: *unnecessary* is one.)

Hyphens are not normally used after words that end in *-ly*. For example, no hyphen should appear in these phrases: *a newly formed organization, rarely spoken words of disgust, the congressionally approved measure,* and *a beautifully painted landscape.*

* **Exercise Eight**

Add hyphens where they are appropriate in the following phrases. (A phrase may call for more than one hyphen or for none.) Use a dictionary *only* if necessary. (Answers may vary, depending upon the dictionary you use.)

1. an up to date film about recently discovered skeletal remains in Thailand

2. a group of Yiddish speaking Jewish immigrants

3. three very positive full length reviews of my friend Mary Ann Watson's newly

   released book on television during the Kennedy years

4. a four year old child

5. a head to head confrontation

6. a bad flare up of that persistent red rash

7. an upper class attitude

8. the soul shaking sounds of Otis Redding

9. to double park your newly purchased van

10. a water repellent coating on the expensive new shoes

Exercise Nine

Continue to follow the directions given for exercise eight.

1. a heart to heart talk with a very close friend

2. the anal retentive chef on "Saturday Night Live"

3. a far reaching decision about the costs and benefits of a strict recycling program

4. a supply side theory of economics

5. a knee jerk reaction to the idea of an on site inspection at your plant

6. four best selling novels about fly fishing in the Rockies

7. making an illegal U turn right in front of a cop

8. a husband who likes to table hop at his favorite Italian restaurant

9. a user friendly computer program

10. a stiffly starched shirt and two nicely ironed skirts

Apostrophes

The apostrophe (') has two main uses: to show possession and to make contractions. We'll first look at how it is used to show possession.

Forming Possessives

Let's say that you want to make a noun possessive—to show that it "owns" something. The basic rules are easy: If the word is singular, you normally add an apostrophe plus *-s*. For example: *the woman's hat, the lawyer's language, the city's reputation*. This goes for indefinite pronouns, too: *somebody's lost glove, everyone's hope, nobody's fault*.

If you want to make a *plural* noun possessive, you normally add just an apostrophe after the *-s* that made the word plural. For example: *both doctors' offices, the two sisters' money-making scheme, the hunters' bad luck*.

But if the noun is an irregular plural—in other words, if it does *not* end in *-s*—then you add an apostrophe plus *-s*, just as if it were a singular noun. For example: *the women's options, the men's business plans, the children's playroom*.

Possessive Pronouns

Possessive pronouns do *not* take apostrophes. Look over these correct examples:

The medicine was *hers*.
The best record in track and field was *ours*.
The lion licked *its* paws.

You might be wondering when *it's* is correct. That word is correct when you mean *it is* and are forming a contraction of those two words. For example:

It's a great day for hot chocolate and a good P.D. James mystery novel.

Let's try a simple exercise.

Exercise Ten   *   PART A

Using the two examples given as your guide, reword the following sets of phrases, adding an apostrophe or an apostrophe plus -s as needed in each case:

    a.   **the duties of one librarian = one *librarian's* duties**
    b.   **the duties of two librarians = two *librarians'* duties**

1. the shoes of a dancer = _____

   the shoes of several dancers = _____

2. the pet lizard of one girl = _____

   the pet lizards of three girls = _____

3. the history of a family = _____

   the histories of two families = _____

4. the imagery of one poet = _____

   the imagery of many poets = _____

5. the schedule of the woman = _____

   the schedules of the women = _____

PART B

Continue to follow the directions given in part A.

1. the secrets of my mother = _____

   the secrets of all mothers = _____

2. the performance of one student = _____

the performance of both students = _____

3. the habits of the child = _____

    the habits of the children = _____

4. the attitude of the man = _____

    the attitude of the men = _____

5. the badge of the police officer = _____

    the badges of the police officers = _____

* Exercise Eleven

Rewrite these phrases so that they require you to add an apostrophe or an apostrophe plus -s

1. the liberation of women = _____

2. the personality of the rabbi = _____

3. the tips of most waiters = _____

4. the strategy of the baseball team = _____

5. soft skin of newborn babies = _____

6. the sleigh of the reindeer = _____

7. the fear of flying of many people = _____

8. the comedy routines of three newcomers = _____

9. the popsicles of the children = _____

10. the views of Sister Souljah = _____

Two Fine Points About Proper Nouns that End in -s

Before you study this section, ask your teacher's advice. He or she may want you to stick to the basic rules already described and not worry about the fine points for now. In that case, you could proceed directly to exercise twelve.

    The rules for using an apostrophe to show possession involve a number of special cases and exceptions, but if you follow the basic rules you just learned you'll be able to avoid making errors when you show possession in your writing. There are two fine points, or options, that you might want to consider if you have the basic rules down pat. Both involve proper nouns (words with capitalized first letters).

1. The first option concerns proper nouns that end in -s. Accepted practice is to add an apostrophe plus -s when making proper nouns that end in -s possessive. But simply adding an apostrophe is gaining popularity. For example, you might write *Chris's shell collection* or *Chris' shell collection;* you might write *Jaws's popularity* or *Jaws' popularity.* Your safest bet is to stick with the accepted practice in your college writing, but if you prefer the other style, use it in your personal writing. The important thing is this: Whichever style you choose, be consistent throughout each piece of writing.

2. The second point relates to pronunciation. If a proper noun already ends in -s, you might want to use the apostrophe alone, omitting the -s added to show possession if that extra -s makes pronunciation difficult. Two proper names—*Moses* and *Jesus*—are always treated this way. Examine this incorrect example:

   Unless they found water for themselves and their livestock, the Israelites planned to rebel against *Moses's* leadership.

   Adding the *'s* to *Moses,* creates three *z* sounds in a row, resulting in an awkward and hard-to-pronounce word. So, instead, we simply write *Moses' leadership.*

Exercise Twelve   *   PART A

Read this material on the Medal of Honor and add apostrophes (or an apostrophe plus -s) where they belong. Use context clues to decide whether a possessive word is singular or plural. Some sentences may call for no apostrophes.
   Caution: **Don't be tricked into adding an apostrophe to every word that ends in the letter -s. Ask yourself what it owns, if anything.**

1. At the time of this writing, only one woman has ever been awarded the Congressional Medal of Honor, this nations highest military decoration.

2. Since the Medal of Honor was established in 1861, 3,410 medals have been awarded, with 3,409 of them honoring mens acts of courage in battle.

3. The one woman to be so decorated was Mary E. Walker, who served as a civilian surgeon during the American peoples most traumatic internal conflict, the Civil War.

4. To add insult to injury, Walkers award was rescinded by a review board in the early part of this century.

5. President Jimmy Carters decision to restore the Medal of Honor to Walker was applauded by womens groups, veterans organizations, and other interested parties.

PART B

Continue to add apostrophes (or an apostrophe plus -s) where needed.

1. Technically, under law, the Medal of Honor is awarded for "gallantry in action" and is given to individuals who have performed heroically while "engaged in an action against an enemy of the United States."

2. A classic example of this type of heroic action would be a soldier throwing his body on top of a grenade or performing some other battlefield feat aimed at saving comrades lives.

3. Since women soldiers traditionally have been barred from combat but have performed other types of heroic deeds, many people think that—to be fair to women—the definition of heroism implicit in the law that created the Congressional Medal of Honor should be broadened.

4. Women, after all, have performed many heroic actions in their countrys service over the years, but often not on the front lines and often not in the same style and manner as their male comrades.

5. On the other hand, representatives of the Womens Overseas Service League, an organization of women veterans, have pointed out that in the past there have been instances in which nurses actions should have qualified them for consideration— even under the original wording of the law.

* PART C

Add apostrophes (or an apostrophe plus -s) where needed.

1. For example, in the Second World War, there were incidents in which military hospitals were stormed by the enemy and patients lives were endangered;

American nurses were known to have thrown themselves on top of their soldier-patients in an effort to protect them.

2. Later, in Vietnam, a war that lacked the starkly drawn lines of previous conflicts, many nurses found themselves very close to the action; medical personnels major contributions were generally made in field hospitals, which were not located in protected areas.

3. More recent conflicts, such as the Gulf War, threaten to pull women even closer to combat or at least to frontline duties, but that seems to be how many women in the military want it: They believe that an individuals contribution and performance should not be determined or evaluated on the basis of gender.

4. Currently, there are efforts underway, headed by Michigans Representative Paul Henry, to change the wording of the law that determines a persons suitability for consideration for the Medal of Honor.

5. There is also a project, headed by the Womens Overseas Service League, to check with all U.S. congressional districts to try to discover deserving women who may have been nominated for the medal but unfairly denied it.

Exercise Thirteen   PART A

Read this short piece on the Salem witchcraft trials and add apostrophes (or an apostrophe plus -s) where they are needed. Use context clues to help you make your decisions.

1. The infamous period of witchcraft hysteria in and around Salem in the Massachu-setts Bay Colony was one of this nations strangest interludes, and it is a subject that continues to hold students attention, generation after generation.

2. According to Tom Burnam, the author of *The Dictionary of Misinformation*, in the seventeenth century, peoples minds were generally quite open concerning the possibility of the existence of witches.

3. In fact, some historians point out that, when the alleged witches accusers were later tried, there was less argument over the question of whether or not witches actually existed than over the various judges sometimes unconventional courtroom procedures.

4. The person who may have triggered the Salem witchcraft hysteria, which led to the deaths of 19 people and the imprisonment of about 150 others, was Samuel Parris, the minister of Salem Village, who, along with his supporters, led the witch hunt in 1692.

5. Many of Parris parishoners were poor farmers and villagers who felt threatened by the more progressive and prosperous people of nearby Salem.

* PART B

Add apostrophes (or an apostrophe plus -s) where needed.

1. A good number of the witch-hunters victims were people of Salem Village who had made the mistake of rejecting Parris and his traditional ways or who were somehow associated with the business life and generally nonagrarian concerns of Salem.

2. It all started when a number of girls began to act in unexplained ways: The girls behavior ranged from speaking in an unintelligible manner to getting down and crawling around on all fours.

3. Before long, the youngsters odd behavior led to several accusations of withcraft, then to convictions and death sentences.

4. The average persons misconceptions about the Salem witchcraft trials include the notions that all the so-called witches were women and that the accused were burned at the stake.

5. In reality, both men and women—plus two dogs—were convicted of witchcraft during the year-long reign of terror.

PART C

Add apostrophes (or an apostrophe plus -s) where needed.

1. And the dogs fate, like the fate of the women and all but one of the men, was to be hanged, *not* burned.

2. That one man was Giles Corey, whose story is a striking example of bravery under torture and a strong testimony to a fathers love and concern for his childrens welfare.

3. Under the laws of the period, Coreys only chance of ensuring that his heirs would not be deprived of his property was to "stand mute," which meant neither confessing to nor denying the charges of witchcraft.

4. His offsprings inheritance was guaranteed only if he died saying nothing at all about his guilt or innocence.

5. This lone defendants death came by "pressing" rather than hanging, and as the heavy stones were placed on his chest one by one, Coreys last defiant words were "More weight!"

Forming Contractions

Apostrophes also can be used to make contractions, which are most often found in informal writing. Some of the writing you do for your college courses—research papers, for example—is too formal for the use of contractions. But in less formal writing, and especially in dialogue, contractions sound very natural and appropriate.

A contraction is simply a shortened form of two words. The apostrophe is placed where one or more letters have been omitted. For example, *I am* becomes *I'm,* and *I have* becomes *I've.*

Exercise Fourteen   ∗   PART A

Make contractions of the following pairs of words.

1. you are = _____

2. are not = _____

3. could have = _____

4. he is = _____

5. were not = _____

6. I am = _____

7. had not = _____

8. I would = _____

9. did not = _____

10. was not = _____

PART B

Make contractions of the following pairs of words.

1. she will = _____

2. who is = _____

3. it is = _____

4. would not = _____

5. they have = _____

6. is not = _____

7. there is = _____

8. you had = _____

9. should not = _____

10. they are = _____

Other Uses

The apostrophe sometimes is used not to make a contraction of two words, but simply to show that a letter or letters have been dropped from one word. For example, in *Howlin' Wolf*, the name of the great blues musician, the apostrophe replaces the letter *g*. Similarly, *rock and roll* can be written as *rock 'n' roll*.

    The apostrophe also may be used to make unusual plurals. For example, to avoid confusion when single lowercase letters are used as nouns, an apostrophe precedes the *-s* to form plurals. For example:

    "Why are all the *k's* and *w's* on this page so light?"

Abbreviations with periods also take an apostrophe in plural form. Again, this style is used for clarification:

    "Is there a ceremony for granting *M.A.'s* and *Ph.D.'s?*"

However, if letters used as words, figures or dates, or other special terms are *not* unclear when only *-s* is added to form the plural, no apostrophe is needed. Note these examples:

"Now I know my *ABCs.*"

Elvis Presley first gained popularity in the *1950s*, but he still has loyal fans in the *1990s*.

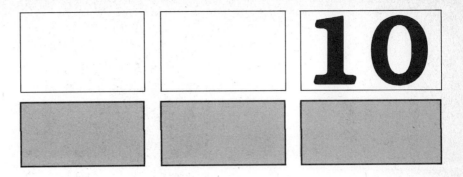

Solving Common Problems in Combining and Punctuating Sentences

UNIT 1:   Run-ons and Comma Splices

In chapter 9, you learned a wide variety of techniques for combining clauses and punctuating sentences. Now we're going to look at some of the most common problems that are solved by those techniques.

The two most common errors that occur during the process of combining clauses are *run-ons* and *comma splices*. Contrary to what many students think, run-ons have nothing to do with writing too much or "running on at the mouth," as one student put it. *A run-on is simply two or more independent clauses that run into each other without connection.* These incorrectly combined clauses can be short or long. Let's look at a typical example.

> **Run-on error:**   Joseph Pulitzer was a Hungarian immigrant he became a major American newspaper publisher.

Can you see how this sentence fits the description of a run-on? It has two independent clauses—*Joseph Pulitzer was a Hungarian immigrant* and *he became a major American newspaper publisher*—that bump into each other without any connection. To solve the problem, you can use some of the sentence-combining and punctuation techniques you learned in chapter 9. Here are a few solutions:

1. **Add a conjunction between the clauses:**
    Joseph Pulitzer was a Hungarian immigrant, and he became a major American newspaper publisher.
2. **Make one of the clauses a relative or dependent clause:**
    a. Joseph Pulitzer, who became a major American newspaper publisher, was a Hungarian immigrant.
    b. Joseph Pulitzer, who was a Hungarian immigrant, became a major American newspaper publisher.
    c. Joseph Pulitzer became a major newspaper publisher after he immigrated to the United States from Hungary.
3. **Compress the information into one clause:**
    a. The Hungarian immigrant Joseph Pulitzer became a major American newspaper publisher.
    b. Joseph Pulitzer emigrated from Hungary to the United States and became a major newspaper publisher.
    c. Joseph Pulitzer came to the United States from Hungary, eventually becoming one of the major American newspaper publishers.
4. **Use a semicolon to link the clauses:**
    Joseph Pulitzer was a Hungarian immigrant; he became a major American newspaper publisher.
5. **Adjust the sentence so that you can use a colon:**
    When Hungarian immigrant Joseph Pulitzer began working as a laborer in St. Louis, Missouri, no one could have guessed what he would eventually become: one of the giants of the American newspaper business.

Don't Use a Comma to Solve a Run-on

Notice that none of the solutions given to correct our example run-on calls simply for a comma between the independent clauses. If you insert a comma, you simply trade one error—a run-on—for another—a comma splice.

> **Comma splice error:** Joseph Pulitzer was a Hungarian immigrant, he became a major American newspaper publisher.

The word *splice* means to combine or fuse, so *comma splice* is a good name for the error of trying to join independent clauses with a comma. In the conventions of the English language, the comma is not that strong; it can do a lot, but it can't link clauses. This is important to know, because comma splices are probably the number one technical error in student writing.

Check It Out

Here are a few simple problem sentences. So you can check your understanding before you go on, label each one as *okay, ro* for run-on, or *cs* for comma splice.

a. _____ He cooked she cleaned.

b. _____ Several times I asked about the possible effects of the two medications no one ever took my questions seriously.

c. _____ The butterscotch pudding was hot, and it burned my tongue.

d. _____ People can be cold, they can be cruel.

e. _____ The phone rang the sound made us all jump.

f. _____ Roses are red, violets are blue.

g. _____ Clinging to their last hope, the search party began one final trek up the mountainside.

[ANSWERS: a. ro;   b. ro;   c. okay;   d. cs;   e. ro;   f. cs;   g. okay.]

Making Separate Sentences

How about using a period and capital letter to break up the independent clauses of a run-on or a comma splice? For instance:

> Joseph Pulitzer was a Hungarian immigrant. He became a major American newspaper publisher.

It's not wrong to do this, but it's often not the best choice for an adult writer. Why not? Because, where a younger writer tends to present each fact or thought as an individual or discrete unit, an adult writer most often wants to show *connections* and *relationships* between ideas, and one good way to do that is to combine small units (clauses) into larger units (compound or complex sentences or other more complicated sentence structures). So *most* of the time you'll want to combine clauses rather than separate them.

Of course, as always, there are exceptions. Writers sometimes create short, choppy sentences for a desired effect—for emphasis, suspense, humor, or variety. In the following passage, notice how Barbara Jordan, formerly a U.S. Representative and later a professor of public affairs at the University of Texas, balances short and long sentences for variety and emphasis. Underline her shorter sentences and notice how they create a strong, assertive effect:

> Texas is more than a place. It is a frame of mind. A Texan believes that the individual is powerful. Texas has that rugged individualism. It may not be polished, may not be smooth, and it may not be silky, but it is there. I believe that I get from the soil and the spirit of Texas the feeling that I, as an individual, can accomplish whatever I want to and that there are no limits, that you can just keep going, just keep soaring. I like that spirit.

In the next passage, notice that baseball player Dave Heaverlo uses short sentences to create a comic rhythm as he explains how he finally got the Oakland Athletics to trade him:

> I tried growing a beard. That didn't work. I became the player rep. That didn't work. Then I bought a house. That worked.

Generally then, you should solve run-ons and comma splices by combining rather than separating clauses. But when you have a good rhetorical reason for writing short sentences, feel free to do so.

The Role of Pronouns

Notice how often in the exercises that follow and in your own papers the subject of the second clause in a run-on or comma splice is a pronoun. For example:

> Elton John began his career as a backup singer *he* provided background vocals for American soul stars on tour in England.

Using the pronoun gives some writers the false sense that they are connecting their clauses because the subject of the later clause is not understandable without reference to information in the preceding clause. But that fact does not connect the clauses in a grammatical sense. Watch for how and where you use pronouns (especially *he, she, we, they, this, that,* and *it*) in your writing. You want to make sure you aren't creating comma splices and run-ons with them.

The Role of the Adverb *Then*

Watch for the word *then*. Writers often think they're linking clauses when they use *then* at the head of the second one. However, *then* is just an adverb: It can describe the time an action happened, but it cannot link clauses. For example:

> **Wrong:**   Alfred Bernhard Nobel invented dynamite in 1867, *then* later he
>   used $9 million of his fortune to establish the Nobel prizes.

A semicolon inserted before *then* would be one good solution here.

Exercises

* **Exercise One**

Some of the following items are perfectly okay; they are not run-ons or comma splices. Label them *okay*. Other items are run-ons or comma splices. Label them *ro* or *cs* and mark an X at every problem spot.
   Next, solve the run-ons and comma splices using the techniques learned in chapter 9. Please don't use a period and a capital letter to break them into separate sentences. Use this exercise to practice your new skills in *combining* clauses.

For revisions that don't fit on the page—those that involve more than the insertion of a conjunction or a change of punctuation—use your own paper.

1. _____ Michael Dorris is a novelist and a professor of anthropology at Dartmouth University he wrote *The Broken Cord,* a riveting book about his adopted son and the tragedy of fetal alcohol syndrome.

2. _____ Currently there are about 30,000 centenarians in the United States their number is expected to grow to 100,000 by the year 2000.

3. _____ In 1874, Levi Strauss made the first blue jeans, he charged customers $13.50 a dozen for them.

4. _____ The legendary Bigfoot, who supposedly has been spotted at least 750 times in the past century, walks upright, has 18-inch feet, and gives off a foul odor.

5. _____ Pluto is the smallest and coldest of the planets it is also the most distant from the earth.

6. _____ Lizzie Borden, who was accused of the ax murder of her father and stepmother, is considered one of America's most famous criminals, actually she was acquitted at her trial.

7. _____ Skateboarding, which is a hobby enjoyed by about twenty million Americans, causes more injuries than football but fewer injuries than bike riding.

8. _____ If you stacked up all the hamburgers that McDonald's sold in the company's first 25 years of business, you'd have 20 piles of burgers, and each pile would be as tall as the Sears Tower in Chicago.

9. _____ During the 1960 Olympics, Wilma Rudolph, Tennessee's star sprinter, was dubbed "La Chattanooga Choo Choo" by the French newspapers she won three gold medals that year.

10. _____ The shortest verse in the Bible is John, chapter 11, verse 35, the verse reads simply, "Jesus wept."

Exercise Two

Label each item as *okay, ro,* or *cs.* Continue to revise problem sentences.

1. _____ Only moments before he was murdered, Malcolm X had walked onto the stage of New York's Audubon Ballroom, greeting the assembled crowd with "As-salaam aleikum" ("Peace be unto you"), they had answered, "Wa-alei-kum salaam" ("And unto you be peace").

2. _____ The colors of the interlocking rings on the Olympic flag are black, blue, red, green, and yellow, at least one of those colors appears on every national flag in the world.

3. _____ In addition to writing *Alice in Wonderland*, Lewis Carroll also invented the miniature chess set for travelers and a forerunner of "Scrabble."

4. _____ The words to "Amazing Grace," one of America's oldest and best loved hymns, were written by John Newton, an eighteenth-century British slave trader who later became a dedicated abolitionist.

5. _____ Arthritis afflicts more than 31 million Americans it is painful and often disabling it strikes people of all ages.

6. _____ The comic actress Mae West once said, "It's not the men in my life; it's the life in my men" at one point in her life West was the highest paid woman in the United States.

7. _____ For years polygamy was legal but not widely practiced in the United States, then it was made illegal in 1882.

8. _____ Now known to most of his fans as Bob Dylan, Robert Zimmerman grew up in Hibbing, Minnesota.

9. _____ Scientists know that rapid eye movement always accompanies dreaming they have been aware of this fact since the early 1950s.

10. _____ Even in the coldest places in the world, penguins have greater difficulty

keeping cool than keeping warm these animals can suffer from the heat if the temperature goes above freezing.

* Exercise Three

Label each item as *okay, ro,* or *cs* and revise problem sentences. This time you won't be working with unrelated bits of information; the subject of this exercise is a study of men, women, and loneliness.

1. _____ Ladd Wheeler and Harry Reis, both psychologists at the University of Rochester in New York, are the authors of an intriguing study.

2. _____ Their study is called "Loneliness, Social Interaction and Sex Roles" it is based on an examination of the social interactions of about one hundred female and male seniors at the University of Rochester.

3. _____ The men and women who participated in the study kept a record of all social interactions that lasted more than ten minutes they kept the record for two weeks.

4. _____ The students' records suggested something very interesting women generally make better friends than men.

5. _____ The study found that people of both genders are lonelier if they socialize mostly with men they are less lonely if they socialize primarily with women.

6. _____ According to Reis and Wheeler, women seem to make better friends because they are more intimate and revealing in their conversations, and they tend to enter social interactions at a deeper level than men.

7. _____ Men, on the other hand, traditionally have had a strong tendency to spend most of their time in conversation talking about less personal matters, Wheeler says many men spend a substantial amount of time talking about sports and joking around.

8. _____ The study acknowledges, of course, that men are not all alike and indicates that "more sharing" men are happier in their social lives than "less sharing" men.

9. _____ The authors of the study believe that the most effective way to fight

loneliness is to spend meaningful personal time with other people, it doesn't have to

be a lot of time.

10. _____ There are things that men can teach women, and there are things that women

can teach men, at this point in human history, it looks as if women can teach men

how to be friends.

Editing for Run-ons and Comma Splices in Context

At this point, you probably have a good deal of skill spotting and revising run-ons and comma splices. But to transfer this skill to your own writing, it's essential that you be able to spot them in a larger context. Exercise four will help you make this transfer.

Exercise Four   PART A

With an *X*, mark each spot where a run-on or comma splice occurs. Then use a variety of techniques to correct the problems. You can break items into separate sentences occasionally, but try mostly to combine clauses. If there is not enough room to make some revisions between the lines, use the margins or your own paper.
   The topic is an outstanding hero of our era, Raoul Wallenberg; the information is derived from a variety of sources.

1   For all of its horrors, the twentieth century has no shortage of heroes. Some are

2   well-known to us, others are largely unknown. One of the least visible but most

3   dramatic heroes of our era is Raoul Wallenberg, a young diplomat who used everything

4   from personal charm to commando tactics to save the lives of tens of thousands of Jews

5   in the final months of World War II.

6   Wallenberg was a member of the most privileged class in Sweden he was from a

7   wealthy, aristocratic family that had made major contributions in literature, law,

8   shipping, banking, government, and religious life. Although the young Wallenberg had

9   an artistic and imaginative temperament, his grandfather encouraged him to prepare for

10   a career in the world of banking and business. As part of his plan to help his grandson

11   become a broad-minded, liberally educated man of the world, the older Wallenberg sent

12   him to the United States to travel and observe, then to study architecture at the

13   University of Michigan there he flourished in both academics and social life.

14   After he returned to Europe, Wallenberg followed his grandfather's wishes and

15   began to work his way up in the banking business he clearly did not have his heart in

16   finance. Eventually, circumstances conspired to draw him into one of the most amazing

17   and inspiring episodes of the entire war. A man named Iver Olsen represented the

18   American War Refugee Board in Stockholm. Olsen asked Wallenberg to go to Budapest

19   it was the only place in Europe that still had a sizable population of Jews, they were in

20   tremendous danger because those who controlled the Nazi war machine were bent upon

21   one last paroxysm of destruction.

* PART B

Continue to follow the directions given in part A.

1   Raoul Wallenberg did not consider himself a particularly brave man, but he readily

2   . agreed to go to the capital of Hungary and do what he could. In Budapest, Wallenberg

3   began his work by designing the *Schutzpass,* this was an official-looking passport that put

4   its holder under the protection of Wallenberg's nation of birth, Sweden. Since Sweden

5   was a neutral country, any Hungarian Jew who held such a document could claim that he

6   or she was planning to immigrate to Sweden, that person could then no more be

7   from German-occupied Hungary to a death camp than any Swedish citizen. (The Jews

8   could not actually escape to Sweden because of wartime restrictions on travel, plus

9   generally the lack of other means to do so.)

10   One of the most fascinating aspects of Wallenberg's scheme is that the *Schutzpass*

11   actually had no basis or precedent in international law, but the German Nazis accepted

12   it as authentic and authoritative. Why did they accept the *Schutzpass?* One expert on the

13   subject is journalist Elenore Lester she points out that Wallenberg was an extremely

14   imaginative man he succeeded where a more conventional thinker almost certainly

15   would have failed. Wallenberg seemed to understand that to save any lives at all, he

16   could not use logical or ethical pleas, it would be more advantageous to try to think like

17 the Nazis, to enter into their psychopathology. If the German Nazis in Hungary

18 represented a formal government that believed it had the right to kill innocent men,

19 women, and children for no other reason than their Jewish heritage, then obviously they

20 could not be reasoned with. Wallenberg decided to assume the role of the formal

21 diplomat who says, "Oh, yes, of course I see that you have your rules, but where there

22 are rules, there are always exceptions."

PART C

Continue to follow the directions given in part A.

1   Although officially Wallenberg was limited to issuing only five thousand *Schutz-*

2   *passe,* he actually distributed around twenty thousand. How did his system work?

3   Typically, when a deportation was scheduled, Wallenberg knew about it through his

4   spies within the Nazi bureaucracy. He would arrive at the train station along with

5   members of his staff, then he would set up an office. He would unfold a portable table,

6   pull up a chair, and open a notebook he would announce that those who held *Schutzpasse*

7   should step forward and produce them. As Wallenberg proceeded to check names off a

8   list, people would begin to catch on that some of those who were stepping forward and

9   who would soon be leaving with Wallenberg did not actually have Swedish passports.

10 Unlike the Nazi guards milling about, some detainees quickly realized that Wallenberg

11 was accepting whatever anyone waved before him, these items included forged

12 passports, old eyeglass prescriptions, letters, and receipts. When he was occasionally

13 challenged by a Nazi soldier, Wallenberg would claim that whatever had been handed to

14 him was at the very least a preliminary application for a Swedish passport. Wallenberg

15 did whatever worked to keep alive as many as possible of the Nazis' intended victims.

16 It didn't matter what was legal, proper, or believable it only mattered what worked.

17   For a while, Wallenberg used this approach with some success, then the

18 Hungarian Nazis, also known as the Arrow Cross government, came to power in

19   October of 1944. In some ways, that regime turned out to be worse than the German

20   government of occupation. From then on, Wallenberg could rely less and less on

21   diplomatic ploys and the appearance of officialdom he had to begin to depend more and

22   more on his considerable personal charisma, boldness, and ingenuity. Once the Arrow

23   Cross government was installed, criminals and psychopaths swarmed into the streets to

24   pull Jews out of hiding, they even wrenched Jewish children from protective hideouts

25   inside Budapest churches. Again and again, Wallenberg came upon situations where he

26   had to resort to commando tactics for example, more than once he placed himself

27   between intended victims and Hungarian Nazi teenagers who were armed with machine

28   guns. Wallenberg would shout in German that he would have to report the teenagers to

29   "higher authorities" if they did not disperse immediately. Of course, those higher

30   authorities would have sided with the thugs, not with Wallenberg, but he operated with

31   such force and conviction that often he could make black seem white.

* PART D

Continue to follow the directions given in part A.

1   Wallenberg's exploits often went beyond the realm of documents and bureaucratic

2   stratagems. He once stood on the roof of a train, ducking Nazi bullets and supplying

3   passports to the Jews who were being crammed into cattle cars below, they were about

4   to be deported to concentration camps.

5   On another occasion, he pulled a young man from the armed Nazis who held him.

6   The young man did not have a *Schutzpass* his older brother did. The older brother would

7   not leave the train without him. Seeing the situation, Wallenberg told the Nazis, "He is

8   working for me," in reality Wallenberg had never seen him before. Both brothers left

9   the train and returned to the temporary safety of home.

10   In 1944, thousands of Jews—mostly women, children, and old men—were pulled

11   off the streets and out of their homes and forced to walk 125 miles to the city of

12   Hegyeshalom on the Austrian border. (Most younger and middle-aged men had long

13   since been deported.) There the survivors of the march would be forced to build

14   fortifications. Many of the women were still in the high heels and dresses they had been

15   wearing when they were taken. They walked for a week with almost no food, thousands

16   died before they reached their destination. Some became weak they were shot. Others

17   threw themselves into the Danube. Although many lives were lost, in this case also,

18   Wallenberg managed to intervene. At the 1961 trial of Adolph Eichmann, who

19   masterminded Hitler's program of deportation, an assistant to Wallenberg told how

20   Wallenberg had sent him to the border with hundreds of blank immunity documents and

21   a typewriter. In this way, Wallenberg was able to save a good number of Jews from sure

22   death on the way to or in Hegyeshalom.

23   On January 16, 1945, about fifty Jewish residents of Budapest were brought to the

24   courtyard of the Swedish embassy in the city, they were stripped of their wedding rings

25   and other jewelry and their remaining food. They stood before a large group of Nazi

26   soldiers, these soldiers were armed with machine guns. Suddenly Wallenberg stormed

27   in. One woman later recalled that he appeared like an angel of mercy, he shouted that

28   it was an extraterritorial building, little by little, the Nazis dispersed, they left without

29   taking the loot they had collected. Years later, the survivor of this encounter said that

30   people could not believe their eyes. Wallenberg had triumphed again through sheer

31   willpower and his belief in the rightness of his actions.

PART E

Continue to follow the directions given in part A.

1   What happened to this amazing man, a man who did so much when so many did

2   nothing? In a sense, what follows is "part two" of this riveting story.

3   On the very day after he rescued the people from the courtyard of the Swedish

4   embassy, Raoul Wallenberg was arrested by officials of the Soviet Army, the Soviets

5   had just liberated Budapest. Ironically, Wallenberg was happy to see the Russians enter

6   the city and was anxious to present to them his ideas on its rehabilitation. It is impossible

7   to say exactly why, but the Russians took him into their custody and sent him to

8   Lubyanka prison in Moscow. Some say it was a simple mistake, they say that pride later

9   kept the Soviets from admitting that Wallenberg should not have been arrested. Others

10 say that he was suspected of being a spy for the United States, and the Russians wanted

11 to prevent a strong American influence in post-war Hungary. At any rate, he vanished

12 from Budapest on January 17, 1945.

13   Wallenberg was never seen again, at least not outside Soviet prisons or mental

14 hospitals. For decades, this extraordinary human being was little-known beyond the

15 circle of Budapest Jews whose lives he saved. Although his mother, Maj von Dardel,

16 and other members of his family kept the search going in the early years, the

17 government of Sweden made few inquiries, the United States also failed him. It was not

18 until 1981, after Elenore Lester's book, *Wallenberg: The Man in the Iron Web,* created

19 a storm of interest, that an international commission to find Wallenberg was formed.

20 The Soviet Union, which earlier had claimed that Wallenberg died of a heart attack at the

21 age of 35, eventually opened selected prison archives, many people remained skeptical

22 that the full truth would ever emerge.

23   What is known for sure is that there is "compelling" evidence that Wallenberg was

24 still alive in the 1960s this evidence comes from released prisoners and Soviet

25 dissidents. According to the international commission, there is even "credible"

26 evidence that he was alive into the 1980s.

27   Why was no one looking for Wallenberg for so many years? Elie Wiesel has put

28 forth a troubling explanation, Wiesel is a survivor of Auschwitz and Buchenwald,

29 chronicler of the Holocaust and winner of the Nobel Peace Prize. He maintains that, for

30   a long time, there was little or no discussion of Wallenberg because people were simply

31   embarrassed they were embarrassed that one person had done so much to fight evil. If

32   it was true that Wallenberg had averted death for tens of thousands of innocent human

33   beings, then it could not also be true that it was impossible to do something, that the

34   force of evil was too strong, that it was utterly paralyzing. Raoul Wallenberg proved that

35   it *was* possible and *is* possible to resist evil.

36   The case of Raoul Wallenberg nags at the conscience, perhaps the best way to

37   honor his memory is to try to learn the truth about his incarceration and emulate his

38   courage in our personal and political lives. As Wiesel has reminded us, "We must always

39   say to one another, 'I am responsible for you, and you for me, but I more so.' " In living

40   out the words of Elie Wiesel, we can realize the legacy of Raoul Wallenberg.

UNIT 2:   Fragments

What is a fragment? As you might expect, it is a *piece* of something—not the whole thing. It's a piece of a sentence that the writer treats as a complete sentence. Here's a more formal definition: *A fragment is a group of words placed between a capital letter and a period even though it does not have all three requirements of a sentence: (1) a subject, (2) a predicate, and (3) a sense of independence.*

In unit 1, you learned that run-ons and comma splices are not necessarily long; here you'll see that fragments are not necessarily short. And, like comma splices and run-ons, fragments can be solved by adding punctuation or using sentence-combining techniques.

Intentional Fragments

As in so many other things, here also what is usually considered an error in writing is sometimes not an error at all. Highly skilled writers sometimes use fragments to create a feeling of incompleteness. Thus, on occasion, a fragment may be an intentional deviation from the norm rather than a mistake. A writer who skillfully and consciously uses an occasional fragment does not need this unit. The discussion and the exercises here are for students who haven't yet achieved that level of control.

Types of Fragments

Sentence fragments appear in a number of different forms in the writing of adults. Let's take a look at the most common types of fragments.

Type 1: Fragments That Begin with Subordinating Conjunctions

The first type of fragment is the simplest kind, and it should be easy to solve because you've already worked with complex sentences. In this type of fragment, there is a subject and there is a predicate, but there is no sense of independence. The subordinating conjunction creates a dependent clause that must be attached to an independent clause. Here are some examples:

a. Because the voice of the late Sarah Vaughn spanned four octaves.
b. If gravity can be fully understood.
c. Although fashion designer Geoffrey Beene was once asked to lend his name to a perfume for puppies.

In each case, the conjunction leads the reader to expect more. For a sense of independence and wholeness, each of these clauses needs to be combined with an independent clause. Another solution would be simply to drop the conjunction from each clause. Choose any one of the three fragments and solve it in two ways. First, drop the conjunction; second, add an independent clause:

Solution one: _____

_____

Solution two: _____

_____

Type 2: Fragments Related to Embedding

Writers make another type of fragment when they slip up in the process of embedding one clause within another. For example:

a. Little Richard, who gave up his career in music to become a minister. Traded rock and roll for the Rock of Ages.

b. The fact that Elvis Costello was once a computer programmer. Is probably unknown to most of his fans.

c. Many of Elizabeth Catlett's sculptures and lithographs, which can be seen in museums all around the world. Portray the lives of black women.

You've already worked with embedded elements in sentences, so these fragments will be easy for you to solve. Each example contains *two* fragments, and each can be solved by making changes in punctuation and capitalization. Make those changes now in examples a, b, and c.

This type of fragment takes another slightly different form, too. Here are two examples:

d. For over forty years, the coach of the baseball team at Grambling State University in Louisiana was Ralph Waldo Emerson Jones. Who was also the university's president.

e. Only seven percent of all nudists suffer from hypertension. Which afflicts seventeen percent of the general population.

Again, these fragments are simple to solve by changing capitalization and punctuation. Make those changes for examples d and e.

To avoid making this type of fragment, follow an easy rule of thumb: If you're starting a sentence with a relative pronoun or embedding word, then normally you should be writing a question (for example, "Which one looks best?" "Who wants to walk with me?")—or else you're going to have a fragment.

Type 3: Fragments with -ing Verbs

The third type of fragment has a subject and a verb but lacks a sense of independence. The problem is that the verb is not *finite* or finished. It leaves the reader hanging. This fragment usually has an *-ing* verb used alone (in other words, used without a helping verb) in the single clause of the sentence. Here are some examples:

a. Billy Joel *crusading* against teen suicide.
b. At their peak, the buffalo *forming* the largest herds of mammals in the history of the earth.
c. Eddie Rommel *being* the first major league umpire to wear glasses.

The possible solutions to these fragments range from adding a helping verb to changing the verb to a form that does not have an *-ing* ending. In example a, for instance, shifting to the verb *crusades* or *crusaded* would solve the problem; forming the verb phrase *is crusading* would also work. For b, *forming* could become *formed*. For c, you can't add a helping verb, but you can change *being* to another form of the verb *to be;* for instance, *being* could become *was*. Another solution is to keep *being* but not rely on it as the verb in the main clause. For example:

> Eddie Rommel, being the first major league umpire to wear glasses, adopted that habit on April 18, 1966, for a game between the New York Yankees and the Washington Senators.

Solve the following fragment in two different ways:

A typical hot fudge sundae *equaling* about 500 calories.

Solution one: _____

_____

Solution two: _____

_____

Type 4: Fragments That Are Cut-off Phrases

The fourth kind of fragment lacks either a subject or a verb. It is a phrase, not a clause. Usually when it appears in a student's writing, it needs to be connected to the preceding or following sentence. Occasionally, it can become a sentence on its own. Here are some examples:

a. *Fearing a breakdown in morality.* Many people cannot support some school systems' policy of making free condoms available to students.

b. The oldest surviving pop music group is The Four Tops. *Going all the way back to 1953.*

c. *Unsure of the exact cause of multiple sclerosis.* Some researchers see a possible link between the disease and close contact with dogs.

Solve each fragment in examples a, b, and c by making changes in punctuation and capitalization.

How About Sentences That Begin with But?

Earlier, you worked with the coordinating conjunctions—*and, but, or, nor, so, for,* and *yet.* Normally, these words draw two clauses together to form a compound sentence. But sometimes they are used at the beginning of a sentence (this one, for example), and that use is okay, too. A quick look at a few stories in today's newspaper will show you that *but* is often used as the first word in a sentence because it's effective in signalling a contrast with the preceding sentence. The other coordinating conjunctions are also used this way from time to time, although *and* is used less frequently as the first word in a sentence. Still, you'll sometimes find *and* in that position, especially when the writer wants to connect two ideas and yet create a hard, dramatic stop between them. For our purposes, let's agree that, in the following exercises, the sentences that begin with coordinating conjunctions should not be identified as fragments.

* **Exercise One**

Label each item as *okay* or *f* for fragment. Then solve the fragments, using a variety of techniques: make changes in capitalization, punctuation, and verb forms or do a larger revision. Lengthy rewrites can go in the margins or on your own paper.

1. _____ 7X being the code name of Coca Cola's secret ingredient.

2. _____ Mt. Ararat, which is traditionally thought to be the resting place of Noah's Ark.

3. _____ Because the Orient Express ran from Paris to Istanbul.

4. _____ The world loved the "Ebony Express." Which was the nickname of track star Jesse Owens.

5. _____ Although he suffered seven broken bones in his career with the New York City Ballet, Edward Vilella never cancelled a performance, and for that reason some observers have called him the greatest athlete in the world.

6. _____ The average American eating nine pounds of pasta a year.

7. _____ When Wilfred J. Funk claimed that the most beautiful word in the English language is *chimes.*

8. _____ The psychologist Bruno Bettelheim believed that fairy-tale characters such as wicked witches, cruel kings, and evil stepmothers play a healthy role in the development of children. Helping them deal with negative feelings about their parents.

9. _____ Jimi Hendrix, possibly the greatest rock and roll guitarist of all time, was once the opening act for the Monkees.

10. _____ One of the many coincidences surrounding the deaths of Abraham Lincoln and John Kennedy is the fact that Lincoln was warned not to go to the Ford Theater by his secretary. A woman named Kennedy. President Kennedy, in turn, was advised against going to Dallas. By his secretary, whose name was Lincoln.

Exercise Two

Label each item as *okay* or *f*. Then solve the fragments by making changes in capitalization, punctuation, or verb forms or by doing a larger revision. Lengthy rewrites can go in the margins or on your own paper. Our subject here is Babe Didrikson Zaharias (1911?–1956), who is often called the greatest female athlete in history.

1. _____ Babe Didrikson Zaharias being the first all-around great woman athlete in American history.

2. _____ She had almost unbelievable versatility. Excelling at track and field, basketball, baseball, swimming, diving, tennis, billiards, and bowling.

3. _____ Since she won two Gold Medals at the 1932 Olympics.

4. _____ At the 1932 games, she set new world records in the high jump, the javelin throw, and the 80-meter hurdles.

5. _____ As a teenager, Babe Didrikson Zaharias once scoring 106 points in a basketball game.

6. _____ Officially entering 634 track and field events throughout her career. She won all of them except 12.

7. _____ This amazing athlete taking the U.S. Amateur golf title in 1946, the British Amateur title in 1947, and women's professional titles in 1948, 1950, and 1954.

8. _____ At one time, she toured the United States with a mostly male baseball team.

9. _____ The fact that she once threw a third strike past Joe Di Maggio.

10. _____ She was a woman who enjoyed great success in almost everything she tried.

Editing Fragments in Context

As usual, the best way to transfer your skill in solving fragments in exercises to solving or avoiding them in your essays is to find and fix fragments in a larger piece of writing.

Exercise Three   *   PART A

Underline each fragment in the following essay. Then solve each one by making it a full sentence or attaching it to a full sentence in a logical way. Use the margins or your own paper for lengthy rewrites.

This exercise concerns the language of the deaf, and much of the information in it is derived from *Seeing Voices: A Journey into the World of the Deaf* **by Oliver Sacks.**

1   Neurologist Oliver Sacks became interested in the deaf when he was asked to

2   review publications on the subject. Dr. Sacks, the author of several books of his own,

3   including *Migraine, Awakenings, A Leg to Stand On,* and *The Man Who Mistook His Wife*

4   *for a Hat,* soon became haunted by the image of deaf people. Who lived their lives in

5   total or near total isolation. Failing to acquire any kind of language and being thwarted

6   in their intellectual, emotional and social development. He began to wonder how

7   language develops and how necessary it actually is to our fulfillment as human beings.

8   Eventually, his research led him to write the book *Seeing Voices: A Journey into the*

9   *World of the Deaf.*

10   In his research, Dr. Sacks met many deaf people and deaf educators. Many of

11   those he met had acquired Sign. A powerful language that allows a kind of thinking and

12   perceiving that probably can't be fully imagined by hearing people. While retaining a

13   medical view of the deaf as a physician might be expected to do, Dr. Sacks also came to

14   see them in what he calls an "ethnic light." In other words, he began to understand them

15   as a people. Who had their own culture, language, and sensibility. In fact, Dr. Sacks is

16   not alone in viewing the Deaf as an ethnic group: He found that many deaf people use the

17   lower case *d* when employing the word *deaf* to describe their audiological condition, and

18   the uppercase *D* when speaking of themselves as a community with particular linguistic

19   and cultural characteristics.

20   The hearing world often regards deafness as little more than a nuisance, but in

21   reality deafness from birth is far more devastating—at least potentially—than blindness

22   at birth. Deaf children can't hear their parents and, unless their parents are proficient in

23   Sign, deaf babies are at great risk of becoming deprived in language and in everything

24   that language brings with it.

25   Although only 0.1 percent of the population is congenitally deaf, any study of this

26   group raises issues that are important to everyone. Especially the question of how we

27   become fully human. That process is not automatic or purely biological. On the contrary,

28   Dr. Sacks asserts, much of what defines and creates our humanity is a social and

29   historical gift that is passed from one generation to the next through the vehicle of

30   language. The threat to the deaf is that this gift, which is dependent upon language, may

31   be withheld. If the natural language strengths of the deaf are ignored, devalued, or

32   discouraged. Sadly, throughout history that often has been the case.

PART B

Continue to follow the directions given in part A.

1   Before 1750, the plight of people who were born deaf was tragic. They were

2   rarely able to acquire speech and were therefore usually judged to be "dumb" or stupid.

3   All uses of Sign were vehemently prohibited, and the prelingually deaf were therefore

4   cut off from language almost completely. (The prelingually deaf are those who were

5   born deaf or who lost their hearing before any speech was acquired.) In rare cases, the

6   deaf children of wealthy nobility were educated to speak and read. So that they could

7   attain legal status and inherit their parents' land and money. Those who could not speak

8   were labeled "mutes" and were not recognized as persons under the law. In general,

9   the deaf living their lives in isolation.

10   According to Dr. Sacks, it took centuries for philosophers of language and

11   educators of the deaf to realize that language could be something other than speech.

12   One of the greatest figures in this discovery and in the education of the deaf was the

13   Abbé de l'Epée. A humble man with a superb mind. He was insistent that the

14   poverty-stricken deaf who lived in the streets of Paris should have the chance to hear

15   the Word of God. This motivation led him to study the deaf closely, learn their language

16   of signs, and connect it to a system of signed French grammar. De l'Epée, who was one

17 of the very first hearing persons to learn Sign, used it to teach deaf students to read. By

18 associating three things: signs, pictures, and written words. In 1755, he opened a

19 school for the deaf. Probably the first such school to receive public support. By the time

20 de l'Epée died in 1789, he had created 21 schools for the deaf in Europe and had trained

21 a vast number of teachers for the deaf. De l'Epée's work emancipated the deaf and for

22 the first time made possible the existence of deaf writers, philosophers, engineers, and

23 intellectuals. Which before that time had been absolutely inconceivable.

24   About thirty years later, another Frenchman important in the education of the deaf

25 came to the United States. He was Laurent Clerc, and before his arrival in 1816

26 Americans had never been exposed to a deaf intellectual. A person of great and obvious

27 gifts. Who could neither hear nor speak. Clerc, like de l'Epée, advanced the cause of the

28 deaf tremendously. With Thomas Gallaudet, Clerc established the American Asylum for

29 the Deaf in Hartford, Connecticut. The success of the Hartford school, which employed

30 many deaf teachers, was spectacular. Its success leading very quickly to the

31 establishment of many other schools for the deaf. Clerc brought with him the French

32 sign system that de l'Epée had helped to create, and it very quickly combined with the

33 language of the local deaf communities and evolved into American Sign Language (ASL).

* PART C

Continue to follow the directions given in part A.

1   One of the fascinating things about the early years of the Hartford asylum involved

2 a group of deaf students from Martha's Vineyard. An island about four miles off the

3 southeastern coast of Massachusetts. These students already had a powerful sign

4 language that became an essential part of ASL. Dr. Sacks first became aware of the

5 Martha's Vineyard story. When he read the book *Everyone Here Spoke Sign Language:*

6 *Hereditary Deafness on Martha's Vineyard* by Nora Ellen Groce. In her book, Groce

7 explains how a recessive gene, brought out through the intermarriage of close relatives,

8   caused hereditary deafness in a significant percentage of the population of Martha's

9   Vineyard over a period of about 250 years. After the first deaf settlers arrived on the

10   island in the late seventeenth century. By the 1850s, in some villages on the island

11   every fourth person was deaf.

12   But on Martha's Vineyard the deaf were fully integrated into the normal flow of

13   life. Not isolated or considered handicapped in any way. This was probably because

14   almost everyone on the island had deaf relatives, in-laws, friends, neighbors, or

15   co-workers, and most hearing people grew up with Sign. For her book, Groce

16   interviewed elderly islanders who talked in great detail and with no shortage of affection

17   about their former acquaintances. Without ever mentioning their deafness. (The last

18   deaf resident of the island died in the early 1950s.) It was only in response to Groce's

19   question that the interviewee would confirm that, yes, the person under discussion had

20   indeed been deaf. On Martha's Vineyard, the deaf were set apart only in the sense that

21   they were generally the most learned people in the island's fishing villages. Having been

22   sent to the Hartford asylum for their education.

23   When Dr. Sacks finished Groce's book, he was so excited that he jumped into his

24   car with nothing but his toothbrush, camera, and tape recorder. Heading straight for

25   Martha's Vineyard. He wanted to see this magical island for himself, and he was not

26   disappointed. Upon his arrival, he came upon a group of six old folks gossiping on the

27   front porch of a general store. They spoke with great animation, and then suddenly they

28   began to sign. As Dr. Sacks described the extraordinary scene, "They signed for a

29   minute, laughed, then dropped back into speech" (36). Later, he met a hearing woman

30   in her nineties who talked to herself in Sign. Her daughter told the doctor that her

31   mother, as she sat peacefully resting, sometimes made what appeared to be knitting

32   motions, but in reality she was talking to herself in Sign. The old woman sometimes

33   even dreaming in Sign.

34 Dr. Sacks deduced from his visit to this amazing community, years after its

35 heyday as a well-mixed community of deaf and hearing, that if Sign is once learned as a

36 primary language, it will be retained and used freely for its own special purpose and

37 beauty. Even when a person is physically able to rely solely on speech. He concluded,

38 "Sign, I was now convinced, was a fundamental language of the brain" (36).

PART D

Continue to follow the directions given in part A.

1 As Dr. Sacks argues in *Seeing Voices,* Sign, the natural language of the deaf, shows

2 the astonishing potential of the human brain and the almost limitless versatility and

3 flexibility of the nervous system. The acquisition and structure of Sign are examples of

4 human strengths. Which are unexpected, mysterious, and undreamt of by most of us.

5 The language experiences of the deaf have important implications for the deaf and the

6 hearing.

7 So how did Sign ever fall into disfavor, as it did for many years? To understand this

8 tragic reversal. We must return to a time not long after Laurent Clerc and Thomas

9 Gallaudet established their school for the deaf in Hartford. By 1869, over 40 percent of

10 the teachers of the deaf in the United States were deaf themselves. In 1864, Congress

11 made the Columbia Institution for the Deaf and Blind in Washington the first college for

12 the deaf in the nation. At its head was Thomas Gallaudet's son, Edward. (Later it was

13 renamed Gallaudet College and then, finally, Gallaudet University.) Sign, which was

14 widely accepted in deaf education, began to empower large numbers of deaf students

15 who previously had had no access to higher learning.

16 Then suddenly in the last quarter of the nineteenth century, the tide turned.

17 Taking with it almost a century of progress. Dr. Sacks maintains that the disfavor into

18 which Sign fell was just one of many manifestations of the oppressive and conformist

19 trends of the Victorian age. Little tolerance was shown to any minority group or its

20 values and practices. Also, there had been for some time a growing feeling among

21 parents and teachers of the deaf that deaf children should learn to speak or they would

22 be limited to life in a very small world. The world of other deaf people who knew Sign.

23 As Dr. Sacks says, this was and still is a genuine dilemma. In the late nineteenth

24 century, the dilemma led to a movement called *oralism*.

25   But according to Dr. Sacks, oralism did not work. Under the oralist approach, it

26 took years and years of arduous one-on-one instruction for one teacher to help one deaf

27 student acquire any significant degree of speech. Furthermore, the time and energy

28 that went into learning speech took away from learning about the rest of the world.

29 About history, literature, math, science, and politics. Previously, schools that employed

30 Sign had produced students. Who were every bit as educated and accomplished as

31 hearing students. Schools that banned the use of Sign, on the other hand, produced

32 frustrated students who had to put all or most of their energy into making headway in

33 speech and lip reading.

∗ PART E

Continue to follow the directions given in part A.

1   One of the most fascinating aspects of the war between the advocates of Sign and

2   the oralists is the role of Alexander Graham Bell. The inventor of the telephone. Bell

3   had unusual personal reasons for entering the debate on the oralist side. For one thing,

4   he came from a family with a strong history of teaching elocution and working with

5   speech problems. For another, both Bell's wife and mother were deaf but never

6   admitted it. Bell had an aversion to the use of Sign and became a strong supporter of

7   oralism. His prestige giving the stamp of approval to the oralist camp. Soon the

8   movement toward oralism began to have drastic practical effects. At the International

9   Congress of Educators of the Deaf in Milan in 1880, a vote was taken. Prohibiting the

10 use of Sign in schools for the deaf. (Deaf teachers were denied the right to vote in

11   Milan.) Dr. Sacks notes that it was typical of the Victorian age, with its emphasis on the

12   power of science, that deaf students should be forcibly turned from their natural

13   language and forced to learn a language—speech—that for them was unnatural.

14   It is Dr. Sacks's position that this would not have been a problem if oralism had

15   worked to expand the world of the deaf, but it did not. In fact, it actually constricted

16   their world. Because immense resources had to be directed toward acquiring speech

17   and away from enjoying the pleasures that language, once acquired through Sign, could

18   bring. The reign of oralism that began in the late nineteenth century lasted for many,

19   many years. Bringing with it devastating effects. For example, in 1972, a study showed

20   that in the United States the typical deaf 18-year-old high school graduate had a

21   fourth-grade reading level. A later study in England showed similar results.

22   It was not until the 1960s that an outcry arose from teachers and parents of deaf

23   children. Who were joined by historians and psychologists. In 1970, Joanne Greenberg's

24   novel *In This Sign* brought the situation to the attention of a wide audience, and years later

25   Mark Medoff's play and movie *Children of a Lesser God* also made an enormous

26   impression. Both works opened many eyes and ears, and along with other forces, helped

27   create an atmosphere for the reemergence of Sign. The truest and most natural language

28   of the deaf.

29   Dr. John Hughlings-Jackson, another neurologist, observes, "We speak not only

30   to tell other people what we think, but to tell ourselves what we think. Speech is a part

31   of thought" (qtd. in Sacks 19). Intelligence may be locked up, unusable, and

32   inaccessible. If language is not available. Through Sign, language becomes present for

33   the deaf, and their intelligence breaks through, flourishes, ascends.

UNIT 3:   Misplaced and Dangling Modifiers

In constructing sentences, writers sometimes put their modifiers in the wrong places. Generally, a modifying word or phrase should be as close as possible to whatever it describes. Sometimes it should precede what it describes, and sometimes it should follow it; you'll need to figure out appropriate placement for each case.

Misplaced Modifiers

Misplaced modifiers are a single word or a phrase that is not in the best spot in the sentence; technically, a misplaced modifier describes something other than what the writer intended. In student writing, the word *only* often is misplaced. Here's a classic example:

> **Wrong:**   Maxwell only drinks on the weekends.

At first glance, this sentence probably seems fine, but if you stop to think about it, should *only* describe *drinks,* which it does because of its placement? Does the writer mean that Maxwell *only drinks* on weekends and does nothing else? He doesn't take a shower, eat, see a movie, talk with anybody? It's possible that this is what the writer means, but it's not likely. This word order conveys what the writer probably meant:

> **Right:**   Maxwell drinks only on the weekends.

In other words, *only* should modify the time of the action, not the action itself.
Analyze and correct this sentence:

> **Wrong:**   On her diet, Tess *only* ate strawberries for three days.
>
> **Right:**   _____
>
>   _____

This error might seem fairly trivial, and it *is* if it happens only once in a great while, but if it occurs a couple or a few times in each paper you write, it creates a minor dissonance you can well do without.

Other single-word modifiers that create the same difficulty include *almost, just, even,* and *nearly.* Try to place these right before the word they describe.

Phrases and clauses also can be misplaced modifiers. Here are two examples to analyze and revise:

> **Wrong:**   Lee planned to spend Saturday afternoon lying on the sandy
>
>   beach and reading a book *about ten feet from the good-looking*
>
>   *new lifeguard* by Hegel.

Right: _____

_____

Can you see how the phrase *about ten feet from the good-looking new lifeguard* needs to be moved away from *book* and placed in a clearer relationship to *lying on the sandy beach?*

Wrong: We watched the play at a beautiful outdoor theater, *which ran*

for two hours and fifteen minutes.

Right: _____

_____

In this example, it sounds as if the theater somehow "ran for two hours and fifteen minutes."

A number of old jokes are based at least in part on misplaced modifiers; for example, you may have heard the expression "Throw Momma *from the train* a kiss."

Dangling Modifiers

Dangling modifiers don't clearly modify any word that is actually in the sentence. They modify something that is implied but not stated. Let's look at some examples.

Wrong: *Plagued by hearing problems for many years,* the Ninth Symphony was written during a time of almost total deafness.

You can see that the modifier *Plagued by hearing problems for many years* does not logically describe anything in this sentence. Who was plagued by these problems? You know it has to be a person, but no person's name is in the sentence. It certainly can't be that the *Ninth Symphony* had hearing problems, although that's what the construction of the sentence would lead a reader to expect. Here is one way to correct the sentence:

Right: *Plagued by hearing problems for many years,* Ludwig van Beethoven wrote the Ninth Symphony when he was almost completely deaf.

In this next example, the dangling modifier is at the end of the sentence:

Wrong: Her projects include both the black granite *V* of the Vietnam Veterans Memorial and the inscribed granite disk of the

Alabama Civil Rights Memorial, *intending her works to be experienced by people's hearts and hands.*

Any reader would have to ask, *"Who* was intending her works to be experienced by people's hearts and hands?" The modifier that begins with *intending* dangles out there in space, not logically attached to anything in the sentence. Compare the corrected sentence with its original version:

Right: Architect Maya Lin, *intending her works to be experienced by people's hearts and hands,* created both the black granite *V* of the Vietnam Veterans Memorial and the inscribed granite disk of the Alabama Civil Rights Memorial.

Exercises

Exercise One * PART A

The following are real examples from student writing. Each contains a misplaced or dangling modifier. (Some might be in need of revision for other reasons, too.) *These examples may be used for class discussion, or your teacher might ask you to rewrite them.*

If you are asked to rewrite the examples, do the following: (a) Underline the part of the sentence that needs changing. (It's not so important to distinguish between the two types of errors—misplaced and dangling modifiers; it's much more useful simply to see that something is out of place and figure out how to fix it.) (b) Rewrite each sentence, solving whatever problems exist. You can change the wording in any way you wish, just as long as you preserve the sense of the writer's intended meaning. For lengthier rewrites, use your own paper.

As you read these items, and perhaps find yourself smiling occasionally, you'll see how misplaced and dangling modifiers often create effects that the writer did not intend. You'll also notice that a modifier error sometimes creates a very hard-to-follow sentence and other times does little damage.

1. Growing up on the west side of Detroit, the life is kind of rough.

2. From that time on, I only purchased fresh fruits and vegetables, and I avoided the canned stuff.

3. The girls' exhibition basketball tournament was a friendly way to start off each season, consisting of ten schools in different divisions.

4. Too angry to cry and too hurt not to, the hot tears finally began to roll down my cheeks.

5. Gazing upon the moonlit sky, the promise that I had made to my grandfather began to echo in my head.

6. I grabbed my suitcase out of the closet that I had packed earlier.

7. In comparing high school to college, the dream was to go to college and find some freedom.

8. Harsh and inhuman treatment, such as whippings and lynchings, were used to keep slaves who initiated protest and who influenced others to follow them in their places.

9. In seeing recurring patterns, the natural laws of physics are formulated.

10. With the pressure that is put on a young lady by her friends or boyfriend nowadays, it is really difficult for her to wait until she is married to refrain from sex.

PART B

Continue to follow the directions given in part A.

1. Dangling from my silky earlobes, my friends could not help but envy my new double-ring super-big gold and silver hoops.

2. A quick flashback ran through her head to her junior high school days, and she remembered how much she had feared one particular teacher.

3. I maintained a G.P.A. of 3.4 throughout my days at North Central High School, which was above average.

4. As a child, my grandmother warned me not to eat too much starchy food.

5. John started stealing and fighting white kids, which were usually of a racial nature.

6. In all those years of knocking ourselves out and doing what the debate coach said, we came close to only winning the state championship once.

7. Religious identity is a very important factor in a person's life that must be taught.

8. In tremendous pain from an infection in my inner ear, my father got me to the hospital emergency room as fast as he could.

9. Although I was only auditioning for a minor role in the play *Oliver*, I was nervous and hesitant because I did not think that I would get the part.

10. I had my mind set on nothing but boxing out, getting the rebound, and scoring the whole week before the game.

* Exercise Two

Some sentences in this exercise may be perfectly fine; label them *okay*. Others contain a dangling or misplaced modifier. Label the sentences that contain these errors with an *X* and underline the modifier that needs to be changed. Then, on your own paper, rewrite the problem sentences, clarifying relationships and putting the modifiers in their proper places.

1. _____ Playing outfield for the Cleveland Indians in 1947, Lawrence Eugene Doby became the first African-American player in the American League.

2. _____ FDR's Secretary of Labor from 1933–1945 was Frances Perkins, which was the first cabinet post to be filled by a woman in U.S. history.

3. _____ The National Collegiate Athletic Association once temporarily banned the dunk while Kareem Abdul-Jabbar was playing at UCLA, whose height of seven feet and two inches was considered an unfair advantage.

4. _____ Introduced to candy lovers in 1937, the Sky Bar contained separate segments of caramel, vanilla, peanuts, and chocolate fudge.

5. _____ It is not true that a person can win a Nobel Prize for any great achievement. The Nobel Prizes are only given for outstanding accomplishments in six areas: chemistry, economics, literature, physics, physiology or medicine, and world peace.

6. _____ Having graduated at the bottom of his West Point class, it is amazing that George Armstrong Custer became a general at the tender age of 23.

7. _____ The black crayon is one of the two colors that get used up the quickest in a

typical child's box of Crayolas, being in great demand for outlining. (The other color is red.)

8. _____ Flannery O'Connor, one of the century's outstanding short-story writers and the author of two novels, only wrote in the mornings; because she was in a weakened condition from lupus, a serious disease which eventually took her life, she had to limit her writing time and finish by noon.

9. _____ Catering to the whims and wishes of Jackie Gleason, the CBS television network, which sponsored "The Honeymooners," built a TV studio right next to his favorite golf course in Florida.

10. _____ Using the stage name of Harry Houdini, Ehrich Weiss's reputation as a magician and escape artist grew until it was unrivaled in the entire world.

Exercise Three

Because so many problems occur when an introductory modifier fails to describe the subject of the sentence or the action of the subject, let's try an exercise in which you are given the modifier and you have to add the independent clause. Choose five of the following items and finish the sentences so that the modifiers are logically attached.

1. Kicked off the soccer team, _____

   _____ .

2. Determined to succeed, _____

   _____ .

3. Often called the top musician of the 1990s, _____

   _____ .

4. Planning for a crowd of one hundred or more, _____

   _____ .

5. Surprised by the demands of college courses, _____

   _____ .

6. Decorated with whipped cream and chocolate bits, _____

_____ .

7. Unable to function properly, _____

_____ .

8. Having lost his appetite, _____

_____ .

9. Worried about drinking too much coffee, _____

_____ .

10. Criticized by most students of color on campus, _____

_____ .

Exercise Four

Some of these sentences about women's health may be perfectly fine; label them *okay*. Others contain a dangling or misplaced modifier. Label the sentences that have these errors with an *X* and underline the modifier that needs to be changed. Then, rewrite problem sentences, clarifying relationships and putting the modifiers in their proper places. For lengthier rewrites, use your own paper.

1. _____ Now facing many of the same pressures as men, medical experts say that women are also beginning to experience the same health problems.

2. _____ Warning women to pay attention to the possible costs of their hard-won gains, some doctors predict significant negative trends in women's health over the next decade.

3. _____ There is no guarantee, for instance, that women will continue to hold an advantage in longevity, currently outliving men by an average of 5.7 years.

4. _____ The number of women who are suffering from peptic ulcers, long regarded as a male illness, is up 13 percent.

5. _____ Alarmed about the implications, high blood pressure, lung cancer, and emphysema also have been on the increase among females.

6. _____ The American Cancer Society estimates that by the year 2000 women will succumb to lung cancer at the same rate as men, basing its prediction on the high number of young female smokers.

7. _____ Rising at an alarming rate, administrators at both public and private psychiatric hospitals have seen the number of female admissions almost double in the last twenty years.

8. _____ It was once men who primarily committed suicide, but a rise in female suicide also has been documented.

9. _____ Experts say that these negative effects are not only felt among women who work outside the home; women who work exclusively in the home also are suffering more and more stress-related health problems.

10. _____ Threats to women's health must be recognized and addressed, which are unintended but real by-products of the successes of the women's movement.

UNIT 4:   Problems in Coordination and Parallelism

Students are often frustrated when teachers write *awkward* in the margins of a paper. What precisely does *awkward* mean, and what is a student writer supposed to do about it?

Awkward describes a multitude of hard-to-define problems, but sometimes what's really wrong with an awkward sentence can be solved easily—and powerfully—if you know something about coordination and parallelism.

Both of these have to do with the *sound* of your sentences. You create good coordination and parallelism in your writing by putting bits of information into matching grammatical forms and listening to the rhythm of your words. **To do well with these skills, you need to read your work aloud.**

Coordination

Coordination means pulling together and creating similarity or harmony in *two* parts of a grammatical construction. The problem—called *lack of coordination* or *faulty coordination*—can show up in a variety of ways, but often it's two predicates, parts of two predicates, or two whole clauses that would be stronger and clearer if they were more similar in structure. Let's take a simple example:

Wrong: Herbie Pischler, of New York's Costello Restaurant, a man who has been called the world's worst waiter, once *tripped* on a carpet and *was spilling* soup on the Prince of Wales.

You can see right away that the verb forms in this sentence clash. Here are two ways to create coordination:

Right: a. Herbie Pischler, of New York's Costello Restaurant, a man who has been called the world's worst waiter, once *tripped* on a carpet and *spilled* soup on the Prince of Wales.
   b. Herbie Pischler, of New York's Costello Restaurant, a man who has been called the world's worst waiter, once *tripped* on a carpet, *spilling soup on the Prince of Wales.*

Revision a solves the problem of faulty coordination by making the verb forms similar: *tripped* and *spilled*. Revision b works differently, solving the problem by creating a sentence in which no one would expect the verbs to be similar. The second revision works not by making things similar, but by making them harmonious.

Let's look at another example of faulty coordination.

Wrong: Stuttering *affects* about two million adult Americans, and four times as many males as females *would be affected* by stuttering.

This time the problem is bigger: The verb forms *affects* and *would be affected* clash, and the first clause of the sentence is active, while the second clause is passive. Here are two good revisions:

Right: a. Stuttering affects about two million adult Americans, and that includes four times as many males as females.
   b. Stuttering affects about two million adult Americans, including four times as many males as females.

Exercise One

Fix these problems in coordination in students' drafts by crossing out problem words and phrases and writing your improvements in the space available or on your own paper. As you create better coordination, you'll see chances to cut down on wordiness and make crisper sentences, too.

1. It would not be long before Grandpa went back to his usual activities

   such as gambler at the nearby park and visiting his lady friend, Rosalee.

2. My boyfriend and I like some of the same things, such as having an

intimate picnic at our favorite park overseeing a lake, or just take a stroll through the city on a cool starry night.

3. As part of his discipline, the coach assigns the penalty mile. The penalty mile is simply meeting at the track at 6:30 A.M. and run a mile and a half every Tuesday and Thursday until we're making our assigned times.

4. In the new "Star Trek," when an enemy alien is shot, the special effects show the alien actually blowing up or disintegrate in accurate detail.

5. I was always the first one in my family to offer my apologies and would be willing to try to make up.

Parallelism

Good parallelism is essentially the same thing as good coordination, but the term *parallelism* usually refers to similarity or harmony among three or more items rather than just two. Here is an obvious example of faulty parallelism:

Wrong: When it comes to basketball, Chicago's Michael Jordan, one of the NBA's perennial top scorers, does almost everything well: *runs, shooting, gets rebounds,* and *can pass.*

It is simple to find a solution to this problem sentence: All you have to do is pull the verbs into the same form. A possible solution is

Right: When it comes to basketball, Chicago's Michael Jordan, one of the NBA's perennial top scorers, does almost everything well: *running, shooting, rebounding,* and *passing.*

You might find a number of other ways to achieve parallelism in the Michael Jordan sentence. Create one other solution, and compare notes with other students:

_____

_____

_____

Good Examples for Discussion

Parallelism should be a powerful tool in your repertoire of writing skills. Before you start the exercises, take a few minutes to examine and enjoy some good examples of parallelism from professional writing.

a.   Nathan Pine, a bookseller, once offered this observation: "There's something special about people who are interested in the printed word. They are a species all their own—learned, kind, knowledgeable and human."

b.   *Detroit Free Press* columnist James Ricci claims, "You just can't tell me that basketball, with its stylized imagery, ritualized movements and dance-like disciplines, is not quasi-mystical."

c.   In the 1941 movie *The Big Store,* Groucho Marx was supposed to be madly in love with a very rich lady. "Martha dear," he said, "there are many bonds that will hold us together through eternity: your savings bonds, your Liberty bonds, and your government bonds."

d.   In his book *The Burning Season: The Murder of Chico Mendes and the Fight for the Amazon Rain Forest,* Andrew Revkin writes, "He [Mendes] was to the ranchers of the Amazon what César Chávez was to the citrus kings of California, what Lech Walesa was to the shipyard managers of Gdansk."

Creating a Setup for the Parallel Items

An easy way to create parallelism is to build in a setup before your items and then check to see that each item is readable with the setup. For example, let's imagine that you wanted to revise this sentence from an early draft of a paper:

> Runners should warm up properly, following a safe route, to vary their speed, and a soft surface like grass or sand is preferable to pavement.

If you consider *Runners should* as your setup, you can read each item in the list after it and quickly see that they don't read right. (For example, you'd have *Runners should warm up, Runners should following, Runners should to vary* and so forth). Taken one by one, the listed items definitely don't sound right when they follow *Runners should.* But in the following revision, notice that each item in the list *does* read well with *Runners should:*

> Runners should warm up properly, follow a safe route, vary their speed, and use a soft surface like grass or sand rather than pavement.

To double-check yourself, you can say, *Runners should warm up, Runners should follow, Runners should vary,* and *Runners should use.* They all work; you have created parallelism.

Let's try an exercise.

* Exercise Two

Underline and correct problems in parallelism. Don't rewrite the entire item if only a section needs to be improved. Remember: This is a chance to attack wordiness, too. Use your own paper for lengthier rewrites.

1. The demographic information that is used to set the prices and time slots for television advertising is broken down into a number of categories, including gender,

the age of the viewers, how much income they have, racial, and their educational level.

2. In his book *Bouncing Back: How a Heroic Band of POWs Survived Vietnam,* Geoffrey Norman documents how ingenuity, solid training, teamwork, and a spirit of resistance helped American prisoners of war survive years of imprisonment in North Vietnam. One example of their ingenuity involves a tap code they developed. Of course, they used it to talk, but also to conduct poetry readings, wine appreciation classes were held, played games to maintain and improve concentration, and they would tell plot summaries of novels they had read. These activities were so crucial that a later study showed that the prisoners' IQ scores generally improved while the men were in captivity.

3. Unemployment obviously imposes financial hardships on its victims, but according to experts, it also has other effects. One study of 250 unemployed workers discovered higher than normal blood pressure, having marital conflicts, parents would typically have more serious problems with their children, smoked more, and a higher level of cholesterol often was found during a period of unemployment.

Exercise Three

Continue to follow the directions given for exercise two.

1. Although his name is not widely known in the United States, Noam Chomsky is a professor at MIT, being the father of modern linguistics, he is a prolific writer, and to be considered a major international figure in radical political thought.

2. Dr. Sonya Friedman, the psychologist and author of *On a Clear Day You Can See Yourself: Turning the Life You Have into the Life You Want,* believes that every woman should have a "totem." By this, she means something that represents the major themes of your life—who you really are, the lessons you've learned, the miracles you've witnessed, and the turning points you've experienced. Dr.

Friedman's totem is a necklace with five gold charms: one is an *S* that represents herself; luck is symbolized by a pair of dice; praying hands suggesting God; another charm is a subway token to recall her New York City roots; and her integrity being signified by the words "Trust Me."

3. In *The Joy of Sports,* Michael Novak asserts that each one of the major American sports is analagous to a type of music: Baseball is like chamber music, a comparison can be made between football and a symphony, and jazz is the music that most closely resembles basketball.

* Exercise Four

Continue to follow the directions given for exercise two.

1. Robin Williams, star of *Dead Poets Society, Hook, Awakenings,* and *Good Morning, Vietnam,* expends a great deal of physical energy in both his movies and in his stand-up comedy routines. To maintain his energy, Williams follows certain practices: He does not smoke, enjoying skiing and surfing, a strict vegetarian, runs, and regular workouts in a gym.

2. Dr. Barry Lester, a professor of psychiatry and pediatrics at Brown University, examined the crying patterns of more than 150 babies, half of whom had ingested cocaine before birth. He found that some cocaine-affected infants were sluggish, and depressed features showing in them. Other babies were tense, and there was excitability and jittery. And a third group of babies manifested all of these signs.

3. According to the U.S. Census Bureau, almost forty million Americans change their residence every year, and that means, of course, that many children find themselves in new schools. Researchers say that children who change schools frequently may face difficult adjustments. The symptoms parents should watch for include a drop in academic performance, a child might withdraw, to rebel at school or at home, sometimes running away, and become involved with drugs or alcohol.

UNIT 5:   Passive Sentences

You know that the word *passive* ordinarily means inactive or weak. A passive person, to take one example, waits for things to happen instead of trying to make them happen.

The *passive voice* in writing is similar. Although they are not technically incorrect, passive sentences are often a poor choice. They're dead, flat, weak. Their subjects do not act; they are acted upon. Often, you'll create much crisper, stronger writing if you do the opposite and use the active voice. Let's look some examples.

> **Passive:** A *turkey* rather than an eagle was first suggested by Benjamin Franklin as the U.S. national symbol.

Do you see how awkward and flat this sentence is? Why put *turkey* in the subject position? Wouldn't *Benjamin Franklin* be a more logical choice? After all, he is the one who *suggested* something; he is, therefore, the logical subject of the verb. Here is a good revision of this sentence:

> **Active:**   Benjamin Franklin first suggested a turkey rather than an eagle as the U.S. national symbol.

In this example, as is often the case when you switch a sentence from the passive to the active voice, the word that was the *subject* in the passive version *(turkey)* becomes the *direct object* in the active rewrite.

Also, by moving to the active voice, you reduce wordiness. In our example, we dropped the preposition *by* and reduced the verb phrase *was suggested* to the single-word verb *suggested*.

An Exercise

Exercise One   *   PART A

Some of the following sentences—or clauses within them—are in the passive voice. Others are in the active voice. Label each sentence *p* for passive or *a* for active. Then, convert the passive sentences to the active voice.

1. _____ Rockets are built, aviation is studied, and chemistry experiments are

   performed by ninth-grade girls in the University of Michigan's annual Summer-

   science Program, which exists to support young women in science.

2. _____ According to one of the strange but persistent myths of the publishing world,

   not much money is ever made by a writer of a book that has a green cover.

3. _____ From 1960 through 1981, Muhammad Ali amassed a record-breaking $71 million in his boxing career.

4. _____ The distinction of being the first woman in Italy to graduate from medical school was earned by Maria Montessori, who is known all over the world for her achievements in early childhood education.

5. _____ Seventeen different kinds of smiles—some sincere and some artificial—have been described by Dr. Paul Ekman, a psychologist and the director of the Human Interaction Laboratory at the University of California medical school in San Francisco.

PART B

Continue to follow the directions given in part A.

1. _____ A job as reporter in the London office of the *New York Tribune* was once held by Karl Marx.

2. _____ Although equal rights and civil liberties were championed by Thomas Jefferson, the third president of the United States, at one time about 130 slaves were owned by him.

3. _____ A comeback is being made by the lowly leech. The leech has been found by plastic surgeons and specialists in microsurgery to provide a great natural source of relief for venous congestion in certain cases involving reattachment of amputated body parts or transplanted tissue.

4. _____ The artist Georgia O'Keefe, who was born in Sun Prairie, Wisconsin, had a deep and lifelong love of the landscape and people of the Southwest.

5. _____ For a variety of reasons, not enough interest in environmental issues is shown by most people of color, according to Amos Bankston, an African American who heads the conservation department of the United Auto Workers. It is said by Bankston that environmental activism is wrongly considered a "white" issue by

some minority groups, in part because they have so many other pressing social

concerns.

Justifiable Passives

Are there any good reasons for using the passive voice? Sure. Sometimes—for example, when a writer does not know who the subject of the action is—the passive voice is necessary. You might write this sentence about a book whose author is unknown: "This masterpiece was written in the fourteenth century." If no one knows who wrote the book, all you can say is that it *was written*.

Similarly, the passive voice is sometimes used when a writer or speaker wants to *conceal* who did what. Analysts of the famous Watergate tapes found an unusual number of passive-voice sentences in those recorded Oval Office conversations. (Presumably, the need to conceal won't often be a factor in your writing, but it's an interesting bit of trivia anyway.)

And sometimes you'll have a sentence in which it's not important to show who did a particular action. For instance, after a party, you might comment that "All the shrimp and cheese snacks were eaten first." The point is to tell what food was the most popular, not who ate it.

Or you might write a sentence in which it's rhetorically effective to show someone in a passive position. In other words, the passive voice of the sentence might somehow match or echo the passive nature of whatever is under discussion. For example, you might write, "The people were deprived of their basic human rights by a tyrannical leader." Here you want the emphasis on the powerlessness of the people, so you have a rhetorical reason—a reason "bigger" than grammar, you might say—for casting your sentence in the passive voice.

The important thing is not to eliminate the passive voice from your writing entirely, but to avoid weak, unnecessary uses of it so that your writing is as lively, active, and strong as possible.

Finding Passive Sentences in Context

In exercises two and three, you'll look for passive sentences in the context of two longer pieces of writing. As usual, this kind of exercise helps you transfer the skills learned in this unit to the editing of your own work.

Exercise Two   *   PART A

Read this short piece on Jim Thorpe and underline and revise weak, unnecessary uses of the passive voice. In the margins, mark "good passives" for class discussion. Expect a little disagreement: This is a matter of judgment, and decisions will probably differ from student to student.

1   Jim Thorpe has been called by many people the greatest athlete who ever lived.

2   A Sac and Fox Indian and the great-grandson of Black Hawk, Thorpe was born in

3   Oklahoma in 1888. At Carlisle Indian Industrial School in Pennsylvania, he was known

4   as an excellent athlete, especially on the football field. As a standout tackler, runner,

5   and place kicker, Thorpe led Carlisle to national honors in football. Then, in 1912, he

6   stunned the entire world with his performance at the Olympic Games in Stockholm,

7   Sweden. Gold medals in both the pentathlon and decathlon were won by him. This

8   achievement has never been duplicated by another athlete in the history of the Olympic

9   Games and probably never will since nowadays one athlete does not enter both events.

10   The world was stunned again a year later—this time unhappily—when it was

11 learned by the International Olympic Committee (IOC) that money had been accepted

12 by Thorpe to play minor league baseball in Rocky Mountain, North Carolina, in 1911.

13 Although the money received by Jim Thorpe was only $2.00 a game, still Thorpe was

14 judged by the Amateur Athletic Union to have been a professional athlete at the time he

15 had competed in Stockholm. Professional status, of course, equaled Olympic ineligibil-

16 ity. Jim Thorpe's gold medals were stripped from him by Olympic officials, and his

17 achievements were erased from the record books. Two personal trophies that had been

18 awarded to Thorpe—and that have been appraised by some experts as having a current

19 value of $7 million—were also confiscated by Olympic officials.

PART B

Continue to follow the directions given in part A.

1   Although the loss of his Olympic gold medals was a great personal sorrow, Jim

2   Thorpe went on to enjoy great success in both baseball and football. An outfield position

3   was played by Thorpe for three major league baseball teams from 1913 to 1919. Later

4   he played professional football for 15 years, and in 1920 the presidency of the American

5   Professional Football Association—later renamed the National Football League—was

6   assumed by him. In fact, he was the association's first president.

7   But the anger felt by many Americans over what happened to Jim Thorpe's

8   Olympic records and medals was deep and abiding. People did not forget. Eventually, a

9   crusade to restore full honors to him was headed by Robert Wheeler, who—strangely

10   enough—first became interested in Thorpe when a town named "Jim Thorpe" was seen

11   by Wheeler on a road map while Wheeler was on vacation in Pennsylvania. Wheeler

12   went to work and had no difficulty coming to certain conclusions. In an interview, the

13   point was made by him that Thorpe was really guilty of only one thing: honesty. Back in

14   those days, assumed names sometimes had been taken by other athletes so that they

15   could play sports for money and then later compete in the Olympics, and those athletes

16   had suffered no such penalties. It was also true that Thorpe had been sent to Rocky

17   Mountain by his coach, Glenn "Pop" Warner. The suggestion has been made by

18   Wheeler and many others throughout the years that Thorpe was penalized for his

19   youthful mistake at least in part because he was a Native American and his superior

20   performances were difficult for some to accept.

21   Finally, in 1982, the announcement was made by the IOC that Jim Thorpe's amateur

22   status had been restored, that his name would be reentered in the official record books,

23   and that his medals and trophies would be returned to his family. Four decades after his

24   death in 1953, the Olympic records established by Jim Thorpe stand once again.

Exercise Three   *   PART A

Here is a description of major events in the life of Nelson Mandela. Continue to follow the directions given for exercise two.

1   Nelson Rolihlahla Mandela was born on July 18, 1918, in Mbhashe near Umtata in

2   South Africa's rural Transkei homeland. In his youth, cattle and goats were herded by

3   the young Mandela, whose great-great-grandfather was a famous Transkeian king. His

4   father, Henry Mandela, was taken from young Nelson by death when the son was only

5   ten. At that point, his uncle assumed responsibility for his education, and, after spending

6   his earlier years in church-run schools, Nelson Mandela was sent to be educated at Fort

7   Hare University, a black institution, in eastern Cape Province.

8   After a marriage was arranged for him by his uncle, and the prospective bride was

9   found to be unacceptable by Mandela, the young man left Fort Hare and fled to

10 Johannesburg. There he found work as a guard in a gold mine, where his skill in boxing

11 was a useful asset. Soon he met Walter Sisulu, a real estate agent who would become

12 a lifelong friend and colleague. Mandela was encouraged by Sisulu to study for a career

13 in law. Before long, the top black law office in South Africa was opened by Mandela and

14 his former schoolmate, Oliver Tambo.

15   Soon Mandela, Sisulu, and Tambo became involved in the African National

16 Congress (ANC). In 1944, the Youth League of the ANC was formed by Mandela and

17 others. As an organization, the ANC had long been dominated by older leaders and

18 members, but now large numbers of young black South Africans were drawn to it

19 because of the charisma and vision of Nelson Mandela and other young leaders.

20   The National Party of South Africa had come to power in 1948, and a series of laws

21 requiring racial segregation in virtually every aspect of life—housing, recreation,

22 hospitals, and personal relationships—had been enacted by the National Party. Mandela

23 participated in the Defiance Campaign, the first large-scale organized protest against

24 apartheid in South Africa's history; in fact, many of the almost nine thousand volunteers

25 who were arrested had been recruited by the young Mandela. Although the Defiance

26 Campaign and other activities were essentially nonviolent, Mandela was arrested and

27 subjected to a very difficult four-year trial for treason.

PART B

Continue to follow the directions given in part A.

1   One incident that marked a sudden and irrevocable turning point in Nelson

2   Mandela's life and in the nature of the ANC was the Sharpeville Massacre of 1960 in

3 which 69 people, who were peacefully protesting South Africa's pass laws, were brutally

4 murdered by police. This is the point at which a complete commitment to the philosophy

5 of nonviolent civil disobedience that had been epitomized by Mohandas Ghandi in India

6 and that also had inspired the vision of Dr. Martin Luther King, Jr., in the United States

7 was veered away from by the ANC.

8   In 1961, ties with the British Commonwealth were broken by South Africa, and

9 South Africa became an independent republic. It was feared by many black leaders that,

10 on its own, South Africa would become even more oppressive. In that same year in

11 Pietermaritzburg, at his last public appearance until his release from prison almost three

12 decades later, Nelson Mandela proposed a nonracial, democratic, constitutional

13 government for South Africa. Soon there was a warrant for his arrest, and Mandela

14 went underground. The communications made by him to journalists were completed

15 from telephone boxes, and soon he was dubbed the "Black Pimpernel" (after the Scarlet

16 Pimpernel of the French Revolution).

17   It was not long before an armed wing of the ANC was formed: *Umkhonto*

18 *we Sizwe,* Spear of the Nation. Emphasis was put by this group on sabotage of

19 South African government installations; the aim was to damage property, not

20 people. During this volatile time, Mandela traveled on an Ethiopian passport under

21 the name of David Motsamayi. In addition to experiencing all the effects of apart-

22 heid that other black South Africans endured, Mandela also had been prohibited from

23 attending political gatherings and leaving Johannesburg from 1952 to 1961. So it is

24 easy to understand why it has been said by Mandela that his travels as David

25 Motsamayi represented the first real freedom he had ever experienced. He visited

26 many parts of Africa, went to England, and in Algeria guerrilla training was received

27 by him.

28   Back in his homeland, one day he went out in the guise of a chauffeur, was stopped

29 at a roadblock, arrested again, and this time imprisoned for most of the next three

30 decades. Reports say that he was betrayed by informers.

* PART C

Continue to follow the directions given in part A.

1   During Mandela's trial for sabotage, the accusation was made by Prime Minister

2 Hendrik Verwoerd that Nelson Mandela was a "communist criminal." Mandela's

3 response? Yes, he said, in order to reach common goals—African unity and full human

4 rights for African people—he *had* formed alliances with communist groups. Then he

5 reminded all in the courtroom that so had Winston Churchill and Franklin Roosevelt in

6 World War II. In spite of what observers called a brilliant defense of his own actions and

7 black resistance in general, Nelson Mandela was found guilty on all counts and received

8 a sentence of life plus five years.

9   For a long time, Mandela broke rocks in a limestone quarry at Robben Island in the

10 extreme cold of the South Atlantic. He could see his wife only rarely and briefly, and

11 they were always separated by a glass wall. Mandela has been quoted as saying that

12 among the things he missed most during his 27 years in prison were music, movies,

13 boxing, holding hands with his wife, and what he movingly called the greatest of all

14 moments shared by husband and wife—the closing of the bedroom door. In spite of all

15 his deprivations, according to Mandela, depression was never experienced by him. He

16 has said that he always knew he would win.

17   Although he suffered greatly and lost fifty pounds, Mandela made good use of

18 whatever time he could control. Daily he rose at 3:30, exercised for two hours, and

19 wrote to his wife. He studied in areas of special interest to him and his work: law,

20 history, economics, and poetry. Because such tremendous admiration was felt for

21 Mandela by younger prisoners, many of whom were sent to Robben Island after the

22 Soweto Uprising of 1976, Mandela was moved to Pollsmoor Prison. Later he was

23 transferred to Victor Verster Prison.

PART D

Continue to follow the directions given in part A.

1   As Mandela became older and began to take on the aura of a mythic figure, South

2 African government leaders faced a dilemma: Should they keep him in prison and face

3 the wrath and contempt of most of the world when he died there, or should they release

4 him and risk that he would galvanize black South Africans and millions of other people of

5 all colors and in all parts of the world?

6   In the 1970s, an offer was made to release Mandela if he would return to the

7 Transkei homeland. This offer was refused by Mandela because to return to the

8 homelands would be to say yes to apartheid; it was claimed by Mandela that *he* should

9 be the one to decide where to live. In 1985, another offer of freedom was made to

10 Mandela. This time President P.W. Botha promised that Mandela could be free only if

11 a renunciation of the use of violence to achieve political aims was made by him. Again,

12 Mandela said no, and through his daughter, Zindziswa Mandela, he released this

13 statement, which she read before a crowd of ten thousand in Soweto, the largest

14 segregated black township in South Africa:

15   Let him [Botha] renounce violence. Let him say that he will dismantle apart-

16   heid. Let him unban the people's organization, the African National Congress. Let

17   him guarantee free political activity so that the people may decide who will govern

18   them.

19   I cherish my own freedom, but I care even more for your freedom. Too

20   many have died since I went to prison. I owe it to their widows, to their orphans,

21   to their mothers and to their fathers who have grieved and wept for them. . . . I

22   will return.   (*Detroit Free Press* 20 June 1990)

23   Five years and one day later, Mandela was freed by order of South African

24 President F.W. de Klerk and, in a deeper sense, by his own perseverance and courage.

25 On February 11, 1990, after 27 years, Nelson Mandela walked out of Victor Verster

26 Prison and returned to the world—and the world, hungry for heroes, rejoiced.

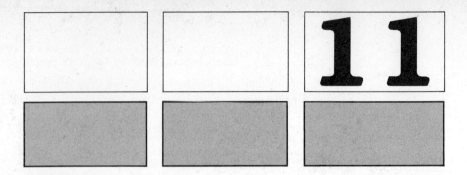

Solving Problems at the Word Level

This chapter deals with a variety of problems that occur at the word level; they are not essentially sentence-structure or clause-related problems. One student might find it helpful to work in one or two units, another in all the units, and another in none. Your writing teacher can help you decide in which units you need to work.

The units in chapter 11 are all independent and self-contained, so you can approach them in any order.

UNIT 1: Subject–Verb Agreement

We all follow a system of subject–verb agreement, even if we can't define the term *subject–verb agreement*. If you listen to your speech and the speech of your family and friends, you'll find that most people adhere to a fairly consistent pattern. For instance, a person typically might say *She smiles* and *He laughs* or *She smile* and *He laugh.* In other words, most of us generally follow a set of rules about using an *-s* or not using an *-s* on the end of present-tense verbs. We learned these patterns early in life and follow them in a mostly unconscious manner.

The potential problem is that the rules you follow may vary from the rules for subject–verb agreement that are considered standard for academic writing. To learn the rules for academic writing, you will have to become conscious of this aspect of your language.

If you're an adult learning a new system of subject–verb agreement (rather than just reviewing it or brushing up on a few fine points), the work you do in this unit will be very important to your academic success, and you might need to reinforce it with other work. When you finish this unit, your teacher may suggest more activities for practicing subject–verb agreement (there are extra exercises in the *Instructor's Manual*). After doing those, perhaps you'll make up your own exercises, following the patterns shown in this unit. But you can achieve success in this skill—there's no doubt about that. Subject–verb agreement will simply become one important thing you look for when editing your written work.

The Standard Pattern

Subject–verb agreement is basically a problem only in the present tense. (The exceptions are the past tense verbs *was* and *were*.) Here are the standard rules:

If the subject is singular, add -*s* or -*es* to the verb.

For example:

> s v
> According to researchers, a newborn **baby** often **experiences** homesickness for the mother's womb.

The subject—*baby*—is singular, so we add -*s* to the verb, and we form *experiences*.

If the subject is plural, add no ending to the verb.

For example:

> s v
> According to researchers, newborn **babies** often **experience** homesickness for the mother's womb.

The word *babies* is plural, so the verb—*experience*—has no added ending. It's either *a baby experiences* or *babies experience*.

A Device to Help You Remember

Some students use this device to help them remember the rules:

> *If the subject is singular, put -s on the verb. (s . . . s)*
> *If the subject is plural, keep the verb plain. (pl . . . pl)*

* Exercise One

To reinforce the standard rules and to check your understanding of them, let's do one very basic exercise. Fill in the blank with the form of the verb that agrees with the subject in these simple sentences. This exercise is a diagnostic tool to help determine whether or not you need more work on this skill at this level.

1a. An ice cube _____ (*melt/melts*) slowly.

b. Ice cubes _____ (*melt/melts*) slowly.

2a. A good father _____ (*protect/protects*) his children.

b. Good fathers _____ (*protect/protects*) their children.

3a. IQ tests _____ (*fail/fails*) to measure intelligence accurately.

b. An IQ test _____ (*fail/fails*) to measure intelligence accurately.

4a. An average-sized apple _____ (*equal/equals*) about eighty calories.

b. Apples typically _____ (*equal/equals*) about eighty calories each.

5a. Children _____ (*need/needs*) tender loving care.

b. A child _____ (*need/needs*) tender loving care.

If You Had Errors on Exercise One

If you had any trouble at all with exercise one, then you probably should practice more on this level before going on. If that's the case, ask your teacher for additional work in basic subject–verb agreement. He or she will find more exercises of this type in the *Instructor's Manual* that accompanies this text.

The Verbs To Be and To Have

Here's an easy way to approach subject–verb agreement when the verb is a form of *to be* or *to have*. Just as with regular verbs, the form to match a singular subject will end in -*s*. The form to match a plural subject will not end in -*s*. Study these correct examples:

Singular subject	**Plural subject**
The dessert *is* delicious.	The desserts *are* delicious.
The song *was* beautiful.	The songs *were* beautiful.
She *has* soul.	They *have* soul.

Notice that all the verb forms that agree with singular subjects end in -*s: is, was,* and *has.* The verbs that agree with plural subjects—*are, were,* and *have*—do not have an -*s* ending.

Exercise Two

Fill in the blank with the form of the verb that agrees with the subject. This exercise also can help you assess whether you need more practice.

1a. A food allergy _____ (*are/is*) most likely to be triggered by eggs, milk, fish, nuts, wheat, peas, or soybeans.

b. Food allergies _____ (*are/is*) most likely to be triggered by eggs, milk, fish, nuts, wheat, peas, or soybeans.

2a. Sunday's crossword puzzles _____ (*was/were*) easy.

b. Sunday's crossword puzzle _____ (*was/were*) easy.

3a. A good teacher _____ (*has/have*) a great deal of power.

  b. Good teachers _____ (*has/have*) a great deal of power.

4a. Mail carriers _____ (*are/is*) not just fair-weather friends.

  b. A mail carrier _____ (*are/is*) not just a fair-weather friend.

5a. The firm's policies _____ (*was/were*) very effective.

  b. The firm's policy _____ (*was/were*) very effective.

If You Had Errors on Exercise Two

As with exercise one, if you had any trouble with exercise two, you should do more work at this level before you continue in the unit. Ask your teacher to duplicate extra exercises from the *Instructor's Manual.*

Important Points

Two Exceptions: The Pronouns I and You as Subjects

There are two important exceptions to the rules as they have been described. Those exceptions are the pronouns *I* and *you.* The word *I,* of course, is always singular, while the word *you* can refer to one person or more than one. But both *I* and *you* are always treated as plural subjects, so they are always used with the base verb.

   These are correct examples:

s   v
I give blood regularly.
s   v
You decide what to do.

When And or Or Appears Between Key Words in the Subject

Two singular subjects joined by the word *and* form a plural subject. Singular subjects separated by the word *or* remain singular subjects. Consider these correct examples:

s   s   v
Aspirin *and* **acetaminophen work** equally well for many people.
s   s   v
Aspirin *or* **acetaminophen works** equally well for many people.

   The idea is clearest in a contrasting pair of sentences such as *John and Mary help me every Saturday* and *John or Mary helps me every Saturday.* In the first case, they both help. In the second case, one or the other helps.

When Prepositional Phrases Appear in the Subject

The key word in the subject of a sentence will never be inside a prepositional phrase. (See pages 211–212 for a list of prepositions.) Remember: Prepositional phrases are modifiers, and they have a decorative rather than structural role in a sentence. A prepositional phrase will not contain the subject, but it will often describe the subject.

When you are looking for the key word in the subject—the word with which the verb must agree—you might find it helpful, as many other students do, to draw parentheses around prepositional phrases or even cross them out. Consider these correct examples:

                                    s   **v**

a.   Rock and roll **festivals are** a common feature of summertime entertainment in the United States.

               s   **v**

b.   Any **history** of rock and roll festivals **is** likely to begin with Woodstock.

If a writer does not mentally set off the prepositional phrase *of rock and roll festivals,* she might mistakenly use the verb *are* in b, thinking that the word *festivals* is the key word in the subject.

The word to watch most closely is *of.* It seems to be the preposition that most often leads writers into making an error in subject–verb agreement. In this unit's exercises, you'll work with quite a few sentences with *of* in the subject part of the clause.

When the Subject Is Delayed

Sometimes the subject of a clause is delayed; in other words, the verb comes first. This happens in clauses that begin with the words *here* and *there* and in questions. Look at these examples:

             v   **s**

1a.   There **was** a serious **problem** with the script.

             v   **s**

  b.   There **were** serious **problems** with the script.

          v   **s**

2a.   Here **is** your **answer.**

           v   **s**

  b.   Here **are** your **answers.**

          v   **s**

3a.   What **is** his **goal?**

           v   **s**

  b.   What **are** his **goals?**

           v   **s**

4a.   Where **is** your **friend?**

           v   **s**

  b.   Where **are** your **friends?**

You'll also find sentences with unusual word order like these:

                      v   s

5a.   Two minutes later, in **walks** my **brother.**

                       v   s

   b.   Three minutes later, in **walk** my **sisters.**

More Exercises

* ## Exercise Three

Complete each of these sentences on various bits of trivia by filling in the blank with the form of the verb that agrees with the subject. Write s over the subject. Draw a line through prepositional phrases or put them within parentheses.

1. People from 45 independent African states ＿＿＿＿＿＿ (*was/were*) in part the topic of Dr. Betty Shabazz's doctoral dissertation. Dr. Shabazz, the widow of Malcolm X, ＿＿＿＿＿＿ (*has/have*) earned both a master's degree in health administration and a doctorate in higher education and curriculum development since her husband's assassination in 1965.

2. According to a national poll of speech teachers, one of the worst-sounding words in the English language ＿＿＿＿＿＿ (*are/is*) phlegmatic.

3. Each year, citizens of this country ＿＿＿＿＿＿ (*spend/spends*) over $31 billion of their hard-earned money on fast food.

4. The five nations of the Iroquois League ＿＿＿＿＿＿ (*include/includes*) the Cayuga, the Mohawk, the Oneida, the Onondaga, and the Seneca.

5. Country singer Waylon Jennings and bluesman B.B. King ＿＿＿＿＿＿ (*has/have*) at least one thing in common: They ＿＿＿＿＿＿ (*was/were*) both disc jockeys earlier in their careers.

6. Year after year, Americans' top five flavors of ice cream ＿＿＿＿＿＿ (*are/is*) vanilla, chocolate, neopolitan, chocolate chip, and strawberry—in that order.

7. The smallest star of all the detected stars in the heavens ＿＿＿＿＿＿ (*was/were*) given the name "Wolf 457."

8. An objection to too much explicit sex on television or a complaint about excessive violence in the movies _____ (*are/is*) often registered in today's editorial pages.

9. The process of embalming bodies, among other practices of the U.S. funeral industry, _____ (*receive/receives*) a very critical evaluation from Jessica Mitford in *The American Way of Death*.

10. Roughly one in every twelve American marriages _____ (*break up/breaks up*) because of alcohol abuse.

Exercise Four

Continue to follow the directions given for exercise three.

1. In 1974, the full-size Chevrolet Impala, the Caprice, and the Bel Air _____ _____ (*was/were*) the best-selling cars in the United States, averaging 10 miles per gallon. In 1990, there_____ (*was/were*) close competitors, but the Honda Accord _____ (*was/were*) the top seller. The Accord _____ (*get/gets*) between 24 and 30 miles per gallon.

2. One slice of American cheese or a single tablespoon of butter _____ (*equal/equals*) about one hundred calories.

3. There _____ (*was/were*) many performers introduced to a national audience by Dick Clark and his "American Bandstand." That list of performers _____ (*include/includes*) Paul Anka, Chuck Berry, Johnny Cash, Neil Diamond, The Four Tops, and Gladys Knight and the Pips.

4. Whirlaway and Citation _____ (*was/were*) the only two horses ever to be ridden to Triple Crown victories by the same jockey; that achievement _____ (*belong/belongs*) to Eddie Arcaro.

5. Only one in every ten thousand college basketball players ultimately _____ (*make/makes*) it as a pro in the National Basketball Association.

6. A careful examination of the bones of ancient skeletons _____ (reveal/reveals) valuable information about the eating habits, illnesses, and longevity of prehistoric people.

7. According to researchers in the field, forgetting where your car keys _____ (are/is) _____ (are/is) not a sign that you _____ (has/have) Alzheimer's disease. But forgetting what car keys _____ (are/is) for can be a sign.

8. In the original version of Cinderella, the glass slipper_____ (was/were) not glass at all; it _____ (was/were) made of fur.

9. In the United States, the first black artists to record their music _____ (was/were) the Dinwiddie Quartet in 1902. They _____ (was/were) on the Monarch label.

10. According to the standards set by the Public Health Service, the defect level for coffee beans _____ (are/is) ten percent. In other words, if a batch of coffee beans _____ (are/is) over ten percent insect-infected, molded, or damaged in some other way, it _____ (are/is) considered unfit for human consumption. Coffee with fewer defects _____ (pass/passes) muster. (Enjoy your morning cup.)

* **Exercise Five**

Complete each of these sentences on SAT results by filling in the blank with the form of the verb that agrees with the subject. Write _s_ over the subject. Draw a line through prepositional phrases or put them within parentheses.

1   The topic of gender differences _____ (are/is) always controversial

2   and fascinating. The most talked-about gender discrepancy in academics today _____

3   (show up/shows up) in recent SAT scores. There _____ (has/have) been—in

4   the past two decades—a general tendency for males, as a group, to outscore females,

5   as a group, on both the math and verbal portions of the test. Males' scores

6 _____ (*are/is*) only slightly higher on the verbal side, and this difference in

7 results on the language-oriented section of the test _____ (*has/have*)

8 been in evidence only since 1972. The patterns of performance in math

9 _____ (*has/have*) a longer history.

10   Possible explanations from the world of research _____ (*range/*

11 *ranges*) from innate biological differences between men and women, to cultural biases

12 in the tests, to socioeconomic factors among the test takers. As time _____

13 (*go/goes*) by, socioeconomic factors _____ (*seem/seems*) to be taken more

14 and more seriously. According to a recent *Newsweek* article entitled "Guns and Dolls,"

15 studies _____ (*show/shows*) that women who _____ (*take/takes*)

16 the Scholastic Aptitude Test _____ (*tend/tends*) to be from less advantaged

17 backgrounds than the men who _____ (*take/takes*) the test. Females

18 _____ (*were/was*) found to take the test in greater numbers and to be at a

19 distinct disadvantage according to three measurements: parents' income, private school

20 attendance, and father's level of education.

Exercise Six   PART A

Complete each of the sentences by filling in the blank with the form of the verb that agrees with the subject. The topic here is birth order and its effects on creative, revolutionary thinking in scientists. The source for most of this information is a *Newsweek* article, "The Order of Innovation."

1   Are you the oldest child in your family? A middle child? The youngest? Or perhaps

2 an only child? Whatever your answer _____ (*happen/happens*) to be, you

3 probably _____ (*has/have*) some interest in the subject of birth order. In

4 fact, the effects of birth order _____ (*has/have*) been studied by researchers

5 for years, and many popular books and articles exploring birth order's signifi-

6 cance _____ (*are/is*) available.

7   However, some recent studies within the field of social science _____

8 (*suggest/suggests*) that birth order possibly _____ (*are/is*) not as crucial as

9 many once had thought. For example, there _____ (*was/were*) two studies

10 in the 1980s that concluded birth order _____ (*have/has*) no effect on the

11 development of personality or _____ (*have/has*) an effect only in certain

12 situations. Cecile Ernst and Jules Angst, two Swiss psychologists, published *Birth*

13 *Order* in 1983. In that book, they _____ (*examine/examines*) all earlier

14 studies and _____ (*conclude/concludes*) that the consequences of birth

15 order _____ (*are/is*) minimal in the personality development of most people.

16 More recently, Judith Blake, a sociologist at UCLA, came to the conclusion that only a

17 family with more than seven children _____ (*contend/contends*) with this

18 phenomenon. In smaller families, she observed, birth order _____ (*play/*

19 *plays*) little, if any, role.

* PART B

Continue to follow the directions given in part A.

1 Into this recently formulated picture, which for the most part _____

2 (*deemphasize/deemphasizes*) birth order's importance, _____ (*enter/enters*)

3 Frank J. Sulloway. Sulloway, an MIT historian with a special interest in scientific

4 revolutions, _____ (*has/have*) spent twenty years determining the impact of

5 birth order in the lives of 2,784 scientists from the sixteenth century to the present.

6 Both birth order and its impact _____ (*was/were*) important in his study,

7 which focused on 28 major scientific revolutions. In each case, Sulloway _____

8 (*see/sees*) an individual scientist as either supporting the old guard or helping to usher in

9 a new era. According to Sulloway's findings, a tendency to challenge established beliefs

10 _____ (*was/were*) least likely to be found in the scientists who _____

11 (*was/were*) firstborn children. Next in line in terms of conservatism in their scientific

12 thinking _____ (*was/were*) those who _____ (*was/were*) the only

13 children in their families. The most radical scientific thinker in any given revo-

14 lution _____ (*was/were*) likely to be a younger son who had at least

15 one older brother. (Sulloway confined his study to male scientists.) Of the 28

16 major revolutions, 23 _____ (*was/were*) led by rebellious "later-

17 borns."

PART C

Continue to follow the directions given in part A.

1   If there _____ (*are/is*) any valid correlations between birth order and

2 radical scientific innovation, what _____ (*are/is*) the principles or mecha-

3 nisms at work? Sulloway _____ (*say/says*) it's really quite simple: The oldest

4 child among a family's several children often _____ (*identify/identifies*) with

5 his or her parents more readily than the other children. After all, the firstborn child

6 frequently must care for the younger siblings and in many families _____

7 (*become/becomes*) a representative or an extension of parental authority. Because the

8 oldest child so often _____ (*play/plays*) this role, he or she more easily

9 _____ (*accept/accepts*) the conventions and values of the establishment.

10 Younger children in a family, on the other hand, often _____ (*push/pushes*) to

11 see how far they can go in any given situation. If these laterborns_____

12 (*venture/ventures*) into science, they _____ (*tend/tends*) to test the limits

13 there, also.

14   Charles Darwin, who discovered the principle of natural selection, _____

15 (*fit/fits*) perfectly into Sulloway's theory. Darwin's theories about evolution _____

16 (*was/were*) not only revolutionary but also an affront to the religious beliefs of the

17 Victorian age. It should come as no surprise that this epitome of radical thinkers

18 _____ (*was/were*) the fifth among six children.

* PART D

Continue to follow the directions given in part A.

1   There _____ (*are/is*) exceptions to every rule, of course, and in this

2 case, Albert Einstein, a firstborn child, _____ (*are/is*) an obvious one. But

3 Sulloway _____ (*point/points*) out that most of the brilliant people who

4 surrounded and assisted Einstein _____ (*was/were*) laterborn children within

5 their respective families.

6   In our time, the theories of Sigmund Freud, the father of psychoanalysis, still

7 _____ (*has/have*) enormous power. Freud proved difficult to classify for the

8 purposes of Sulloway's birth order research. Why? Freud had two stepbrothers, but

9 they _____ (*was/were*) already living outside the family home when Freud

10 _____ (*was/were*) born, so in a sense he _____ (*was/were*) raised as

11 a firstborn. However, during the first three years of his life he was constantly in the com-

12 pany of the son of one of his stepbrothers, and this son was older than Sigmund. Therefore,

13 in one way, he _____ (*fit/fits*) into the category of the firstborn, but in another

14 way he _____ (*qualify/qualifies*) as a laterborn with an older surrogate brother.

15   Where _____ (*do/does*) Frank Sulloway, MIT's premier science

16 historian, fall within the order of children in his own family? As you might have guessed,

17 he is not a conservative firstborn. In fact, the author of this and other fascinating studies

18 _____ (*are/is*) number three in a set of four.

UNIT 2: Consistency of Verb Tense

What's wrong with this sentence?

    I am walking down the street, and suddenly I saw him.

The writer starts out in a form of the present tense—with *am walking*—and then, for no apparent reason, switches into the past tense—with the verb *saw*. The next sentence has the same problem:

I was walking down the street and suddenly I see him.

In the second example, the writer begins with the past tense and switches into a form of the present. Here are two good revisions:

Present: I *am walking* down the street, and suddenly I *see* him.
Past: I *was walking* down the street, and suddenly I *saw* him.

Tense Problems: A Source of Incoherence

Although at first glance, inconsistent and illogical verb tenses may seem a trivial concern, they actually present a major problem for many student writers. If they occur often enough, tense problems are frequently the real culprit when a paper seems to be lacking in coherence or slightly disorganized.

Which Verb Tenses to Use

When do you use the various verb tenses? It's mostly a matter of common sense when you check over your final drafts. Here are the basic guidelines: (1) The present tense is appropriate when you're writing about what's currently going on or what's always the case. (2) The past tense is used for anything that happened before the time of your writing, whether it's events in your life or someone else's life, research that was conducted in the past, views that were held in the past, and so forth. (3) The future tense is used when you're writing about what you know or believe will happen in the future.

These are the three basic verb tenses you'll work with most of the time: present, past, and future. But there are other verb tenses, and soon we'll look at a couple of fine points concerning them.

Logical Changes in Verb Tense

Is it ever appropriate to switch tenses? Yes, it's correct whenever you have a logical reason. Here's a very basic example:

I *was born* in Wahpeton, North Dakota, but now I *live* in Ann Arbor, Michigan.

The first clause refers to the past, the second clause to the present. So here it would be illogical *not* to make a switch in verb tense.

Using the Helping Verb Had to Show an Earlier Time in the Past

The helping verb *had* is used when you have been using the past tense and you wish to indicate that something happened *even earlier* in the past. Here is a simple example:

a. By the time Mother *started* to cook breakfast at 6:45 this morning, she *had washed* two loads of clothes and read a chapter in her anthropology text.

And here are two more correct examples:

b. The song "We Shall Overcome" *became* an anthem of the civil rights movement in the early 1960s, but a decade earlier it *had gained* popularity as a union song during a bitter strike against the American Tobacco Company in Charleston, South Carolina.
c. Before Pete Seeger *popularized* "We Shall Overcome" in the early 1960s, the song *had been known* in a slightly different version as the traditional hymn "I'll Be All Right."

In each example, the writer began in the past tense and then wished to show something that had happened at an *earlier* time in the past.

Using the Helping Verb Would When There's a Condition to Be Met

The helping verb *would* is often misused. Generally, it should be reserved for situations in which there is a condition to be fulfilled. In many cases, the presence of the word *if* in the sentence is a tip-off that there is a condition to be fulfilled and the use of *would* is appropriate. For example:

If Molly really worked on her tennis game, she *would be* great.

Here there is a condition to be fulfilled: Molly would be great *if* she first fulfilled the condition of working on her game.

You probably won't have problems with *would* if you avoid using it in situations when you're describing something that happened repeatedly in the past. For example:

When we were little, we *would play* tennis all the time.

Here there is no condition to be fulfilled. The writer is simply describing something that happened often in the past. It would be better to say simply:

When we were little, we *played* tennis all the time.

Can/Could and Will/Would

The helping verb *could* is the past tense of *can*. Similarly, *would* is the past tense of *will*. These are both correct:

Present: At this point in her career, Suzanne *can pitch* like a twenty-year-old.

Past: When she was a kid, Suzanne *could pitch* better than anyone she knew.

Writing About Literature, Films, Television Shows, and So Forth

You often have interesting choices concerning verb tense when you are writing about literature, movies, television shows, and similar cultural products. Usually, you can write about these things in either the present or the past tense, but the important thing is to make a conscious choice of verb tense and then be consistent throughout an entire piece of writing.

Even though either tense is usually correct as long as you're consistent, experienced writers often choose the present tense because its use seems to suggest that the story, play, novel, poem, movie, or TV show is a continually living or eternal thing, not something that existed only or even primarily in the past. Art lives *now;* its life span is not limited to the time it was created or the time the writer encountered it. The present tense expresses this idea.

Compare the two following paragraphs. Both versions are acceptable because each is consistent in verb tense, but can you see how the version that is basically in the present tense has virtues that the past-tense version lacks?

PRESENT

In Bernard Malamud's magical short story "Angel Levine," a tailor named Manischevitz, who *believes* he *has lost* or *is* about to lose almost everything worth living for, *faces* a difficult decision: The forlorn tailor *is visited* by a black man who *claims* to be a Jew and an angel of God. The man, who *says* his name *is* Alexander Levine, suddenly *appears* sitting at a table in Manischevitz's living room and *offers* to help the tailor in his time of trouble, although by Levine's own admission he *is* on probation and *has* limited powers. *Can* it be that Levine really *is* an angel? If Manischevitz *chooses* to believe, Levine *says* he *can* be found in Harlem.

PAST

In Bernard Malamud's magical short story "Angel Levine," a tailor named Manischevitz, who *believed* he *had lost* or *was* about to lose almost everything worth living for, *faced* a difficult decision: The forlorn tailor *was visited* by a black man who *claimed* to be a Jew and an angel of God. The man, who *said* his name *was* Alexander Levine, suddenly *appeared* sitting at a table in Manischevitz's living room and *offered* to help the tailor in his time of trouble, although by Levine's own admission he *was* on probation and *had* limited powers. *Could* it be that Levine really *was* an angel? If Manischevitz *chose* to believe, Levine *said* he *could* be found in Harlem.

Each paragraph about the Malamud story is correct and consistent in terms of verb tense. But many readers would probably agree that the present-tense version has more pizzazz and a slightly more sophisticated sound than the past-tense version. It has more immediacy, and its writer seems to affirm that the story "Angel Levine" is as alive today as it was the day Malamud finished writing it.

Let's try an exercise.

* **Exercise One**

Here are five sentences about Shakespearean plays. Examine the underlined verbs and change *some* of them to create consistency in verb tense. (Not all underlined verbs should be changed.) Some students may choose to convert an entire sentence to the present while others opt to use the past throughout. The important thing is to be consistent.

1. In the play *King Lear,* Shakespeare <u>explores</u> many universal concerns: He <u>analyzed</u> the nature of absolute power, <u>studies</u> the complexities of relationships, and <u>reaffirmed</u> the healing power of unselfish love.

2. Hamlet <u>decided</u> not to kill Claudius when he <u>has</u> the chance; that <u>is</u> the crucial decision that Hamlet <u>made</u>, and it <u>proves</u> to be his undoing.

3. Contrary to some critical interpretations, jealousy <u>is</u> perhaps not really Othello's tragic flaw; after all, he <u>observed</u> very eloquently in Act V that he <u>is</u> a man "not easily jealous, but being wrought, perplex'd in the extreme . . ."

4. Shakespeare's *Henry V,* which <u>reflects</u> important Tudor philosophies, <u>presented</u> a profile of an ideal king, <u>explored</u> soldiers' responsibilities in war, and comically <u>stereotypes</u> several nationalities.

5. It <u>is</u> most certainly not ineffective bleach about which Lady Macbeth <u>is</u> distressed when she vehemently <u>exclaimed</u>, "Out damned spot."

Exercise Two

In these short passages, all verbs that are not underlined are correct. Use them as context clues to help you make choices about the verbs that are underlined. Revise *some* of the underlined verbs to solve inconsistencies in tense.

1. President Franklin D. Roosevelt initiated the United States Selective Service on October 29, 1941. That was the day he <u>reached</u> into an enormous bin and <u>pulls</u> out a capsule that <u>contained</u> a slip of paper marked with the number "158." On the other side of the country, in Los Angeles, a Mexican American by the name of Pedro Aguilar Despart <u>checks</u> his draft card and <u>realized</u> that he was the very first American man <u>selected</u> for the draft in the Second World War.

2. One of the all-time classic spots on Public Television's *Sesame Street* shows Bo Jackson, who is a running back for the Oakland Raiders and an outfielder for the Kansas City Royals, being approached by a little girl who <u>was</u> carrying a crooked stick and is followed by a couple of sheep. The little girl <u>extends</u> her hand and <u>introduced</u> herself: "Bo," she <u>said</u>, "you don't know Peep."

Jackson, who <u>would be</u> almost as famous for his "Bo Knows" commercials as for his versatility in pro sports, then introduces himself to the sheep. He says, "Bo."

They <u>answer</u>, "Baaa."

And so it <u>went</u>—"Bo," "Baaa," "Bo," "Baaa."

3. Anna Maria Van Schurman, who lived from 1607 until 1678, was a leading scholar of her day. She mastered Greek and Latin and <u>would study</u> astronomy, mathematics, geography, and music. The author of works of theology and a major treatise on the right of women to be educated, Van Schurman <u>immerses</u> herself in the study of Hebrew, Arabic, Ethiopian, and other languages. In fact, she <u>creates</u> an Ethiopian grammar for her own use. She had contact with other European women scholars of the seventeenth century, including Princess Elizabeth of Bohemia, Queen Christine of Sweden, Bathsua Makin, and Dorothea Moor, and <u>encountered</u> problems that <u>are</u> common in the lives of most early female scholars. In a sense, one example <u>tells</u> the tale: When she studied at the university in the city of Utrecht in the Netherlands, her mentor, Rector Gisbertus Voetius, was concerned that if a woman appeared in a university classroom, that odd sight <u>would disturb</u> the other students, who—it probably <u>goes</u> without saying—were all men. Voetius therefore arranged for her to sit in a specially built cubicle that <u>opens</u> into his lecture hall so that she <u>can see</u> but not be seen.

∗ Exercise Three

Examine all the verbs in this brief description of a baseball scandal. Then make necessary revisions in verb tenses wherever needed. This exercise and exercise four are a bit more demanding than earlier ones.

1   Never has there been a World Series as controversial and infamous as the thrown

2   World Series of 1919. In spite of the fact that the Chicago White Sox were favored five

3   to one, Jack Doyle, the head of a major betting operation in New York City, said that

4   about two million dollars had been wagered on the series, almost all of it on the

5   Cincinnati Reds to win. "You couldn't miss it," Doyle recalls later. "The thing had an

6   odor." However, the fact that the World Series was fixed was not generally known until

7   the fall of the next year, which was September 1920.

8   Actually, to most observers at the time, the series seemed quite aboveboard,

9   with the Reds winning it five games to three. (This was in the era of the best-of-nine

10   series.) The Reds won the first two games, but the White Sox win game three. The

11   Reds then take games four and five, but the White Sox bounce back for games six and

12   seven. The Reds finally wrap it all up with a 10–5 victory in the eighth game.

13   The day after the series ended, Hugh Fullerton, a sportswriter, suggested in his

14   column that something was perhaps not quite right, but he is generally ignored. Charles

15   Comiskey, who owned the White Sox at the time, offered a cash reward to anyone who

16   can prove that the series was fixed. Some of the innocent White Sox players who had

17   not been part of the plan to throw the game expressed just as much disbelief as the

18   team's owner.

19   Almost a year later, three men—Eddie Cicotte, Lefty Williams, and Joe

20   Jackson—signed confessions and admit that there had been a fix and that they, along

21   with others, had been in on it. But just before they were to go to trial, their confessions

22   mysteriously disappear from the office of the Illinois State's Attorney. When the case

23   finally reached court, the three men denied ever making any confessions, and the case

24 is dropped. But K.M. Landis, the baseball commissioner at the time, bans the three

25 from all major-league parks for life.

Exercise Four   PART A

For your final workout on this skill, read the following essay on the subject of psychopaths and criminal justice and, as you read, correct inconsistent and illogical verb tenses. Exercise three, concerning an historical event and therefore generally calling for the past tense, was quite a bit easier than this exercise. Here you have a complicated mix: Some statements concern events that occurred and theories that were formulated in the past; other statements concern present and eternal truths; still others project into the future.

1   Experts from the worlds of psychology and criminal justice say that as we move

2 closer to the end of the twentieth century the incidence of psychopathy is almost

3 certainly on the rise. What is *psychopathy?* Most of us are more familiar with other forms

4 of the word, such as *psychopath* and *psychopathic. Psychopathy* is simply the name of the

5 disease that afflicts the psychopath, a person who is unable to experience compassion

6 or pangs of conscience. Psychopathy is an emotional defect that currently afflicted at

7 least two to three percent of the population, and there is strong evidence that those

8 numbers are increasing. Federal statistics, for example, suggest that criminals are

9 becoming younger, are increasingly detached from their victims, and were more likely

10 to use brutal force when committing crimes.

11   What are the characteristics of psychopaths? In an article in *The New York Times,*

12 Daniel Goleman cites experts who say that psychopaths are manipulative con artists

13 who are callous and selfish. They are good talkers and smooth liars who practically ooze

14 charm. Characterized by grandiosity (extreme self-importance), lack of guilt, impulsive-

15 ness, and the inability to make long-term plans, psychopaths were irresponsible rule

16 breakers in almost every aspect of life. This is not news to people in the mental health

17 field. In fact, this is the picture of psychopaths that is widely known since ground-

18 breaking work on the illness was done in the 1940s.

Which Verb Tenses to Use

* PART B

Continue to correct problems in verb tenses.

1   But now, in the 1990s, much more is known, and the new information for the most

2   part adds to, rather than contradicted, the earlier picture. For example, recent research

3   indicates that in the psychopath the part of the brain that would control language often

4   functions abnormally. After twenty years of studying psychopaths, Dr. Robert Hare, a

5   psychologist at the University of British Columbia, has found that although in most

6   right-handed people the language center is in the left hemisphere of the brain, in

7   right-handed psychopaths, language seemed controlled equally by the left and right

8   halves of the brain.

9   Dr. Hare's discovery may indicate that there is a neurological basis for at least

10   some of the differences between the language of healthy people and the language of

11   psychopaths. Psychopaths are smooth, facile talkers who are rarely or never at a loss

12   for words but who seem disconnected from the emotional impact of what they were

13   saying. One recent experiment suggests that normal people react differently to neutral

14   words than they do to emotionally loaded words, and this difference could be measured

15   by examining brain-wave patterns. For example, a healthy person reacts very

16   differently to words like *love* and *death* than to words like *refrigerator* and *lamppost*. A

17   classic psychopath, on the other hand, had the same reaction to both types of words.

18   One possible conclusion is that the psychopathic personality understands things at a

19   shallow and superficial level.

20   A psychopath, for example, can talk about love for hours, but without any

21   evidence that he or she has ever experienced it. Similarly, in talking to a physician, the

22   psychopath may use highly technical medical language and seemed not to care at all

23   about using it erroneously. If caught lying, the psychopath may change the subject and

24   continue on as if he or she had not been caught.

Copyright © 1993 by HarperCollins College Publishers.

PART C

Continue to correct problems in verb tenses.

1   Do differences in the brain explain the psychopath completely? Researchers say

2   no. Childhood experiences may play a major role. Dr. William H. Reid, a psychiatrist at

3   the University of Texas Medical School in San Antonio, would say that psychopaths, in

4   spite of their normally suave facades, are like little children standing outside a window

5   looking at a happy family gathered around the fireplace inside. One program of therapy,

6   in fact, was geared directly toward what the psychopathic person probably missed in

7   childhood. In that treatment program, an afflicted person may stay for years at a

8   treatment center that resembles a tightly structured home environment with clear and

9   unbendable rules. This atmosphere provided the sense of order, organization, and

10   protection that may have been missing in a psychopath's early life, leaving

11   the individual in an early stage of moral and emotional development.

12   As part of the treatment in such a setting, a psychopath may receive

13   psychotherapy. In the past, this approach was thought to be useless because experts

14   believe that a psychopath could not form the kind of bond necessary for talk therapy to

15   be effective. But some therapists have changed their minds on this point. If all goes

16   well, what could a psychopath accomplish in therapy? Psychotherapists say

17   that if these very ill people are ever to have any hope of getting better, they must

18   confront an overwhelming, profound despair at their own inability to connect emotion-

19   ally with other human beings. If they can do that, there is hope that they can enter a

20   world in which words have meaning and people had love.

UNIT 3:   Adding -d and -ed Endings

As you know from chapter 8, the first chapter in section II, verbs are either
regular or irregular. If a verb is regular, its past tense and variations of the past
tense will end in *-d* or *-ed*. Remembering to add the *-d* or *-ed* ending in the writing
or editing process takes practice for some students. If you're one of them, the

series of editing exercises in this unit will help you learn to recognize when you need to add an ending to a verb.

An irregular verb presents a different challenge. Take *eat,* for example. We say *I eat, I ate, I have eaten.* The forms of the verb must be memorized. This is a good time to turn back to the full list of irregular verbs on pages 202–204 to see if there are any you still need to work on.

A regular verb, on the other hand, is just that—regular. Where the irregular verb changes form in the various tenses, the regular one follows a predictable pattern. Take *learn,* for example: We say *I learn, I learned, I have learned.*

Three Important Tenses

Most students who have trouble putting their verbs into the past tense have the most difficulty not with the regular past tense—as in "Yesterday the Vikings *played* the Packers"—but with the other verb forms that are more complex and subtle. There are three verb forms in the English language that are variations of the past tense. Each one shows a more complex time relationship than the simple past, and each one can cause trouble. Let's look at examples of each:

Present perfect	Past perfect	Future perfect
has/have decided	had decided	will have decided
has/have purchased	had purchased	will have purchased
has/have jumped	had jumped	will have jumped
has/have stopped	had stopped	will have stopped

The *present perfect*—with the helping verb *has* or *have*—is used to describe an action that is completed at the present time. For example:

a. Throughout my life I *have encountered* both saints and sinners.
b. Suzanna can take a break because she *has finished* the entire exercise.

The *past perfect*—with the helping verb *had*—was discussed in unit 2 in reference to consistency in verb tenses. This tense is used when the writer is already in the past tense and wants to show that another action happened at an even earlier time or, you might say, in the more distant past. For example:

c. Before the woman became a helicopter pilot, she *had worked* as a medic.
d. By the time the firefighters arrived, the home *had been destroyed.*

The *future perfect*—with the helping verbs *will have*—is used to show a time in the future when a particular act will already be completed. For example:

e. By six o'clock tonight, we *will have watched* the news on CNN for a full twelve hours.
f. When Edie is ready for college, her parents *will have saved* most of the money needed for tuition and room and board.

To test your understanding of these three tenses, fill in the blanks in these sentences:

g. When Lenny saw the book advertised at a fifty percent discount on Wednesday, he was furious because he _____ (*has purchased/had purchased/will have purchased*) it at the full price on Monday.

h. Two months from now, her parents _____ (*have been married/had been married/will have been married*) for half a century.

i. Jack should try something new; I'm sure he _____ (*has rented/had rented/will have rented*) the same movie from the video store ten times in a row.

[ANSWERS: g. had purchased (past perfect);   h. will have been married (future perfect);   i. has rented (present perfect).]

Modal Auxiliaries

In addition to the three verb tenses just described, writers can use a number of other ways to combine verbs and helping verbs to create verb phrases. The modal auxiliaries—especially *could, would, might,* and *should*—also combine with *have* to form verb phrases in which the last (and main) verb often must end in *-d* or *-ed.* For example:

a. If I had known you were coming, I *would have baked* a cake.
b. He *should have looked* around before he made his choice.
c. Actually she *might have appeared* in as many as forty films.

It's good to keep these types of verb phrases in mind as you edit your written work to make sure you have the *-d* and *-ed* endings attached.

Passives

In chapter 10, we looked at passive sentences. This might be a good time to review that discussion. When you use the passive voice with regular verbs, you need to make sure that you've added the *-d* or *-ed* ending to the verb.

Remember that where the active voice says, "I *dressed* the baby," the passive voice says, "The baby *was dressed* by me." Although you have learned to avoid the passive voice unless you have a good reason to use it, when you *do* have a good reason for using it, make sure that your verbs have the right endings.

Verb phrases in the passive voice will begin with the helping verbs *am, is, are, was,* and *were.* For example:

a. The speech *was delivered* in a strong voice.
b. In the third scene of Act II, she *is abused* by an absolute brute.
c. The sundaes *were drenched* with caramel sauce and *covered* with salty chopped peanuts.

Spelling Changes

When it comes to adding *-d* and *-ed* endings to verbs, some verbs will require no other change than the addition of the *-d* or *-ed.* But other verbs do require a spelling change:

1. **When a verb ends in the long *i* sound represented by the letter *y*, you generally change the *y* to *i* before you add *-ed.*** For example: cry → cried; try → tried; identify → identified.
2. **When the base verb ends in a consonant that is preceded by a short vowel, you usually double the consonant before adding *-ed.*** (A short vowel would be the *a* sound in *cat,* the *e* sound in *get,* the *i* sound in *sit,* the *o* sound in *mop,* and the *u* sound in *nut.*) For example: bat → batted; net → netted; rip → ripped; spot → spotted; cup → cupped.

If you are in doubt about whether to change a *y* to *i* or to double a consonant, consult your dictionary.

Adjectives Made from Verbs

Another problem for many students is the adjective that is made from a verb and ends in *-d* or *-ed.* Here are some examples—first, of the past-tense verb, then second, of the adjective derived from that verb:

a. **Past tense:** Yesterday I *fried* a chicken.
   Adjective: I made *fried* chicken.
b. **Past tense:** They *completed* the quilt.
   Adjective: They gave the *completed* quilt to the museum.
c. **Past tense:** We *softened* the ice cream for the recipe.
   Adjective: We needed *softened* ice cream for the recipe.

Summary

To sum up, these are the three basic situations in which *-d* and *-ed* endings are most likely to be left out in writing:

1. in regular past tense verbs;
2. at the ends of verb phrases (those made from the present perfect, the past

perfect, and the future perfect tenses; those made with modal auxiliaries; those made for the passive voice, and so forth); and

3. in adjectives made from verbs.

With all this in mind, let's try an exercise.

Exercise One   *   PART A

Add -*d* and -*ed* endings where needed in each of the following sentences. Make whatever spelling changes become necessary when you add -*d* or -*ed*. In the blank after each sentence, write the reason for the change: *past* (regular past tense verb), *vp* (end of a verb phrase), or *adj* (adjective made from a verb).

1. When he was a kid, the rap star Hammer (a.k.a. M.C. Hammer) work as a bat boy

   for the Oakland A's. _____

2. For his successes in the first modern Olympics in 1896, the Greek Marathon

   champion Spiridon Loues was honor with the gold medal, 365 free meals, and a

   lifetime supply of shoe-polishing services. _____

3. Septima Clark, who was call "Mother Conscience" by her admirers in the civil rights

   movement, trained voter-registration workers and teachers of basic literacy at the

   Highlander Folk School in Tennessee in the 1950s. _____

4. A nationally recognize medical journalist by the name of William Rubin has written

   eloquently on the "pariah syndrome," the phenomenon in which people avoid

   contact with the sick or dying because they don't know what to say or they fear

   facing their own mortality. _____

5. Singer and songwriter Paul Anka serve as an usher in a movie theater at the

   beginning of his show business career. _____

PART B

Continue to follow the directions given in part A.

1. Pete Gray, a one-arm baseball player, was an outfielder for the St. Louis Browns in

   1945 and batted .218. _____

2. Rosabeth Moss Kanter, a Harvard Business School professor and the first female

editor of the *Harvard Business Review,* has publish ten books while—in addition to her teaching—serving as co-director of a consulting firm and raising a son.

_____

3. King Solomon rule Israel for about forty years and had approximately seven hundred wives. _____

4. One of America's oldest comics, George Burns, was originally name Nathan Birnbaum. _____

5. According to the National Assessment of Educational Progress, only seven percent of all 17-year-olds in the United States have sufficiently advance science skills that they should be able to perform well in college-level science courses. _____

Exercise Two

Choose five words from the following list and write two sentences with each word, using its *-d* or *-ed* form. Label your use of the words as *past, vp,* or *adj.* For example, here are three possibilities for the verb *waste:*

    a. He *wasted* his time. (*past*)
    b. They *have wasted* a tremendous amount of lab equipment. (*vp*)
    c. She thought it was largely a *wasted* effort. (*adj*)

Use your own paper, please.

decrease	assume	love
patch	raise	butter
fail	satisfy	prejudice
ruin	improve	lighten
announce	haunt	fry

Avoiding Common Errors

Before you do any more exercises, it may be a good time to point out that many students make *-d* and *-ed* errors on certain key words and phrases. The following are the most common problems: *old-fashioned, prejudiced, used to* and *supposed to.*

   Old-fashioned is an adjective that always ends in *-ed;* it's as simple as that.

   Prejudice is a noun, and *prejudiced* is an adjective. An easy way to keep them straight is to substitute the noun *hate* for the noun *prejudice* and the adjective *hateful* for the adjective *prejudice.* (Although prejudice and hate aren't exactly the same thing, they're close enough for our purposes here.) These are correct examples:

Noun: *Prejudice* (or hate) has tragic effects.
Adjective: The speech contained several *prejudiced* (or hateful) remarks.

Used to is a verb phrase that often appears with its *-d* missing. Make sure you attach the *-d* when you're using the phrase to mean that you did something repeatedly in the past. Many writers drop this *-d* because very few of us pronounce it. (In fact, it would sound strange if we did.) These are correct examples:

I *used to* be afraid of flying.
He *used to* work for General Motors.
As kids, we *used to* dream about going to Disneyland.

Suppose and *supposed* are easy to keep straight if you substitute *assume* for *suppose*, and *assumed* for *supposed*. For example, "I was *supposed* to be the leader" is roughly equivalent to "I was *assumed* to be the leader." In any sentence, if *assumed* is correct, then *supposed* is correct. If *assume* is correct, then *suppose* is correct. For example, the sentence "*Suppose* for a moment that the earth is not round" is basically the same as "*Assume* for a moment that the earth is not round."

To check your understanding, add *-d* or *-ed* endings where they belong in these sentences:

a.   Mr. Jameson use to be a priest.

b.   Robert has a lot of old-fashion ideas.

c.   We are suppose to be in Reno by midnight.

d.   They have rather prejudice attitudes on that issue.

e.   Do you suppose we can get some fresh spinach?

f.   Prejudice is something we all have to confront in ourselves.

g.   What use to drive me crazy was his constant punning.

h.   I think they were suppose to stop the test after page six.

i.   I don't believe this is an exceptionally prejudice community.

[ANSWERS: a. used;   b. old-fashioned;   c. supposed;
d. prejudiced;   e. no change;   f. no change;   g. used;   h. supposed;
i. prejudiced.]

Exercise Three

On your own paper, write a paragraph on one of these subjects:

   a. what you did to get ready to go to college;
   b. your role in a particular athletic event (such as a big game, track event, tennis tournament) or in a project at work;
   c. what you did to get ready for a certain date, wedding, or other special occasion;
   d. what you accomplished this morning before noon; or
   e. a summary of the action of your favorite movie.

Check your paragraph for words that end in *-d* and *-ed.* Try to label each usage as *past, vp,* or *adj.*

Exercise Four   *   PART A

Add *-d* and *-ed* endings and make spelling changes where needed in this series of sentences on César Chávez and union organizing. Some sentences may require no change.

1. According to publish accounts of his life, César Chávez was born in 1927 on a farm near Yuma, Arizona.

2. When he was a boy, his parents lost their farm, and to support themselves the family became migrant workers.

3. Chávez began organizing farm workers in 1962, which was the same year he establish the National Farm Workers Association.

4. The organization use to be known—at various stages—under different names, but it eventually end up as the United Farm Workers of America.

5. Chávez develop a strong reputation for his ability to organize strikes and boycotts; the labor actions that were suppose to gain workers benefits from well-establish grape and lettuce growers were among the most well-known.

6. In an interview with John R. Moyer some years ago, Chávez discuss various aspects of his philosophy and several of the principles of good organizing he has follow throughout his life.

7. For one thing, he told Moyer that although it is always a gamble, it is not really

difficult to organize people as long as they have a share goal and a few things are kept in mind and emphasize.

8. Chávez maintain, for instance, that benefits and incentives must be disburse even in the formative stages of building a labor organization; it is not effective to rely entirely on promises of payoffs in the future.

9. Another point that Chávez raise was that, in the early stages of building a solid organization, it is more crucial to find organizers than to enroll members.

10. To get them, Chávez recall encountering many failures; he sometimes knock on forty to sixty doors to get the one sincere, commit volunteer he really need.

PART B

Continue to add -*d* and -*ed* endings and make whatever spelling changes your new endings necessitate.

1. That Chávez is a man of great humility was evident in some of the things he reveal to Moyer, his interviewer.

2. Chávez said that, even after he had achieve many successes, he never arrive at the point where he believe that he knew everything.

3. No matter how experience he became, he tried to remain open-minded and not become prejudice; he realize, for instance, that he could always learn from new members of the migrant workers' organization, and that those new members, like the older, more experience ones, must be allow a high degree of freedom to act because if they were require to be puppets, in the long run their contributions would be very constrain.

4. He also told of working hard to find just the right job for each person; he has a strong belief that there is an optimum role for each person to play in a well-form organization, and that the right role is the one that taps into the person's greatest power or most highly develop skill.

5. To Chávez, time is and always was more highly value than money.

6. The impact of an individual who gives time to a cause is much greater than that of an individual who simply contributes money: The worker's impact can be multiply many times as he or she draws others into support of a boycott or strike.

7. In Chávez's view, students and other young people are instrumental because, in spite of how full their lives can be, they still have time, especially compare to many of the union members and supporters who might be middle-age or older.

8. Simplicity is another highly regard virtue in any organizing campaign, according to Chávez; in fact, in both organizing and in education, he believes that one of the greatest dangers is that things can get so complicated and involve that people can become confuse and sometimes even paralyze.

9. Finally, the work of César Chávez has always been admire for its high level of commitment to a philosophy of nonviolence; his is one of the few organizations or movements on behalf of the poor and disenfranchise that has never veer from its state belief in the value of nonviolence.

10. The interview conclude with Chávez telling John Moyer that the organize migrant farm workers never have been committed to nonviolence because it is the easy way, nor because it is the cowardly way; they are dedicate to nonviolence because it is the powerful way. It works.

* Exercise Five

Add -*d* and -*ed* endings where they are needed in this short piece on childbirth. Make whatever other spelling changes are necessary due to the new endings.

1   For many years, most women in Western cultures have deliver their babies lying

2 down. But it wasn't always that way. It use to be consider normal for women to give

3 birth in a standing or sitting position—that is, until the eighteenth century. The ancient

4 Greeks, for example, use a birthing chair with a crescent-shape opening. In medieval

5   Europe, new brides from wealthy families often receive jewel-trim birthing chairs as

6   wedding gifts.

7   With the approval and encouragement of enlighten physicians, the sit-down

8   method, which for so long was consider old-fashion, is making a modest comeback. The

9   Century Manufacturing Company of Nebraska has design a modern birthing chair that is

10   fully motorize so that it can be raise, lower, or tilt to suit the needs of the mother and

11   her doctor or midwife.

12   One of the biggest benefits of the chair is that it takes advantage of the force of

13   gravity, which is suppose to help along a woman's contractions; her second-stage labor

14   therefore often can be reduce from sixty or ninety minutes to an average of thirty

15   minutes. With the chair, there is also less pressure on the back and a decrease risk of

16   blood clots in the legs.

17   A few objections, however, have been raise by some obstetricians who find it

18   easier to listen to an infant's heartbeat or to use forceps when the mother is lying down.

19   Some doctors feel that they are allow less freedom to maneuver when the mother is

20   sitting down. On the other hand, some medical professionals are moving in the direction

21   of reevaluating the possibly somewhat prejudice views they've held on this subject in

22   the past. New York's Dr. Warner Nash is quote by *Newsweek* as saying, "It's

23   embarrassing for us . . . to finally learn what nature told us many years ago. Most of

24   womankind will give birth in the vertical position if there's no interfering physician to

25   make them lie down."

UNIT 4:   Forming Plural Nouns

Some writers have to work hard at forming the standard plural nouns—nouns
that indicate more than one thing or person. If you're one of these writers, this
unit should be of help.

The great majority of plural nouns in English end in *-s* or *-es;* for example,
books, flowers, stars, hopes, developments. The exceptions—nouns that do not
become plural by the addition of *-s* or *-es*—are very few. Here are some of the
most common *irregular* nouns:

Singular form	Plural form
man	men
woman	women
businessman	businessmen
congresswoman	congresswomen
child	children
tooth	teeth
mouse	mice
sheep	sheep
ox	oxen
phenomenon	phenomena
medium	media
crisis	crises
basis	bases
analysis	analyses
species	species

You can add to this list as you discover the odd word here and there that does not take the addition of an -s or -es for its plural form.

It's a good idea to pay special attention to the word *people.* This word is already plural, but an -s is added in those rare situations where you're grouping various races or nationalities together, such as in "all the *peoples* of the world." But in the most common usages—for example, "Many people are perfectionists"—the word is plural without the -s ending.

There are also a few irregular plural nouns, such as *police,* that don't have a singular form. One might say that the singular forms of *police* are *police officer, policewoman,* and *policeman.* But *police* itself is plural.

Noun Markers

When students have trouble knowing where to add the -s or -es—and this is often the case when English is not the student's first language—it's helpful to learn some of the most common noun markers. These are words or phrases that signal when a noun is about to appear. The noun marker used most often—*the*—is not very helpful because it signals both singular and plural nouns. But most other noun markers clearly send the reader a signal to get ready for either a singular noun or a plural noun. Here are many of the most common noun markers divided into their two groups:

Noun markers that signal singular nouns

a	one
an	this
each	that
every	

Noun markers that signal plural nouns

a few	several
all	some
many	these
most	those
one of the	two, three, four, and so on

A plural noun marker that deserves special attention is the phrase *one of the*. The word *one* might fool you, but remember that, when you use this expression, you're going to follow it with a plural word because you're speaking of one of a group or collection of things. Consider these correct phrases:

> one of the *things* I like about you
> one of the *perfumes* on sale
> one of the best *nose tackles* in pro football

The noun markers *these* and *those* also deserve special mention. Remember that they're plural. A common error is to use them before a singular noun such as *type*. For example:

> **Wrong:** *These type* of fashion designers are interesting to watch.
> **Right:** *These types* of fashion designers are interesting to watch.

Another correct way of wording this example is

> **Right:** *This type* of fashion designer is interesting to watch.

When you do the editing exercises in this unit, come back frequently to the lists of noun markers. The more you review the two categories of noun markers and use them to help you find plural nouns, the faster you'll progress in identifying which nouns are plural and which are single.

When There Is No Noun Marker

Sometimes there is no marker before a noun. When this happens in English, most often the noun will be plural. For example, "In France, *researchers* believe that they have found an important clue." If the writer had used the singular form of the noun, it would have been preceded by a noun marker: for example, "In France, *a* researcher . . ." or "In France, *the* researcher . . ."

Are there exceptions? Yes. Here's one example: "I want *chocolate cake,* and I want it now!" But this is an unusual sentence. In general, singular nouns are preceded by noun markers while plural nouns may or may not be.

Spelling Changes

When you form regular plurals, sometimes you have to make small changes in the spelling of a word.

Adding -es

If the singular noun ends in *ch, s, sh, x,* or *z,* you need to add *-es* when you form the plural. This aids in pronunciation. For example:

Singular	Plural
church	churches
punch	punches
glass	glasses
brush	brushes
fox	foxes
Ortiz (a family name)	the Ortizes

You also add *-es* to *some* nouns that end in an *o* preceded by a consonant. For example, *hero* becomes *heroes,* and *tomato* becomes *tomatoes.* But, unfortunately, there are a good number of exceptions to this rule—for example, *pro* becomes *pros,* and *memo* becomes *memos*—so, on this point, you may need to rely on a dictionary.

Changing y to i and Adding -es

If the singular form of a noun ends in a *y* that is preceded by a consonant, you need to change the *y* to *i* and add *-es.* For example:

Singular	Plural
fly	flies
story	stories
worry	worries
luxury	luxuries
company	companies
identity	identities

This rule does not apply to proper (capitalized) nouns. For example, you'd write, "How many *Marys* were in the class?" It would be incorrect to change the *y* on *Mary* to an *i.*

Changing f to v

With some nouns that end in *f* or *fe* in their singular form, you change the *f* to *v* before you add the *-s* or *-es.* For example, *life* becomes *lives,* and *scarf* becomes *scarves.* This switch aids in pronunciation. There are plenty of exceptions—*belief* becomes *beliefs,* and *proof* becomes *proofs*—so again you may need to use a dictionary.

When a Singular Noun Ends in st

Singular nouns that end in *st* are tricky for some writers. Don't forget to add the *-s* that is needed to make the word plural. For example:

Singular	Plural
scientist	scientists
analyst	analysts
breast	breasts
hypnotist	hypnotists

Exercises

* ### Exercise One

Add -*s* or -*es* to the regular plural nouns in these brief paragraphs. Make appropriate spelling changes where needed.

In this exercise, and in those that follow, occasionally you'll find words that could be left singular or made plural because either way would be correct in the context of the sentence.

1. Expert agree that friendship are absolutely essential to the psychological health and stability of people of all age—children, teenager, and adult. In *Among Friends,* one of the many book she has written, author Letty Cottin Pogrebin says that most people have between three and seven close friend, around fifteen more casual friend (usually people they know from work), and five hundred to twenty-five hundred acquaintance.

2. In wartime, one of the thing that pilot must learn is how to manage their fear. Many veteran flier say that their worst problem is not the fear they feel during mission over enemy territory; the most nerve-racking experience are the often inevitable attempt to refuel in midair and to land on aircraft carrier. In fact, a study was conducted to determine the specific event that cause the greatest stress to flier. During the Vietnam War, a number of Navy pilot were asked to wear heart monitor during their sortie. As it turned out, most pilots' heart beat faster during their attempt to land on naval aircraft carrier than during their attack on various target within enemy territory.

Exercise Two

Add -*s* or -*es* to the regular plural nouns in these paragraphs. Make appropriate spelling changes where needed.

1. Gerald Tomlinson's *Speaker's Treasury of Sports Anecdotes, Stories & Humor* is a wonderful source of quote, anecdote, and one-liner about both famous and little-known personality in the world of sports. In his book, he tells of a Scottish blacksmith by the name of Kirkpatrick Macmillan, who added foot pedals to the bicycle about 150 year ago. With this technological addition, he was able to rev up his own bike to the then-astonishing speed of 14 mile an hour. As Tomlinson points out, at that speed the blacksmith often left local stagecoach in the dust, terrifying their driver and passenger. In fact, Macmillan was arrested at least once for what the police termed "furious driving on the road."

2. It used to be that kaleidoscope were just for kid, who could pick them up easily for a few penny at the local dimestore. Nowadays, discerning men and women—including many serious art collector—have shown a strong interest in acquiring the most elegant version of these formerly humble toy. In fact, in the past ten year or so, artist from many part of the world began to create handmade kaleidoscope, the best of which are sold primarily in art gallery. These kaleidoscope, sometimes called "art scope" or simply "scope," have exterior made of fine material such as gold, silver, ceramic, and stained glass. Their interior are filled with such thing as butterfly wing, herb, seed, dried flower, semiprecious stone, and colored liquid held within tiny bit of blown glass. Viewer peer into a world of beautiful shape and luscious color reflected in an intricate system of mirror. Some of the most lavish art scope now sell for $5,000 to $10,000, and, at art auction, bid of up to $60,000 for an antique kaleidoscope have been turned down as too low. Why the sudden interest in kaleidoscope? That is anybody's guess, but some observer point out that these are very stressful time, and the kaleidoscope, which is a type of mandala—a circle within a circle—may provide a meditative, therapeutic, healing experience. (At $10,000 or more, who would expect anything less?)

Exercise Three   *   PART A

Add -s or -es to the regular plural nouns in this short piece on an important figure in American folk music. Make spelling changes as needed.

1   One of the most colorful and influential figure in the history of American folk music

2   is Alan Lomax, a man perhaps few people in the general public have heard of. Lomax

3   sees folklorist as people who make vital connection between the larger culture and

4   musician who otherwise might remain obscure. With a special interest in the way

5   African and European influence mixed and combined to form American folk music,

6   Lomax started recording folk tune in the deep South in 1933. Along with his father, John

7   Lomax, he discovered or introduced many of the greatest folk musician the United

8   States—and possibly the world—has ever known. The Lomax, father and son,

9   discovered Leadbelly in a Louisiana prison, and Alan Lomax used his radio show to

10   introduce such major singer-songwriter as Woody Guthrie and Pete Seeger. Another of

11   his most lasting accomplishment was to encourage the folk in Washington, specifically

12   the decision maker at the Library of Congress, to add folk music to its many collection.

PART B

Continue to follow the directions given in part A.

1   On his PBS television series called "American Patchwork," Lomax, now in his

2   seventy, brings to life many chapter in the history of American music. Some of these

3   episode are thrilling, others quirky, and a few tragic. To some observer, the history of

4   American folk music is a microcosm of the history of America. On a show that traces the

5   various origin of Cajun music, Lomax tells one of the grimmest story imaginable. It's the

6   true story of one of the greatest accordian player who ever lived, Amadie Ardoin. Year

7   ago, after a performance, Ardoin was beaten, and he later died from his injury. What

8   brought on the attack? Ardoin was a black man and, while he was playing, a white

9   woman used her handkerchief to wipe the sweat from his brow.

UNIT 5: Pronoun Problems

Pronouns can present a number of problems for writers, but they're all easily solved. We'll focus on those problems that crop up often.

Pronoun-Antecedent Agreement

You know that subjects have to agree with verbs. Pronouns also have to agree, but not with verbs. Pronouns replace nouns, and they must agree in number with the nouns they replace. A noun that a pronoun replaces or refers to is called an *antecedent,* and it normally appears *before* the pronoun. (If you're a poker player, you should have no trouble remembering what *antecedent* means; just think about how you ante up before you play a hand.) If the antecedent noun is singular, it can be replaced only by a singular pronoun; if it's plural, it can be replaced only by a plural pronoun.

For example, if you're writing about *Gregory* and you use the pronoun *he* to mean Gregory, then you have no problem. Your pronoun—*he*—agrees with your antecedent—*Gregory*—because they're both singular.

Disagreement most often occurs when you're writing about something like "the ideal family man" or "the typical father," and after using *he* once or twice—correctly, because your antecedent is singular—you switch to *they.* Why would you switch to *they?* Because, first of all, your mind is on the content of your sentence, not the grammar. And second, although you're writing about something singular, in a sense you probably mean "all ideal family men" or "typical fathers everywhere." So it's easy to slip.

Here is another example of pronoun–antecedent disagreement:

Wrong: The *mail* came late, but *they* always do on Mondays.

In this case, the plural pronoun *they* can't logically replace the singular antecedent *mail.* The writer is using a singular word—*mail*—but is probably picturing something plural—like letters. Here's one solution:

Right: The *mail* came late, but *it* always does on Mondays.

(Notice that, in this case, changing the pronoun from plural to singular also means changing the verb from *do* to *does.*) This is another good revision:

Right: The *letters* came late, but *they* always do on Mondays.

Avoiding he or she *When You Can*

In English, unfortunately, we have no singular third person pronoun that's genderless. Instead, we have *he* and *she* and their variants: *him* and *her; his* and *hers;* and *himself* and *herself.* Before writers became sensitive to issues of sexism in language, most used the masculine pronouns in a universal sense, but many women felt—and still feel—excluded by that usage, even when the writer did not intend to discount or devalue females.

To avoid devaluing or stereotyping through pronoun usage, writers sometimes, as you know, employ *he or she* or *he/she*. These choices are fine, but they can get messy. For example:

> A good *student* knows that if *he or she* does not keep on top of *his or her* assignments, *he or she* will find *himself or herself* jammed up at the end of the academic term.

Any sentence like this one is, of course, ridiculously wordy and awkward (although technically correct) and should be avoided. The simplest solution here—and in many situations—is to convert to the plural:

> Good *students* know that if *they* do not keep on top of *their* assignments, *they* will find *themselves* jammed up at the end of the academic term.

Converting to the plural is a good solution when you can do it, but there may be times when it's important to you to stay in the singular. In a given situation, for example, you might want to write about "the three-year-old," not "three-year-olds." In that case, go ahead and use "he or she" or "he/she" if you so desire, but avoid long, convoluted constructions.

Another option is to use *he* in one section and *she* in another. More and more writers are doing this, and readers seem to perceive quickly what the writer means, namely, that some subjects (teachers, doctors, lawyers, or students, for instance) are male and some are female. For example, in a paper about the ideal engineer, the writer might use the masculine pronouns in one part of the paper and then, when it is not likely to cause confusion or seem in error, switch to the use of feminine pronouns in another part.

Or you can do as some writers do and continue to use the masculine pronouns in a universal sense. You might also use the feminine pronouns in a universal sense. This is a decision that you have to make for yourself.

Singular Collective Nouns

Words such as *group, family, team,* and *association* are normally considered singular. Each of these collective nouns refers to *one* thing, even though it may bring to mind a number of people or a number of parts. So *a team,* for example, is considered an *it,* not a *they*. For example:

> *Rolling Stone* magazine once called *R.E.M.* "the best rock and roll band in America"; years later, the magazine called *it* "the most resourceful rock and roll band in America."

There might be a temptation to use the pronoun *they* for a band because it's natural to picture its various members, but a band—like a team or an organization—is singular. It's an *it.*

Note: There's an interesting fine point about certain collective nouns, such as *family* and *committee*. If they're imagined as functioning as one, united thing—everybody's in agreement, let's say, or voting the same way—considered singular. (This goes for subject–verb agreement as well as for pronoun-antecedent agreement.) But if the components of a collective noun are imagined as functioning separately, the noun is considered plural. So these are both correct:

> My *family* is very eccentric, and *it* is often the talk of the town.
> The *family* are expected to arrive by four this afternoon, and *they* will be coming from all four corners of the country.

Prepositional Phrases

Some pronoun–antecedent mistakes involve prepositional phrases. The antecedent is the noun *before* a prepositional phrase, not the noun inside a prepositional phrase. Fill in the blank with the correct pronoun and verb choice:

> In recent years the number of women in the banking business has risen
>
> tremendously, and _____ (*it is/they are*) expected to continue
>
> to rise for some time.

Did you choose *it is?* That's the correct choice because the antecedent is *number*. The *number* is expected to continue to rise. The word *women* is not the antecedent because it is in a prepositional phrase—*of women*—and, being inside a prepositional phrase, it has a modifying function in the sentence.

Indefinite Pronouns as Antecedents

Sometimes you'll find that the antecedent of your pronoun is actually another pronoun—an indefinite one. Remember that indefinite pronouns, such as *anyone, anybody, anything, somebody, someone,* or *nobody,* are singular in number. So are *each* and *each one.*

Nonstandard Pronouns

Nonstandard pronouns appear once in a while in student writing, and, because they are not standard, they should be avoided in your academic work. Unless you use these pronouns for a stylistic reason, such as in quoted dialogue, *hisself, theirselves,* and *themself* should be replaced with the standard forms *himself* and *themselves.*

* Exercise One

Fill in the blank with the correct pronoun or pronoun and verb choice. Write *ante* (for antecedent noun) over the noun that agrees in number with the

pronoun you choose. When necessary, in those rare cases where it doesn't work to switch everything to the plural, *he or she* and its variations will be the option chosen in this unit's exercises.

1. When comedian W.C. Fields, whose real name was Claude William Dukenfield, died in 1946, he was mourned at three burial services. _____ (*It/They*) included a nonsectarian ceremony headed by the ventriloquist Edgar Bergen, a Catholic service arranged by Mrs. Fields, and a spiritualist reading organized by a companion of many years, Carlotta Monti.

2. In Faye Wattleton, the Planned Parenthood Federation of America, the nation's largest family-planning agency, had _____ (*its/their*) first woman president.

3. Critic and reformer John Ruskin once said, "When a man is wrapped up in _____ (*himself/themselves*), _____ (*he makes/they make*) a pretty small package."

4. According to a recent interview, the American misfit is the role Jodie Foster loves to play. _____ (*It/They*) might be a runaway teen, a child prostitute, a vulnerable but tough FBI trainee, or a carnival hustler, but she always plays a disenfranchised character and brings _____ (*her/them*) to life in a way few other young actresses can.

5. Not wanting to relinquish their independence, in 1912 about two thousand members of the Cherokee tribe refused to claim _____ (*its/their*) land allotments. Historian Angie Debo points out that many proud Cherokees made this choice even though the tribe found _____ (*itself/themselves*) in the most destitute poverty imaginable.

6. The English wit Oscar Wilde once said, "The advantage of the emotions is that _____ (*it leads/they lead*) us astray."

7. The American Film Institute, an organization of 35,000 professionals, students, and

amateur filmmakers, issued _____ (*its/their*) own list of the best movies ever made in the United States: *Gone With the Wind* came in number one, *Citizen Kane* was number two, and *Casablanca* was number three.

8. "Sports do not build character," said journalist Heywood Hale Broun. "_____ (*It reveals/They reveal*) it."

9. Here's a homespun quip from a journalist by the name of Edgar Howe: "Put cream and sugar on a fly, and _____ (*it tastes/they taste*) very much like a black raspberry."

10. Ever since Wild Bill Hickok was shot and killed in a card game on August 2, 1876, the poker hand that he was holding has been called the "dead man's hand." _____ (*It/They*) consisted of two pairs—aces and eights.

Exercise Two

Fill in the blank with the correct pronoun or pronoun and verb choice. Write *ante* over the noun that agrees in number with the pronoun you choose.

1. Henrik Ibsen, the great Norwegian playwright, once said, "It is inexcusable for scientists to torture animals; let _____ (*him or her/them*) make _____ (*his or her/their*) experiments on journalists and politicians."

2. The number of child-abuse cases seems to increase each year, but some experts say that this number may not actually reflect more abuse; _____ (*it/they*) may reflect better reporting of such incidents.

3. According to Mary Field Belenky, Blythe McVicker Clinchy, Nancy Rule Goldberger, and Jill Mattuck Tarule, the authors of *Women's Ways of Knowing: The Development of Self, Voice, and Mind*, a woman is more likely than a man to define _____ (*herself/themselves*) in terms of _____ (*her/their*) relationships to other people.

4. Each year, more than a million young people between the ages of 10 and 17 run

away from home. One youngster out of every two is running away from physical

abuse by _____ (*his or her/their*) parents.

5. Gioacchino Antonio Rossini, an Italian composer of operas, once boasted, "Give me

a laundry list and I'll set _____ (*it/them*) to music."

6. In defense of the humble pun, Oscar Levant once said, "A pun is the lowest form of

humor—when you don't think of _____ (*it/them*) first."

7. The League of Women Voters is famous for many of _____ (*its/their*)

functions, but _____ (*it is/they are*) probably most well-known for

sponsoring presidential debates in national elections.

8. According to experts in nutrition, the average American eats about thirty tons of

food during _____ (*his or her/their*) lifetime.

9. Here is a classic sexist observation from the eighteenth-century English man of

letters, Samuel Johnson: "Nature has given women so much power that the law has

very wisely given _____ (*her/them*) little." Dr. Johnson is the same poor,

misguided soul who said, "A man is in general better pleased when _____

(*he has/they have*) a good dinner upon _____ (*his/their*) table than when

_____ (*his/their*) wife talks Greek."

10. Abraham Lincoln is reported to have said, "Whenever I hear anyone arguing for

slavery, I feel a strong impulse to see it tried on _____ (*him/them*)

personally."

Two More Problems

Two other pronoun problems concern antecedents. They occur less often than
pronoun-antecedent disagreement, so we'll take a very brief look at each.

Pronouns that Don't Have Antecedents

Make sure all your pronouns actually do have antecedents. Sometimes, in both
conversation and writing, we tend to speak of an unknown *they* or *it* without first

making it clear (through the use of a noun antecedent) who *they* or *it* is. (Other pronouns are misused this way, too, but *they* and *it* are the culprits most of the time.)

Here's a classic error of this type:

> The Names Project AIDS Memorial Quilt became so significant that in 1988 *they* nominated it for the Nobel Peace Prize.

No doubt you can see the problem clearly: Who's *they?* One solution is to name *they.* But if you don't know who nominated the quilt project or you don't wish to say, how else can you revise the sentence? Using the passive voice is one possibility, and you can probably think of others.

Unclear Pronouns

The other problem is simple to fix. Look at this example:

> In 1989, a film about the quilt was produced by Bill Couturie and narrated by Dustin Hoffman. *He* did a magnificent job.

What is the noun antecedent of *He?* Is it *Bill Couturie* or *Dustin Hoffman?* Technically, it's *Dustin Hoffman* because his name directly precedes the pronoun. But is that the writer's intention? Obviously, the sentence should be a little more clear. How can you revise it?

Pronoun Case

I and *me* are two different cases of the same pronoun. So are *she* and *her,* and *he* and *him.* When we use pronouns alone, we normally use the correct cases automatically. But when a pronoun is paired with a noun or another pronoun, mistakes happen easily. For example:

> **Right:**   *He* is a good friend of mine.
> **Wrong:**   Megan and *him* are good friends of mine.

He is the correct case of the third person singular pronoun to use in the subject position of a clause, and it doesn't matter if it's used alone or with another pronoun or a noun.

To avoid this error, simply omit the other noun or pronoun and see which case sounds correct when used alone. In our example, you'd omit *Megan* and ask yourself if "Him is a good friend of mine" sounds right. (You'll notice that we had to adjust the verb from *are* to *is* to make the test.) *He* is the correct pronoun to use in the subject position in our example. In other words, it should be "Megan and *he* are good friends of mine."

* **Exercise Three**   PART A

Fill in the blanks with the correct case of the pronoun.

1. It's important to Charlene and _____ (*I/me*).

2. Patty and _____ (*I/me*) will definitely be there.

3. What will you do with Caitlin and _____ (*he/him*)?

4. We're very happy for the Wilsons and _____ (*them/they*).

5. Elaine and _____ (*he/him*) have been planning their wedding for years.

PART B

Continue to fill in the blanks with the correct pronouns.

1. I am sure that Richard and _____ (*them/they*) would be happy to do it for you.

2. When my mother-in-law and _____ (*I/me*) get together, we always have a wonderful time.

3. Remember the Miracles? I'll always love Smokey Robinson and _____ (*them/they*).

4. The Joneses and _____ (*us/we*) used to live right next door to each other.

5. Rita and _____ (*her/she*) have always been best friends.

UNIT 6:   Homonyms and Other Easily Confused Word Pairs

Fran Healy, a catcher-turned-sportscaster, was once covering a game between the Yankees and the Blue Jays when he spotted a flock of ducks on the field. "That's the first time," he told fans, "I've ever seen a *fowl* in fair territory."

If you intentionally use one word in place of another, as Healy did, you have no problem in your sentence. With language, as long as you have a logical reason for doing it, you can get away with almost anything. You can use a fragment, a comma splice, a different system of subject–verb agreement, or *fowl* instead of *foul*. The problem occurs only when you do any of these things unintentionally.

Sometimes the wrong word sneaks into a piece of writing unbidden. This unit reviews some of the word pairs that are easy to confuse and often appear in the wrong spots in college students' writing. To the twenty listed, you can add any other pairs that give you trouble, and you can make up your own exercises to help you with them.

Some of these problem words are *homonyms*—words that sound alike but have different meanings and different spellings—and some are pairs of words that are confused for other reasons. We'll focus on these words in this unit:

a/an	it's/its
accept/except	passed/past
affect/effect	principal/principle
amount/number	than/then
bare/bear	their/there/they're
coarse/course	threw/through
conscience/conscious	to/too/two
finally/finely	weather/whether
have/of	who's/whose
hear/here	you're/your

Please read the following explanations before you do the exercises. Consult a dictionary if you need more help than given in the brief discussions here.

A/An

The words *a* and *an* are both markers for singular nouns. *A* is used before nouns that begin with a consonant, and *an* is used before words that begin with a vowel or a vowel sound. For example:

a chance	an opportunity
a lucky guess	an educated guess

When a noun begins with the letter *u,* you use *a* before it when the *u* is long. (When *u* is long, it sounds like the *y* in *yellow.*) You use *an* when the *u* is short. These are correct examples:

a united effort	an uncle from Texas
a union meeting	an uninspiring lecture

When the first letter of a noun is a sounded *h,* you use *a* before the noun. When the first letter is a silent *h,* you use *an* because the noun actually starts with a vowel sound and *an* will make the combination easier to pronounce. For example:

a heaven on earth   an hourly rate
a high-flying hawk   an herbal shampoo

Accept/Except

Accept is the verb form of *acceptance,* and it means to receive something, not to reject it. The word *except* is a preposition related to the noun *exception,* as in the phrase "an exception to the rule." For example:

He can *accept* a compliment fairly well.
She loves every dance *except* the polka.

Affect/Effect

Effect is the noun. *Affect* is the verb, and it is the one you'll use in various forms: *affects, affected, is affecting,* and so forth. One easy way to distinguish between these two words is to consider their meanings: *Effect* is an end result, and *affect* means to *act* on. Just remember **end result = effect,** and **act on = affect.** For example:

The *effect* of the drug was immediately apparent.
The drug could *affect* her breathing.

(There is a verb *effect* also, but it has a little different meaning and is used much less often than the noun *effect.* We won't take it up here.)

Amount/Number

The word *amount* is used with substances that can't be counted. The word *number* is used with substances that can be counted—even when you don't know the number. For example:

the amount of love   the number of kisses
the amount of mashed potatoes   the number of baked potatoes

Also, the words *less* and *much* work in the same way as *amount.* The words *fewer* and *many* work in the same way as *number.* For example:

the amount of humor   the number of jokes
less humor   fewer jokes
much humor   many jokes

Bare/Bear

The word *bare* is an adjective that means naked, plain. It's also a verb that means to reveal. The word *bear* means the animal, of course, but it also means to give birth, carry a burden, or endure something. For example:

Your paper is a little *bare* in spots; it could use more detail.
In the sacrament of reconciliation in the Catholic Church, penitents *bare* their souls to a priest.
In Montana's Glacier National Park, the grizzly *bear* is able to roam free.
How many children did the woman *bear?*
I don't know if I can *bear* to hear that joke one more time.

Coarse/Course

The word *coarse* means rough; it can describe anything from the texture of fabric to a kind of language. *Course* is used in the expression *of course* and has a number of other meanings, such as a path or a route. For example:

The language was too *coarse* for your delicate ears.
The material of the shirt was so *coarse* that it irritated his skin.
Of *course,* I'll be there tonight.
Throughout the *course* of history, wars seem to erupt over the same conflicts again and again.

Conscience/Conscious

Conscience is a noun; it's what bothers you when you've violated your own sense of right and wrong. The word *conscious* is an adjective related to the noun *consciousness,* and it means to be aware. For example:

A psychopathic person lacks a well-formed *conscience.*
She made a *conscious* attempt to show him more love.

Finally/Finely

Finally means at last. *Finely* means delicately or in small pieces. For example:

The pen pals *finally* met.
Add some *finely* chopped onions to the salad, please.

Have/Of

The error relating to this word pair is a little different. Here are two examples: *must of looked* and *would of run.* This is not a matter of mixing up two words, but of using *of* when *have* is required in a verb phrase. The only reason writers ever make this mistake is that *have* can sound like *of* if said quickly after certain auxiliary verbs. For example:

Wrong: I could *of* died.
Right: I could *have* died.
Wrong: You should *of* seen it.
Right: You should *have* seen it.

Hear/Here

The verb *hear* means to listen. *Here* is an adverb that designates a place. For example:

I *hear* the song every day.
Put the plates *here*.

It's/Its

It's is the contraction of *it is*. *Its* is the possessive pronoun. Some students have trouble with *its* because possessive nouns take an apostrophe, but possessive pronouns do not. For example:

Will you tell me when *it's* midnight?
The statue fell off *its* base.

Passed/Past

Passed is the past tense of the verb *pass* and an adjective derived from that verb. *Past* is (1) the noun that means the opposite of the future; (2) an adjective derived from that noun; and (3) a preposition meaning beyond. For example:

Verb: I *passed* him on the street yesterday.
Adjective: A *passed* ball is the catcher's fault, while a wild pitch is the pitcher's fault.
Noun: There is no sense living in the *past*.
Adjective: Why torture yourself over *past* mistakes?
Preposition: It's a little *past* noon.

Principal/Principle

The noun *principal,* as all students know, means the head of a school. (The principal is your pal, right?) But *principal* has other related meanings, too. For example, as a noun it also means a sum of money that earns interest. As an adjective, the word means most important, main, central.

The word *principle* is a noun and nothing but a noun. It means a basic truth, law, rule, ideal, or standard. (Like *rule, principle* ends in *-le*—that's one way of remembering.) For example:

The *principal* is also the history teacher.
Did the bank tell you how much you earned on your *principal?*
Her *principal* asset is her zest for life.
We're studying the *principle* of supply and demand.

Than/Then

Than is used to make comparisons. *Then* is an adverb that describes the time of an action and often is used in conjunction with *if*. For example:

> My mouth was working faster *than* my brain.
> When she was young, she hated westerns, but *then* she saw *High Noon*.
> If you care about yourself, *then* please don't drink and drive.

One more note: The word *than* should not follow the word *different*. The expression *different from* is preferred.

Their/There/They're

Their is a possessive pronoun. *There* is an adverb showing location, and it's also sort of an empty sentence starter, as in "There is still a chance we can work this out." *They're* is the contraction of *they* and *are*. For example:

> *Their* hearts were heavy.
> Put the pizza over *there*.
> *There* is a little something I want to discuss with you.
> I wonder how *they're* planning to get here.

Threw/Through

Threw is the past tense of the verb *throw*. *Through* is a preposition. For example:

> Who *threw* out the leftovers?
> Let's go *through* the tunnel of love.

To/Too/Two

The word *to* can be part of an infinitive verb phrase, as in "I want to go" or a preposition, as in "Send a message to Mary."

The word *two* is a noun ("the two of hearts"), a plural pronoun ("We'd like two, please."), or an adjective ("See section two.") It always refers to the number between one and three.

The word *too* is the one that causes trouble. *Too* precedes adjectives and intensifies them. Roughly, it means excessively, as in "It's too cold for me." *Too* also means also, as in "Let me go, too." For example:

> **Part of a verb phrase:**   She wants *to* sing.
> **Preposition:**   The road *to* heaven is rough.
> **Intensifier of an Adjective:**   You're *too* cute for words.
> **Also:**   Give me an apple, *too*.
> **Number:**   Marriage unites *two* people.

Weather/Whether

Weather, of course, refers to the climate. *Whether* is a conjunction used in such sentences as "I don't know whether I should leave now or wait another hour." For example:

The *weather* had a big effect on the band's marching.
It doesn't matter *whether* or not I push down on the pedal.

Who's/Whose

Who's is the contraction of *who* and *is. Whose* is a possessive pronoun. For example:

Who's afraid of the big bad wolf?
Whose yogurt is this?
She's a woman *whose* whole life was planned out for her.

You're/Your

You're is the contraction of *you* and *are. Your* is a possessive pronoun. For example:

You're too hot to handle.
Your salad is perfect.

Exercises

If you're unclear about the correct usage of any of these words, look them up in the dictionary and consult your teacher.

Exercise One   *   PART A

Here are some *old* vaudeville jokes. Fill in the blanks with the correct word choices.

1. When I saw my father all dressed up, I said, "Hey, that suit _____

   (*you're/your*) wearing fits like a glove."

      "Yeah," he said, "I know. I wish I could _____ (*have/of*) found one

   that fit like a suit."

2. "Excuse me," the man said, "but you look like Helen Green."

"Well," I replied, "I know _____ (*it's/its*) not my best color, but really!"

3. Did you _____ (*hear/here*) this one? _____ (*It's/Its*) supposed to be the first joke ever told:

   Adam: "Do you really love me?"

   Eve: "Who else?"

4. _____ (*Their/There/They're*) is poor, and then _____ (*their/there/they're*) is poor. My neighbor used to say that you know _____ (*you're/your*) really poor when the only thing you can pay is attention.

5. *Question:* What did the beauty columnist in the newspaper say when she was asked, "How can _____ (*a/an*) individual avoid falling hair?"

   Answer: "Jump out of _____ (*it's/its*) way."

6. "Can you tell me," asked the man, "_____ (*weather/whether*) or not _____ (*their/there/they're*) is _____ (*a/an*) English word that contains all the vowels in the language?"

   "Unquestionably," I replied.

7. After _____ (*their/there/they're*) honeymoon, Harry told Harriet that he felt like a new man. Harriet said she did, _____ (*to/too/two*).

8. The man looked right at me and said, "I never forget a face, but in _____ (*you're/your*) case, I'll try to make _____ (*a/an*) exception."

9. Judging by the _____ (*amount/number*) of divorces nowadays, a lot of people who said "I do" didn't.

10. My parents will _____ (*have/of*) been married fifty years tomorrow, and they've had only one argument. Of _____ (*coarse/course*), it started on _____ (*their/there/they're*) wedding day and _____ (*it's/its*) not over yet.

PART B

Can you stand more vaudeville jokes? Fill in the blanks.

1. _____ (*Hear/Here*) are _____ (*to/too/two*) definitions of gos-

    sips: people who have a good sense of rumor, and people who believe more

    _____ (*than/then*) they hear.

2. Did you _____ (*hear/here*) the one about the cannibal who went to see a

    psychiatrist? The poor guy had _____ (*finally/finely*) gotten fed up with

    people.

3. One day, my mother-in-law dropped in, and I asked her to settle _____

    (*a/an*) argument for us. "Last night," I said, "we had _____ (*a/an*) ele-

    gant formal dinner, and _____ (*your/you're*) son had a fit because I served

    boiled eggs. What do you think?"

    "Well, dear," my mother-in-law replied, "this time I'm on _____

    (*you're/your*) side. I think you should _____ (*have/of*) served anyone who

    showed up."

4. _____ (*It's/Its*) a fact that _____ (*a/an*) officer of the law in

    this town recently_____ (*passed/past*) out thirty parking tickets within

    five minutes. _____ (*Than/Then*) he realized he was in a drive-in movie.

5. Aunt Tilly: "_____ (*You're/Your*) not going _____ (*to/too/two*)

    believe this, but I heard that Ida got _____ (*a/an*) engagement ring from

    that X-ray technician she's been going out with."

    Aunt Milly: "Really? I can't figure out what he sees in her."

6. After I had been waiting for the bus for _____ (*a/an*) hour or more, I

    _____ (*finally/finely*) gave up and asked a man if he would please call me

    a cab.

    "Sure, lady," he said, "_____ (*you're/your*) a cab."

7. Maybe _____ (*you're/your*) right. Maybe I should _____

(*have/of*) been insulted when the mind reader charged me half-price.

8. I never did figure out why the class laughed when the professor asked me if I

believed in the _____ (*principal/principle*) of the two-party system. "Of

_____ (*coarse/course*)," I said, "one on Friday night, and another on

Saturday."

9. Aunt Milly: "_____ (*Who's/Whose*) that lady with the little wart?"

Aunt Tilly: "Would you watch what _____ (*you're/your*) saying?

That's Gertie and her husband."

10. Did you _____ (*hear/here*) about the dentists who lost _____

(*their/there/they're*) patients because they couldn't stop telling jokes while they were

working? I guess they pulled _____ (*to/too/two*) many good ones.

Exercise Two   *   PART A

Fill in the blanks with the correct word choices.

1. Novelist Walker Percy once said, "A good title should be like a good metaphor: It

should intrigue without being _____ (*to/too/two*) baffling or _____

(*to/too/two*) obvious."

2. Another writer, Robert Benchley, apparently thought of giving up the writing life

but had already _____ (*passed/past*) the point of no return. In his words,

"It took me fifteen years_____ (*to/too/two*) discover I had no talent for

writing, but I couldn't give it up because by that time I was _____

(*to/too/two*) famous."

3. _____ (*Hear/Here*) is a story that might be titled "A Woman for

All Seasons." Amy Cook of Chaminade High School in Los Angeles might

_____ (*have/of*) looked like the typical homecoming queen when she was

crowned at halftime during Chaminade's homecoming game against St. Bernard's—

_____ (*accept/except*) this particular teen queen was also Chaminade's place kicker. She was nervous that the halftime festivities would have a negative _____ (*affect/effect*) on her game, but that didn't turn out to be the case. She traded her white sequined dress and high-heeled shoes for a uniform, pads, cleats, and a helmet, and _____ (*than/then*) kicked an extra point to come within six points of the California state record for girls on high school varsity football teams. According to the Associated Press, Harry Cook, Amy's father and _____ (*principal/principle*) fan, proudly summed it all up: "Everybody thinks she's just a jock. But hey, she's also a pretty, feminine girl."

4. In the recent _____ (*passed/past*), Andrew Dice Clay was roundly criticized for _____ (*coarse/course*) language and insensitivity towards women in his stand-up routines.

5. President Harry Truman had some interesting advice on raising children, _____ (*accept/except*) that one might fault it as just a bit _____ (*bare/bear*) on the specifics: "Find out what they want," he urged, "and _____ (*than/then*) advise them to do it."

PART B

Continue to fill in the blanks with the correct word choices.

1. The last time you _____ (*threw/through*) away your gum, did you check it first to see if it had anything to tell you? If you were chewing Stress Gum, which is made in Japan, you should have because _____ (*it's/its*) main purpose is to make you _____ (*conscience/conscious*) of what _____ (*affect/effect*) stress is having on _____ (*you're/your*) health. If it turns pink, everything's okay. If it turns green, _____ (*you're/your*) in trouble.

2. When European immigrants arrived in California in large numbers in the mid-1800s, they were taught a great _____ (*amount/number*) of things by the Mexi-

can Americans who had already settled _____ (*their/there/they're*). They were taught, for instance, a _____ (*principal/principle*) by which mercury could be used to separate silver from ore; cattle branding and the taming of wild horses; and techniques for planting and irrigating that helped the newcomers adjust to the _____ (*weather/whether*) conditions in the West. All these things made the hardships of immigrant life much easier to _____ (*bare/bear*).

3. If yesterday's sorrows _____ (*affect/effect*) you more _____ (*than/then*) they should, _____ (*hear/here*) is a beautiful quote from Eva Jessye: "They say you should not suffer _____ (*threw/through*) the _____ (*passed/past*). You should be able to wear it like a loose garment, take it off, and let it drop."

4. In _____ (*a/an*) interview about his experience playing the title role in Franco Zeffirelli's film version of *Hamlet,* Mel Gibson said that he identified with the character of Hamlet in a number of ways. For one thing, Hamlet admires people who are not controlled by _____ (*their/there/they're*) passions, and Gibson does, _____ (*to/too/two*). "Emotions are fleeting things, aren't they?" asked Gibson. "They wear off and then you have a _____ (*conscience/ conscious*)." He also identifies with the sensibility that underlies Hamlet's famous "To be or not to be" speech. Says Gibson, "_____ (*You're/Your*) never really supremely happy, _____ (*accept/except*) in short spurts in _____ (*you're/your*) life."

5. These are the words of author and educator Richard White: "_____ (*Hear/Here*) is a _____ (*principal/principle*) for _____ (*principals/principles*): If you have a real English teacher on _____ (*you're/your*) team, treat her or him as you would the spotted owl, the snail darter, and the whooping crane. For you are entrusted with _____ (*a/an*) endangered species.

Survival is in _____ (*you're/your*) hands—and in the best interests

of those you serve."

UNIT 7:   Capitalization

These basic guidelines should meet the needs of most college writers.

1. *Brand names* are always capitalized. For example: Nike running shoes; Head & Shoulders shampoo; Bisquick baking mix; Apple software.
2. *Buildings and institutions* are capitalized. For example: the White House; St. Francis Hospital; the University of Iowa; the Smithsonian Institution.
3. *Companies and corporations* are capitalized. For example: The Gillette Company; Lockheed Aircraft Corporation; Clinique Laboratories, Inc.
4. *Days of the week and months of the year* are always capitalized. For example: Monday, Tuesday; July, August. The seasons usually are not capitalized. For example: Let's go to Vermont in the fall and Wyoming in the spring.
5. *Direction words* are capitalized only when they refer to an entire region. They remain lower case when they merely show relationships. Correct examples:

   a. The South fought the North in the Civil War.
   b. I live two blocks south of Main.

6. *Geographical locations* are capitalized. This includes cities, counties, states, nations, lakes, rivers, oceans, mountain ranges, parks, continents, planets, and so forth. For example: Ithaca, New York; the Pacific Ocean; the Allegheny Mountains; Germany; Jupiter. (The word *earth* is capitalized only when it is used specifically as the name of the planet; for example, "The Earth is not the largest planet.") Terms derived from the names of geographical locations are also capitalized. For example: German shepherd, a New Yorker.
7. *Historical periods* are usually capitalized. For example: the Renaissance, the Pleistocene Age, Victorian manners, the Middle Ages. There are exceptions, so please check your dictionary.
8. *Holidays and holy days* are capitalized. For example: Thanksgiving, the Fourth of July, Yom Kippur, Easter.
9. *I*—the first person singular pronoun—is always capitalized.
10. *Mother and father* (and similar words, such as *grandmother*) are capitalized when they are used as a person's name. Correct examples:

    a. I called *Mother* from the car phone.
    b. I called *my mother* from the car phone.

Let's say your mother's name is Elaine. In a, the word *Mother* substitutes for *Elaine*. If you use *Elaine* in b, however, it doesn't work: you end up with *my Elaine*.

Similarly, *professional titles*—president, mayor, doctor, judge, professor, dean, queen, and so on—are capitalized only when they precede a person's name or are used as a substitute for the name. For example:

a. He wants to see Professor Smith.
b. May I speak to you, Professor?
c. He needs to see his professor.

11. *Names of people and pets* are capitalized. For example: Jackie, Bradley; Snoopy, Killer.
12. *One-of-a-kind events* are usually capitalized. For example: the Orange Bowl, the World Series, the War of 1812.
13. *Organizations, associations, and political parties* are capitalized. For example: the American Civil Liberties Union, the National Aeronautics and Space Administration, the Democratic party.
14. *Races and ethnic groups* and words derived from them usually are capitalized. For example: Thais, Polish Americans, African Americans, Native Americans. Normally, the words *black* and *white,* when used to denote the races, are lower case, but you may choose to capitalize them for rhetorical or stylistic reasons.
15. *Religions* and words derived from them are capitalized. For example: Catholic practices, Jewish customs, a Baptist minister, the study of Islam.
16. *The first word in a sentence* is capitalized; this includes the first word in a quoted sentence within another sentence. For example: The note said, "Your books are overdue. Please return them and pay your fine."
17. *Titles of poems, stories, plays, books, newspapers, magazines,* and *movies* begin with a capital letter. Also capitalize the last word and any word that is *not* a coordinating conjunction, preposition, or article, or the *to* in an infinitive verb phrase. The titles of poems, songs, short stories and television shows also are placed within double quotation marks. Other titles are underlined or italicized. For example: "The Love Song of J. Alfred Prufrock"; "Jake and the Fatman"; *Pro Football Digest; The Silence of the Lambs.*

Exercises

* Exercise One

Make appropriate changes in capitalization.

1. Valentine's day, celebrated with lacy hearts and chocolate candies every february

   14, probably has several origins. One that's particularly strange may go back to the ancient romans, whose "lupercalia" festival fell on february 15. The purpose of the festival, according to *the world book encyclopedia,* was to seek protection from wolves. On this day, young men whipped people with strips of hide, and women cooperated in the strange rite, believing that the whippings increased their fertility. After britain was conquered by the romans, many roman practices—and variations thereof—made their way into british life, and according to speculation, valentine's day is one of them.

2. In 1963, leroi jones, later to be known as amiri baraka, wrote a book that has come to be something of a classic—*blues people: the negro experience in white america and the music that developed from it.* Most of the book traces the development of jazz and the blues, but in one chapter the author describes how the imagery in the christianity of early african americans reflected an identification with the oppression of the jews during biblical times. In particular, he mentions the spirituals "go down moses," "I'm marching to zion," and "walk into jerusalem just like john."

Exercise Two

Make appropriate changes in capitalization.

1. A survey that was recently conducted by r.h. bruskin associates found that most american adults spend so much of their weekends on household chores that, when monday morning rolls around, they are more worn out than they were on friday night. In fact, the survey, which queried 1,008 adults from across the united states, determined that the average adult spends 14 hours per weekend on household chores and errands.

2. In the early 1940s, enzo ferrari built his first race cars. The first model to have the legendary ferrari name was the 125 sport, which came out in 1947. Later, ferrari was also the force behind several high-performance V12 touring cars, among them the berlinetta boxer, the daytona, the gto, and the testarossa. In italy, ferrari was

a larger-than-life figure whom people often compared to the pope; in fact, one newspaper account tells of a time when pope john paul II couldn't get an audience with enzo ferrari. (Ferrari was sick with the flu.) But in spite of his mystique, ferrari was an unassuming, humble man. He once told *car and driver* magazine, "I'm just a simple artisan. We have no computers, no wall-to-wall carpeted offices. In fact, I don't even know how to use a slide rule; I use the multiplication table."

* Exercise Three

Make appropriate changes in capitalization.

1. The north country trail association has its national headquarters in an old one-room schoolhouse on the edge of the manistee national forest in michigan. At the top of the schoolhouse is a sign that points in two directions—to crown point, new york, 1,603 miles to the southeast, and to lake sakakwea, north dakota, 1,633 miles to the northwest. The trail system now runs through seven states, and someday, when it's complete, it will hook up with the appalachian trail in the east and the lewis and clark trail in the west. On that great day, hikers will be able to walk a scenic route from the atlantic to the pacific.

2. In an article entitled "when the stars go to bed, viewers often go to sleep," diana e. lundin of *the los angeles daily news* observes that, in the television sitcoms that rely on a loving but combative relationship between a female and a male character, once the sexual tension is gone, the ratings will probably drop. In her analysis, she discusses the characters david and maddie on abc's "moonlighting," sam and diane on nbc's "cheers," and hannah and marty on abc's "anything but love." When couples stop fighting and start loving, writers lose a rich source of story lines, and viewers reach for the remote control. Lundin calls it the "consummation equals cancellation" syndrome.

Exercise Four

Make appropriate changes in capitalization.

1. The american indian movement (a.i.m.) was founded in 1968 in minneapolis, minnesota, and spread quickly to other urban areas in the midwest. The group began as a regional civil rights organization, grew to encompass the entire united states, and by the mid-1970s, served to unite and represent the needs of indian women and men in the entire western hemisphere.

2. Not too long ago, construction workers were busy at the site of a new sewage treatment center to be built on deer island, a small island in boston harbor, when they made a startling discovery. The workers turned up the bones of thousands of irish immigrants who came within four miles of america's shores but died before they saw their dream come true.

   These immigrants, who numbered over four thousand, were fleeing famine in ireland in the mid-nineteenth century. Many of them were poor, sick, and debilitated after a month or more crossing the atlantic aboard inhumanly crowded "coffin ships." As mayor raymond flynn of boston pointed out, they were generally the poorest of the poor, immigrants who had no connections in america, no one waiting for them, no one to plead their case. Fearing disease, massachusetts authorities created a quarantine hospital on deer island, where many of the immigrants were detained until they died. Almost 150 years later, the construction workers found the immigrants' remains in mass graves—lime-lined trenches that held close to a dozen bodies each.

   The mayor and other boston city officials have declared that these immigrants symbolize all who have come to america's shores and that they deserve to be remembered in a more respectful manner. Plans are underway to landscape the gravesite and erect a sculpture and a celtic cross. These attempts to honor over four thousand would-be irish americans will be part of boston's "great hunger memorial project," which is the first memorial in u.s. history to pay tribute to the victims of the potato famine and to all who are hungry on the face of the earth.

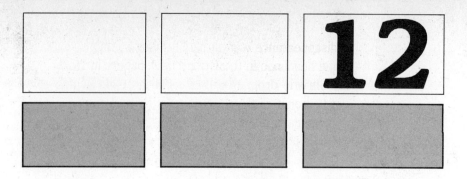

Exercises in Sentence Combining

No matter what your strengths and weaknesses are, the exercises in this chapter will reinforce and help you continue to practice everything you've learned in section II. They will be especially valuable in helping student writers tighten their wording and achieve greater flexibility and variety in their sentence structures. Sentence-combining exercises are great, too, if you need to practice punctuation, parallelism, or converting passives to actives.

How Sentence Combining Works

To understand how these exercises work, please read this passage carefully:

> Agatha Christie disappeared in 1924. She was a famous mystery writer. She was missing for ten days. Her disappearance made headlines in the British newspapers. It made the front page.

If these five sentences appeared in a college student's paper, they would be judged as choppy and overly simple. On the other hand, if they appeared in the writing of a ten-year-old, they would seem just fine. Adult writers combine clauses more often than do younger writers and, in doing so, their language structures reflect their greater ability to see relationships and connections in the world. Short sentences are fine, but not in abundance. Save them for special effects: variety, balance, suspense, humor, and so forth.

A skillful adult writer might combine the five short simple sentences in our passage in any one of a number of ways. For example:

a. Agatha Christie, a famous mystery writer, was missing for ten days in 1924, and her disappearance made front-page headlines in the British newspapers.

b. The ten-day disappearance of Agatha Christie, a famous mystery writer, made front-page headlines in the British newspapers in 1924.

c. When Agatha Christie dropped out of sight in 1924, British newspapers made the disappearance of the great mystery writer front-page news until she resurfaced ten days later.

d. In 1924, banner headlines in British newspapers announced the ten-day disappearance of the famous mystery writer, Agatha Christie.

e. Missing for ten days in 1924, Agatha Christie, a woman who was already famous for her whodunits, found herself front-page news in the British press.

f. The ten-day disappearance of Agatha Christie, a famous mystery writer, was well covered by the British press in 1924; in fact, the story made front-page headlines.

And on and on we could go. Notice that the word order, sentence structure, and punctuation change in each rewrite. Sometimes the actual word choice changes, too. Feel free to use different words in your rewrites as long as you preserve the basic meaning of a sentence.

As you combine sentences, you'll often use sentence patterns that you've worked with earlier in section II. Sometimes, too, you'll come up with wonderful structures that were not addressed explicitly in this book.

Reversing the Process

When you edit your essays and other written work, you may find that your sentences are not too short, but too long. If the longer ones seem a little weak or twisted, try "sentence combining in reverse." Break a long problem sentence into small simple sentences and start over. Eventually, you'll find a number of good ways to recombine the clauses.

Don't Let It Be Busywork—and Other Important Instructions

Some students love sentence combining; others hate it. To get the most out of it, don't let it get monotonous and boring. Don't work at it for more than twenty or thirty minutes at a time, and, if an item seems impossible, move on. Your teacher will let you know how many combinations you should try to create for each numbered item in an exercise. Sometimes only one combination will seem right for a numbered item, but usually you can create at least two.

Also, if a numbered item contains only one sentence (for example, item 2 in exercise one), it should be left alone, not combined with any other sentence.

You may use the space provided in the exercises to draft your combinations, but for your final rewrites, use your own paper. Good luck!

Exercises

Exercise One: Robert Johnson and the Roots of Rock and Roll

1. Robert Johnson died almost twenty years before Elvis Presley or Chuck Berry had sung a single note. Many music fans have never heard Johnson's name. He had an enormous influence on rock and roll.

2. Who was he?

3. Robert Johnson has been called the king of the Delta blues singers. He has also been called the true father of rock and roll. Johnson was born on May 8, 1911. He was born in Hazelwood, Mississippi.

4. Johnson was a gifted composer. He was a superb guitar player. He also had a great voice.

5. The songs he wrote include "Crossroad Blues," "Stop Breaking Down Blues" and "Terraplane Blues." Another is "I Believe I'll Dust My Broom." "They're Red Hot" is one of his creations. "Hellhound on My Trail" is his, too. He's also the author of "Sweet Home Chicago."

6. Some of his songs were recorded decades later by major figures in rock and roll. Eric Clapton was one. The Rolling Stones also recorded Robert Johnson tunes. So did Fleetwood Mac. And Z.Z. Top did Johnson material. George Thorogood did, also. Johnson's music was sung by Led Zeppelin's Robert Plant.

7. Johnson's life was short. It was productive. It was tempestuous. It had its mythic elements.

8. He died on August 16, 1938. He died near Greenwood, Mississippi. He died after drinking whiskey. The whiskey had been poisoned. It apparently had been poisoned by a jealous husband.

9. Johnson's influential body of work is now available on the Columbia label. It's called *Robert Johnson: The Complete Recordings*. It includes 41 performances.

10. One critic has said that listening to Johnson's songs is like something else. It's like

stumbling onto the blueprints for rock and roll. That critic's name is J.D. Considine.

Considine writes for *The Baltimore Sun*.

Exercise Two: A "Favorite Oddity of All Time"

1. *The Book of Lists* describes many strange and wondrous things. It is a fascinating book.

2. The book even has a list of favorite oddities of all time. One oddity concerns three dates. One is December 5, 1664. One is December 5, 1785. One is December 5, 1860.

3. On each of those dates, somewhere in the world a ship sank. Each time there was only one survivor. Each time that survivor was a man. In each incident, the lone survivor's name was Hugh Williams.

Exercise Three: Everybody's All-American

1. Charles Leerhsen was asked to write an article. It was an article for a special issue of *Newsweek* magazine. The issue focused on American teenagers.

2. His assignment was to discover the heroes of American teenagers. He didn't want to rely on the traditional statistical surveys.

3. He visited five schools. During his visits, he talked with the students. He also handed out index cards. He asked students to write the names of their heroes on the cards.

4. Leerhsen visited Culver Academies. Culver is a military school for boys and an academy for girls. It is located in Culver, Indiana. He also went to Rolling Meadows High School. It is in Rolling Meadows, Illinois. He went to the Hockaday School. It is a school for girls. It is in North Dallas, Texas. He went to Immaculate Conception School. It is in the South Bronx in New York City. He went to the Red Cloud School. It is on the Pine Ridge Indian Reservation. The reservation is in South Dakota.

5. The students at the five schools mentioned a wide variety of heroes and role models.

Their lists included some of the standard names that made similar lists decades ago. One was John F. Kennedy. Another was Martin Luther King, Jr. Elvis Presley and James Dean were included. So was Anne Frank.

6. But their lists also included some new names. One was Mother Theresa. One was Chuck Yeager. Chief Red Cloud and Fools Crow were mentioned. So was Jane Goodall. Sinead O'Connor and Arsenio Hall also made the list.

7. The lists also included some offbeat names. One example was Winnie the Pooh. Another was Bart Simpson.

8. There was a great deal of variety among all these runners-up. But there was no doubt about who came in number one.

9. Among students in all five schools, one person stood head and shoulders above the rest. That person was Michael Jordan.

10. According to Leerhsen, Jordan did not rank first because of his athletic ability. He was not chosen because of all the money he makes. He was selected because students admire two things. They admire his work on behalf of charities. They also admire his work against drugs.

Exercise Four: Women on Top

1. Marija Gimbutas is a world-famous archeologist. She is a professor at UCLA. She is the author of twenty books. She reads more than twenty languages. She has directed numerous archeological excavations.

2. Gimbutas has become a heroine to many people. They include feminists, social critics, theologians, and artists.

3. She is celebrated for her theory of Stone Age culture. The Stone Age was from about 7000 to 3500 B.C. It was a European culture. Its rulers were women.

4. Gimbutas believes that this society revolved around women. The society was matrilineal. People worshipped goddesses.

5. Women did not dominate men. Men did not dominate women. People lived in harmony. They treated each other and the earth with reverence.

6. Then everything changed. Between 4000 and 3500 B.C., the society was invaded. The invaders came from the Russian steppes. They shattered the peace and harmony of the "Great Goddess" culture.

7. Patriarchy replaced sexual equality. Hierarchy replaced egalitarianism.

8. Gimbutas has her supporters. She also has her critics. Most of her critics do not believe that the "Great Goddess" society ever existed.

9. Gimbutus admits that her methods of analysis are not always the accepted ones in her profession. She uses her linguistic abilities. She uses her knowledge of religion. She uses her knowledge of folklore.

10. But even those archeologists who dispute her conclusions have to admit one thing. They have to admit that her ideas stimulate the imagination. Her ideas allow us to imagine a possible future like the possible past.

11. We can imagine a future in which men and women would work together. They would love together. They would care for the earth together.

Exercise Five: Against Our Own—The World War II Internment of Japanese Americans   PART A

1. Many people in the United States thought that war with Japan was inevitable. This was in the fall of 1941. Some wondered if the people of Japanese descent living in the United States would be loyal to the United States.

2. Some suspected that they would be loyal to the emperor of Japan instead. They worried that these loyalists might function as "an enemy within."

3. It was about this time that Curtis B. Munson was assigned to write a report. He was an official of the State Department. It was a secret investigative report. It was to

assess the loyalty of Japanese Americans. It was to focus especially on the loyalty of those living on the West Coast and in Hawaii.

4. Munson completed his research. He wrote his report. His report established indisputably the loyalty of Japanese Americans to the United States. It also cleared them of any involvement in sabotage. It cleared them of all accusations of collaboration with agents of Japan.

5. Munson's report was shared with the State Department. It was shared with the Department of War. It was also shared with the Department of Navy. The report was returned to President Franklin D. Roosevelt's desk by February 5, 1942.

6. One week later, Roosevelt signed Executive Order 9066. This order gave the U.S. military complete authority to designate certain parts of the country as military areas. It also gave the U.S. military complete power to remove any and all persons from those areas. This was in spite of Munson's findings.

7. In reality, Executive Order 9066 enabled the U.S. military to ignore the constitutional rights of over 120,000 Japanese Americans. It empowered the military to remove completely innocent people from their homes. The order allowed the military to place them in internment camps.

8. The order also applied to German and Italian nationals. But that was primarily in theory. In practice, it affected very few people who were not of Japanese descent.

PART B

1. What had happened between the filing of Munson's report and FDR's signing of Executive Order 9066 was something momentous. It was the bombing of Pearl Harbor by Japan on December 7, 1941.

2. The 77th Congress of the United States backed up the president's order. The Congress did so by passing Public Law No. 503. That was on March 19, 1942. Public

Law No. 503 made it a federal offense to violate any restriction by a military commander in a military area.

3. Later, the U.S. Supreme Court upheld the constitutionality of the internment program. It was upheld in a 6–3 decision in the case of *Korematsu v. the U.S.*

4. The court ruled against Fred T. Korematsu. Korematsu was a young Japanese American welder. He was a native of Oakland, California. He was one of several Japanese Americans who fought the evacuation and internment orders in court.

5. So all three branches of the U.S. government contributed to this tragedy. The three branches are the executive, the legislative, and the judicial.

6. Justice Frank Murphy was one of the three dissenters in *Korematsu v. the U.S.* He called the court's decision to affirm the actions of the president and the Congress the "legalization of racism."

PART C

1. A terrible period of confusion followed Executive Order 9066. Japanese Americans' bank accounts were frozen. Their travel was restricted. They had to observe curfews.

2. Ultimately, they were told to dispose of all property that they could not carry by hand. Then they were ordered to turn themselves in to authorities.

3. There were no exceptions. Even the Japanese Americans who had proven their loyalty by fighting for the United States in World War I were not exempt.

4. Some evacuees had non-Japanese friends or neighbors who were willing to look after their property. Most were not so lucky.

5. In either case, postwar records are shocking. They show that a full eighty percent of all the internees' goods that were stored privately met one of two fates by the end of the war. They were completely ruined, or they disappeared.

6. Most of the evacuees were taken to existing structures. These included livestock pavilions and stables. They included racetracks and fairgrounds.

7. Conditions were crowded. Facilities were often unclean. They were freezing cold in the winter. They were unbearably hot in the summer.

8. People were given too little to eat. There was little variety. Not much of the food was fresh.

9. For a long time, there were no partitions between toilets in the communal bathrooms. Men and women were denied their privacy.

10. Young children in the internment camps often begged their parents to take them back to America. Parents had to tell their children reluctantly, "This *is* America."

PART D

1. Against this grim background, there were heroes.

2. There was Fred T. Korematsu. There were also the other Japanese Americans who resisted in court.

3. There were religious groups. The Society of Friends was an especially strong force. They are also known as the Quakers.

4. They and other religious groups fought relentlessly for the release of internees. They also fought with some success for improved conditions at the camps.

5. There was also a lawyer. His name was Wayne M. Collins. After the war, he helped Japanese Americans with serious legal problems. He was strongly supported by the Northern California branch of the American Civil Liberties Union.

6. Then there was Dr. Robert Gordon Sproul. He was the president of the University of California at Berkeley. He fought for a scholarship program for Japanese-American students whose educations had been interrupted by internment.

7. Such a scholarship program was created. It was funded through private sources. It helped to restore the faith of Japanese Americans in the goodwill of other Americans.

8. There was also the 442nd Regimental Combat Team. This was an all Japanese-American unit of the U.S. Army.

9. The men of the 442nd were allowed to fight only against Europeans. They suffered heavy casualties.

10. They fought and died while their families were denied their freedom back home. The unit's motto was "Go for Broke."

PART E

1. In 1988, the U.S. Congress passed legislation that apologized to the Japanese-American community for their treatment during World War II.

2. The legislation said that the internment had three main causes. One cause was racial prejudice. One was wartime hysteria. Another was a failure of political leadership.

3. In 1989, a vote passed 74–22 in the U.S. Senate. It was a vote to compensate Japanese Americans for their internment during World War II.

4. The Senate voted to make payments of $20,000. These would go to each of approximately 80,000 eligible Japanese Americans.

5. In 1990, the program began. It began with a ceremony at the Department of Justice. The Department of Justice is in Washington, D.C.

6. At the ceremony, each of nine elderly Japanese Americans received a check for $20,000. Each also received a letter from the president. These were presented by U.S. Attorney General Dick Thornburgh.

7. The first check was presented to the Reverend Mamoru Eto. He was 107 years old. He was in a wheelchair. Thornburgh presented the check to Rev. Eto on bended knee.

8. Some survivors insisted that the money could not erase or even lessen their pain and outrage. Others felt that finally justice was being done.

9. But all will remember the image of the government's official representative on bended knee. That image—over the years—may begin to heal what money alone cannot.

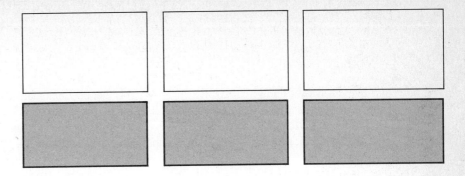

Answer Key

Chapter 8, Unit 1

Exercise One, pages 191–192

If some of your answers for the exercises in this unit vary a bit from those shown, you're not necessarily wrong. In marking clauses, some differences in how much one includes are inconsequential and to be expected. For example, in sentence 6, it's fine to identify *Music lovers* or simply *lovers* as the subject. In sentence 9, the object complement can be marked as *short* or *very short*. Generally, the Answer Key gives the shortest possible answers. If you're in doubt about an item, consult your teacher.

1. s = motive; v = was; c = mysterious.
2. s = I; v = bought; do = suit.
3. s = woman; v = coughed.
4. s = Caroline; v = gave; io = Steven; do = choice.
5. s = nectarines; v = feel; sub com = ripe.
6. s = lovers; v = named; do = Aretha; ob com = Queen of Soul.
7. s = patient; v = improved.
8. s = teacher; v = lent; io = Katherine; do = tape.
9. s = She; v = made; do = skirt; ob com = short.
10. s = father; v = frosted; do = cupcakes.

Exercise Three, PART A, pages 193–194

Here again, expect some variations. For example, in sentence 1, it's okay to label *a superb major league pitcher* as the object complement. In sentence 6, the subject complement might be identified as *a thing of the past*. Master the big picture. Don't worry about minor differences.

1. s = fans; v = consider; do = Nolan Ryan; ob com = pitcher.
2. s = Ryan; v = endures, improves.
3. s = pitcher; v = shows; io = hitters; do = best stuff.

4. s = season; v = was; sub com = twenty-fourth.
5. s = He; v = was; sub com = 43 years old, better than ever.
6. s = problems; v = became; sub com = thing.
7. s = fastballs; v = reached; do = speeds.
8. s = fastball; v = made; do = curveball; ob com = more effective.
9. s = Batters; v = braced.
10. s = he; v = slipped; io = them; do = curve.

Exercise Four, page 195

1. s = Tu Dil Hil I; v = is; sub com = name.
2. s = "Yo! MTV Raps"; v = draws; do = audience.
3. s = trucks; v = brought; io = Americans; do = "Chicken Dinners."
4. s = industry; v = uses; do = materials.
5. s = quiltmakers; v = are; sub com = famous.
6. s = George Bush; v = vomited, collapsed.
7. s = Jack Agueros; v = is; sub com = author.
8. s = Madonna; v = played; do = roles.
9. s = students; v = elected; do = Barack Obama; ob com = president.
10. s = Americans; v = walk.

Chapter 8, Unit 2

Exercise One, page 197

The nouns are these: (1) beginning; (2) prediction; (3) organization; (4) liar; (5) gentleness; (6) decision; (7) allowance; (8) reliability; (9) collection; (10) defiance.

Exercise Four, pages 200–201

1. s = To work hard today (INFINITIVE VERB PHRASE).

2. s = Banning the book (GERUND PHRASE).
3. s = To say yes to Kit (INFINITIVE VERB PHRASE).
4. s = What the world needs now (CLAUSE).
5. s = At the very beginning of a string of commercials (PREPOSITIONAL PHRASE).
6. s = Tracking students into so-called ability groups (GERUND PHRASE).
7. s = To kiss him once (INFINITIVE VERB PHRASE).
8. s = That you would revise this paper four times (CLAUSE).
9. s = Outside that crazy office (PREPOSITIONAL PHRASE).
10. s = What a racist or sexist joke reveals about its teller (CLAUSE).

Chapter 8, Unit 3

Exercise One, pages 204–205

1. s = deprivation; v = can prevent; do = retention.
2. s = tongue; v = has given; io = doctors; do = mirror.
3. s = Malcolm X; v = had made; do = trips; v = had altered; do = position.
4. s = *Nintendo Power* magazine; v = is published.
5. s = Vincent van Gogh; v = painted; do = suns; ob com = yellow.
6. s = Competition; v = has been defined.
7. s = Chester F. Carlson; v = should have named; do = invention; ob com = after himself.
8. s = mannequins; v = wear; do = size 40 regular.
9. s = size; v = has been decreasing.
10. s = people; v = should blame; do = diet.

Chapter 8, Unit 4

Exercise One, page 207

The adjectives are these: (1) polished, oak; (2) biggest, small; (3) negative, best; (4) deep, raspy; (5) persistent, drastic; (6) supporting, historical; (7) crystal, big; (8) tallest, old-fashioned, blackberry; (9) final, difficult, challenging; (10) dramatic, sunburnt, pale, white.

Exercise Three, PART A, page 209

In each item in this exercise, the words between the commas form the appositive, and the labeled parts of the clause form the kernel.
1. George Washington, the first president of the United States, loved peanut soup. s = George Washington; v = loved; do = peanut soup.
2. John Quincy Adams, the sixth president, liked swimming in the nude in the Potomac River every morning at five o'clock. s = John Quincy Adams; v = liked; do = swimming.

3. Zachary Taylor, a career officer in the army for most of his life, voted for the first time at the age of 62. s = Zachary Taylor; v = voted.
4. James Buchanan, president from 1857 to 1861, was a bachelor throughout his entire life. s = James Buchanan; v = was; sub com = bachelor.
5. Abraham Lincoln, an extremely persistent individual, won the presidency in 1860 after eight election losses in a row. s = Abraham Lincoln; v = won; do = presidency.

Exercise Four, pages 212–213

After you have crossed out the modifying elements, the remaining components that form the kernels are these:
1. s = Robin Burns; v = is; sub com = officer.
2. s = Babe Ruth; v = pitched.
3. s = number; v = exceeded; do = number.
4. s = color; v = has been; sub com = blue.
5. s = Treasury Department; v = dry-cleaned; do = money.
6. s = female tree frog; v = recognizes; do = connection.
7. s = headquarters; v = has; do = waterbed.
8. s = matter; v = is; sub com = *duff*.
9. s = size; v = is; sub com = 5 feet and 7 inches and 135 pounds.
10. s = record; v = was; sub com = "I'll Never Get Out of this World Alive."

Chapter 8, Unit 5

Exercise One, PART A, page 214

Minus the modifying elements, the key structural parts are these:
1. s = students; v = have been; sub com = poets, philosophers, psychologists, historians, folks.
2. s = Some; v = have noticed; do = differences.
3. s = women; v = make; do = decisions.
4. s = field-workers; v = took; do = stopwatch.
5. s = they; v = made; do = discovery.
6. s = intentions; v = were formed.
7. s = Women; v = are; sub com = slower, cautious.
8. s = reason; v = is; sub com = importance.
9. s = Men; v = seem; sub com = concerned.
10. s = Women; v = judge; do = men; ob com = attractive or unattractive.

Exercise Two, PART A, page 216

Minus the modifying elements, the key structural parts are these:
1. s = Rosa Parks; v = is; sub com = mother.
2. s = movement; v = was born.
3. s = Mrs. Parks; v = had been altering; do = clothing.
4. s = she; v = felt; do = pains.

5. s = She; v = climbed; do = steps; v = paid; do = fare; v = took; do = seat.
6. s = Mrs. Parks; v = recognized; do = driver.
7. s = J.P. Blake; v = had ejected; do = Mrs. Parks.
8. s = no places; v = remained.
9. s = Blake; v = wanted; do = seat.
10. s = That she and three other black passengers move to the back of the bus; v = was; sub com = demand. (Sentence 10 has a "whole clause" subject.)

Exercise Two, PART C, page 217

1. s = Mrs. Parks; v = was booked, fingerprinted, jailed.
2. s = mother; v = contacted; do = E.D. Nixon.
3. s = Nixon; v = was; sub com = activist.
4. s = Nixon, Clifford Durr; v = became; sub com = involved; v = posted; do = bail.
5. s = Mrs. Parks, E.D. Nixon, Clifford Durr, Virginia Durr; v = arrived, were greeted.
6. s = Nixon, the Durrs; v = explained; do = use.
7. s = Mrs. Parks; v = discussed; do = situation.
8. s = Both; v = wanted; do = end; v = were; sub com = upset.
9. s = Raymond Parks; v = feared; do = possibility.
10. s = Mrs. Parks; v = chose; do = path.

Exercise Two, PART E, pages 218–219

1. s = Mrs. Rosa Parks; v = was convicted.
2. s = population; v = began; do = boycott.
3. s = Montgomery Improvement Association; v = was formed.
4. s = boycott; v = became; sub com = success.
5. s = action; v = ballooned.
6. s = people; v = formed; do = car pools; v = gave; io = friends, neighbors; do = rides.
7. s = Others; v = pedaled; do = bicycles; v = walked.
8. s = companies; v = charged; io = customers; do = bus fare.
9. s = people; v = raised; do = money.
10. s = Boycotters; v = endured; v = denied; io = bus company; do = profits. (In sentence 10, the verb *endured* is complete by itself; it does not have an object. The verb *denied* has both direct and indirect objects.)

Chapter 9, Unit 1

Exercise One, pages 224–225

If you have questions about the key parts of the clauses, please consult your teacher. Entire sentences are not reproduced here; rather, the words before and after the conjunction are shown.
1. 32 minutes, *and* 40 percent (COMPOUND)
2. teams, *but* now (COMPOUND)

3. Ku Klux Klan, *and* I (COMPOUND)
4. no comma (SIMPLE)
5. daylight, *or* they (COMPOUND)
6. no comma (SIMPLE)
7. letters, *yet* the (COMPOUND)
8. Buddy Holly, *and* his (COMPOUND)
9. makeup, *nor* do (COMPOUND)
10. way, *so* she (COMPOUND)

Exercise Two, PART B, pages 226–227

1. children, *but* this (COMPOUND)
2. problems, *for* women (COMPOUND)
3. legislation, *or* they (COMPOUND)
4. no comma (SIMPLE)
5. Washington, *but* government (COMPOUND)
6. range land, *and* he (COMPOUND)
7. North, *and* the Choctaws (COMPOUND)
8. lands, *and* they (COMPOUND)
9. relatives, *or* they (COMPOUND)
10. policy, *and* reform (COMPOUND)

Chapter 9, Unit 2

Exercise One, pages 230–231

CONJ is the abbreviation for *conjunction*.
1. 1969, they (CONJ = *Although*)
2. no comma (CONJ = *until*)
3. book, I (CONJ = *When*)
4. no comma (CONJ = *as soon as*)
5. it, I (CONJ = *If*)
6. no comma (CONJ = *after*)
7. feet, it (CONJ = *Unless*)
8. calories, eating (CONJ = *Because*)
9. no comma (CONJ = *that*)
10. you, you (CONJ = *When*)

Exercise Five, pages 238–239

1. s of main clause = Women; embedded clause = who have heart attacks; no commas.
2. President McKinley, who took a car ride in 1900, was the first U.S. president to travel in an automobile.
3. s of main clause = one; embedded clause = who does not have a beard; no commas.
4. Charlie Chaplin, who was widely imitated, once entered a Charlie Chaplin look-alike contest and came in in third place.
5. A child's first teacher, who may be good or bad or in-between, is certainly bound to have a strong impact.
6. s of main clause = Everyone; embedded clause = who works in the domain of fiction; no commas.
7. s of main clause = Those; embedded clause = who attended the Mad Hatter's tea party; no commas.
8. My paternal grandmother, who left Poland in her late teens, never returned to her homeland.

9. s of main clause = man; embedded clause = who does not read good books; no commas.
10. Al McGuire, who coached the Marquette University Warriors to an NCAA basketball championship before the start of his television sports-announcing career, once gave this answer . . .

Chapter 9, Unit 3

The answers shown here represent the punctuation choices that Louise Erdrich made in *Love Medicine*. In some cases, other choices are also good options that reflect different oral readings of the sentences. If in doubt about your decisions, consult your teacher. Where possible, answers are given without duplicating the original sentence in its entirety.

Exercise One, page 244

1. pattern, I
2. concentration, patting
3. breasts, like overfilled inner tubes, strained
4. confidence, he
5. slowness, now
6. power, this
7. windows, black
8. flashed, now wolf white and sharp, in
9. elevator, he
10. on, even

Exercise Three, pages 245–246

1. Muffled, slogged in pillows, she
2. thieves, she
3. sister, stealing duck eggs, blowing crabgrass between their thumbs, chasing
4. jars, pouring
5. Flylike, glued to him by suction, we rode as one person, whipping
6. dress, I
7. wavering, fringed like a flower's mouth, was
8. black, sly, snapping
9. her, hopeless
10. Watching Zelda walk in front of me, so sure of herself and thin, with a cutting edge, with a mind that wasn't made up, with pure white anklets and careful curls, I felt an amazement.

Chapter 9, Unit 4

Exercise One, PART A, pages 248–249

As you know, the comma before the *and* that links the last two items in a series is optional, but it is often desirable for clarity. For this reason and for the sake of simplicity, it is always included in the Answer Key.

1. booed, cheered, cut, sold, traded, and
2. hot dogs, hamburgers, tuna fish sandwiches, jawbreakers, and

3. weaving, farming, gathering, temple maintenance, and
4. Aaron, Art, Charles, and
5. Joe Martinez, Manuel Pérez, Sylvester Herreras, Macario García, and

Exercise Two, page 251

1. (a) no comma; (b) interesting, thought-provoking.
2. (a) crisp, crumbly; (b) no comma.
3. (a) patient, well-trained; (b) no comma.
4. (a) no comma; (b) sinister, bleak.
5. (a) no comma; (b) inexpensive, unpretentious.

Exercise Four, page 252

1. no comma
2. mysterious, mischievous
3. murderous, sadistic
4. no comma
5. no comma
6. no comma
7. churning, twisting
8. slick, flat-faced
9. no comma
10. enthusiastic, energetic

Chapter 9, Unit 5

Once again, answers are usually shown in the shortest possible way. In some cases, for clarity, an entire sentence or a large part of it may appear.

Exercise One, pages 254–255

1. On January 25, 1989, Michael Jordan scored his ten-thousandth point in the National Basketball Association, and on January 26, 1990, he
2. others, but
3. sang, songs
4. Michael Newman, who was a protege of W.H. Auden and is currently an editor of *The Paris Review*, has
5. Arnold Schwartzenegger, in a quest to terminate flab, has
6. myth, there is no way to increase the body's rate of burning up one-half ounce of alcohol per hour, not
7. Johnny Ace, an important figure in early rock and roll, died backstage in the Houston City Auditorium on December 24, 1954, while
8. no commas
9. alcoholism, men drink because it makes them feel more masculine, and
10. sheep, not

Exercise Three, page 256

The abbreviation *OP*. indicates optional punctuation. Answers are given on a line-by-line basis, showing only the relevant parts of sentences.

Line 1: anyway, the
Line 3: whisker, for example, grows
Line 4: much, but
Line 5: week, devoting ·
Line 6: lifetime, (OP.) that's
Line 9: shaving cream, and
Line 11: activity, American
Line 12: products, and
Line 13: 15, his

Exercise Five, page 257

Line 1: *Great American Sports Book,* the
Line 2: Chicago, Illinois, on
Lines 3–4: July 9, 1871. Before a crowd of five hundred, the Uniques, who were black, beat the Alerts, who were white, by

Chapter 9, Unit 6

Exercise One, page 259

1. die; they
2. kids; it
3. die; they
4. farm; it
5. legs; she
6. driver; he
7. is; he
8. world; she
9. die; they
10. die; they

Exercise Four, pages 262–263

1. century; she
2. concerns; the
3. In 1840, (OP.) she and her husband traveled to London for the World Anti-Slavery Convention; however, the
4. For years, (OP.) Stanton
5. After the Civil War, however, she
6. Later, (OP.) Elizabeth Cady Stanton joined ranks with Susan B. Anthony; together, (OP.) they
7. On behalf of women, (OP.) Stanton used all her persuasive powers on California's Senator Aaron A. Sargent; as a result, he
8. 1919; then
9. "The Solitude of the Self"; it
10. In it, (OP.) Stanton argues that throughout life each human being is alone in an essential way; consequently, each individual should come to "own" as much of herself or himself as possible. (OPTION: In sentence 10, you can set off *throughout life* by enclosing the phrase within two commas.)

Chapter 9, Unit 7

Exercise One, page 266

1. Recently, (OP.) Video Storyboard Tests named the five most believable celebrities in television commercials: Bill Cosby, James Garner, Bruce Willis, Cher, and Linda Evans. (This sentence is also correct with no colon. If you omit the colon, you're probably reading the sentence the way you'd read "We declared her the top candidate." In other words, the celebrities' names can be considered object complements. But it's a stronger sentence with the colon.)
2. When Kevin Costner's *Dances with Wolves* was released, many critics called it the first truly sympathetic movie about Native Americans. But some film historians mentioned several earlier films with a pro-Indian point of view: *The Vanishing American, Massacre, Broken Arrow, The Big Sky, Apache, Run of the Arrow, Cheyenne Autumn,* and *Little Big Man.*
3. The five general categories of arthritis are rheumatoid arthritis, osteoarthritis, gout, septic arthritis, and ankylosing spondylitis. (no colon)
4. Research at Ohio State University shows that eight- to twelve-year-olds use over 500 different stress-reducing techniques, including nail biting, lip chewing, thumb sucking, hair twisting, exercising, praying, teasing, and being aggressive. (no colon)
5. The Olympic decathlon is made up of ten events: the 110-meter hurdles, the 100-meter dash, the 400-meter dash, the 1500-meter run, the long jump, the high jump, the pole vault, the javelin throw, the discus, and the shot put.

Exercise Five, page 268

As noted in the unit, if the part after the colon is a full sentence, you may begin it with a capital letter. The Answer Key shows the capitalization option.
1. one-liner: "All things . . . Philadelphia."
2. blue whale: A single
3. revolution: no violence
4. disability: He
5. history: miraculous

Chapter 9, Unit 8

Exercise One, page 271

1. Harold had always dreamed of being an attorney for a nudist colony, but there was just one problem: They didn't allow suits. (Students often use a semicolon in this kind of sentence, but a full colon is much preferred when a clear explanation or definition is involved. In this case, the word *problem* is explained by the words that follow it.)
2. husband, but

3. no punctuation
4. Ernie, the electrician down the block, says that he has a valid professional reason for reading the newspaper every day: He needs to keep up on current events.
5. manicurist, but
6. archeologist: Archeologists
7. no punctuation
8. When Barney announced that he wanted to become a chimney sweep, his father said, "Soot yourself."
9. If you're in the offshore drilling business, it's always the same old thing: oily to bed and oily to rise.
10. trombone player: He (In sentence 10, *trombone player; he* is also correct.)

Exercise Three, pages 272–273

1. Freiberg; however, he
2. planet, completing
3. Ellen DeGeneres, a stand-up comic, claims that her grandmother started walking five miles a day when she was sixty. "She's 97 today," says DeGeneres, "and we don't know where the hell she is."
4. no punctuation
5. experience, and experience
6. In order from one to ten, the most consumed foods in the United States are these: milk and cream, potatoes, beef, refined sugar, canned vegetables, fresh noncitrus fruits, pork, chicken, eggs, and fresh citrus fruits.
7. "As the World Turns," which premiered on April 2, 1956, was
8. According to *Newsweek* magazine, Nebraska, Arkansas, Idaho, and
9. When men and women graduate from college, they can expect to earn roughly the same salaries only if they majored in accounting or engineering; in other fields, men
10. statistic: Over

Exercise Five, page 275

1. Although most people associate croissants with the French, those flaky little pastries are actually Austrian in origin. Invented in the seventeenth century, croissants were made in the shape of a crescent because the bakers of Vienna wanted to celebrate the city's successful defense against the Turks. A crescent shape was a prominent part of the Turkish flag; consequently, an Austrian who ate a croissant was symbolically demolishing and consuming the enemy.
2. Alice Paul, the founder of the National Woman's Party, marched on Washington with five thousand others in 1913, demanding the right of women to vote. Although their efforts were later successful, on the day of the march, (OP.) the women and their supporters were laughed at, spit upon, hit, and burned by the lighted cigars of bystanders. Paul was also the person who submitted the first version of the Equal Rights Amendment to the U.S. Congress ten years later.
3. When Berry Gordy founded the Motown record company in Detroit in 1963, few could have predicted how many musicians his organization would catapult to success. Some of the most famous acts on the Motown label were Diana Ross and the Supremes, Martha and the Vandellas, Gladys Knight and the Pips, the Four Tops, the Temptations, Smokey Robinson, and Jr. Walker and the All Stars.

Exercise Seven, pages 276–278

1. The Volstead Act, which banned the manufacture, transportation, sale, use, and import or export of alcohol, became the 18th Amendment to the U.S. Constitution, (OP.) in spite of a veto by President Woodrow Wilson. Prohibition became official on January 17, 1920, and ironically, (OP.) that date was also Alphonse Capone's twenty-first birthday. Who was Alphonse Capone? Better known as Al Capone, he was for many years America's most celebrated criminal, and he made a multimillion dollar fortune on bootleg whiskey. At its height, (OP.) his empire included brothels, breweries, gambling casinos, and speakeasies. Capone, who had a certain way with words, once said, "Everybody calls me a racketeer. I call myself a businessman. When I sell liquor, it's bootlegging. When my patrons serve it on a silver tray on Lake Shore Drive, it's hospitality."
2. Buddy Holly, an important early figure in rock and roll, became a sort of mythic figure and permanent symbol of the 1950s when he died in a plane crash on February 3, 1959, while en route from Clear Lake, Iowa, to Fargo, North Dakota. Along with Ritchie Valens and J.P. Richardson, also known as "The Big Bopper," Holly originally had planned to travel by bus, but at the last minute, (OP.) he and his companions chartered the ill-fated plane. Why were they in a hurry? They wanted to get to Fargo in time to do laundry and catch up on their mail before their next performance. Buddy Holly, the co-composer and voice of "Peggy Sue" and "That'll Be the Day," was only 22 when he died.
3. Dr. James P. Comer, a professor of child psychiatry at the Yale University Medical School, is one of the brightest lights in education today. Dr. Comer was one of five children of an East Chicago steel-mill worker, and after their father's early death, all five children went on to complete college. After he graduated from the medical school at Howard University in Washington, D.C., Dr. Comer entered the field of psychiatry, looking for ways to alleviate some of the

hopelessness and depression he witnessed among the poor in the nation's capital. His educational model, which is now being implemented in many urban schools, is based on a simple idea: A good school is run like a good family. A school in the Comer model forms a "governance team" of parents, teachers, psychologists, administrators, and representatives from such groups as the cafeteria and custodial staffs. The team plans academic and social events that ensure a great deal of parent involvement and create an atmosphere in which reading, writing, and math skills blossom right along with fuller, richer self-esteem for the children.

Exercise Eight, PART B, page 279

Because of the length of some context exercises, they are not shown in full here. Rather, shortest possible answers are given on a line-by-line basis.
Line 2: members; however, field workers
Line 4: law, migrant farm workers, as of the early 1990s, are (OPTION: Two commas or none may be used around *as of the early 1990s.*).
Line 7: (EPA), which
Line 8: use, falls
Line 11: guidelines, however, are
Line 15: phosdrin, an
Line 16: warfare; some
Line 19: food, especially in produce. But as Dr. Moses has pointed out, the (OPTION: A comma may be inserted after *But.*)
Line 22: and, in doing so, protect

Chapter 9, Unit 9

Exercise One, page 282

As noted in Unit 9, you may close up or add a space on each side of a dash, but be consistent. Here, spaces are closed up. Only relevant parts of sentences are shown.
1. stage—a period
2. "We are so busy obsessing over what is wrong with us—whether it's our weight, misproportion, wrinkles, pimples, excess hair, or functional limitations—that we fail to develop our potential as human beings."
3. Sarah Vaughan—bebop—was
4. *The People Shall Continue*—all
5. "The students who know her—black and white—respect . . ."

Exercise Three, pages 283–284

Keep in mind that the way the following exercise is punctuated is not the only correct way to do it. If you have variations, they may be right or wrong. Dashes permit some room for differences because of variations

in writers' intentions. Check with your teacher if you have questions.

One caution is important: When you begin to use dashes, don't start using them where you would normally use commas. For example, in the first sentence of this exercise, the words *an attorney in the nationally known accounting firm of Price Waterhouse* can be viewed as an appositive (a noun phrase that follows and describes another noun or noun phrase) or as a reduction of the relative clause *who is an attorney in the . . . Price Waterhouse.* Such elements and all "extra" relative clauses (those not needed to limit or make sense of the subject) normally should be set off with commas, not dashes. In other words, keep your comma rules in mind and follow them. Use dashes sparingly.
Line 1: 1983, (OP.) Ann Hopkins, an
Line 2: Waterhouse, could make an impressive claim: She
Line 3: success, she (OPTION: Use a comma after *But.*)
Line 5: men, and ironically, (OP.) it
Line 6: Hopkins—that she smoked cigarettes, drank beer at lunch,
Line 7: cursed, wore no makeup or jewelry, carried a briefcase instead of a purse, and
Line 8: man—held no weight with U.S. District Judge Gerhard Gesell, who
Line 12: promotion, she
Line 13: decided—as a divorced mother of three—to (OPTIONS: You can use commas instead of dashes around *as a divorced mother of three.* It's also fine to omit punctuation directly before and after this phrase.)

Chapter 9, Unit 10

If your answers vary from those shown here, check with your teacher.

Exercise One, PART A, pages 284–285

1. 1990s, there is no doubt about one simple fact: Rap
2. is, however, a
3. Gil Scott-Heron, the Sugar Hill Gang, and
4. James Brown, the cadences of gospel preaching, the ritualized insults of the dozens, and the storytelling tradition of the blues—these
5. "Toasting," a little-known influence of both Jamaican and African-American origin, involves
6. rap music, other observers point to African-American literary influences, including poets such as Don L. Lee, Nikki Giovanni, and
7. Some critics, most notably Jon Pareles of *The New York Times,* have (OPTION: The commas in sentence 7 can be replaced by dashes for emphasis.)
8. characteristics: fast-paced rhythms, unexpected juxtapositions, diverse material, and
9. it; inner-city (OPTION: You can use a dash after *it* instead of a semicolon.)

10. rap, which was initially expected to be a short-lived fad, by

Exercise One, PART C, pages 286–287

1. responsible, socially conscious rap is September 10, 1987
2. Kool Moe Dee, BDP, Doug E. Fresh, and others appeared at the Nassau Coliseum in Long Island, New York
3. music; they
4. over, a number of people had been stabbed; the
5. no punctuation
6. By the next day, representatives of three of the major branches of the media—the newspapers, radio, and television—had almost unanimously found their scapegoat for the tragedy at the Nassau Coliseum: the music itself. (OPTION: A dash instead of a colon is okay before *the music itself,* but the colon looks better because dashes are already used in the sentence.)
7. violence, a group
8. Nelson George, who edited a recent book on this chapter in the history of rap, the movement had three main goals: to create awareness of the causes and costs of black-on-black crime, to raise money for the fight against illiteracy and crime in the inner-city, and
9. "Self-Destruction," which
10. Before long, "Self-Destruction" had sold over half a million copies, generating more than $200,000 for community programs run by the National Urban League and creating the possibility of a new direction for rap—away from the glorification of the self and toward the regeneration of the community. (OPTION: A colon after *rap* also works.)

Exercise Two, PART B, pages 288–289

1. medicine, and though obstacles included both age and gender, many
2. no punctuation
3. 60, and this view reflects a common pattern in American Indian societies: Women (OPTION: The colon is preferred to the dash because sentence 3 is quite formal in tone.)
4. woman, regardless of her age, could (OPTION: Dashes instead of commas are also okay.)
5. Occasionally, (OP.) a woman gained her healing gifts after she had met two conditions: first, she had been chosen and instructed as the successor of an elderly woman doctor, and second, she
6. Pretty-shield, a medicine woman of the Sore-lip clan of the Crows, had
7. alive, the future medicine woman wandered alone in the hills and mountains of Montana for more than two months, eating

8. Finally, according to Pretty-shield's account, physical deprivation induced a dream in which a woman appeared and helped Pretty-shield ask for the power she needed; this
9. nature, many readers might find it difficult to imagine how ants could assist a doctor, but Pretty-shield believed firmly that they spoke to her throughout her life, often
(Incidentally, Pretty-shield, whose story is told in a fascinating oral history by Frank B. Linderman, was the wife of Goes-ahead, one of Custer's scouts at the Battle of the Little Bighorn on June 25, 1876.)
10. accept; for example, Otsani, a Blackfoot wise woman, enjoyed

Chapter 9, Unit 11

Exercise One, pages 296–297

1. i
2. d   Fondly recalling his parents, comedian Rodney Dangerfield once claimed, "They sent me to a child psychiatrist, but what can I say? That kid didn't help me at all."
3. d   "What are you rebelling against?" Marlon Brando was asked in the movie *The Wild Ones* in 1953.
    "What've you got?" he answered.
4. i
5. i   (OPTION: It's also okay to enclose *medium* within quotation marks, even though in a general sense Fred Allen is being paraphrased in sentence 5.)
6. d   Once . . . cooking. "Did you find that interesting?" the first one asked the second one when the show was over.
    "No," replied the second muppet. "Actually, I was smorgasbord."
7. d   Years ago, the writer Oscar Wilde made a wonderfully cynical comment about Niagara Falls: "Every American bride . . . married life."
8. i
9. d   Here's a fellow comedian's description of Jack Benny: "He was not one who said funny things, but one who said things funny."
10. d   A man asked the preacher, "Do you save bad women?"
    "Yes," replied the preacher, "I surely do."
    "In that case," responded the man, "would you save me two for Thursday night?"

Exercise Three, pages 299–300

1. So I went to my doctor, and he said, "Have you ever had this before?"
I said, "Yes, I have."
He said, "Well, you've got it again."

2. So I went to my doctor, and I said, "Doctor, I broke my arm in three places."
   She said, "Oh yeah? Well, stay out of those places."
3. So I went to my doctor, and I said, "Doctor, it hurts when I do this."
   He said, "Well then, don't do that." (OPTION: He said, "Well, then don't do that.")
4. So I went to my doctor, and she said, "You're sick."
   I said, "I want a second opinion."
   "Okay," she said, "you're ugly, too."
5. So I went to my dentist, and I said, "I've got yellow teeth. What should I do?"
   He said, "Wear a brown tie."
6. So I went to my pharmacist, and I said, "Which way to the talcum powder?"
   She said, "Walk this way."
   I said, "If I could walk that way, I wouldn't need the talcum powder."
7. So I went to my doctor, and I said, "I got the bill for my surgery."
   He said, "Oh, good."
   I said, "Yeah, now I know why you were wearing a mask."
8. So I went to my doctor, and I said, "Now don't tell me I'm overweight."
   "Okay," she said, "you're four inches too short."
9. So I went to my doctor, and I said, "After this operation, will I be able to play the violin?"
   He said, "Certainly."
   I said, "That's funny. I could never play it before."
10. So I went to my doctor, and she said, "I've got some good news and some bad news. The bad news is that you owe me $1,000 a month for the next 12 months."
    "So," I said, "what's the good news?" (OPTION: So I said, "What's the good news?")
    She said, "You've got only six months to live."

Exercise Six, pages 301–302

1. Eva Jessye recalled one of the barriers that existed in the early days of her career: "In New York at the radio they used to say, 'Well, we don't have any need for your music.' They thought the Negro didn't know anything except spirituals. Radio was an area black people hadn't broken into and it hadn't been opened for them."
2. *Newsweek* magazine reported that after listening to negotiations over the dates of a meeting between two world powers, U.S. Representative Patricia Schroeder said, "I feel like you're listening to a fight between two three-year-olds. 'No, I will not. No, I will. Na na na.'"
3. In *I Dream a World,* actress Cicely Tyson remembers how her mother taught embroidery to her children: "She would buy these huge things, tablecloths,

bedspreads—whatever—and she would give each of us a corner to work (the fourth corner was hers). 'When I get back,' she would say, 'I want you to have finished this much right here.' Today we each have several of these beautiful pieces—remembrances of Mama's efforts to keep her family harmonious."
4. In his book *Humor and Social Change in Twentieth-Century America,* Joseph Boskin explains, "Although it is possible to categorize and characterize the diversity of humor, its nature and meaning remain elusive. E.B. White once wrote, 'Essentially, it is a complete mystery.'"
5. "The women I meet are *so* self-absorbed," said comedian Garry Shandling in a recent interview. "For example, I met this blonde today at a barbecue. At least I *think* she was blonde—her hair was on fire—anyway, she couldn't stop talking about herself. You know, 'Help *me, I'm* on fire, put *me* out . . .'"

Exercise Eight, pages 306–307

Answers are based on entries in *Webster's Ninth New Collegiate Dictionary*. Some words require hyphens but probably will not appear in any dictionary (see items 2 and 8, for example). Common sense is your guide on these items.
1. up-to-date
2. Yiddish-speaking
3. full-length
4. four-year-old
5. head-to-head
6. flare-up
7. upper-class
8. soul-shaking
9. double-park
10. water-repellent

Exercise Ten, PART A, page 308

1. a dancer's shoes; several dancers' shoes
2. one girl's pet lizard; three girls' pet lizards
3. a family's history; two families' histories
4. one poet's imagery; many poets' imagery
5. the woman's schedule; the women's schedules

Exercise Eleven, page 309

1. women's liberation
2. the rabbi's personality
3. most waiters' tips
4. the baseball team's strategy
5. newborn babies' soft skin
6. the reindeer's sleigh
7. many people's fear of flying
8. three newcomers' comedy routines
9. the children's popsicles
10. Sister Souljah's views

Exercise Twelve, PART A, pages 310–311

1. nation's
2. men's
3. people's
4. Walker's
5. Carter's; women's; veterans'

Exercise Twelve, PART C, pages 311–312

1. patients'
2. personnel's
3. individual's
4. Michigan's; person's
5. Women's

Exercise Thirteen, PART B, pages 313–314

1. witch-hunters'
2. girls' behavior (There is no apostrophe on the first *girls* in sentence 2.)
3. youngsters'
4. person's
5. no apostrophe

Exercise Fourteen, PART A, page 315

1. you're
2. aren't
3. could've
4. he's
5. weren't
6. I'm
7. hadn't
8. I'd
9. didn't
10. wasn't

Chapter 10, Unit 1

Exercise One, pages 320–321

In the answers for this unit, an X is inserted to show the problem spot in each run-on or comma splice. Ask your writing teacher or classmates to check your rewrites.

1. ro   University   X   he
2. ro   United States   X   their
3. cs   blue jeans,   X   he
4. okay
5. ro   planets   X   it
6. cs   criminals,   X   actually
7. okay
8. okay
9. ro   newspapers   X   she
10. cs   verse 35,   X   the

Exercise Three, pages 323–324

1. okay
2. ro   "Loneliness, Social Interaction and Sex Roles"   X   it

3. ro   minutes   X   they
4. ro   interesting   X   women
5. ro   men   X   they
6. okay
7. cs   matters,   X   Wheeler
8. okay
9. cs   people,   X   it
10. cs   men,   X   at

Exercise Four, PART B, pages 325–326

Line 3: *Schutzpass*,   X   this
Line 6: Sweden,   X   that
Line 13: Lester   X   she
Line 14: man   X   he
Line 16: pleas,   X   it

Exercise Four, PART D, pages 327–328

Line 3: below,   X   they
Line 6: *Schutzpass*   X   his
Line 8: "He is working for me,"   X   in
Line 15: food,   X   thousands
Line 16: weak   X   they
Line 24: city,   X   they
Line 26: soldiers,   X   these
Line 27: mercy,   X   he
Line 28: building,   X   little by little, the Nazis dispersed,   X   they

Chapter 10, Unit 2

Exercise One, page 334

Please ask your teacher or classmates to check your revisions. For items in which there is a whole sentence and a fragment, the fragment is shown within parentheses.

1. f
2. f
3. f
4. f (Which . . . Owens.)
5. okay
6. f
7. f
8. f (Helping . . . parents.)
9. okay
10. f (A . . . Kennedy. *and* By . . . Lincoln.)

Exercise Three, PART A, pages 335–337

Lines 4–5: Who . . . isolation.
Lines 5–6: Failing . . . development.
Lines 11–12: A powerful . . . people.
Line 15: Who . . . sensibility.
Lines 26–27: Especially . . . human.
Lines 31–32: If . . . discouraged.

Exercise Three, PART C, pages 338–340

Lines 2–3: An island . . . Massachusetts.
Lines 5–6: When . . . Groce.

Lines 9–10: After . . . century.
Line 13: Not . . . way.
Line 17: Without . . . deafness.
Lines 21–22: Having . . . education.
Lines 24–25: Heading . . . Vineyard.
Lines 32–33: The old . . . Sign.
Line 37: Even . . . speech.

Exercise Three, PART E, pages 341–342

Line 2: The inventor . . . telephone.
Line 7: His prestige . . . camp.
Lines 9–10: Prohibiting . . . deaf.
Lines 16–18: Because . . . bring.
Line 19: Bringing . . . effects.
Line 23: Who . . . psychologists.
Line 27: The truest . . . deaf.
Line 31: If . . . available.

Chapter 10, Unit 3

Exercise One, PART A, pages 345–346

Here is one revision for each sentence, and there are *many* other good possibilities. These revisions address problems with misplaced and dangling modifiers, but in some cases other small improvements are also evident. Ask your teacher or classmates to review your rewrites.

1. Growing up on the west side of Detroit, I found life to be kind of rough.
2. From that time on, I purchased only fresh fruits and vegetables, and I avoided the canned stuff.
3. The girls' exhibition basketball tournament, consisting of ten schools in different divisions, was a friendly way to start off each season.
4. For a while, I was too angry to cry and too hurt not to, but finally the hot tears began to roll down my cheeks.
5. Gazing upon the moonlit sky, I remembered the promise I had made to my grandfather.
6. I went to the closet and grabbed the suitcase that I had packed earlier.
7. I dreamed of going to college because it offered more freedom than high school offered.
8. Slaveholders used whippings, lynchings, and other forms of harsh and inhuman treatment to try to control slaves who initiated protest and influenced others to follow them.
9. By observing recurring patterns in nature, scientists are able to formulate the laws of physics.
10. Because of the pressure that is put on a young lady by her friends or boyfriend nowadays, it is really difficult for her to refrain from sex until she is married.

Exercise Two, pages 347–348

Ask your teacher or classmates to check your rewrites.
1. okay

2. X
3. X
4. okay
5. X
6. X
7. X
8. okay or X (Sentence 8 is a tricky item. If the writer means that O'Connor wrote but did no other activities before noon, then the sentence is fine as it is. But if the writer means that O'Connor wrote in the mornings and at no other times, then a better word order is *wrote only in the mornings.*)
9. okay
10. X

Chapter 10, Unit 4

Exercise Two, pages 353–354

Here is one good rewrite for each item; there are other effective strategies. The key shows only the part of each item that needs to be revised because of problems in parallelism.

1. The demographic . . . categories, including viewers' gender, age, income, race, and education.
2. Of course, they used it to talk, but also to conduct poetry readings, hold wine appreciation classes, play games to maintain and improve concentration, and tell plot summaries of novels they had read.
3. One study of 250 unemployed workers discovered that, during a period of unemployment, people often experienced increases in blood pressure, marital conflicts, problems with children, smoking, and cholesterol levels.

Exercise Four, page 355

1. To maintain his energy, Williams follows certain practices: He is a nonsmoker and a strict vegetarian who enjoys skiing, surfing, running, and working out in a gym.
2. He found that some cocaine-affected infants were sluggish and depressed; others were tense, excitable, and jittery; a third group manifested all of these signs.
3. Parents should become concerned if their child begins to do poorly in school, withdraws, rebels at school or at home, runs away, or becomes involved with drugs or alcohol.

Chapter 10, Unit 5

Exercise One, PART A, pages 356–357

Your active-voice rewrites may differ slightly from those given here and still be correct. If yours vary, ask your teacher or classmates to check them.
1. p   *active rewrite:* In the University of Michigan's

annual Summerscience Program, which exists to support young women in science, ninth-grade girls build rockets, study aviation, and perform chemistry experiments.

2. p   *active rewrite:* According to one of the strange but persistent myths of the publishing world, a writer never makes much money from a book that has a green cover.

3. a

4. p   *active rewrite:* Maria Montessori, who is known all over the world for her achievements in early childhood education, was the first woman in Italy to graduate from medical school.

5. p   *active rewrite:* Dr. Paul Ekman, a psychologist and the director of the Human Interaction Laboratory at the University of California medical school in San Francisco, has described seventeen different kinds of smiles—some sincere and some artificial.

Exercise Two, PART A, pages 358–359

Listed below are the weakest and most unnecessary uses of the passive voice in Exercises two and three. Remember that occasionally a passive sentence is rhetorically effective, and a few others may be debatable. Also, it's possible for a sentence to be passive in more than one clause. Ask your writing teacher or classmates to evaluate your rewrites.

Line 1: Jim Thorpe . . . lived.
Line 7: Gold medals . . . him.
Lines 10–12: The world . . . 1911.
Lines 13–15: Although . . . Stockholm.
Lines 16–17: Jim Thorpe's gold medals . . . books. (This sentence may be seen as a justifiable passive. Why?)
Lines 17–19: Two . . . officials.

Exercise Three, PART A, pages 360–361

Lines 2–3: In . . . king.
Lines 3–5: His father . . . ten. (It would probably be better to make this sentence active, but why might some writers consider the passive form justified in this case?)
Lines 8–10: After . . . Johannesburg.
Lines 12–13: Mandela . . . law.
Lines 13–14: Before . . . Tambo.
Lines 16–17: In 1944 . . . others.
Lines 20–22: The National Party . . . the National Party.

Exercise Three, PART C, pages 363–364

Lines 1–2: During . . . "communist criminal."
Lines 14–15: In . . . him.
Lines 20–22: Because . . . Pollsmoor Prison.

Chapter 11, Unit 1

Exercise One, pages 367–368

1. (a) melts (b) melt
2. (a) protects (b) protect
3. (a) fail (b) fails
4. (a) equals (b) equal
5. (a) need (b) needs

Exercise Three, pages 371–372

In the answers, the subject appears first, even in the few cases in which it follows the verb in the exercise sentence.

1. People **were**; Dr. Shabazz **has**
2. one **is**
3. citizens **spend**
4. nations **include**
5. Waylon Jennings and B.B. King **have**; They **were**
6. flavors **are**
7. star **was**
8. objection or complaint **is**
9. process **receives**
10. one **breaks up**

Exercise Five, pages 373–374

The line number indicates the line in which you fillled in the verb in the exercise. (Sometimes the subject is on another line.)

Line 1: topic **is**
Line 2: discrepancy **shows up**
Line 3: tendency **has** (inverted word order in sentence)
Line 6: scores **are**
Line 7: difference **has**
Line 8: patterns **have**
Line 10: explanations **range**
Line 12: time **goes**
Line 13: factors **seem**
Line 15: studies **show**; women **take**
Line 16: women **tend**
Line 17: men **take**
Line 18: Females **were**

Exercise Six, PART B, pages 375–376

Line 1: picture **deemphasizes**
Line 2: Frank J. Sulloway **enters** (inverted word order in sentence)
Line 4: Sulloway **has**
Line 6: birth order and impact **were**
Line 7: Sulloway **sees**
Line 10: tendency **was**; scientists **were**
Line 12: those **were** (inverted word order in sentence); those **were**
Line 14: thinker **was**
Line 16: 23 (revolutions) **were**

Exercise Six, PART D, page 377

Line 1: exceptions **are** (inverted word order in sentence)
Line 2: Albert Einstein **is**
Line 3: Sulloway **points**
Line 4: people **were**
Line 7: theories **have**

Line 9: they **were**
Line 10: Freud **was**; he **was**
Line 13: he **fits**
Line 14: he **qualifies**
Line 15: Frank Sulloway **does** (inverted word order in sentence)
Line 18: author **is**

Chapter 11, Unit 2

Exercise One, page 381

The answers for Exercise one are given in the present tense. If you were consistent in using the past tense instead of the present for any given sentence in this exercise, that's fine, too.
1. explores; analyzes; studies; reaffirms
2. decides; has; is; makes; proves
3. is; observes; is
4. reflects; presents; explores; stereotypes
5. is; is; exclaims

Exercise Three, pages 383–384

The arrow indicates the correct change in the verb tense. If your answers vary, check with your teacher. There's a certain amount of gray area where verb tense is concerned, and occasionally other answers also may be correct.
Line 5: recalls → recalled
Line 10: win → won
Line 11: take → took; bounce → bounced
Line 12: wrap → wrapped
Line 14: is → was
Line 16: can → could; was → had been
Line 20: admit → admitted
Line 22: disappear → disappeared
Line 24: is → was; bans → banned

Exercise Four, PART B, page 385

Basically, Exercise four should be in the present tense. You have learned that *could* is the past tense of *can* and that *would* is the past tense of *will*. In some sentences in this exercise, you see the verb *may*, which is correct; it should not be changed to its past tense, *might*. Note, however, that the difference between *may* and *might* is considered small compared with the difference between *can* and *could* or *will* and *would*. One standard dictionary says that *may* and *might* differ mostly in intensity rather than in time. *May* is considered stronger in expressing possibility ("The only bank in the neighborhood may close before August.") and permission ("You may go.").
Line 2: contradicted → contradicts
Line 3: would control → controls
Line 7: seemed → seems
Line 12: were saying → are saying (OPTION: were saying → say)

Line 14: could be → can be
Line 17: had → has
Line 22: seemed → seem (OPTION: seemed → may seem)
Line 24: had → has

Chapter 11, Unit 3

Exercise One, PART A, page 390

1. work → worked (past)
2. was honor → was honored (vp)
3. was call → was called (vp)
4. recognize → recognized (adj)
5. serve → served (past)

Exercise Four, PART A, pages 393–394

1. publish → published
2. no change
3. establish → established
4. use → used; end → ended
5. develop → developed; suppose → supposed; well-establish → well-established
6. discuss → discussed; has follow → has followed
7. share → shared; emphasize → emphasized
8. maintain → maintained; disburse → disbursed
9. raise → raised
10. recall → recalled; knock → knocked; commit → committed; need → needed

Exercise Five, pages 395–396

Line 1: have deliver → have delivered
Line 2: use → used; consider → considered
Line 4: use → used; crescent-shape → crescent-shaped
Line 5: receive → received; jewel-trim → jewel-trimmed
Line 7: enlighten → enlightened
Line 8: consider → considered; old-fashion → old-fashioned
Line 9: has design → has designed
Line 10: motorize → motorized; raise → raised; lower → lowered; tilt → tilted
Line 13: is suppose → is supposed
Line 14: reduce → reduced
Line 15: decrease → decreased
Line 17: have been raise → have been raised
Line 19: are allow → are allowed
Line 21: prejudice → prejudiced
Line 22: is quote → is quoted

Chapter 11, Unit 4

Exercise One, page 400

1. SENTENCE 1: Expert → Experts; friendship → friendships; age → ages; teenager → teenagers; adult → adults.
SENTENCE 2: book → books; friend → friends; friend → friends; acquaintance → acquaintances.
2. SENTENCE 1: thing → things; pilot → pilots; fear → fears (OPTION: no change on *fear*).

SENTENCE 2: flier→fliers; mission→missions; experience → experiences; attempt → attempts; carrier → carriers.

SENTENCE 3: event → events; flier → fliers.

SENTENCE 4: pilot→pilots; monitor→monitors; sortie → sorties.

SENTENCE 5: heart → hearts; attempt → attempts; carrier → carriers; attack → attacks; target → targets.

Exercise Three, PART A, page 402

Line 1: figure → figures
Line 3: folklorist → folklorists; connection → connections
Line 4: musician → musicians
Line 5: influence → influences
Line 6: tune → tunes
Line 7: folk musician → folk musicians
Line 8: The Lomax → The Lomaxes
Line 10: singer-songwriter → singer-songwriters
Line 11: accomplishment→accomplishments; folk→folks (OPTION: No change on *folk*. This word has two plural forms: *folk* and *folks*.)
Line 12: decision maker → decision makers; collection → collections

Chapter 11, Unit 5

Exercise One, pages 405–407

In the answers for Exercise one, the antecedent appears in parentheses before the pronoun (or pronoun and verb combination) with which it agrees in number.
1. (services) They
2. (Planned Parenthood Federation of America) its
3. (man) himself, he makes
4. (role) It; (character) her
5. (two thousand members) their; (tribe) itself
6. (emotions) they lead
7. (American Film Institute) its
8. (Sports) They reveal
9. (fly) it tastes
10. (poker hand) It

Exercise Three, PART A, page 410

1. me
2. I
3. him
4. them
5. he

Chapter 11, Unit 6

Exercise One, PART A, pages 416–417

1. you're; have
2. it's
3. hear; It's
4. There; there; you're
5. an; its

6. whether; there; an
7. their; too
8. your; an
9. number
10. have; course; their; it's

Exercise Two, PART A, pages 419–420

1. too; too
2. passed; to; too
3. Here; have; except; effect; then; principal
4. past; coarse
5. except; bare; then

Chapter 11, Unit 7

Exercise One, pages 423–424

The answers show the words that you should have capitalized. (Words that are already capitalized in the exercises are correct and shouldn't be changed.)
1. SENTENCE 1: Valentine's Day; February 14.
   SENTENCE 2: Romans; "Lupercalia"; February 15.
   SENTENCE 3: *The World Book Encyclopedia.*
   SENTENCE 4: no change.
   SENTENCE 5: Britain; Romans; Roman; British; Valentine's Day.
2. SENTENCE 1: LeRoi Jones; Amiri Baraka; *Blues People: The Negro Experience in White America and the Music That Developed from It.* (The word *The* that follows the colon is capitalized because it is the first word in a subtitle.)
   SENTENCE 2: Christianity; African Americans; Jews.
   SENTENCE 3: "Go down Moses"; "I'm Marching to Zion"; "Walk into Jerusalem Just like John."

Exercise Three, page 425

1. SENTENCE 1: North Country Trail Association; Manistee National Forest; Michigan.
   SENTENCE 2: Crown Point, New York; Lake Sakakwea, North Dakota.
   SENTENCE 3: Appalachian Trail; East; Lewis and Clark Trail; West.
   SENTENCE 4: Atlantic; Pacific.
2. SENTENCE 1: "When the Stars Go to Bed, Viewers Often Go to Sleep"; Diana E. Lundin; *The Los Angeles Daily News.*
   SENTENCE 2: David; Maddie; ABC's; "Moonlighting"; Sam; Diane; NBC's; "Cheers"; Hannah; Marty; ABC's; "Anything but Love."
   SENTENCES 3 and 4: no change.

Chapter 12

Please ask your writing teacher or classmates to evaluate your sentence-combining work in Chapter 12.

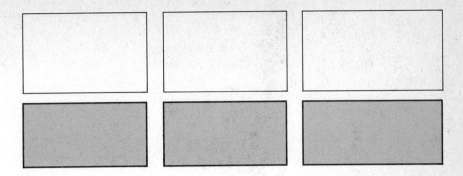

Sources

I express grateful acknowledgment to the following sources:

"Acquired Taste: Let Them Eat Croissants." *Time* 12 April 1982.

Adams, Cecil. *The Straight Dope: A Compendium of Human Knowledge.* New York: Ballantine Books, 1984.

"The Agony of Talking: Stuttering's Causes Are Baffling, But Its Misery Is Clear." *Detroit Free Press* 4 October 1988, sec. C: 1+.

Allen, Dick, qtd. in *Speaker's Treasury of Sports Anecdotes, Stories, and Humor.* Gerald Tomlinson. Englewood Cliffs, New Jersey: Prentice Hall, 1990: 20

Allen, Fred, qtd. in *You Can't Show Kids in Underwear, And Other Little-Known Facts about Television.* Barbara Seuling. New York: Doubleday and Co., Inc., 1982: 14.

Allen, Paula Gunn. "Who Is Your Mother? Red Roots of White Feminism." *The Graywolf Annual Five: Multi-Cultural Literacy.* Eds. Rick Simonson and Scott Walker. St. Paul: Graywolf Press, 1988. 13–27

Alvarez, Julia, qtd. in *The Writer's Craft.* 2nd ed. Glenview, Illinois: Scott, Foresman, and Company, 1989: 39.

American Psychological Association. *Publication Manual of the American Psychological Association.* Washington, D.C.: APA, 1984.

Angier, Natalie. "The Ideal Mate." *Ann Arbor News* 31 May 1990, sec. E: 1+.

"Annenberg America's Most Generous." *Ann Arbor News* (AP) 26 December 1990.

Antoinette, Marie, qtd. in "Deathbed Words Vary from Pleas to Plaints." *Milwaukee Sentinel* 26 October 1982, sec. 3: 1.

Applebome, Peter. "American Blacks Talk of Change as Main Legacy of Mandela Visit." *New York Times* 1 July 1990, sec. Y: 1+.

Atkinson, Rick. "Gulf on Brink of War: World Watches, Waits." *Ann Arbor News* (Washington Post) 15 January 1991, sec. A: 1+.

Automobile Manufacturers Association, Inc. *Automobiles of America.* Detroit: Wayne State University Press, 1968.

Bailey, Moira. "Pez, a Sweet Taste of the Past, Is Popping up All Over." *Detroit Free Press* (Orlando Sentinel) 18 January 1988.

Baldwin, James. "A Talk to Teachers." *The Graywolf Annual Five: Multi-Cultural Literacy.* Eds. Rick Simonson and Scott Walker. St. Paul: Graywolf Press, 1988: 6–7.

Bankston, Amos, qtd. in "Earthly Causes Lack Minority Input, Activists Say." Michael Betzold. *Detroit News and Free Press* 7 April 1990, sec. A: 1.

Banta, Martha. *Imaging American Women: Idea and Ideals in Cultural History.* New York: Columbia University Press, 1987.

Bass, Janet. "By 2001, Women to Outrank PhD Men." *Detroit Free Press* (UPI) 27 December 1990.

Beck, Joan. "2 Live Crew Is More Offensive than Obscene." *Detroit Free Press* 25 June 1990.

Beck, Roy Howard. "Heroism Notwithstanding, Only 1 Woman Has Ever Won Medal of Honor." *Ann Arbor News* 7 May 1989, sec. A: 7.

Beethoven, Ludwig van, qtd. in "Memorable Putdowns." Robert Wells. *Milwaukee Journal* 14 January 1982, sec. B: 1.

Begley, Sharon. "Scratch 'n' Sniff Science." *Newsweek Special Issue* Fall/Winter 1990: 24+.

Belenky, Mary Field, et al. *Women's Ways of Knowing: The Development of Self, Voice, and Mind.* New York: Basic Books, Inc., Publishers, 1986.

Benchley, Robert, qtd. in *The Dictionary of Humorous Quotations.* Ed. Evan Esar. New York: Bramhall House, 1949: 28.

Bennett, Jr., Lerone. *Before the Mayflower: A History of Black America.* 5th ed. New York: Penguin Books, 1962, 1988.

Berkow, Ira. "Ryan Wincing His Way to 300th." *New York Times* 22 July 1990, sec. 1: 25–26.

Bloodworth-Thomason, Linda, qtd. in "A Winner Made in the Shade." Harry F. Waters and Lynda Wright. *Newsweek* 17 December 1990: 64.

Boehm, David A., ed. *Guinness Sports Record Book 1990–91.* New York: Sterling Publishing Co., Inc., 1990.

Bouton, Katherine. "Painful Decisions: The Role of the Medical Ethicist." *New York Times Magazine* 5 August 1990: 22+.

Boyer, Paul. "Salem Witchcraft Trials." *World Book Encyclopedia.* 1988 ed.

Branch, Taylor. *Parting the Waters: America in the King Years, 1954–63.* New York: Simon and Schuster, 1988.

Brando, Marlon, qtd. in *Rock 'n' Roll: The First 25 Years.* John Tobler and Pete Frame. Feltham, Middlesex, England: The Hamlyn Publishing Group Limited, 1981: 12.

Braun, Dick. "Why Does that 'Hic' Come Up?" *Detroit Free Press* 14 June 1988.

Brink, J.R., ed. *Female Scholars: A Tradition of Learned Women Before 1800.* Montreal: Eden Press Women's Publications, 1980: 68–85 and 95.

Brody, Jane E. "A Universal Feeling, Jealousy Can Wreak Havoc in Relationships." *Ann Arbor News* (New York Times) 19 January 1988.

Brooks, Gwendolyn, qtd. in *I Dream a World: Portraits of Black Women Who Changed America.* Brian Lanker. New York: Stewart, Tabori & Chang, 1989: 43.

Brothers, Joyce. "How Women Love." *Parade Magazine* 9 April 1989, supplement to *The Forum* [Fargo, North Dakota, and Moorhead, Minnesota]: 4–7.

Broun, Heywood Hale, qtd. in *Speaker's Treasury of Sports Anecdotes, Stories, and Humor.* Gerald Tomlinson. Englewood Cliffs, New Jersey: Prentice Hall, 1990: 58.

Brown, Les. *The New York Times Encyclopedia of Television.* New York: Times Books-The New York Times Book Co., 1977.

Bruchac, Joseph. *Iroquois Stories: Heroes and Heroines, Monsters and Magic.* Freedom, California: The Crossing Press, 1985.

Burke, Don. "A Crusade for the Return of Thorpe's Medals." *Milwaukee Journal* 24 June 1982.

Burnam, Tom. *The Dictionary of Misinformation.* New York: T.Y. Crowell, 1975.

Burnham, Whitey, qtd. in *Speaker's Treasury of Sports Anecdotes, Stories, and Humor.* Gerald Tomlinson. Englewood Cliffs, New Jersey: Prentice Hall, 1990: 80.

Burns, George, qtd. in "Replays." *Chicago Tribune Sunday Magazine* 24 April 1988: 6.

Butterfield, Fox. "Review Picks Black to Lead." *Detroit Free Press* (New York Times) 6 February 1990.

"Campus Life: Miami of Ohio Plagiarism Is Rampant, a Survey Finds." *New York Times* 1 April 1990, sec. 1, part 2: 36.

Cantu, John Carlos. "AIDS Quilt Warms the Emotions." *Ann Arbor News* 18 November 1990, sec. E: 6.

Capone, Al, qtd. in *Newsday.* Los Angeles Times and Washington Post News Service, reprinted in *Journal Herald* [Dayton, Ohio]. George Dewan. 5 June 1982.

Carlton, Michael. "US Seeking Wilderness' Last Remains." *Milwaukee Journal* 9 May 1982. Copyright © *The Denver Post.*

Catlin, Roger. "A 'Rilly Big Show' Launched Fab Four." *Detroit News* (Hartford Courant) 9 February 1989, sec. D: 3.

Charlton, James, ed. *The Writer's Quotation Book: A Literary Companion.* Wainscott, New York: Pushcart Press, 1980, 1985.

Chávez, César, qtd. in "A Conversation with César Chávez." John R. Moyer. *Readings on La Raza: The Twentieth Century.* Ed. Matt S. Meier. New York: Hill and Wang, 1974: 249.

Christie, Agatha, qtd. in *The Writer's Quotation Book: A Literary Companion.* Ed. James Charlton. Wainscott, New York: Pushcart Press, 1980, 1985: 62.

Churchill, Winston, qtd. in *The Second Book of Insults.* Nancy McPhee. New York: St. Martin's Press, 1981: 28.

Cicero, qtd. in *The Writer's Quotation Book: A Literary Companion.* Ed. James Charlton. Wainscott, New York: Pushcart Press, 1980, 1985: 9.

Cohn, Victor. "Facing the Pariah Syndrome: If a Friend Is Gravely Ill or Grieving, Why Shun Them?" *Ann Arbor News* (Washington Post) 19 June 1990.

Collins, Glenn. "No Regrets: At 81, Feisty Bette Davis Is Still Speaking Her Mind." *Ann Arbor News* (New York Times) 23 April 1989, sec. D: 2.

Considine, J.D. "Robert Johnson: Rock's Mysterious, Pervasive Influence." *Ann Arbor News* (Baltimore Sun) 15 September 1990, sec. D: 3.

"Conversation from the '20s." *Milwaukee Journal* 25 February 1982.

Cook, Harry, qtd. in "Homecoming Queen Makes Her Point." *Ann Arbor News* (AP) 7 November 1990, sec. D: 1.

Cooper, Abraham. "Wallenberg, Raoul." *World Book Encyclopedia.* 1988 ed.

Corey, Giles, qtd. in *The Dictionary of Misinformation.* Tom Burnam. New York: T.Y. Crowell, 1975: 291.

Cornwell, George W. "Amazing Grace: Documentary Explores History of Poignant Hymn." *Ann Arbor News* (AP) 8 September 1990, sec. A: 12.

———. "Episcopalians Help Rule the Capitol Roost." *Detroit News* (AP) 21 January 1989.

Coward, Noel, qtd. in "Memorable Putdowns." Robert Wells. *Milwaukee Journal* 14 January 1982, sec. B: 1.

Crump, Constance. "Fill 'Er Up at the Drive-In." *Ann Arbor News* 26 March 1989, sec. E: 1–2.

———. "Ode to the Open Road." *Ann Arbor News* 18 December 1988, sec. F: 1–2.

———. "Sarah Vaughan Still Sassy." *Ann Arbor News* 1 July 1988.

"A Crusade for the Return of Thorpe's Medals." *The Milwaukee Journal* 24 June 1982.

Cullen, Sandy. "Kaleidoscopes Take on Value, Beauty for Serious Collectors." *Ann Arbor News* 5 December 1989.

Dangerfield, Rodney, qtd. in "Even So, He's Built a Respectable Career." *Milwaukee Journal* (New York Times Service) 19 May 1982, sec. Green sheet: 1.

Daubenmier, Judy. "Martha Griffiths Reflects on Feminist Role, ERA, and Sex Discrimination." *Ann Arbor News* (AP) 26 March 1989, sec. E: 1.

Davidson, Marshall B. *A History of Art: From 25,000 B.C. to the Present.* New York: Random House, 1984.

Davis, Sandra D., and Monice Mitchell. "Rap and Responsibility." *Detroit Free Press* 15 June 1990.

Debo, Angie. *A History of the Indians of the United States.* Norman, Oklahoma: University of Oklahoma Press, 1970.

DeGeneres, Ellen, qtd. in "Women Who Kill—Nightly." Charles Leerhsen. *Newsweek* 15 June 1992: 53.

Demarest, Michael. "It's a Pasta Avalanche!" *Time* 26 April 1982.

Dennis, Henry C. *The American Indian 1492–1970.* Dobbs Ferry, New York: Oceana Publications, Inc., 1977.

Dickerson, A.J. "Tension Part of Fabric of Life for Detroit's Arab-Americans." *Ann Arbor News* (AP) 14 September 1989, sec. A: 6.

Disraeli, Benjamin, qtd. in *The Writer's Quotation Book: A Literary Companion.* Ed. James Charlton. Wainscott, New York: Pushcart Press, 1980, 1985: 66.

Dix, Jennifer. "Medicine Rehabilitates Lowly Leech." *Ann Arbor News* 8 December 1987, sec. B: 1–2.

Doyle, Jack, qtd. in *The Great American Sports Book.* George Gipe. Garden City, New York: Dolphin-Doubleday & Company, Inc., 1978: 22.

Drewry, John Eldridge. "Pulitzer, Joseph." *World Book Encyclopedia.* 1988 ed.

Dreyfous, Leslie. "Boston Discovers Graves of Immigrants Who Saw, But Never Entered, America." *Ann Arbor News* (AP) 7 July 1990.

Dunham, Molly. "Books for Young Readers Help Dispel Stereotypes about American Indians." *Ann Arbor News* (Baltimore Evening Sun) 18 November 1990, sec. E: 4.

"Eating Habits." *Newsweek Special Issue* Winter/Spring 1990: 79.

Edwards, Lee R. *Psyche as Hero: Female Heroism and Fictional Form.* Middletown, Connecticut: Wesleyan University Press, 1984: 11.

Ehrenreich, Barbara, qtd. in "A Thousand Points of Blight," by H. Jack Geiger. Rev. of *The Worst Years of Our Lives: Irreverent Notes from a Decade of Greed,* by B. Ehrenreich. *New York Times Book Review* 20 May 1990: 9.

Elbow, Peter. *Writing with Power: Techniques for Mastering the Writing Process.* New York: Oxford University Press, 1981.

Eliot, T.S., from *Murder in the Cathedral,* pt. 1, 1935, qtd. in *The Great Quotations.* George Seldes. Secaucus, New Jersey: Castle Books-Book Sales Inc., 1960, 1966: 230.

Elizabeth I, Queen, qtd. in "Deathbed Words Vary from Pleas to Plaints." *Milwaukee Sentinel* 26 October 1982, sec. 3: 1.

Epstein, Aaron. "Woman Wins Partnership in Bias Case." *Detroit Free Press* 16 May 1990, sec. A: 3+.

Erdrich, Louise. *Love Medicine.* Toronto: Bantam Books, 1984.

Eskenazi, Gerald. "When Athletic Aggression Turns into Sexual Assault." *New York Times* 3 June 1990, sports sec.: 27+.

"Events in the Life of Nelson Mandela." *Detroit Free Press* 20 June 1990, sec. S: 2.

Fechtner, Leopold. *5,000 One and Two Liners for Any and Every Occasion.* West Nyack, New York: Parker Publishing Co., Inc., 1973.

Ferber, Edna, qtd. in *The Writer's Quotation Book: A Literary Companion.* Ed. James Charlton. Wainscott, New York: Pushcart Press, 1980, 1985: 63.

Ferrari, Enzo, qtd. in "Enzo Ferrari Was Simply a Legend." Lienert, Paul, and Anita Pyzik Lienert. *Detroit Free Press* 19 August 1988.

Fields, W.C., qtd. in "Only in L.A." Steve Harvey. *Los Angeles Times* 17 April 1992, Metro edition, B: 2.

Fleming, Suzanne. "Spangles and Sparkles." *Ann Arbor News* 28 June 1990, sec. B: 1+.

France, Anatole, qtd. in *The Writer's Quotation Book: A Literary Companion.* Ed. James Charlton. Wainscott, New York: Pushcart Press, 1980, 1985: 58.

Fraser, Antonia. *Love Letters: An Anthology.* New York: Alfred A. Knopf, 1977.

Friedman, Sonya. "Rap Lyrics Reflect Society's Problems." *Detroit Free Press* 20 June 1990.

———. qtd. in "Stand for Something: Sonya Friedman Makes One Last Try at Bringing Women out of the Doldrums." Ellen Creager. *Detroit Free Press* 29 January 1991, sec. C: 1–2.

Gallagher, Terry. "Wiesel to Present 1st Wallenberg Lecture." *University Record* [Ann Arbor, Michigan] 17 September 1990: 3.

Garcia, Homer D.C. "Mexican Americans." *World Book Encyclopedia.* 1988 ed.

Gardner, John. *The Art of Fiction: Notes on Craft for Young Writers.* New York: Vintage Books-Random House, 1984, 1985.

———. *On Becoming a Novelist.* New York: Perennial Library-Harper & Row, 1983, 1985: 12–14.

Gates, David. "The Voices of America: Tuning in to Mr. Folklore." *Newsweek* 16 July 1990: 60.

Gates, Max. "Many More Americans May Lead Good Lives Past Age 100." *Ann Arbor News* 15 May 1990.

George, Maryanne. "Camp Helps Girls Imagine New Careers." *Detroit Free Press* 27 June 1990.

George, Nelson, ed. *Stop the Violence: Overcoming Self-Destruction.* New York: Pantheon Books, 1990. (© 1990 by The National Urban League).

Gershenfeld, Matti, qtd. in "Even as Adults, Some of Us Find It Hard to Please Our Parents." Lawrence Kutner. *Ann Arbor News* 13 January 1991, sec. D: 6.

Gibaldi, Joseph, and Walter S. Achtert. *MLA Handbook for Writers of Research Papers.* New York: The Modern Language Association of America, 1988.

Gibbs, Jewelle Taylor, qtd. in "Tense Times." Julie Kosterlitz. *National Journal* 45.2 (11 November 1989): 2784.

Gibson, Mel, qtd. in "I Admire People with Self-Control." Michael Ryan. *Parade Magazine* 3 March 1991, supplement to *Ann Arbor News:* 10.

Gide, André, qtd. in *The Writer's Quotation Book: A Literary Companion.* Ed. James Charlton. Wainscott, New York: Pushcart Press, 1980, 1985: 88.

Gimbutas, Marija, qtd. in "When Women Ruled the World . . ." Peter Steinfels. *Ann Arbor News* (New York Times) 1 March 1990, sec. B: 1–2.

Gipe, George. *The Great American Sports Book.* Garden City, New York: Dolphin-Doubleday & Company, Inc., 1978.

Goldberg, Michael. "Performance: ZZ Top." *Rolling Stone* 24 January 1991: 13.

———. "Red Hot Lollapalooza." *Rolling Stone* 30 April 1992: 23.

Goleman, Daniel. "In the Psychology of Smiles, Not All Are Created Equal." *Ann Arbor News* (New York Times) 8 December 1987, sec. B: 2.

———. "Special Abilities of the Sexes: Do They Begin in the Brain?" *Psychology Today* November 1978: 48.

———. "What Makes Psychopaths Tick?" *Ann Arbor News* (New York Times) 2 September 1987, sec. B: 1+.

Golovko, Vilen, qtd. in "Daring the Impossible." Glenn Collins. *New York Times Magazine* 30 December 1990: 12.

Gordon, Suzanne. "Anger, Power, and Women's Sense of Self." *Ms.* July 1985: 42–44.

Groce, Nora Ellen. *Everyone Here Spoke Sign Language: Hereditary Deafness on Martha's Vineyard.* Cambridge: Harvard University Press, 1985.

Hacker, David. "Parish Aims to Recognize Indian Spirituality." *Detroit Free Press* 26 December 1990.

Hager, Mary, and Tom Warnke. "Broken Circuitry." *Newsweek* 18 December 1989.

Hamilton, Marsh. "Soviets Allow Search for Wallenberg." *Ann Arbor News* (Los Angeles Times) 21 October 1989.

Handelman, David. "Sold on Ice." *Rolling Stone* 10 January 1991: 38+.

Hare, Robert, qtd. in "What Makes Psychopaths Tick?" Daniel Goleman. *Ann Arbor News* (New York Times) 2 September 1987, sec. B: 1+.

Harjo, Suzan Shown. "I Won't Be Celebrating Columbus Day." *Newsweek.* Columbus Special Issue. Fall/Winter 1991: 32.

"Harper's Index." *Harper's Magazine* November 1988.

Hart, Michael H. *The 100: A Ranking of the Most Influential Persons in History.* New York: Hart Publishing Company, 1978.

Harvey, Randy. "Events that Changed Sports." *Ann Arbor News* (Los Angeles Times) 25 December 1990.

Healy, Fran, qtd. in *Speaker's Treasury of Sports Anecdotes, Stories, and Humor.* Gerald Tomlinson. Englewood Cliffs, New Jersey: Prentice Hall, 1990: 211.

Heaverlo, Dave, qtd. in *Speaker's Treasury of Sports Anecdotes, Stories, and Humor.* Gerald Tomlinson. Englewood Cliffs, New Jersey: Prentice Hall, 1990: 233.

Herrmann, Dorothy. *With Malice toward All.* New York: G.P. Putnam's Sons, 1982.

Hirshey, Gerri. *Nowhere to Run: The Story of Soul Music.* New York: Penguin Books, 1984, 1985.

Holden, Stephen. "Nevilles Make a Political Statement." *Ann Arbor News* (New York Times) 8 September 1990.

———. "Strike the Pose: When Music Is Skin Deep." *New York Times* 5 August 1990, sec. 2: 1+.

Howe, Edgar Watson, qtd. in *The Dictionary of Humorous Quotations.* Ed. Evan Esar. New York: Bramhall House, 1949: 99.

Humphrey, Hubert H., qtd. in "Says Who? New Book Sets the Quote Record Straight." Randolph E. Schmid. *Ann Arbor News* (AP) 22 February 1990, sec. B: 7.

Hungry Wolf, Beverly. *The Ways of My Grandmothers.* New York: Quill-William Morrow and Company, 1982.

Hutchinson, Marcia Germaine, qtd. in "Poor Body Image Can Impair Social, Professional Life." Jane Brody. *Ann Arbor News* (New York Times) 27 October 1988, sec. D: 3.

Ibsen, Henrik, qtd. in *The Dictionary of Humorous Quotations.* Ed. Evan Esar. New York: Bramhall House, 1949: 110.

"Illini's Galloping Ghost Helped Put Struggling NFL on Its Feet." *Detroit Free Press* 29 January 1991.

"In Pennsylvania: The Amish . . . " *Time* 19 April 1982.

Irons, Peter. *Justice at War.* New York: Oxford University Press, 1983.

"Is the Party Finally Over?" *Time* 26 April 1982.

Jackson, Bo, qtd. in "Deep Down, Bo the Man Still Bo the Kid." Mike Downey. *Ann Arbor News* 30 October 1990, sec. B: 1.

Jessye, Eva, qtd. in *I Dream a World: Portraits of Black Women Who Changed America.* Brian Lanker. New York: Stewart, Tabori & Chang, 1989: 20.

Johnson, Samuel, qtd. in *The Dictionary of Humorous Quotations.* Ed. Evan Esar. New York: Bramhall House, 1949: 117.

Jones, LeRoi. *Blues People: The Negro Experience in White America and the Music that Developed from It.* New York: Morrow Quill Paperbacks, 1963.

Jordan, Barbara, qtd. in *I Dream a World: Portraits of Black Women Who Changed America.* Brian Lanker. New York: Stewart, Tabori & Chang, 1989: 31.

Kaiser, Charles. "A Roach Clip with Every Paid Subscription." Rev. of *Rolling Stone Magazine: The Uncensored History,* by Robert Draper. *New York Times Book Review* 17 June 1990.

Kantrowitz, Barbara, and Pat Wingert. "A Dismal Report Card." *Newsweek* 17 June 1991: 64+.

Kaufman, George S., qtd. in *With Malice toward All.* Dorothy Herrmann. New York: G.P. Putnam's Sons, 1982: 58 and 61.

Kemp, Jack, qtd. in *Speaker's Treasury of Sports Anecdotes, Stories, and Humor.* Gerald Tomlinson. Englewood Cliffs, New Jersey: Prentice Hall, 1990: 186.

Kernan, Michael. "The Sweet History of Candy Bars." *Ann Arbor News* (Washington Post) 10 May 1988, sec. D: 1+.

Kessler, Lauren. "Women's Magazines' Coverage of Smoking Related Health Hazards." *Journalism Quarterly* Summer 1989: 316.

"Kids Start Dealing with Stress at Age 8." *Detroit News* 27 April 1989.

Kilborn, Peter T. "Brave New World Seen for Robots Appears Stalled by Quirks and Costs." *New York Times* 1 July 1990, sec. Y: 14.

Kilpatrick, James J. "900,000 Forgotten Americans: American Indians Are an Overlooked, Neglected Minority." *Detroit Free Press* (Universal Press Syndicate) 27 June 1990.

King, Jr., Martin Luther. "Letter from Birmingham Jail" (16 April 1963). *The Harper & Row Reader: Liberal Education through Reading and Writing.* 2nd. ed. Wayne C. Booth and Marshall W. Gregory. New York, Harper & Row, 1988: 438.

Kinget, G. Marian. *On Being Human.* Lanham, Maryland: University Press of America, 1987: 113.

Kinkopf, Eric. "Reflections of a Pilot." *Detroit Free Press* 26 February 1991, sec. D: 1+.

Knutson, Lawrence L. "WW II Internees to Receive Reparations." *Ann Arbor News* (AP) 30 September 1989.

Kohn, Alfie. "Nobody Wins when Everybody Is Called upon to Compete." *Detroit Free Press* 13 March 1988, sec. D: 1+.

Kolata, Gina. "What Women Need to Take to Heart." *Detroit Free Press* (New York Times) 24 November 1987, sec. 2: B.

Kool Moe Dee. "Self-Destruction." *Knowledge Is King.* Jive-RCA, 1182-2, 1989.

Kozol, Jonathon. *Illiterate America.* Garden City, New Jersey: Anchor Press-Doubleday, 1985.

Laitner, Bill. "Take Your Medicine with a Good Joke." *Detroit Free Press* 8 September 1989.

Lanker, Brian. *I Dream a World: Portraits of Black Women Who Changed America.* New York: Stewart, Tabori & Chang, 1989.

Lardner, Ring, qtd. in *The Writer's Quotation Book: A Literary Companion.* Ed. James Charlton. Wainscott, New York: Pushcart Press, 1980, 1985: 73.

Layton, Lynne, qtd. in "Madonna Just a Mix of Identities." Ellen Goodman. *Ann Arbor News* (Boston Globe, distributed by the Washington Post Writers Group) 7 December 1990.

Lazarus, Edward. *Black Hills, White Justice: The Sioux Nation Versus the United States, 1775 to the Present.* New York: HarperCollins, 1991.

Leerhsen, Charles. "The Year's Role Model." *Newsweek Special Issue* Summer/Fall 1990: 44–47.

Leerhsen, Charles, and Elizabeth Schaefer. "Pregnancy + Alcohol = Problems." *Newsweek* 31 July 1989: 57.

Leslie, Connie. "James P. Comer: Help for No-Hope Kids." *Newsweek* 2 October 1989: 50.

Lester, Barry, qtd. in "More Data about Cocaine, Newborns." Nancy Ross-Flanigan. *Detroit Free Press* 29 January 1991, sec. D: 3.

Lester, Elenore. *Wallenberg: The Man in the Iron Web.* Englewood Cliffs, New Jersey: Prentice-Hall, Inc., 1982.

Levant, Oscar, qtd. in *The Dictionary of Humorous Quotations.* Ed. Evan Esar. New York: Bramhall House, 1949: 130.

Lewis, Peter H. "Poet's Tool Transforms Thoughts into Rhymes with Ease." *Ann Arbor News* (New York Times) 28 September 1988, sec. B: 3.

Liberace, qtd. in *You Can't Show Kids in Underwear, And Other Little-Known Facts about Television.* Barbara Seuling. New York: Doubleday and Co., Inc., 1982: 33.

Lincoln, Abraham, qtd. in *The Dictionary of Humorous Quotations.* Ed. Evan Esar. New York: Bramhall House, 1949: 131.

———. qtd. in "Veni, Vidi, Visa: We Came, We Saw, We Went Shopping." *Chicago Tribune* 15 September 1986, sec. Perspective: 15.

Linderman, Frank B. *Pretty-Shield: Medicine Woman of the Crows.* Lincoln: University of Nebraska Press, 1932, 1972.

Littwin, Mike. "NFL's Penalties Don't Fit the Crime." *Ann Arbor News* (Baltimore Sun) 28 November 1990, sec. D: 1+.

Loh, Jules. "They Call Him the World's Worst Waiter." *Ann Arbor News* (AP) 6 March 1989, sec. B: 1.

Lovenheim, Barbara. "A Thorny Human Drama: Writer Examines Date Rape." *Ann Arbor News* (New York Times) 12 May 1991, sec. D: 3.

Lowell, James Russell, qtd. in *The Writer's Quotation Book: A Literary Companion.* Ed. James Charlton. Wainscott, New York: Pushcart Press, 1980, 1985: 89.

Lucaire, Edward. *Celebrity Trivia.* New York: Warner Books, Inc., 1980.

Lundin, Diana E. "When the Stars Go to Bed, Viewers Often Go to Sleep." *Ann Arbor News* (Los Angeles Daily News) 3 March 1991, sec. E: 3.

Lustig, Jay. " 'Chess Box' Captures Highlights of Bo Diddley's Early Recordings." *Ann Arbor News* 29 September 1990.

Malamud, Bernard. "Angel Levine." *The Stories of Bernard Malamud.* New York: Farrar, Straus and Giroux, 1983: 277–289.

Mandela, Nelson, qtd. in "Leader's Family Has Shared in the Struggle." Michele Chandler. *Detroit Free Press* 20 June 1990, sec. S: 3.

Mansfield, Katherine, qtd. in *The Writer's Quotation Book: A Literary Companion.* Ed. James Charlton. Wainscott, New York: Pushcart Press, 1980, 1985: 27.

Martin, Steve, qtd. in *The Writer's Quotation Book: A Literary Companion.* Ed. James Charlton. Wainscott, New York: Pushcart Press, 1980, 1985: 56.

Marx, Groucho, qtd. in "A 'Marxist' Theory of Humor Celebrates Start of 2nd Century." Lee Mitgang. *Ann Arbor News* 1 October 1990.

———. qtd. in "Civility Deserves Support, But We Need More Fine Insults, Too." Emmett Watson. *Seattle Times* 24 September 1991, sec. C: 1.

Mathews, Tom. "The Custer Syndrome: What's the Right Answer to 'Who Owns the West?' " *Newsweek* 30 September 1991: 34–35.

———. "Fine Art or Foul?" *Newsweek* 2 July 1990: 46–52.

Mathews, Tom, et al. "The Leader No One Knows." *Newsweek* 19 February 1990: 44+.

Matthews, Anne. "The Poppers and the Plains." *New York Times Magazine* 24 June 1990: 24+.

Matthiessen, Peter. *In the Spirit of Crazy Horse.* New York: Viking Press, 1980, 1983.

McAllister, Bill. "Obscure Workplace Hero Gets Stamp of Recognition." *Ann Arbor News* 9 October 1988.

McDowell, Edwin. "In Publishing, Maxims Are Made to Be Broken." *Ann Arbor News* (New York Times) 5 March 1989.

McGuire, Al, qtd. in *Speaker's Treasury of Sports Anecdotes, Stories, and Humor.* Gerald Tomlinson. Englewood Cliffs, New Jersey: Prentice Hall, 1990: 93.

McKelvey, Bob. "True Lit." *Detroit Free Press* 4 October 1988, sec. B: 1–2.

McNally, Owen. "Today's Jazz Musicians Moving Away from Junkie Image." *Ann Arbor News* (Hartford Courant) 11 August 1990, sec. B: 1.

McPhee, Nancy. *The Second Book of Insults.* New York: St. Martin's Press, Inc., 1981: 31.

McWhirter, Norris, et al. *Guinness Book of Sports Records, Winners, and Champions, 1982–83.* New York, Sterling Publishing Co., 1983.

Mencken, H.L., qtd. in "Book Puts Words in the Right Mouth." *Chicago Tribune* (AP) 21 March 1990, final edition, sec. sports: 25.

Miel, Rhoda. "North Quest: 3,000-Mile Trail Links State with N.D., N.Y." *Ann Arbor News* 18 August, 1990, sec. C: 1–2.

Mizner, Addison, and Wilson Mizner, qtd. in *With Malice toward All.* Dorothy Herrmann. New York: G.P. Putnam's Sons, 1982: 158.

"Modern Americans Have Cut Calories but Not Fat." *Detroit Free Press* 5 June 1990.

Morris, William, ed. *The American Heritage Dictionary.* Boston: Houghton Mifflin Company, 1980.

Morrison, Toni, qtd. in *I Dream a World: Portraits of Black Women Who Changed America.* Brian Lanker. New York: Stewart, Tabori & Chang, 1989: 32.

Moyer, John R. "A Conversation with César Chávez." *Readings on La Raza: The Twentieth Century.* Ed. Matt S. Meier. New York: Hill and Wang, 1974: 248–254.

Murphy, Caryle. " 'We Shall Overcome': Traditional Hymn Became a Civil-Rights Anthem." *Ann Arbor News* (Washington Post) 19 January 1988.

Murphy, Frank, qtd. in *Years of Infamy.* Michi Weglyn. New York: William Morrow and Company, Inc., 1976: 74.

Nash, Warner, qtd. in "Childbirth Sitting Up." Matt Clark with Mariana Gosnell. *Newsweek* 2 March 1981: 79.

Niethammer, Carolyn. *Daughters of the Earth: The Lives and Legends of American Indian Women.* New York: Collier Books-Macmillan Publishing Company, 1977.

Noble, Jeanne. *Beautiful, Also, Are the Souls of My Black Sisters: A History of the Black Woman in America.* New York: Prentice-Hall. 1978.

Norman, Geoffrey. *Bouncing Back: How a Heroic Band of POWs Survived Vietnam.* Boston: Houghton Mifflin Company, 1990.

North, Stephen M. *The Making of Knowledge in Composition: Portrait of an Emerging Field.* Portsmouth, New Hampshire: Boynton/Cook-Heinemann, 1987.

Novak, Michael. *The Joy of Sports: End Zones, Bases, Baskets, Balls, and the Consecration of the American Spirit.* New York: Basic Books, 1976.

NYU Medical Center. "More Women in Medicine." *Ann Arbor News* 15 July 1990,, sec. D: 5.

Olmstead, Larry. "Mandela Has Played Key Role in Movement Since Mid-1940s." *Detroit Free Press* 20 June 1990, sec. S: 2.

Panati, Charles. *Breakthroughs.* Boston: Houghton Mifflin Company, 1980.

Pang, Kevin, qtd. in " 'Oracle Bones' Hint at Earth's Rotation Rate." Nancy Ross-Flanigan. *Detroit Free Press* 13 June 1989.

Pareles, Jon. "How Rap Moves to Television's Beat." *New York Times* 14 January 1990, sec. 2: 1+.

Parker, Jo Goodwin. "What Is Poverty?" *75 Readings: A Freshman Anthology.* New York: McGraw-Hill Book Company, 1987: 143–147.

Pascal, Blaise, qtd. in *The Writer's Quotation Book: A Literary Companion.* Ed. James Charlton. Wainscott, New York: Pushcart Press, 1980, 1985: 9.

Pasta, Elmer. *Complete Book of Roasts, Boasts, and Toasts.* West Nyack, New York: Parker Publishing Company, Inc., 1982.

Percy, Walker. *Lost in the Cosmos: The Last Self-Help Book.* New York: Farrar, Straus & Giroux, 1983.

———. qtd. in *The Writer's Quotation Book: A Literary Companion.* Ed. James Charlton. Wainscott, New York: Pushcart Press, 1980, 1985: 27.

Perry, Bruce, ed. *Malcolm X: The Last Speeches.* New York, Pathfinder, 1989: 175.

Pine, Nathan, qtd. in *The Writer's Quotation Book: A Literary Companion.* Ed. James Charlton. Wainscott, New York: Pushcart Press, 1980, 1985: 13.

Pines, Maya. "Invisible Playmates." *Psychology Today* September 1978: 38.

Pogrebin, Letty Cottin. *Among Friends: Who We Like, Why We Like Them, and What We Do with Them.* New York: McGraw-Hill, 1987.

Pogrebin, Robin. "On Her Own: Veronica, as Snooty and Male-Obsessed as Ever, Goes Solo in a New Archie Comic." *Ann Arbor News* (New York Times) 2 March 1989, sec. B: 4.

"Psychological Dwarfism: The Link between Emotions and Growth." *Ann Arbor News* 31 May 1990, special advertising supplement: 4+.

"Random Violence Drives Many People out of Cities." *Ann Arbor News* (AP) 14 December 1990.

Rasky, Susan F. "Apache Land Undergoes 'Linguistic Remapping.' " *Detroit Free Press* (New York Times) 5 August 1988.

The Reader's Digest Association, Inc. *Strange Stories, Amazing Facts.* Pleasantville, New York: The Reader's Digest Association, Inc., 1976.

"Real 'Rain Man': Man Knows Facts, Figures, but Reasons Poorly." *Ann Arbor News* (AP) 19 February 1989.

Reid, William H., qtd. in "What Makes Psychopaths Tick?" Daniel Goleman. *Ann Arbor News* (New York Times) 2 September 1987, sec. B: 1+.

Reinhardt, Paul, qtd. in "The Professor in the Blue-Denim Suit." *Newsweek on Campus* November 1983: 16.

Revkin, Andrew, qtd. in "Why They Killed Chico Mendes" by James Brooke. Rev. of *The Burning Season: The Murder of Chico Mendes and the Fight for the Amazon Rain Forest* by Andrew Revkin, and *The World Is Burning* by Alex Shoumatoff. *New York Times Book Review* 19 August 1990: 7.

Rexford, Peter. "Mistakes on Stamps and Coins May Prove to Be Quite Valuable." *Ann Arbor News* 18 December 1988, sec. F: 4.

Ricci, James. "Isiah's Play Is Almost Mystical." *Detroit Free Press* 14 June 1990, sec. A: 1+.

Rinehart, Mary Roberts, qtd. in *The Writer's Quotation Book: A Literary Companion.* Ed. James Charlton. Wainscott, New York: Pushcart Press, 1980, 1985: 80.

Rodriguez, Richard, qtd. in *The Writer's Craft.* 2nd ed. Glenview, Illinois: Scott, Foresman, and Company, 1989: 59.

Roethke, Theodore. "I Knew a Woman." *The Collected Poems of Theodore Roetke.* Garden City, New York: Anchor-Doubleday, 1975: 122.

Ross-Flanigan, Nancy. "Klutzy? Blame Bad Design." *Detroit Free Press* 14 June 1988.

Rossini, Gioacchino Antonio, qtd. in *The Dictionary of Humorous Quotations.* Ed. Evan Esar. New York: Bramhall House, 1949: 170.

Rubin, Neal. "Celebrity Pitch." *Detroit Free Press* 24 May 1988, sec. B: 1+.

Ruskin, John, qtd. in *The Dictionary of Humorous Quotations.* Ed. Evan Esar. New York: Bramhall House, 1949: 174.

Sacks, Oliver, qtd. in "More Than a Shtick Figure." Joe Morgenstern. *New York Times Magazine* 11 November 1990: 33.

———. *Seeing Voices: A Journey into the World of the Deaf.* Berkeley: University of California Press, 1989: 31.

Sanders, Thomas E., and Walter W. Peek. *Literature of the American Indian.* Beverly Hills: Glencoe Press, 1973.

Schifrin, Matthew, with Peter Newcomb. "A Brain for Sin and a Bod for Business." *Forbes* 1 October 1990: 162+.

Schneider, Keith. "Migrant Worker Group Is Subject of Wide Study." *New York Times* 19 August 1990, sec. Y: 12.

Schroeder, Jay, qtd. in *Speaker's Treasury of Sports Anecdotes, Stories, and Humor.* Gerald Tomlinson. Englewood Cliffs, New Jersey: Prentice Hall, 1990: 177.

Scribner-Bantam English Dictionary. New York: Scribner, 1977.

Scruggs, Otey M. "Tubman, Harriet." *World Book Encyclopedia.* 1988 ed.

Seldes, George. *The Great Quotations.* Secaucus, New Jersey: Castle Books-Book Sales Inc., 1960, 1966.

Seuling, Barbara. *You Can't Show Kids in Underwear, And Other Little-Known Facts about Television.* New York: Doubleday and Co., Inc., 1982.

Sforim, Mendele Mocher, qtd. in *The Writer's Quotation Book: A Literary Companion.* Ed. James Charlton. Wainscott, New York: Pushcart Press, 1980, 1985: 85.

Shalala, Donna, qtd. in "Big Campus, Big Issues." Bonnie Angelo. *Time* 23 April 1990: 11+.

Shandling, Garry, qtd. in "Comedian Working Up New Material." Kevin Ransom. *Ann Arbor News* 2 October 1990, sec. D: 6.

Shapiro, Laura. "Guns and Dolls." *Newsweek* 28 May 1990: 56+.

Shapiro, Peter. "These Poems Shoot Guns." *Michigan Daily* 24 October 1990.

Shook, Robert L. *The Book of Why.* Maplewood, New Jersey: Hammond, 1983.

Singer, Isaac Bashevis, qtd. in *The Writer's Quotation Book: A Literary Companion.* Ed. James Charlton. Wainscott, New York: Pushcart Press, 1980, 1985: 44.

Sloan, Irving J., ed. *Blacks in America 1492–1970: A Chronology and Fact Book.* Dobbs Ferry, New York: Oceana Publications, Inc., 1976.

Smith, Red, qtd. in *The Writer's Quotation Book: A Literary Companion.* Ed. James Charlton. Wainscott, New York: Pushcart Press, 1980, 1985: 55.

Smith, Vern E., et al. "Rediscovering Malcolm X." *Newsweek* 26 February 1990: 68–69.

Sochen, June. "Stanton, Elizabeth Cady." *World Book Encyclopedia.* 1988 ed.

"Soviets Open Files in Case of WWII Hero." *Detroit Free Press* (Free Press Wire Services) 28 August 1990.

Spears, Gregory. "Lincoln Exhibit Shows Assassination Artifacts." *Detroit Free Press* 3 October 1990.

Specter, Michael. "Smoking Cuts Male Lives by 18 Years, Study Says." *Ann Arbor News* (Washington Post) 13 May 1990.

Sperling, Dan. "Work Doesn't End When the Weekend Begins." *Detroit News* (Gannett News Service) 7 March 1989.

"Splitting Hairs on an Old Chore." *Milwaukee Journal* 25 May 1982.

Sporkin, Elizabeth. "USA Is Swathed in Quilting's Warmth." *USA Today* 5 July 1982.

Standing Bear, Chief Luther, qtd. in *Literature of the American Indian.* Thomas E. Sanders and Walter W. Peek. Beverly Hills: Glencoe Press-Benziger Bruce & Glencoe, Inc., 1973, 1976: 176.

Steinem, Gloria, qtd. in "Overheard." *Newsweek* 18 December 1989: 19.

Stieglitz, Alfred, qtd. in "Juicy O'Keeffe Biography Gives Art Short Shrift." Misha Berson. *Seattle Times* 18 August 1991, sec. L: 3.

Storr, Anthony. *Solitude: A Return to the Self.* New York: Ballantine Books, 1988.

Story, Ralph D. "Gender and Ambition: Zora Neale Hurston in the Harlem Renaissance." *The Black Scholar* Summer/Fall 1989: 30.

"Stress Gum Tells if Life's Too Hectic." *Ann Arbor News* 19 March 1990.

Sulloway, Frank J., qtd. in "The Order of Innovation." Kenneth L. Woodward and Lydia Denworth. *Newsweek* 21 May 1990: 76.

Terry, Wallace. "She Helps Make Winners." *Parade Magazine* 27 May 1990, supplement to *Ann Arbor News*: 24.

"Tired of Hearing about Firsts? Read On." *Milwaukee Journal* 23 September 1982.

Tobler, John, and Pete Frame. *Rock 'n' Roll: The First 25 Years.* Feltham, Middlesex, England: The Hamlyn Publishing Group Limited, 1981.

Tomlinson, Gerald. *Speaker's Treasury of Sports Anecdotes, Stories, and Humor.* Englewood Cliffs, New Jersey: Prentice Hall, 1990.

Truffaut, François, qtd. in *The Writer's Quotation Book: A Literary Companion.* Ed. James Charlton. Wainscott, New York: Pushcart Press, 1980, 1985: 68.

Truman, Harry S., qtd. in "Overheard." *Newsweek Special Issue* Winter/Spring 1990: 10.

Turan, Kenneth. "Condom Industry Makes Good Reading." Rev. of *The Condom Industry in the United States,* by James S. Murphy. *Ann Arbor News* (Los Angeles Times) 27 December 1990.

Twain, Mark, qtd. in *The Writer's Quotation Book: A Literary Companion.* Ed. James Charlton. Wainscott, New York: Pushcart Press, 1980, 1985: 13, 40.

Tyson, Cicely, qtd. in *I Dream a World: Portraits of Black Women Who Changed America.* Brian Lanker. New York: Stewart, Tabori & Chang, 1989: 27.

The University of Chicago. *The Chicago Manual of Style.* 13th ed. Chicago: The University of Chicago Press, 1982.

"U.S. Kneels to Apologize: Japanese Americans Imprisoned in World War II Are Compensated." *Detroit Free Press* (AP and UPI) 10 October 1990.

Uslan, Michael, and Bruce Solomon. *Dick Clark's The First 25 Years of Rock & Roll.* New York: Delacorte Press, 1981.

Vann, Sonya. "Rap for Pride." *Detroit Free Press* 13 July 1990, sec. D: 1.

Varasdi, J. Allen. *Myth Information.* New York: Ballantine Books, 1989.

Walker, Alice, qtd. in *I Dream a World: Portraits of Black Women Who Changed America.* Brian Lanker. New York: Stewart, Tabori & Chang, 1989: 24.

Wallechinsky, David, and Irving Wallace. *The People's Almanac.* Garden City, New York: Doubleday & Company, Inc., 1975: 1320.

Wallechinsky, David, Irving Wallace, and Amy Wallace. *The Book of Lists. New York: William Morrow and Company, Inc., 1977: 463.*

Warner, Judith. "Board Games People Play Mirror '80s Preoccupations." *Ann Arbor News* (New York Times) 18 December 1988, sec. F: 2.

Washington, Mary Helen. "Her Mother's Gifts." *Ms.* June 1982: 38.

Waters, Muddy, qtd. in "Eric Clapton: The Importance of Being a Gentleman." Hillel Italie. *Ann Arbor News* (AP) 7 July 1990, sec. F:2.

Weglyn, Michi. *Years of Infamy.* New York: William Morrow and Company, Inc., 1976.

Weisbrot, Robert. *Freedom Bound: A History of America's Civil Rights Movement.* New York: Norton, 1990.

Wellington, Duke of, qtd. in "Throwing in the Towel . . . " Michael J. Goodman. *Los Angeles Times Sunday Magazine* 16 February 1992: 18.

"What Americans Drove: The Best-Selling Cars." *New York Times* 18 November 1990, sec. 3: 1+.

Wheeler, Ladd, and Harry Reis, qtd. in "Buddies: Women Make Better Friends, Study Says." *Milwaukee Journal* 23 May 1982.

Wheeler, Thomas C. *The Immigrant Experience: The Anguish of Becoming American.* Baltimore: Penguin Books, Inc., 1971, 1972.

White, E.B., qtd. in *Humor and Social Change in Twentieth-Century America.* Joseph Boskin. Boston: Trustees of the Public Library, 1979.

White, Richard. "Real English Teachers Are an Endangered Species." *Today's Catholic Teacher* October 1990.

Wiesel, Elie. "A Passion for Memory": University of Michigan Wallenberg Lecture. University of Michigan, Ann Arbor. 25 September 1990.

Wilde, Oscar, qtd. in *The Great American Sports Book.* George Gipe. Garden City, New York: Dolphin-Doubleday & Company, Inc., 1978: 335.

———. qtd. in *The Dictionary of Humorous Quotations.* Ed. Evan Esar. New York: Bramhall House, 1949: 215.

Wilford, John Noble. "Skeletal Remains Can Tell Life Stories." *Detroit Free Press* (New York Times) 17 November 1987.

———. "Today's Teeth Tiny by Neanderthal Standards, Says U-M Study." *Ann Arbor News* 15 September 1988.

Wilmington, Michael. " 'Dances with Wolves' Not Alone in Its Positive Depiction of American Indians." *Ann Arbor News* (Los Angeles Times) 22 December 1990, sec. E: 6.

Wolf, Bob. "Thorpe, Jim." *World Book Encyclopedia.* 1988 ed.

Woodward, Kenneth L., and Lydia Denworth. "The Order of Innovation." *Newsweek* 21 May 1990: 76.

Worth, Fred L. *The Trivia Encyclopedia.* Los Angeles: Brooke House, 1974.

Wright, B.H. "The Effects of Racial Self-Esteem on the Personal Self-Esteem of Black Youth." *The International Journal of Intercultural Relations* 9.1 (1985): 19–30.

Wu, Cheng-Tsu, ed. *"Chink!" A Documentary History of Anti-Chinese Prejudice in America.* New York: World Publishing Company-Times Mirror, 1972.

Wu, Shanlon. "In Search of Bruce Lee's Grave." *New York Times Magazine* 15 April 1990.

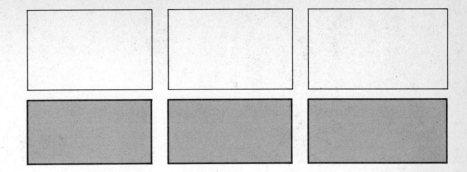

Index

Note: Included among the more traditional topics are entries for students whose writing appears in the book and for all sources quoted on the subject of writing; individuals quoted on or discussed in reference to other topics are not included here.

A/an, 411–412
Absolutes, 246–247
Abstract language, 12–18. *See also* Diction
Accept/except, 412
Action verbs, 184
Active voice, 356–365
Adjectives, 206–207
Adverbs, 207–208
  errors with hyphens, 306
  then as a factor in run-ons and comma splices, 320
Affect/effect, 412
Alli, Reneé A., 129–130
Alojipan, Junaur, 41–43, 126
Alvarez, Julia, 283
Amanze, Adanna Chioma, 79–80
Amount/number, 412
Answers for exercises in section II
  in-text key, 439
  system explained, 191
APA parenthetical citation system, 164–165
Apostrophes
  for contractions, 314–315
  for miscellaneous purposes, 315–316
  for possession, 307–314
Appositives, 208–210
Argumentative writing
  documentation in, 151–165
  examples of student work, 165–178
  suggested topics for, 178–180
  treatment of opposing views in, 154–155
Audience, 72–73
  examples from student writing, 73–80
  exercises, 76–80
Auxiliary verbs. *See* Helping verbs

Barajas, Sally, 31–35
Bare/bear, 412–413
Barksdale, Lisa M., 15, 105–106
Bell, Andrea L., 68
Benchley, Robert, 419
Bidol, Jonathon Sung, 143–144
Bidol, Molly Jung, 43–44
Bivins, Bishari, 174–176

Block quotes. *See* Quoting
Bowen, Roxanne, 127–128
Brackets, 304
Brainstorming, 6
Brooks, Gwendolyn, 63

Campbell, William, 15, 22–23
Can/could. *See* Modal auxiliary verbs
Capitalization, 422–427
Cause and effect essays, 136–137
  examples from student writing, 139–151
  suggested topics for, 137–139
Cauterucci, Daniel R., 118
Chinnukroh, Salina S., 78
Cicero, 255
Citations. *See* APA parenthetical citation system *and* MLA parenthetical citation system
Clauses, 184. *See also* Dependent clauses, Independent clauses, Relative clauses, Restrictive and nonrestrictive clauses, *and* Simple sentences
  five basic types of, 190–191
  as subjects of other clauses, 200
Clichés. See Diction
Coarse/course, 413
Colons
  before direct quotes, 270, 294–295
  before explanations, 268–269
  before lists, 264–267
Commas
  in adjective pairs, 250–252
  between city and state, 252–253
  in complex sentences with subordinating conjunctions, 229
  in compound sentences, 222–223
  in dates, 253
  in direct address, 253
  before direct quotes, 270, 293–294
  exercises for all comma uses, 254–258
  between items in a series, 248–250
  before and after phrases, 242–248
  with relative clauses, 233–242
  in tag questions, 253

Comma splices, 317–330
Comparison/contrast essays
  controlling purpose of, 101–103, 106–110
  examples from student writing, 103–106
  options for organizing, 102, 106–110
  Pepsi/"Like a Prayer" project, 102–106
  suggested topics for, 107–108
Complements. *See* Object complements *and* Subject complements
Complex sentences
  made with relative pronouns, 232–242
  made with subordinating conjunctions, 228–232
Compound sentences, 222–228
Conclusions. *See* Paragraph organization
Concrete language, 12–18
Condition verbs. *See* Linking verbs
Conjunctions. *See* Coordinating conjunctions *and* Subordinating conjunctions
Conjunctive adverbs. *See* Logical connectives
Conscience/conscious, 413
Contractions. *See* Apostrophes
Controlling purpose
  and audience, 73
  and cause and effect essays, 139
  and comparison/contrast essays, 101–103, 106–110
  and definition essays, 84–85
  and descriptions, 22
  and documented arguments, 151
Cook, Kimberly A., 93–97
Coordinating conjunctions, 222–228
Coordination. *See* Faulty coordination
Coward, Noel, 298
Crick, Ian, 13–14
Cruz, Giovanni, 81–83

-d and -ed endings, 386–396. *See also* Verb tense
Dangling modifiers, 344–350
Dashes, 279–284
Definition essays, 83–86
  examples of student work, 86–101
  suggested topics for, 84–85

Dependent clauses, 228–229. *See also* Complex sentences
Descriptions of people
　examples from student writing, 22–28
　suggested topics for, 35–36
Descriptions of places
　examples from student writing, 28–35, 81–82
　suggested topics for, 36–37
Dialogue, 296. *See also* Maskai, Shyam
Diction, 61
　ambiguity in, 67
　clichés, 61–63
　exercises in, 67–72
　originality in, 14
　overuse of thesaurus, 64–65
　shifts in, 65–66
　slang, 62–63, 65–66
　stereotyping through, 63–64
　wordiness, 66–67
Dilligard III, John, 21
Direct objects, 188–189, 192–193
Direct quotes. *See* Quoting *and* Quotation marks
Disraeli, Benjamin, 230
Dixon, Euniece Lashawn, 74–76
Documented argument essays. *See* Argumentative writing *and* Researched essays
Double quotation marks. *See* Quotation marks

Editing, 3–4, 183. *See also* names of specific skills
Ellipsis points, 303–304
Emphatic verbs. *See* Helping verbs
Endnotes, 163–164
Erdrich, Louise, 243–248
Evidence
　within body paragraphs of an essay, 121–122
　within documented argument essays, 151–152
Exclamation point, 294
Expository writing, 81–83. *See also* names of specific types

Fairness
　in citing sources, 155–156
　in handling opposing views, 154–155
　in making language choices, 63–64
Faulty coordination, 350–352
Faulty parallelism, 352–355
Ferber, Edna, 280
Finally/finely, 413
Fragments, 330–342
Freewriting, 6–10. *See also* Prewriting
Friedenzohn, Daniel, 23

García, Darilís, 24–25
Gardner, John, 14, 62
Garza, Socorro Nieto, 145–147
Gastman, Becky, 47–52, 126–127
Generality in language, 12–18, 117–118, 123–124. *See also* Diction
Generalizations. *See* Logic
Gerunds, 199–200, 205–206
Gide, André, 260

Harrison, Jason H., 15
Hathaway, Regina C., 122
Have/of, 413
Hear/here, 414
Helping verbs, 201–202. *See also* Modal auxiliary verbs

Hennings, Don A., 147–151
Homonyms, 410–422
Hughes, T.S., 139–143
Hyphens, 281, 304–307

Independent clauses, 222. *See also* Compound sentences *and* Simple sentences
Indirect objects, 189–190, 192–193
Indirect quotes. *See* Quoting
Infinitive verb phrases, 199, 205–206
Intransitive verbs, 188
Introductions. *See* Paragraph organization
Irregular verbs, 202–204
It's/its, 414

Journals. *See* Prewriting

Kaufman, George S., 298
Kendrick, Angela, 73–74
Kernels of clauses, 206
Kinget, G. Marian, 269
Kirk, Kristi A., 87–89
Kloubec, Jeremy, 169–171

Laney, Chessada, 25–28
Lang, Tiffanie L., 125, 165–169
Lewis, Sina L., 128
Lincoln, Abraham, 113
Linking verbs, 184–185, 187–188
Logic
　circular reasoning, 113
　exercises for, 112–113, 115–117
　false causes, 113–114
　misdirected attacks on people, 111
　mixing issues, 114–115
　problems stemming from misuse of conjunctions, 115
　problems stemming from personification, 114–115
Logical connectives, 261–262

Makin, Bathsua, 196
Mansfield, Katherine, 11
Martin, Steve, xvi
Maskai, Shyam, 45–47
Matthews II, Michael Z., 67–68
Miranda, Mike, 10
Misplaced modifiers, 343–350
Mizner, Addison and Wilson, 298–299
MLA parenthetical citation system, 157–164
Modal auxiliary verbs, 201
　and consistency of verb tense, 379
　and -d and -ed verb endings, 388
Montgomery, Hakeemeh, 171–173
Moore, Roderick D., 16
Morales, Clarissa, 125

Narrative writing, 37–60
　examples of student work, 38–57
　suggested topics for, 57–58
　value of narrative elements in documented argument essays, 118–119
Note taking, 153–154
Nouns, 196–198
　collective nouns and pronoun-antecedent agreement, 404–405
　plural forms of, 396–402
　substitute forms of, 199–201

Object complements, 190–193
Objects. *See* Direct objects *and* Indirect Objects
Olachea, Enrique Humberto, 28–31

Organization. *See also* Paragraph organization
　beginning in the note-taking stage, 154
　turning research into writing, 156–157

Paragraph organization
　body paragraphs, 120–123
　"closing the circle," 126–127
　conclusions, 123–127
　examples from student writing, 117–135
　exercises for, 127–135
　introductions, 117–120
Parallelism. *See* Faulty parallelism
Paraphrasing. *See* Quoting
Parentheses, 281, 304
Parts of speech, 185–186, 207, 231–232. *See also* names of individual parts
Pascal, 117
Passed/past, 414
Passive voice, 188–189, 356–365
Past participle, 202
Past tense. *See* Verb tense
Peljovich, Adriana, 89–91
Percy, Walker, 305, 419
Persuasion, 136. *See also* Cause and effect essays *and* Documented argument essays
Phrasal prepositions, 212
Phrases, 199, 242–248
Pine, Nathan, 353
Plagiarism, 155–156
Plural nouns. *See* Nouns
Point of view, 19–21
Possession. *See* Apostrophes
Predicate, 184
Prepositional phrases, 200, 211–212
　exercise for identifying, 212–213
　as a factor in pronoun-antecedent agreement, 405
　as a factor in subject-verb agreement, 370
Prepositions, 211–212
Prewriting, 3–11
Principal/principle, 414
Privacy issues in student writing, 5, 10–11, 58
Pronoun-antecedent agreement. *See* Pronouns
Pronoun case. *See* Pronouns
Pronouns, 198
　agreement with antecedent, 403–408
　ambiguous reference of, 409
　and case, 409–410
　demonstrative, 198
　as a factor in run-ons and comma splices, 198, 320
　indefinite, 198, 405
　nonstandard, 405
　omitted antecedents, 408–409
　personal, 198
　possessive, 307–308
　relative, 232–242
Punctuation. *See also* names of specific marks
　cumulative exercises for commas, semicolons, and colons, 269–279
　cumulative exercises for commas, semicolons, colons, and dashes, 283–291

Question mark, 294
Quotation marks. *See also* Quoting
　and block quotes, 302–303
　double, 291–304
　single, 300–302
Quoting. *See also* Quotation marks
　in conclusions of essays, 125–126
　directly and indirectly, 291–293

Quoting (*Continued*)
fairly within context, 154
and keeping records of sources, 154
passages longer than four lines, 302–303

Racist uses of language, 63–64
Rajan, Sivaram, 77–78
References, 164. *See also* APA parenthetical
citation system *and* MLA parenthetical
citation system
Reffigee, Lester, 119
Regular verbs, 202. *See also* -d and -ed end-
ings
Relative clauses, 232–242
Relative pronouns, 232–242
Researched essays, 151–180. *See also* Argu-
mentative writing *and* Plagiarism
avoiding "cut and paste" jobs, 151–152
citing sources for, 157–165
controlling purpose in, 151–153, 157
examples of student work, 165–178
organizing information for, 156–157
suggested topics for, 178–180
Restrictive and nonrestrictive clauses, 236–
238
Riley, Eric K., 86–87
Rinehart, Mary Roberts, 269
Robinson, Dora R., 19–21, 131–135
Rodriguez, Richard, 282
Run-on sentences, 317–330

Semicolons, 258–264
between independent clauses, 258–261
between items in a complex list, 263–264
with logical connectives, 261–262
Sentence combining, 221

free exercises in, 428–437
usefulness in solving run-ons and comma
splices, 319–320
Sentence fragments. *See* Fragments
Sentences, 183–184. *See also* specific type,
e.g., Simple sentences
Sexist uses of language, 63–64, 403–404
Sforim, Mendele Mocher, 281
Sharma, Salig Ram Hutchins, 98–101, 119–
120
Simple sentences, 184
exercises on, 191–195, 200–201, 204–205,
209–210, 212–220
key points about, 194–195
rhetorical reasons for using, 221
Singer, Isaac Bashevis, xv
Single quotation marks. *See* Quotation
marks
Sources, 151–165
Specificity in language, 12–18
Spelling changes, 389, 398–400
"State of being" verbs. *See* Linking verbs
Stephens, Mila L., 176–178
Story, Ralph D., 295
Subject complements, 187–188, 192–193
Subjects of clauses, 184, 186, 192–193
Subject-verb agreement, 186, 366–377
Subordinating conjunctions, 228–232
exercises for, 230–231
list of most common, 230
Surface errors, 183. *See also* names of specific
types
Switching modes of discourse, 85–86, 102

Taylor, Yolanda R., 15–16, 91–92
Than/then, 415
Their/there/they're, 415

Thesis statements, 152–153. *See also* Control-
ling purpose
Threw/through, 415
Topic sentences. *See* Paragraph organization
To/too/two, 415
Transitive verbs, 188
Truffaut, François, 239
Turner II, Clyde F., 14, 38–41
Twain, Mark, 61

Verb phrases, 201–205. *See also* Helping
verbs *and* Modal auxiliary verbs
Verbs, 184–191. *See also* Irregular verbs *and*
Regular verbs
Verb tense, 201
consistency of, 377–386
and -d and -ed endings, 386–396
in framing direct quotes, 302
in present perfect, past perfect, and future
perfect, 387–388
Voice, 61–67

Weather/whether, 416

Weiskopf, Michael G., 52–57

Who's/whose, 416
Williams, Marcus A., 103–105, 125–126
Will/would. *See* Modal auxiliary verbs
Wilson, Chrisalle M., 18–19
Works Cited. *See* MLA parenthetical citation
system
Wright, Stephanie S., 122–123
Writing process, 3–4. *See also* names of spe-
cific stages

You're/your, 416